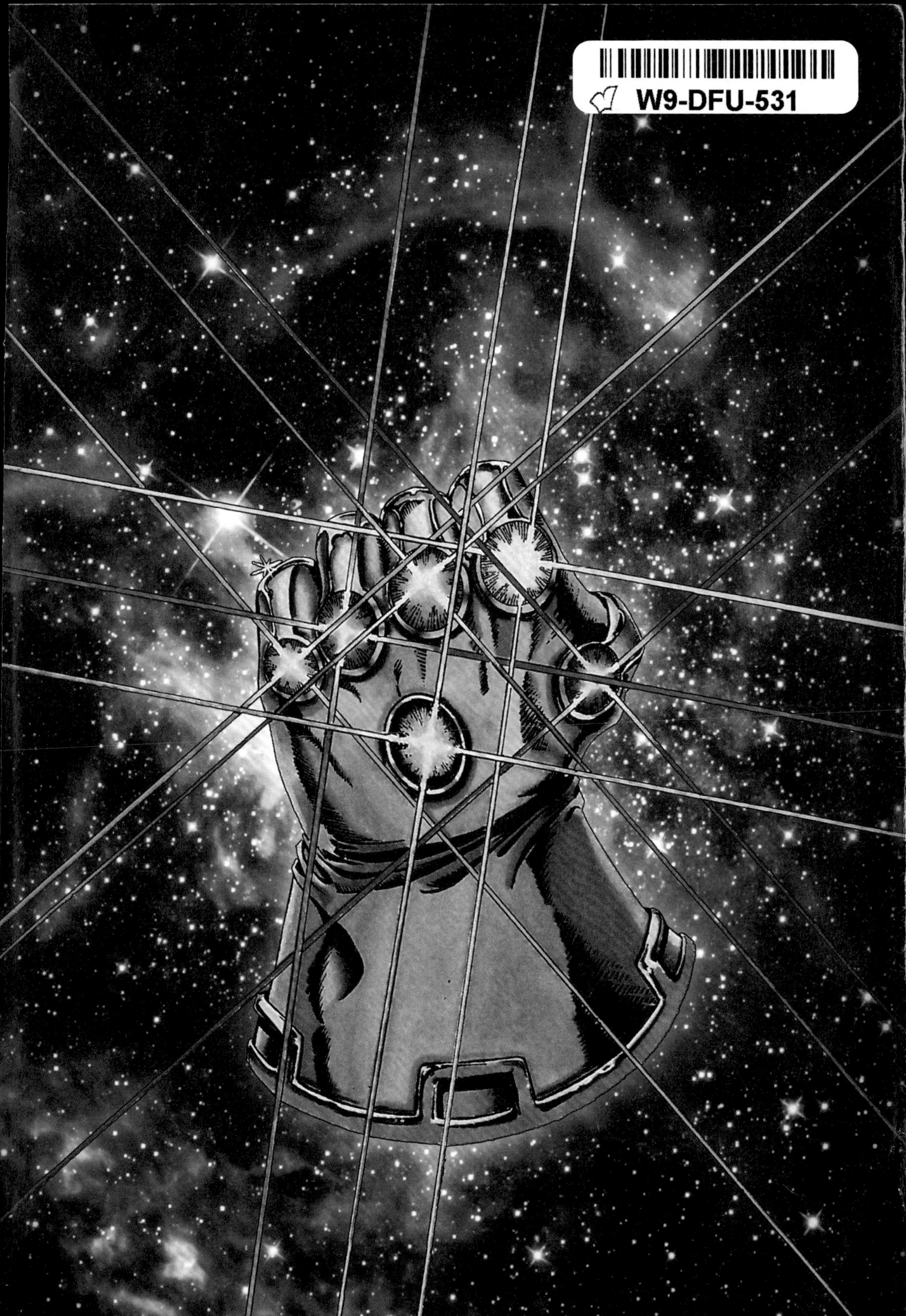

INFINITY GAUNTLET

INFINITY GAUNTLET

WRITER
JIM STARLIN

PENCILERS
GEORGE PÉREZ & RON LIM

INKERS
JOSEF RUBINSTEIN
WITH TOM CHRISTOPHER
& BRUCE SOLOTOFF

COLORISTS
MAX SCHEELE, IAN LAUGHLIN
& EVELYN STEIN

LETTERER
JACK MORELLI

EDITOR
CRAIG ANDERSON

COVER ART
GEORGE PÉREZ

BACK COVER COLORS
THOMAS MASON

COLLECTION EDITOR
MARK D. BEAZLEY

ASSISTANT EDITOR
CAITLIN O'CONNELL

ASSOCIATE MANAGING EDITOR
KATERI WOODY

ASSOCIATE MANAGER, DIGITAL ASSETS
JOE HOCHSTEIN

SENIOR EDITOR, SPECIAL PROJECTS
JENNIFER GRÜNWALD

VP PRODUCTION & SPECIAL PROJECTS
JEFF YOUNGQUIST

SVP PRINT, SALES & MARKETING
DAVID GABRIEL

PRODUCTION
COLORTEK & JOE FRONTIRRE

BOOK DESIGNER
MICHAEL CHATHAM

EDITOR IN CHIEF
C.B. CEBULSKI

CHIEF CREATIVE OFFICER
JOE QUESADA

PRESIDENT
DAN BUCKLEY

EXECUTIVE PRODUCER
ALAN FINE

INFINITY GAUNTLET. Contains material originally published in magazine form as INFINITY GAUNTLET #1-6. Fourteenth printing 2019. ISBN 978-0-7851-5659-8. Published by MARVEL WORLDWIDE, INC., a subsidiary of MARVEL ENTERTAINMENT, LLC. OFFICE OF PUBLICATION: 135 West 50th Street, New York, NY 10020. © 2011 MARVEL No similarity between any of the names, characters, persons, and/or institutions in this magazine with those of any living or dead person or institution is intended, and any such similarity which may exist is purely coincidental. **Printed in Canada.** DAN BUCKLEY, President, Marvel Entertainment; JOHN NEE, Publisher; JOE QUESADA, Chief Creative Officer; TOM BREVOORT, SVP of Publishing; DAVID BOGART, Associate Publisher & SVP of Talent Affairs; Publishing & Partnership; DAVID GABRIEL, SVP of Sales & Marketing, Publishing; JEFF YOUNGQUIST, VP of Production & Special Projects; DAN CARR, Executive Director of Publishing Technology; ALEX MORALES, Director of Publishing Operations; DAN EDINGTON, Managing Editor; SUSAN CRESPI, Production Manager; STAN LEE, Chairman Emeritus. For information regarding advertising in Marvel Comics or on Marvel.com, please contact Vit DeBellis, Custom Solutions & Integrated Advertising Manager, at vdebellis@marvel.com. For Marvel subscription inquiries, please call 888-511-5480. **Manufactured between 1/11/2019 and 2/5/2019 by SOLISCO PRINTERS, SCOTT, QC, CANADA.**

20 19 18 17 16 15 14

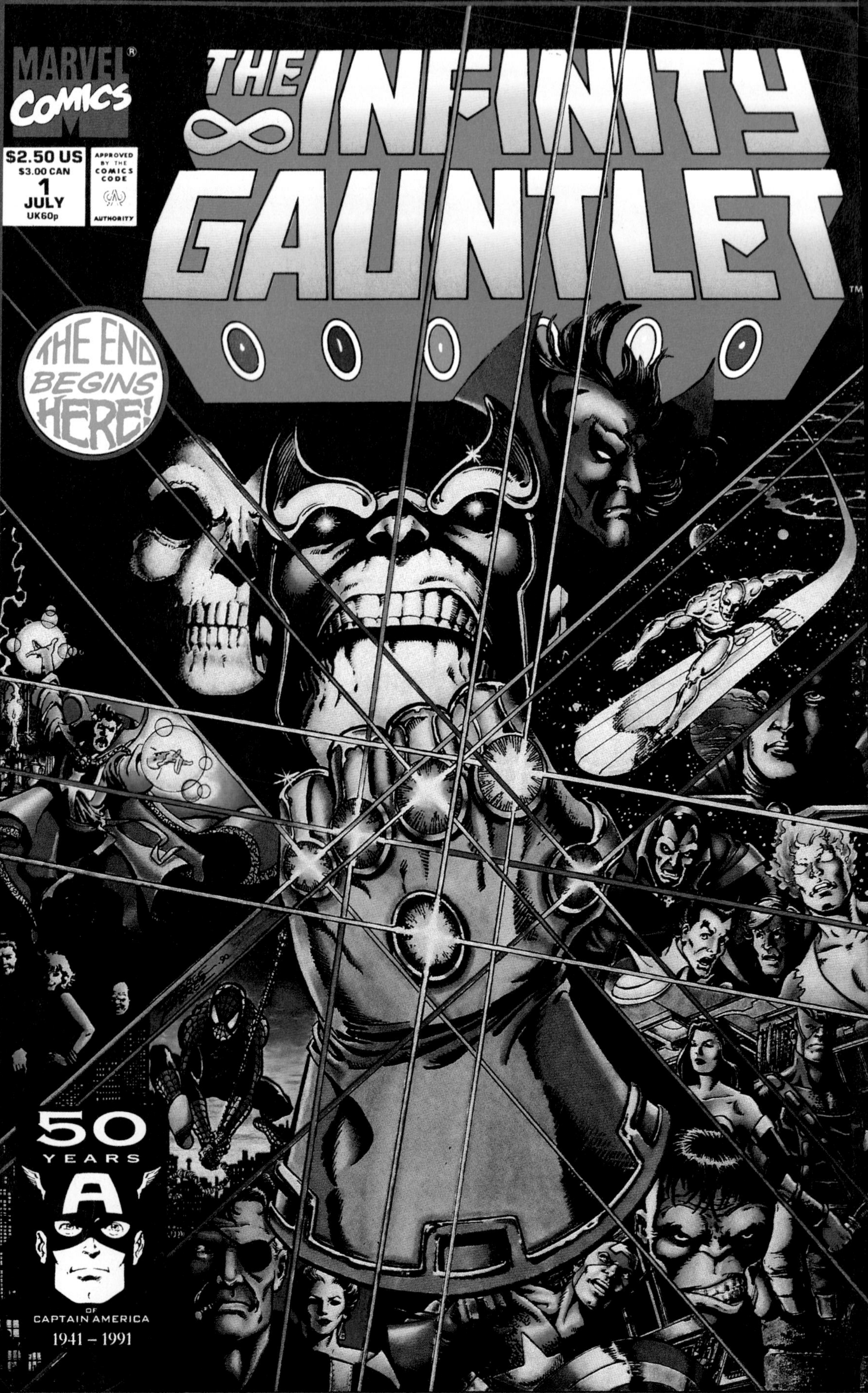
MARVEL COMICS
THE INFINITY GAUNTLET
$2.50 US
$3.00 CAN
1
JULY
UK60p
APPROVED BY THE COMICS CODE AUTHORITY
THE END BEGINS HERE!
50 YEARS
OF CAPTAIN AMERICA
1941 – 1991

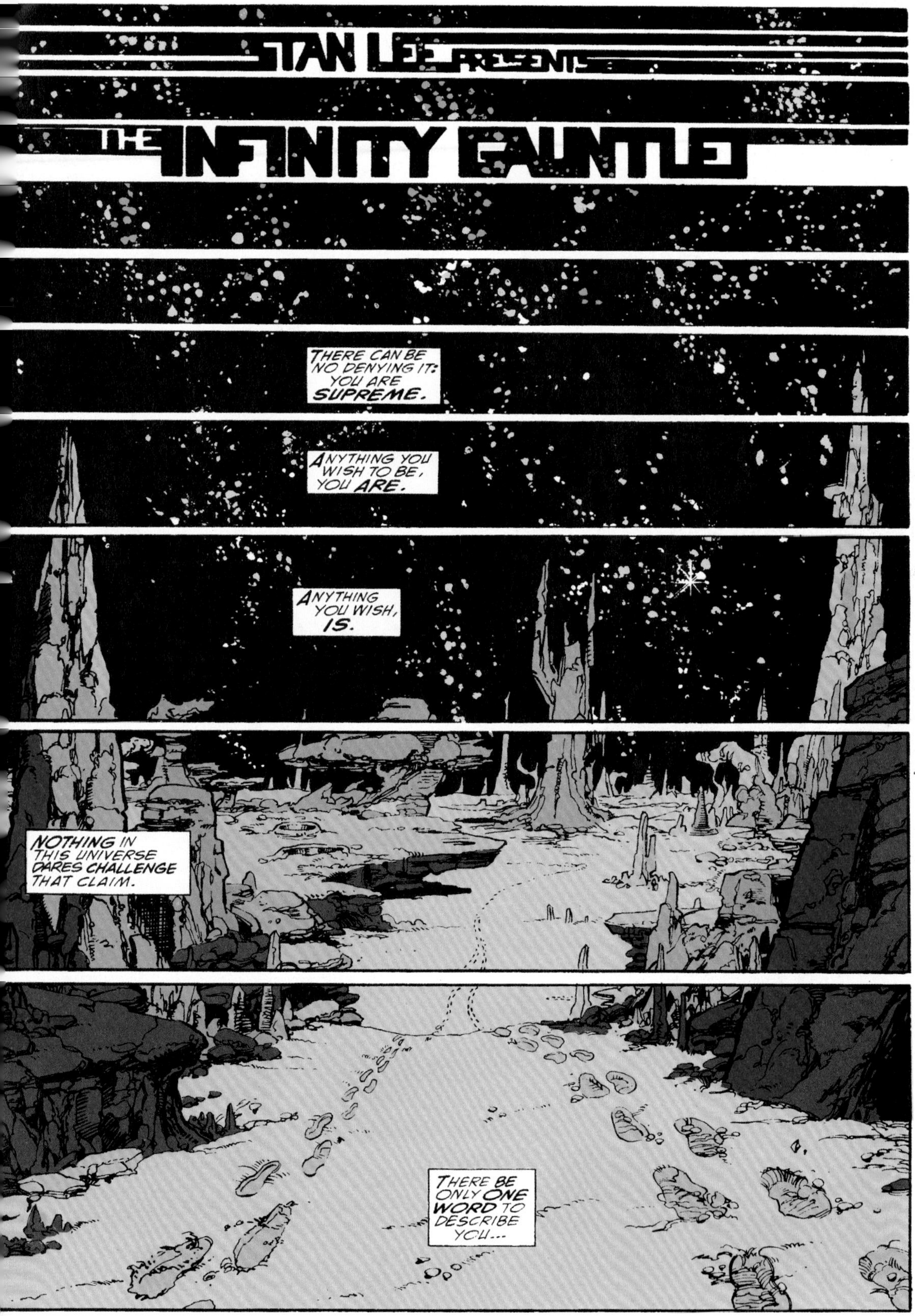
STAN LEE PRESENTS
THE INFINITY GAUNTLET
THERE CAN BE NO DENYING IT: YOU ARE SUPREME.
ANYTHING YOU WISH TO BE, YOU ARE.
ANYTHING YOU WISH, IS.
NOTHING IN THIS UNIVERSE DARES CHALLENGE THAT CLAIM.
THERE BE ONLY ONE WORD TO DESCRIBE YOU...

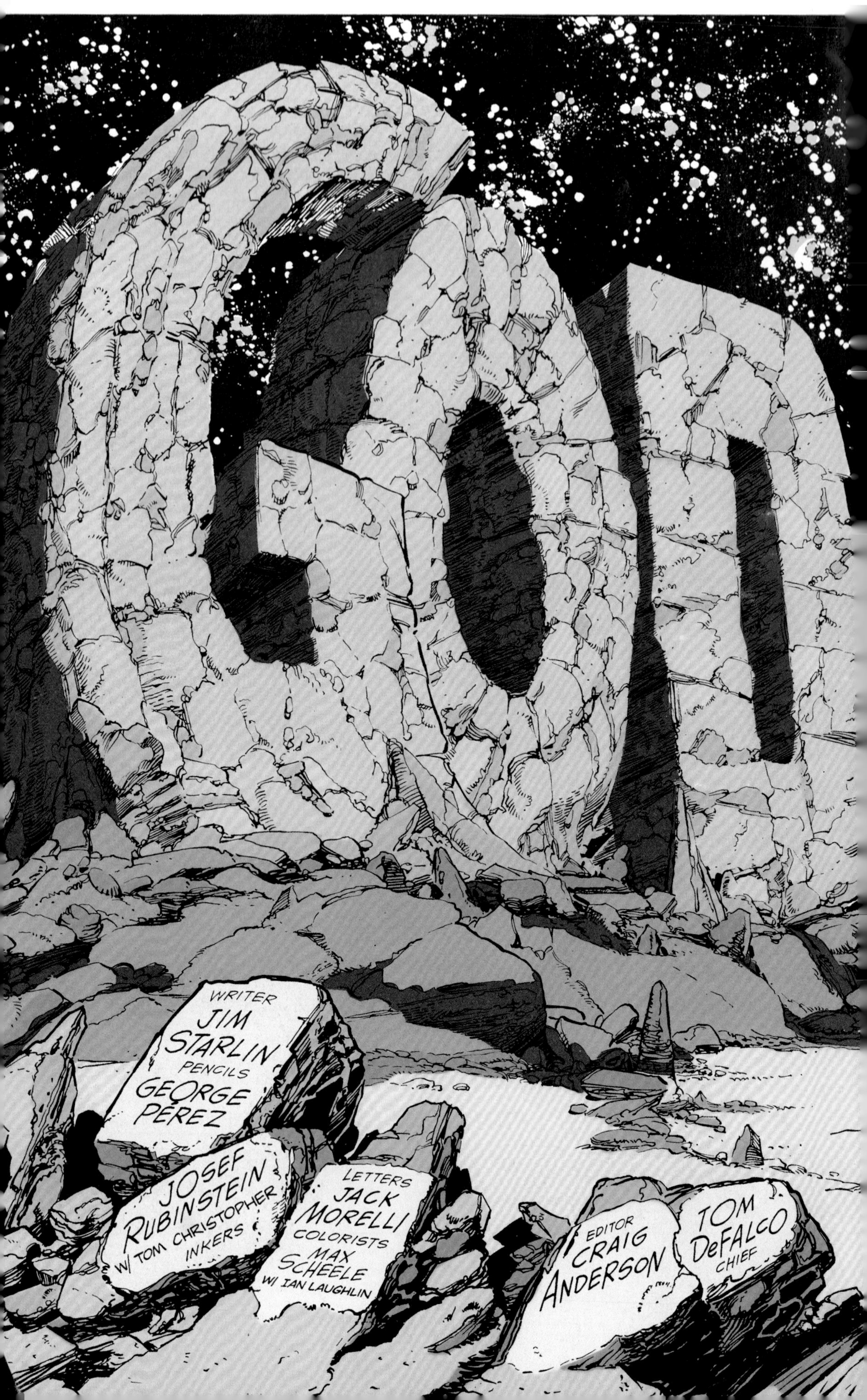

GOD
WRITER
JIM STARLIN
PENCILS
GEORGE PÉREZ
JOSEF RUBINSTEIN
W/ TOM CHRISTOPHER
INKERS
LETTERS
JACK MORELLI
COLORISTS
MAX SCHEELE
W/ IAN LAUGHLIN
EDITOR
CRAIG ANDERSON
TOM DeFALCO
CHIEF

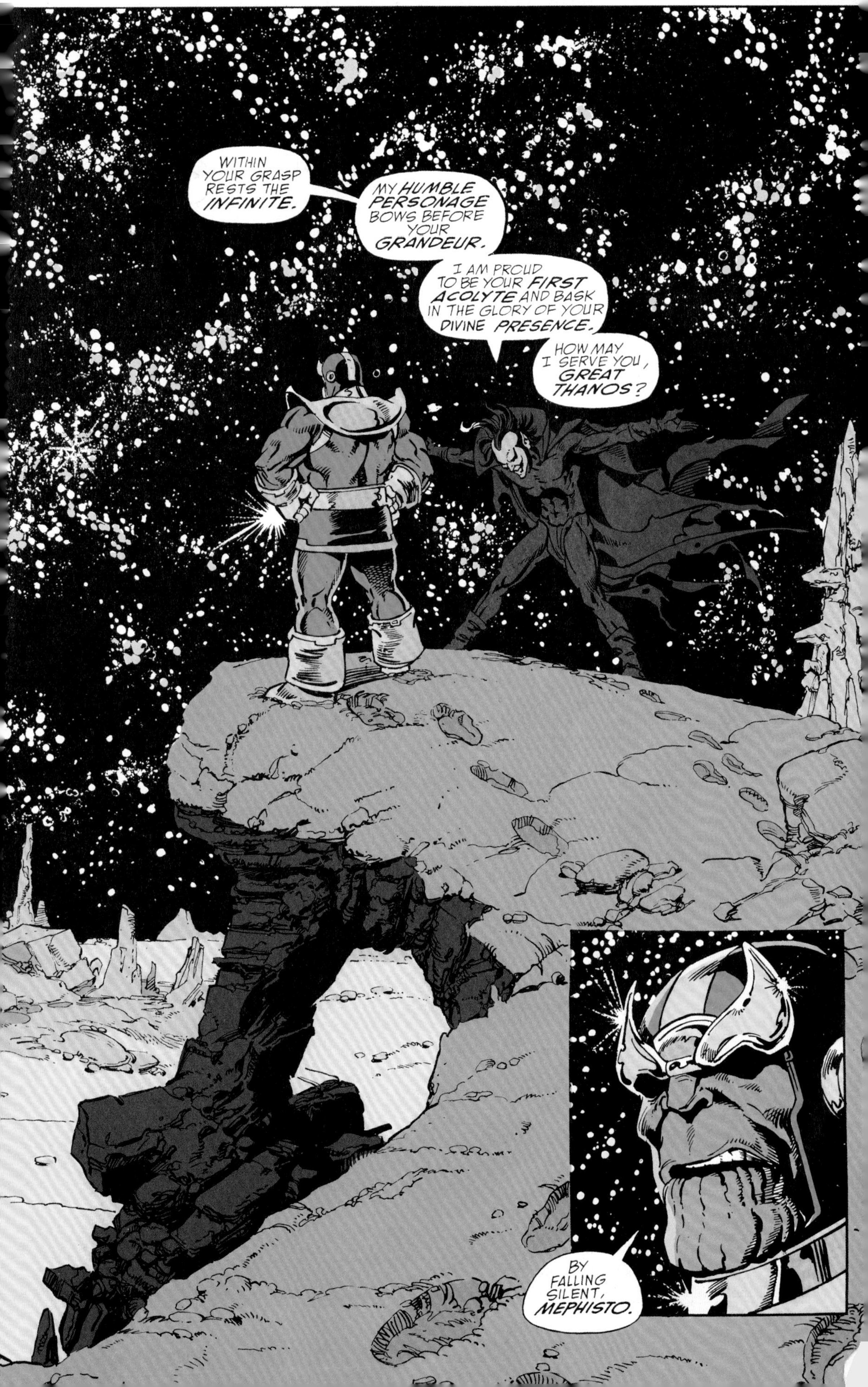

WITHIN YOUR GRASP RESTS THE INFINITE.
MY HUMBLE PERSONAGE BOWS BEFORE YOUR GRANDEUR.
I AM PROUD TO BE YOUR FIRST ACOLYTE AND BASK IN THE GLORY OF YOUR DIVINE PRESENCE.
HOW MAY I SERVE YOU, GREAT THANOS?
BY FALLING SILENT, MEPHISTO.

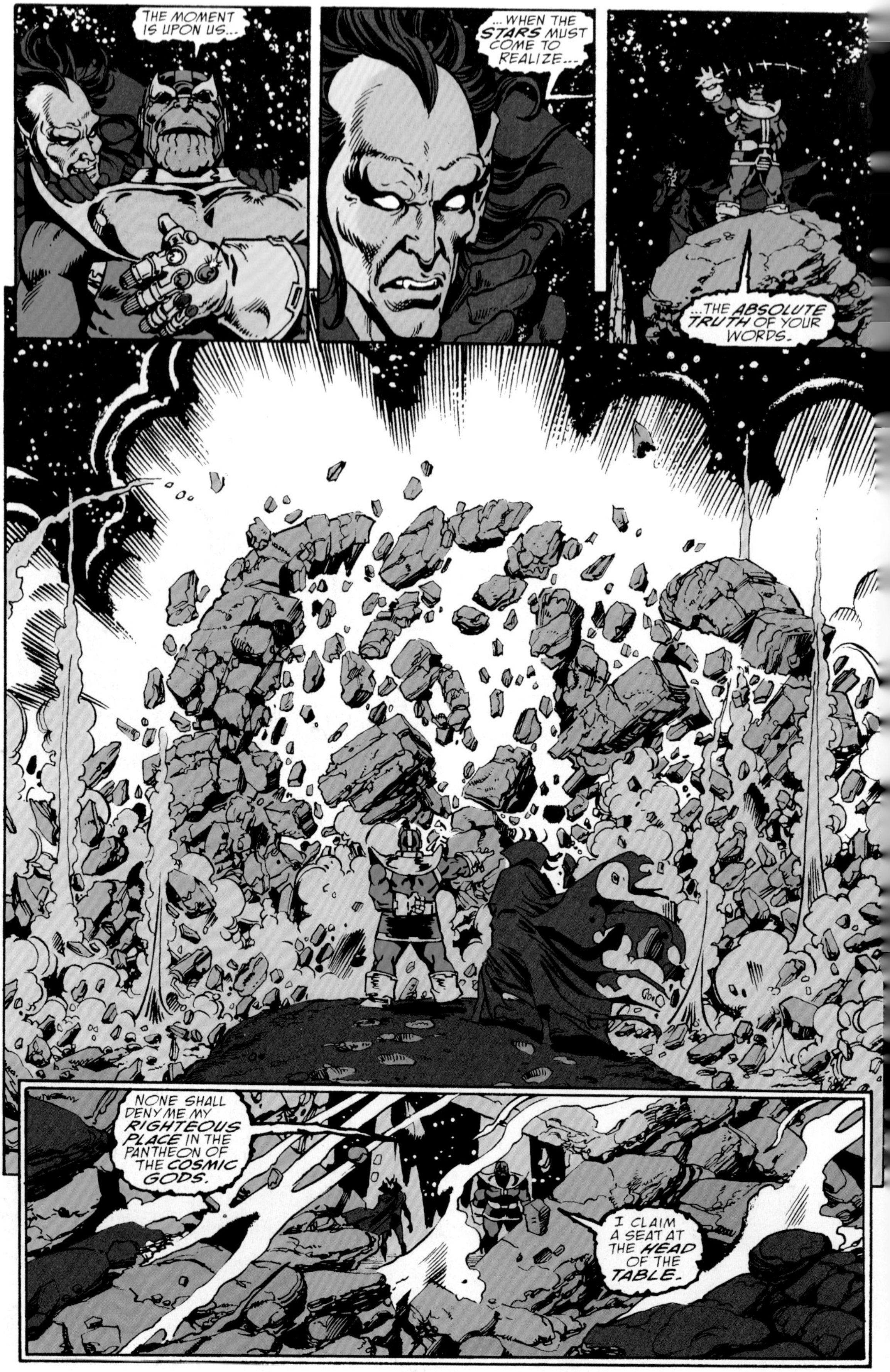
THE MOMENT IS UPON US...
...WHEN THE STARS MUST COME TO REALIZE...
...THE ABSOLUTE TRUTH OF YOUR WORDS.
NONE SHALL DENY ME MY RIGHTEOUS PLACE IN THE PANTHEON OF THE COSMIC GODS.
I CLAIM A SEAT AT THE HEAD OF THE TABLE.

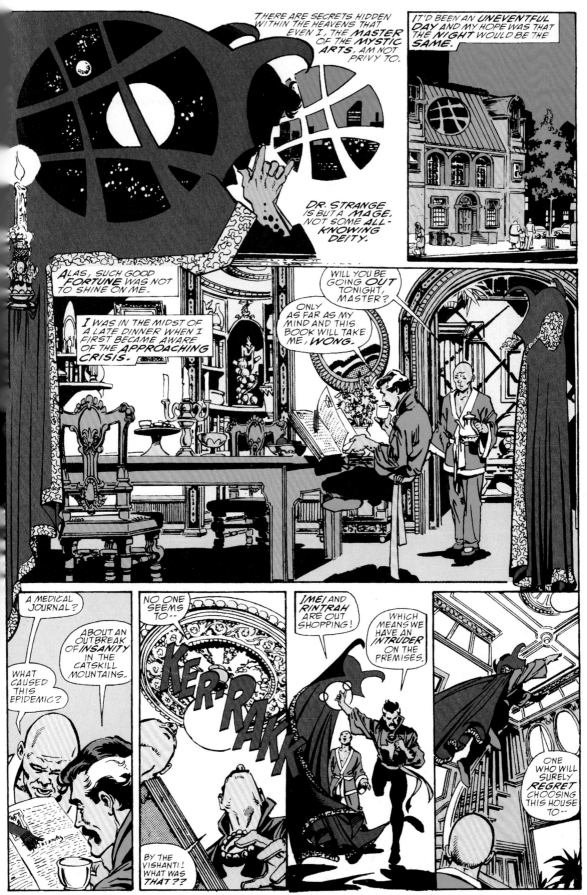

THERE ARE SECRETS HIDDEN WITHIN THE HEAVENS THAT EVEN I, THE MASTER OF THE MYSTIC ARTS, AM NOT PRIVY TO.

IT'D BEEN AN *UNEVENTFUL DAY* AND MY HOPE WAS THAT THE *NIGHT* WOULD BE THE *SAME.*

DR. STRANGE IS BUT A *MAGE,* NOT SOME *ALL-KNOWING DEITY.*

ALAS, SUCH GOOD *FORTUNE* WAS NOT TO SHINE ON ME.

I WAS IN THE MIDST OF A LATE DINNER WHEN I FIRST BECAME AWARE OF THE *APPROACHING CRISIS.*

WILL YOU BE GOING *OUT* TONIGHT, MASTER?

ONLY AS FAR AS MY *MIND* AND THIS *BOOK* WILL TAKE ME, *WONG.*

A MEDICAL JOURNAL?

ABOUT AN OUTBREAK OF *INSANITY* IN THE CATSKILL MOUNTAINS.

WHAT CAUSED THIS EPIDEMIC?

NO ONE SEEMS TO --

KER-RAKK

BY THE *VISHANTI!* WHAT WAS *THAT??*

IMEI AND *RINTRAH* ARE OUT SHOPPING!

WHICH MEANS WE HAVE AN *INTRUDER* ON THE PREMISES.

ONE WHO WILL SURELY *REGRET* CHOOSING THIS HOUSE TO --

9

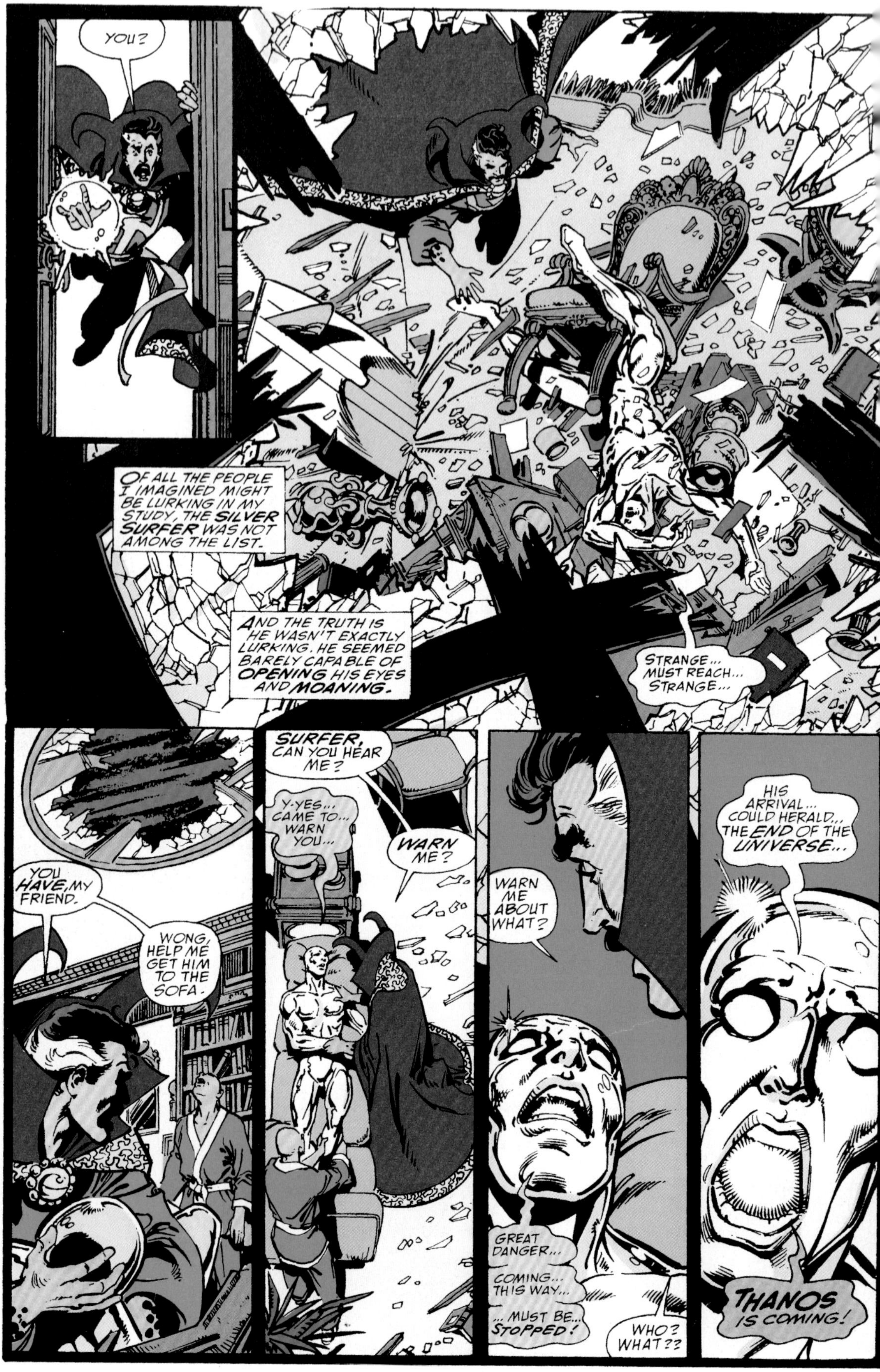
YOU?
OF ALL THE PEOPLE I IMAGINED MIGHT BE LURKING IN MY STUDY, THE SILVER SURFER WAS NOT AMONG THE LIST.
AND THE TRUTH IS HE WASN'T EXACTLY LURKING. HE SEEMED BARELY CAPABLE OF OPENING HIS EYES AND MOANING.
STRANGE... MUST REACH... STRANGE...
YOU HAVE, MY FRIEND.
WONG, HELP ME GET HIM TO THE SOFA.
SURFER, CAN YOU HEAR ME?
Y-YES... CAME TO... WARN YOU...
WARN ME?
WARN ME ABOUT WHAT?
GREAT DANGER...
COMING... THIS WAY...
... MUST BE... STOPPED!
WHO? WHAT??
HIS ARRIVAL... COULD HERALD... THE END OF THE UNIVERSE...
THANOS IS COMING!

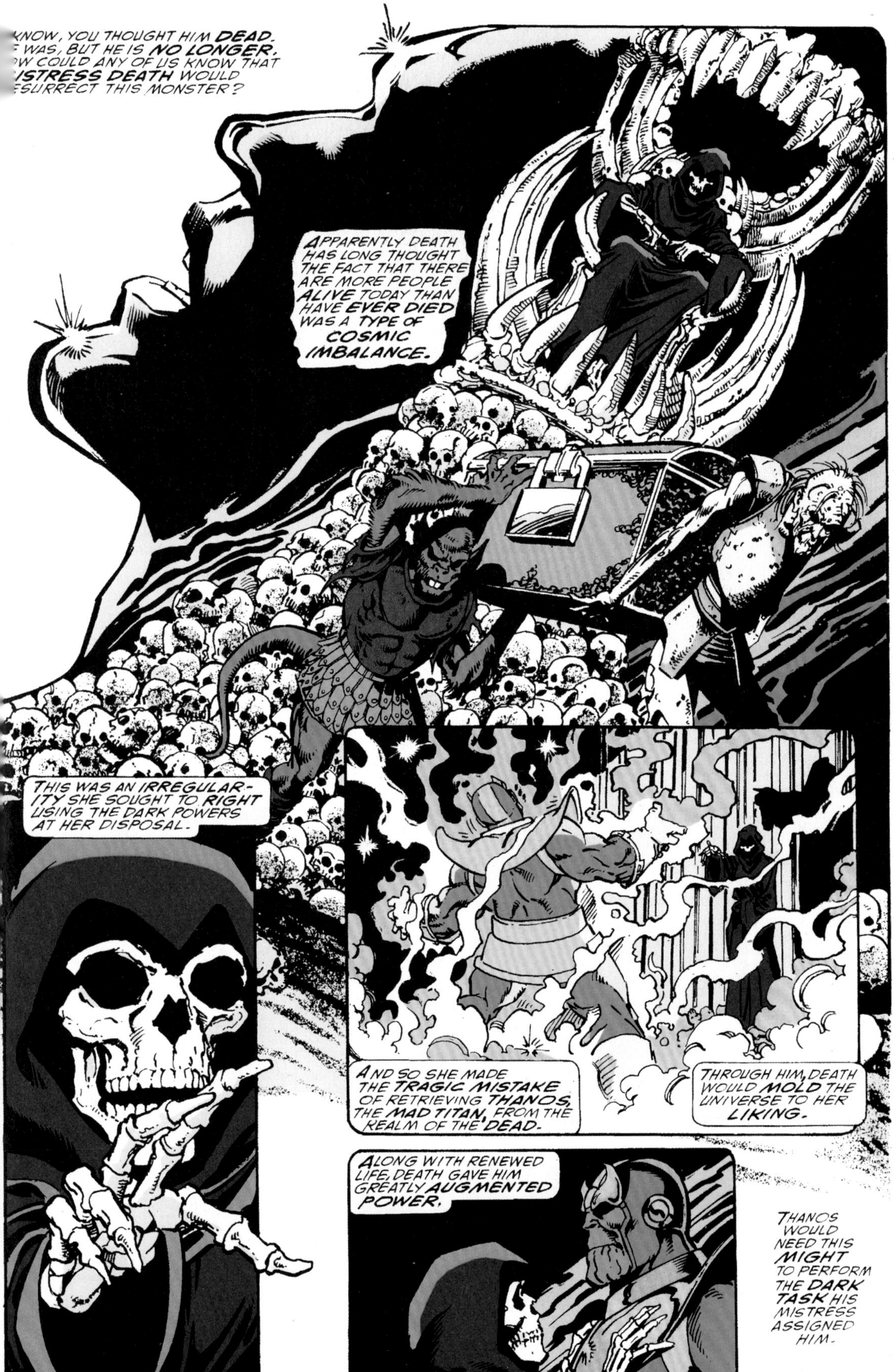
KNOW, YOU THOUGHT HIM DEAD. E WAS, BUT HE IS NO LONGER. W COULD ANY OF US KNOW THAT ISTRESS DEATH WOULD ESURRECT THIS MONSTER?
APPARENTLY DEATH HAS LONG THOUGHT THE FACT THAT THERE ARE MORE PEOPLE ALIVE TODAY THAN HAVE EVER DIED WAS A TYPE OF COSMIC IMBALANCE.
THIS WAS AN IRREGULARITY SHE SOUGHT TO RIGHT USING THE DARK POWERS AT HER DISPOSAL.
AND SO SHE MADE THE TRAGIC MISTAKE OF RETRIEVING THANOS, THE MAD TITAN, FROM THE REALM OF THE DEAD.
THROUGH HIM, DEATH WOULD MOLD THE UNIVERSE TO HER LIKING.
ALONG WITH RENEWED LIFE, DEATH GAVE HIM GREATLY AUGMENTED POWER.
THANOS WOULD NEED THIS MIGHT TO PERFORM THE DARK TASK HIS MISTRESS ASSIGNED HIM.

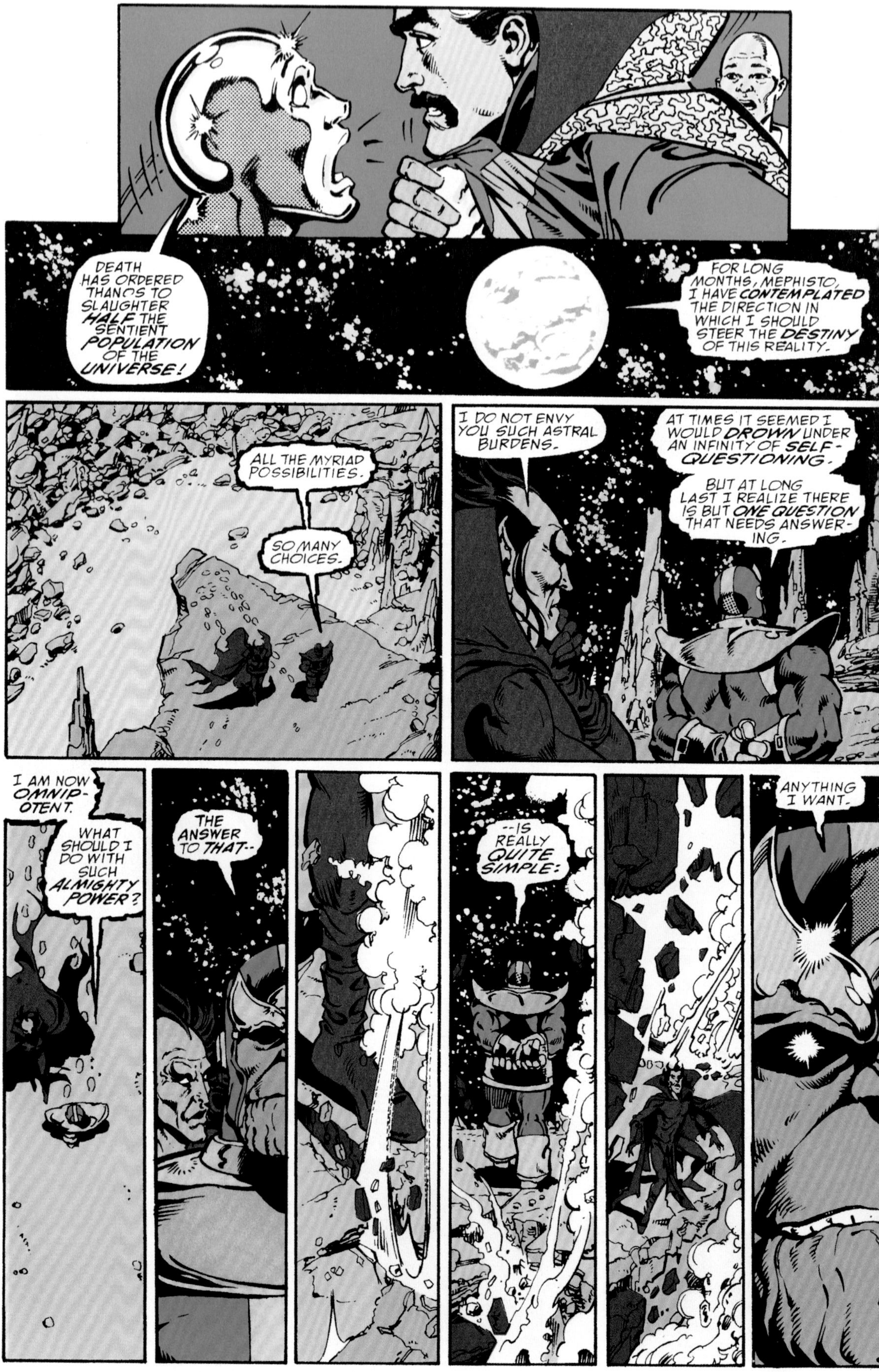
DEATH HAS ORDERED THANOS TO SLAUGHTER HALF THE SENTIENT POPULATION OF THE UNIVERSE!
FOR LONG MONTHS, MEPHISTO, I HAVE CONTEMPLATED THE DIRECTION IN WHICH I SHOULD STEER THE DESTINY OF THIS REALITY.
ALL THE MYRIAD POSSIBILITIES.
SO MANY CHOICES.
I DO NOT ENVY YOU SUCH ASTRAL BURDENS.
AT TIMES IT SEEMED I WOULD DROWN UNDER AN INFINITY OF SELF-QUESTIONING.
BUT AT LONG LAST I REALIZE THERE IS BUT ONE QUESTION THAT NEEDS ANSWERING.
I AM NOW OMNIPOTENT.
WHAT SHOULD I DO WITH SUCH ALMIGHTY POWER?
THE ANSWER TO THAT--
--IS REALLY QUITE SIMPLE:
ANYTHING I WANT.

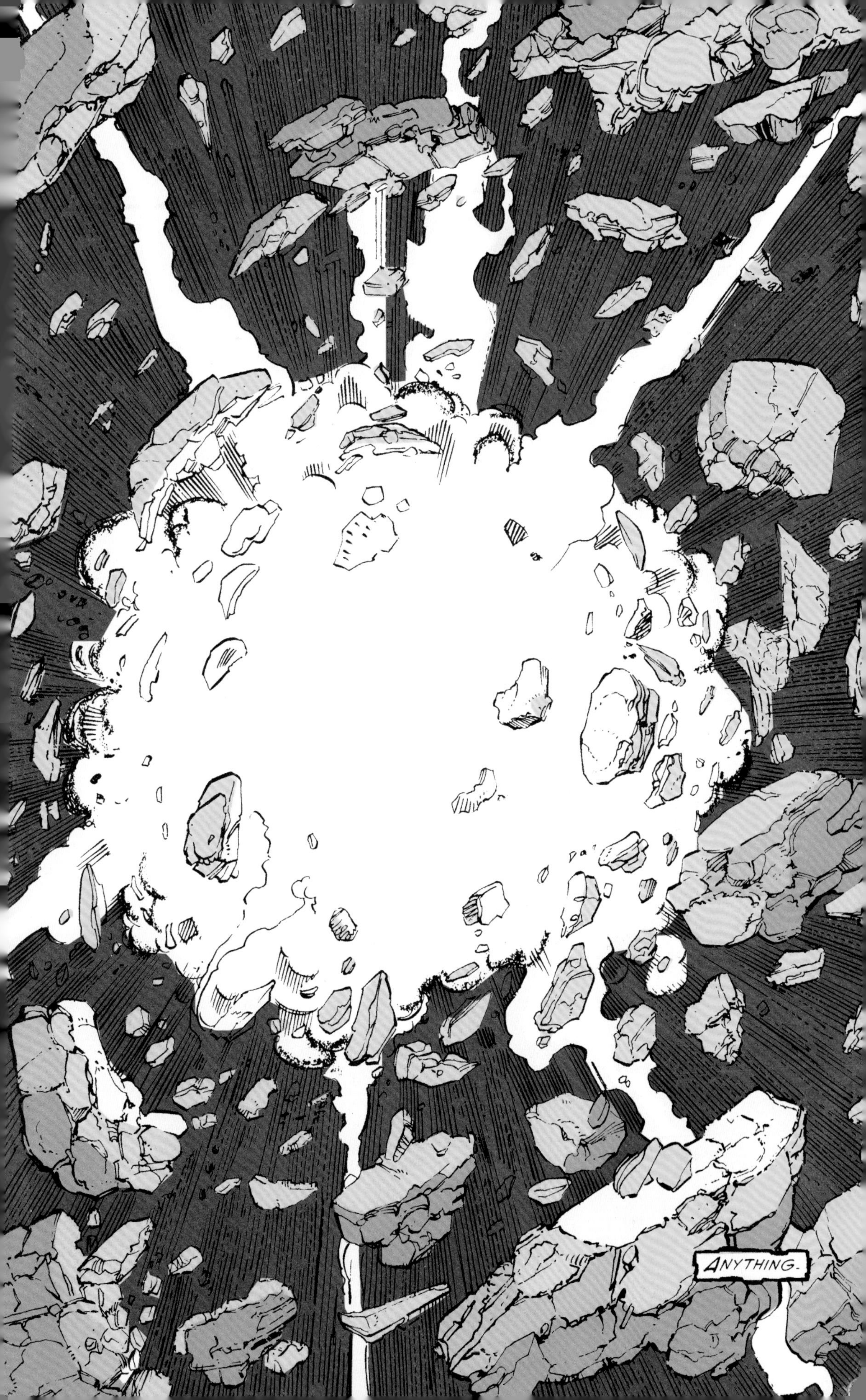
ANYTHING.

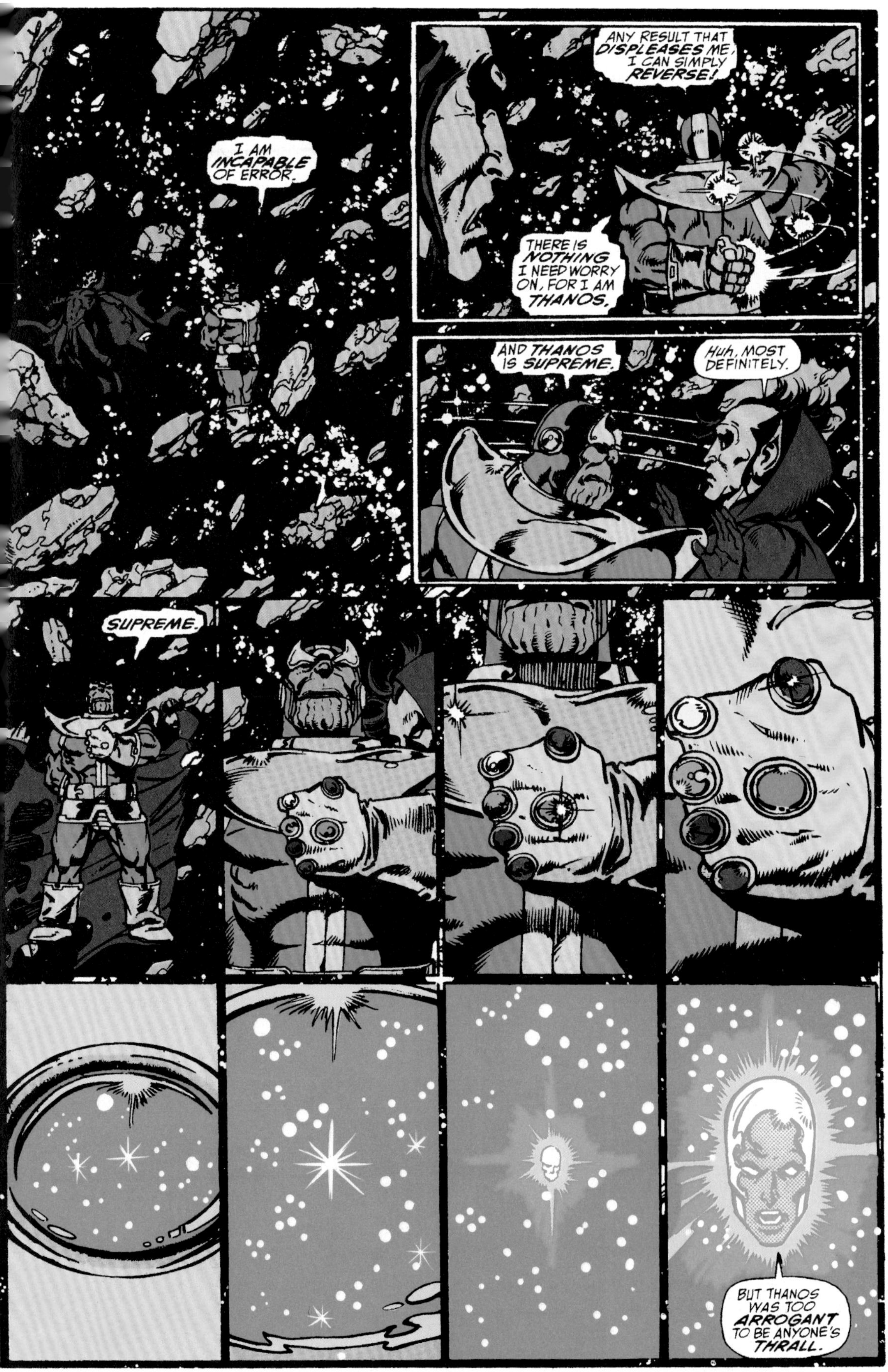

I AM INCAPABLE OF ERROR.
ANY RESULT THAT DISPLEASES ME, I CAN SIMPLY REVERSE!
THERE IS NOTHING I NEED WORRY ON, FOR I AM THANOS.
AND THANOS IS SUPREME.
Huh, MOST DEFINITELY.
SUPREME.
BUT THANOS WAS TOO ARROGANT TO BE ANYONE'S THRALL.

HIS SINISTER SCHEME WAS CONCEIVED WHILE GAZING INTO THE DEPTHS OF DEATH'S *INFINITY WELL.*

NOT EVEN DEATH REALIZED WHAT *LIMITLESS MIGHT* THE MAD TITAN WAS STRIVING FOR. THROUGH CUNNING, SHEER STRENGTH, AND MURDER, THANOS WRESTED THE *INFINITY GEMS* FROM THOSE THAT POSSESSED THEM AND WITH EACH ACQUISITION HE GAINED *MASTERY* OVER...

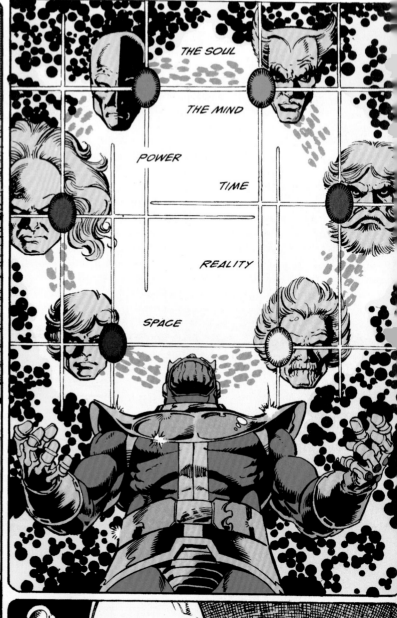

THE SOUL

THE MIND

POWER

TIME

REALITY

SPACE

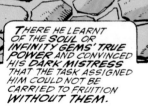

THERE HE LEARNT OF THE *SOUL* OR INFINITY GEMS' TRUE *POWER* AND CONVINCED HIS *DARK MISTRESS* THAT THE TASK ASSIGNED HIM COULD NOT BE CARRIED TO FRUITION *WITHOUT THEM.*

IN OTHER WORDS, THANOS NOW HAS THE UNBRIDLED *POWER* OF A GOD!

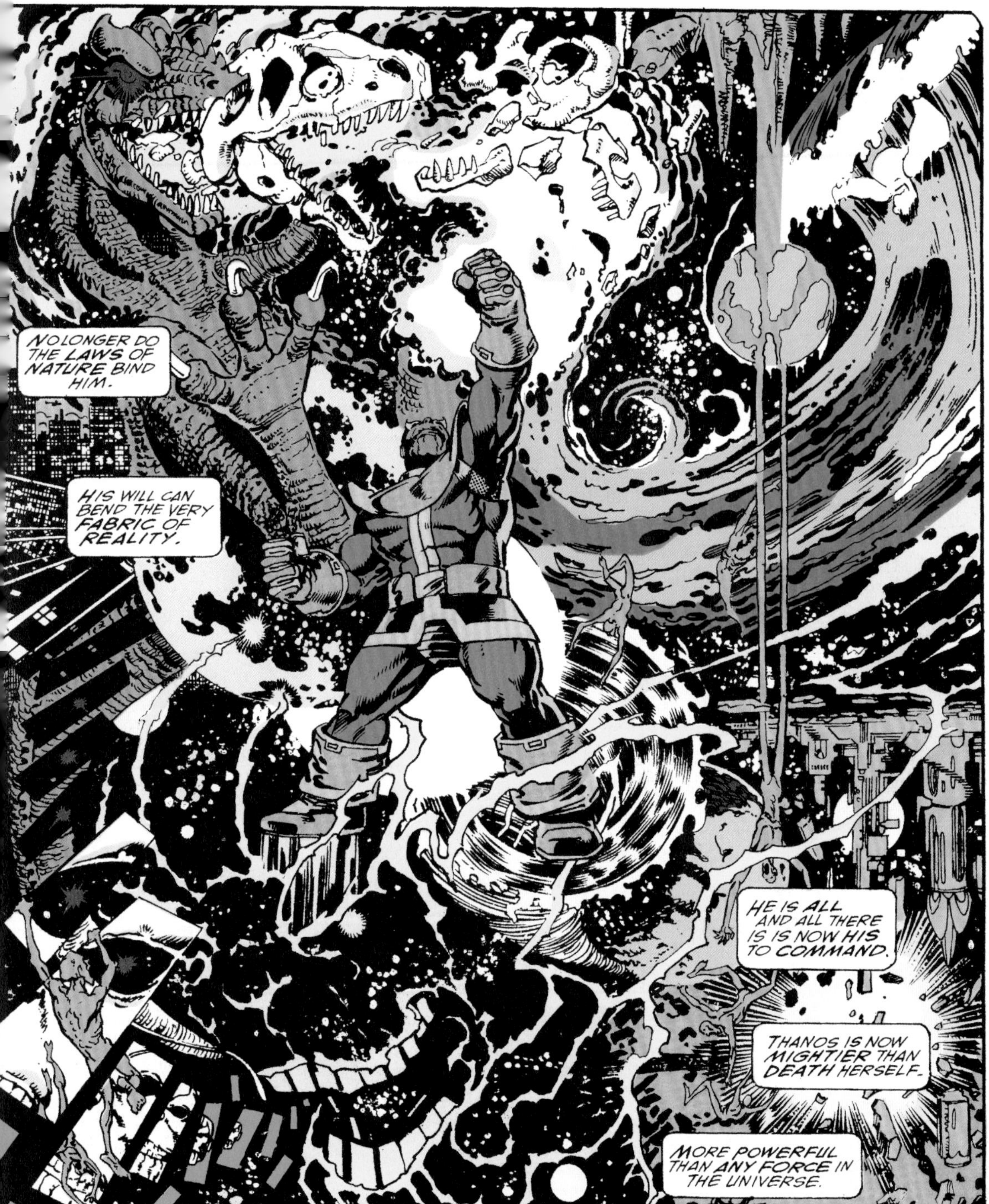
NO LONGER DO THE LAWS OF NATURE BIND HIM.
HIS WILL CAN BEND THE VERY FABRIC OF REALITY.
HE IS ALL AND ALL THERE IS IS NOW HIS TO COMMAND.
THANOS IS NOW MIGHTIER THAN DEATH HERSELF.
MORE POWERFUL THAN ANY FORCE IN THE UNIVERSE.

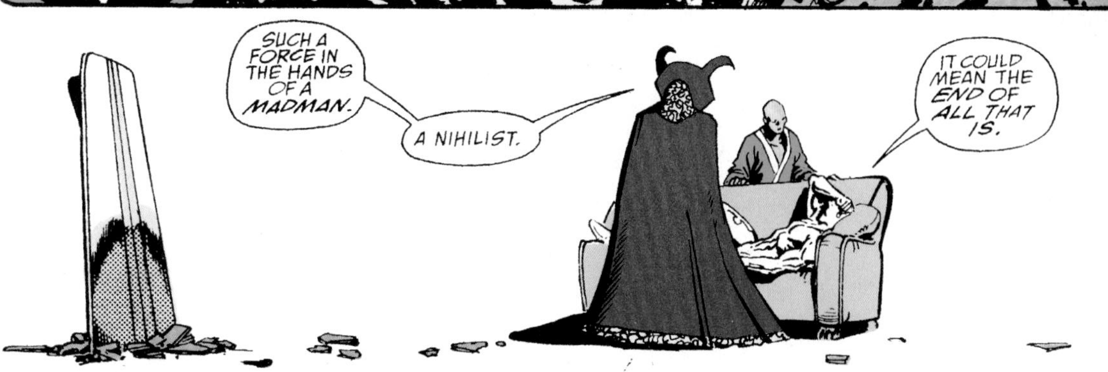
SUCH A FORCE IN THE HANDS OF A MADMAN.
A NIHILIST.
IT COULD MEAN THE END OF ALL THAT IS.

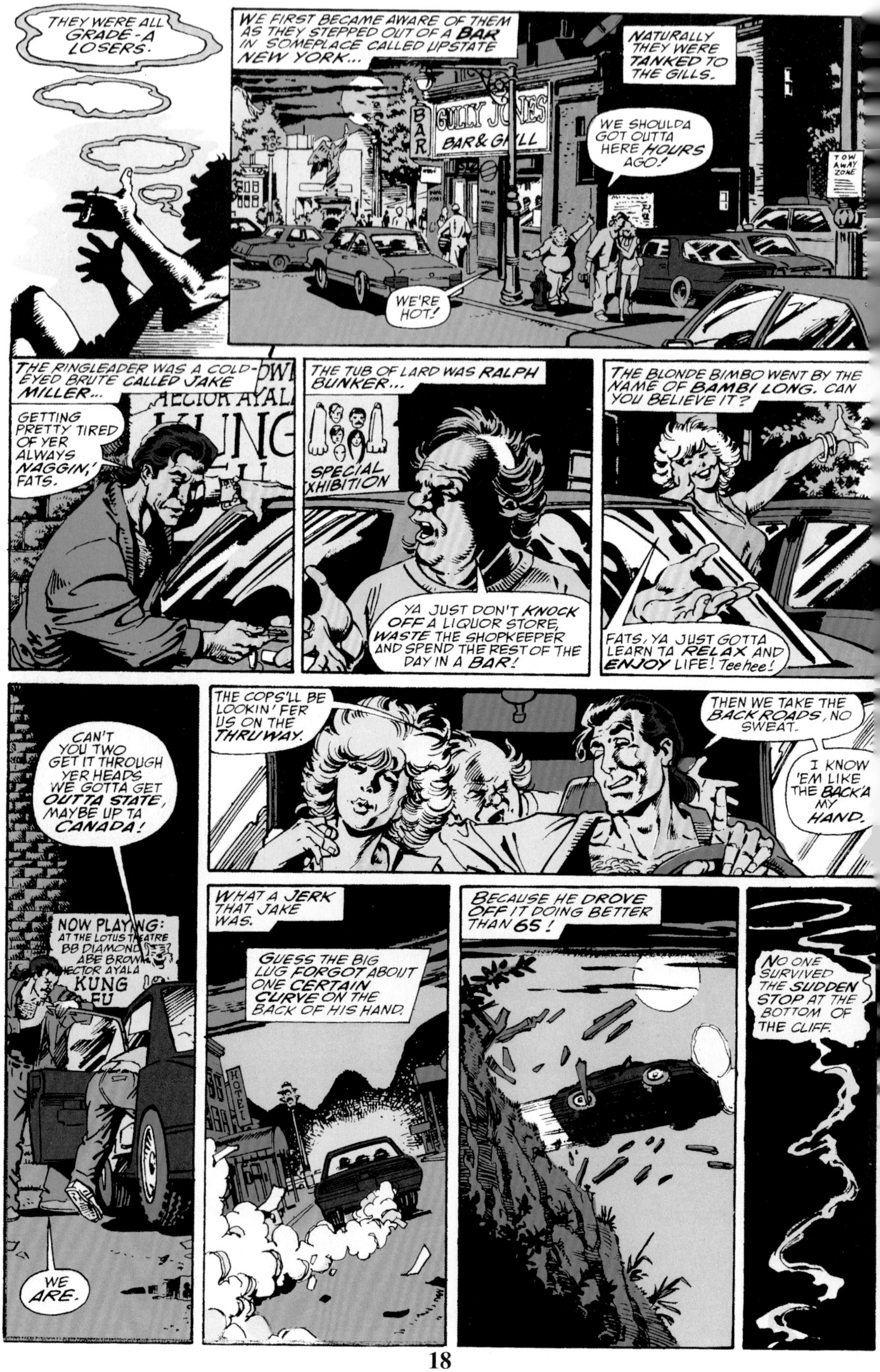
THEY WERE ALL GRADE-A LOSERS.
WE FIRST BECAME AWARE OF THEM AS THEY STEPPED OUT OF A BAR IN SOMEPLACE CALLED UPSTATE NEW YORK...
NATURALLY THEY WERE TANKED TO THE GILLS.
BAR
GULLY JONES
BAR & GRILL
WE SHOULDA GOT OUTTA HERE HOURS AGO!
TOW AWAY ZONE
WE'RE HOT!
THE RINGLEADER WAS A COLD-EYED BRUTE CALLED JAKE MILLER...
GETTING PRETTY TIRED OF YER ALWAYS NAGGIN,' FATS.
THE TUB OF LARD WAS RALPH BUNKER...
SPECIAL EXHIBITION
YA JUST DON'T KNOCK OFF A LIQUOR STORE, WASTE THE SHOPKEEPER AND SPEND THE REST OF THE DAY IN A BAR!
THE BLONDE BIMBO WENT BY THE NAME OF BAMBI LONG. CAN YOU BELIEVE IT?
FATS, YA JUST GOTTA LEARN TA RELAX AND ENJOY LIFE! Teehee!
CAN'T YOU TWO GET IT THROUGH YER HEADS WE GOTTA GET OUTTA STATE, MAYBE UP TA CANADA!
NOW PLAYING: AT THE LOTUS THEATRE BB DIAMOND ABE BROWN HECTOR AYALA KUNG FU
WE ARE.
THE COPS'LL BE LOOKIN' FER US ON THE THRUWAY.
THEN WE TAKE THE BACK ROADS, NO SWEAT.
I KNOW 'EM LIKE THE BACK'A MY HAND.
WHAT A JERK THAT JAKE WAS.
GUESS THE BIG LUG FORGOT ABOUT ONE CERTAIN CURVE ON THE BACK OF HIS HAND.
HOTEL
BECAUSE HE DROVE OFF IT DOING BETTER THAN 65!
NO ONE SURVIVED THE SUDDEN STOP AT THE BOTTOM OF THE CLIFF.

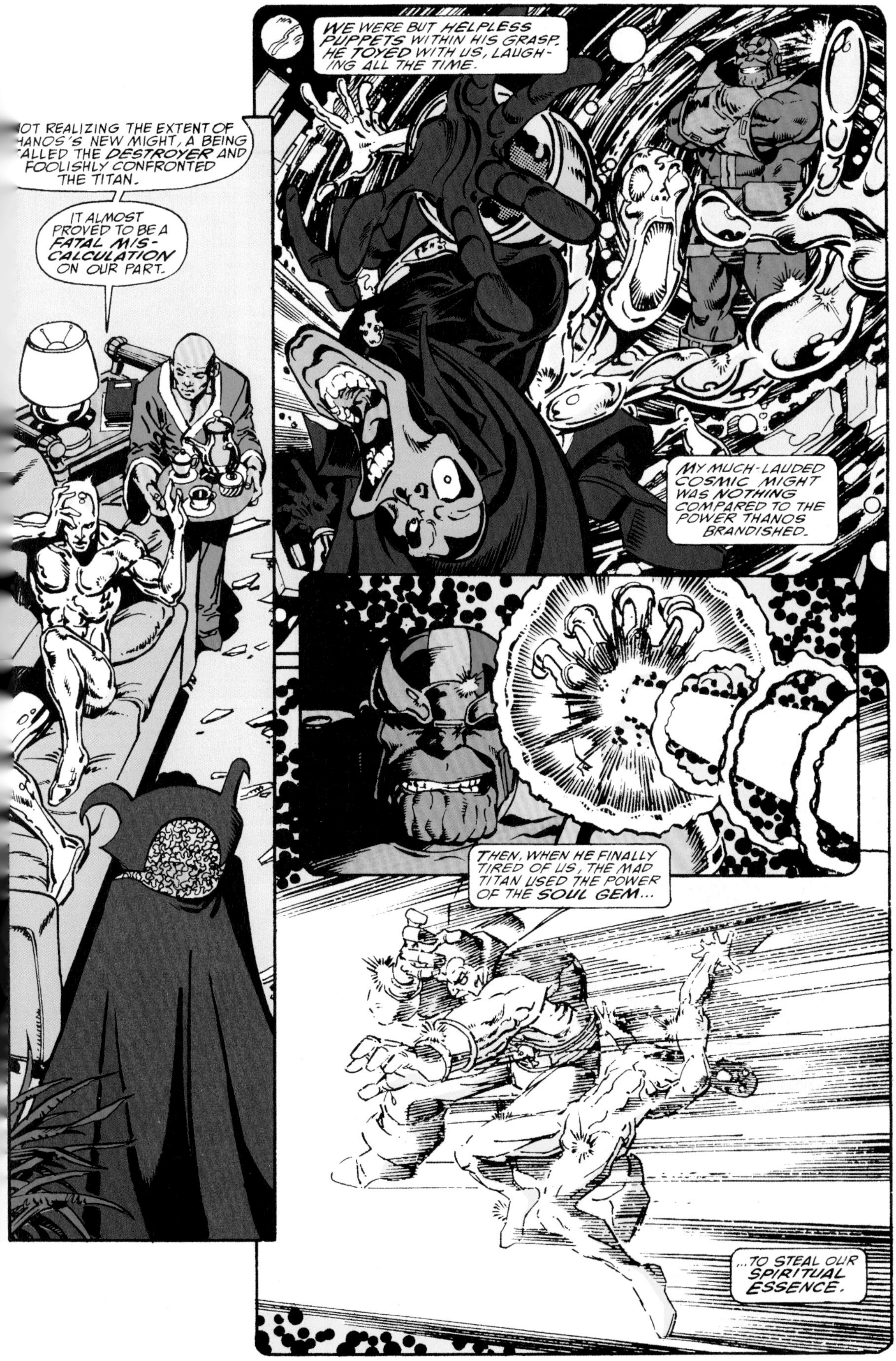
OT REALIZING THE EXTENT OF HANOS'S NEW MIGHT, A BEING ALLED THE DESTROYER AND FOOLISHLY CONFRONTED THE TITAN.
IT ALMOST PROVED TO BE A FATAL MIS-CALCULATION ON OUR PART.
WE WERE BUT HELPLESS PUPPETS WITHIN HIS GRASP. HE TOYED WITH US, LAUGH-ING ALL THE TIME.
MY MUCH-LAUDED COSMIC MIGHT WAS NOTHING COMPARED TO THE POWER THANOS BRANDISHED.
THEN, WHEN HE FINALLY TIRED OF US, THE MAD TITAN USED THE POWER OF THE SOUL GEM...
...TO STEAL OUR SPIRITUAL ESSENCE.

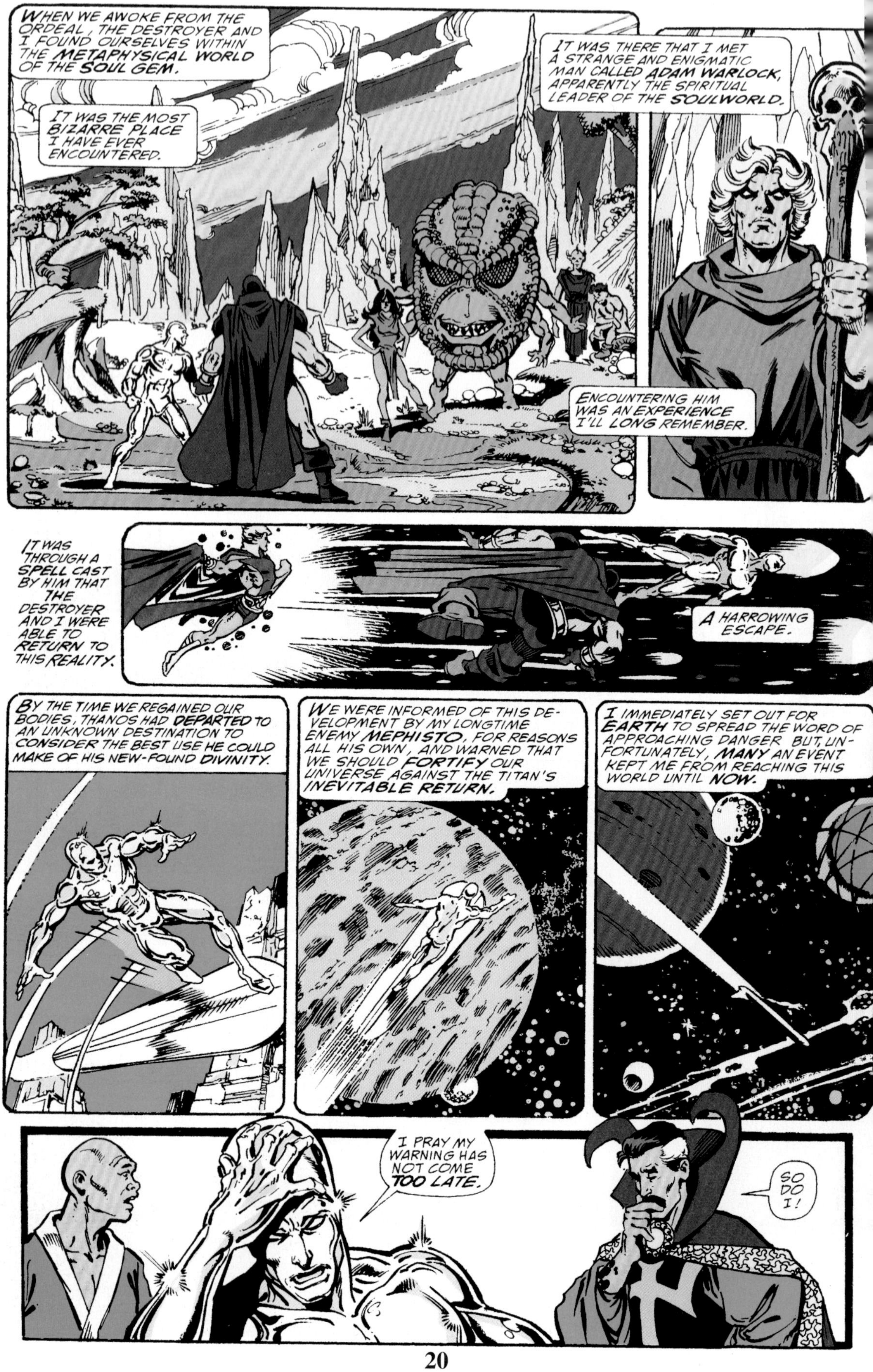
WHEN WE AWOKE FROM THE ORDEAL, THE DESTROYER AND I FOUND OURSELVES WITHIN THE METAPHYSICAL WORLD OF THE SOUL GEM.
IT WAS THE MOST BIZARRE PLACE I HAVE EVER ENCOUNTERED.
IT WAS THERE THAT I MET A STRANGE AND ENIGMATIC MAN CALLED ADAM WARLOCK, APPARENTLY THE SPIRITUAL LEADER OF THE SOULWORLD.
ENCOUNTERING HIM WAS AN EXPERIENCE I'LL LONG REMEMBER.
IT WAS THROUGH A SPELL CAST BY HIM THAT THE DESTROYER AND I WERE ABLE TO RETURN TO THIS REALITY.
A HARROWING ESCAPE.
BY THE TIME WE REGAINED OUR BODIES, THANOS HAD DEPARTED TO AN UNKNOWN DESTINATION TO CONSIDER THE BEST USE HE COULD MAKE OF HIS NEW-FOUND DIVINITY.
WE WERE INFORMED OF THIS DEVELOPMENT BY MY LONGTIME ENEMY MEPHISTO, FOR REASONS ALL HIS OWN, AND WARNED THAT WE SHOULD FORTIFY OUR UNIVERSE AGAINST THE TITAN'S INEVITABLE RETURN.
I IMMEDIATELY SET OUT FOR EARTH TO SPREAD THE WORD OF APPROACHING DANGER BUT, UNFORTUNATELY, MANY AN EVENT KEPT ME FROM REACHING THIS WORLD UNTIL NOW.
I PRAY MY WARNING HAS NOT COME TOO LATE.
SO DO I!

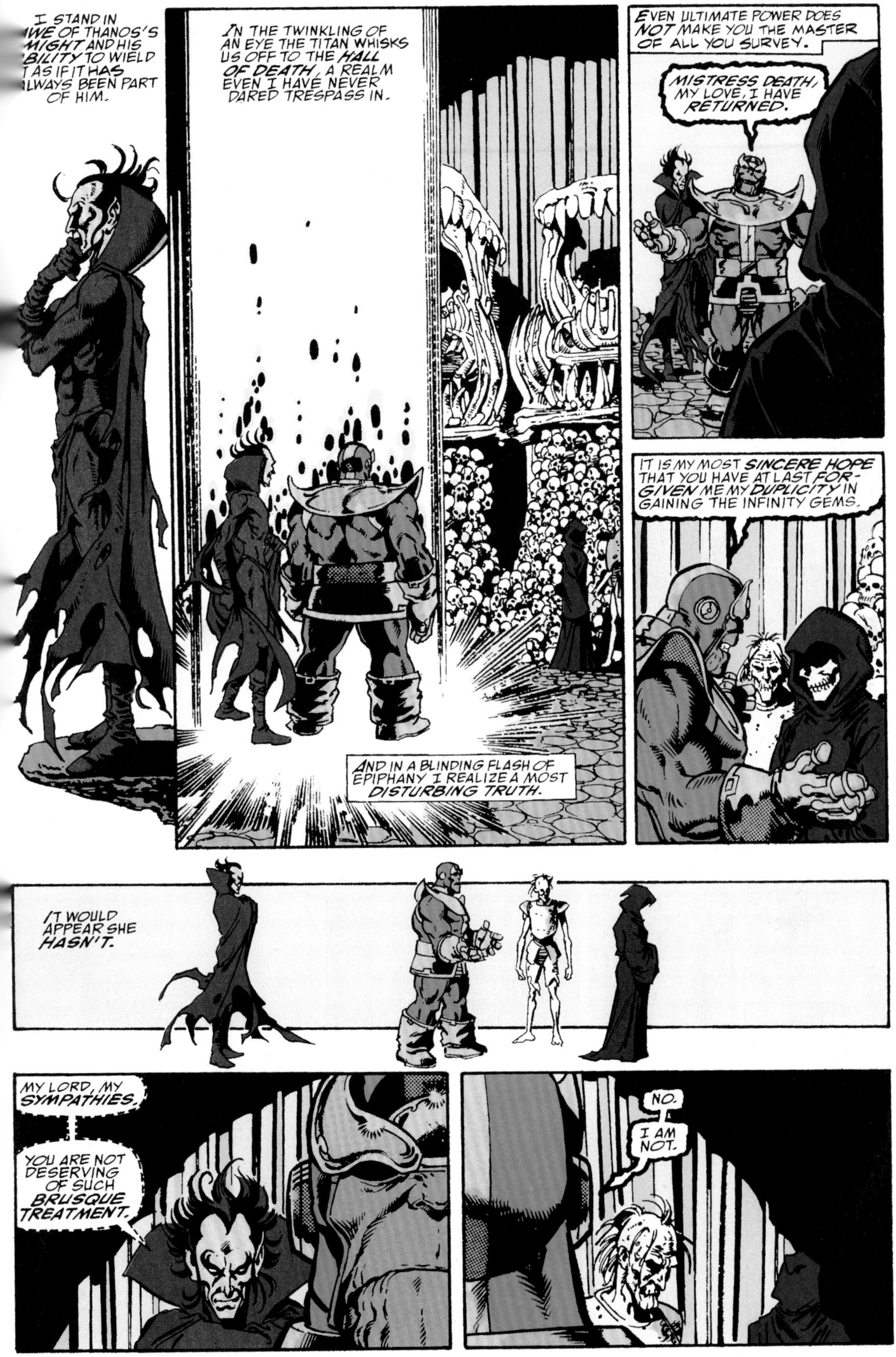
I STAND IN AWE OF THANOS'S MIGHT AND HIS ABILITY TO WIELD IT AS IF IT HAS ALWAYS BEEN PART OF HIM.
IN THE TWINKLING OF AN EYE THE TITAN WHISKS US OFF TO THE HALL OF DEATH, A REALM EVEN I HAVE NEVER DARED TRESPASS IN.
AND IN A BLINDING FLASH OF EPIPHANY I REALIZE A MOST DISTURBING TRUTH.
EVEN ULTIMATE POWER DOES NOT MAKE YOU THE MASTER OF ALL YOU SURVEY.
MISTRESS DEATH, MY LOVE, I HAVE RETURNED.
IT IS MY MOST SINCERE HOPE THAT YOU HAVE AT LAST FORGIVEN ME MY DUPLICITY IN GAINING THE INFINITY GEMS.
IT WOULD APPEAR SHE HASN'T.
MY LORD, MY SYMPATHIES.
YOU ARE NOT DESERVING OF SUCH BRUSQUE TREATMENT.
NO.
I AM NOT.

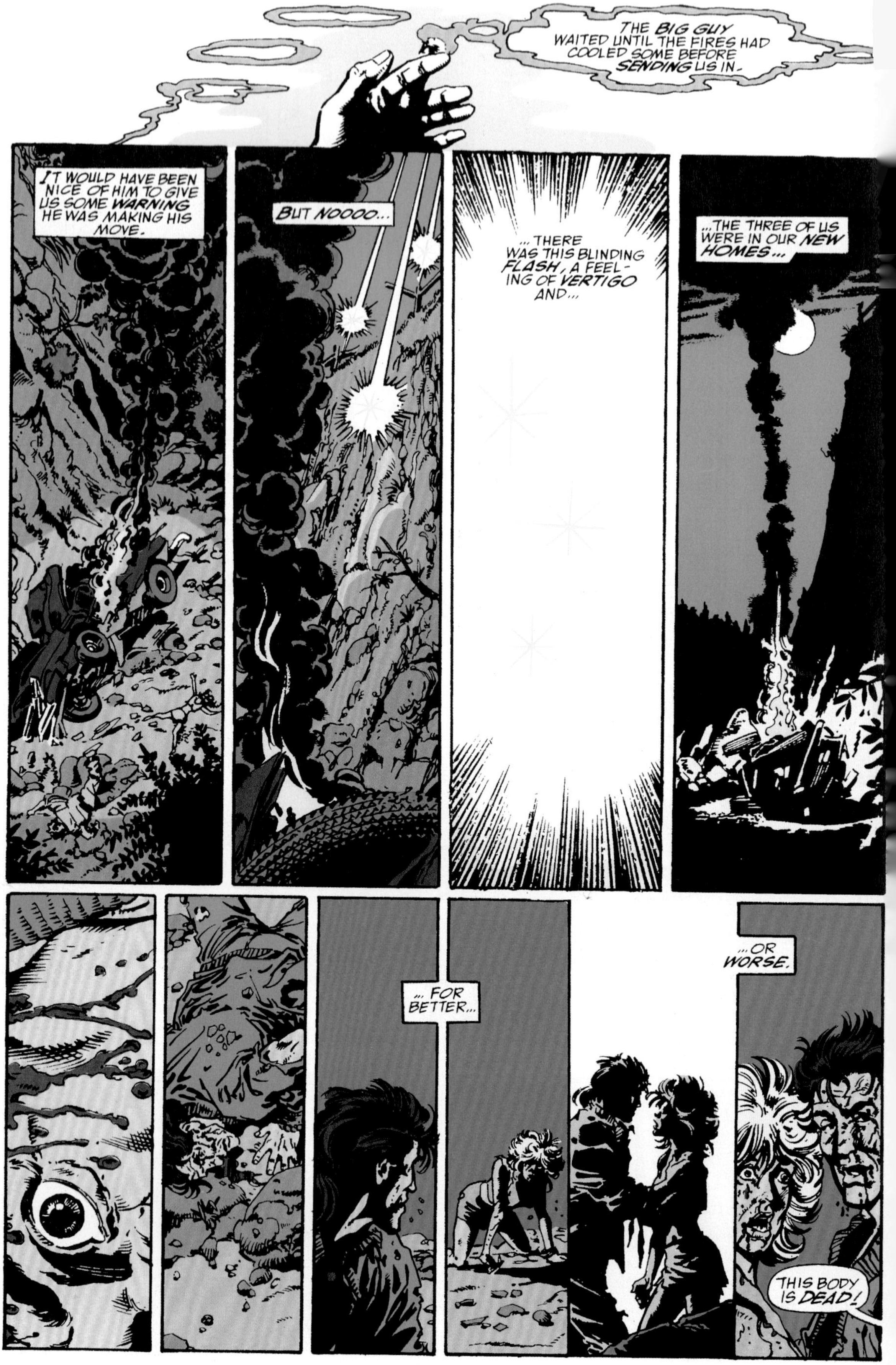
THE BIG GUY WAITED UNTIL THE FIRES HAD COOLED SOME BEFORE SENDING US IN.
IT WOULD HAVE BEEN NICE OF HIM TO GIVE US SOME WARNING HE WAS MAKING HIS MOVE.
BUT NOOOO...
...THERE WAS THIS BLINDING FLASH, A FEELING OF VERTIGO AND...
...THE THREE OF US WERE IN OUR NEW HOMES...
...FOR BETTER...
...OR WORSE.
THIS BODY IS DEAD!

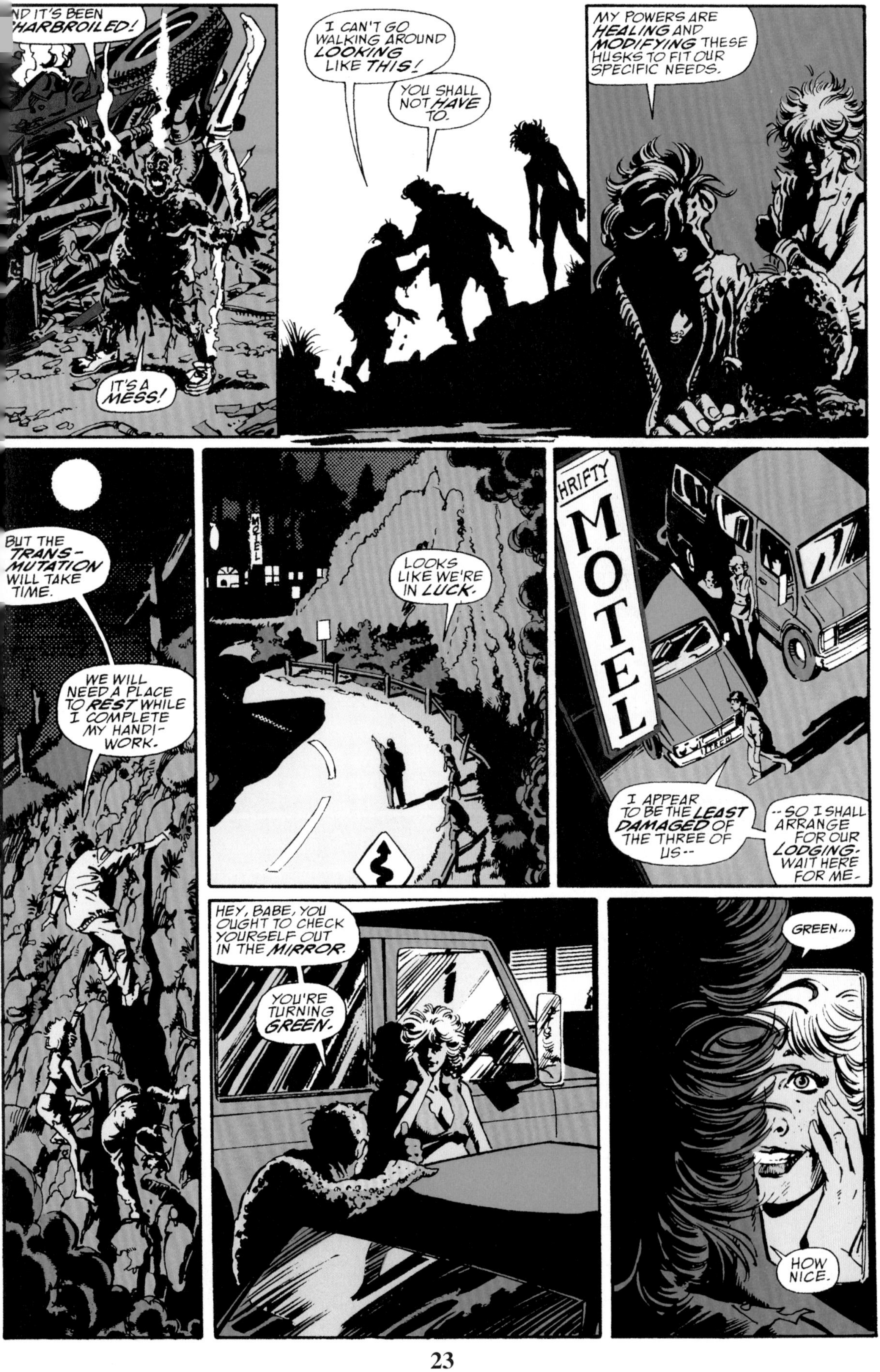
ND IT'S BEEN CHARBROILED!
IT'S A MESS!
I CAN'T GO WALKING AROUND LOOKING LIKE THIS!
YOU SHALL NOT HAVE TO.
MY POWERS ARE HEALING AND MODIFYING THESE HUSKS TO FIT OUR SPECIFIC NEEDS.
BUT THE TRANS-MUTATION WILL TAKE TIME.
WE WILL NEED A PLACE TO REST WHILE I COMPLETE MY HANDI-WORK.
MOTEL
LOOKS LIKE WE'RE IN LUCK.
HRIFTY
MOTEL
I APPEAR TO BE THE LEAST DAMAGED OF THE THREE OF US--
--SO I SHALL ARRANGE FOR OUR LODGING. WAIT HERE FOR ME.
HEY, BABE, YOU OUGHT TO CHECK YOURSELF OUT IN THE MIRROR.
YOU'RE TURNING GREEN.
GREEN....
HOW NICE.

SO MUCH *POWER* IN THE POSSESSION OF ONE WHO HAS BARELY REACHED THE STATUS OF *GODLING.*

THE VERY *THOUGHT* BOGGLES THE MIND.

THANOS COULD DESTROY EVEN *ME* WITH BUT A *THOUGHT,* YET HIS BASIC SOUL REMAINS ON THE EDGE OF *MORTALITY.*

IS HE CAPABLE OF MANAGING THE FORCES NOW UNDER HIS COMMAND?

OR WILL HIS *FRAGILE HEART* BE HIS UNDOING?

DARLING MISTRESS, YOUR *SCORN* WOUNDS ME *DEEPLY.*

IT WAS *NEVER* MY INTENTION TO *WRONG* YOU NOR, DO I BELIEVE, I *HAVE.*

TRUE, I DID USE THE POWERS *YOU* GRANTED ME TO SEEK OUT THE INFINITY GEMS TO BECOME THE *SUPREME BEING* THAT NOW STANDS BEFORE YOU.

BUT I ONLY SOUGHT SUCH *GLORY* IN ORDER TO BECOME *WORTHY* OF YOUR LOVE.

YOUR HEART DESERVES *BETTER* THAN THE *THRALL* I WAS.

I HAD *NO* OTHER *CHOICE* THAN TO BECOME YOUR *EQUAL*.

NOT *EQUAL*...

...*SUPERIOR*.

NOW *MISTRESS DEATH* IS NOTHING MORE THAN *YOUR* LOVE SLAVE.

THAT WAS A *POSITION* YOU *CHAFED* IN.

HOW CAN *SHE* FIND SUCH STATUS ANY LESS *STIFLING*?

BUT SHE IS THE *KEEPER* OF MY *HEART*!

YOUR *LOVE* IS *BONDAGE*.

MY LOVE IS *WORSHIP*!

THE *MISTRESS* OF THE HALL OF DEATH HAS NO NEED FOR *SYCOPHANTS*.

NO!

YOU ARE *WRONG*! DEATH SHOULD BE *REVERED*!

SHRINES SHOULD BE *BUILT* TO HER!

YES...

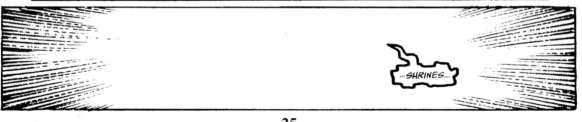

...*SHRINES*...

25

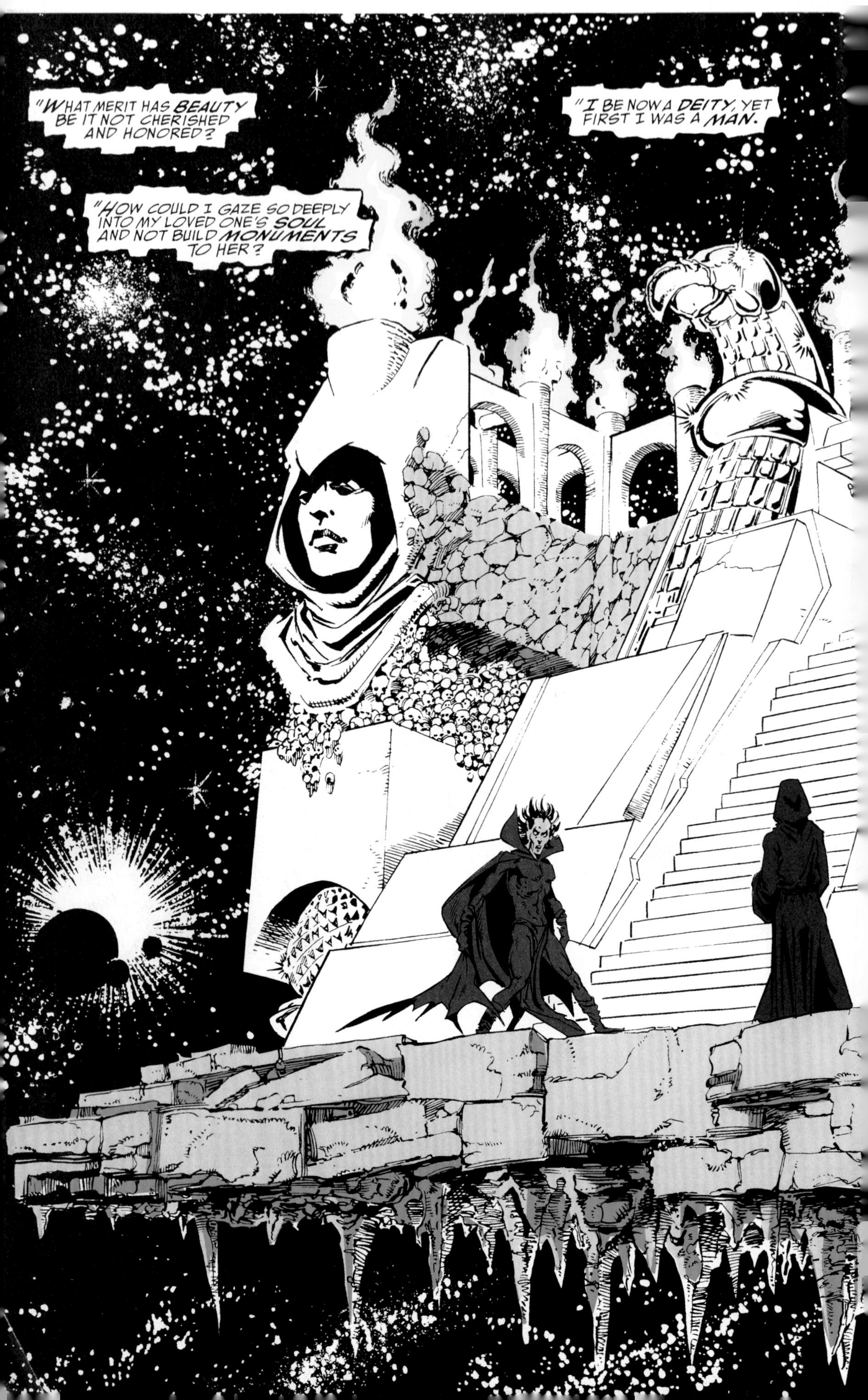
"WHAT MERIT HAS BEAUTY BE IT NOT CHERISHED AND HONORED?
"HOW COULD I GAZE SO DEEPLY INTO MY LOVED ONE'S SOUL AND NOT BUILD MONUMENTS TO HER?
"I BE NOW A DEITY, YET FIRST I WAS A MAN.

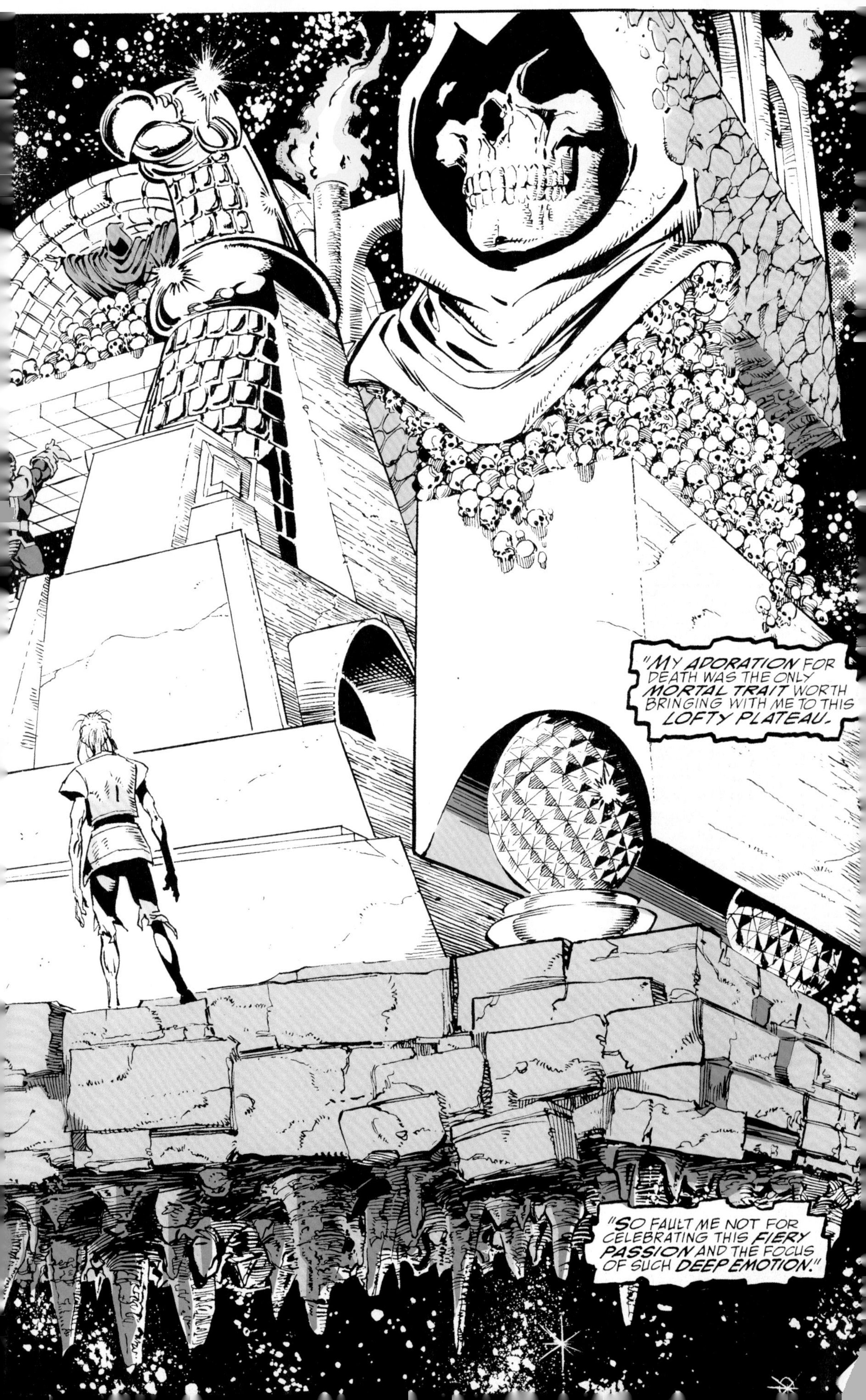
"MY ADORATION FOR DEATH WAS THE ONLY MORTAL TRAIT WORTH BRINGING WITH ME TO THIS LOFTY PLATEAU.
"SO FAULT ME NOT FOR CELEBRATING THIS FIERY PASSION AND THE FOCUS OF SUCH DEEP EMOTION."

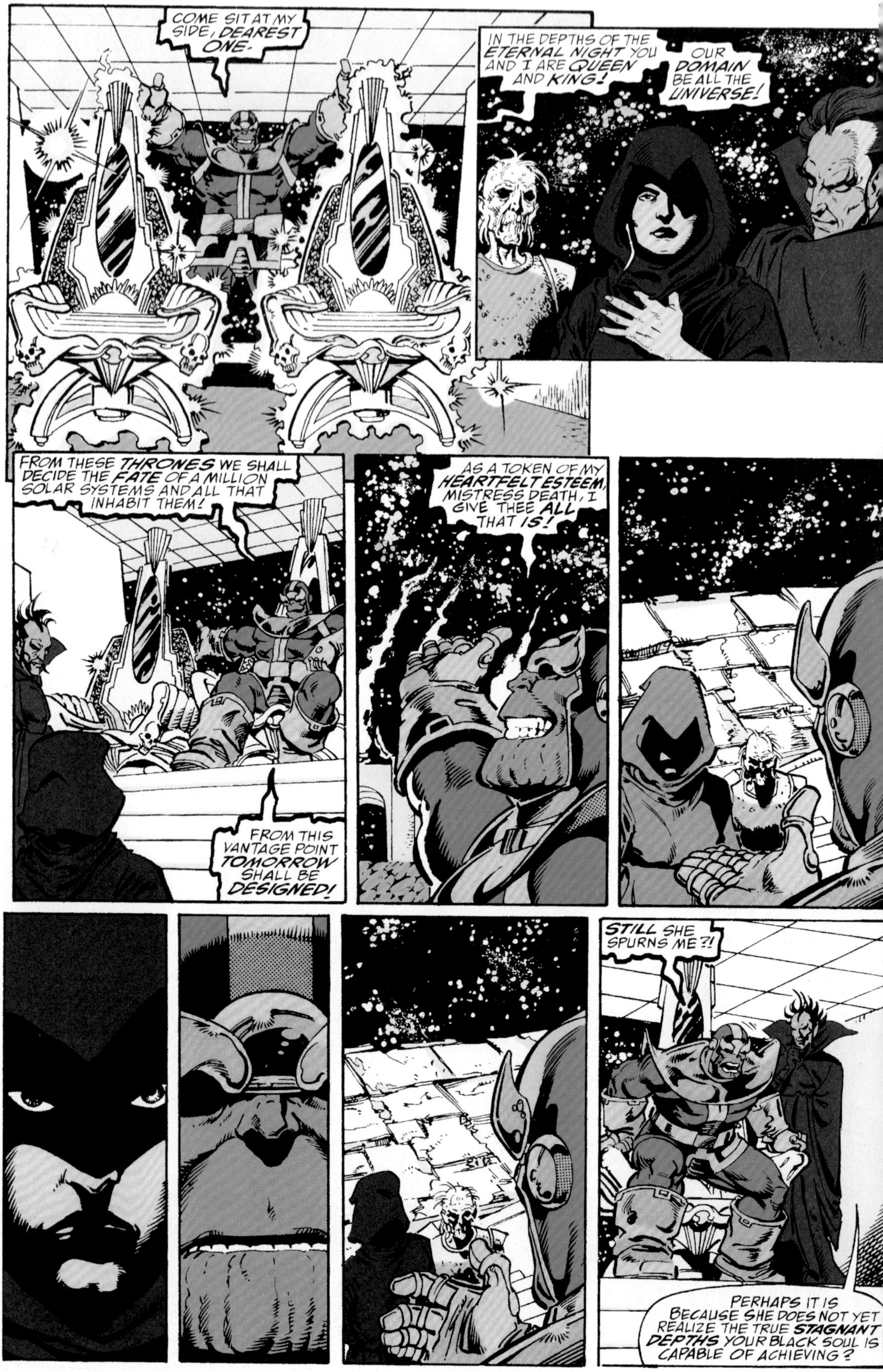
COME SIT AT MY SIDE, DEAREST ONE-
IN THE DEPTHS OF THE ETERNAL NIGHT YOU AND I ARE QUEEN AND KING!
OUR DOMAIN BE ALL THE UNIVERSE!
FROM THESE THRONES WE SHALL DECIDE THE FATE OF A MILLION SOLAR SYSTEMS AND ALL THAT INHABIT THEM!
FROM THIS VANTAGE POINT TOMORROW SHALL BE DESIGNED!
AS A TOKEN OF MY HEARTFELT ESTEEM, MISTRESS DEATH, I GIVE THEE ALL THAT IS!
STILL SHE SPURNS ME?!
PERHAPS IT IS BECAUSE SHE DOES NOT YET REALIZE THE TRUE STAGNANT DEPTHS YOUR BLACK SOUL IS CAPABLE OF ACHIEVING?

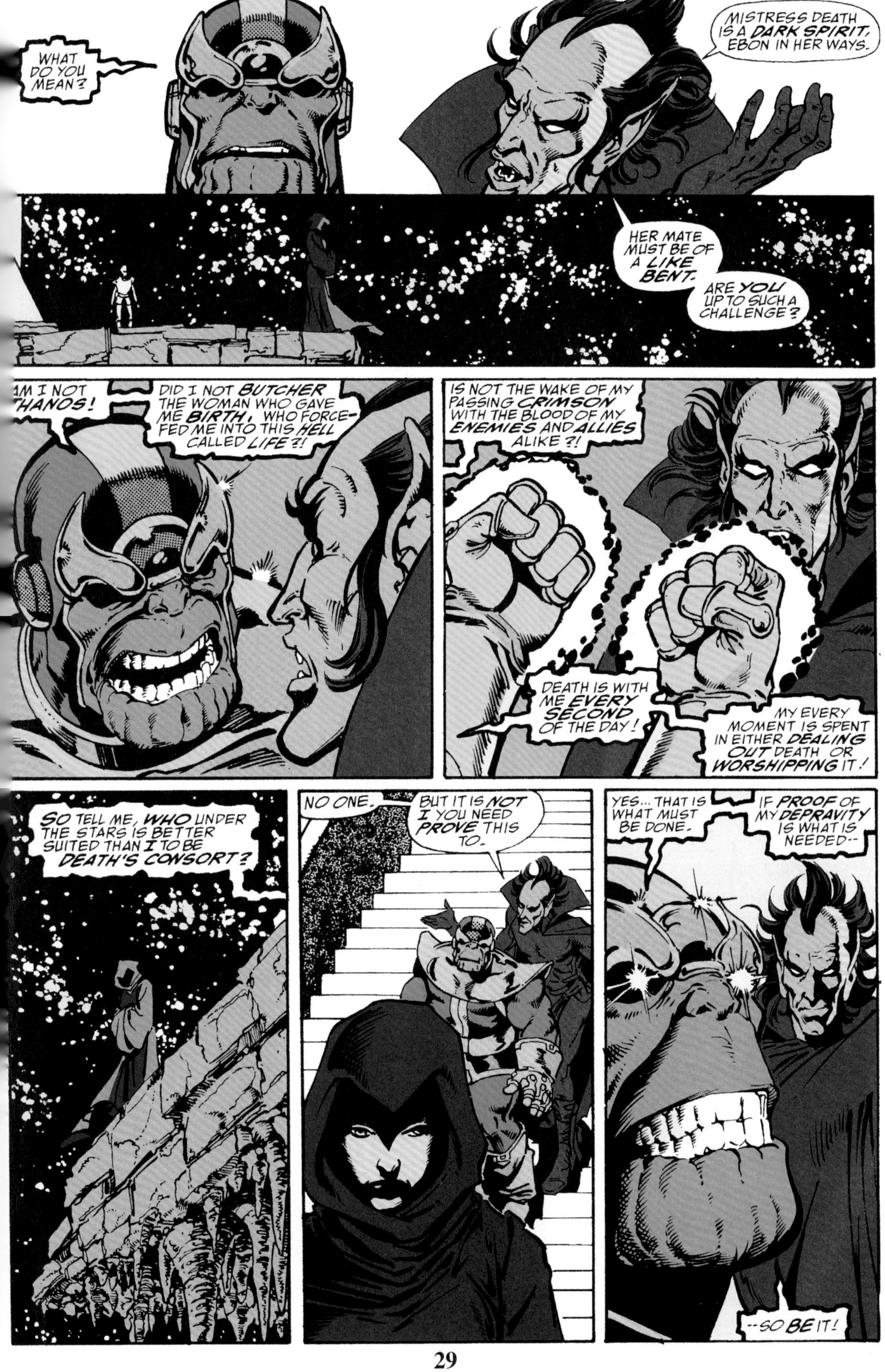
WHAT DO YOU MEAN?
MISTRESS DEATH IS A DARK SPIRIT, EBON IN HER WAYS.
HER MATE MUST BE OF A LIKE BENT.
ARE YOU UP TO SUCH A CHALLENGE?
AM I NOT THANOS!
DID I NOT BUTCHER THE WOMAN WHO GAVE ME BIRTH, WHO FORCE-FED ME INTO THIS HELL CALLED LIFE?!
IS NOT THE WAKE OF MY PASSING CRIMSON WITH THE BLOOD OF MY ENEMIES AND ALLIES ALIKE?!
DEATH IS WITH ME EVERY SECOND OF THE DAY!
MY EVERY MOMENT IS SPENT IN EITHER DEALING OUT DEATH OR WORSHIPPING IT!
SO TELL ME, WHO UNDER THE STARS IS BETTER SUITED THAN I TO BE DEATH'S CONSORT?
NO ONE.
BUT IT IS NOT I YOU NEED PROVE THIS TO.
YES... THAT IS WHAT MUST BE DONE.
IF PROOF OF MY DEPRAVITY IS WHAT IS NEEDED--
--SO BE IT!

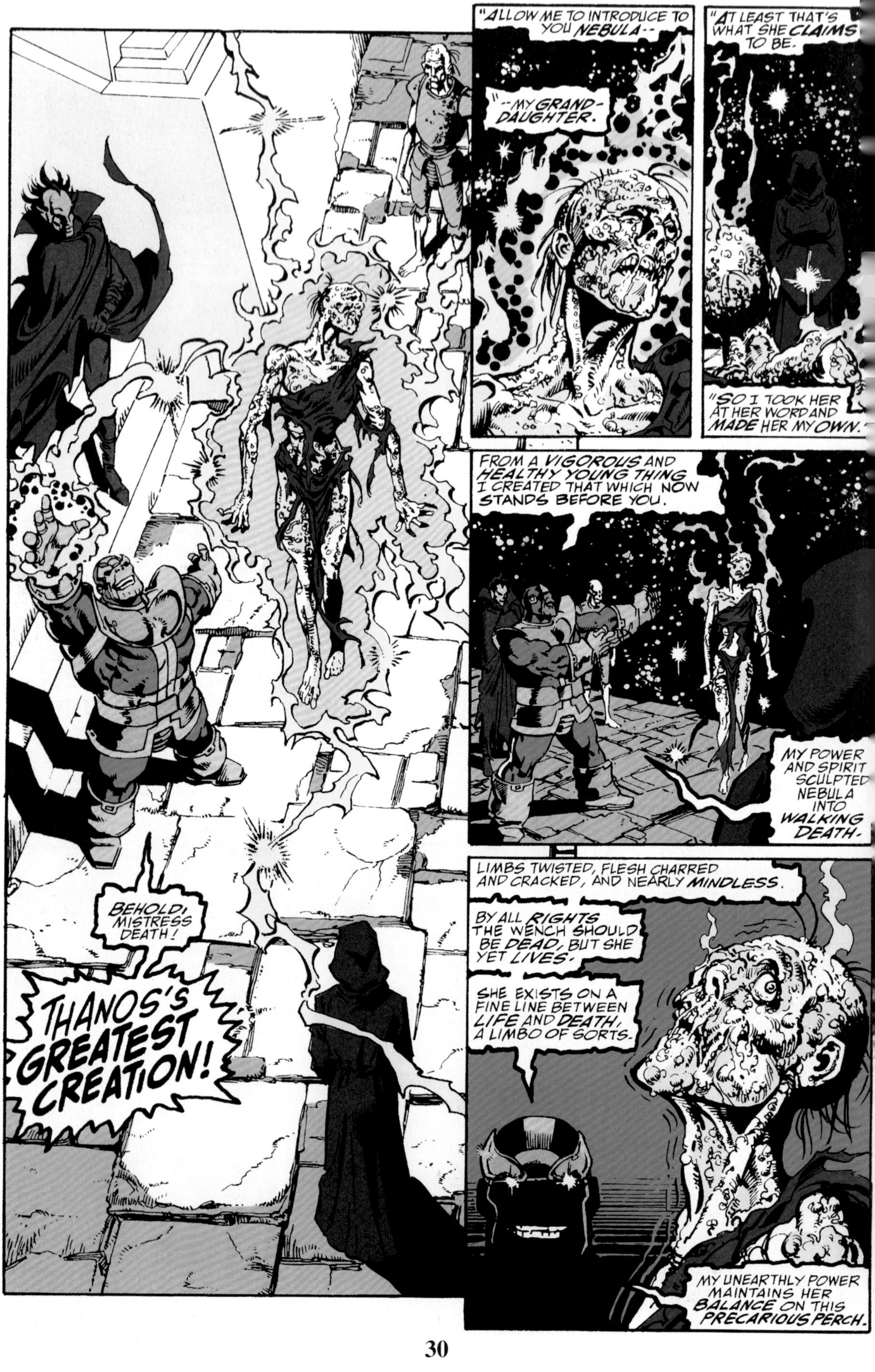

BEHOLD, MISTRESS DEATH!
THANOS'S GREATEST CREATION!
"ALLOW ME TO INTRODUCE TO YOU NEBULA--
"--MY GRAND-DAUGHTER.
"AT LEAST THAT'S WHAT SHE CLAIMS TO BE.
"SO I TOOK HER AT HER WORD AND MADE HER MY OWN.
FROM A VIGOROUS AND HEALTHY YOUNG THING I CREATED THAT WHICH NOW STANDS BEFORE YOU.
MY POWER AND SPIRIT SCULPTED NEBULA INTO WALKING DEATH.
LIMBS TWISTED, FLESH CHARRED AND CRACKED, AND NEARLY MINDLESS.
BY ALL RIGHTS THE WENCH SHOULD BE DEAD, BUT SHE YET LIVES.
SHE EXISTS ON A FINE LINE BETWEEN LIFE AND DEATH, A LIMBO OF SORTS.
MY UNEARTHLY POWER MAINTAINS HER BALANCE ON THIS PRECARIOUS PERCH.

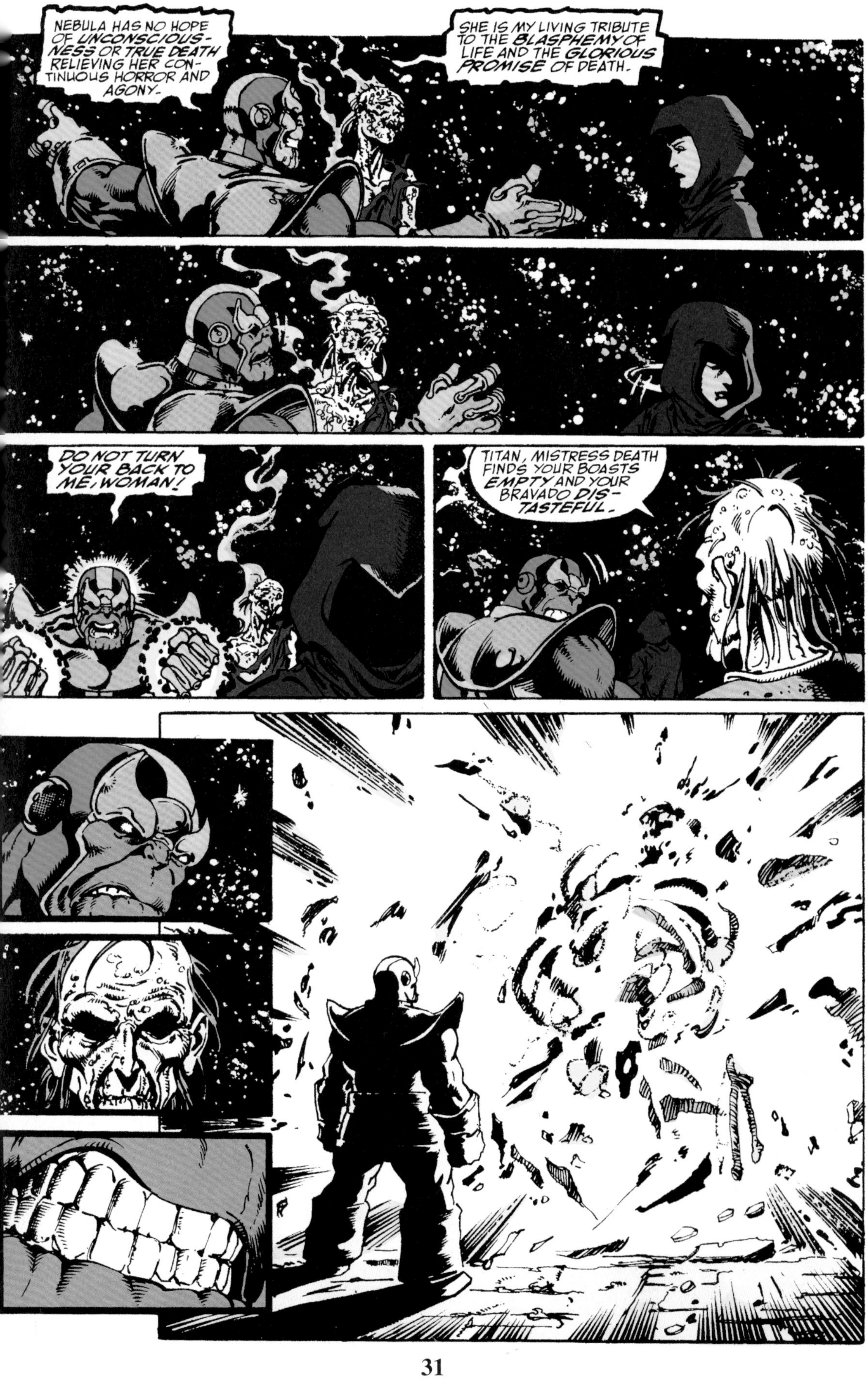

NEBULA HAS NO HOPE OF UNCONSCIOUS-NESS OR TRUE DEATH RELIEVING HER CON-TINUOUS HORROR AND AGONY-
SHE IS MY LIVING TRIBUTE TO THE BLASPHEMY OF LIFE AND THE GLORIOUS PROMISE OF DEATH.
DO NOT TURN YOUR BACK TO ME, WOMAN!
TITAN, MISTRESS DEATH FINDS YOUR BOASTS EMPTY AND YOUR BRAVADO DIS-TASTEFUL.

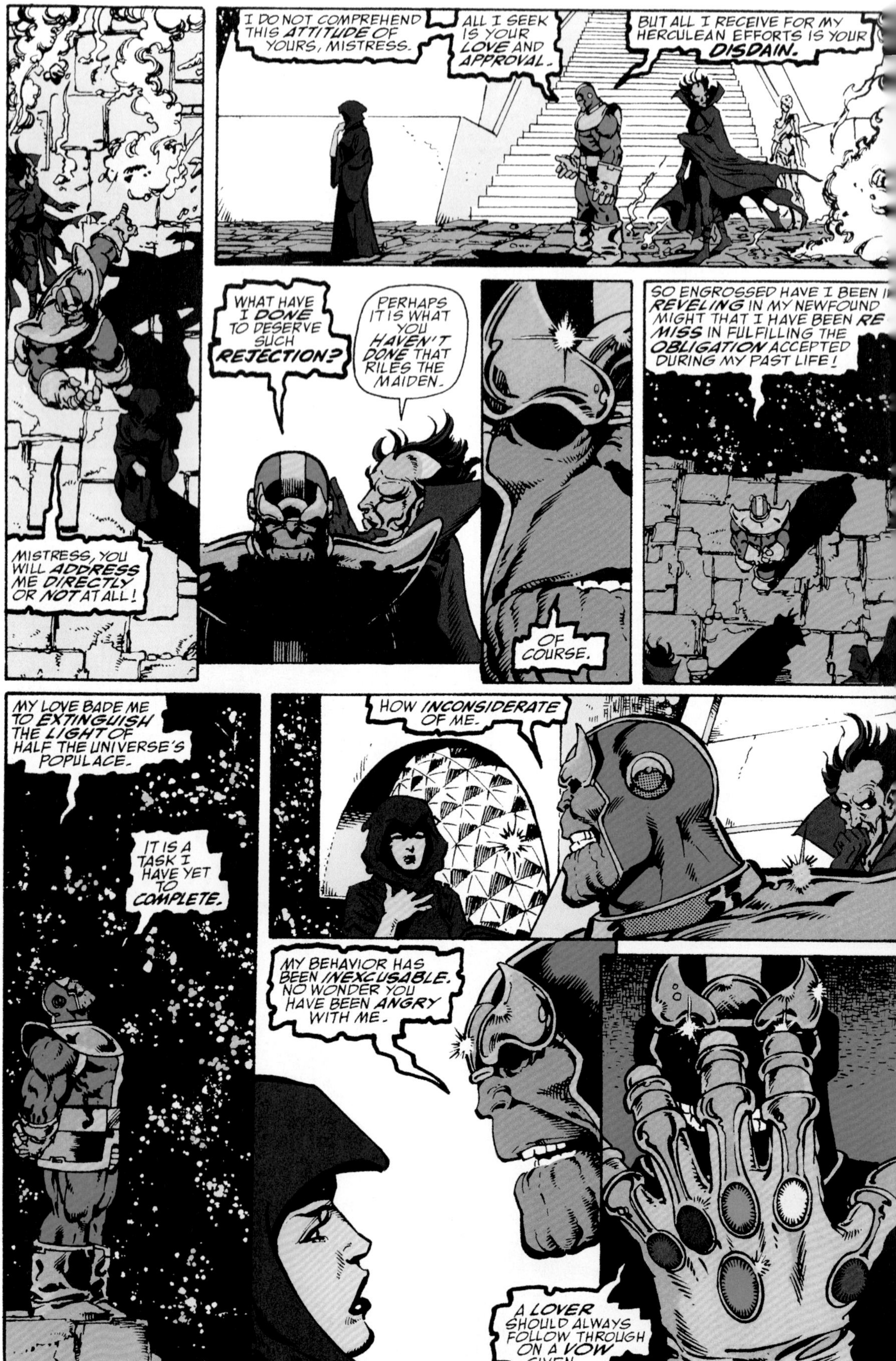

MISTRESS, YOU WILL ADDRESS ME DIRECTLY OR NOT AT ALL!
I DO NOT COMPREHEND THIS ATTITUDE OF YOURS, MISTRESS.
ALL I SEEK IS YOUR LOVE AND APPROVAL.
BUT ALL I RECEIVE FOR MY HERCULEAN EFFORTS IS YOUR DISDAIN.
WHAT HAVE I DONE TO DESERVE SUCH REJECTION?
PERHAPS IT IS WHAT YOU HAVEN'T DONE THAT RILES THE MAIDEN.
OF COURSE.
SO ENGROSSED HAVE I BEEN I
REVELING IN MY NEWFOUND
MIGHT THAT I HAVE BEEN RE
MISS IN FULFILLING THE
OBLIGATION ACCEPTED
DURING MY PAST LIFE!
MY LOVE BADE ME TO EXTINGUISH THE LIGHT OF HALF THE UNIVERSE'S POPULACE.
IT IS A TASK I HAVE YET TO COMPLETE.
HOW INCONSIDERATE OF ME.
MY BEHAVIOR HAS BEEN INEXCUSABLE. NO WONDER YOU HAVE BEEN ANGRY WITH ME.
A LOVER SHOULD ALWAYS FOLLOW THROUGH ON A VOW GIVEN.

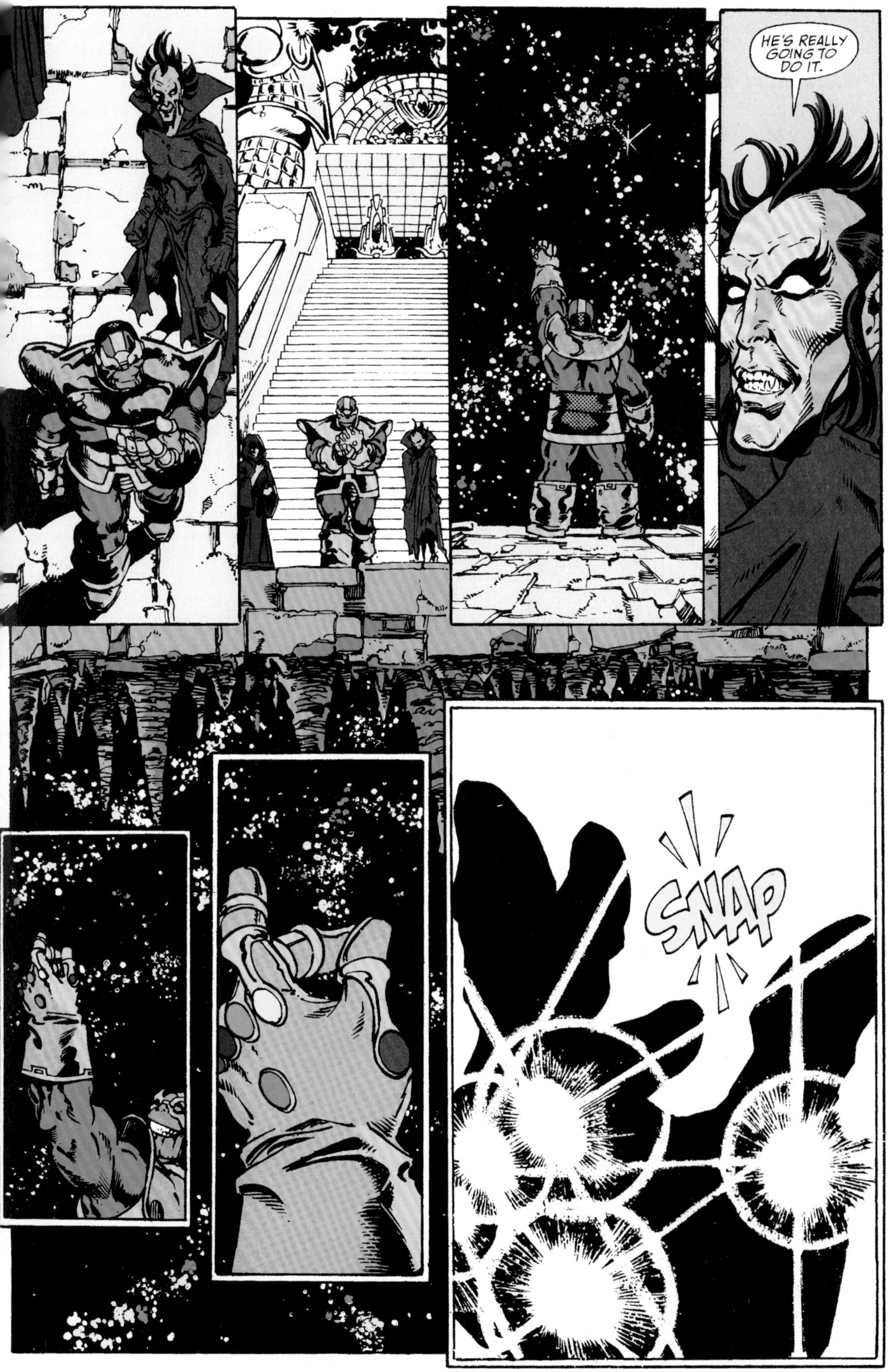
HE'S REALLY GOING TO DO IT.
SNAP

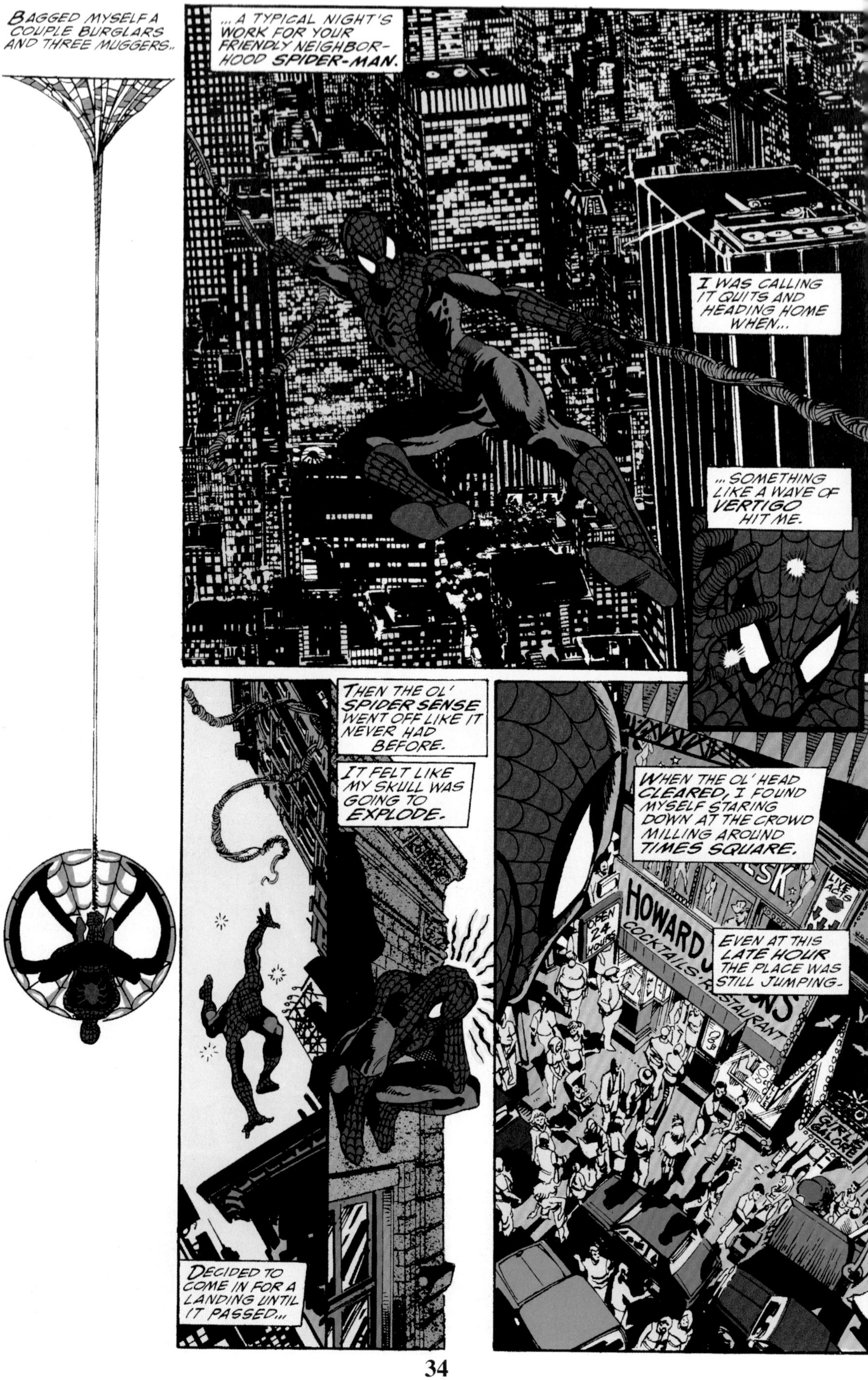
BAGGED MYSELF A COUPLE BURGLARS AND THREE MUGGERS..
...A TYPICAL NIGHT'S WORK FOR YOUR FRIENDLY NEIGHBOR-HOOD SPIDER-MAN.
I WAS CALLING IT QUITS AND HEADING HOME WHEN...
...SOMETHING LIKE A WAVE OF VERTIGO HIT ME.
THEN THE OL' SPIDER SENSE WENT OFF LIKE IT NEVER HAD BEFORE.
IT FELT LIKE MY SKULL WAS GOING TO EXPLODE.
DECIDED TO COME IN FOR A LANDING UNTIL IT PASSED...
WHEN THE OL' HEAD CLEARED, I FOUND MYSELF STARING DOWN AT THE CROWD MILLING AROUND TIMES SQUARE.
EVEN AT THIS LATE HOUR THE PLACE WAS STILL JUMPING.
OPEN 24 HOURS
LIVE ACTS
COCKTAILS RESTAURANT
GIRLS GALORE

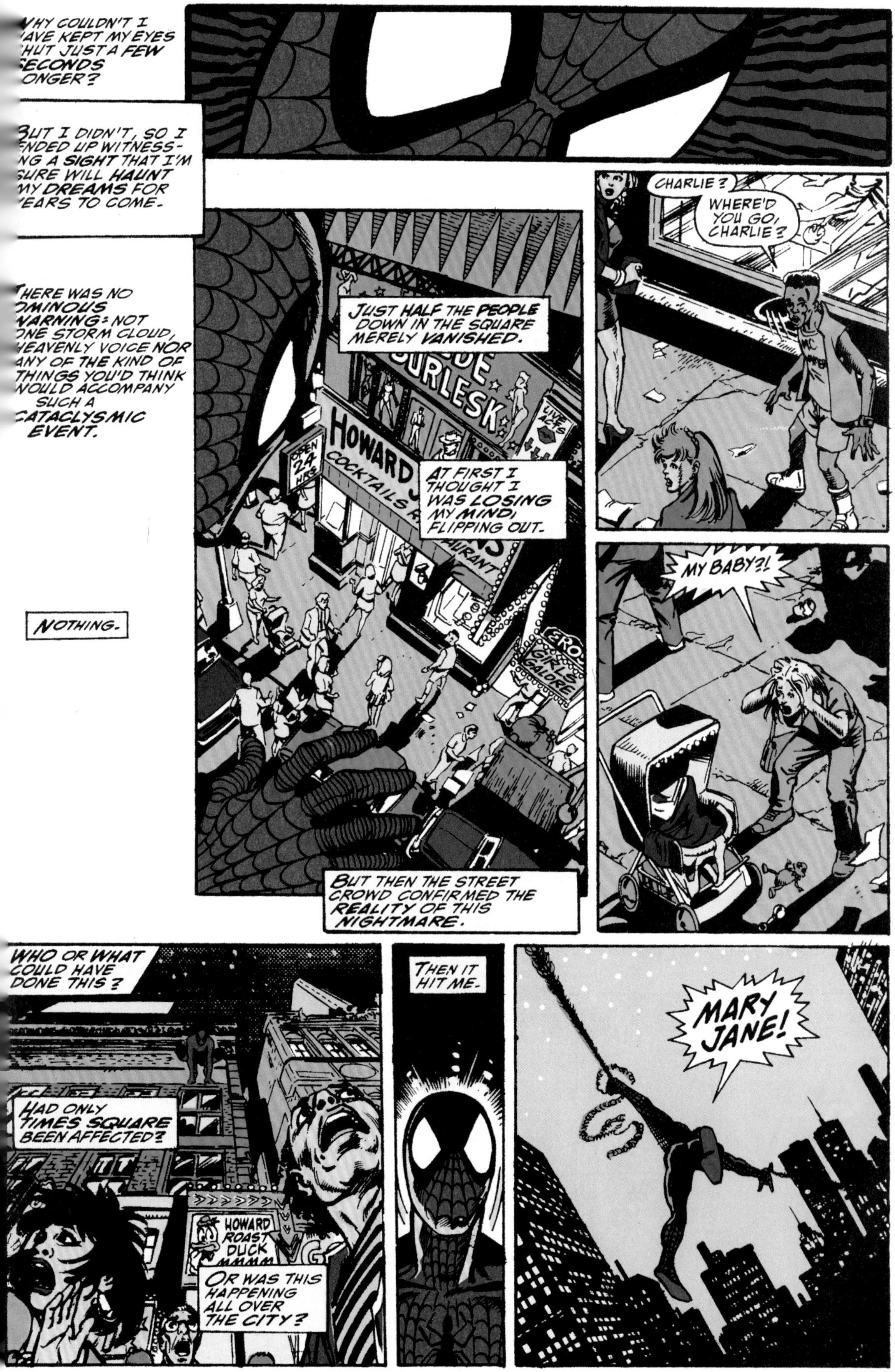
HY COULDN'T I AVE KEPT MY EYES HUT JUST A FEW ECONDS ONGER?
UT I DIDN'T, SO I ENDED UP WITNESS-NG A SIGHT THAT I'M SURE WILL HAUNT MY DREAMS FOR YEARS TO COME.
HERE WAS NO OMINOUS WARNING: NOT ONE STORM CLOUD, HEAVENLY VOICE NOR ANY OF THE KIND OF THINGS YOU'D THINK WOULD ACCOMPANY SUCH A CATACLYSMIC EVENT.
NOTHING.
JUST HALF THE PEOPLE DOWN IN THE SQUARE MERELY VANISHED.
BURLESK
HOWARD
COCKTAILS
OPEN 24 HRS
LIVE ACTS
AT FIRST I THOUGHT I WAS LOSING MY MIND, FLIPPING OUT.
GIRLS GALORE
BUT THEN THE STREET CROWD CONFIRMED THE REALITY OF THIS NIGHTMARE.
CHARLIE?
WHERE'D YOU GO, CHARLIE?
MY BABY?!
WHO OR WHAT COULD HAVE DONE THIS?
HAD ONLY TIMES SQUARE BEEN AFFECTED?
HOWARD ROAST DUCK MMMM
OR WAS THIS HAPPENING ALL OVER THE CITY?
THEN IT HIT ME.
MARY JANE!

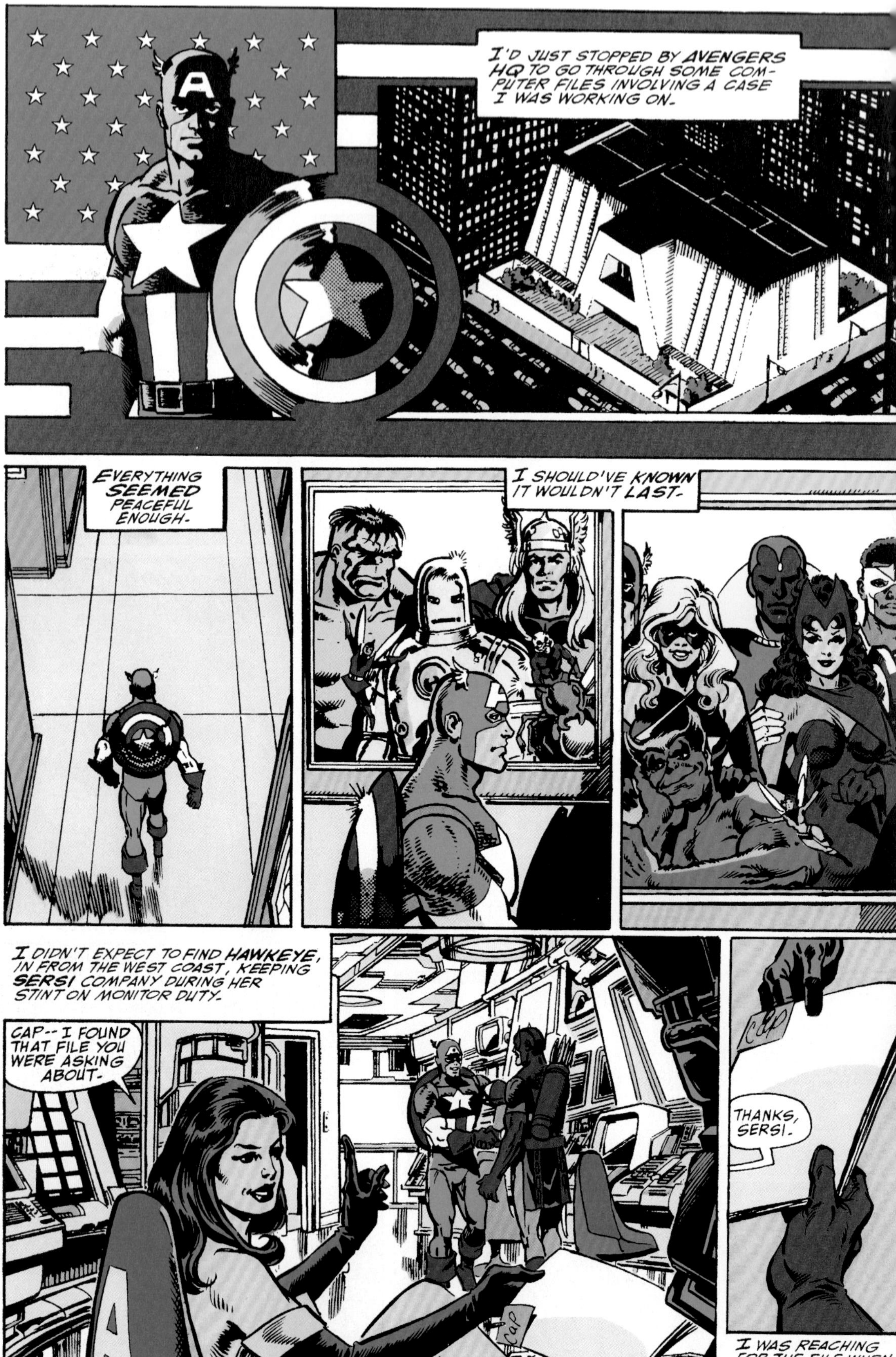
I'D JUST STOPPED BY AVENGERS HQ TO GO THROUGH SOME COM-PUTER FILES INVOLVING A CASE I WAS WORKING ON.
EVERYTHING SEEMED PEACEFUL ENOUGH.
I SHOULD'VE KNOWN IT WOULDN'T LAST.
I DIDN'T EXPECT TO FIND HAWKEYE, IN FROM THE WEST COAST, KEEPING SERSI COMPANY DURING HER STINT ON MONITOR DUTY.
CAP-- I FOUND THAT FILE YOU WERE ASKING ABOUT.
THANKS, SERSI.
I WAS REACHING FOR THE FILE WHEN IT HAPPENED...

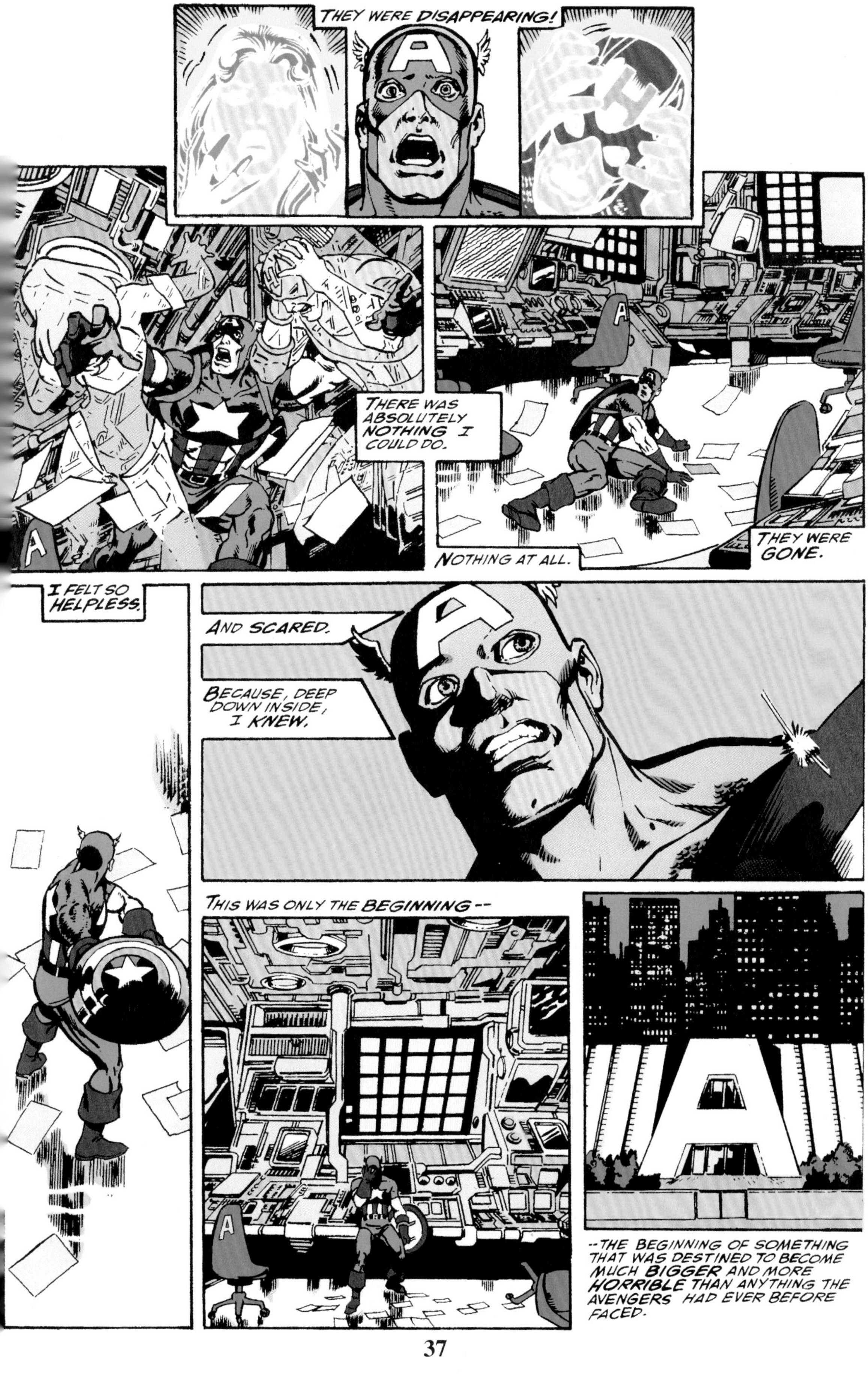
THEY WERE DISAPPEARING!
THERE WAS ABSOLUTELY NOTHING I COULD DO.
NOTHING AT ALL.
THEY WERE GONE.
I FELT SO HELPLESS.
AND SCARED.
BECAUSE, DEEP DOWN INSIDE, I KNEW.
THIS WAS ONLY THE BEGINNING--
--THE BEGINNING OF SOMETHING THAT WAS DESTINED TO BECOME MUCH BIGGER AND MORE HORRIBLE THAN ANYTHING THE AVENGERS HAD EVER BEFORE FACED.

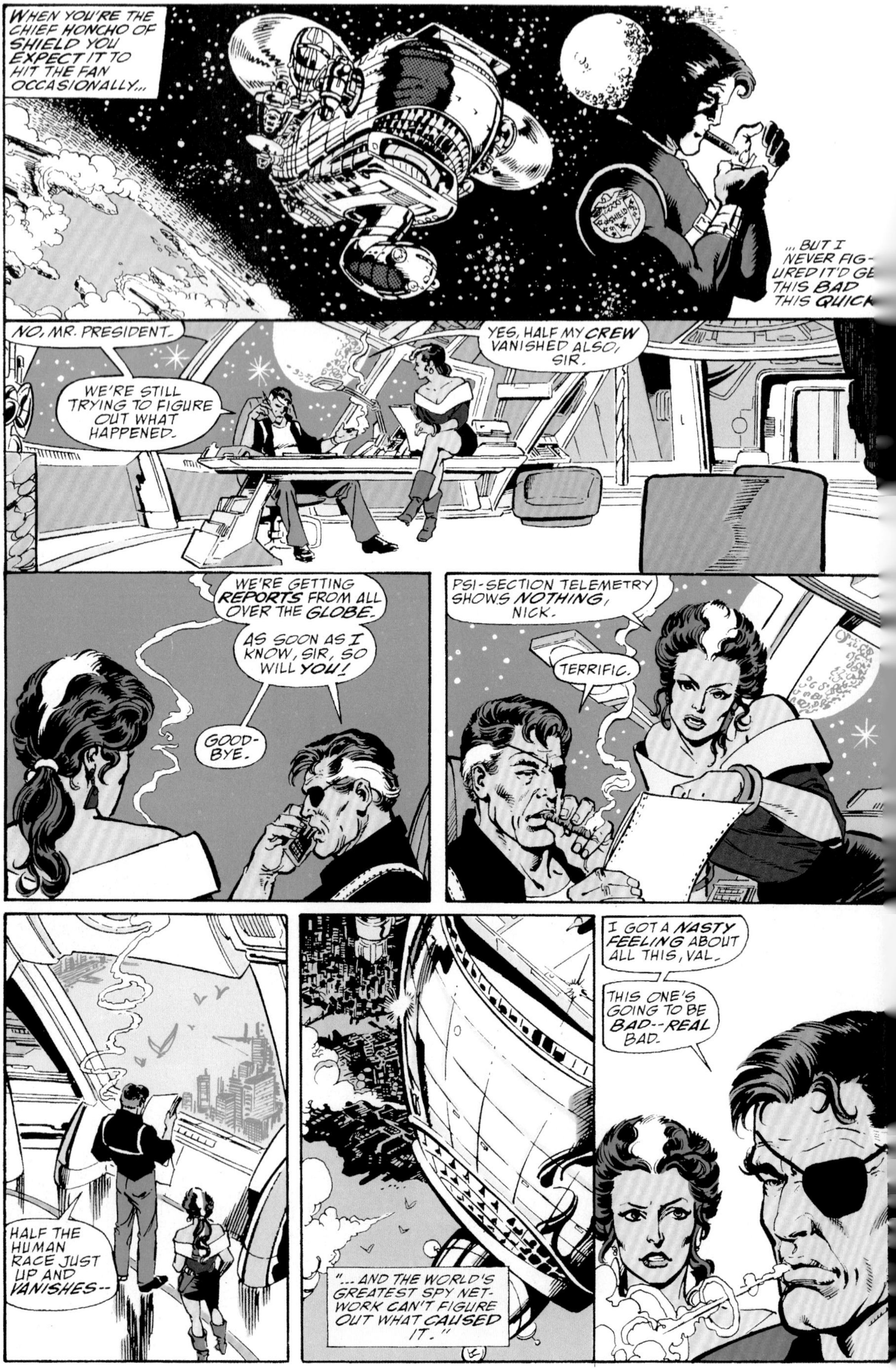
WHEN YOU'RE THE CHIEF HONCHO OF SHIELD YOU EXPECT IT TO HIT THE FAN OCCASIONALLY...
...BUT I NEVER FIGURED IT'D GET THIS BAD THIS QUICK
NO, MR. PRESIDENT.
WE'RE STILL TRYING TO FIGURE OUT WHAT HAPPENED.
YES, HALF MY CREW VANISHED ALSO, SIR.
WE'RE GETTING REPORTS FROM ALL OVER THE GLOBE.
AS SOON AS I KNOW, SIR, SO WILL YOU!
GOOD-BYE.
PSI-SECTION TELEMETRY SHOWS NOTHING, NICK.
TERRIFIC.
HALF THE HUMAN RACE JUST UP AND VANISHES--
"...AND THE WORLD'S GREATEST SPY NETWORK CAN'T FIGURE OUT WHAT CAUSED IT."
I GOT A NASTY FEELING ABOUT ALL THIS, VAL.
THIS ONE'S GOING TO BE BAD--REAL BAD.

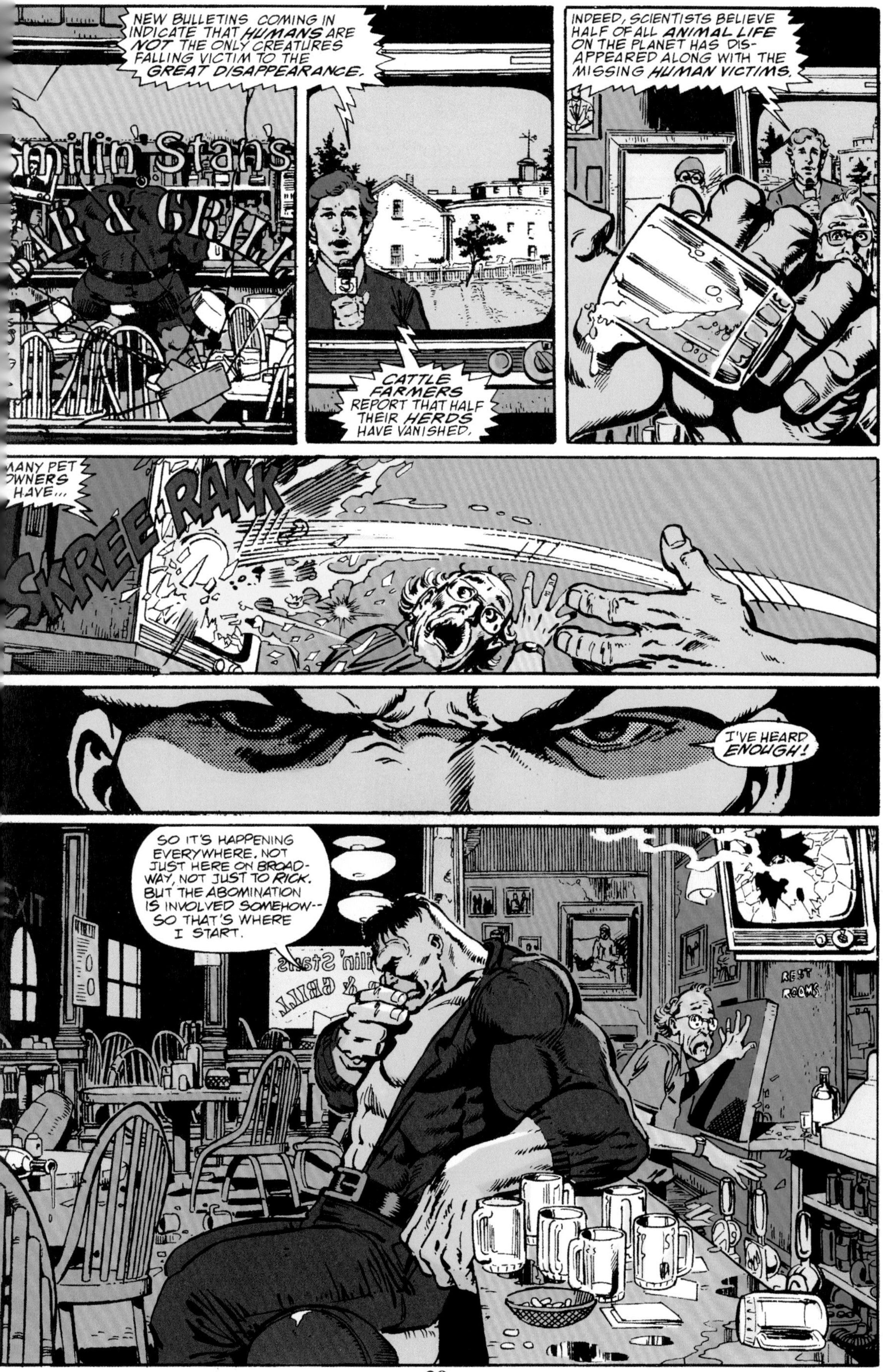
NEW BULLETINS COMING IN INDICATE THAT HUMANS ARE NOT THE ONLY CREATURES FALLING VICTIM TO THE GREAT DISAPPEARANCE.
CATTLE FARMERS REPORT THAT HALF THEIR HERDS HAVE VANISHED.
INDEED, SCIENTISTS BELIEVE HALF OF ALL ANIMAL LIFE ON THE PLANET HAS DISAPPEARED ALONG WITH THE MISSING HUMAN VICTIMS.
MANY PET OWNERS HAVE...
SKREE-RAKK
I'VE HEARD ENOUGH!
SO IT'S HAPPENING EVERYWHERE. NOT JUST HERE ON BROADWAY, NOT JUST TO RICK. BUT THE ABOMINATION IS INVOLVED SOMEHOW-- SO THAT'S WHERE I START.
REST ROOMS

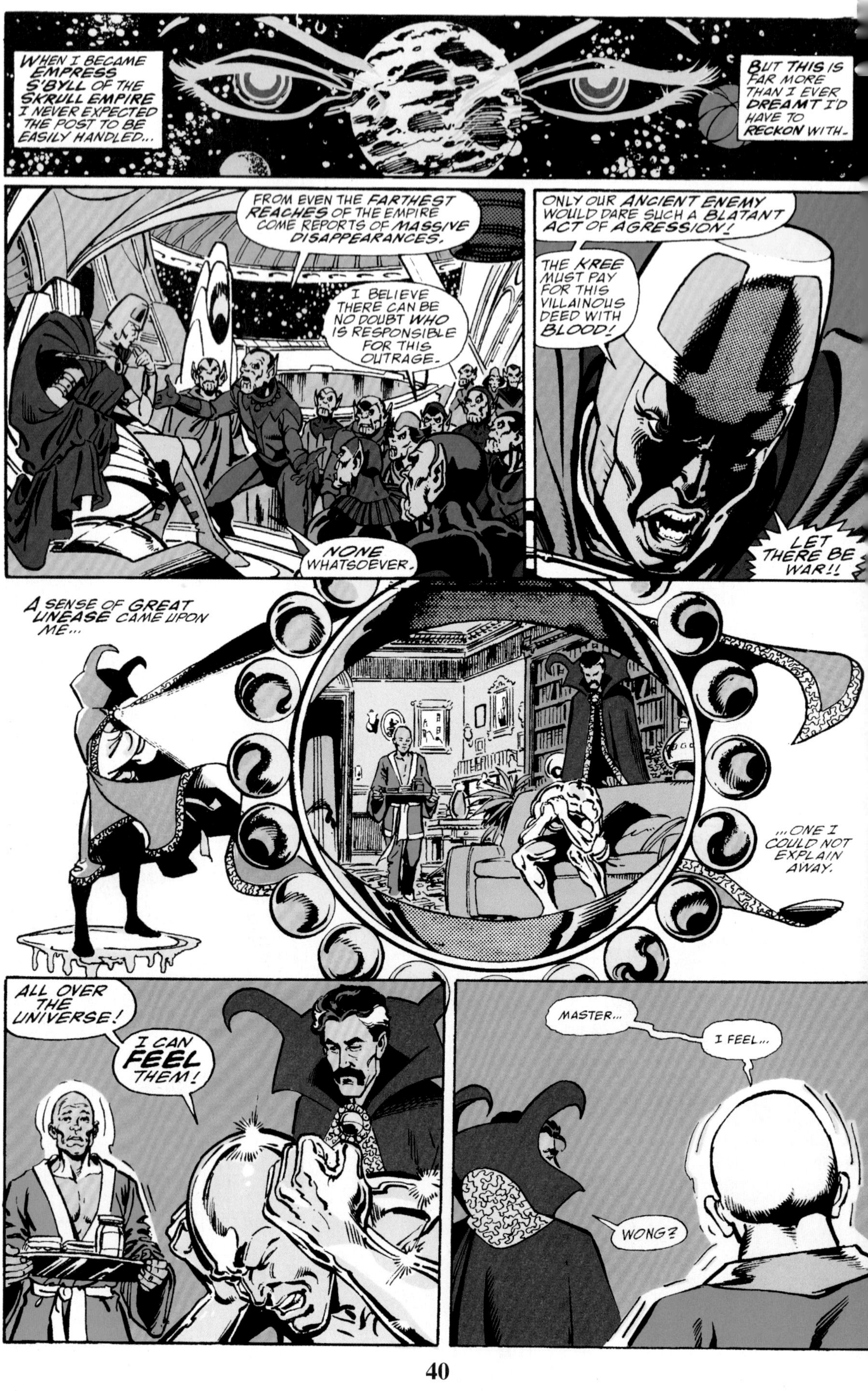

WHEN I BECAME EMPRESS S'BYLL OF THE SKRULL EMPIRE I NEVER EXPECTED THE POST TO BE EASILY HANDLED...
BUT THIS IS FAR MORE THAN I EVER DREAMT I'D HAVE TO RECKON WITH.
FROM EVEN THE FARTHEST REACHES OF THE EMPIRE COME REPORTS OF MASSIVE DISAPPEARANCES.
I BELIEVE THERE CAN BE NO DOUBT WHO IS RESPONSIBLE FOR THIS OUTRAGE.
NONE WHATSOEVER.
ONLY OUR ANCIENT ENEMY WOULD DARE SUCH A BLATANT ACT OF AGRESSION!
THE KREE MUST PAY FOR THIS VILLAINOUS DEED WITH BLOOD!
LET THERE BE WAR!!
A SENSE OF GREAT UNEASE CAME UPON ME...
...ONE I COULD NOT EXPLAIN AWAY.
ALL OVER THE UNIVERSE!
I CAN FEEL THEM!
MASTER...
I FEEL...
WONG?

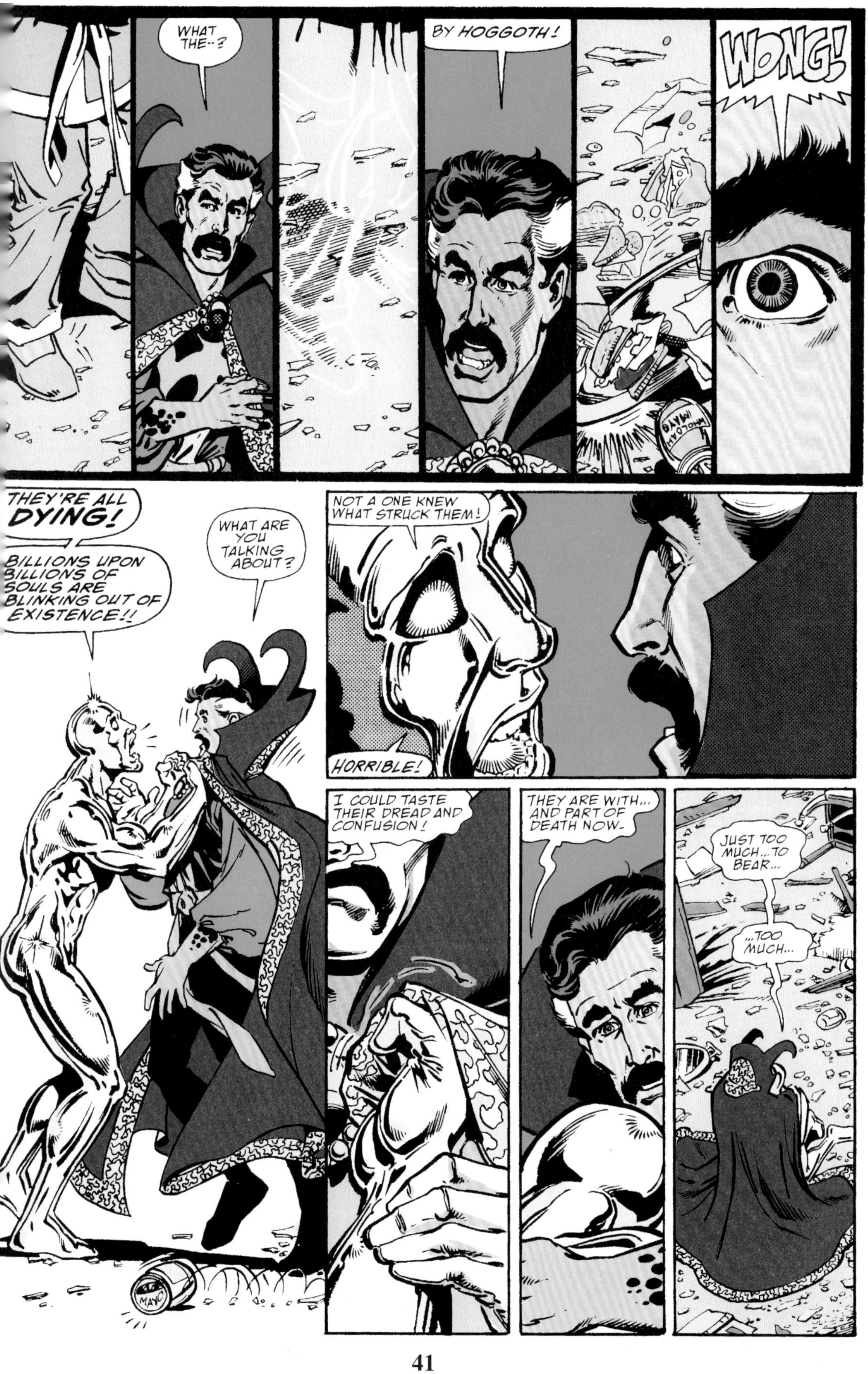
WHAT THE--?
BY HOGGOTH!
WONG!
THEY'RE ALL DYING!
BILLIONS UPON BILLIONS OF SOULS ARE BLINKING OUT OF EXISTENCE!!
WHAT ARE YOU TALKING ABOUT?
MAYO
NOT A ONE KNEW WHAT STRUCK THEM!
HORRIBLE!
I COULD TASTE THEIR DREAD AND CONFUSION!
THEY ARE WITH... AND PART OF DEATH NOW...
JUST TOO MUCH... TO BEAR...
...TOO MUCH...

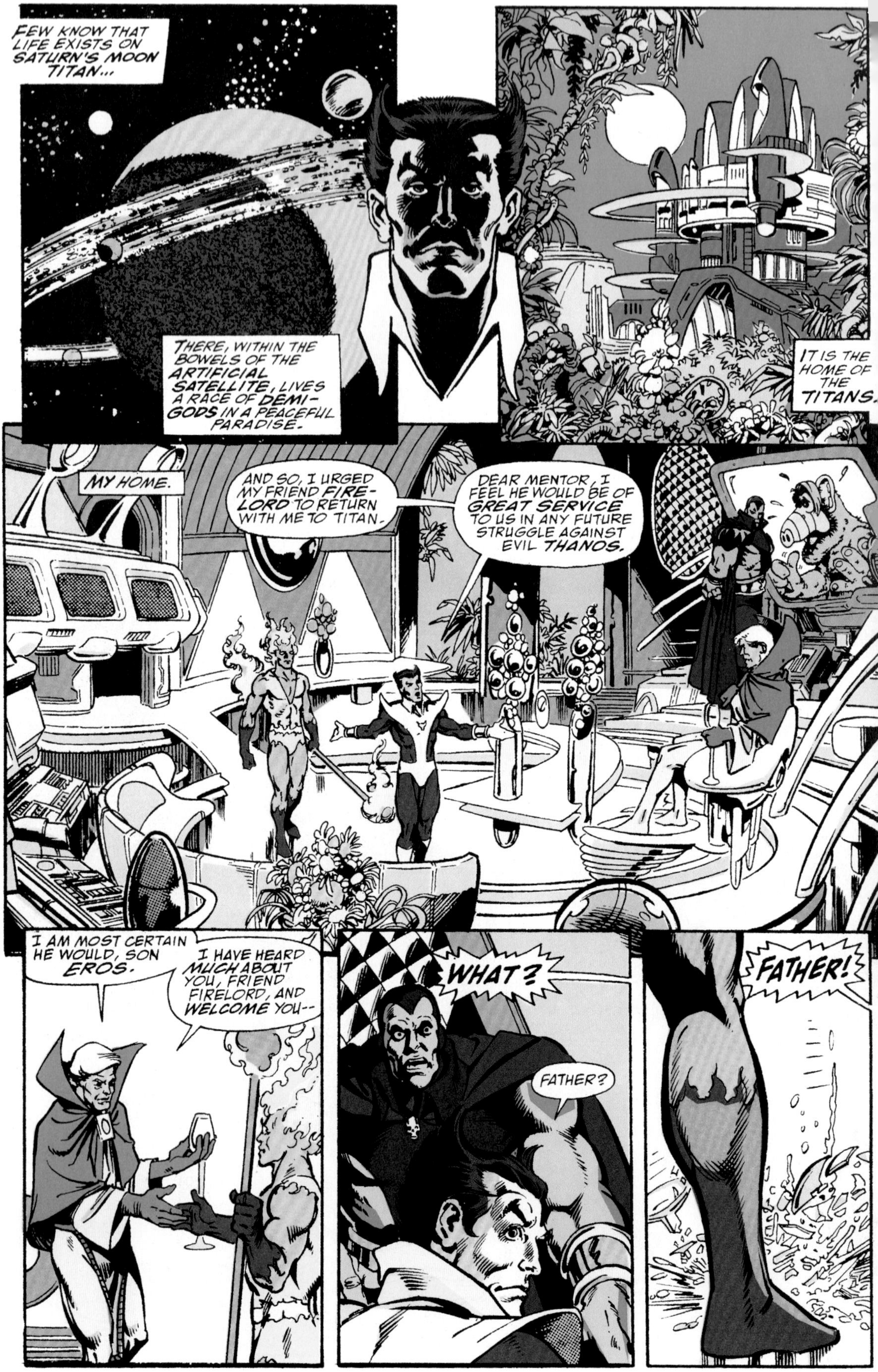
FEW KNOW THAT LIFE EXISTS ON SATURN'S MOON TITAN...
THERE, WITHIN THE BOWELS OF THE ARTIFICIAL SATELLITE, LIVES A RACE OF DEMI-GODS IN A PEACEFUL PARADISE.
IT IS THE HOME OF THE TITANS.
MY HOME.
AND SO, I URGED MY FRIEND FIRE-LORD TO RETURN WITH ME TO TITAN.
DEAR MENTOR, I FEEL HE WOULD BE OF GREAT SERVICE TO US IN ANY FUTURE STRUGGLE AGAINST EVIL THANOS.
I AM MOST CERTAIN HE WOULD, SON EROS.
I HAVE HEARD MUCH ABOUT YOU, FRIEND FIRELORD, AND WELCOME YOU--
WHAT?
FATHER?
FATHER!

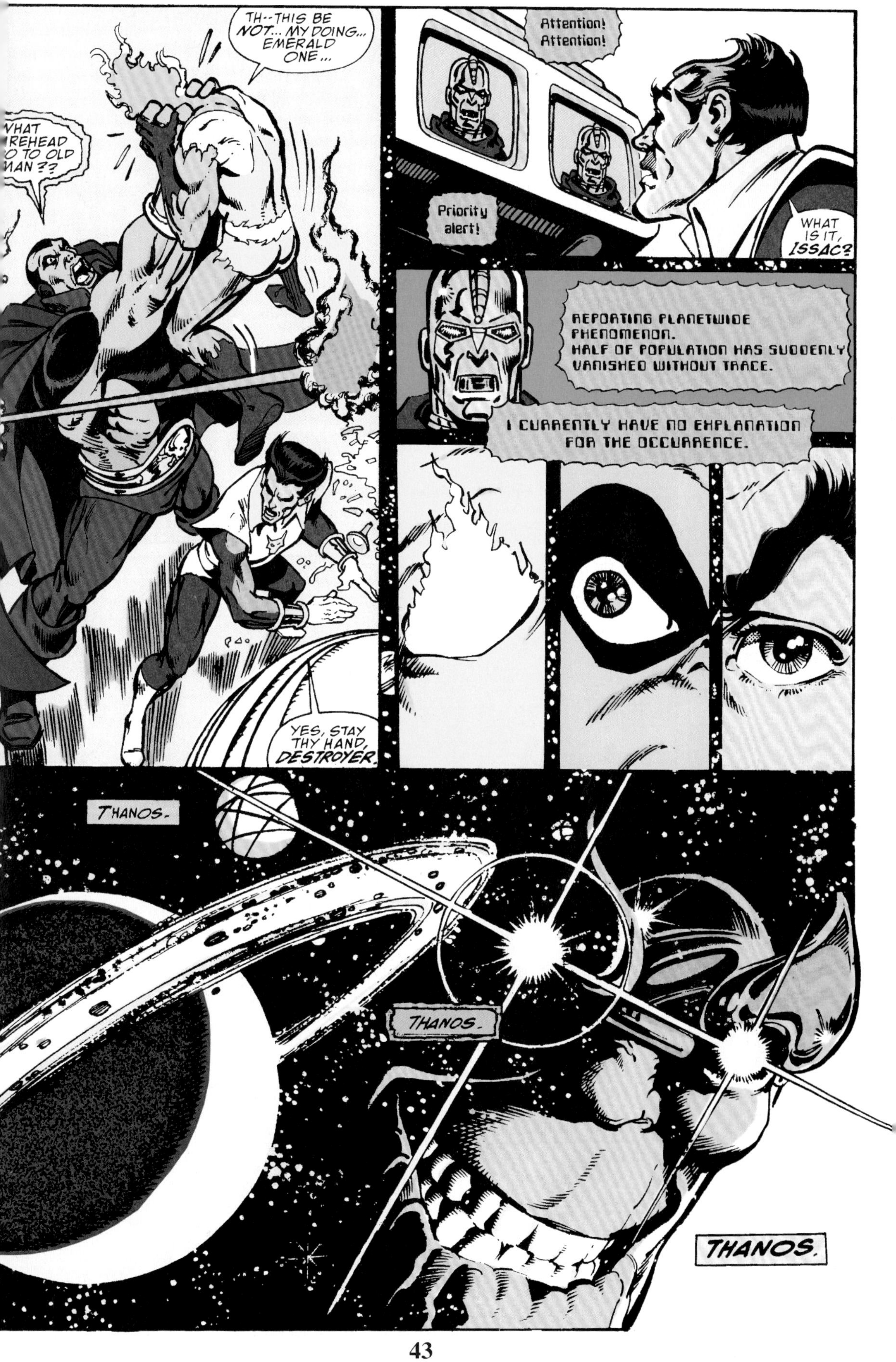
TH--THIS BE NOT... MY DOING... EMERALD ONE...
WHAT REHEAD O TO OLD MAN ??
YES, STAY THY HAND, DESTROYER.
Attention! Attention!
Priority alert!
WHAT IS IT, ISSAC?
REPORTING PLANETWIDE PHENOMENON.
HALF OF POPULATION HAS SUDDENLY VANISHED WITHOUT TRACE.
I CURRENTLY HAVE NO EXPLANATION FOR THE OCCURRENCE.
THANOS.
THANOS.
THANOS.

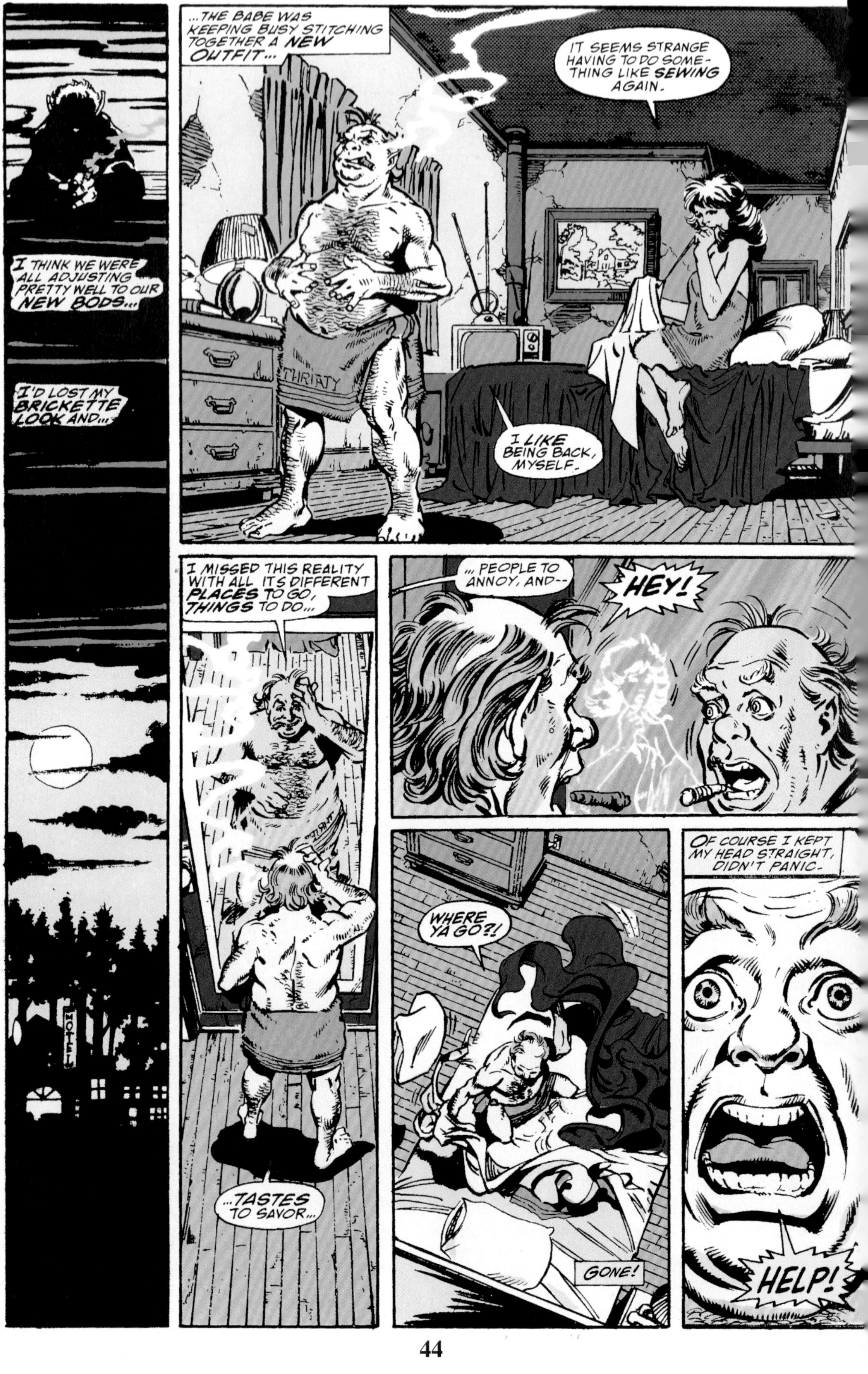
I THINK WE WERE ALL ADJUSTING PRETTY WELL TO OUR NEW BODS...
I'D LOST MY BRICKETTE LOOK AND...
...THE BABE WAS KEEPING BUSY STITCHING TOGETHER A NEW OUTFIT...
IT SEEMS STRANGE HAVING TO DO SOMETHING LIKE SEWING AGAIN.
I LIKE BEING BACK, MYSELF.
THRIFTY
I MISSED THIS REALITY WITH ALL ITS DIFFERENT PLACES TO GO, THINGS TO DO...
...TASTES TO SAVOR...
...PEOPLE TO ANNOY, AND--
HEY!
WHERE YA GO?!
GONE!
OF COURSE I KEPT MY HEAD STRAIGHT, DIDN'T PANIC-
HELP!
MOTEL

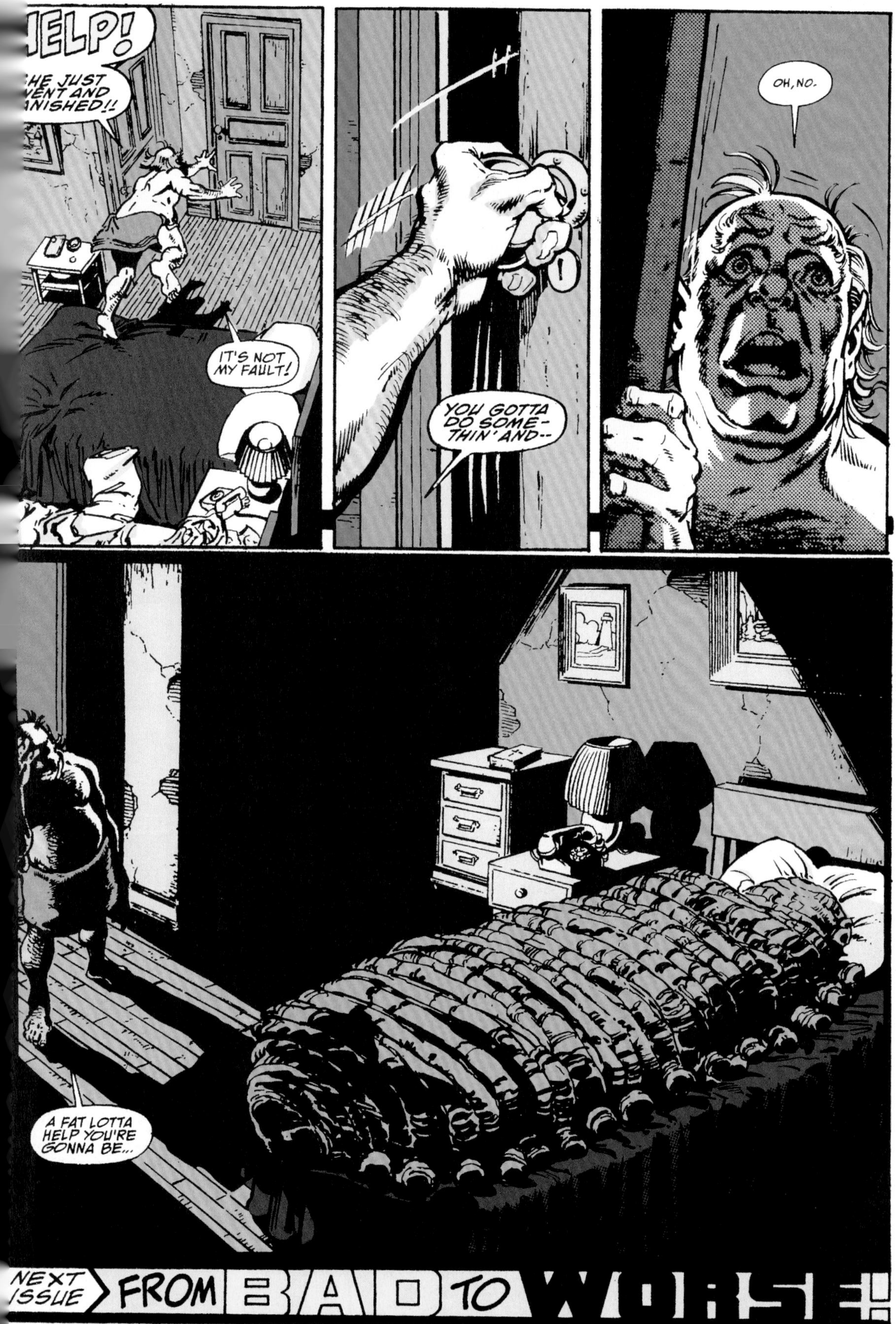
HELP!
HE JUST WENT AND VANISHED!!
IT'S NOT MY FAULT!
YOU GOTTA DO SOME-THIN' AND--
OH, NO.
A FAT LOTTA HELP YOU'RE GONNA BE...
NEXT ISSUE FROM BAD TO WORSE!

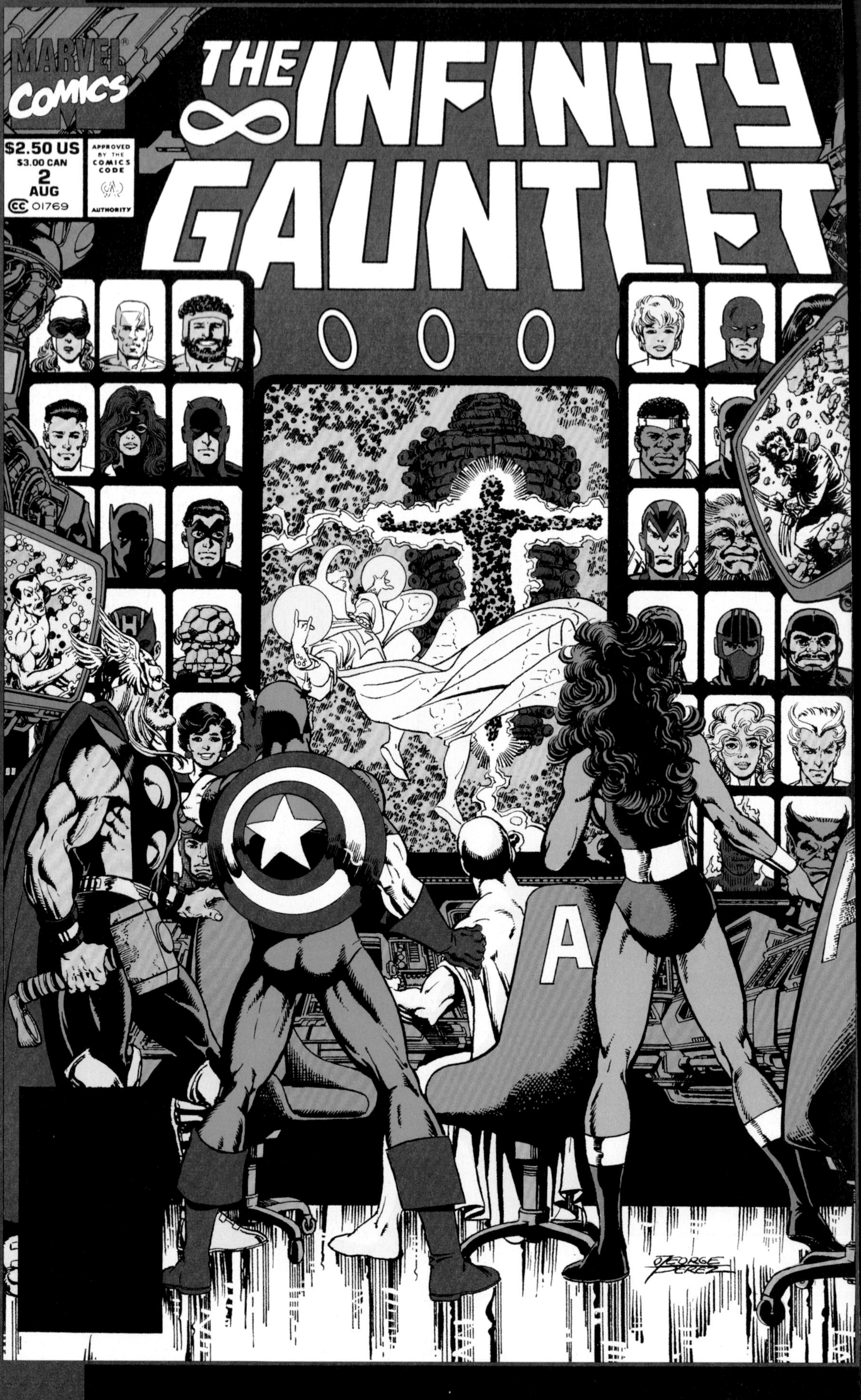

MARVEL COMICS
THE INFINITY GAUNTLET
$2.50 US
$3.00 CAN
2
AUG
CC 01769
APPROVED BY THE COMICS CODE AUTHORITY
A
GEORGE PEREZ

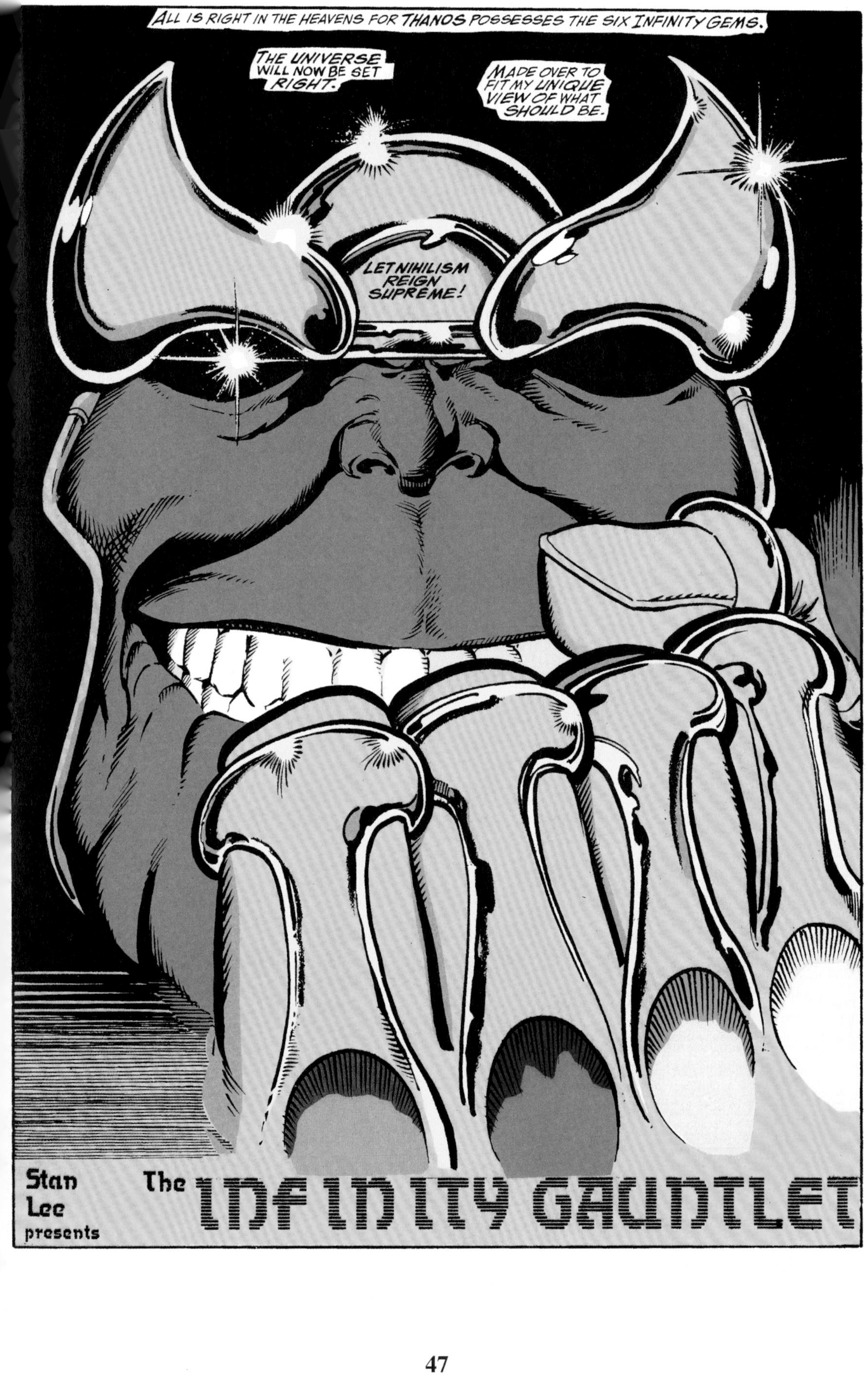

ALL IS RIGHT IN THE HEAVENS FOR THANOS POSSESSES THE SIX INFINITY GEMS.
THE UNIVERSE WILL NOW BE SET RIGHT.
MADE OVER TO FIT MY UNIQUE VIEW OF WHAT SHOULD BE.
LET NIHILISM REIGN SUPREME!
Stan Lee presents
The INFINITY GAUNTLET

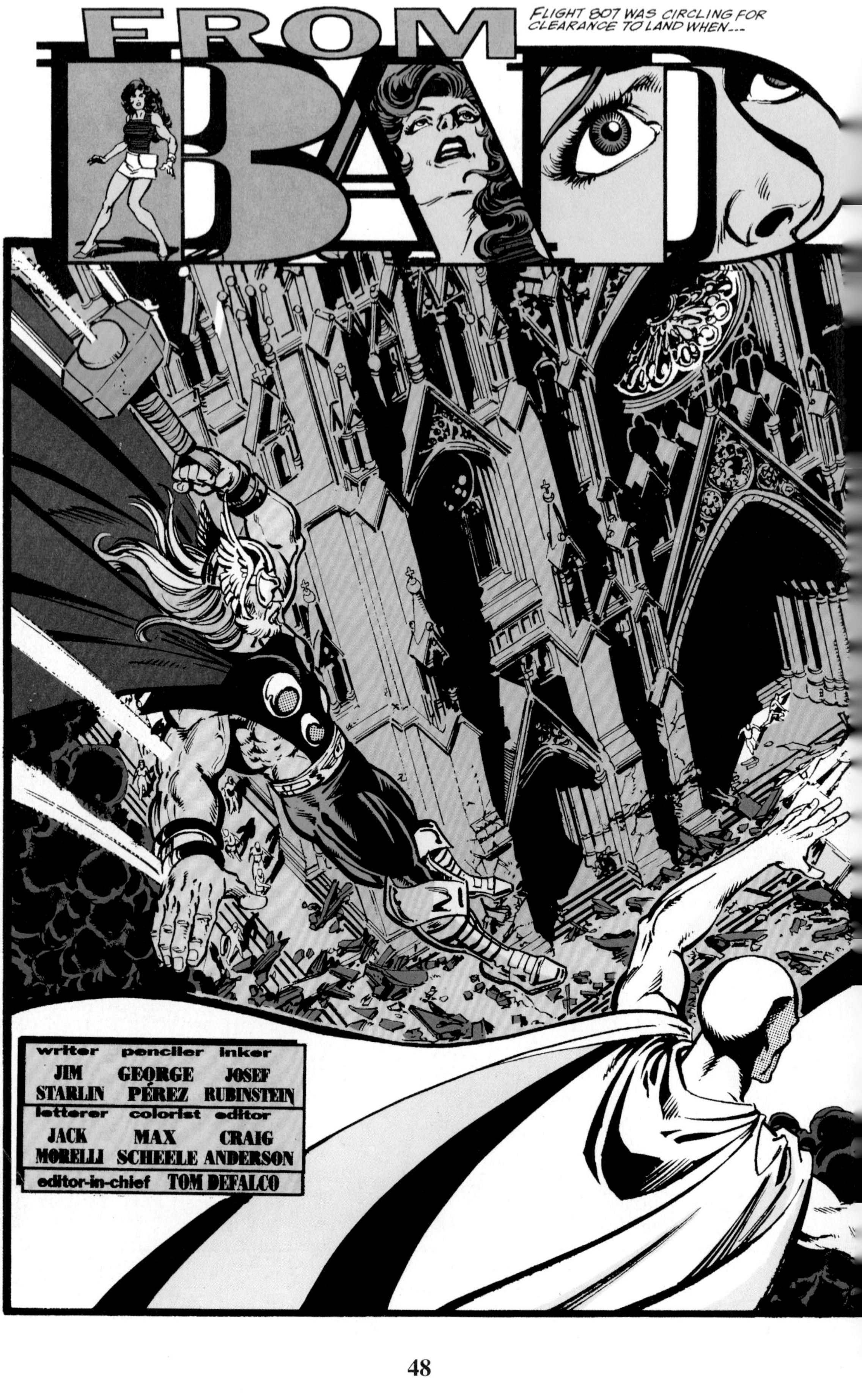
FROM BAD
FLIGHT 807 WAS CIRCLING FOR CLEARANCE TO LAND WHEN---
writer JIM STARLIN
penciler GEORGE PÉREZ
inker JOSEF RUBINSTEIN
letterer JACK MORELLI
colorist MAX SCHEELE
editor CRAIG ANDERSON
editor-in-chief TOM DEFALCO

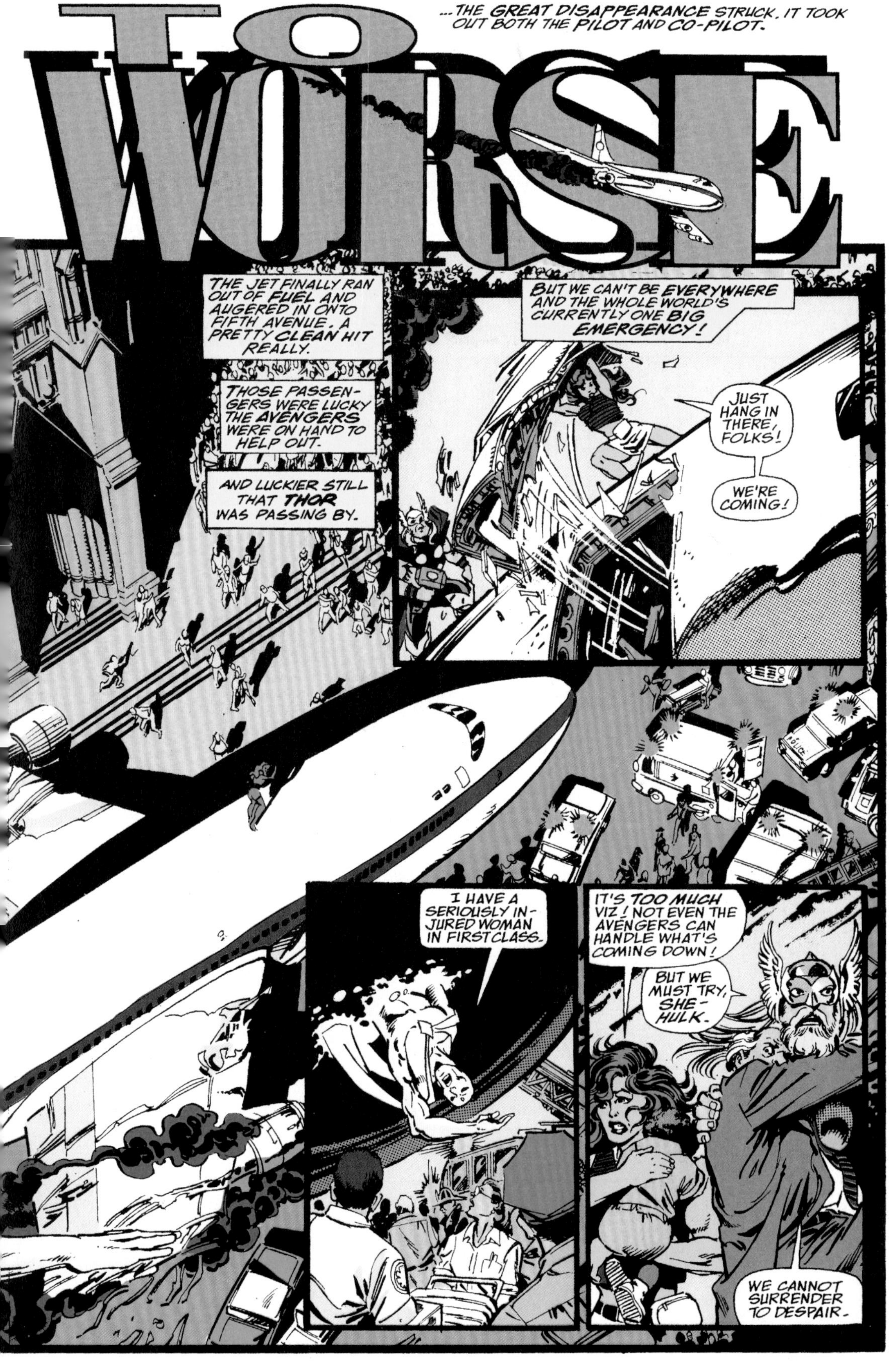
TO WORSE
...THE GREAT DISAPPEARANCE STRUCK. IT TOOK OUT BOTH THE PILOT AND CO-PILOT.
THE JET FINALLY RAN OUT OF FUEL AND AUGERED IN ONTO FIFTH AVENUE. A PRETTY CLEAN HIT REALLY.
THOSE PASSENGERS WERE LUCKY THE AVENGERS WERE ON HAND TO HELP OUT.
AND LUCKIER STILL THAT THOR WAS PASSING BY.
BUT WE CAN'T BE EVERYWHERE AND THE WHOLE WORLD'S CURRENTLY ONE BIG EMERGENCY!
JUST HANG IN THERE, FOLKS!
WE'RE COMING!
I HAVE A SERIOUSLY INJURED WOMAN IN FIRST CLASS.
IT'S TOO MUCH VIZ! NOT EVEN THE AVENGERS CAN HANDLE WHAT'S COMING DOWN!
BUT WE MUST TRY, SHE-HULK.
WE CANNOT SURRENDER TO DESPAIR.

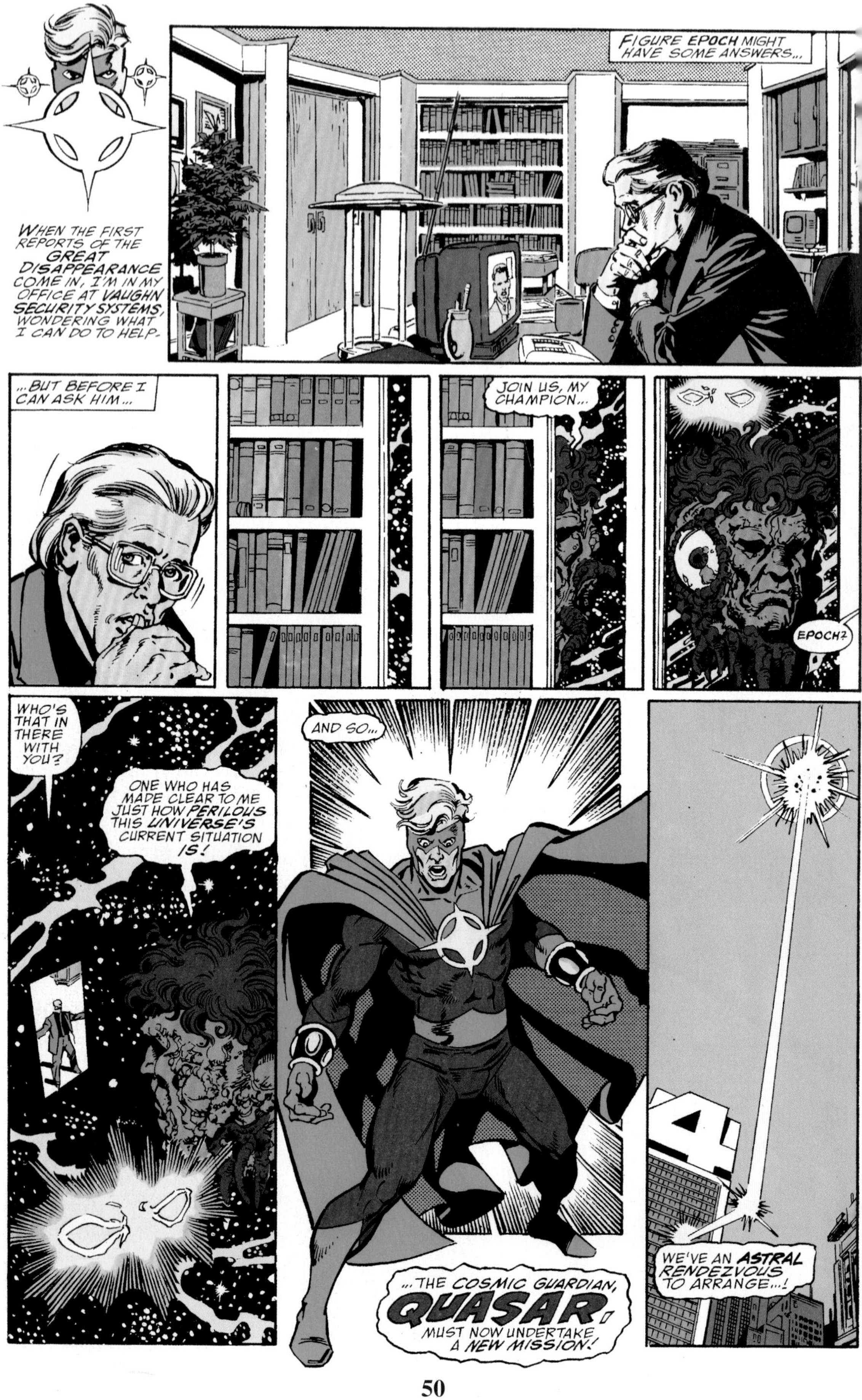
WHEN THE FIRST REPORTS OF THE GREAT DISAPPEARANCE COME IN, I'M IN MY OFFICE AT VAUGHN SECURITY SYSTEMS, WONDERING WHAT I CAN DO TO HELP-
FIGURE EPOCH MIGHT HAVE SOME ANSWERS...
...BUT BEFORE I CAN ASK HIM...
JOIN US, MY CHAMPION...
EPOCH?
WHO'S THAT IN THERE WITH YOU?
ONE WHO HAS MADE CLEAR TO ME JUST HOW PERILOUS THIS UNIVERSE'S CURRENT SITUATION IS!
AND SO...
...THE COSMIC GUARDIAN, QUASAR, MUST NOW UNDERTAKE A NEW MISSION!
WE'VE AN ASTRAL RENDEZVOUS TO ARRANGE...!

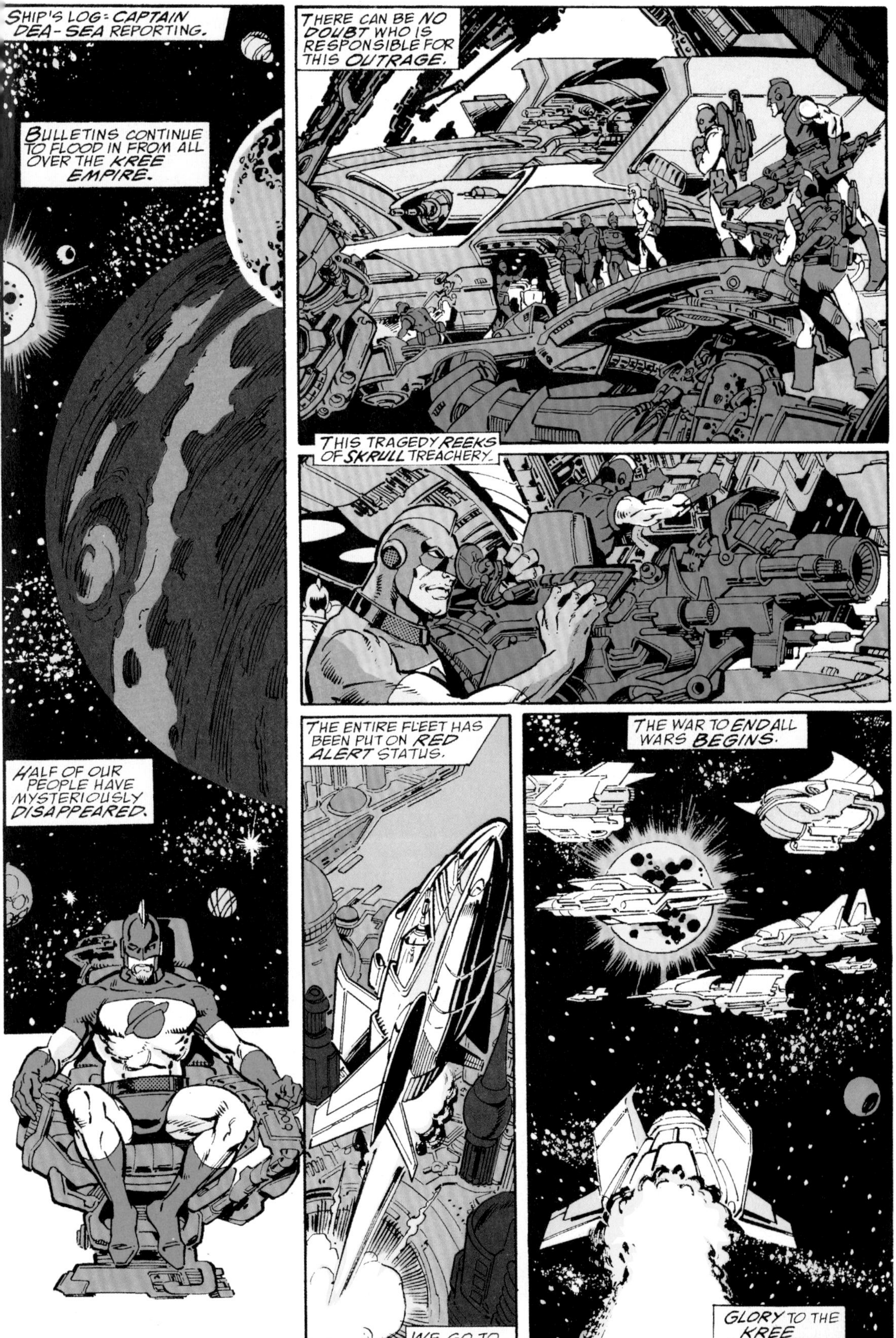
SHIP'S LOG: CAPTAIN DEA-SEA REPORTING.
BULLETINS CONTINUE TO FLOOD IN FROM ALL OVER THE KREE EMPIRE.
HALF OF OUR PEOPLE HAVE MYSTERIOUSLY DISAPPEARED.
THERE CAN BE NO DOUBT WHO IS RESPONSIBLE FOR THIS OUTRAGE.
THIS TRAGEDY REEKS OF SKRULL TREACHERY.
THE ENTIRE FLEET HAS BEEN PUT ON RED ALERT STATUS.
WE GO TO JOIN THE ARMADA.
THE WAR TO END ALL WARS BEGINS.
GLORY TO THE KREE EMPIRE--!

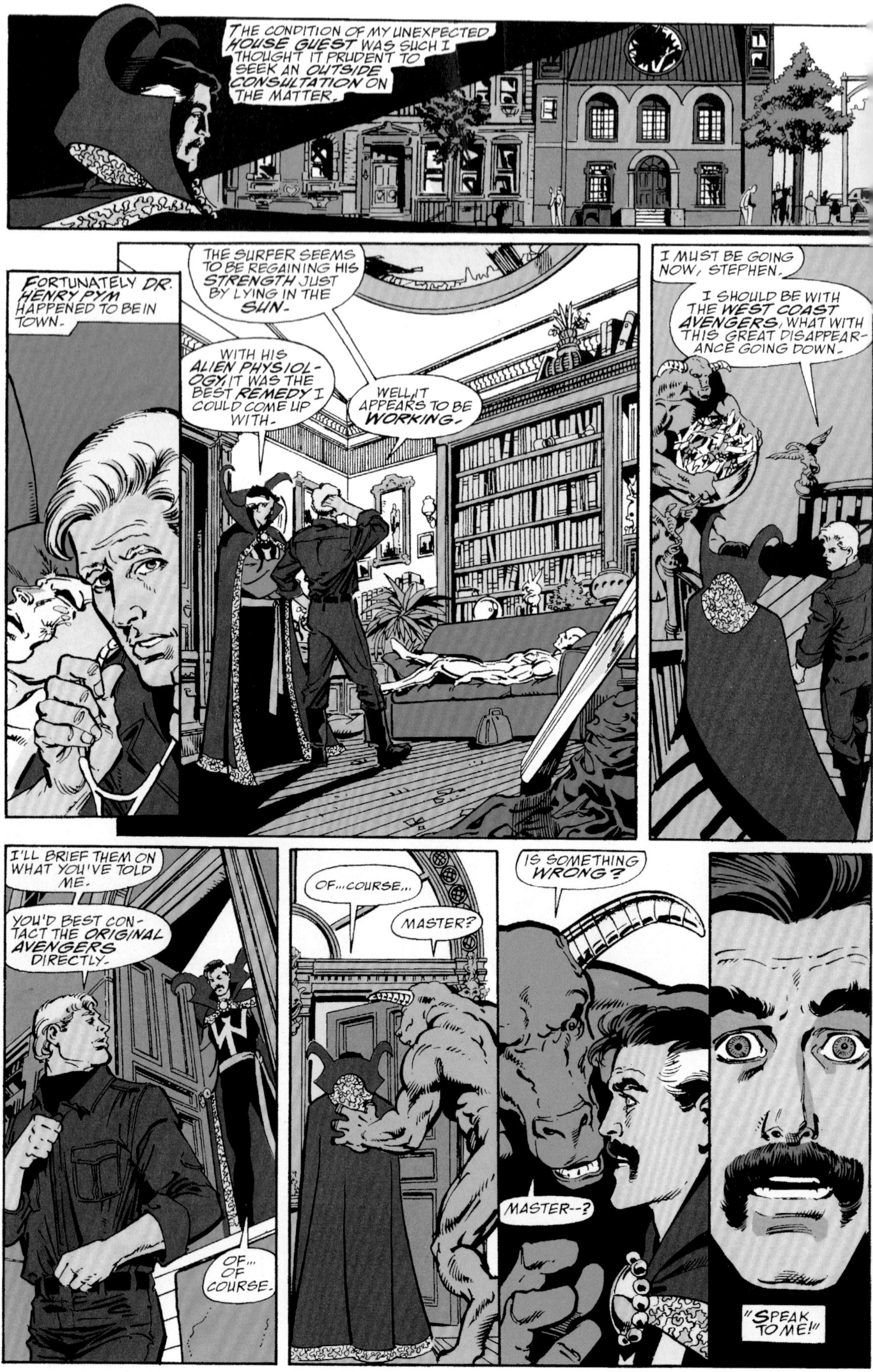
THE CONDITION OF MY UNEXPECTED HOUSE GUEST WAS SUCH I THOUGHT IT PRUDENT TO SEEK AN OUTSIDE CONSULTATION ON THE MATTER.
FORTUNATELY DR. HENRY PYM HAPPENED TO BE IN TOWN.
THE SURFER SEEMS TO BE REGAINING HIS STRENGTH JUST BY LYING IN THE SUN.
WITH HIS ALIEN PHYSIOLOGY, IT WAS THE BEST REMEDY I COULD COME UP WITH.
WELL, IT APPEARS TO BE WORKING.
I MUST BE GOING NOW, STEPHEN.
I SHOULD BE WITH THE WEST COAST AVENGERS, WHAT WITH THIS GREAT DISAPPEARANCE GOING DOWN.
I'LL BRIEF THEM ON WHAT YOU'VE TOLD ME.
YOU'D BEST CONTACT THE ORIGINAL AVENGERS DIRECTLY.
OF... OF COURSE.
OF...COURSE...
MASTER?
IS SOMETHING WRONG?
MASTER--?
"SPEAK TO ME!"

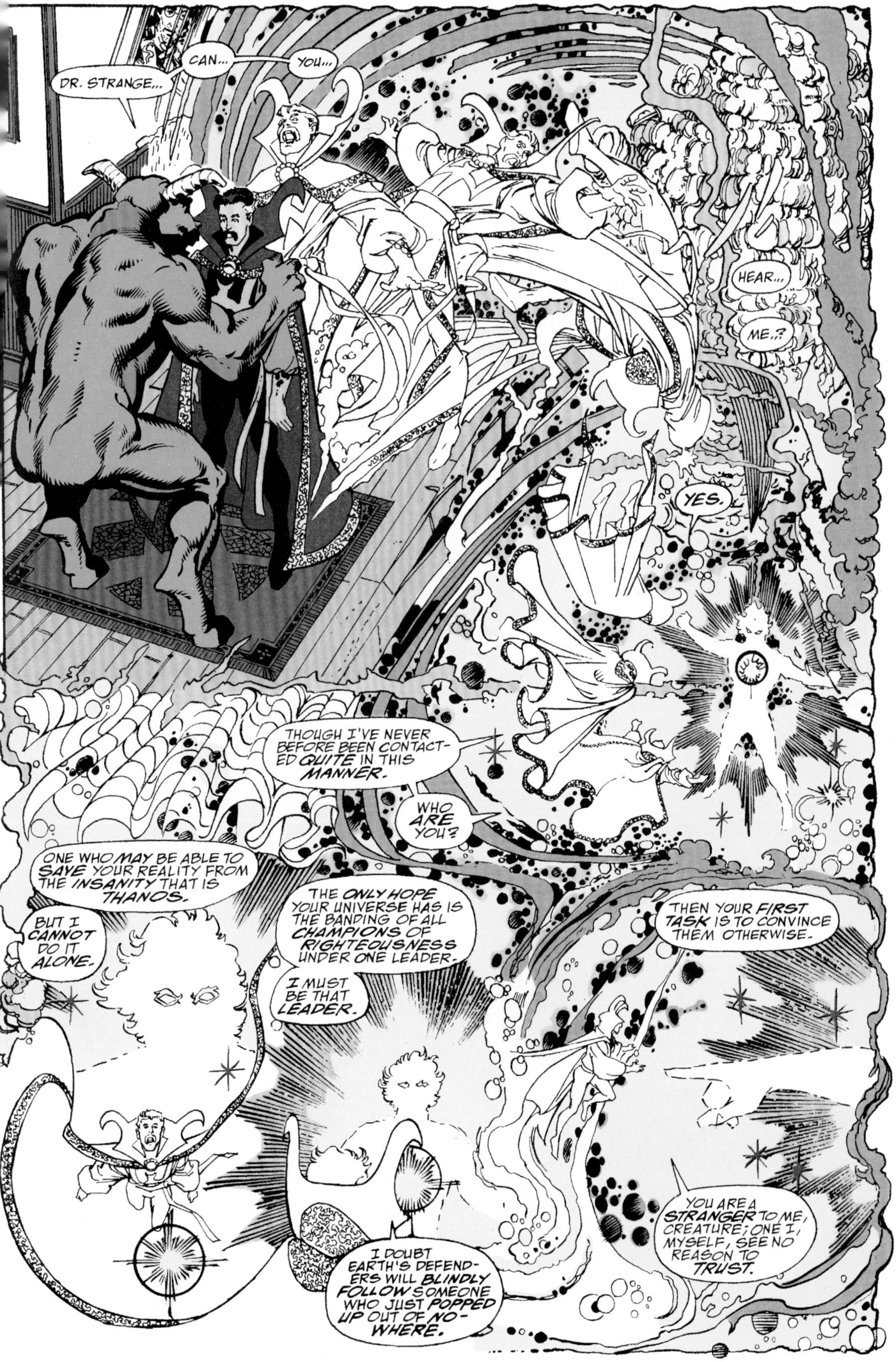

DR. STRANGE...
CAN...
YOU...
HEAR...
ME..?
YES.
THOUGH I'VE NEVER BEFORE BEEN CONTACTED QUITE IN THIS MANNER.
WHO ARE YOU?
ONE WHO MAY BE ABLE TO SAVE YOUR REALITY FROM THE INSANITY THAT IS THANOS.
BUT I CANNOT DO IT ALONE.
THE ONLY HOPE YOUR UNIVERSE HAS IS THE BANDING OF ALL CHAMPIONS OF RIGHTEOUSNESS UNDER ONE LEADER.
I MUST BE THAT LEADER.
THEN YOUR FIRST TASK IS TO CONVINCE THEM OTHERWISE.
YOU ARE A STRANGER TO ME, CREATURE; ONE I, MYSELF, SEE NO REASON TO TRUST.
I DOUBT EARTH'S DEFENDERS WILL BLINDLY FOLLOW SOMEONE WHO JUST POPPED UP OUT OF NOWHERE.

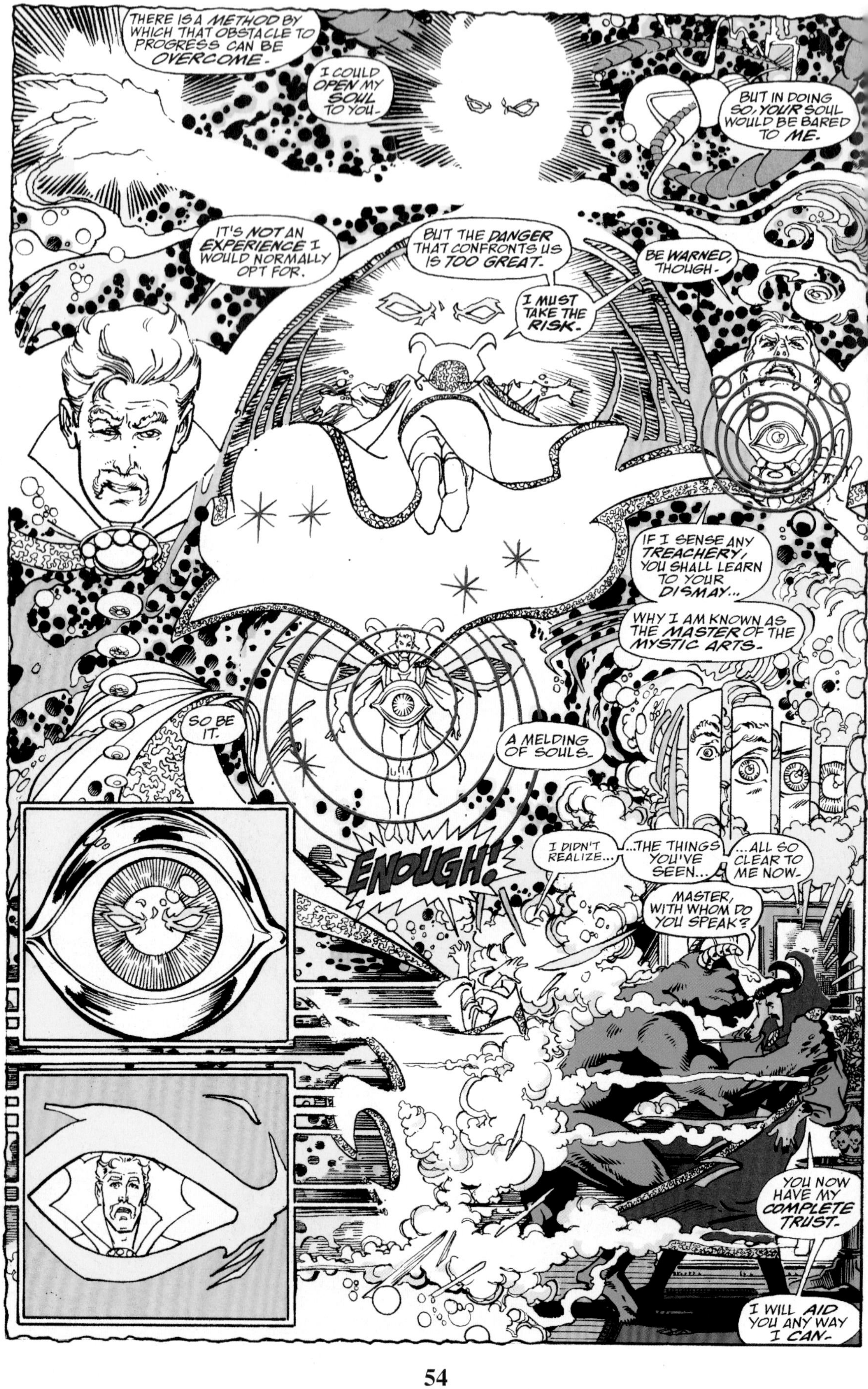
THERE IS A METHOD BY WHICH THAT OBSTACLE TO PROGRESS CAN BE OVERCOME-
I COULD OPEN MY SOUL TO YOU-
BUT IN DOING SO, YOUR SOUL WOULD BE BARED TO ME.
IT'S NOT AN EXPERIENCE I WOULD NORMALLY OPT FOR.
BUT THE DANGER THAT CONFRONTS US IS TOO GREAT-
I MUST TAKE THE RISK-
BE WARNED, THOUGH-
IF I SENSE ANY TREACHERY, YOU SHALL LEARN TO YOUR DISMAY...
WHY I AM KNOWN AS THE MASTER OF THE MYSTIC ARTS-
SO BE IT.
A MELDING OF SOULS-
ENOUGH!
I DIDN'T REALIZE...
...THE THINGS YOU'VE SEEN...
...ALL SO CLEAR TO ME NOW-
MASTER, WITH WHOM DO YOU SPEAK?
YOU NOW HAVE MY COMPLETE TRUST-
I WILL AID YOU ANY WAY I CAN-

MY INSTRUMENTS INDICATE THAT THE *FORCE* RESPONSIBLE FOR THE *GREAT DISAPPEARANCE* ORIGINATED ON THE *FAR SIDE* OF THE *GALAXY*.

I HAVE NEVER BEFORE ENCOUNTERED SUCH *POWERFUL* READINGS!

YET I'M PICKING UP *SIMILAR EMANATIONS* FROM A SMALL TOWN IN UPSTATE NEW YORK.

ODDER STILL...

...THESE TRANSMISSIONS ARE BEING DIRECTED TO THE HOME OF *DR. STEPHEN STRANGE—*

WHAT IS THE CONNECTION?

THIS IS A QUESTION I *MUST* HAVE ANSWERED.

FOR THIS IS *MY UNIVERSE.* THESE ARE *MY PEOPLE* DISAPPEARING.

AND NO ONE SHOULD *DARE TAMPER* WITH WHAT BELONGS TO DOCTOR DOOM!

PLUS, THERE IS THE FACT THAT *GREAT DISASTERS* OF THIS MAGNITUDE ALSO PRESENT A CURIOUS INTELLECT WITH *GREAT OPPORTUNITY.*

A CHANCE TO *EXPAND ON MY SCIENTIFIC KNOWLEDGE* AND...

...PERSONAL POWER.

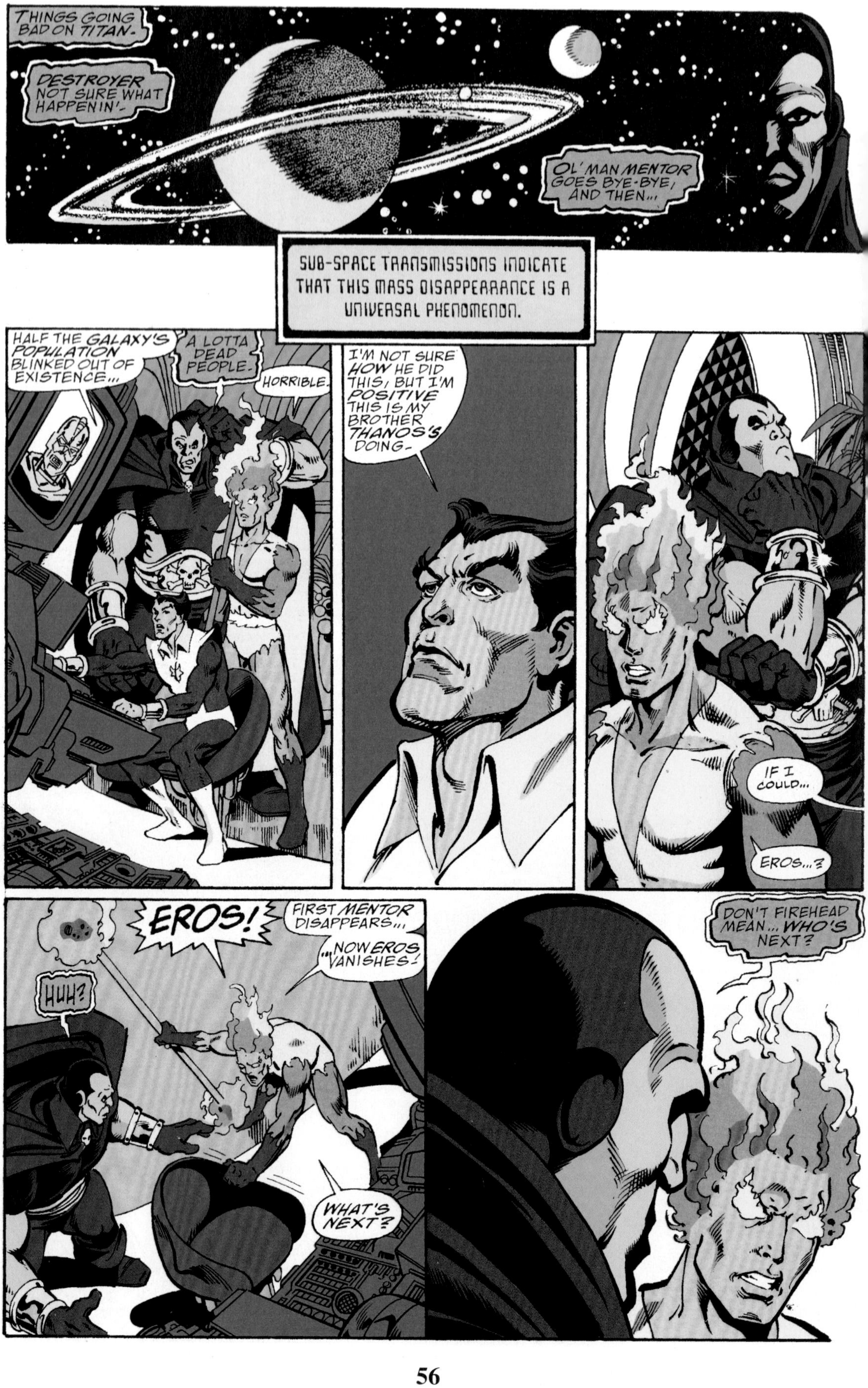
THINGS GOING BAD ON TITAN-
DESTROYER NOT SURE WHAT HAPPENIN'-
OL' MAN MENTOR GOES BYE-BYE, AND THEN...
SUB-SPACE TRANSMISSIONS INDICATE THAT THIS MASS DISAPPEARANCE IS A UNIVERSAL PHENOMENON.
HALF THE GALAXY'S POPULATION BLINKED OUT OF EXISTENCE...
A LOTTA DEAD PEOPLE-
HORRIBLE.
I'M NOT SURE HOW HE DID THIS, BUT I'M POSITIVE THIS IS MY BROTHER THANOS'S DOING-
IF I COULD...
EROS...?
EROS!
HUH?
FIRST MENTOR DISAPPEARS...
...NOW EROS VANISHES!
WHAT'S NEXT?
DON'T FIREHEAD MEAN... WHO'S NEXT?

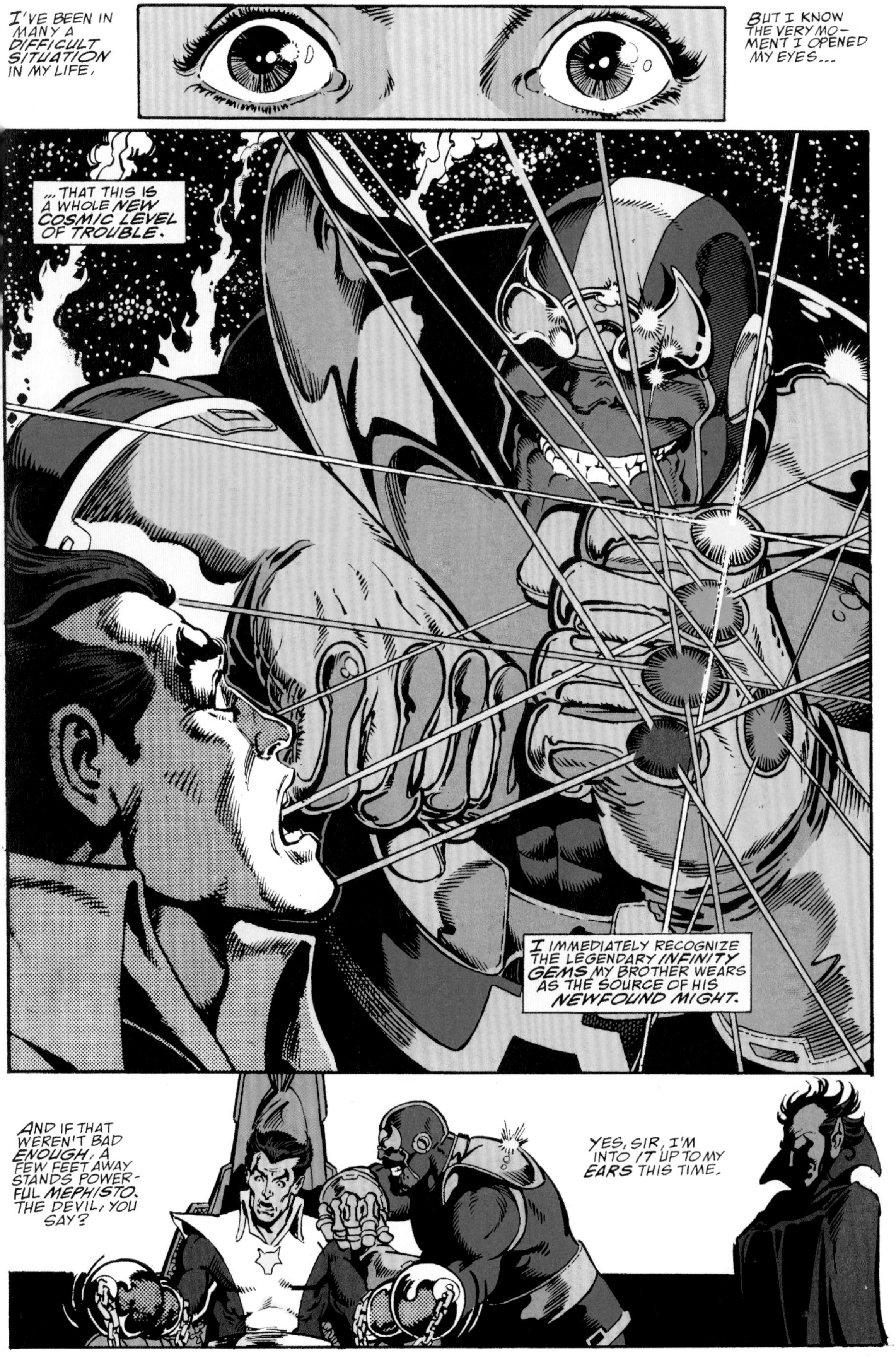
I'VE BEEN IN MANY A DIFFICULT SITUATION IN MY LIFE.
BUT I KNOW THE VERY MOMENT I OPENED MY EYES...
...THAT THIS IS A WHOLE NEW COSMIC LEVEL OF TROUBLE.
I IMMEDIATELY RECOGNIZE THE LEGENDARY INFINITY GEMS MY BROTHER WEARS AS THE SOURCE OF HIS NEWFOUND MIGHT.
AND IF THAT WEREN'T BAD ENOUGH, A FEW FEET AWAY STANDS POWERFUL MEPHISTO. THE DEVIL, YOU SAY?
YES, SIR, I'M INTO IT UP TO MY EARS THIS TIME.

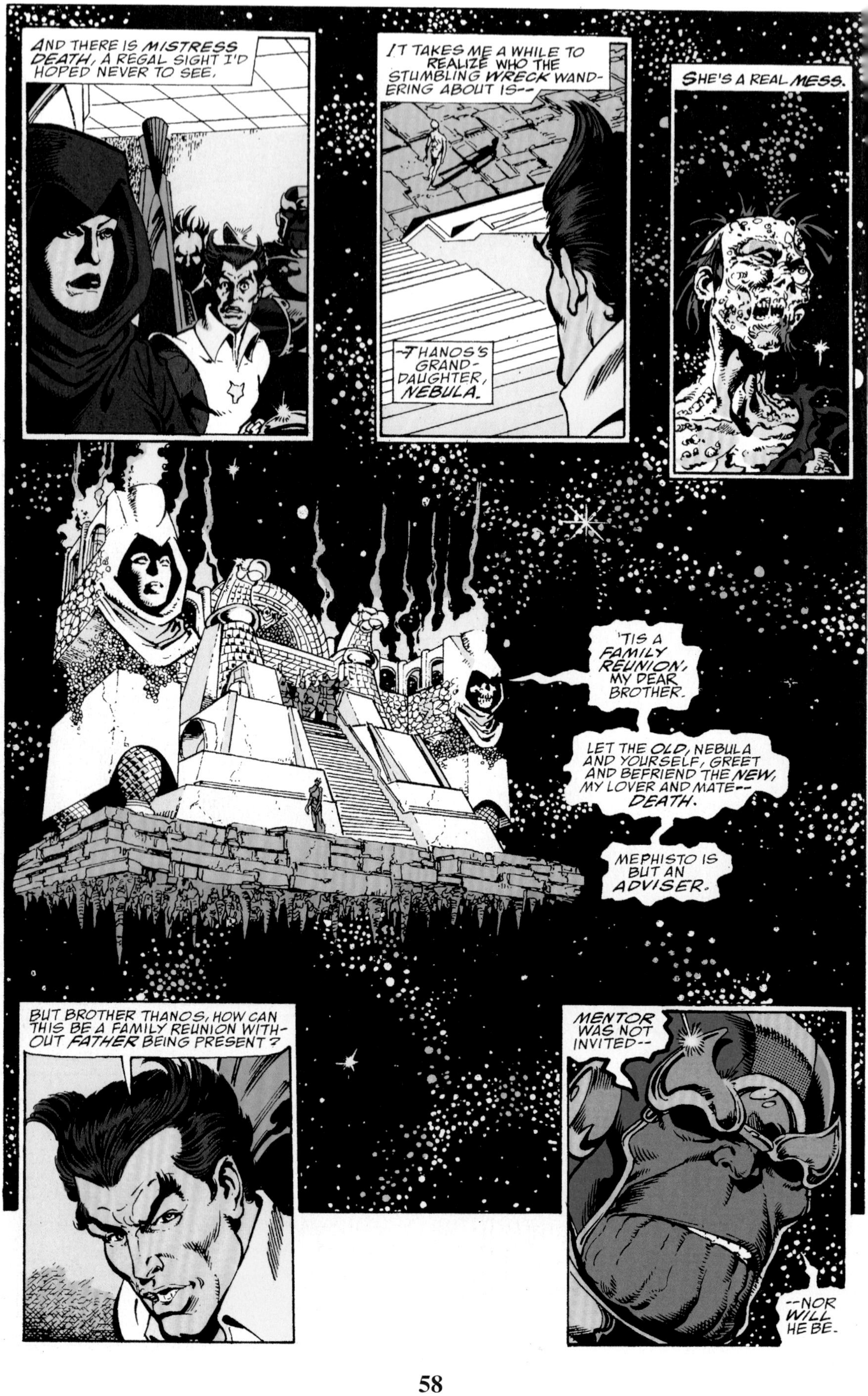
AND THERE IS MISTRESS DEATH, A REGAL SIGHT I'D HOPED NEVER TO SEE.
IT TAKES ME A WHILE TO REALIZE WHO THE STUMBLING WRECK WANDERING ABOUT IS--
--THANOS'S GRAND-DAUGHTER, NEBULA.
SHE'S A REAL MESS.
'TIS A FAMILY REUNION, MY DEAR BROTHER.
LET THE OLD, NEBULA AND YOURSELF, GREET AND BEFRIEND THE NEW, MY LOVER AND MATE-- DEATH.
MEPHISTO IS BUT AN ADVISER.
BUT BROTHER THANOS, HOW CAN THIS BE A FAMILY REUNION WITHOUT FATHER BEING PRESENT?
MENTOR WAS NOT INVITED--
--NOR WILL HE BE.

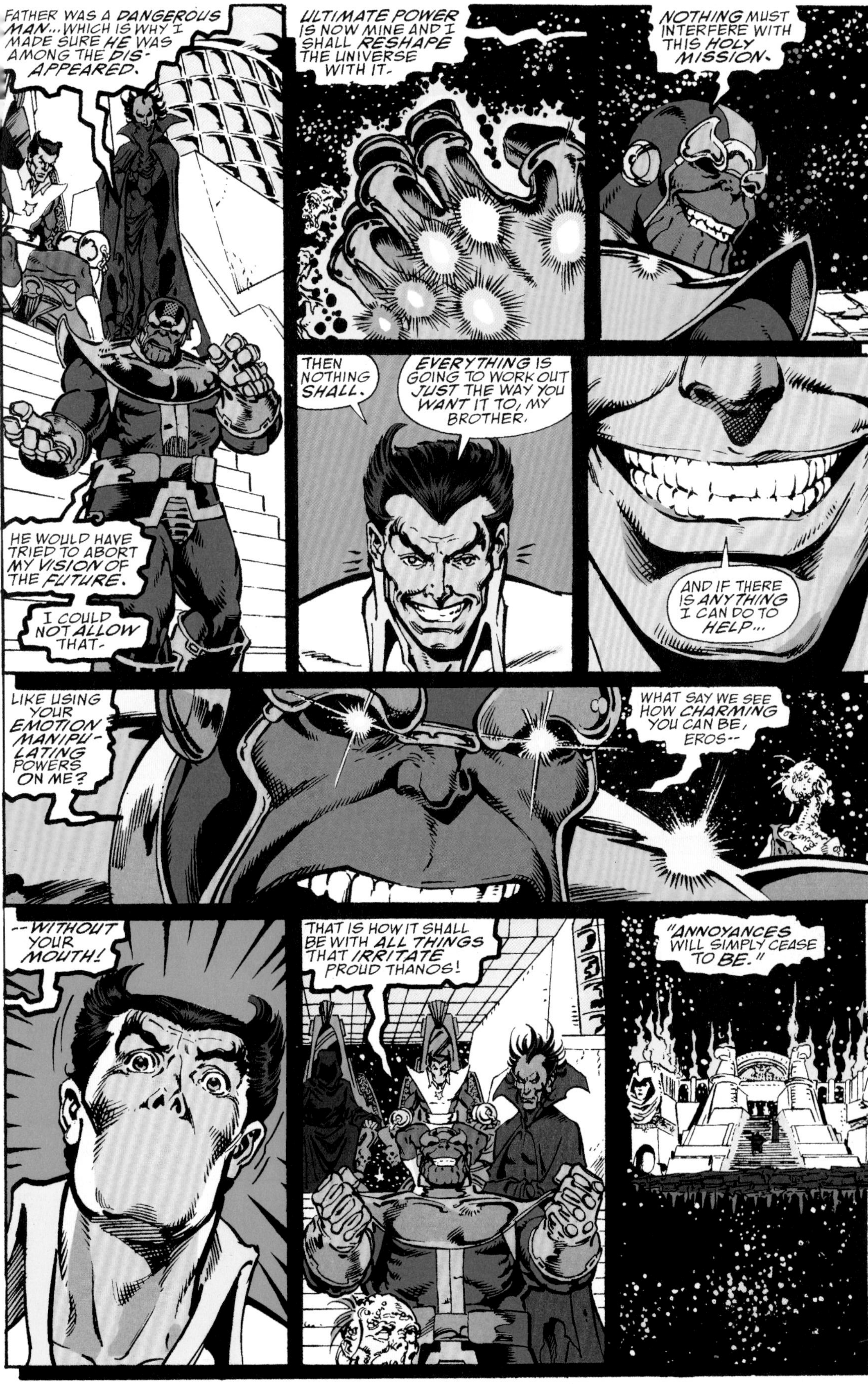
FATHER WAS A DANGEROUS MAN... WHICH IS WHY I MADE SURE HE WAS AMONG THE DIS-APPEARED.
HE WOULD HAVE TRIED TO ABORT MY VISION OF THE FUTURE.
I COULD NOT ALLOW THAT.
ULTIMATE POWER IS NOW MINE AND I SHALL RESHAPE THE UNIVERSE WITH IT.
NOTHING MUST INTERFERE WITH THIS HOLY MISSION.
THEN NOTHING SHALL.
EVERYTHING IS GOING TO WORK OUT JUST THE WAY YOU WANT IT TO, MY BROTHER.
AND IF THERE IS ANYTHING I CAN DO TO HELP...
LIKE USING YOUR EMOTION MANIPU-LATING POWERS ON ME?
WHAT SAY WE SEE HOW CHARMING YOU CAN BE, EROS--
--WITHOUT YOUR MOUTH!
THAT IS HOW IT SHALL BE WITH ALL THINGS THAT IRRITATE PROUD THANOS!
"ANNOYANCES WILL SIMPLY CEASE TO BE."

ARCHANGEL · BEAST · BLACK CAT · BLACK PANTHER · BOX · DAGGER · DAREDEVIL · DIAMOND LIL

FIRESTAR · GUARDIAN · HAWKEYE · HERCULES · HUMAN TORCH · ICEMAN · INVISIBLE WOMAN · MAKKARI

MARVEL BOY · MARVEL GIRL · MR. FANTASTIC · NIGHT THRASHER · NORTHSTAR · POWER MAN · PUCK · QUICKSILVER

SASQUATCH · SERSI · SHAMAN · THING · USAGENT · VINDICATOR · WASP · WINDSHEAR

HERE'S THE UPDATE ON THE TALLY OF DIS-APPEARED SUPER HEROES.

DISAPPEARED—DISAPPEARED—DISAPPEARED

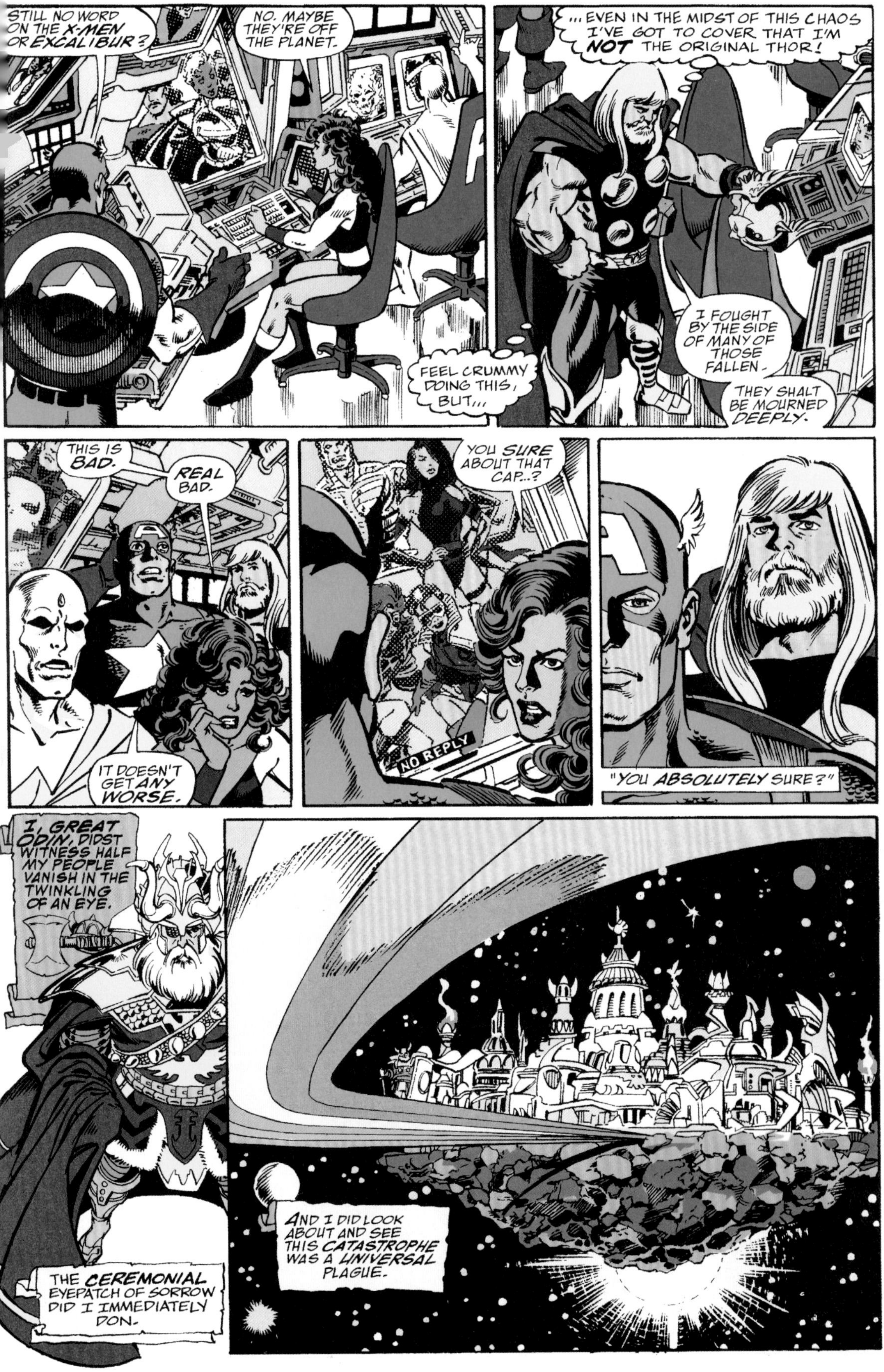
STILL NO WORD ON THE X-MEN OR EXCALIBUR?
NO. MAYBE THEY'RE OFF THE PLANET.
...EVEN IN THE MIDST OF THIS CHAOS I'VE GOT TO COVER THAT I'M NOT THE ORIGINAL THOR!
FEEL CRUMMY DOING THIS, BUT...
I FOUGHT BY THE SIDE OF MANY OF THOSE FALLEN.
THEY SHALT BE MOURNED DEEPLY.
THIS IS BAD.
REAL BAD.
IT DOESN'T GET ANY WORSE.
YOU SURE ABOUT THAT CAP...?
NO REPLY
"YOU ABSOLUTELY SURE?"
I, GREAT ODIN, DIDST WITNESS HALF MY PEOPLE VANISH IN THE TWINKLING OF AN EYE.
THE CEREMONIAL EYEPATCH OF SORROW DID I IMMEDIATELY DON.
AND I DID LOOK ABOUT AND SEE THIS CATASTROPHE WAS A UNIVERSAL PLAGUE.

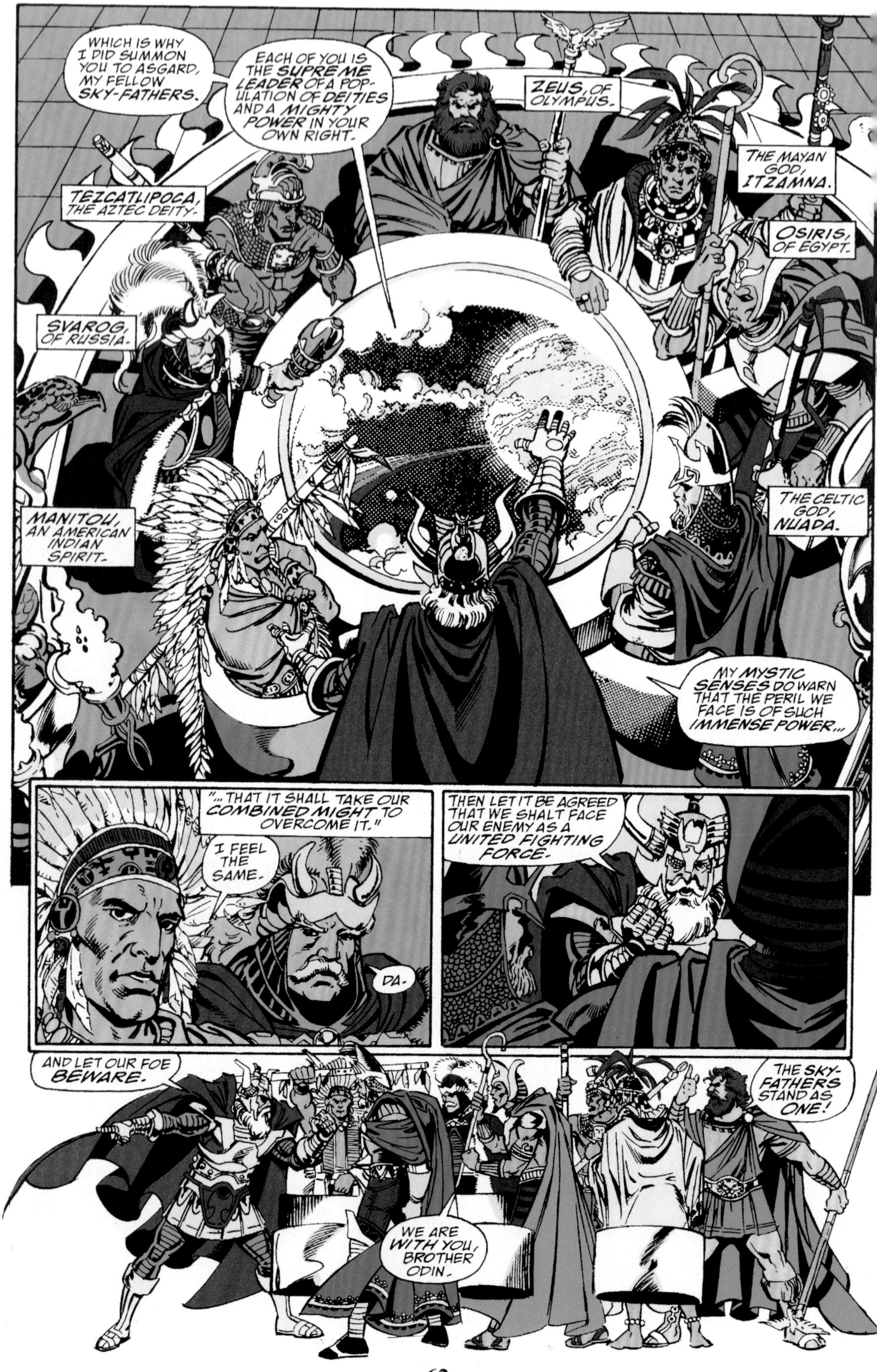

WHICH IS WHY I DID SUMMON YOU TO ASGARD, MY FELLOW SKY-FATHERS.
EACH OF YOU IS THE SUPREME LEADER OF A POPULATION OF DEITIES AND A MIGHTY POWER IN YOUR OWN RIGHT.
ZEUS, OF OLYMPUS.
THE MAYAN GOD, ITZAMNA.
TEZCATLIPOCA, THE AZTEC DEITY.
OSIRIS, OF EGYPT.
SVAROG, OF RUSSIA.
MANITOU, AN AMERICAN INDIAN SPIRIT.
THE CELTIC GOD, NUADA.
MY MYSTIC SENSES DO WARN THAT THE PERIL WE FACE IS OF SUCH IMMENSE POWER...
"...THAT IT SHALL TAKE OUR COMBINED MIGHT TO OVERCOME IT."
I FEEL THE SAME.
DA.
THEN LET IT BE AGREED THAT WE SHALT FACE OUR ENEMY AS A UNITED FIGHTING FORCE.
AND LET OUR FOE BEWARE.
THE SKY-FATHERS STAND AS ONE!
WE ARE WITH YOU, BROTHER ODIN.

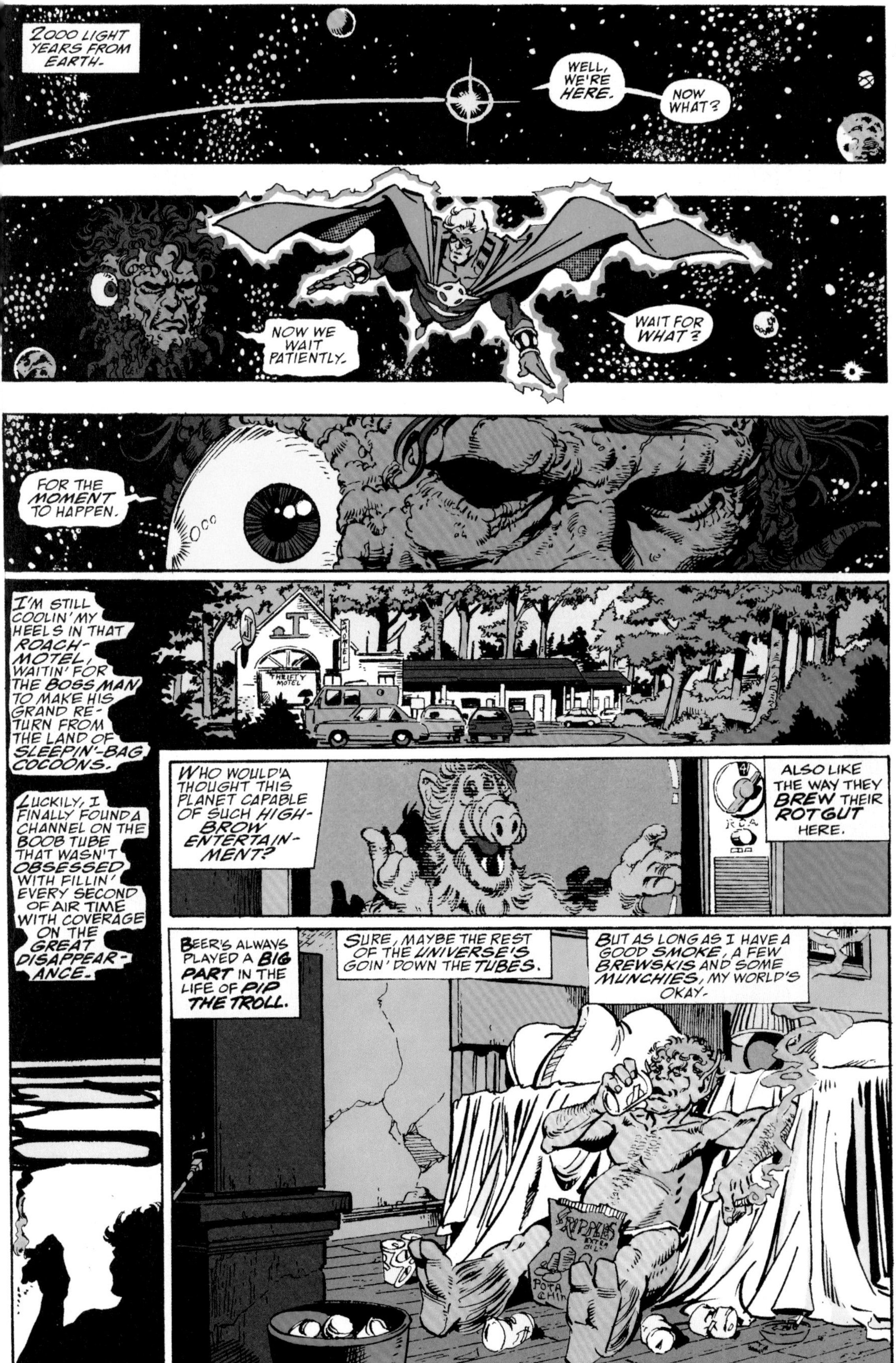
2000 LIGHT YEARS FROM EARTH.
WELL, WE'RE HERE.
NOW WHAT?
NOW WE WAIT PATIENTLY.
WAIT FOR WHAT?
FOR THE MOMENT TO HAPPEN.
I'M STILL COOLIN' MY HEELS IN THAT ROACH-MOTEL, WAITIN' FOR THE BOSS MAN TO MAKE HIS GRAND RETURN FROM THE LAND OF SLEEPIN'-BAG COCOONS.
THRIFTY MOTEL
LUCKILY, I FINALLY FOUND A CHANNEL ON THE BOOB TUBE THAT WASN'T OBSESSED WITH FILLIN' EVERY SECOND OF AIR TIME WITH COVERAGE ON THE GREAT DISAPPEAR-ANCE.
WHO WOULD'A THOUGHT THIS PLANET CAPABLE OF SUCH HIGH-BROW ENTERTAIN-MENT?
ALSO LIKE THE WAY THEY BREW THEIR ROTGUT HERE.
BEER'S ALWAYS PLAYED A BIG PART IN THE LIFE OF PIP THE TROLL.
SURE, MAYBE THE REST OF THE UNIVERSE'S GOIN' DOWN THE TUBES.
BUT AS LONG AS I HAVE A GOOD SMOKE, A FEW BREWSKIS AND SOME MUNCHIES, MY WORLD'S OKAY.

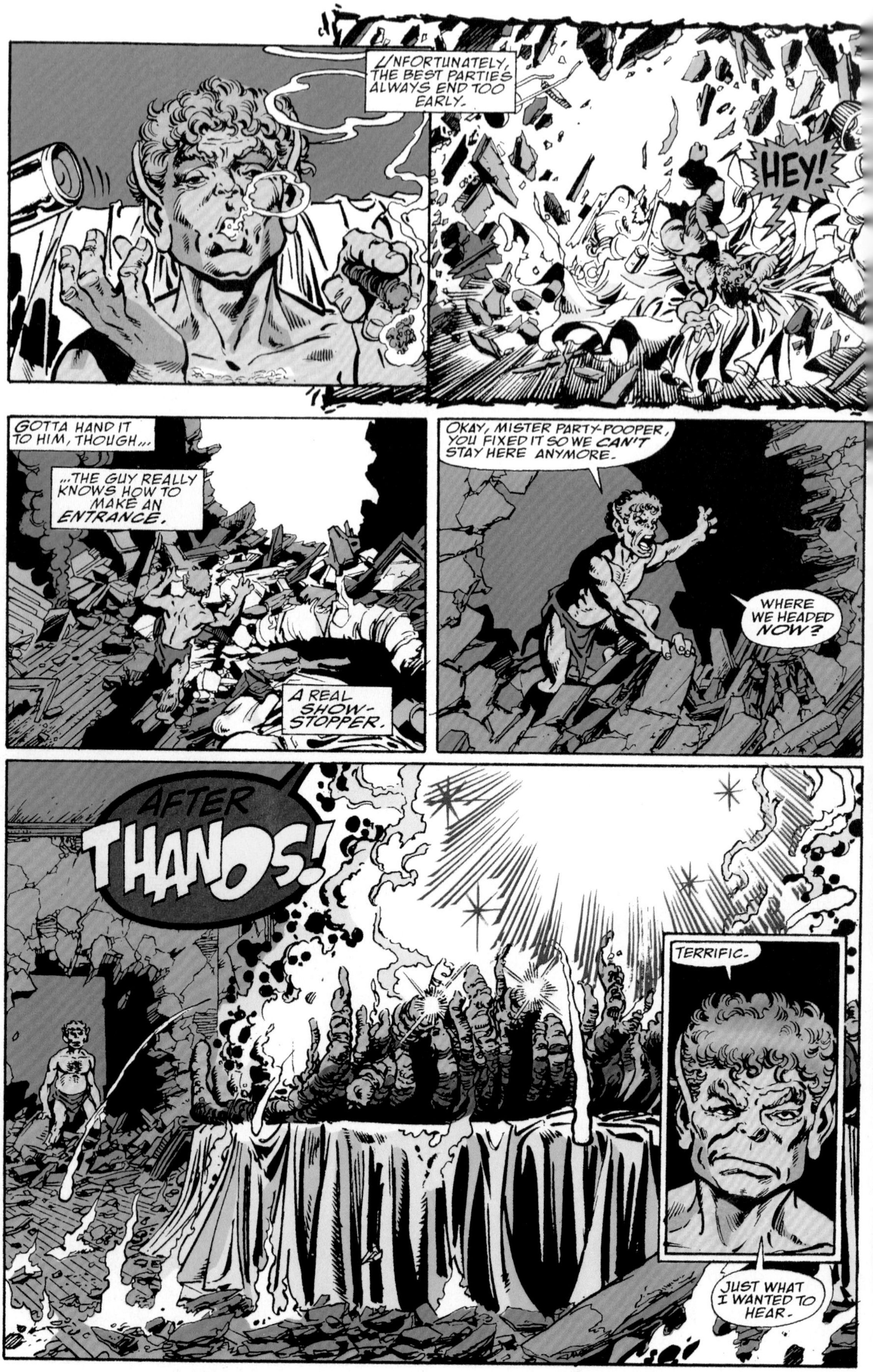
UNFORTUNATELY, THE BEST PARTIES ALWAYS END TOO EARLY.
HEY!
GOTTA HAND IT TO HIM, THOUGH...
...THE GUY REALLY KNOWS HOW TO MAKE AN ENTRANCE.
A REAL SHOW-STOPPER.
OKAY, MISTER PARTY-POOPER, YOU FIXED IT SO WE CAN'T STAY HERE ANYMORE.
WHERE WE HEADED NOW?
AFTER THANOS!
TERRIFIC.
JUST WHAT I WANTED TO HEAR.

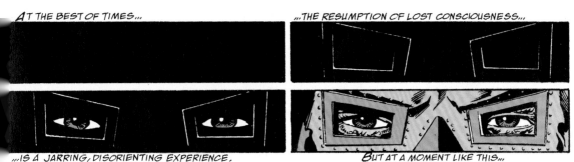

AT THE BEST OF TIMES...

...THE RESUMPTION OF LOST CONSCIOUSNESS...

...IS A JARRING, DISORIENTING EXPERIENCE.

BUT AT A MOMENT LIKE THIS...

WHAT?

...IT CAN BE DEVASTATING.

DR. STRANGE...?

DR. DOOM?

I WARN YOU, DOOM, YOU MEDDLE IN DANGEROUS MATTERS YOU DO NOT FULLY UNDERSTAND!

THEN YOU SHALL ENLIGHTEN ME OR SUFFER FURTHER DISCOMFORT AT MY SERVANTS HANDS.

DOOM! UNHAND MY COMRADE!!

OR I SHALL--

FALL VICTIM TO A SUPERIOR INTELLECT AND POWER AS YOU DID IN OUR LAST ENCOUNTER!

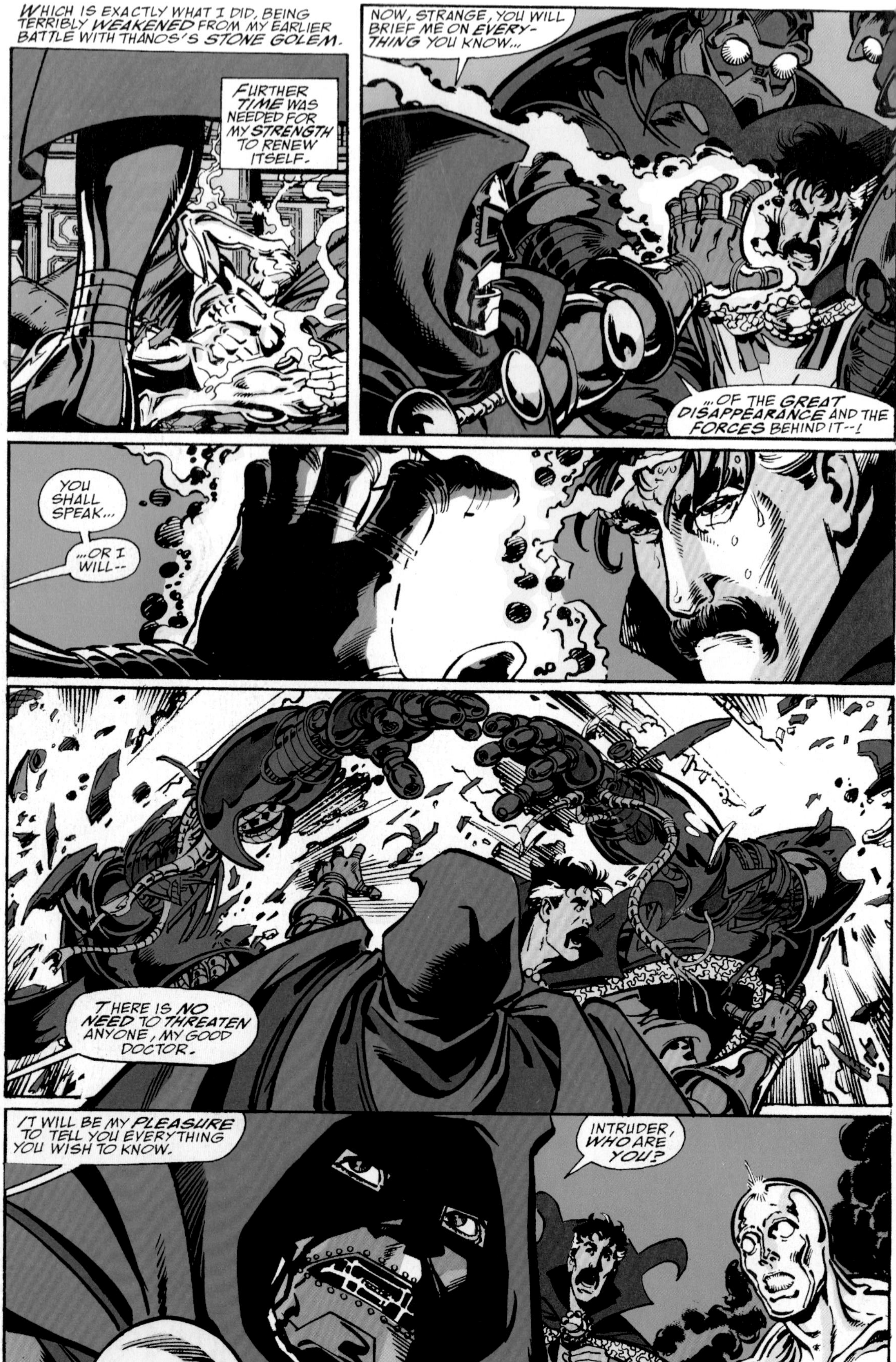

WHICH IS EXACTLY WHAT I DID, BEING TERRIBLY WEAKENED FROM MY EARLIER BATTLE WITH THANOS'S STONE GOLEM.
FURTHER TIME WAS NEEDED FOR MY STRENGTH TO RENEW ITSELF.
NOW, STRANGE, YOU WILL BRIEF ME ON EVERY-THING YOU KNOW...
...OF THE GREAT DISAPPEARANCE AND THE FORCES BEHIND IT--!
YOU SHALL SPEAK...
...OR I WILL--
THERE IS NO NEED TO THREATEN ANYONE, MY GOOD DOCTOR.
IT WILL BE MY PLEASURE TO TELL YOU EVERYTHING YOU WISH TO KNOW.
INTRUDER, WHO ARE YOU?

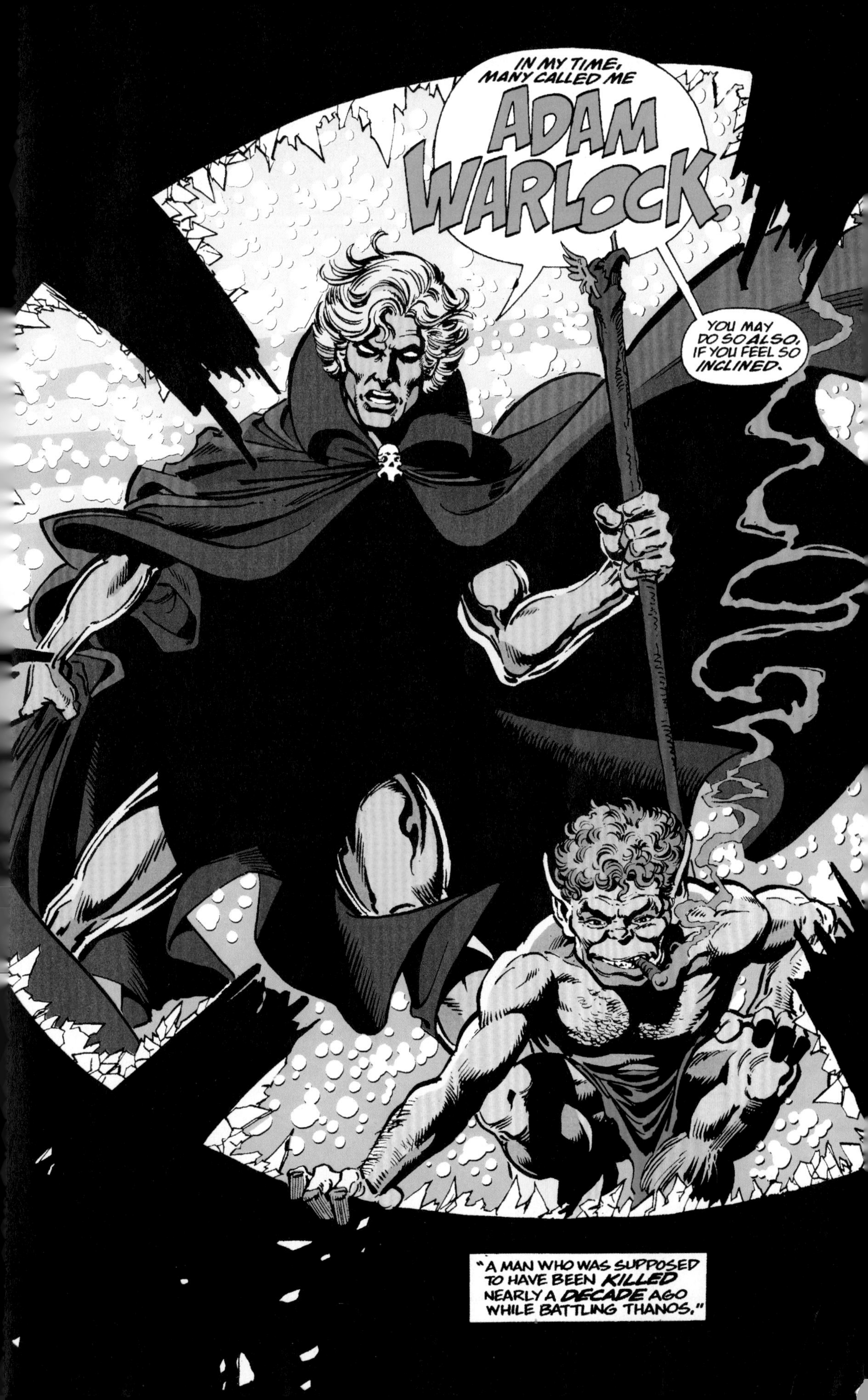
IN MY TIME, MANY CALLED ME ADAM WARLOCK.
YOU MAY DO SO ALSO, IF YOU FEEL SO INCLINED.
"A MAN WHO WAS SUPPOSED TO HAVE BEEN KILLED NEARLY A DECADE AGO WHILE BATTLING THANOS."

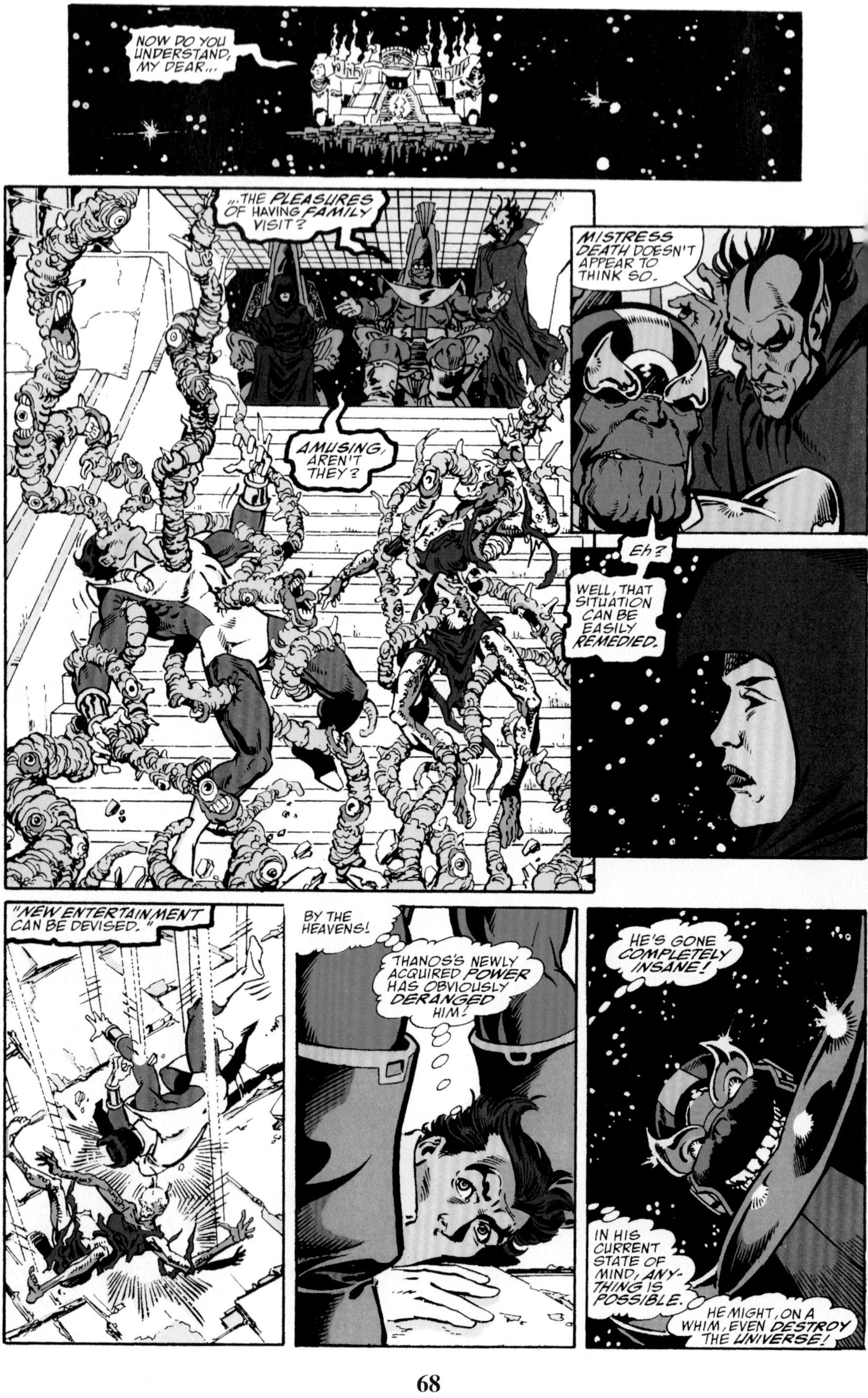
NOW DO YOU UNDERSTAND, MY DEAR...
...THE PLEASURES OF HAVING FAMILY VISIT?
AMUSING, AREN'T THEY?
MISTRESS DEATH DOESN'T APPEAR TO THINK SO.
Eh?
WELL, THAT SITUATION CAN BE EASILY REMEDIED.
"NEW ENTERTAINMENT CAN BE DEVISED."
BY THE HEAVENS!
THANOS'S NEWLY ACQUIRED POWER HAS OBVIOUSLY DERANGED HIM!
HE'S GONE COMPLETELY INSANE!
IN HIS CURRENT STATE OF MIND, ANYTHING IS POSSIBLE.
HE MIGHT, ON A WHIM, EVEN DESTROY THE UNIVERSE!

...AND THAT IS HOW THANOS GAINED HIS VAST POWER AND I CAME TO AID IN THE THWARTING OF HIS MAD SCHEMES.

THEN YOU ARE THE ENTITY I COMMUNICATED WITH EARLIER!

AN AMAZING STORY AND A PERIL THAT RIVALS THE COMING OF THE BEYONDER!

IT IS A CHALLENGE WE MUST MEET AND TRIUMPH OVER.

THERE IS BUT ONE WAY THIS CAN BE ACCOMPLISHED.

I MUST LEAD THE FORCES OF SANITY AGAINST THE MAD TITAN.

BY WHAT RIGHT DO YOU CLAIM THE MANTLE OF LEADERSHIP?!

A MAN WHO WAS SUPPOSED TO HAVE BEEN KILLED NEARLY A DECADE AGO-- WHILE BATTLING THANOS!

PERHAPS. BUT I ALONE AM FAMILIAR WITH THE SECRET WORKINGS OF THE INFINITY GEMS.

THAT KNOWLEDGE IS THIS UNIVERSE'S ONLY HOPE.

A BANNER I WILL GLADLY STAND BEHIND.

WHAT SAY YOU, SURFER?

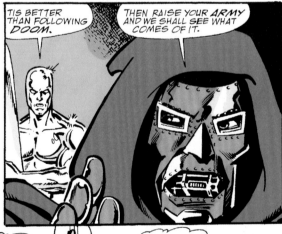

TIS BETTER THAN FOLLOWING DOOM.

THEN RAISE YOUR ARMY AND WE SHALL SEE WHAT COMES OF IT.

BUT IS WARLOCK TRULY THE BEST CHOICE? HE SEEMS MARKEDLY DIFFERENT FROM THE MAN I MET ON SOUL-WORLD.

THERE'S SO LITTLE ANYONE REALLY KNOWS ABOUT HIM. HOW CAN WE BE CERTAIN?

69

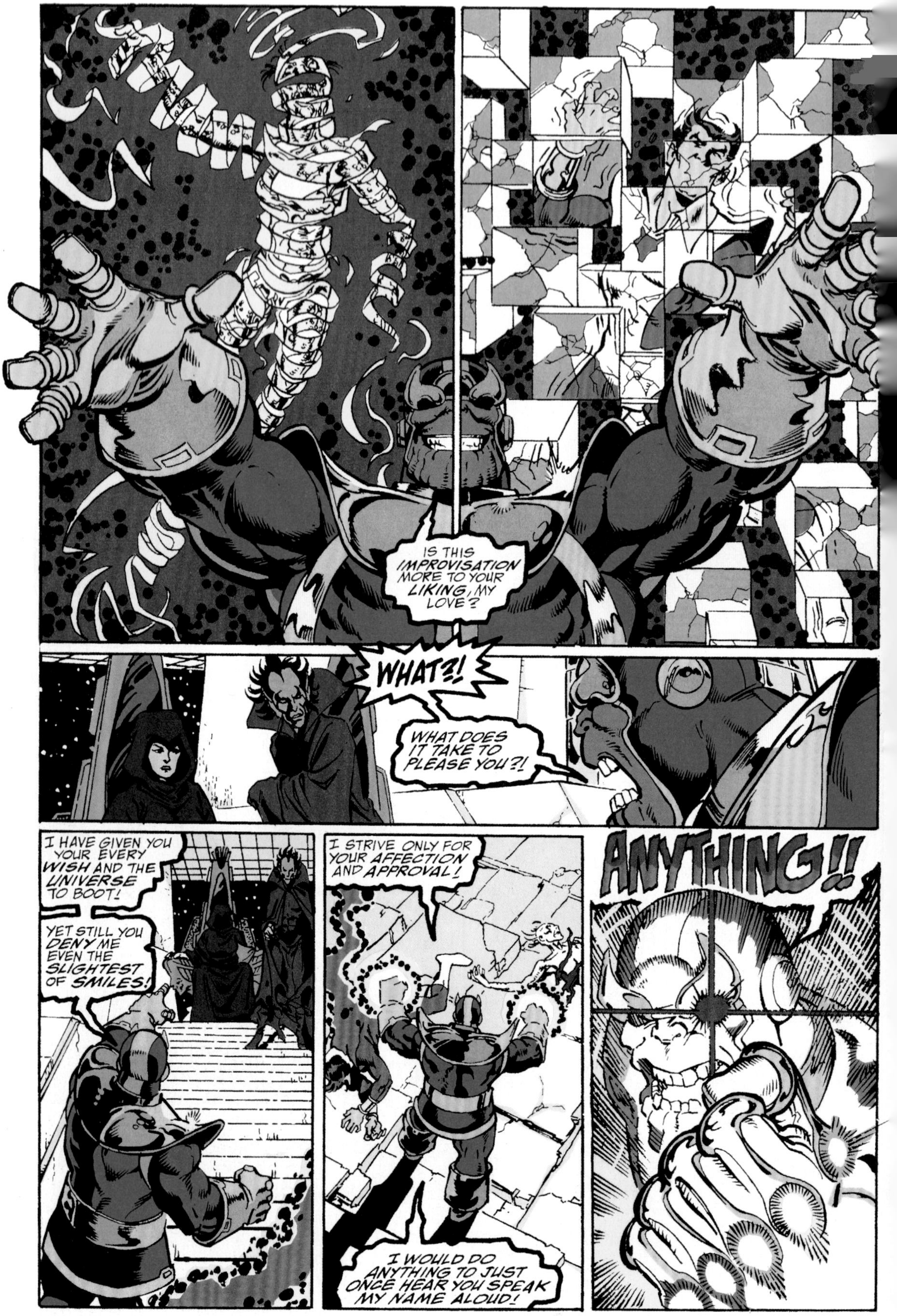
IS THIS IMPROVISATION MORE TO YOUR LIKING, MY LOVE?
WHAT?!
WHAT DOES IT TAKE TO PLEASE YOU?!
I HAVE GIVEN YOU YOUR EVERY WISH AND THE UNIVERSE TO BOOT!
YET STILL YOU DENY ME EVEN THE SLIGHTEST OF SMILES!
I STRIVE ONLY FOR YOUR AFFECTION AND APPROVAL!
I WOULD DO ANYTHING TO JUST ONCE HEAR YOU SPEAK MY NAME ALOUD!
ANYTHING!!

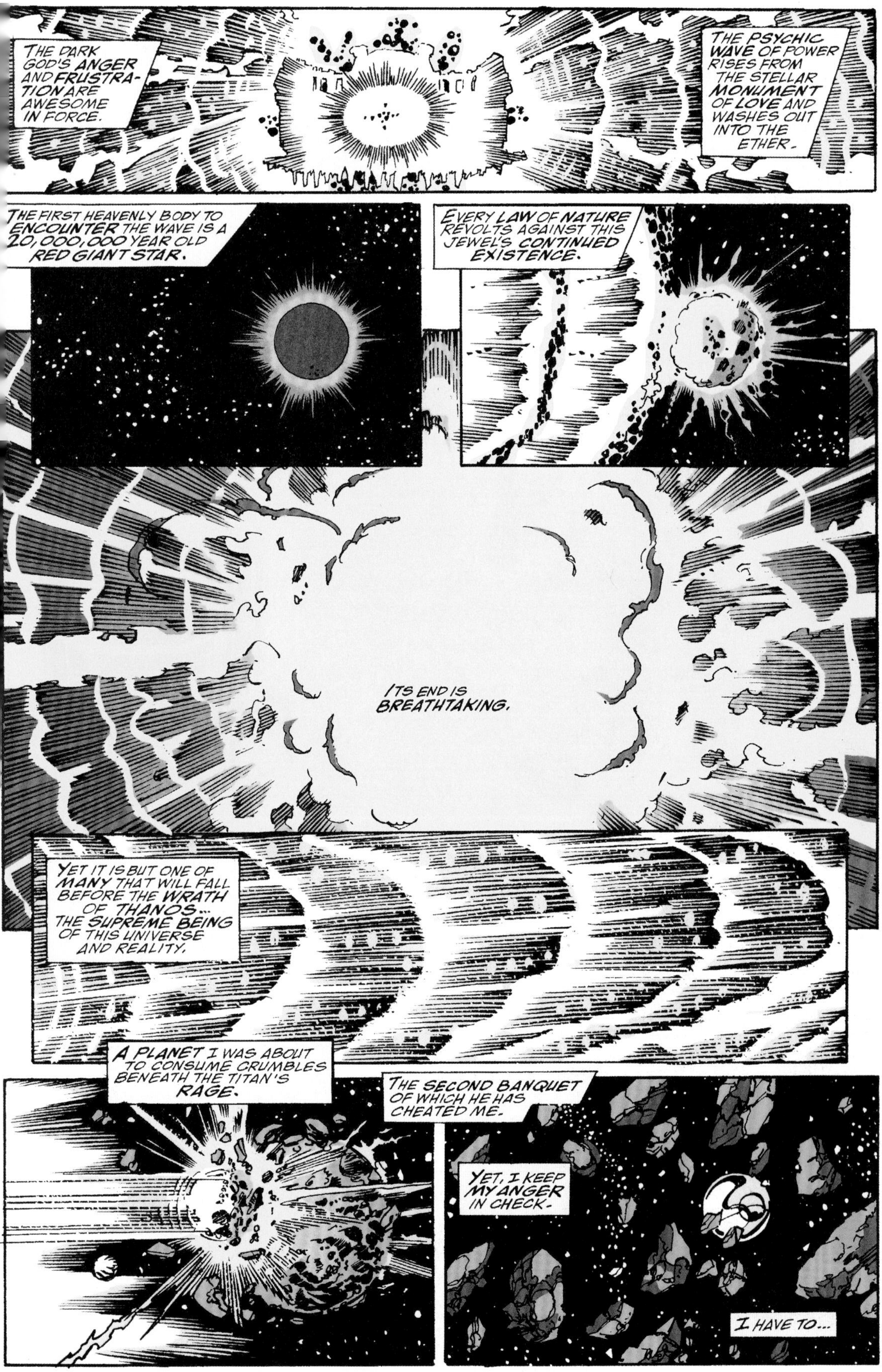
THE DARK GOD'S ANGER AND FRUSTRATION ARE AWESOME IN FORCE.
THE PSYCHIC WAVE OF POWER RISES FROM THE STELLAR MONUMENT OF LOVE AND WASHES OUT INTO THE ETHER.
THE FIRST HEAVENLY BODY TO ENCOUNTER THE WAVE IS A 20,000,000 YEAR OLD RED GIANT STAR.
EVERY LAW OF NATURE REVOLTS AGAINST THIS JEWEL'S CONTINUED EXISTENCE.
ITS END IS BREATHTAKING.
YET IT IS BUT ONE OF MANY THAT WILL FALL BEFORE THE WRATH OF THANOS... THE SUPREME BEING OF THIS UNIVERSE AND REALITY.
A PLANET I WAS ABOUT TO CONSUME CRUMBLES BENEATH THE TITAN'S RAGE.
THE SECOND BANQUET OF WHICH HE HAS CHEATED ME.
YET, I KEEP MY ANGER IN CHECK.
I HAVE TO...

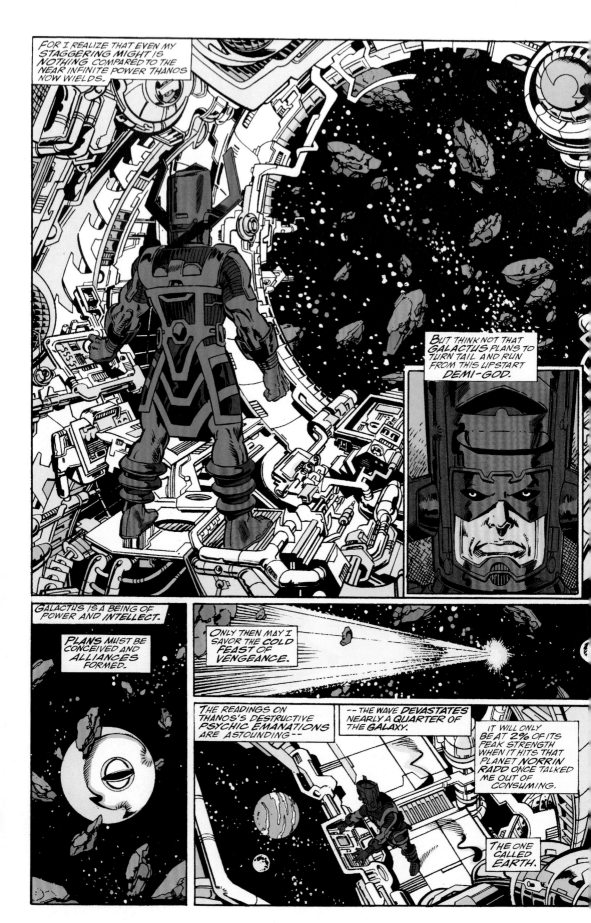

FOR I REALIZE THAT EVEN MY STAGGERING MIGHT IS NOTHING COMPARED TO THE NEAR INFINITE POWER THANOS NOW WIELDS.

BUT THINK NOT THAT GALACTUS PLANS TO TURN TAIL AND RUN FROM THIS UPSTART DEMI-GOD.

GALACTUS IS A BEING OF POWER AND INTELLECT.

PLANS MUST BE CONCEIVED AND ALLIANCES FORMED.

ONLY THEN MAY I SAVOR THE COLD FEAST OF VENGEANCE.

THE READINGS ON THANOS'S DESTRUCTIVE PSYCHIC EMANATIONS ARE ASTOUNDING--

--THE WAVE DEVASTATES NEARLY A QUARTER OF THE GALAXY.

IT WILL ONLY BE AT 2% OF ITS PEAK STRENGTH WHEN IT HITS THAT PLANET NORRIN RADD ONCE TALKED ME OUT OF CONSUMING.

THE ONE CALLED EARTH.

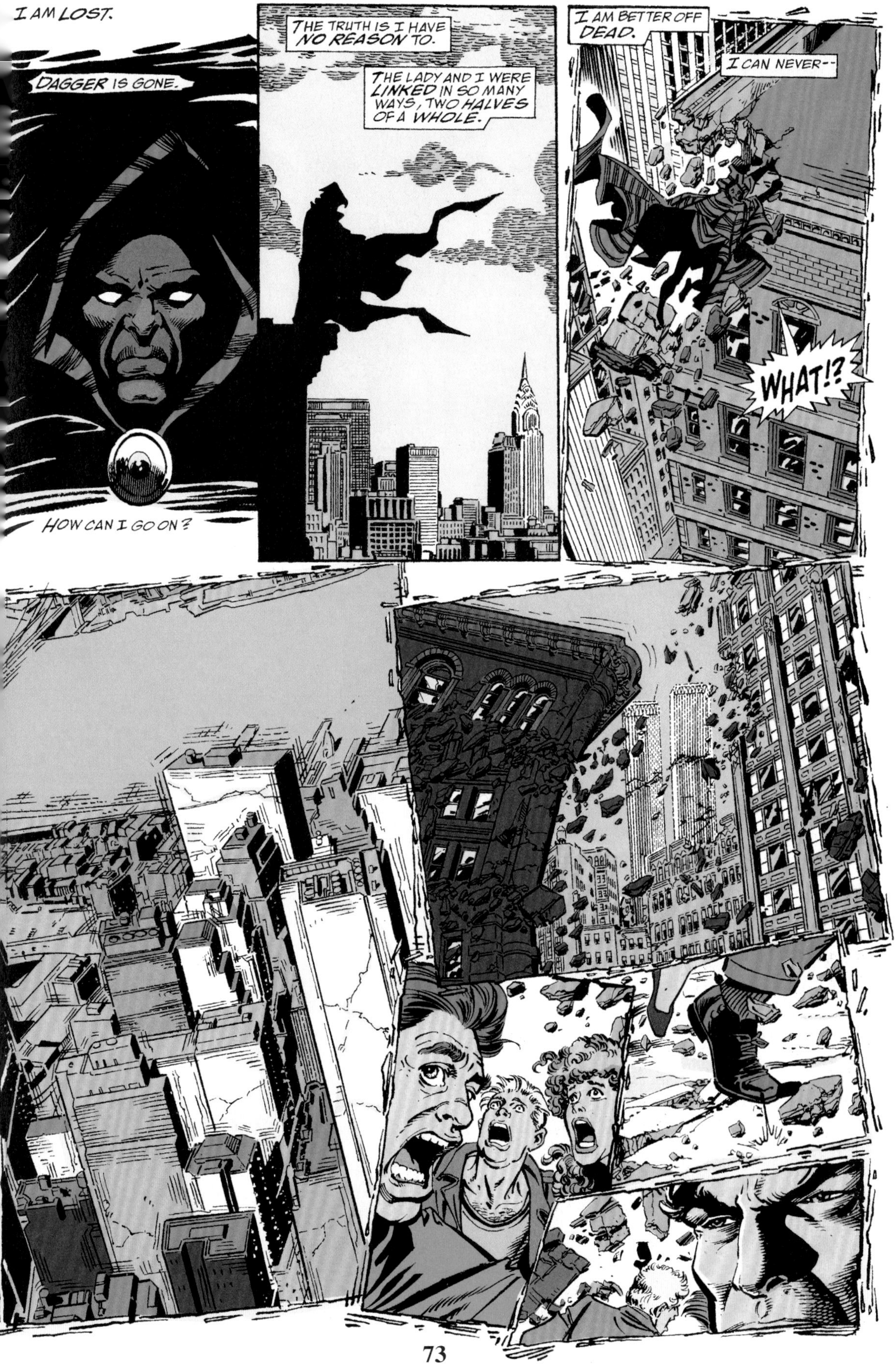
I AM LOST.
DAGGER IS GONE.
HOW CAN I GO ON?
THE TRUTH IS I HAVE NO REASON TO.
THE LADY AND I WERE LINKED IN SO MANY WAYS, TWO HALVES OF A WHOLE.
I AM BETTER OFF DEAD.
I CAN NEVER--
WHAT!?

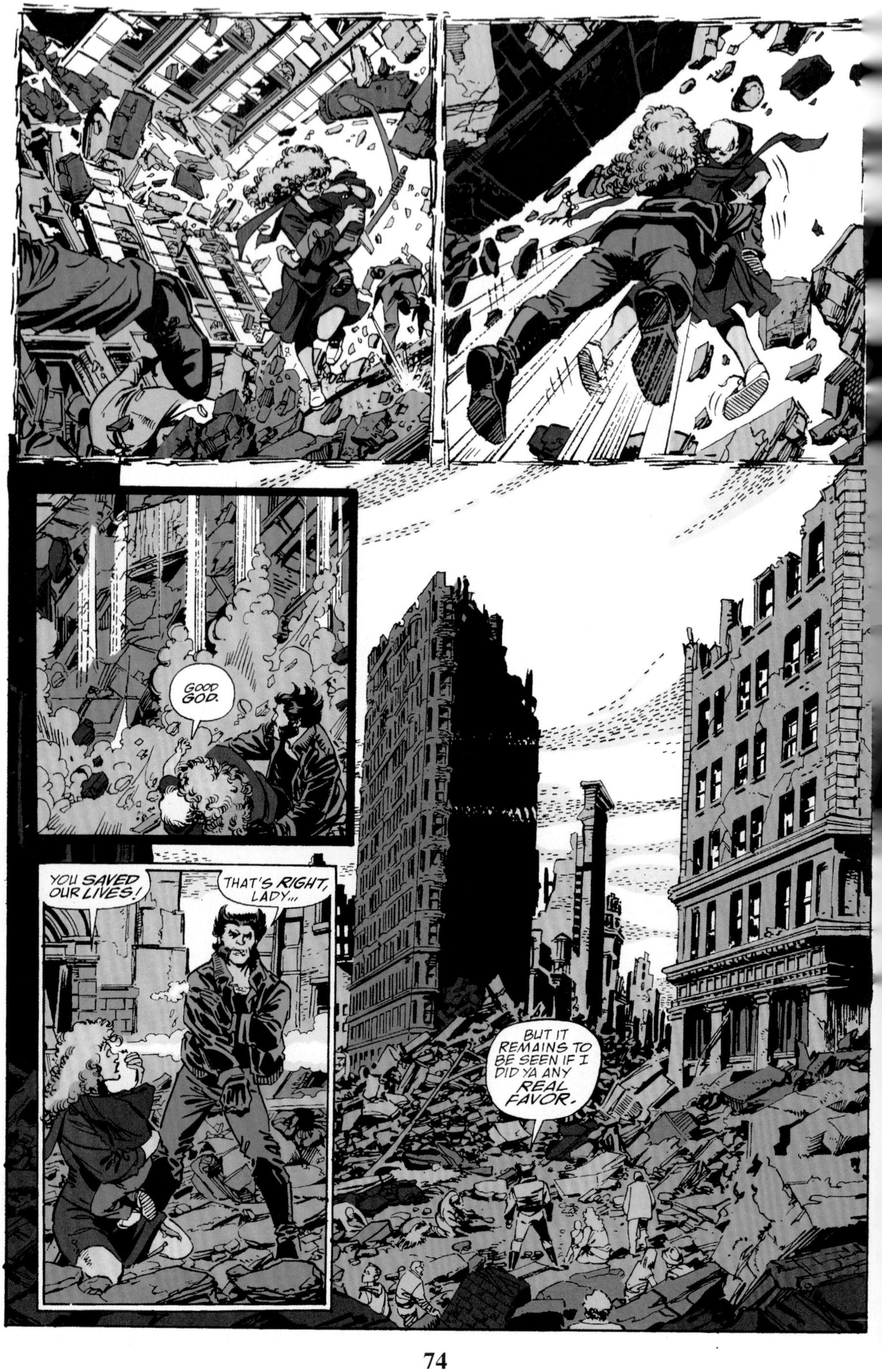
GOOD GOD.
YOU SAVED OUR LIVES!
THAT'S RIGHT, LADY...
BUT IT REMAINS TO BE SEEN IF I DID YA ANY REAL FAVOR.

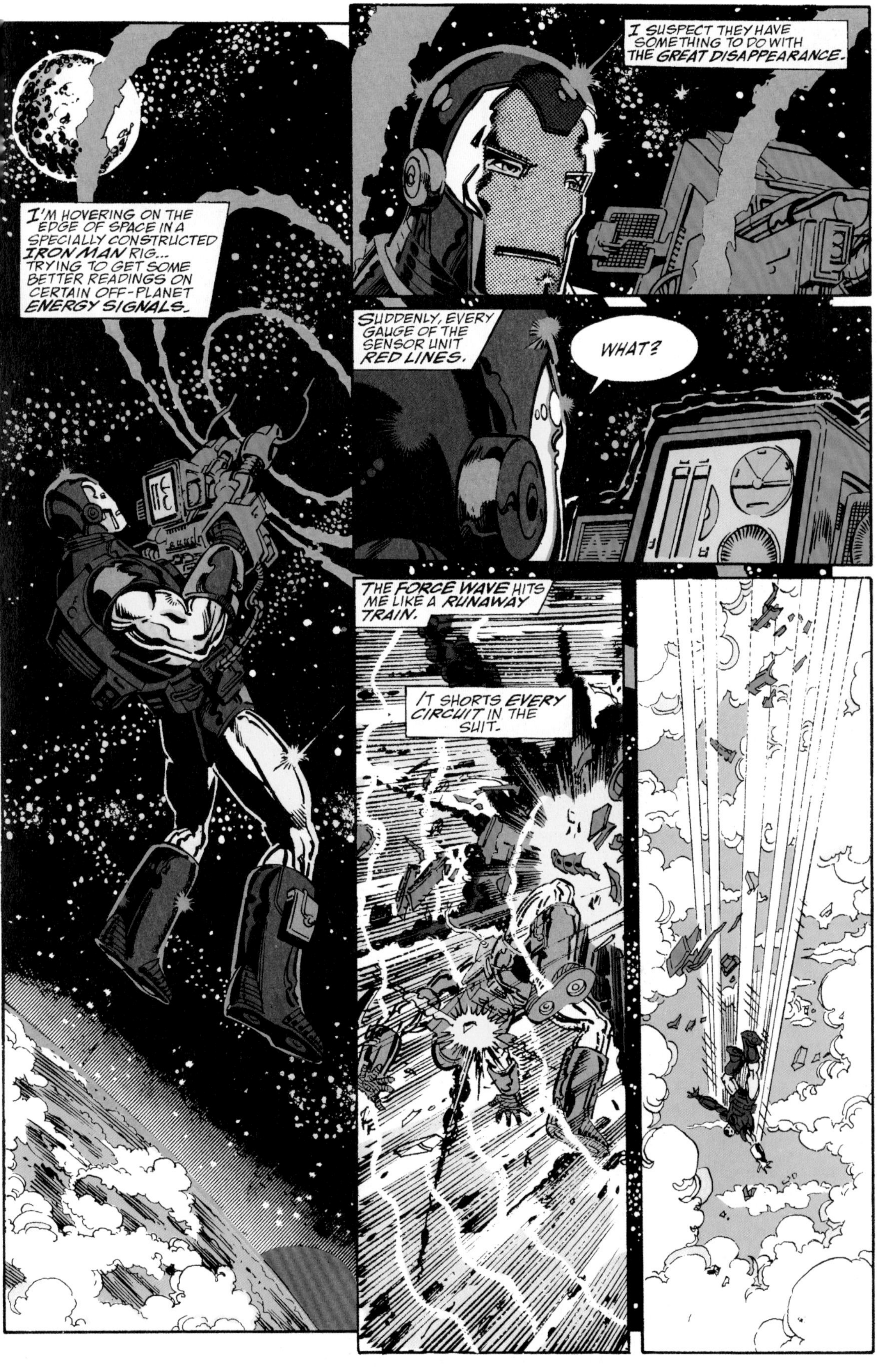
I'M HOVERING ON THE EDGE OF SPACE IN A SPECIALLY CONSTRUCTED IRON MAN RIG... TRYING TO GET SOME BETTER READINGS ON CERTAIN OFF-PLANET ENERGY SIGNALS.
I SUSPECT THEY HAVE SOMETHING TO DO WITH THE GREAT DISAPPEARANCE.
SUDDENLY, EVERY GAUGE OF THE SENSOR UNIT RED LINES.
WHAT?
THE FORCE WAVE HITS ME LIKE A RUNAWAY TRAIN.
IT SHORTS EVERY CIRCUIT IN THE SUIT.

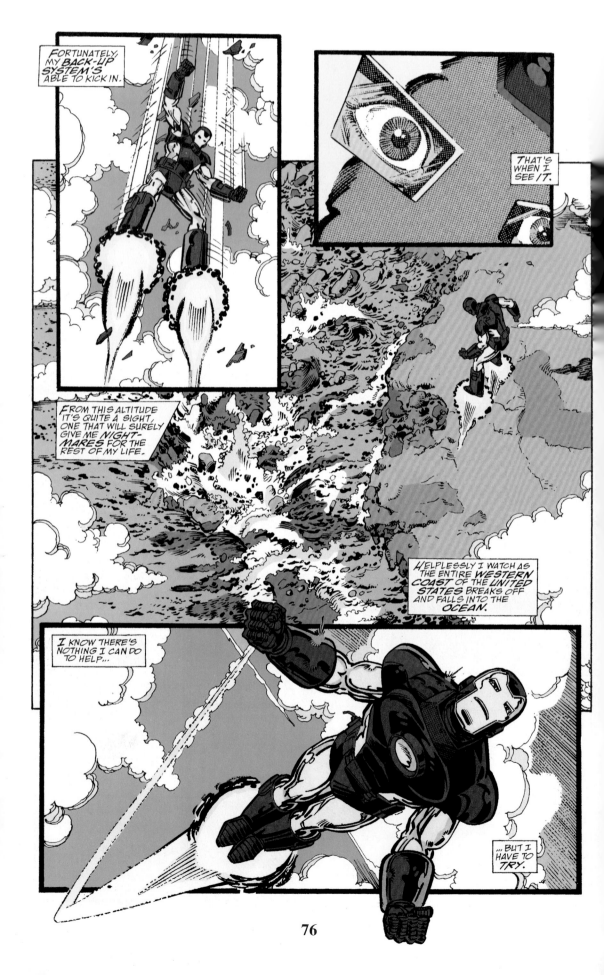

FORTUNATELY, MY *BACK-UP SYSTEM'S* ABLE TO KICK IN.

THAT'S WHEN I SEE *IT.*

FROM THIS ALTITUDE IT'S QUITE A SIGHT, ONE THAT WILL SURELY GIVE ME *NIGHTMARES* FOR THE REST OF MY LIFE.

*H*ELPLESSLY I WATCH AS THE ENTIRE *WESTERN COAST* OF THE *UNITED STATES* BREAKS OFF AND FALLS INTO THE *OCEAN.*

I KNOW THERE'S NOTHING I CAN DO TO *HELP*...

...BUT I HAVE TO *TRY.*

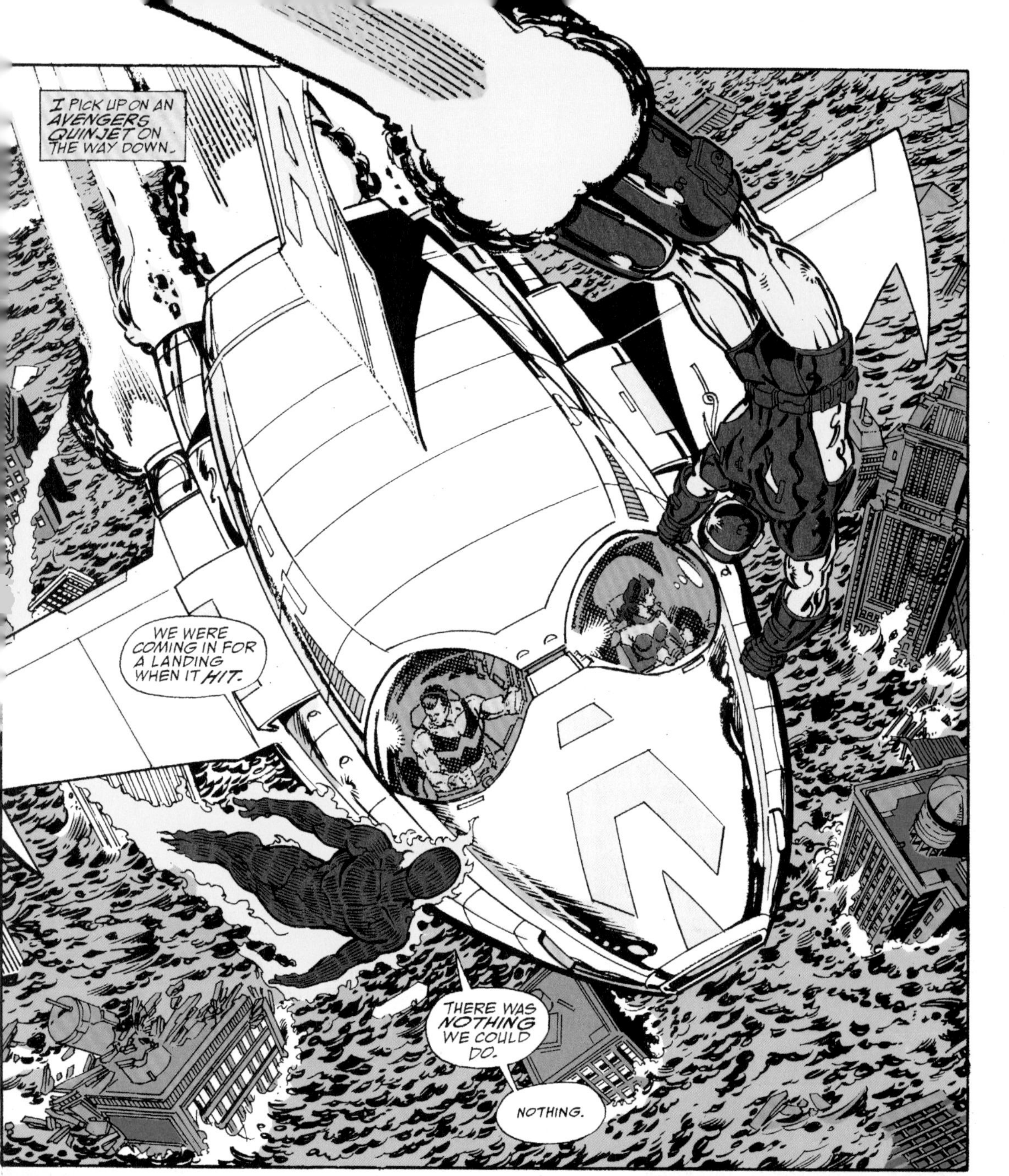
I PICK UP ON AN AVENGERS QUINJET ON THE WAY DOWN.
WE WERE COMING IN FOR A LANDING WHEN IT HIT.
THERE WAS NOTHING WE COULD DO.
NOTHING.

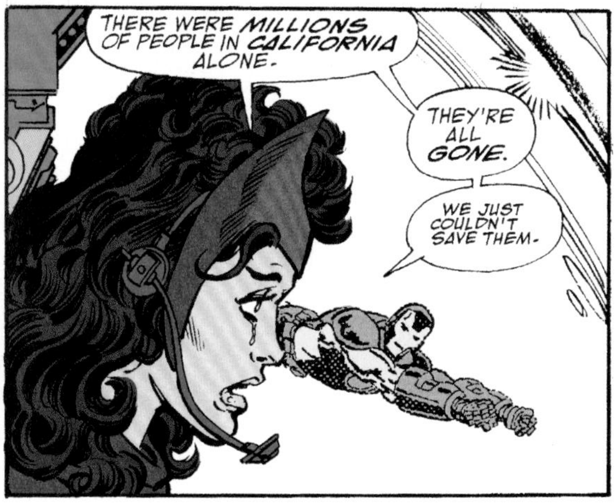
THERE WERE MILLIONS OF PEOPLE IN CALIFORNIA ALONE.
THEY'RE ALL GONE.
WE JUST COULDN'T SAVE THEM.

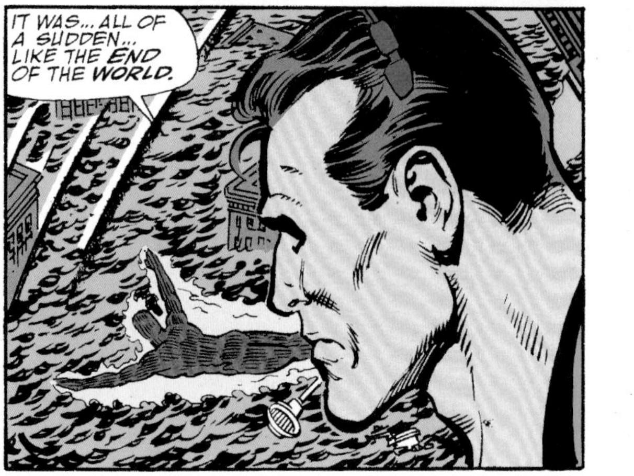
IT WAS... ALL OF A SUDDEN... LIKE THE END OF THE WORLD.

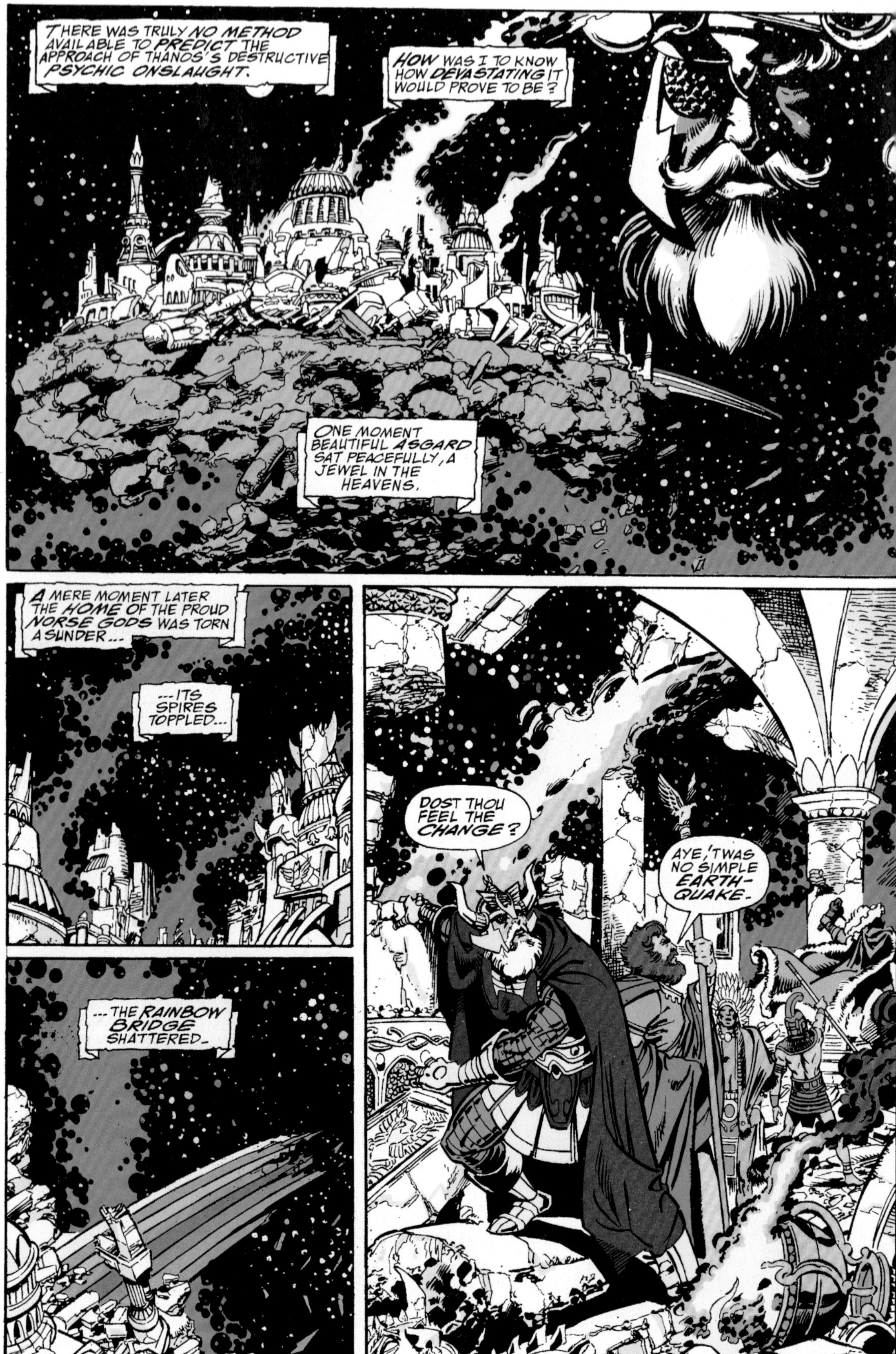
THERE WAS TRULY NO METHOD AVAILABLE TO PREDICT THE APPROACH OF THANOS'S DESTRUCTIVE PSYCHIC ONSLAUGHT.
HOW WAS I TO KNOW HOW DEVASTATING IT WOULD PROVE TO BE?
ONE MOMENT BEAUTIFUL ASGARD SAT PEACEFULLY, A JEWEL IN THE HEAVENS.
A MERE MOMENT LATER THE HOME OF THE PROUD NORSE GODS WAS TORN ASUNDER...
...ITS SPIRES TOPPLED...
...THE RAINBOW BRIDGE SHATTERED.
DOST THOU FEEL THE CHANGE?
AYE, 'TWAS NO SIMPLE EARTH-QUAKE.

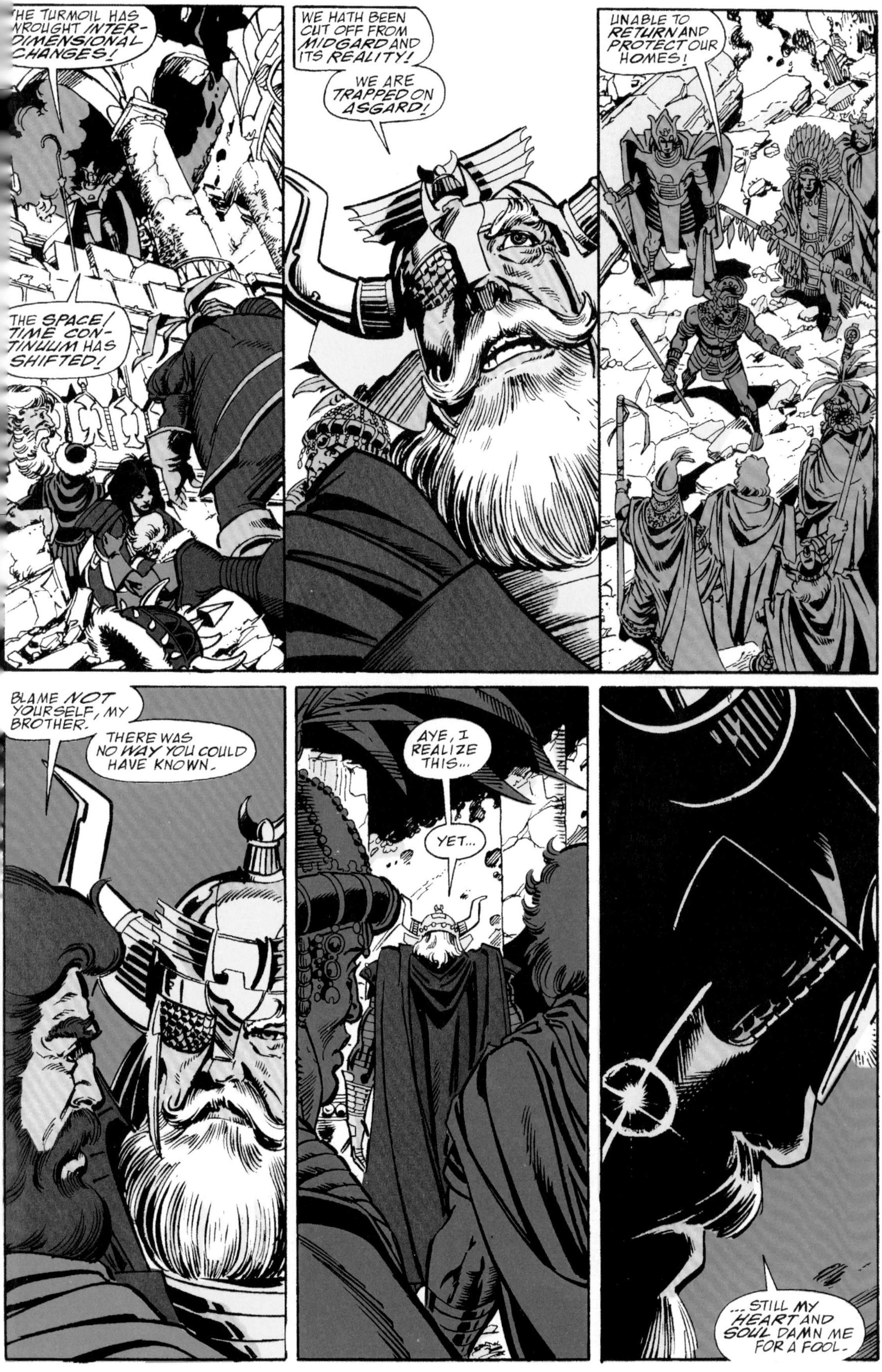
THE TURMOIL HAS WROUGHT INTER-DIMENSIONAL CHANGES!
THE SPACE/TIME CONTINUUM HAS SHIFTED!
WE HATH BEEN CUT OFF FROM MIDGARD AND ITS REALITY!
WE ARE TRAPPED ON ASGARD!
UNABLE TO RETURN AND PROTECT OUR HOMES!
BLAME NOT YOURSELF, MY BROTHER.
THERE WAS NO WAY YOU COULD HAVE KNOWN.
AYE, I REALIZE THIS...
YET...
...STILL MY HEART AND SOUL DAMN ME FOR A FOOL.

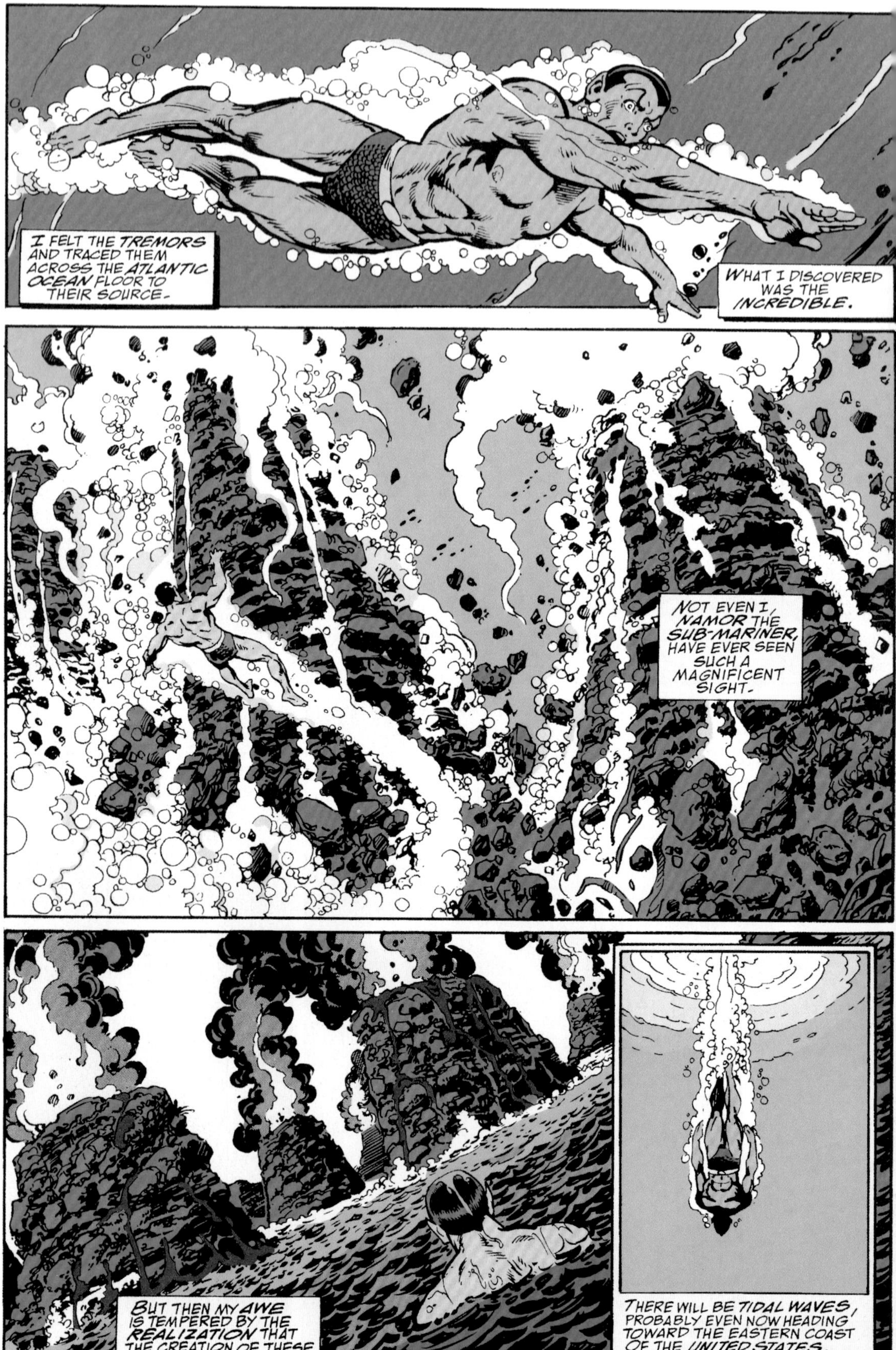
I FELT THE TREMORS AND TRACED THEM ACROSS THE ATLANTIC OCEAN FLOOR TO THEIR SOURCE.
WHAT I DISCOVERED WAS THE INCREDIBLE.
NOT EVEN I, NAMOR THE SUB-MARINER, HAVE EVER SEEN SUCH A MAGNIFICENT SIGHT.
BUT THEN MY AWE IS TEMPERED BY THE REALIZATION THAT THE CREATION OF THESE ISLES WILL HAVE CATA-CLYSMIC RESULTS.
THERE WILL BE TIDAL WAVES, PROBABLY EVEN NOW HEADING TOWARD THE EASTERN COAST OF THE UNITED STATES.

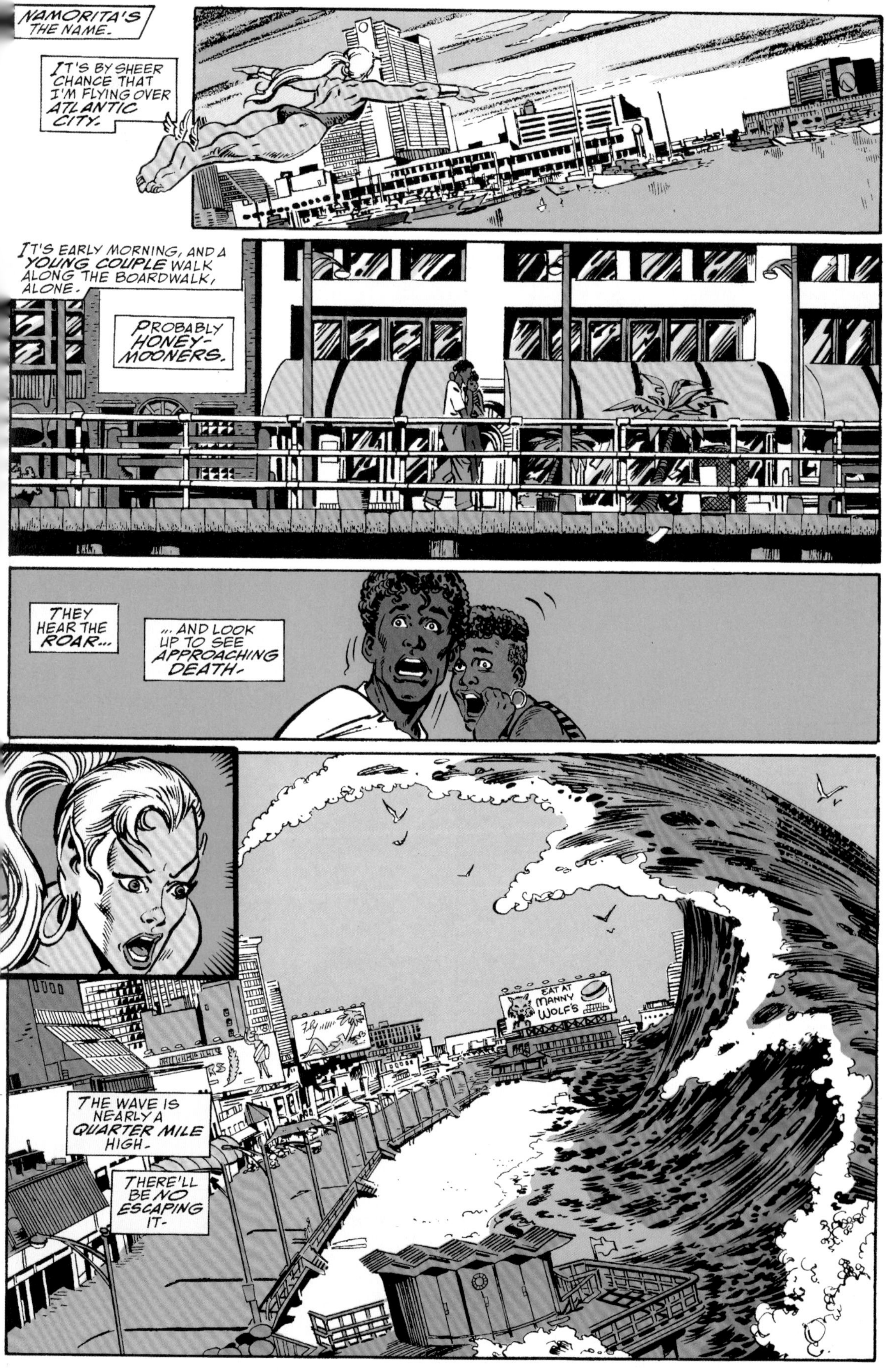
NAMORITA'S THE NAME.
IT'S BY SHEER CHANCE THAT I'M FLYING OVER ATLANTIC CITY.
IT'S EARLY MORNING, AND A YOUNG COUPLE WALK ALONG THE BOARDWALK, ALONE.
PROBABLY HONEY-MOONERS.
THEY HEAR THE ROAR...
...AND LOOK UP TO SEE APPROACHING DEATH.
EAT AT MANNY WOLF'S
THE WAVE IS NEARLY A QUARTER MILE HIGH.
THERE'LL BE NO ESCAPING IT.

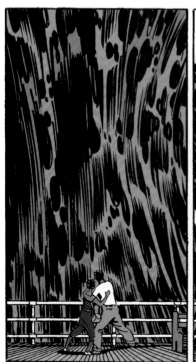

THE YOUNG LOVERS ARE THE ONLY *TWO PEOPLE* I MANAGE TO SAVE.

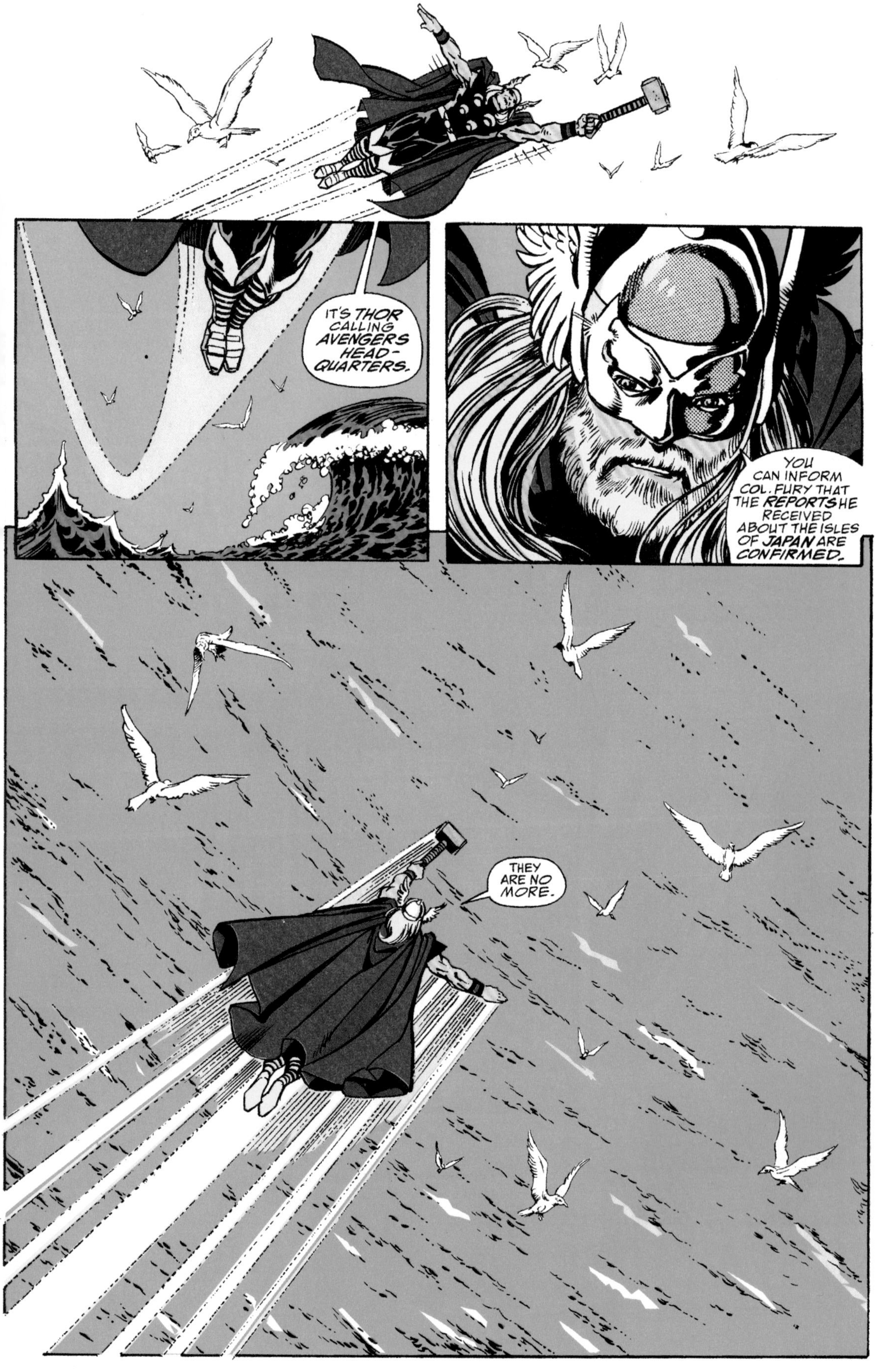
IT'S THOR CALLING AVENGERS HEAD-QUARTERS.
YOU CAN INFORM COL. FURY THAT THE REPORTS HE RECEIVED ABOUT THE ISLES OF JAPAN ARE CONFIRMED.
THEY ARE NO MORE.

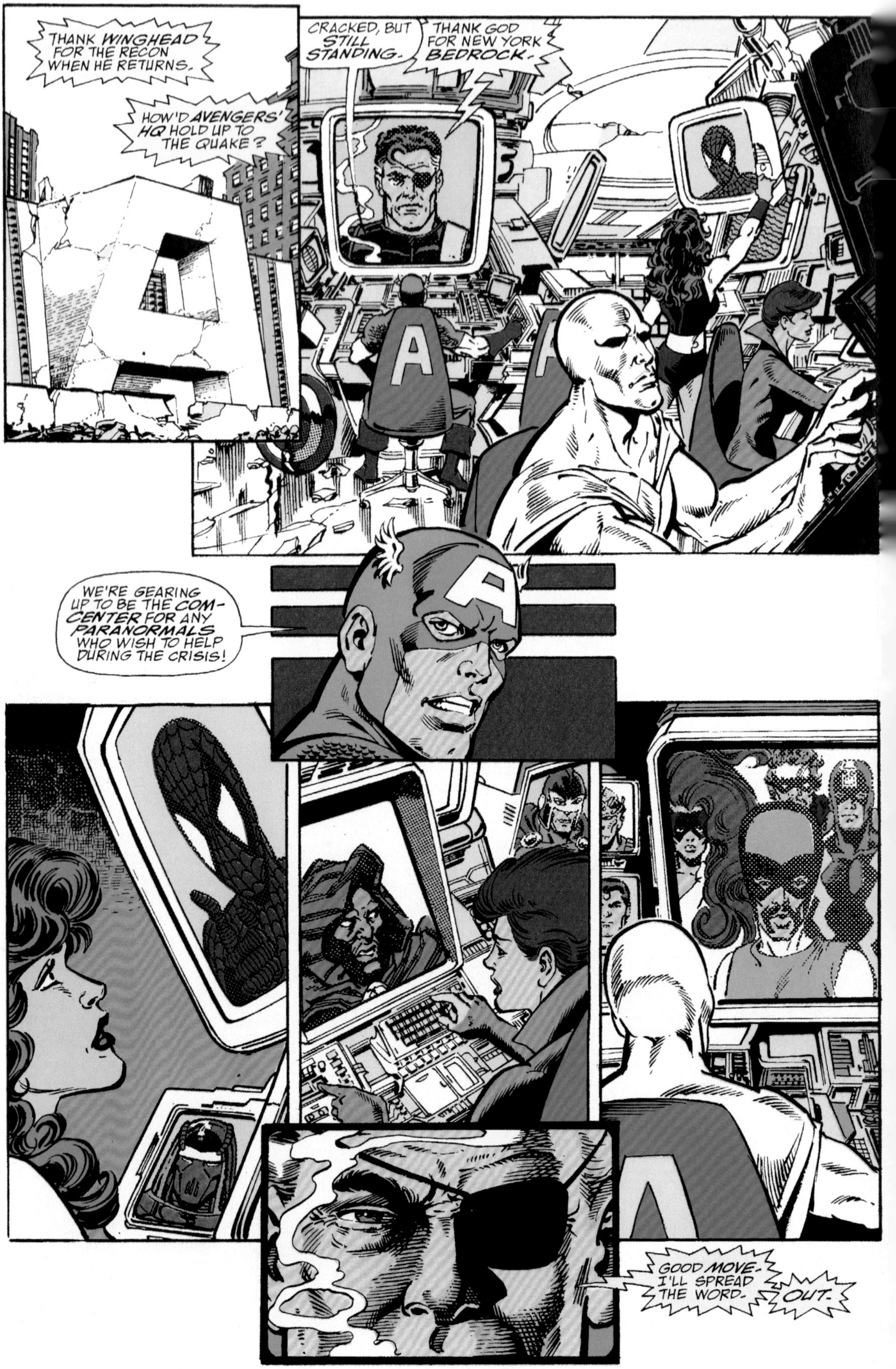
THANK WINGHEAD FOR THE RECON WHEN HE RETURNS.
HOW'D AVENGERS' HQ HOLD UP TO THE QUAKE?
CRACKED, BUT STILL STANDING.
THANK GOD FOR NEW YORK BEDROCK.
WE'RE GEARING UP TO BE THE COM-CENTER FOR ANY PARANORMALS WHO WISH TO HELP DURING THE CRISIS!
GOOD MOVE. I'LL SPREAD THE WORD.
OUT.

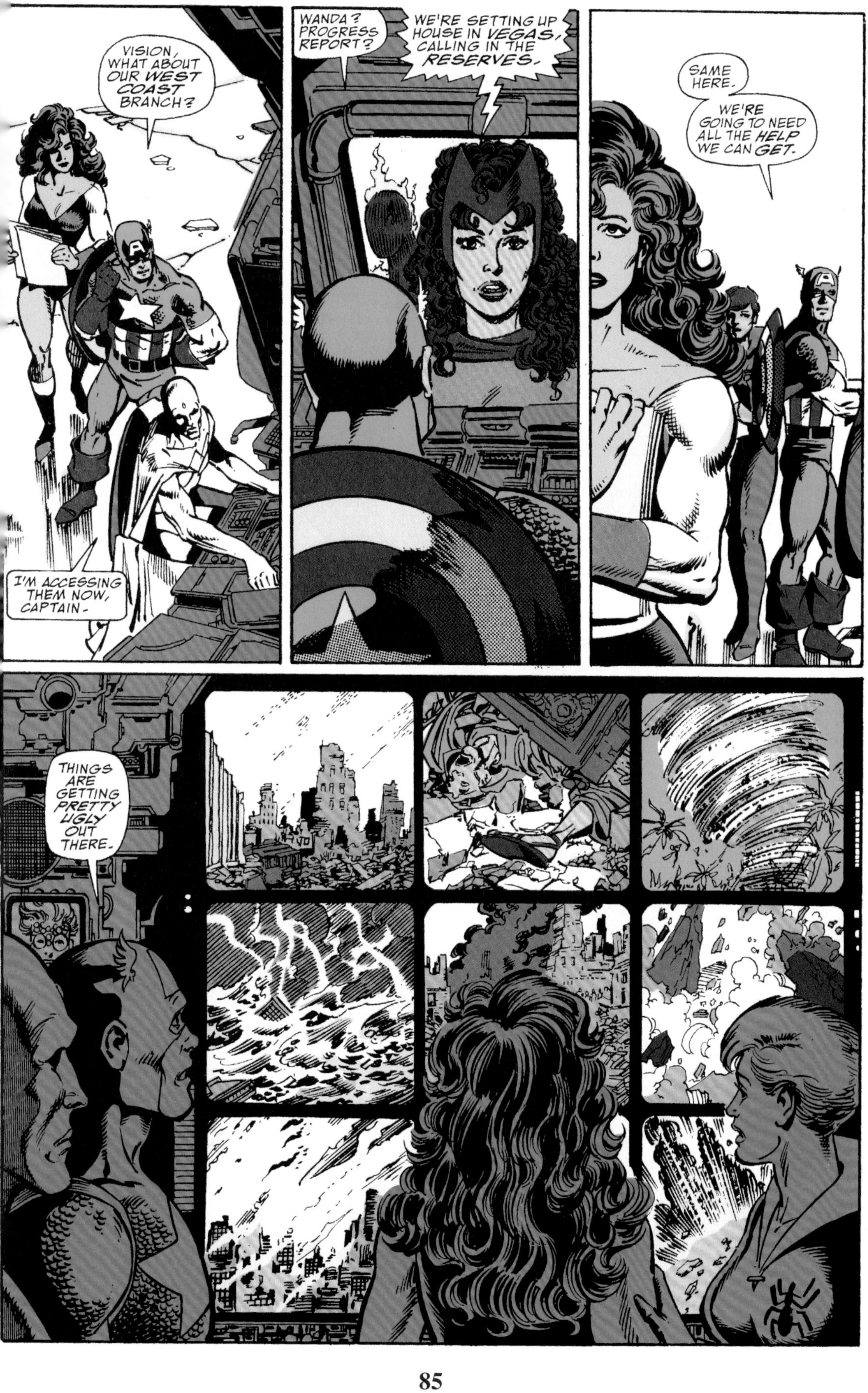
VISION, WHAT ABOUT OUR WEST COAST BRANCH?
I'M ACCESSING THEM NOW, CAPTAIN.
WANDA? PROGRESS REPORT?
WE'RE SETTING UP HOUSE IN VEGAS, CALLING IN THE RESERVES.
SAME HERE.
WE'RE GOING TO NEED ALL THE HELP WE CAN GET.
THINGS ARE GETTING PRETTY UGLY OUT THERE.

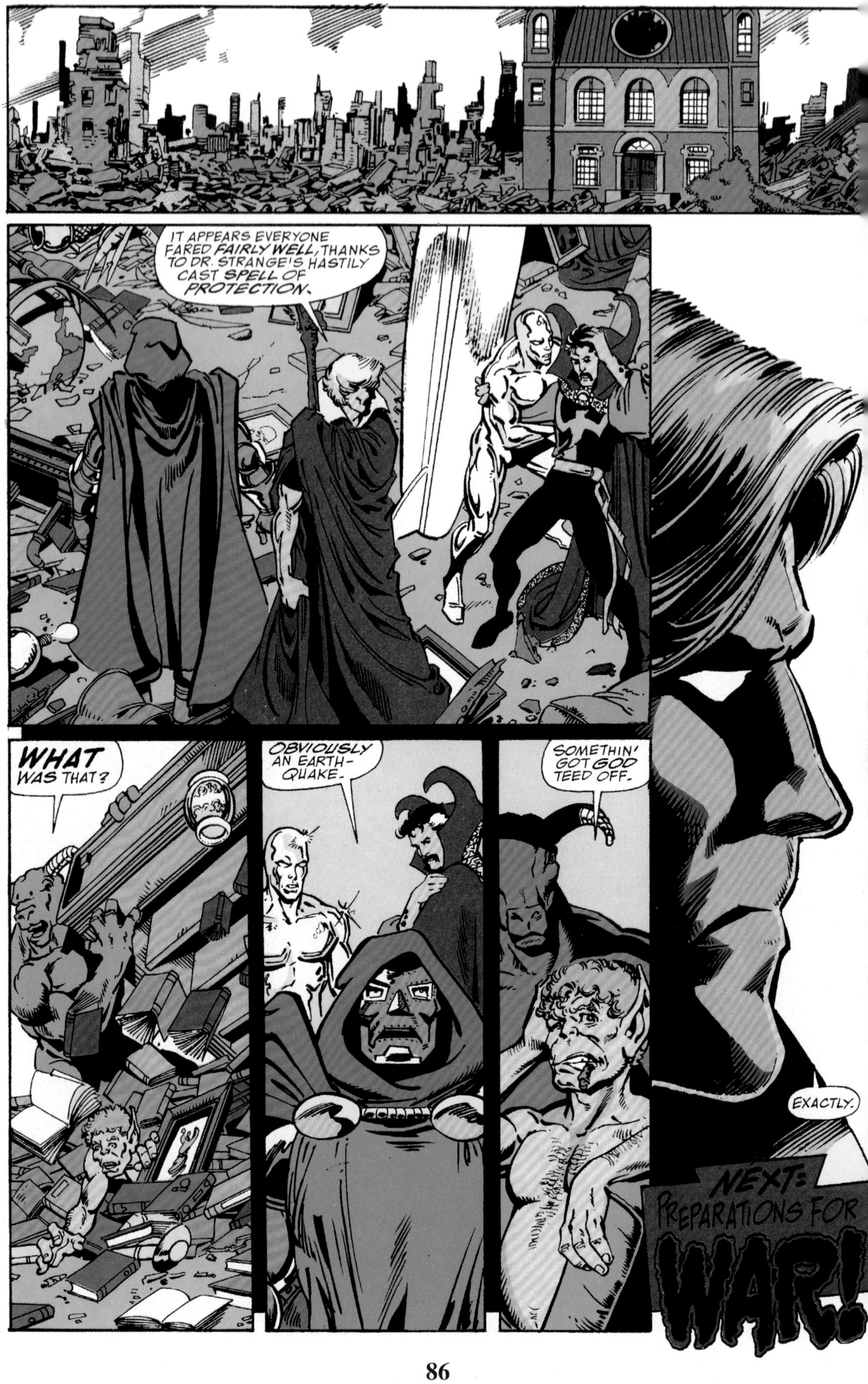
IT APPEARS EVERYONE FARED FAIRLY WELL, THANKS TO DR. STRANGE'S HASTILY CAST SPELL OF PROTECTION.
WHAT WAS THAT?
OBVIOUSLY AN EARTH-QUAKE.
SOMETHIN' GOT GOD TEED OFF.
EXACTLY.
NEXT: PREPARATIONS FOR WAR!

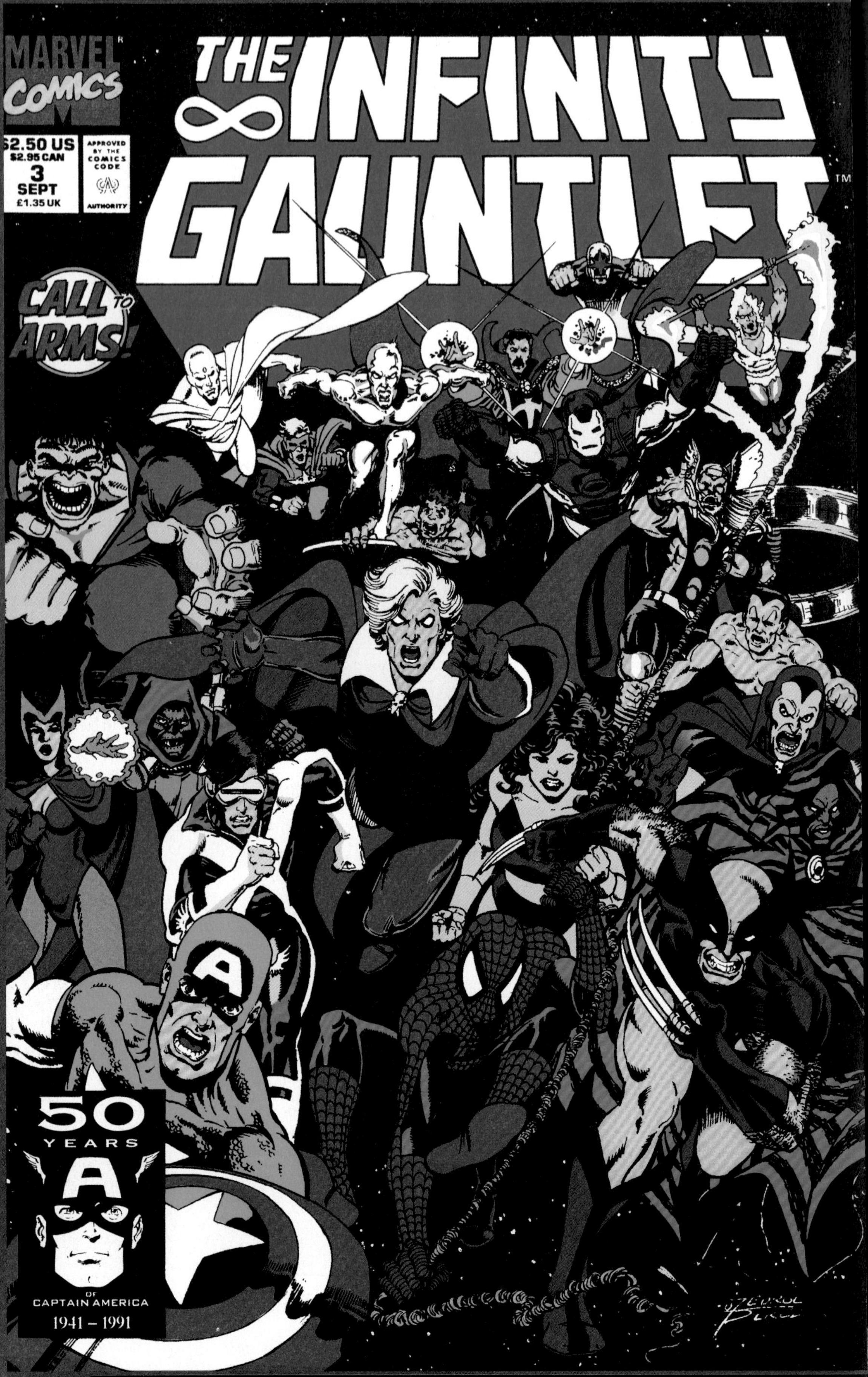
MARVEL COMICS
THE INFINITY GAUNTLET™
$2.50 US
$2.95 CAN
3
SEPT
£1.35 UK
APPROVED BY THE COMICS CODE AUTHORITY
CALL TO ARMS!
50 YEARS OF CAPTAIN AMERICA
1941 – 1991

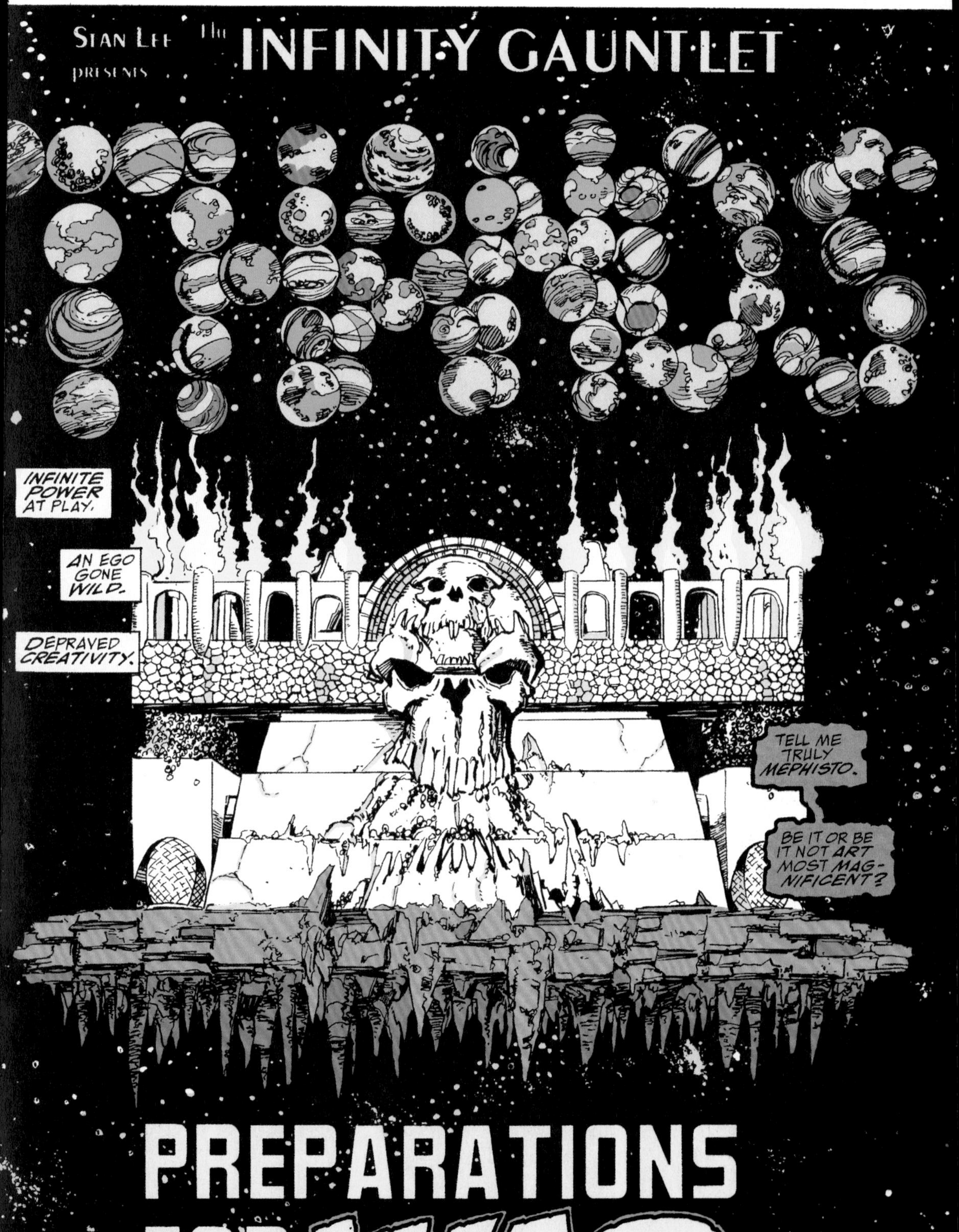

JIM STARLIN WRITER · GEORGE PÉREZ PENCILS · JOE RUBINSTEIN INKS · SCHEELE & LAUGHLIN COLORS · JACK MORELLI LETTERS · CRAIG ANDERSON EDITOR · TOM DeFALCO CHIEF · YES! WE'RE ALL STILL HERE!!

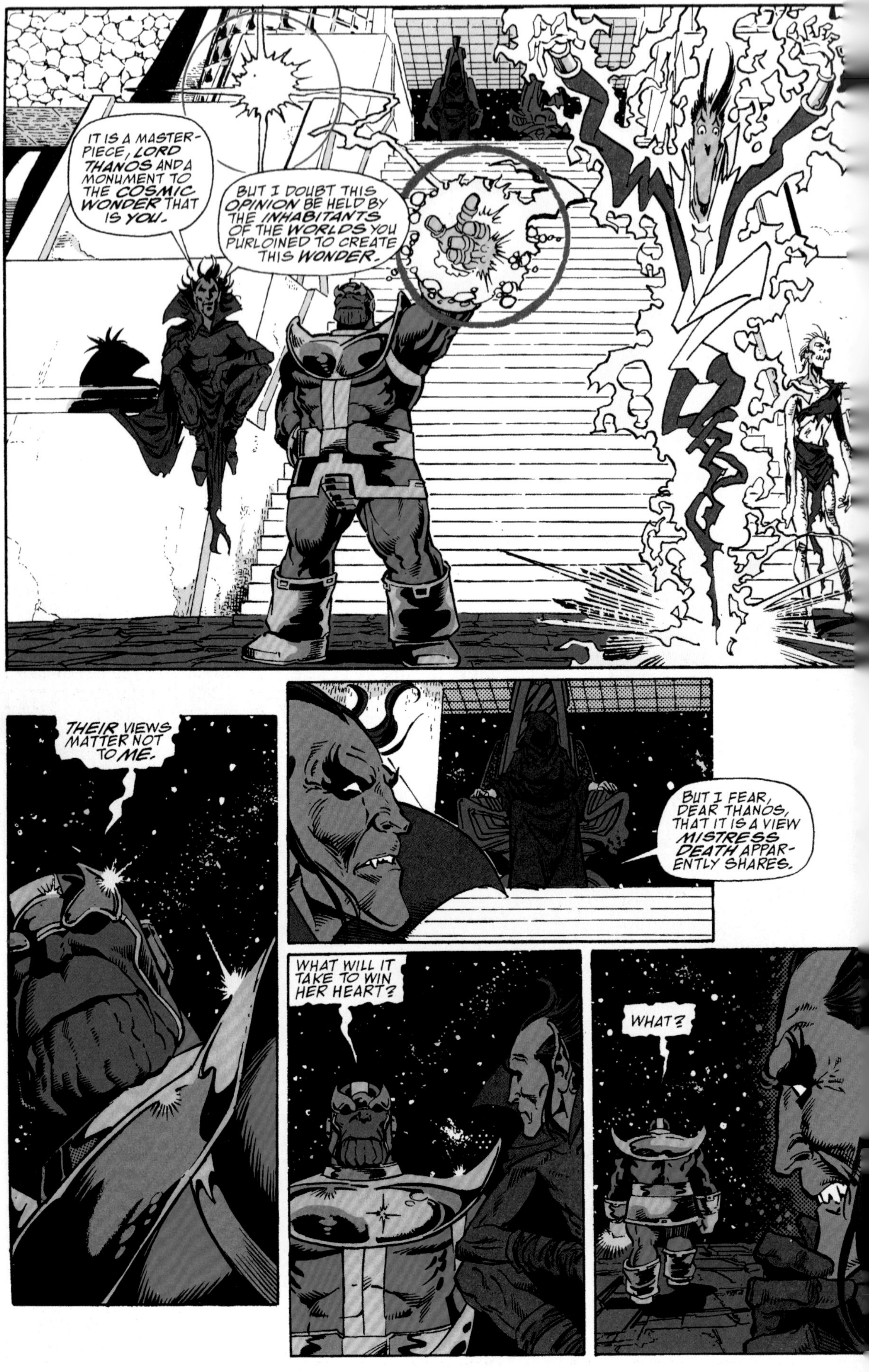

IT IS A MASTER-PIECE, LORD THANOS AND A MONUMENT TO THE COSMIC WONDER THAT IS YOU.
BUT I DOUBT THIS OPINION BE HELD BY THE INHABITANTS OF THE WORLDS YOU PURLOINED TO CREATE THIS WONDER.
THEIR VIEWS MATTER NOT TO ME.
BUT I FEAR, DEAR THANOS, THAT IT IS A VIEW MISTRESS DEATH APPARENTLY SHARES.
WHAT WILL IT TAKE TO WIN HER HEART?
WHAT?

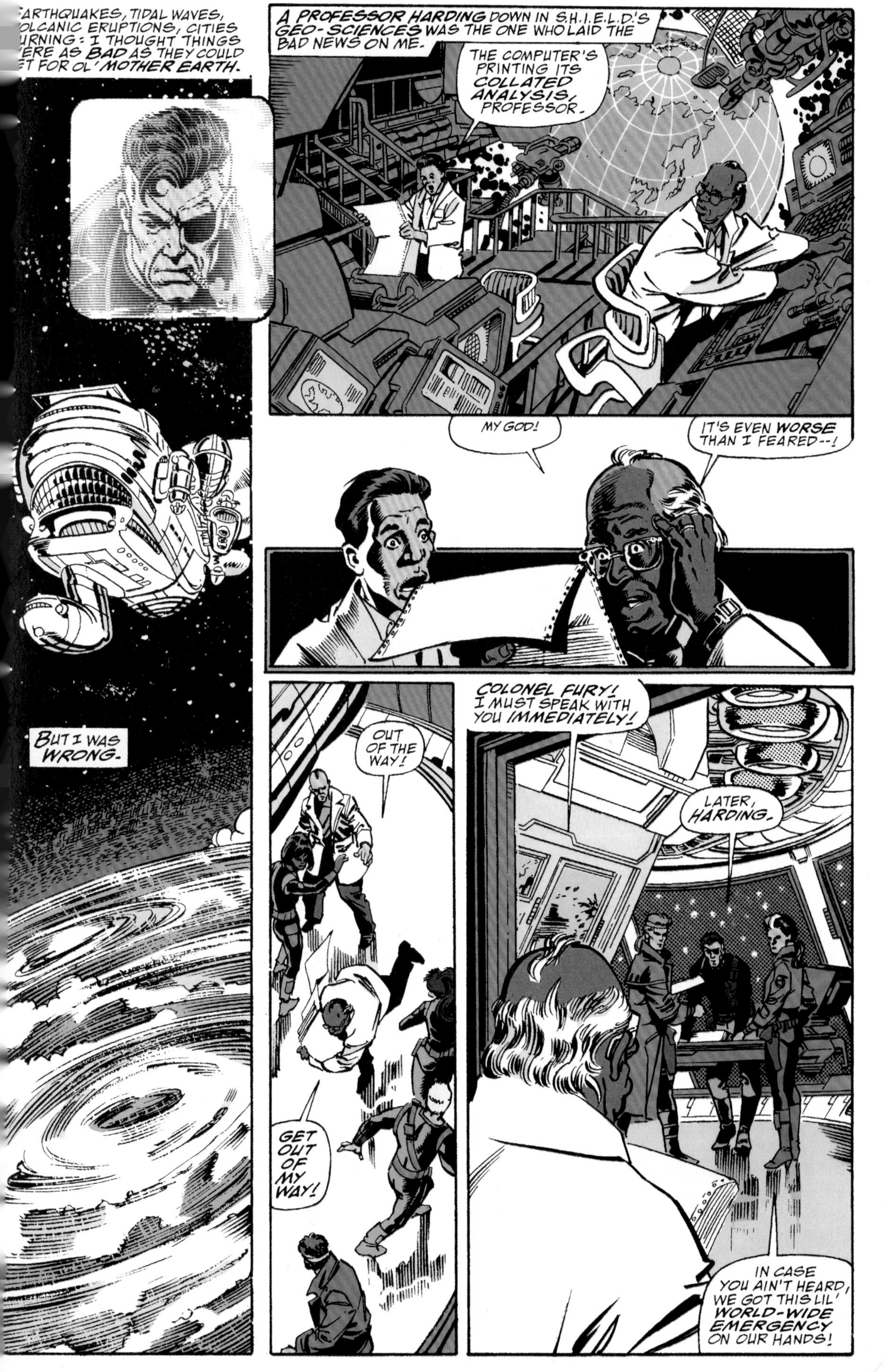
EARTHQUAKES, TIDAL WAVES, VOLCANIC ERUPTIONS, CITIES BURNING: I THOUGHT THINGS WERE AS BAD AS THEY COULD GET FOR OL' MOTHER EARTH.
BUT I WAS WRONG.
A PROFESSOR HARDING DOWN IN S.H.I.E.L.D.'S GEO-SCIENCES WAS THE ONE WHO LAID THE BAD NEWS ON ME.
THE COMPUTER'S PRINTING ITS COLLATED ANALYSIS, PROFESSOR.
MY GOD!
IT'S EVEN WORSE THAN I FEARED--!
OUT OF THE WAY!
GET OUT OF MY WAY!
COLONEL FURY! I MUST SPEAK WITH YOU IMMEDIATELY!
LATER, HARDING.
IN CASE YOU AIN'T HEARD, WE GOT THIS LIL' WORLD-WIDE EMERGENCY ON OUR HANDS!

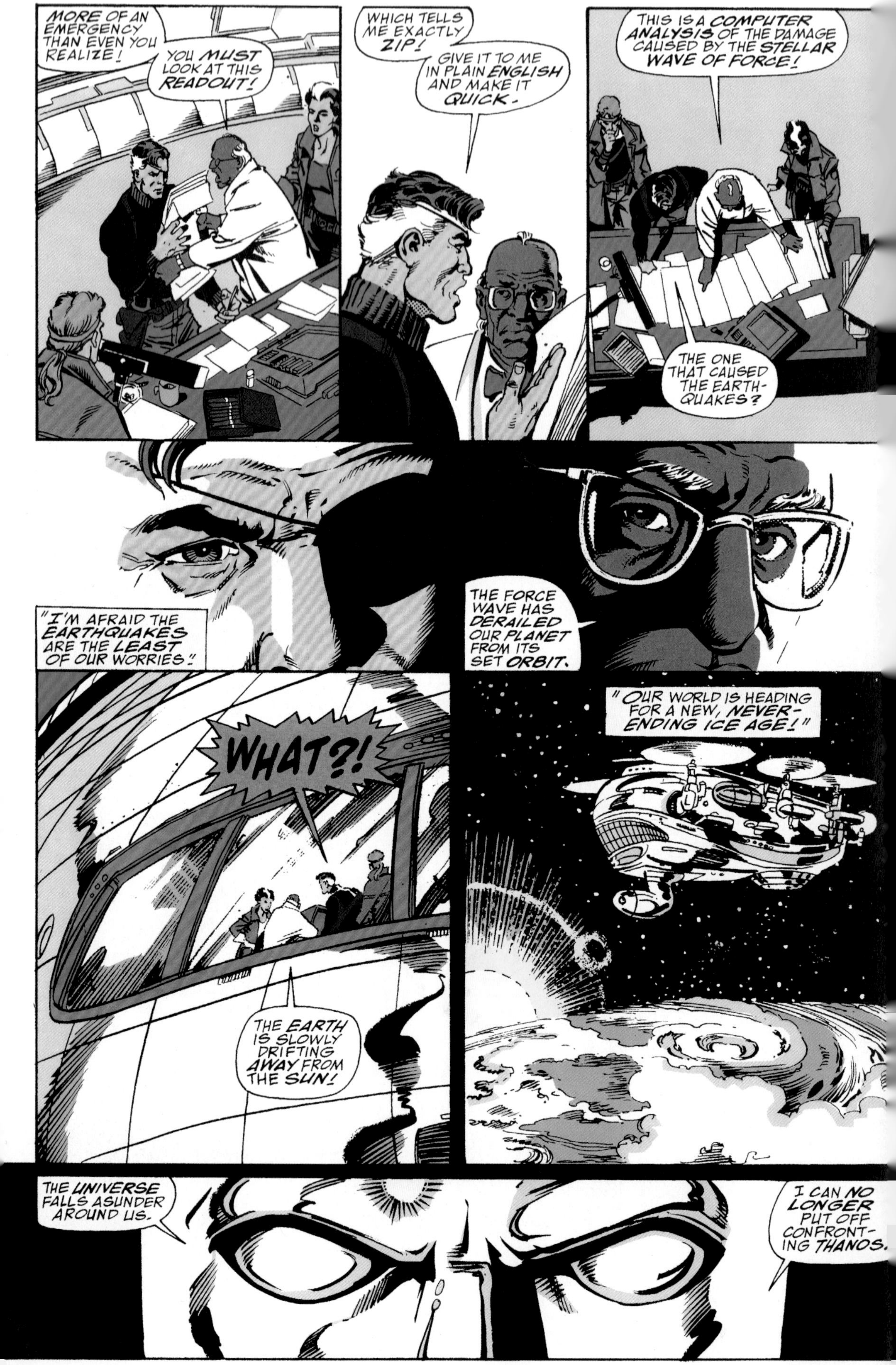
MORE OF AN EMERGENCY THAN EVEN YOU REALIZE!
YOU MUST LOOK AT THIS READOUT!
WHICH TELLS ME EXACTLY ZIP!
GIVE IT TO ME IN PLAIN ENGLISH AND MAKE IT QUICK.
THIS IS A COMPUTER ANALYSIS OF THE DAMAGE CAUSED BY THE STELLAR WAVE OF FORCE!
THE ONE THAT CAUSED THE EARTH-QUAKES?
"I'M AFRAID THE EARTHQUAKES ARE THE LEAST OF OUR WORRIES."
THE FORCE WAVE HAS DERAILED OUR PLANET FROM ITS SET ORBIT.
WHAT?!
THE EARTH IS SLOWLY DRIFTING AWAY FROM THE SUN!
"OUR WORLD IS HEADING FOR A NEW, NEVER-ENDING ICE AGE!"
THE UNIVERSE FALLS ASUNDER AROUND US.
I CAN NO LONGER PUT OFF CONFRONT-ING THANOS.

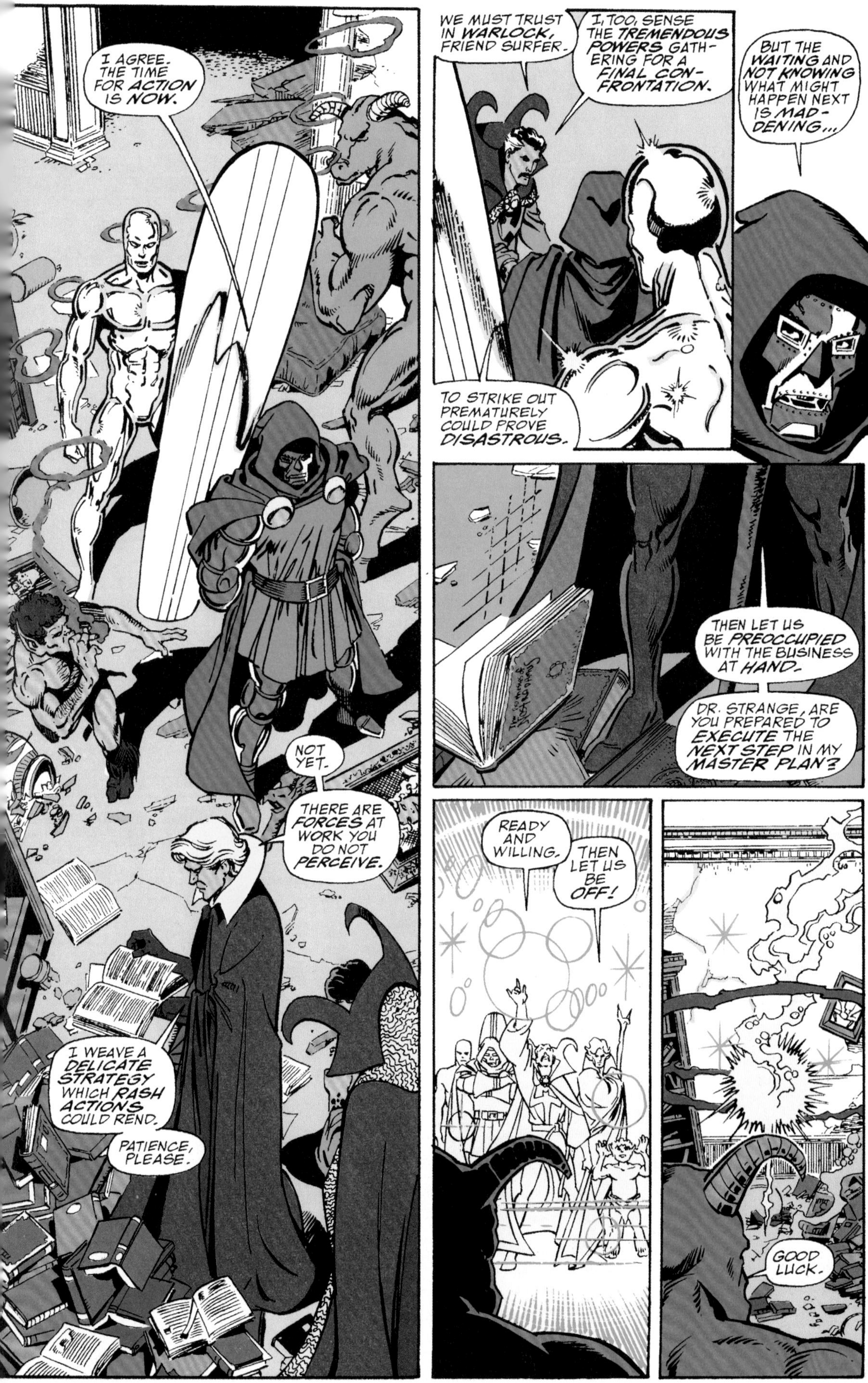
I AGREE. THE TIME FOR ACTION IS NOW.
NOT YET.
THERE ARE FORCES AT WORK YOU DO NOT PERCEIVE.
I WEAVE A DELICATE STRATEGY WHICH RASH ACTIONS COULD REND.
PATIENCE, PLEASE.
WE MUST TRUST IN WARLOCK, FRIEND SURFER.
I, TOO, SENSE THE TREMENDOUS POWERS GATHERING FOR A FINAL CONFRONTATION.
BUT THE WAITING AND NOT KNOWING WHAT MIGHT HAPPEN NEXT IS MADDENING...
TO STRIKE OUT PREMATURELY COULD PROVE DISASTROUS.
THEN LET US BE PREOCCUPIED WITH THE BUSINESS AT HAND.
DR. STRANGE, ARE YOU PREPARED TO EXECUTE THE NEXT STEP IN MY MASTER PLAN?
READY AND WILLING.
THEN LET US BE OFF!
GOOD LUCK.

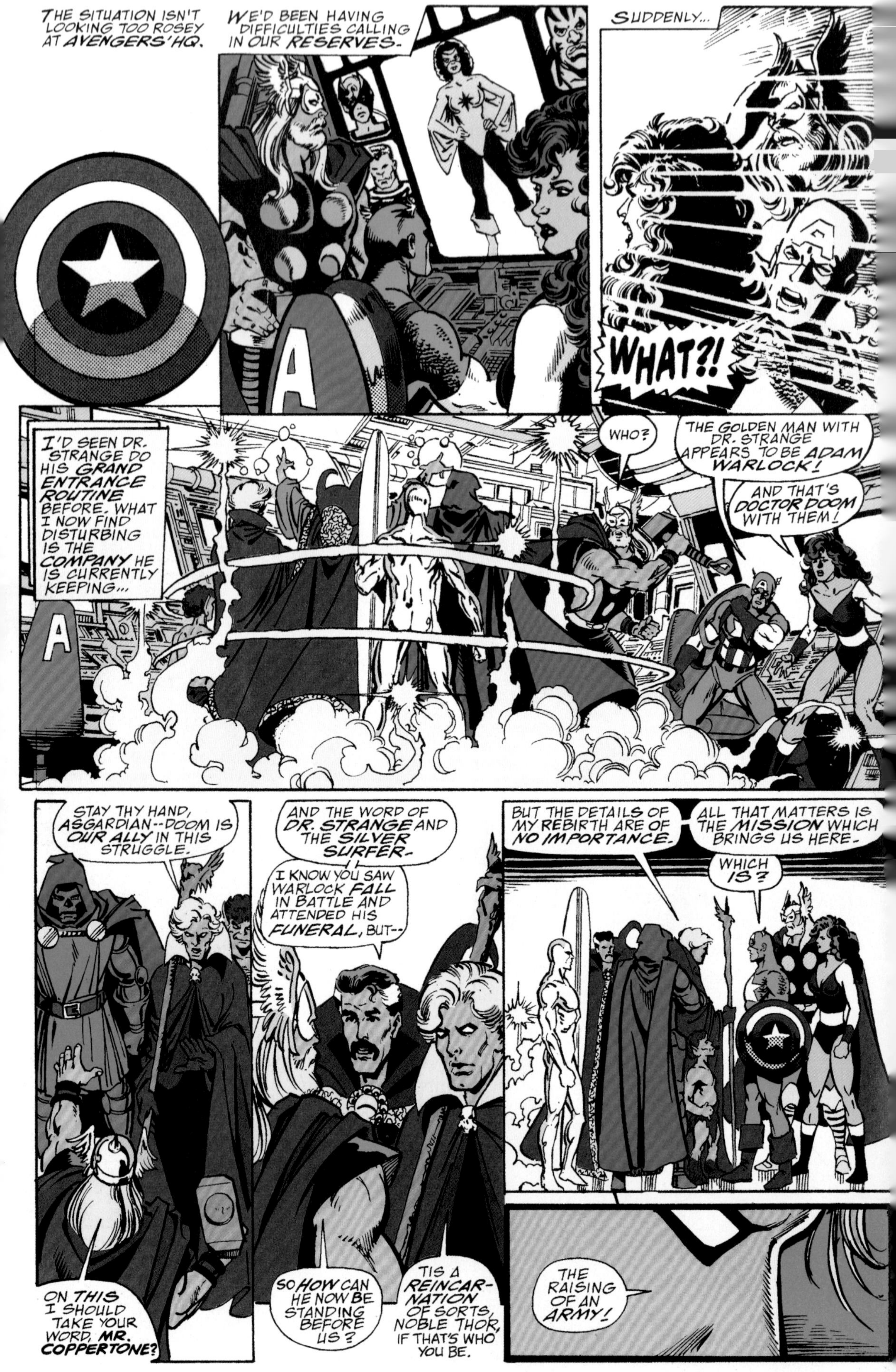
THE SITUATION ISN'T LOOKING TOO ROSEY AT AVENGERS' HQ.
WE'D BEEN HAVING DIFFICULTIES CALLING IN OUR RESERVES-
SUDDENLY...
WHAT?!
I'D SEEN DR. STRANGE DO HIS GRAND ENTRANCE ROUTINE BEFORE. WHAT I NOW FIND DISTURBING IS THE COMPANY HE IS CURRENTLY KEEPING...
WHO?
THE GOLDEN MAN WITH DR. STRANGE APPEARS TO BE ADAM WARLOCK!
AND THAT'S DOCTOR DOOM WITH THEM!
STAY THY HAND, ASGARDIAN--DOOM IS OUR ALLY IN THIS STRUGGLE.
ON THIS I SHOULD TAKE YOUR WORD, MR. COPPERTONE?
AND THE WORD OF DR. STRANGE AND THE SILVER SURFER-
I KNOW YOU SAW WARLOCK FALL IN BATTLE AND ATTENDED HIS FUNERAL, BUT--
SO HOW CAN HE NOW BE STANDING BEFORE US?
TIS A REINCARNATION OF SORTS, NOBLE THOR, IF THAT'S WHO YOU BE.
BUT THE DETAILS OF MY REBIRTH ARE OF NO IMPORTANCE.
ALL THAT MATTERS IS THE MISSION WHICH BRINGS US HERE.
WHICH IS?
THE RAISING OF AN ARMY!

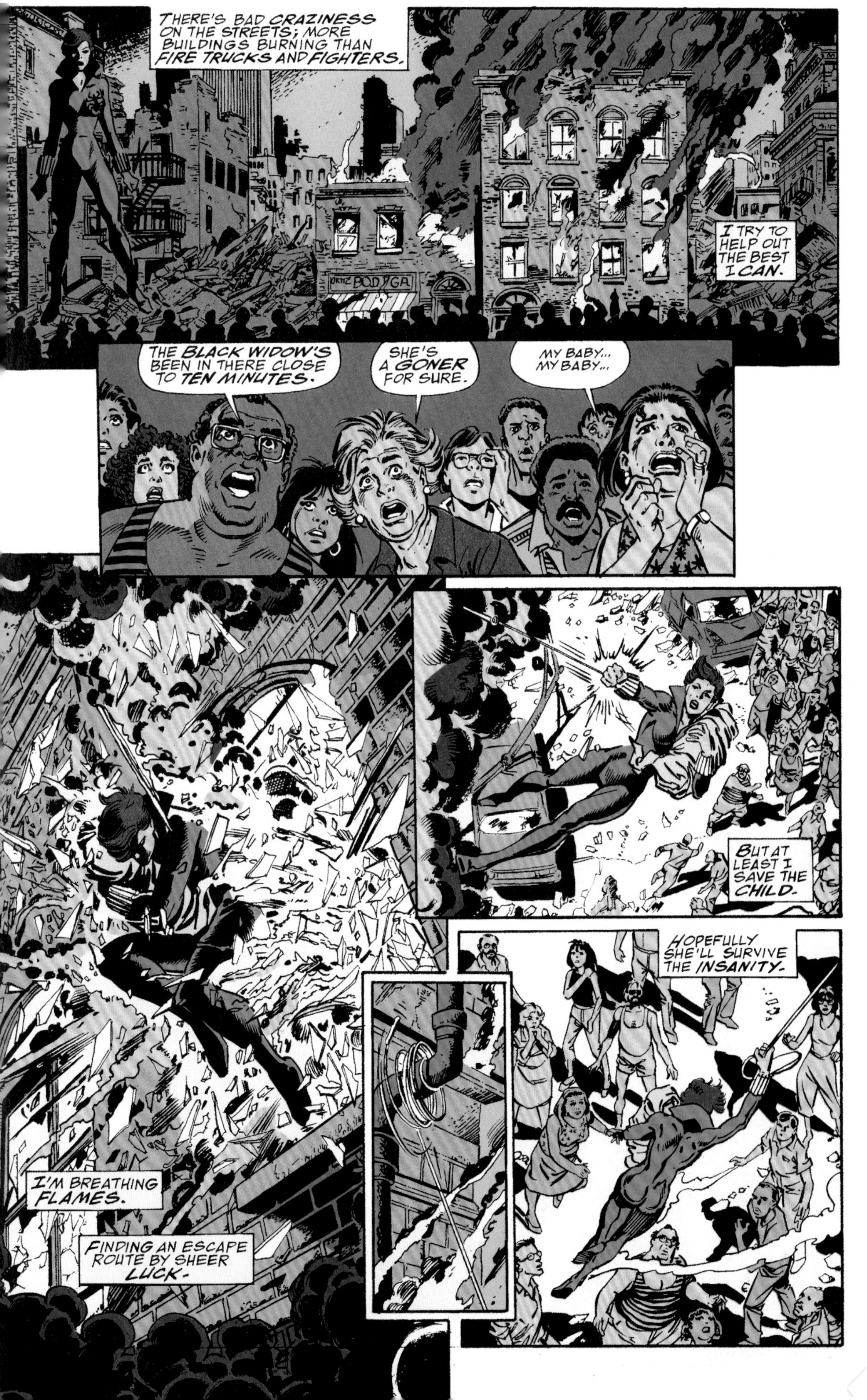
THERE'S BAD CRAZINESS ON THE STREETS; MORE BUILDINGS BURNING THAN FIRE TRUCKS AND FIGHTERS.
I TRY TO HELP OUT THE BEST I CAN.
THE BLACK WIDOW'S BEEN IN THERE CLOSE TO TEN MINUTES.
SHE'S A GONER FOR SURE.
MY BABY... MY BABY...
I'M BREATHING FLAMES.
FINDING AN ESCAPE ROUTE BY SHEER LUCK.
BUT AT LEAST I SAVE THE CHILD.
HOPEFULLY SHE'LL SURVIVE THE INSANITY.

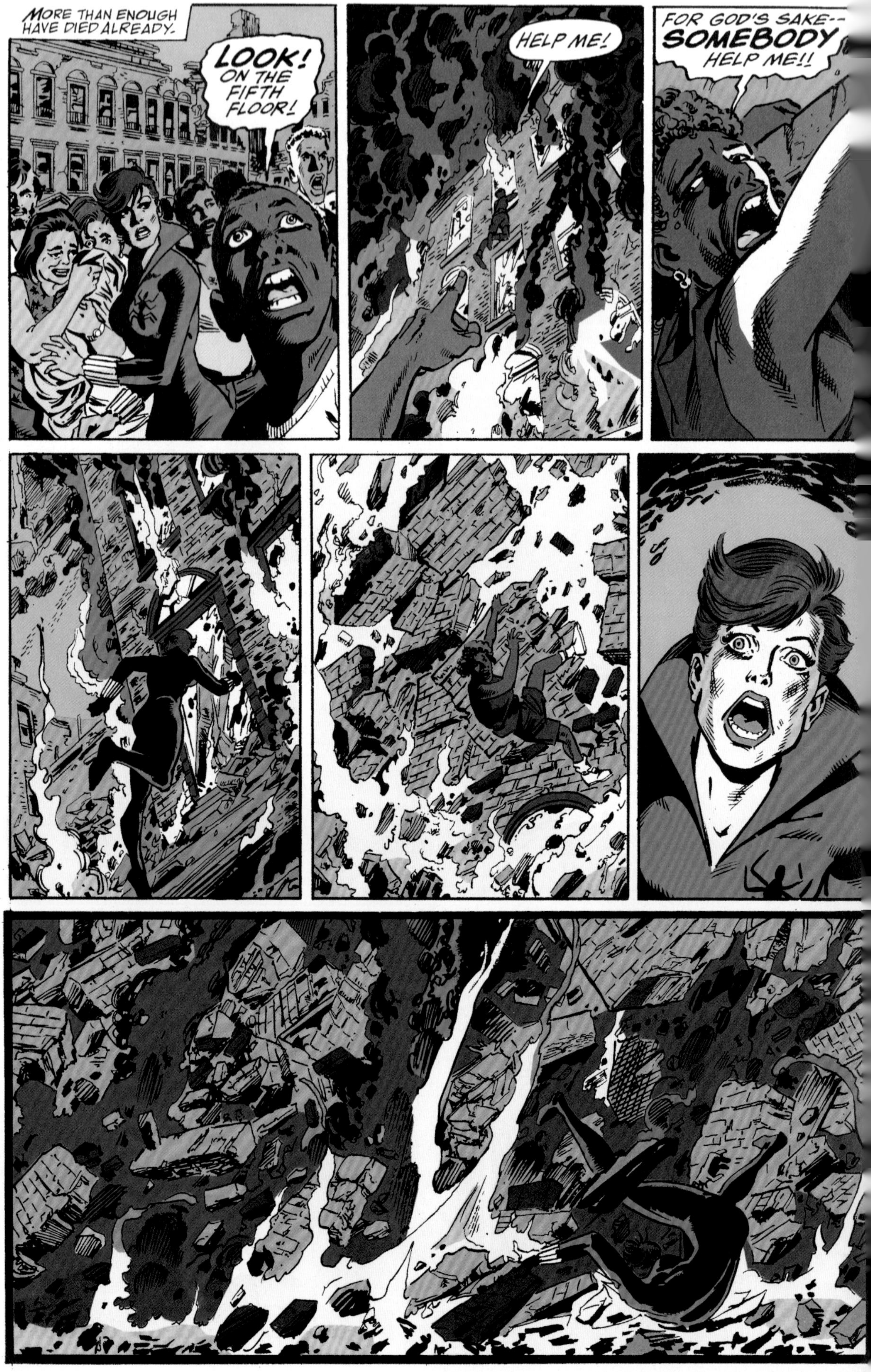
MORE THAN ENOUGH HAVE DIED ALREADY.
LOOK! ON THE FIFTH FLOOR!
HELP ME!
FOR GOD'S SAKE-- SOMEBODY HELP ME!!

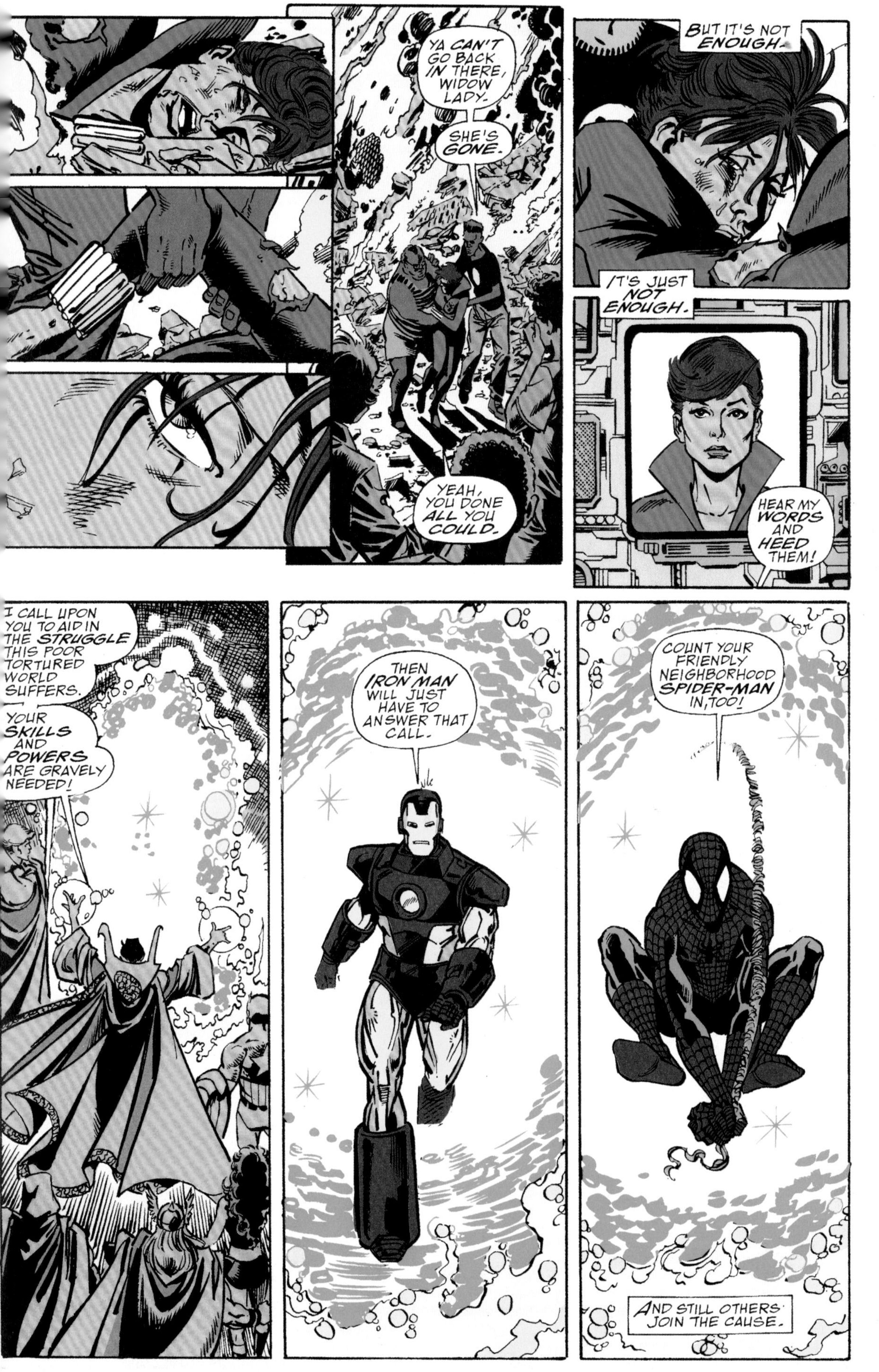
YA CAN'T GO BACK IN THERE, WIDOW LADY.
SHE'S GONE.
YEAH, YOU DONE ALL YOU COULD.
BUT IT'S NOT ENOUGH.
IT'S JUST NOT ENOUGH.
HEAR MY WORDS AND HEED THEM!
I CALL UPON YOU TO AID IN THE STRUGGLE THIS POOR TORTURED WORLD SUFFERS.
YOUR SKILLS AND POWERS ARE GRAVELY NEEDED!
THEN IRON MAN WILL JUST HAVE TO ANSWER THAT CALL.
COUNT YOUR FRIENDLY NEIGHBORHOOD SPIDER-MAN IN, TOO!
AND STILL OTHERS JOIN THE CAUSE.

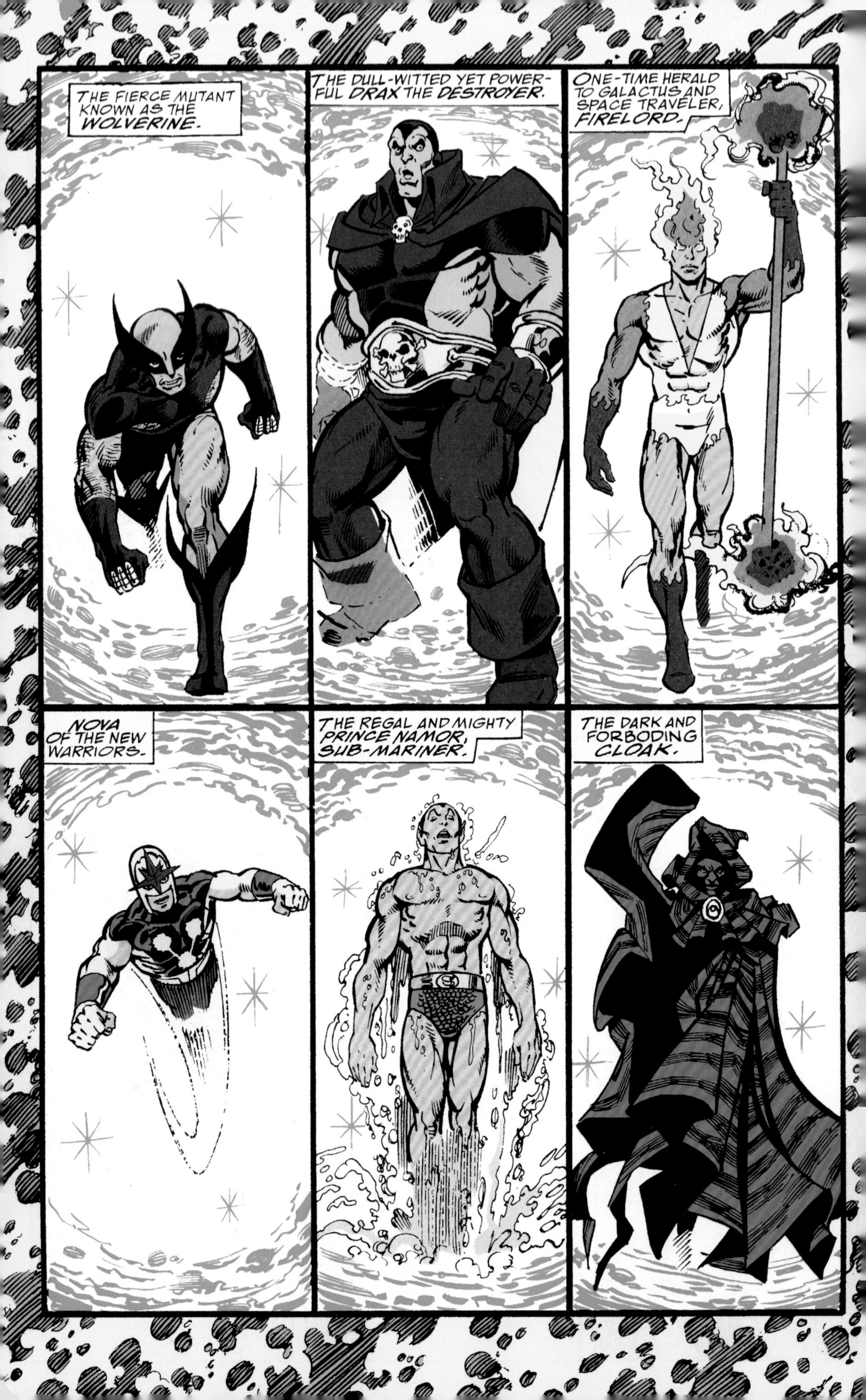
THE FIERCE MUTANT KNOWN AS THE WOLVERINE.
THE DULL-WITTED YET POWERFUL DRAX THE DESTROYER.
ONE-TIME HERALD TO GALACTUS AND SPACE TRAVELER, FIRELORD.
NOVA OF THE NEW WARRIORS.
THE REGAL AND MIGHTY PRINCE NAMOR, SUB-MARINER.
THE DARK AND FORBODING CLOAK.

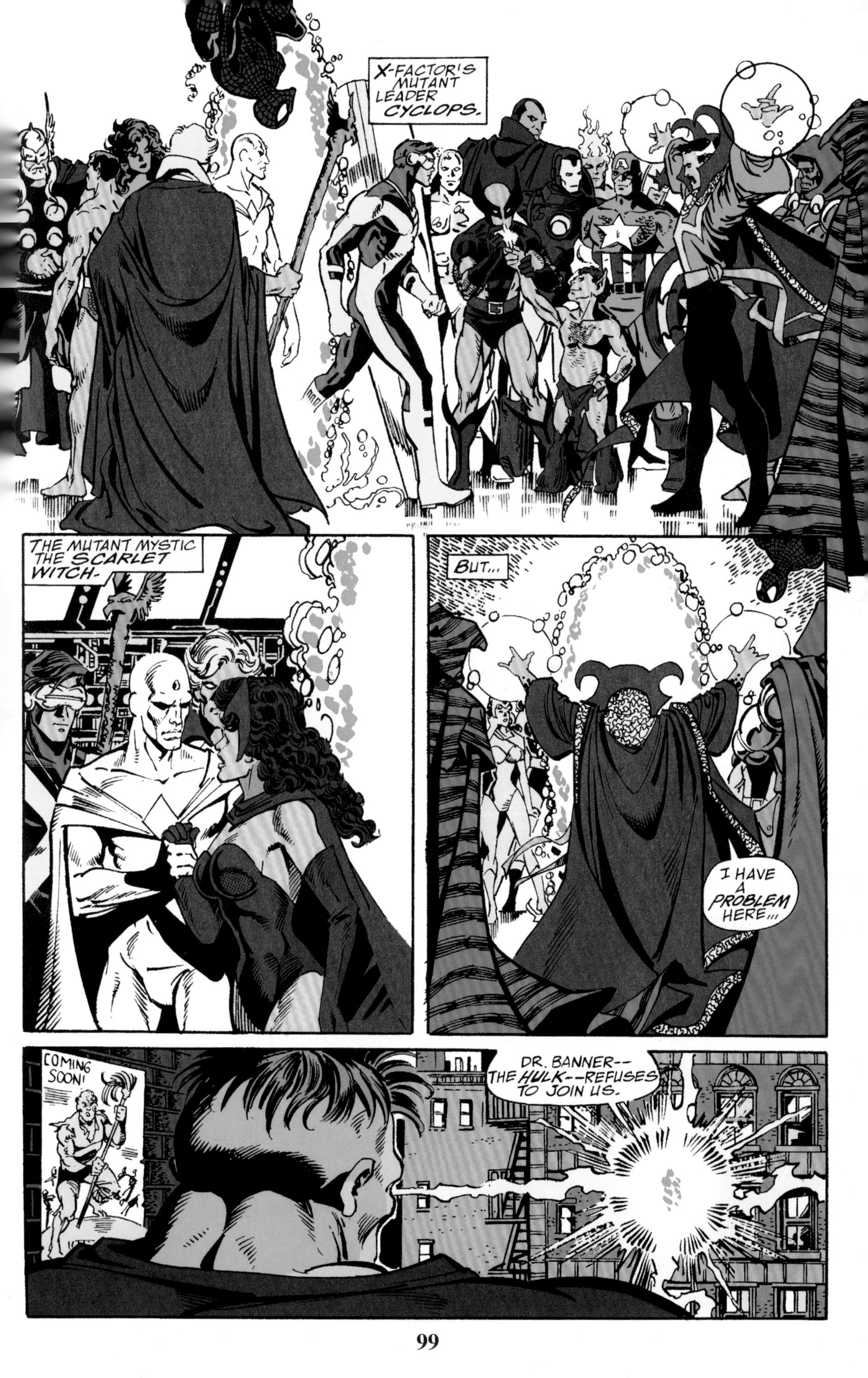
X-FACTOR'S MUTANT LEADER CYCLOPS.
THE MUTANT MYSTIC THE SCARLET WITCH-
BUT...
I HAVE A PROBLEM HERE...
COMING SOON!
DR. BANNER-- THE HULK--REFUSES TO JOIN US.

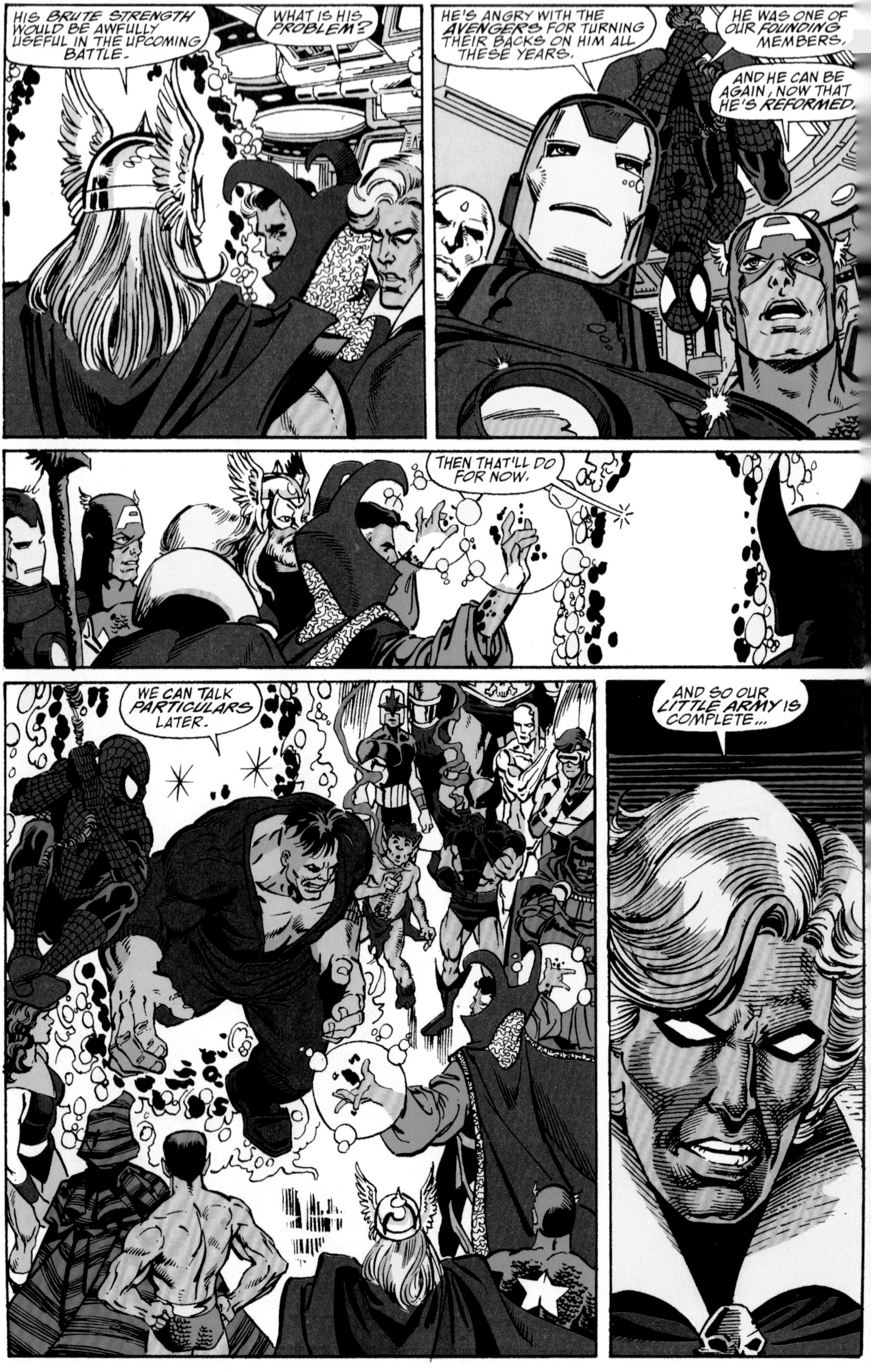
HIS BRUTE STRENGTH WOULD BE AWFULLY USEFUL IN THE UPCOMING BATTLE.
WHAT IS HIS PROBLEM?
HE'S ANGRY WITH THE AVENGERS FOR TURNING THEIR BACKS ON HIM ALL THESE YEARS.
HE WAS ONE OF OUR FOUNDING MEMBERS,
AND HE CAN BE AGAIN, NOW THAT HE'S REFORMED.
THEN THAT'LL DO FOR NOW.
WE CAN TALK PARTICULARS LATER.
AND SO OUR LITTLE ARMY IS COMPLETE...

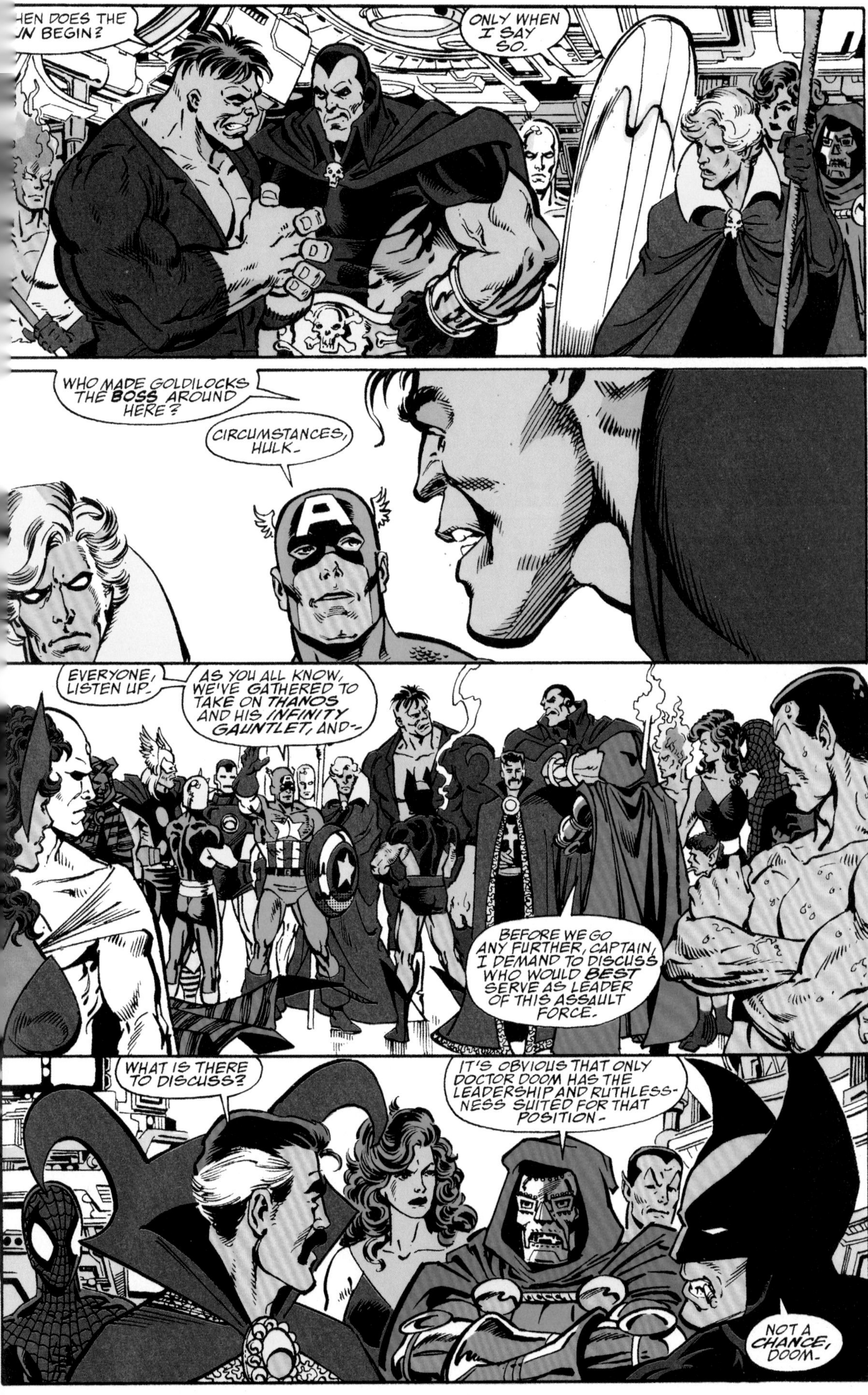
HEN DOES THE
UN BEGIN?
ONLY WHEN I SAY SO.
WHO MADE GOLDILOCKS THE BOSS AROUND HERE?
CIRCUMSTANCES, HULK--
EVERYONE, LISTEN UP--
AS YOU ALL KNOW, WE'VE GATHERED TO TAKE ON THANOS AND HIS INFINITY GAUNTLET, AND--
BEFORE WE GO ANY FURTHER, CAPTAIN, I DEMAND TO DISCUSS WHO WOULD BEST SERVE AS LEADER OF THIS ASSAULT FORCE.
WHAT IS THERE TO DISCUSS?
IT'S OBVIOUS THAT ONLY DOCTOR DOOM HAS THE LEADERSHIP AND RUTHLESS-NESS SUITED FOR THAT POSITION--
NOT A CHANCE, DOOM--

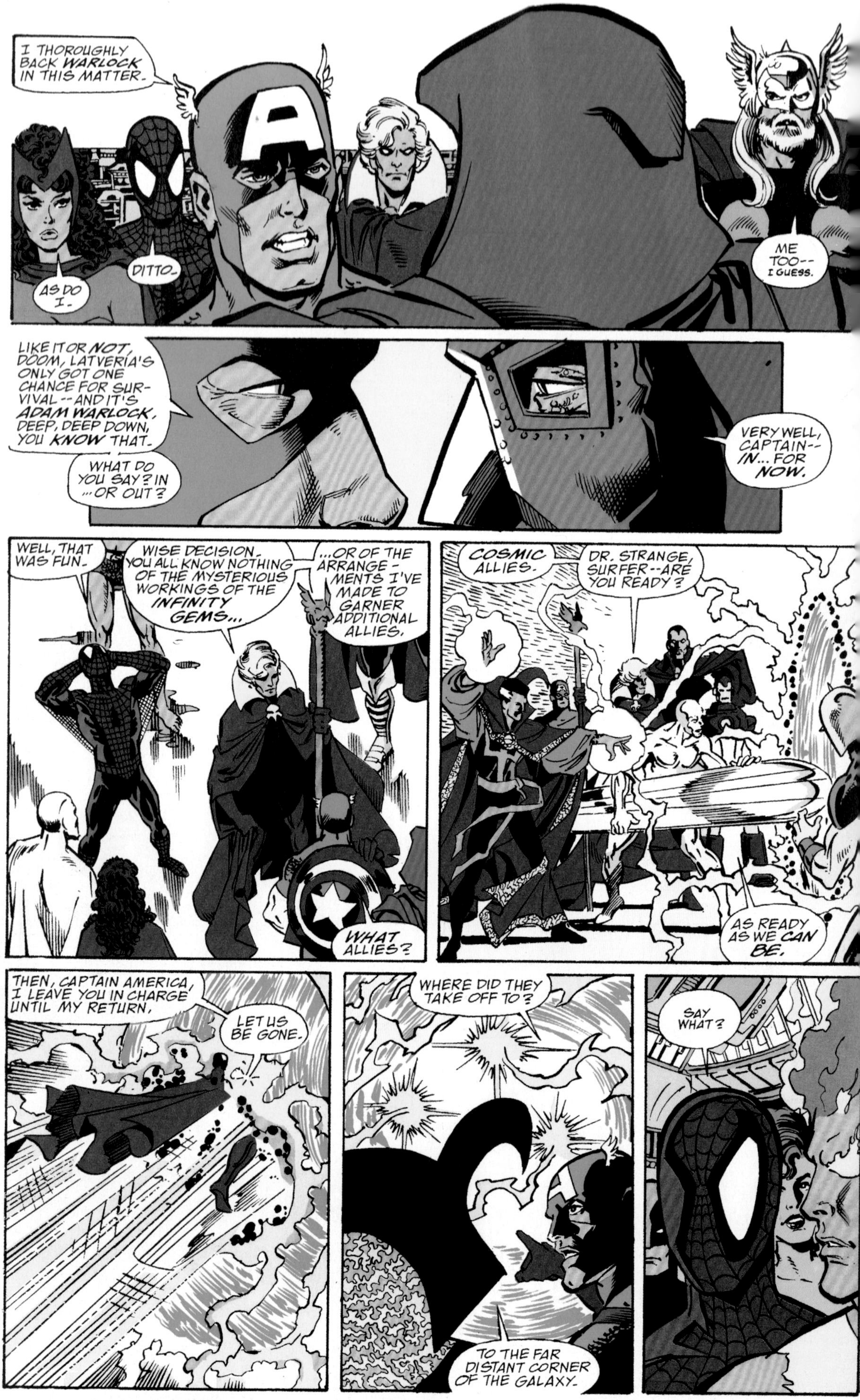

I THOROUGHLY BACK WARLOCK IN THIS MATTER.
AS DO I.
DITTO.
ME TOO-- I GUESS.
LIKE IT OR NOT, DOOM, LATVERIA'S ONLY GOT ONE CHANCE FOR SURVIVAL--AND IT'S ADAM WARLOCK. DEEP, DEEP DOWN, YOU KNOW THAT.
WHAT DO YOU SAY? IN ...OR OUT?
VERY WELL, CAPTAIN-- IN... FOR NOW.
WELL, THAT WAS FUN.
WISE DECISION. YOU ALL KNOW NOTHING OF THE MYSTERIOUS WORKINGS OF THE INFINITY GEMS...
...OR OF THE ARRANGEMENTS I'VE MADE TO GARNER ADDITIONAL ALLIES.
WHAT ALLIES?
COSMIC ALLIES.
DR. STRANGE, SURFER--ARE YOU READY?
AS READY AS WE CAN BE.
THEN, CAPTAIN AMERICA, I LEAVE YOU IN CHARGE UNTIL MY RETURN.
LET US BE GONE.
WHERE DID THEY TAKE OFF TO?
TO THE FAR DISTANT CORNER OF THE GALAXY.
SAY WHAT?

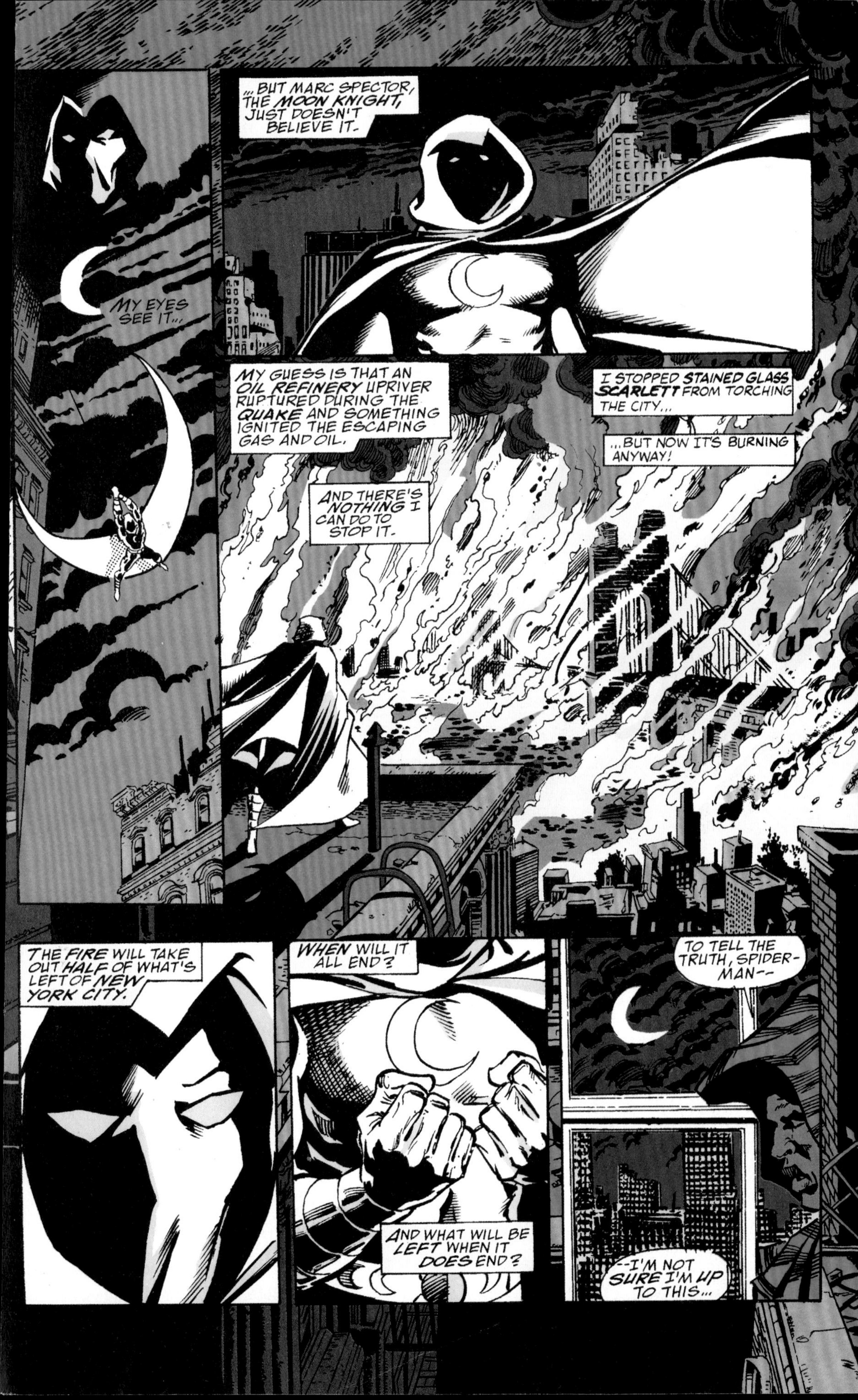
MY EYES SEE IT...
...BUT MARC SPECTOR, THE MOON KNIGHT, JUST DOESN'T BELIEVE IT.
MY GUESS IS THAT AN OIL REFINERY UPRIVER RUPTURED DURING THE QUAKE AND SOMETHING IGNITED THE ESCAPING GAS AND OIL.
AND THERE'S NOTHING I CAN DO TO STOP IT.
I STOPPED STAINED GLASS SCARLETT FROM TORCHING THE CITY...
...BUT NOW IT'S BURNING ANYWAY!
THE FIRE WILL TAKE OUT HALF OF WHAT'S LEFT OF NEW YORK CITY.
WHEN WILL IT ALL END?
AND WHAT WILL BE LEFT WHEN IT DOES END?
TO TELL THE TRUTH, SPIDER-MAN--
--I'M NOT SURE I'M UP TO THIS...

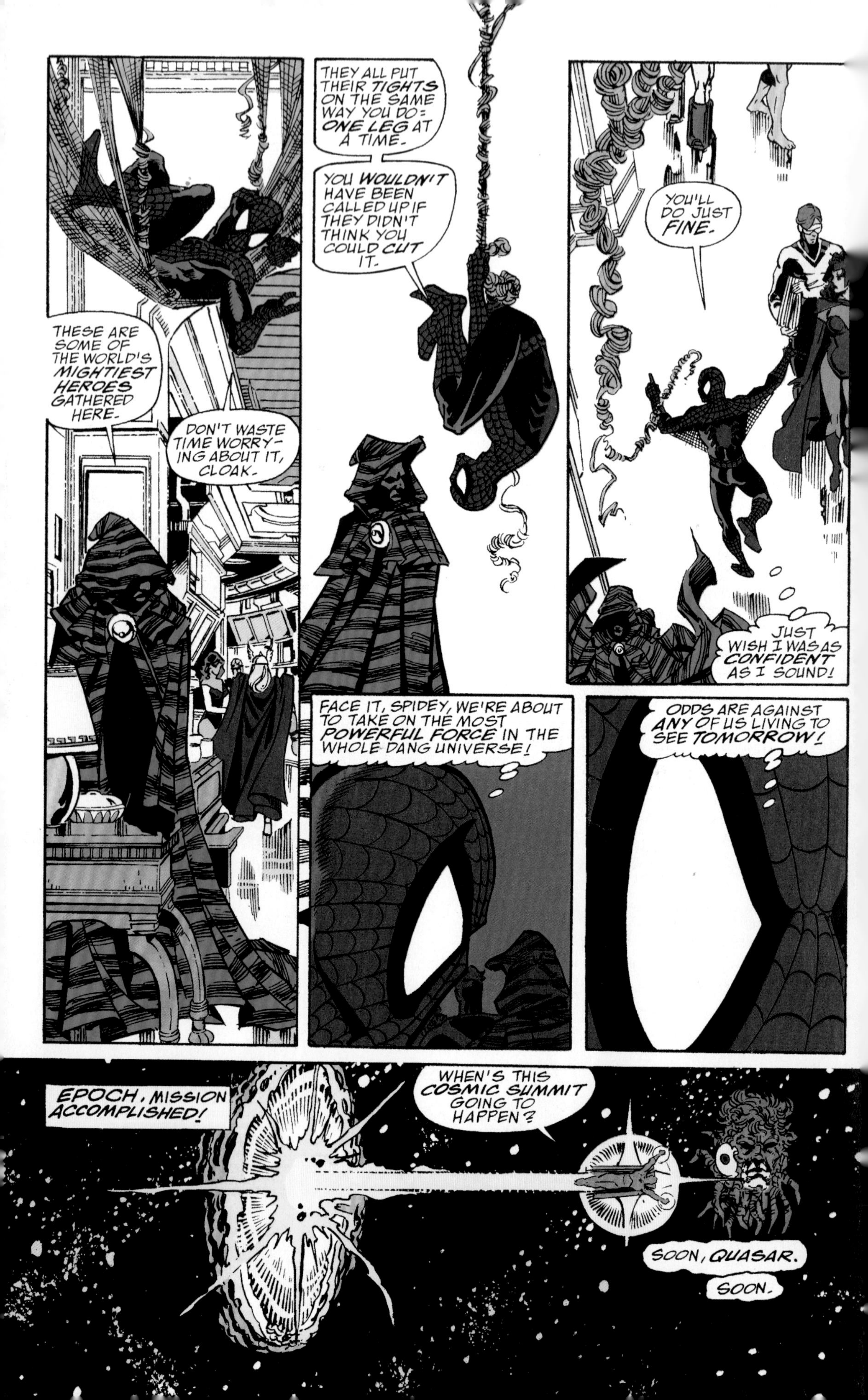
THESE ARE SOME OF THE WORLD'S MIGHTIEST HEROES GATHERED HERE.
DON'T WASTE TIME WORRYING ABOUT IT, CLOAK.
THEY ALL PUT THEIR TIGHTS ON THE SAME WAY YOU DO: ONE LEG AT A TIME.
YOU WOULDN'T HAVE BEEN CALLED UP IF THEY DIDN'T THINK YOU COULD CUT IT.
YOU'LL DO JUST FINE.
JUST WISH I WAS AS CONFIDENT AS I SOUND!
FACE IT, SPIDEY, WE'RE ABOUT TO TAKE ON THE MOST POWERFUL FORCE IN THE WHOLE DANG UNIVERSE!
ODDS ARE AGAINST ANY OF US LIVING TO SEE TOMORROW!
EPOCH, MISSION ACCOMPLISHED!
WHEN'S THIS COSMIC SUMMIT GOING TO HAPPEN?
SOON, QUASAR.
SOON.

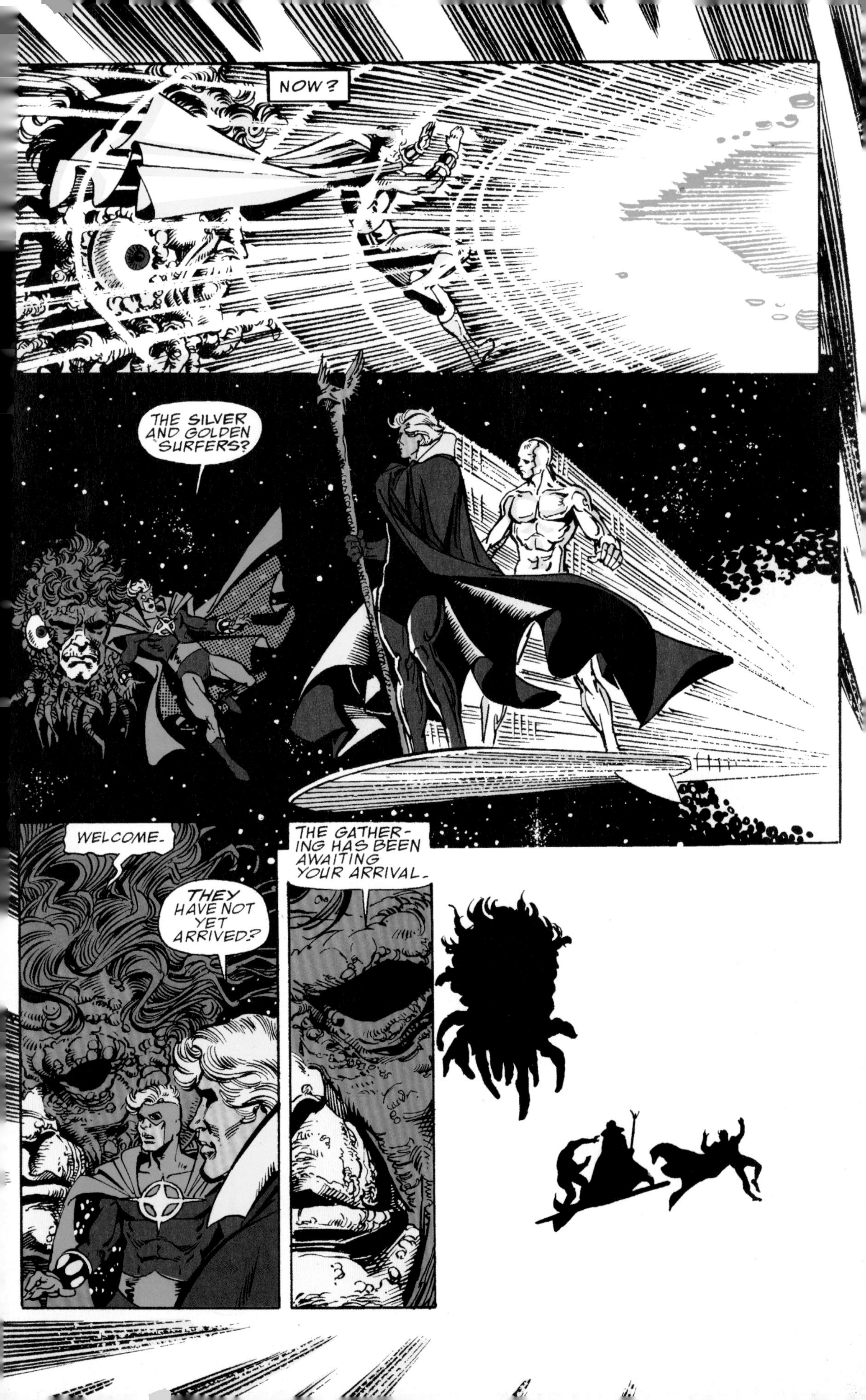
NOW?
THE SILVER AND GOLDEN SURFERS?
WELCOME.
THEY HAVE NOT YET ARRIVED?
THE GATHERING HAS BEEN AWAITING YOUR ARRIVAL.

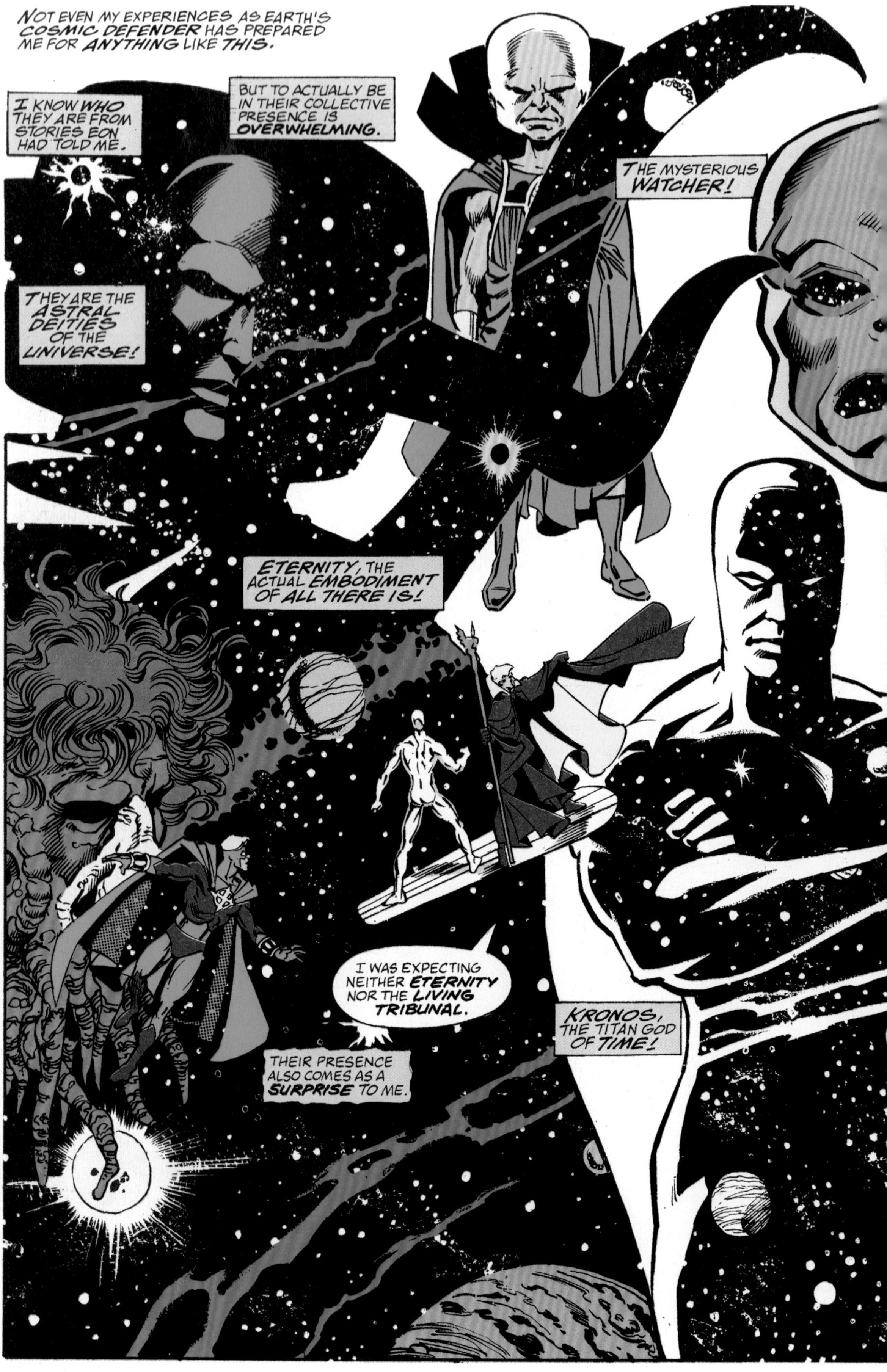
NOT EVEN MY EXPERIENCES AS EARTH'S COSMIC DEFENDER HAS PREPARED ME FOR ANYTHING LIKE THIS.
I KNOW WHO THEY ARE FROM STORIES EON HAD TOLD ME.
BUT TO ACTUALLY BE IN THEIR COLLECTIVE PRESENCE IS OVERWHELMING.
THE MYSTERIOUS WATCHER!
THEY ARE THE ASTRAL DEITIES OF THE UNIVERSE!
ETERNITY, THE ACTUAL EMBODIMENT OF ALL THERE IS!
I WAS EXPECTING NEITHER ETERNITY NOR THE LIVING TRIBUNAL.
KRONOS, THE TITAN GOD OF TIME!
THEIR PRESENCE ALSO COMES AS A SURPRISE TO ME.

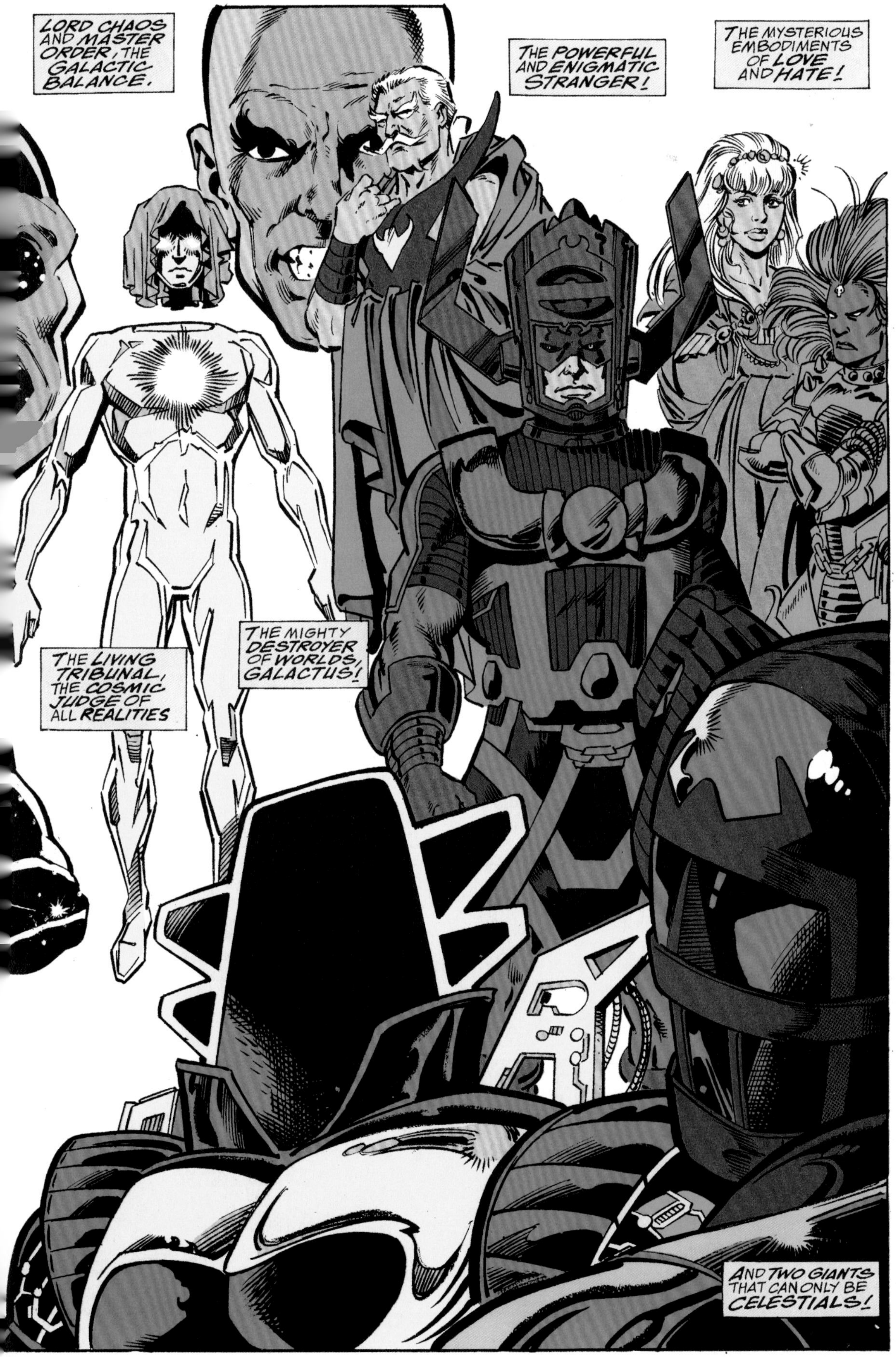
LORD CHAOS AND MASTER ORDER, THE GALACTIC BALANCE.
THE POWERFUL AND ENIGMATIC STRANGER!
THE MYSTERIOUS EMBODIMENTS OF LOVE AND HATE!
THE LIVING TRIBUNAL, THE COSMIC JUDGE OF ALL REALITIES
THE MIGHTY DESTROYER OF WORLDS, GALACTUS!
AND TWO GIANTS THAT CAN ONLY BE CELESTIALS!

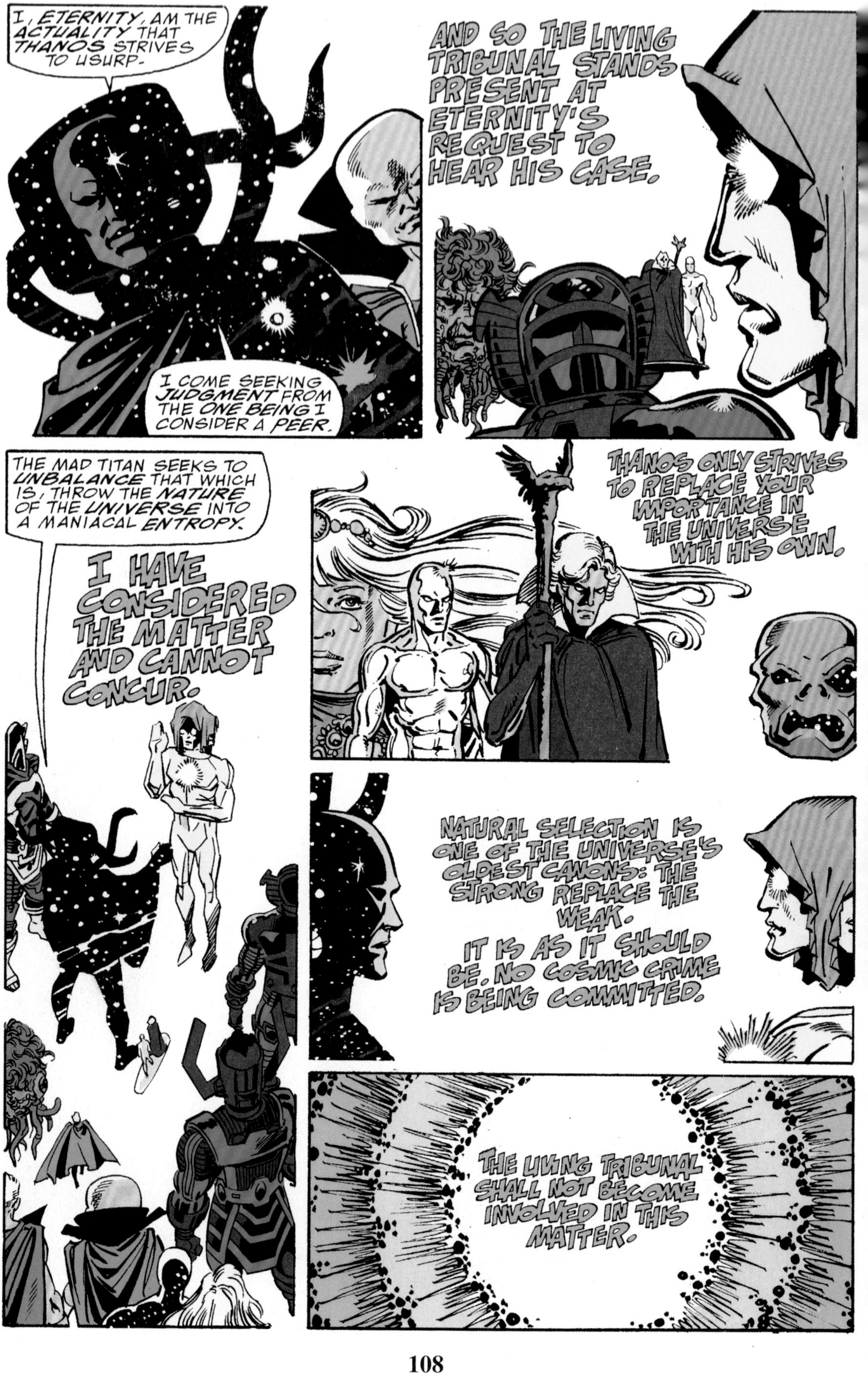
I, ETERNITY, AM THE ACTUALITY THAT THANOS STRIVES TO USURP-
I COME SEEKING JUDGMENT FROM THE ONE BEING I CONSIDER A PEER.
AND SO THE LIVING TRIBUNAL STANDS PRESENT AT ETERNITY'S REQUEST TO HEAR HIS CASE.
THE MAD TITAN SEEKS TO UNBALANCE THAT WHICH IS, THROW THE NATURE OF THE UNIVERSE INTO A MANIACAL ENTROPY.
I HAVE CONSIDERED THE MATTER AND CANNOT CONCUR.
THANOS ONLY STRIVES TO REPLACE YOUR IMPORTANCE IN THE UNIVERSE WITH HIS OWN.
NATURAL SELECTION IS ONE OF THE UNIVERSE'S OLDEST CANONS: THE STRONG REPLACE THE WEAK.
IT IS AS IT SHOULD BE. NO COSMIC CRIME IS BEING COMMITTED.
THE LIVING TRIBUNAL SHALL NOT BECOME INVOLVED IN THIS MATTER.

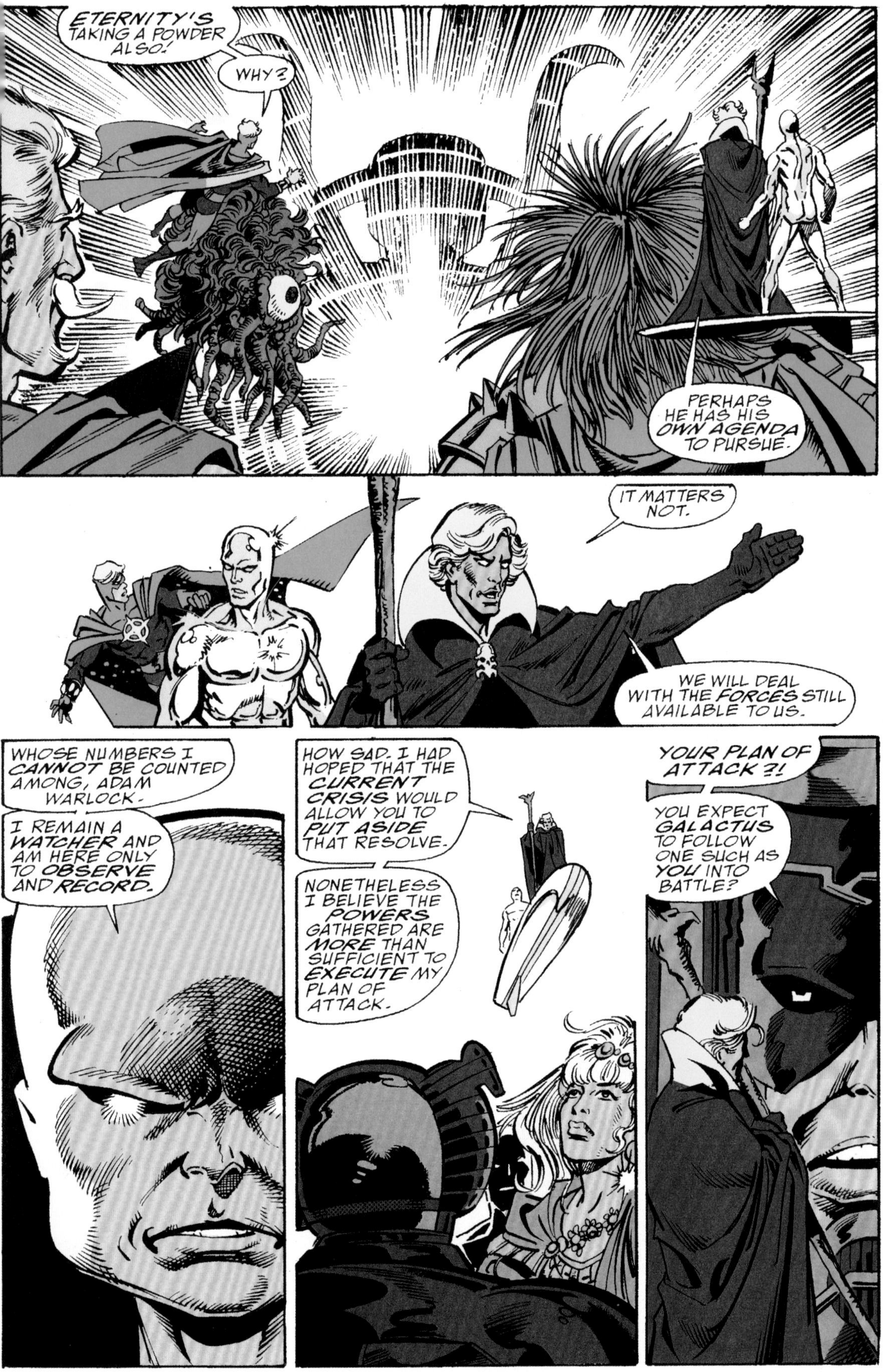
ETERNITY'S TAKING A POWDER ALSO!
WHY?
PERHAPS HE HAS HIS OWN AGENDA TO PURSUE.
IT MATTERS NOT.
WE WILL DEAL WITH THE FORCES STILL AVAILABLE TO US.
WHOSE NUMBERS I CANNOT BE COUNTED AMONG, ADAM WARLOCK.
I REMAIN A WATCHER AND AM HERE ONLY TO OBSERVE AND RECORD.
HOW SAD. I HAD HOPED THAT THE CURRENT CRISIS WOULD ALLOW YOU TO PUT ASIDE THAT RESOLVE.
NONETHELESS I BELIEVE THE POWERS GATHERED ARE MORE THAN SUFFICIENT TO EXECUTE MY PLAN OF ATTACK.
YOUR PLAN OF ATTACK?!
YOU EXPECT GALACTUS TO FOLLOW ONE SUCH AS YOU INTO BATTLE?

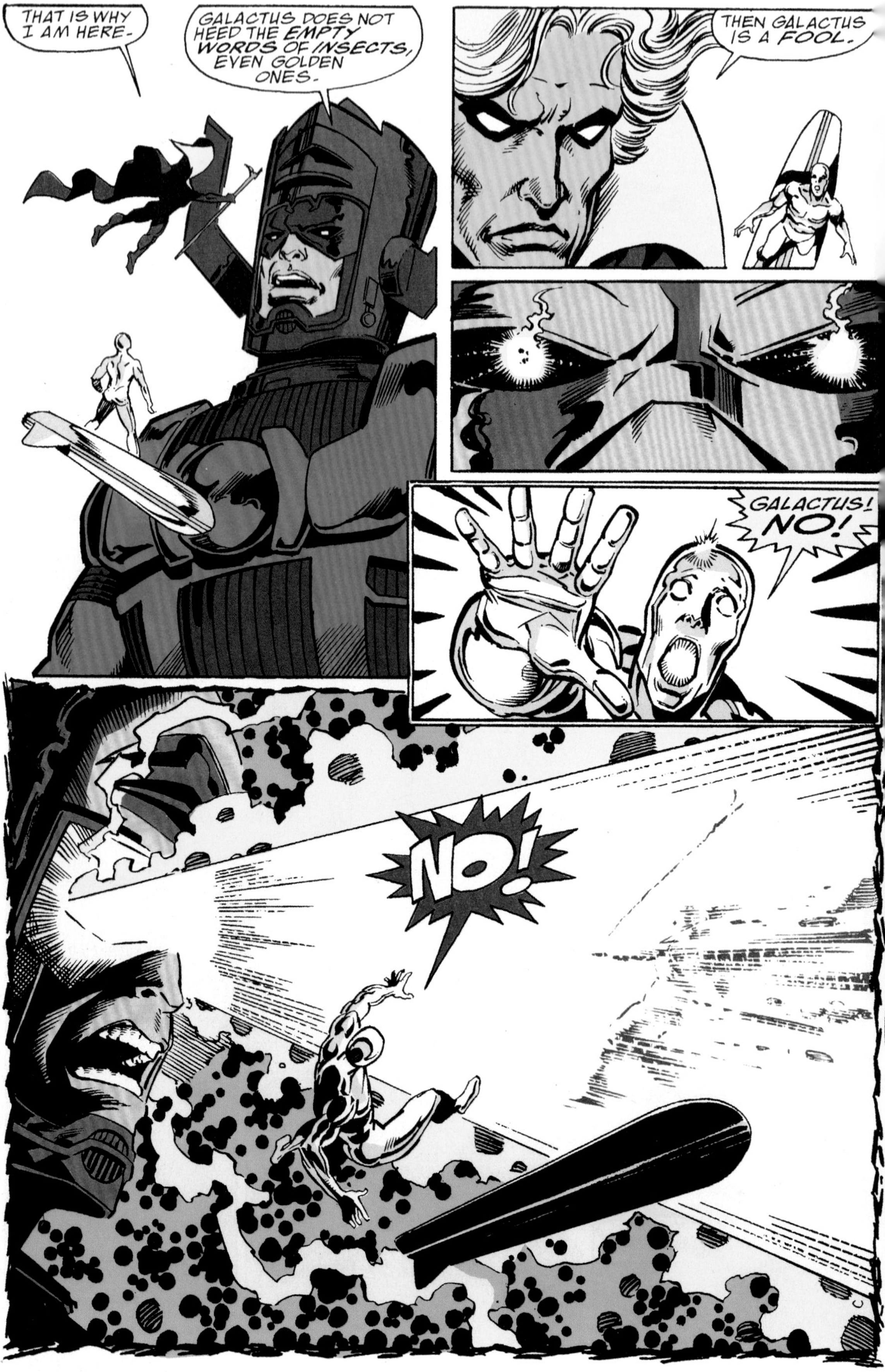
THAT IS WHY I AM HERE-
GALACTUS DOES NOT HEED THE EMPTY WORDS OF INSECTS, EVEN GOLDEN ONES-
THEN GALACTUS IS A FOOL.
GALACTUS! NO!
NO!

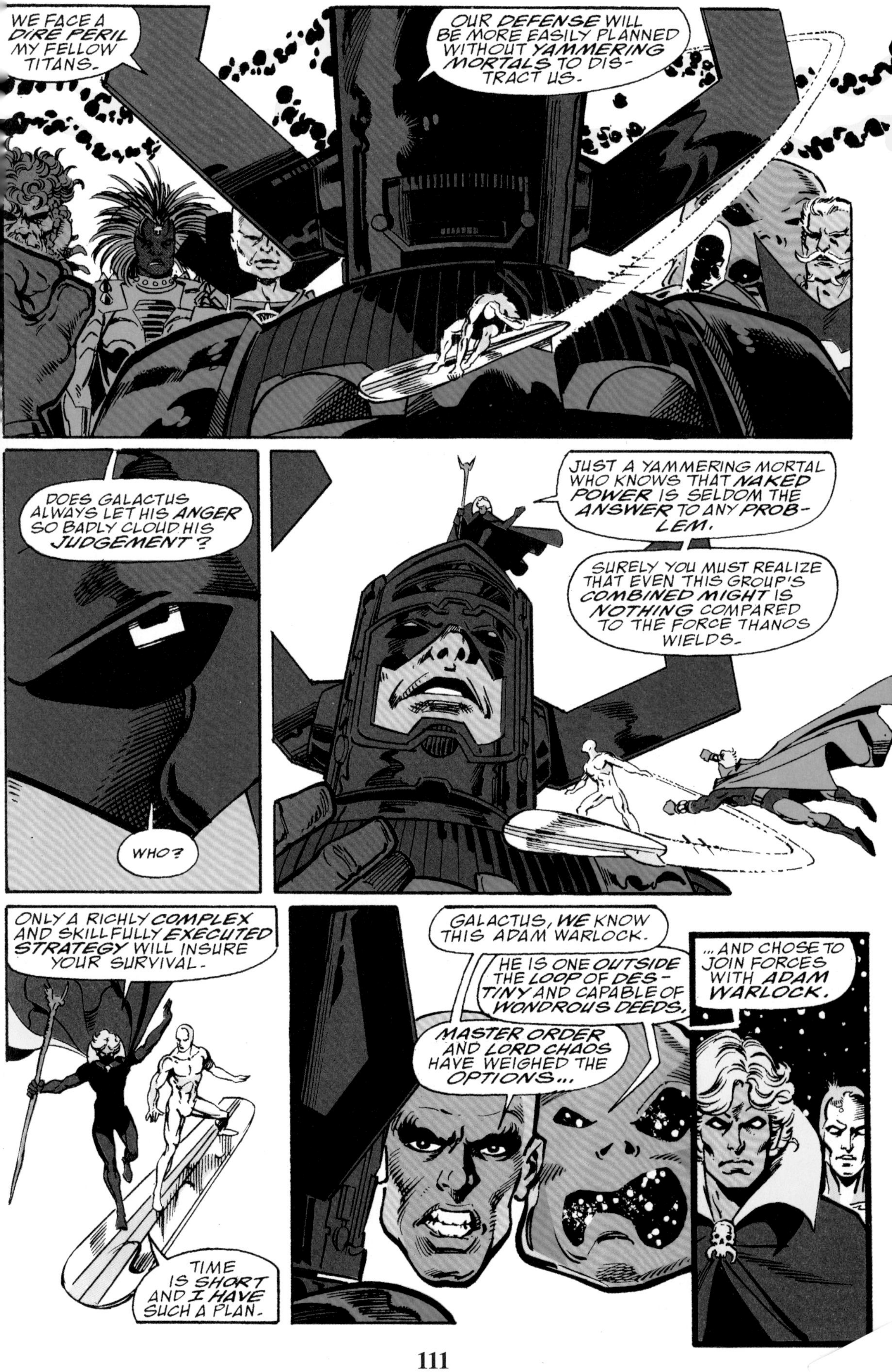
WE FACE A DIRE PERIL MY FELLOW TITANS.
OUR DEFENSE WILL BE MORE EASILY PLANNED WITHOUT YAMMERING MORTALS TO DISTRACT US.
DOES GALACTUS ALWAYS LET HIS ANGER SO BADLY CLOUD HIS JUDGEMENT?
WHO?
JUST A YAMMERING MORTAL WHO KNOWS THAT NAKED POWER IS SELDOM THE ANSWER TO ANY PROBLEM.
SURELY YOU MUST REALIZE THAT EVEN THIS GROUP'S COMBINED MIGHT IS NOTHING COMPARED TO THE FORCE THANOS WIELDS.
ONLY A RICHLY COMPLEX AND SKILLFULLY EXECUTED STRATEGY WILL INSURE YOUR SURVIVAL.
TIME IS SHORT AND I HAVE SUCH A PLAN.
GALACTUS, WE KNOW THIS ADAM WARLOCK.
HE IS ONE OUTSIDE THE LOOP OF DESTINY AND CAPABLE OF WONDROUS DEEDS.
MASTER ORDER AND LORD CHAOS HAVE WEIGHED THE OPTIONS...
...AND CHOSE TO JOIN FORCES WITH ADAM WARLOCK.

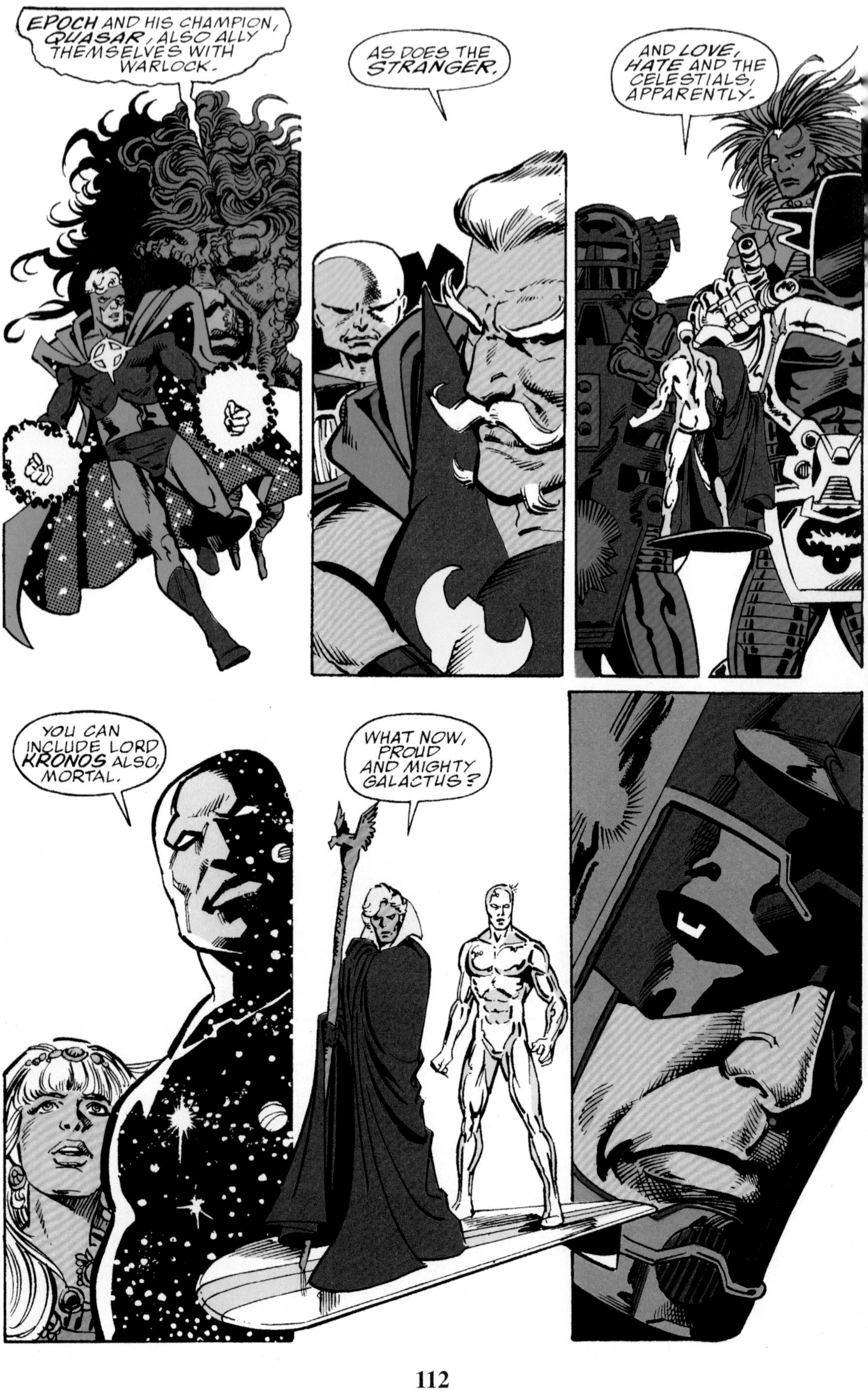

EPOCH AND HIS CHAMPION, QUASAR, ALSO ALLY THEMSELVES WITH WARLOCK.
AS DOES THE STRANGER.
AND LOVE, HATE AND THE CELESTIALS, APPARENTLY-
YOU CAN INCLUDE LORD KRONOS ALSO, MORTAL.
WHAT NOW, PROUD AND MIGHTY GALACTUS?

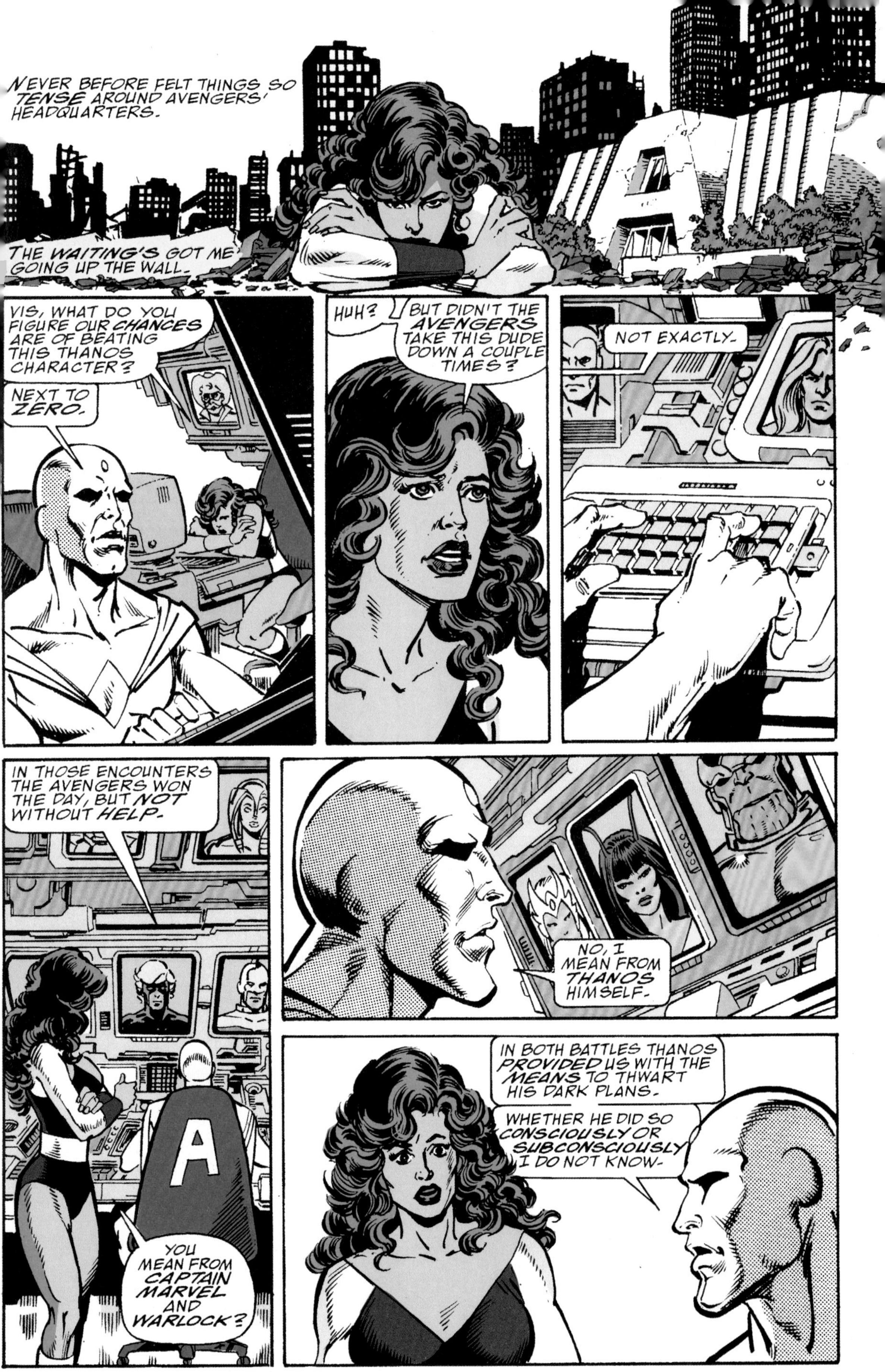
NEVER BEFORE FELT THINGS SO TENSE AROUND AVENGERS' HEADQUARTERS.
THE WAITING'S GOT ME GOING UP THE WALL.
VIS, WHAT DO YOU FIGURE OUR CHANCES ARE OF BEATING THIS THANOS CHARACTER?
NEXT TO ZERO.
HUH?
BUT DIDN'T THE AVENGERS TAKE THIS DUDE DOWN A COUPLE TIMES?
NOT EXACTLY.
IN THOSE ENCOUNTERS THE AVENGERS WON THE DAY, BUT NOT WITHOUT HELP.
YOU MEAN FROM CAPTAIN MARVEL AND WARLOCK?
NO, I MEAN FROM THANOS HIMSELF.
IN BOTH BATTLES THANOS PROVIDED US WITH THE MEANS TO THWART HIS DARK PLANS.
WHETHER HE DID SO CONSCIOUSLY OR SUBCONSCIOUSLY I DO NOT KNOW.

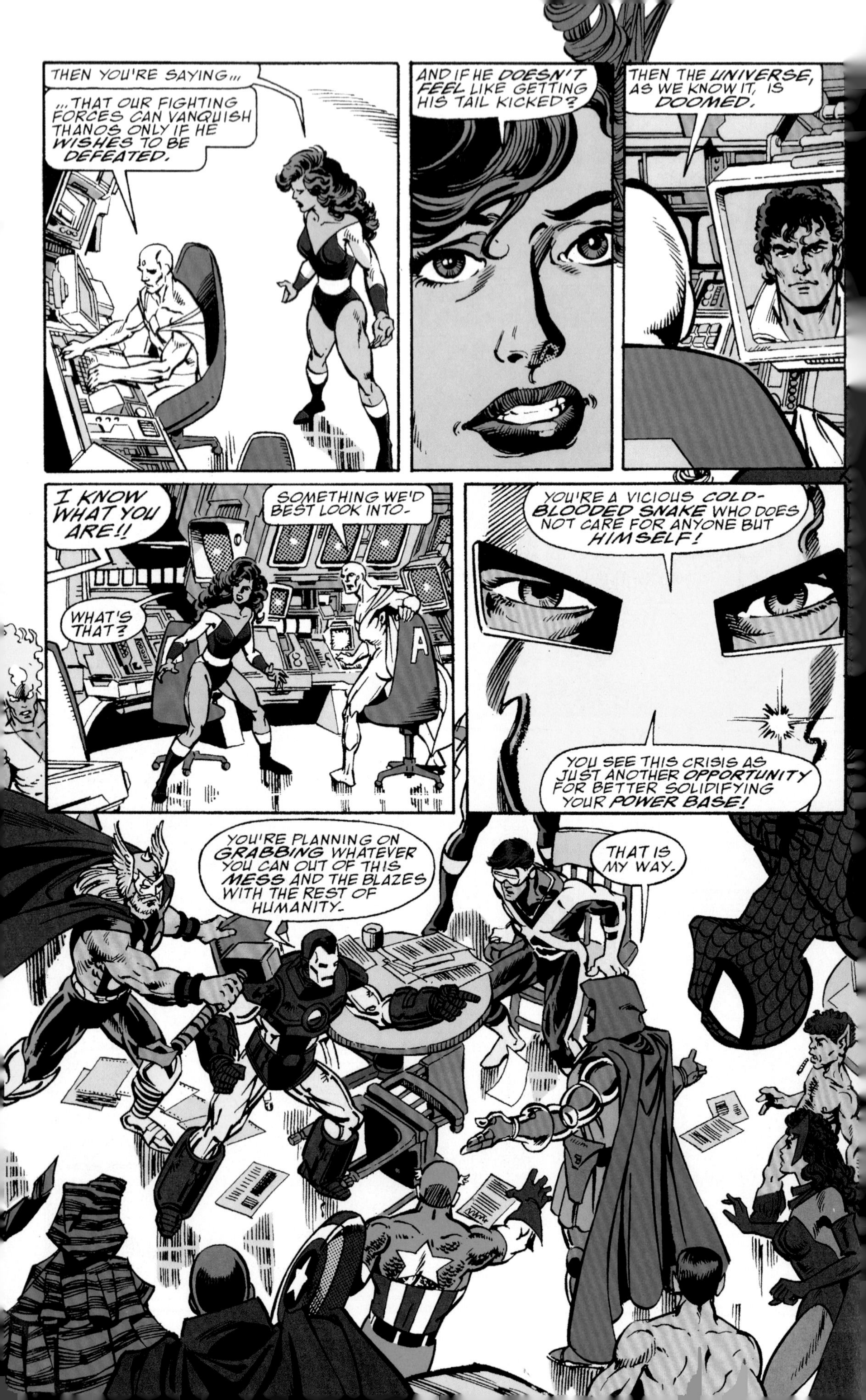
THEN YOU'RE SAYING...
...THAT OUR FIGHTING FORCES CAN VANQUISH THANOS ONLY IF HE WISHES TO BE DEFEATED.
AND IF HE DOESN'T FEEL LIKE GETTING HIS TAIL KICKED?
THEN THE UNIVERSE, AS WE KNOW IT, IS DOOMED.
I KNOW WHAT YOU ARE!!
SOMETHING WE'D BEST LOOK INTO-
WHAT'S THAT?
YOU'RE A VICIOUS COLD-BLOODED SNAKE WHO DOES NOT CARE FOR ANYONE BUT HIMSELF!
YOU SEE THIS CRISIS AS JUST ANOTHER OPPORTUNITY FOR BETTER SOLIDIFYING YOUR POWER BASE!
YOU'RE PLANNING ON GRABBING WHATEVER YOU CAN OUT OF THIS MESS AND THE BLAZES WITH THE REST OF HUMANITY-
THAT IS MY WAY.

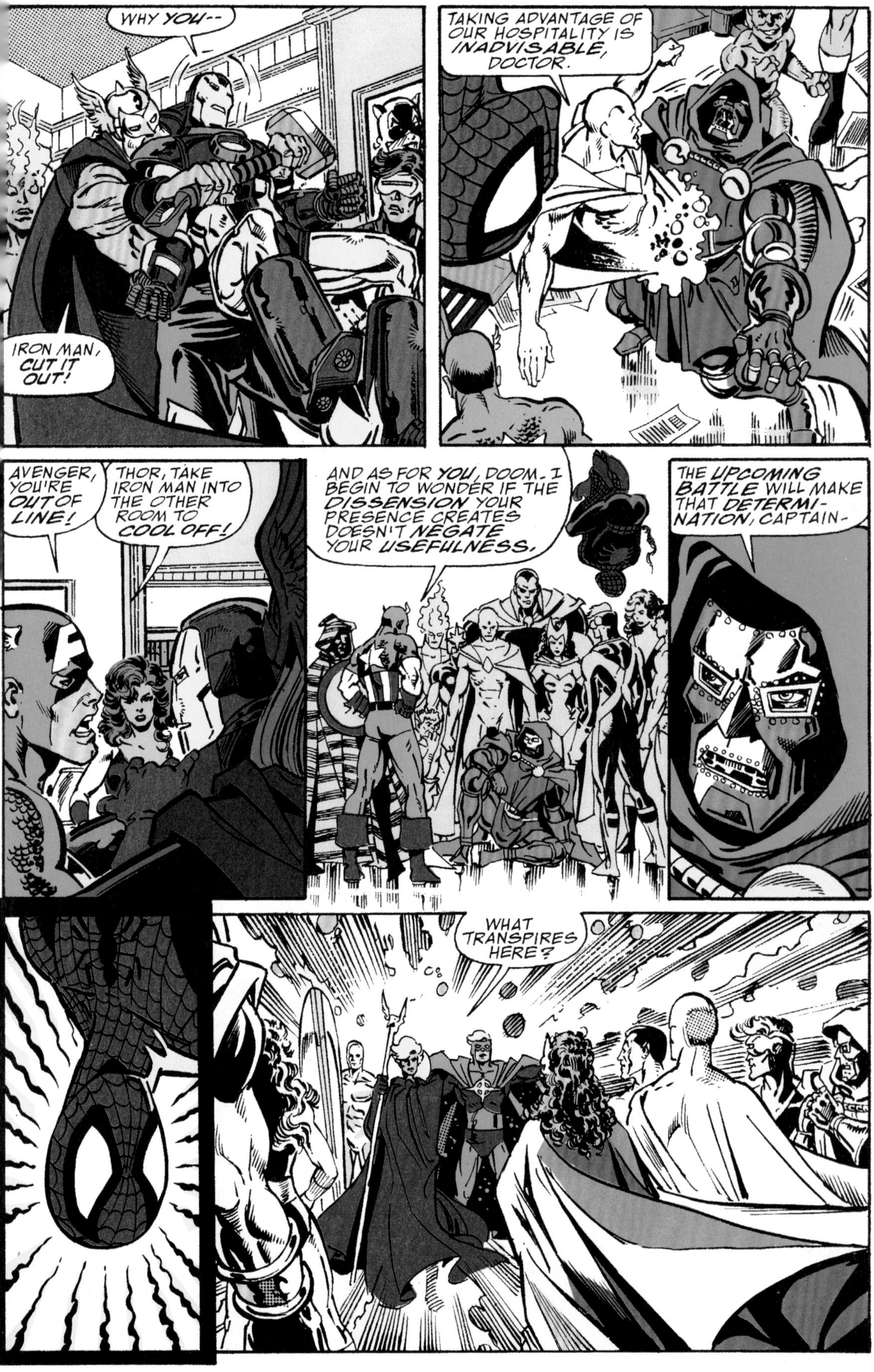
WHY YOU--
IRON MAN, CUT IT OUT!
TAKING ADVANTAGE OF OUR HOSPITALITY IS INADVISABLE, DOCTOR.
AVENGER, YOU'RE OUT OF LINE!
THOR, TAKE IRON MAN INTO THE OTHER ROOM TO COOL OFF!
AND AS FOR YOU, DOOM. I BEGIN TO WONDER IF THE DISSENSION YOUR PRESENCE CREATES DOESN'T NEGATE YOUR USEFULNESS.
THE UPCOMING BATTLE WILL MAKE THAT DETERMINATION, CAPTAIN-
WHAT TRANSPIRES HERE?

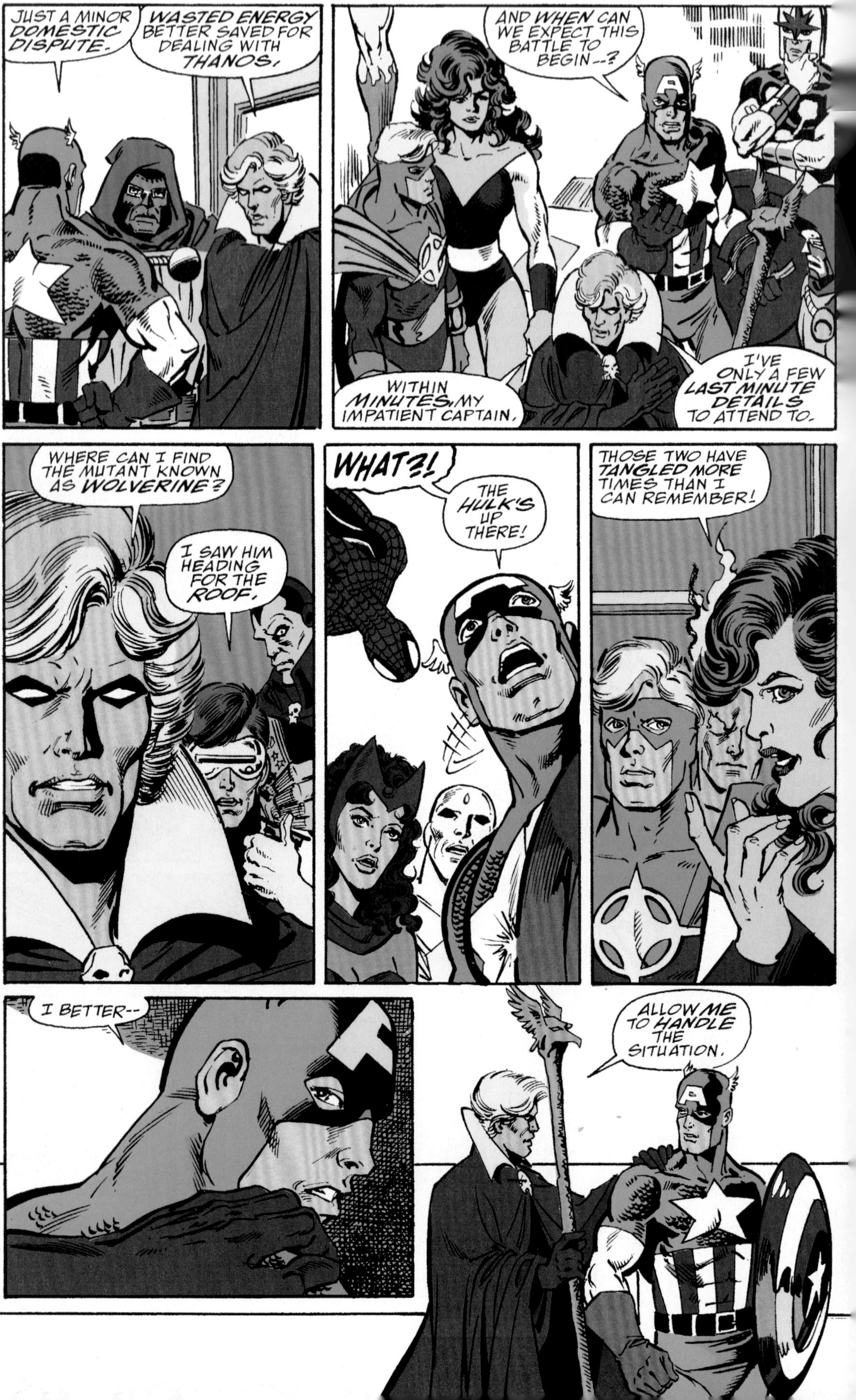

JUST A MINOR DOMESTIC DISPUTE.
WASTED ENERGY BETTER SAVED FOR DEALING WITH THANOS.
AND WHEN CAN WE EXPECT THIS BATTLE TO BEGIN--?
WITHIN MINUTES, MY IMPATIENT CAPTAIN.
I'VE ONLY A FEW LAST MINUTE DETAILS TO ATTEND TO.
WHERE CAN I FIND THE MUTANT KNOWN AS WOLVERINE?
I SAW HIM HEADING FOR THE ROOF.
WHAT?!
THE HULK'S UP THERE!
THOSE TWO HAVE TANGLED MORE TIMES THAN I CAN REMEMBER!
I BETTER--
ALLOW ME TO HANDLE THE SITUATION.

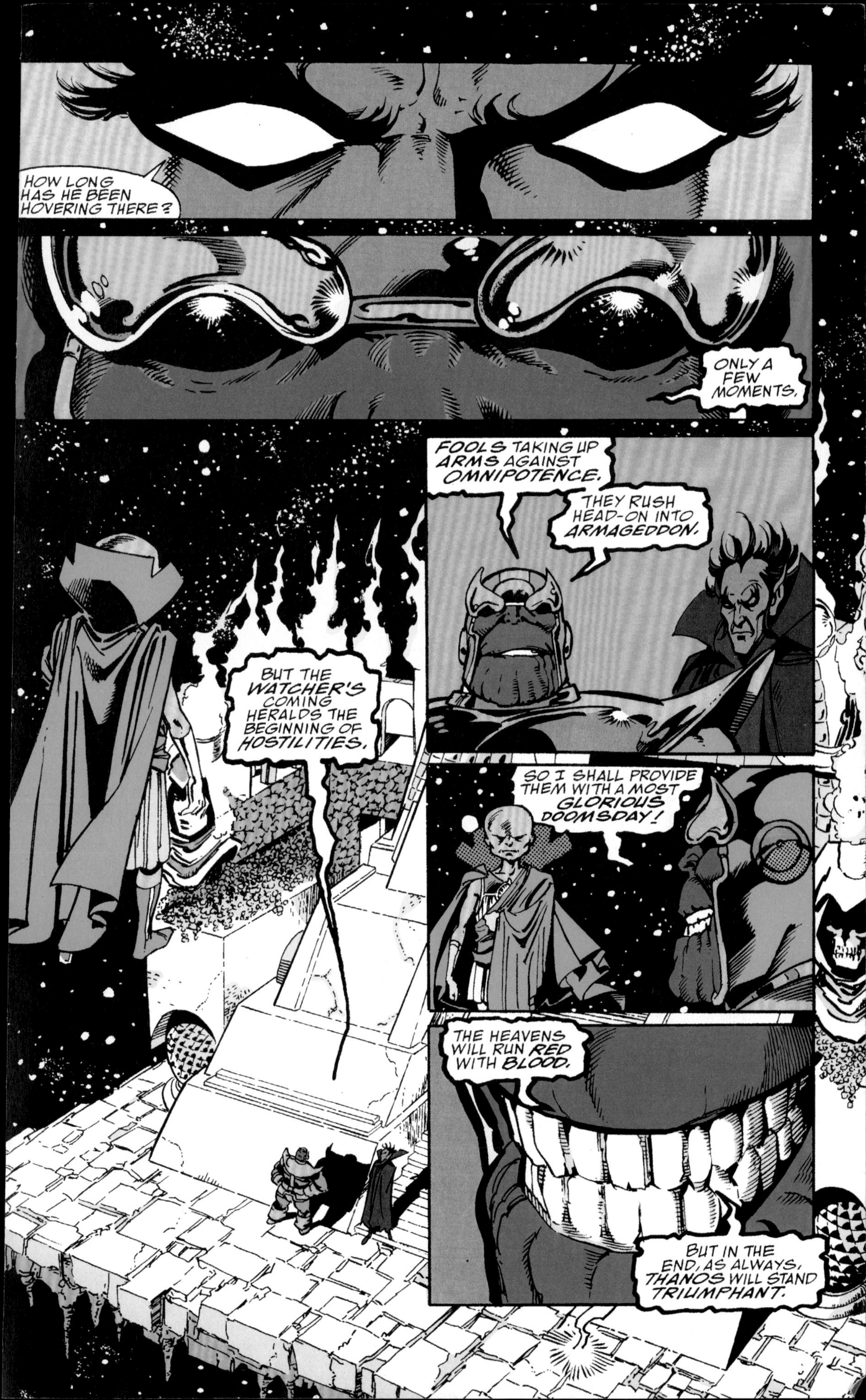
HOW LONG HAS HE BEEN HOVERING THERE?
ONLY A FEW MOMENTS.
FOOLS TAKING UP ARMS AGAINST OMNIPOTENCE.
THEY RUSH HEAD-ON INTO ARMAGEDDON.
BUT THE WATCHER'S COMING HERALDS THE BEGINNING OF HOSTILITIES.
SO I SHALL PROVIDE THEM WITH A MOST GLORIOUS DOOMSDAY!
THE HEAVENS WILL RUN RED WITH BLOOD.
BUT IN THE END, AS ALWAYS, THANOS WILL STAND TRIUMPHANT.

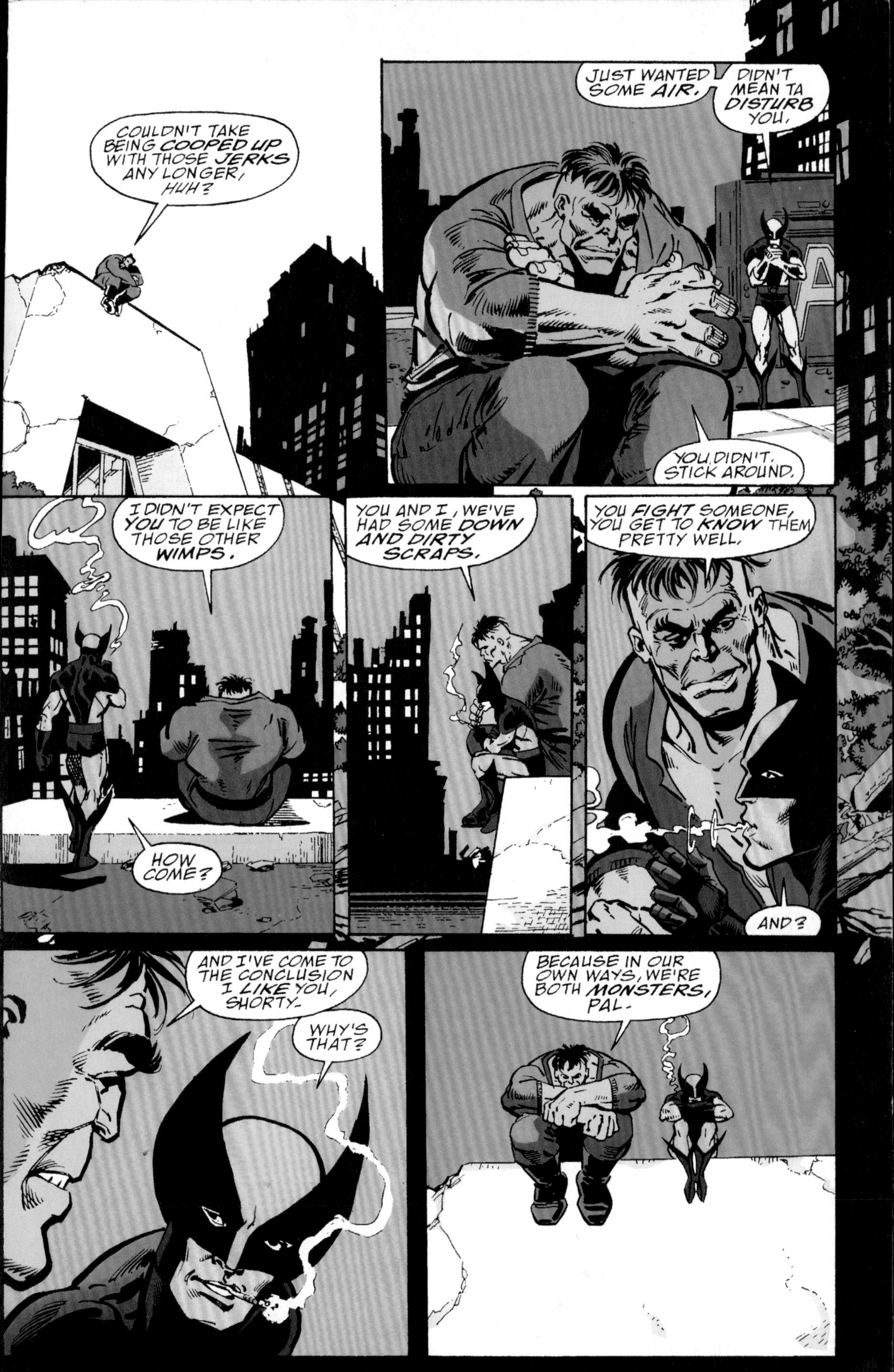

COULDN'T TAKE BEING COOPED UP WITH THOSE JERKS ANY LONGER, HUH?
JUST WANTED SOME AIR.
DIDN'T MEAN TA DISTURB YOU.
YOU DIDN'T STICK AROUND.
I DIDN'T EXPECT YOU TO BE LIKE THOSE OTHER WIMPS.
HOW COME?
YOU AND I, WE'VE HAD SOME DOWN AND DIRTY SCRAPS.
YOU FIGHT SOMEONE, YOU GET TO KNOW THEM PRETTY WELL.
AND?
AND I'VE COME TO THE CONCLUSION I LIKE YOU, SHORTY.
WHY'S THAT?
BECAUSE IN OUR OWN WAYS, WE'RE BOTH MONSTERS, PAL.

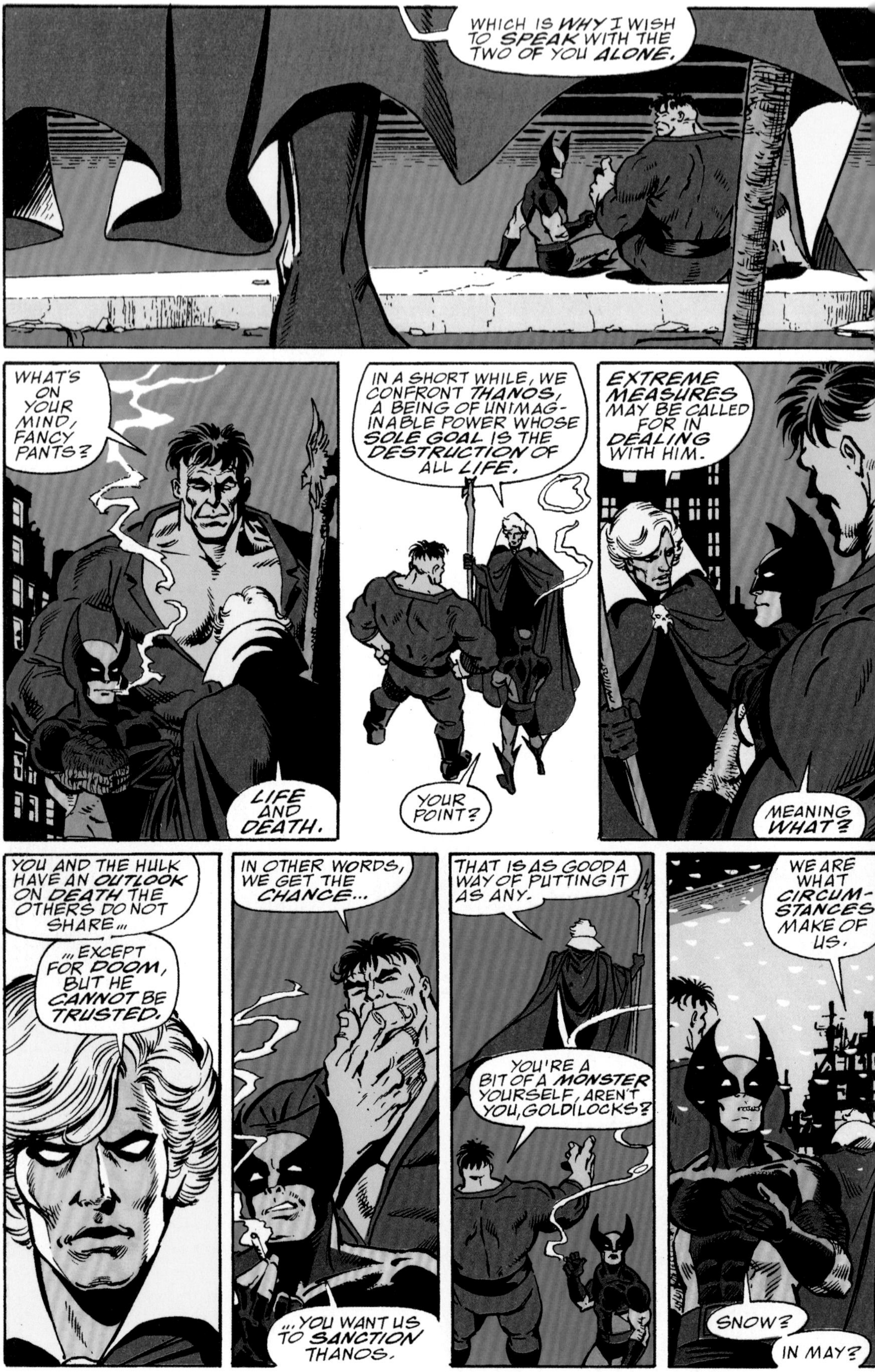
WHICH IS WHY I WISH TO SPEAK WITH THE TWO OF YOU ALONE.
WHAT'S ON YOUR MIND, FANCY PANTS?
LIFE AND DEATH.
IN A SHORT WHILE, WE CONFRONT THANOS, A BEING OF UNIMAG-INABLE POWER WHOSE SOLE GOAL IS THE DESTRUCTION OF ALL LIFE.
YOUR POINT?
EXTREME MEASURES MAY BE CALLED FOR IN DEALING WITH HIM.
MEANING WHAT?
YOU AND THE HULK HAVE AN OUTLOOK ON DEATH THE OTHERS DO NOT SHARE...
...EXCEPT FOR DOOM, BUT HE CANNOT BE TRUSTED.
IN OTHER WORDS, WE GET THE CHANCE...
...YOU WANT US TO SANCTION THANOS.
THAT IS AS GOOD A WAY OF PUTTING IT AS ANY.
YOU'RE A BIT OF A MONSTER YOURSELF, AREN'T YOU, GOLDILOCKS?
WE ARE WHAT CIRCUM-STANCES MAKE OF US.
SNOW?
IN MAY?

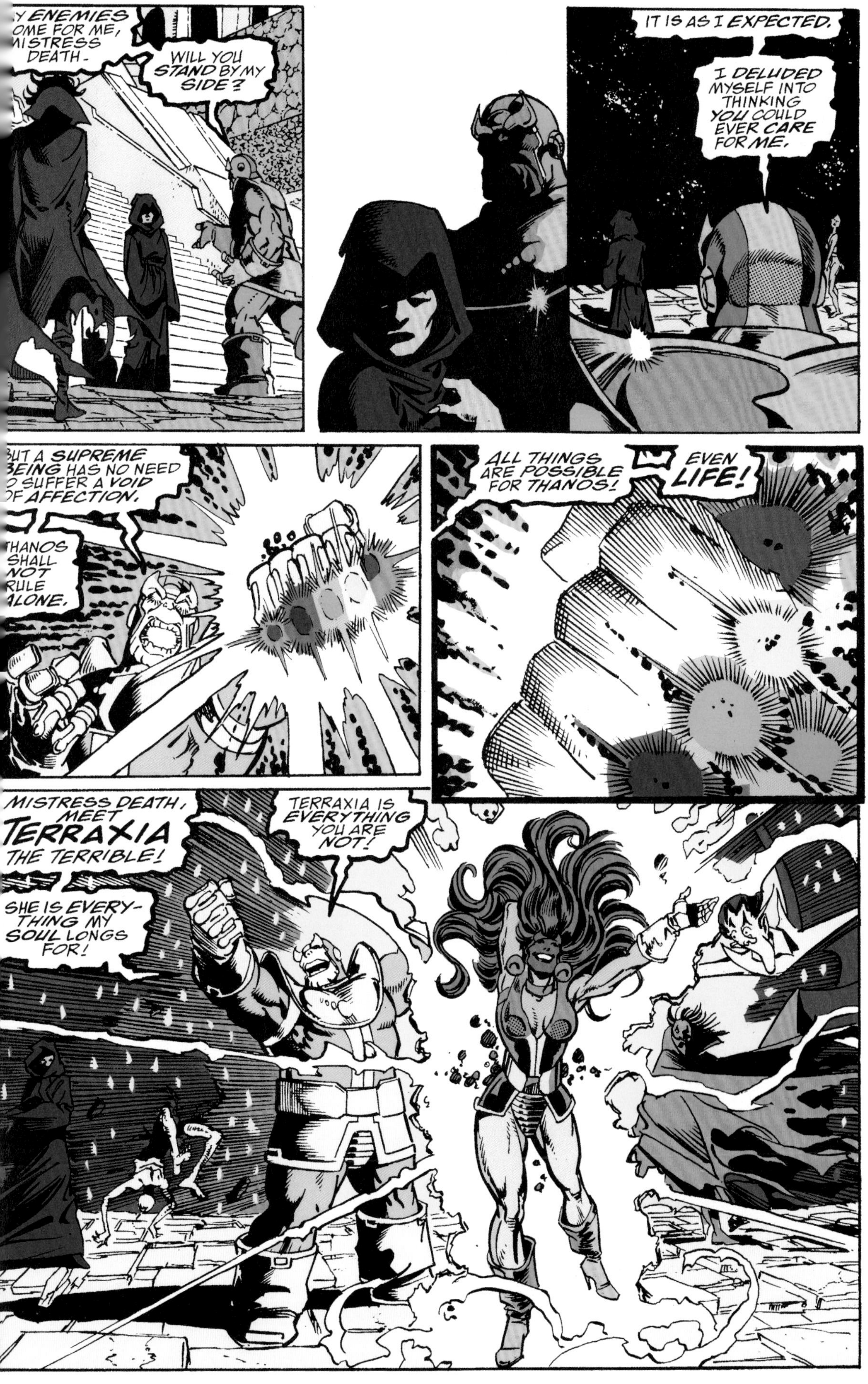

...Y ENEMIES ...OME FOR ME, MISTRESS DEATH.
WILL YOU STAND BY MY SIDE?
IT IS AS I EXPECTED.
I DELUDED MYSELF INTO THINKING YOU COULD EVER CARE FOR ME.
...UT A SUPREME ...EING HAS NO NEED ...O SUFFER A VOID OF AFFECTION.
THANOS SHALL NOT RULE ALONE.
ALL THINGS ARE POSSIBLE FOR THANOS!
EVEN LIFE!
MISTRESS DEATH, MEET TERRAXIA THE TERRIBLE!
TERRAXIA IS EVERYTHING YOU ARE NOT!
SHE IS EVERY-THING MY SOUL LONGS FOR!

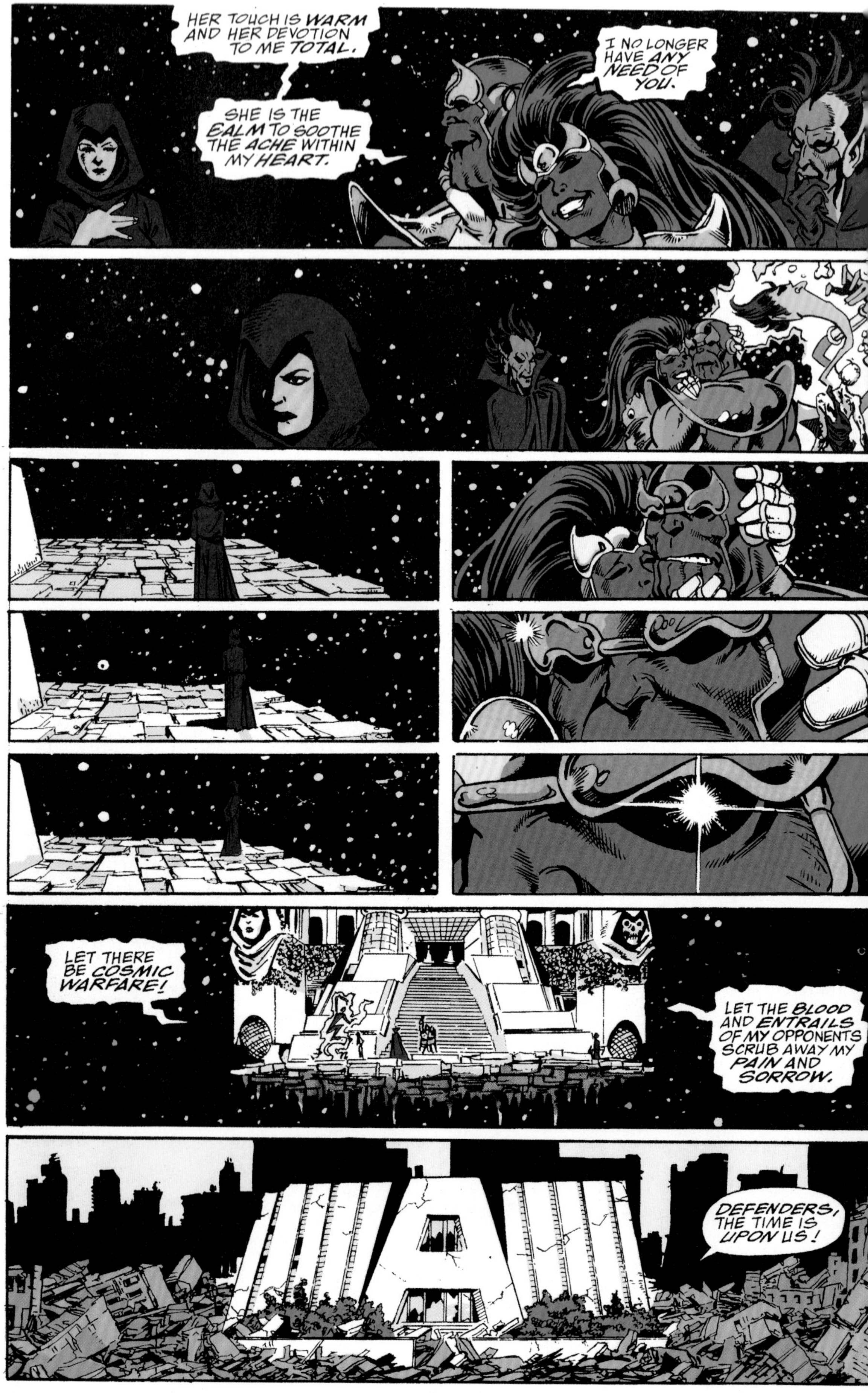
HER TOUCH IS WARM AND HER DEVOTION TO ME TOTAL.
SHE IS THE BALM TO SOOTHE THE ACHE WITHIN MY HEART.
I NO LONGER HAVE ANY NEED OF YOU.
LET THERE BE COSMIC WARFARE!
LET THE BLOOD AND ENTRAILS OF MY OPPONENTS SCRUB AWAY MY PAIN AND SORROW.
DEFENDERS, THE TIME IS UPON US!

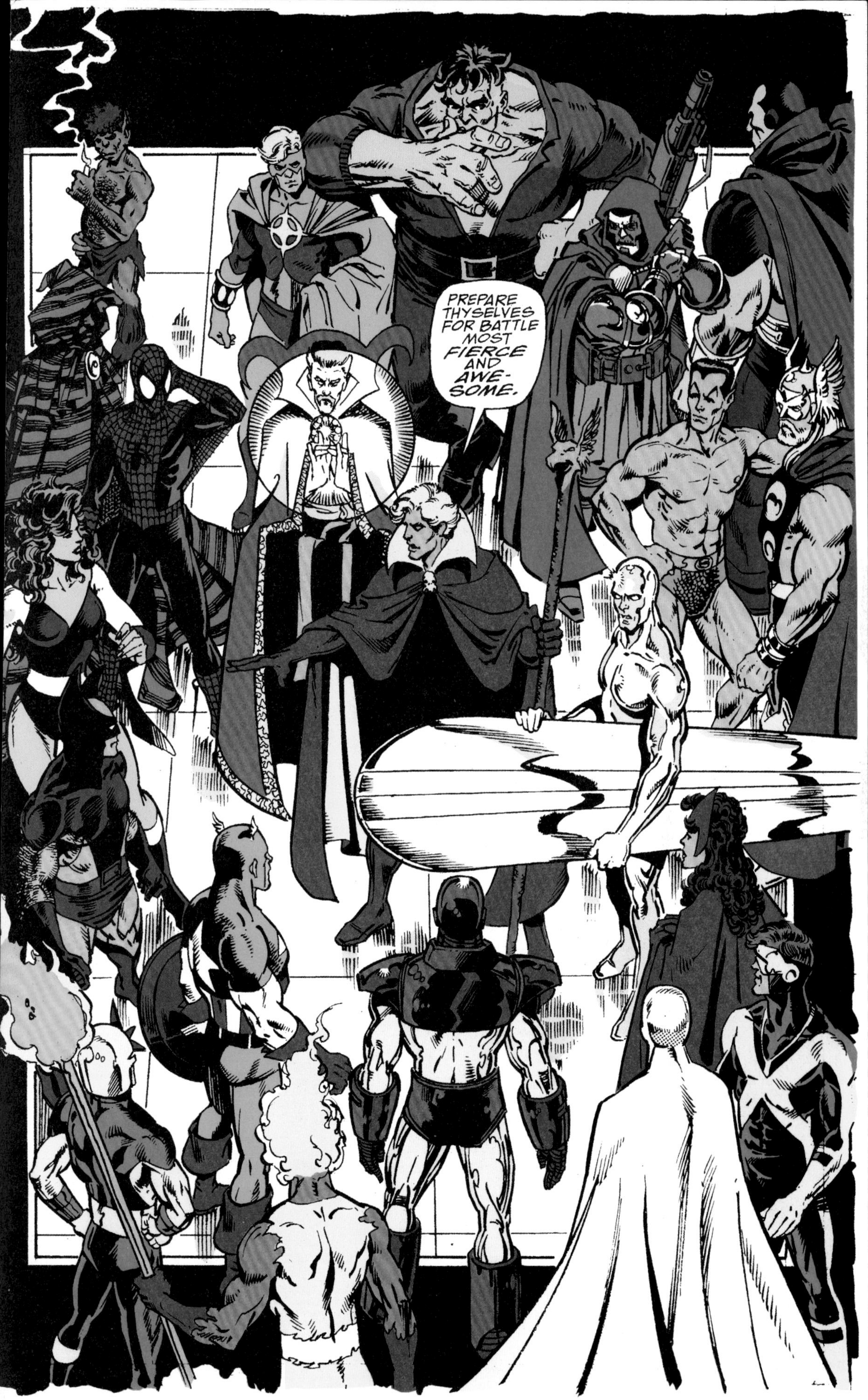
PREPARE THYSELVES FOR BATTLE MOST FIERCE AND AWE-SOME.

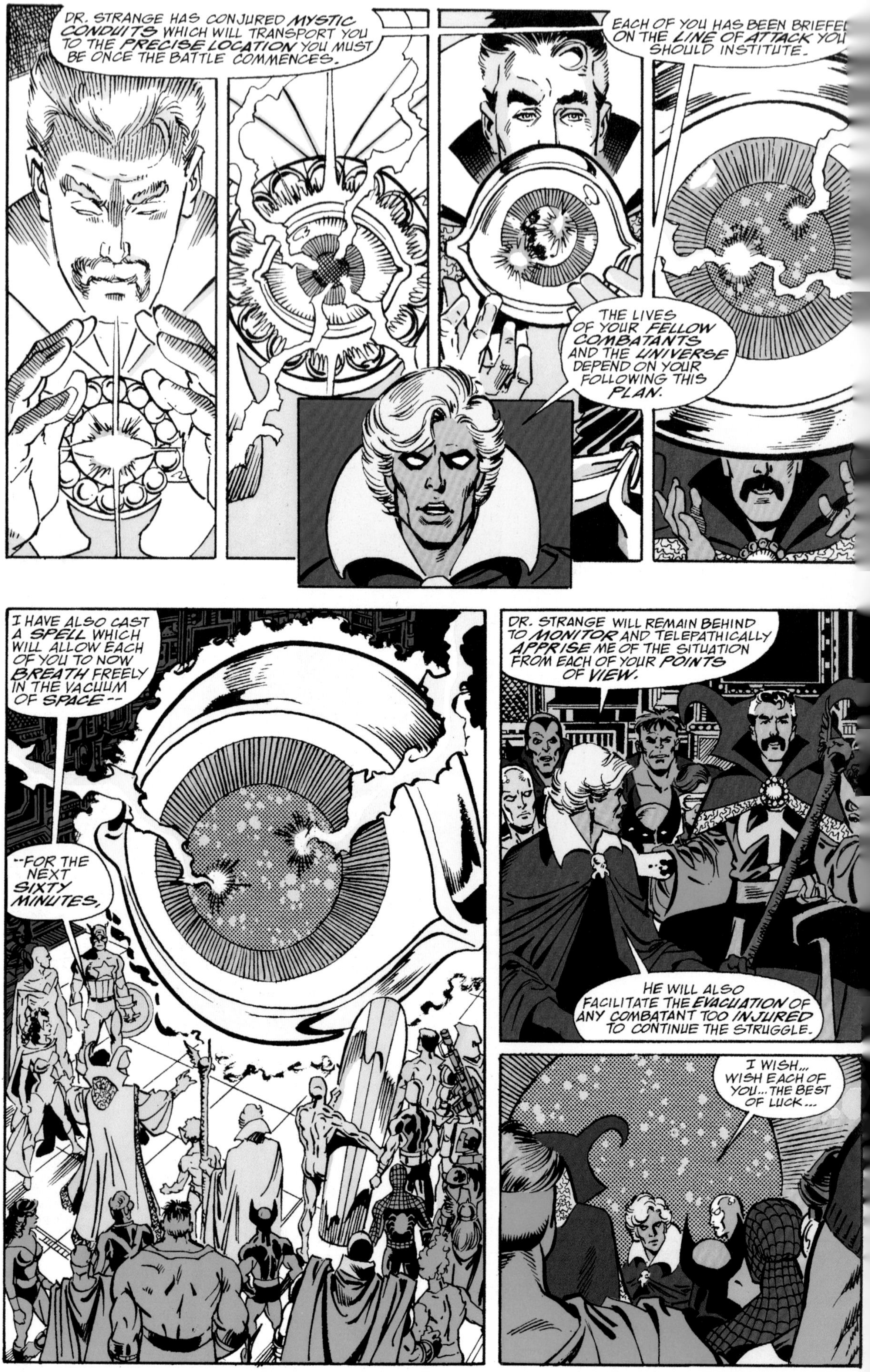
DR. STRANGE HAS CONJURED MYSTIC CONDUITS WHICH WILL TRANSPORT YOU TO THE PRECISE LOCATION YOU MUST BE ONCE THE BATTLE COMMENCES.
EACH OF YOU HAS BEEN BRIEFED ON THE LINE OF ATTACK YOU SHOULD INSTITUTE.
THE LIVES OF YOUR FELLOW COMBATANTS AND THE UNIVERSE DEPEND ON YOUR FOLLOWING THIS PLAN.
I HAVE ALSO CAST A SPELL WHICH WILL ALLOW EACH OF YOU TO NOW BREATH FREELY IN THE VACUUM OF SPACE--
--FOR THE NEXT SIXTY MINUTES.
DR. STRANGE WILL REMAIN BEHIND TO MONITOR AND TELEPATHICALLY APPRISE ME OF THE SITUATION FROM EACH OF YOUR POINTS OF VIEW.
HE WILL ALSO FACILITATE THE EVACUATION OF ANY COMBATANT TOO INJURED TO CONTINUE THE STRUGGLE.
I WISH... WISH EACH OF YOU... THE BEST OF LUCK...

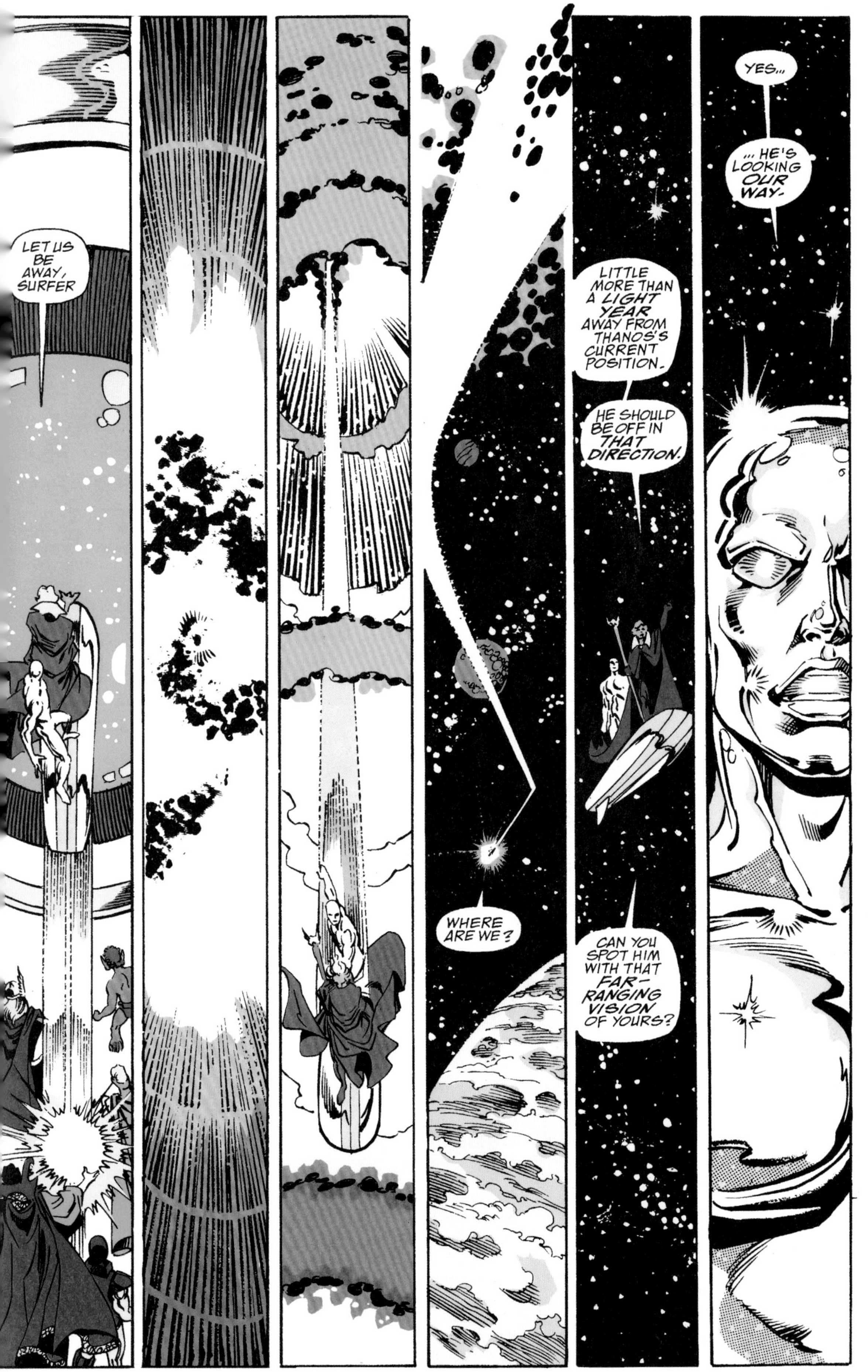
LET US BE AWAY, SURFER
WHERE ARE WE?
LITTLE MORE THAN A LIGHT YEAR AWAY FROM THANOS'S CURRENT POSITION.
HE SHOULD BE OFF IN THAT DIRECTION.
CAN YOU SPOT HIM WITH THAT FAR-RANGING VISION OF YOURS?
YES...
...HE'S LOOKING OUR WAY-

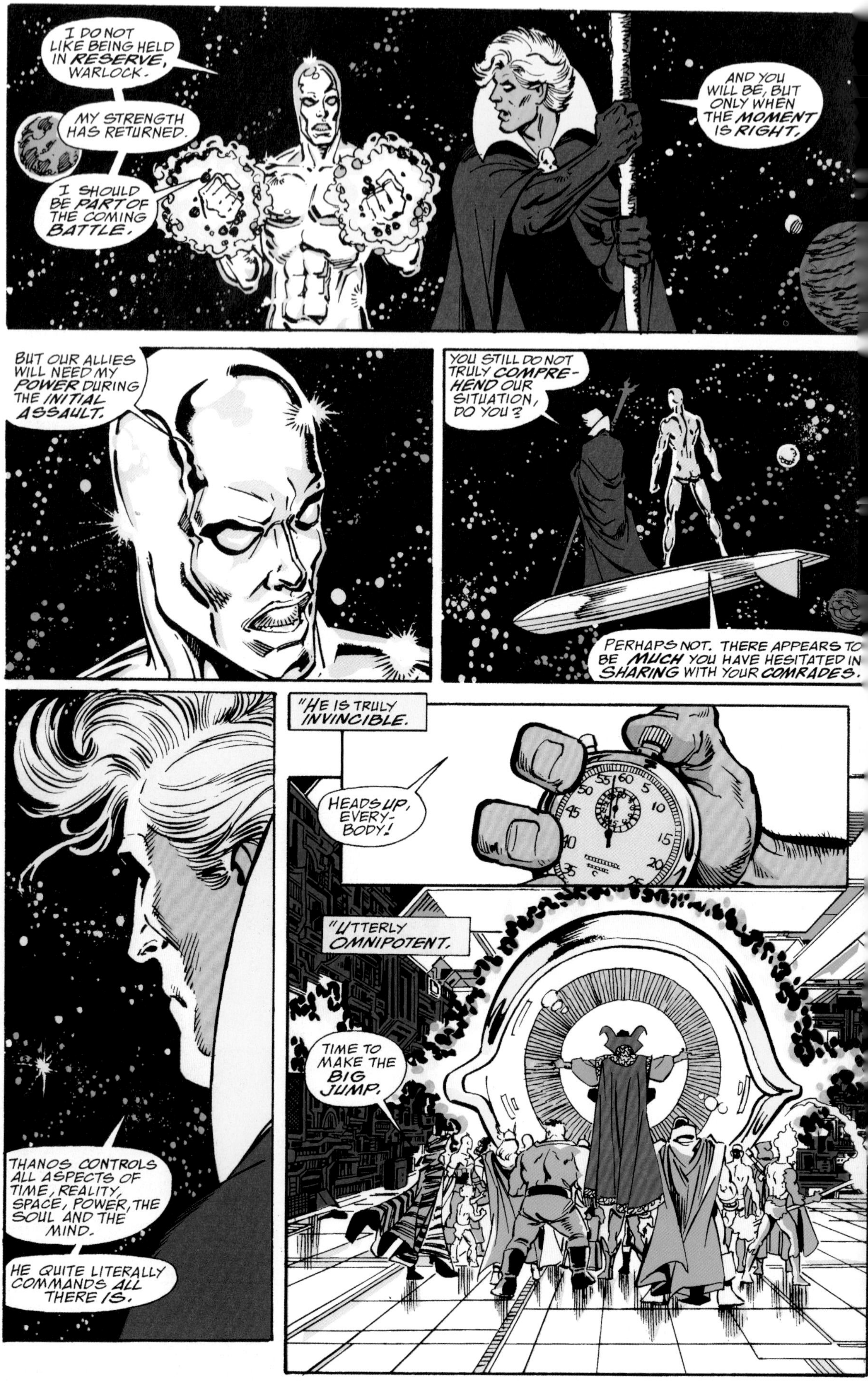
I DO NOT LIKE BEING HELD IN RESERVE, WARLOCK.
MY STRENGTH HAS RETURNED.
I SHOULD BE PART OF THE COMING BATTLE.
AND YOU WILL BE, BUT ONLY WHEN THE MOMENT IS RIGHT.
BUT OUR ALLIES WILL NEED MY POWER DURING THE INITIAL ASSAULT.
YOU STILL DO NOT TRULY COMPRE-HEND OUR SITUATION, DO YOU?
PERHAPS NOT. THERE APPEARS TO BE MUCH YOU HAVE HESITATED IN SHARING WITH YOUR COMRADES.
"HE IS TRULY INVINCIBLE.
HEADS UP, EVERY-BODY!
"UTTERLY OMNIPOTENT.
TIME TO MAKE THE BIG JUMP.
THANOS CONTROLS ALL ASPECTS OF TIME, REALITY, SPACE, POWER, THE SOUL AND THE MIND.
HE QUITE LITERALLY COMMANDS ALL THERE IS.

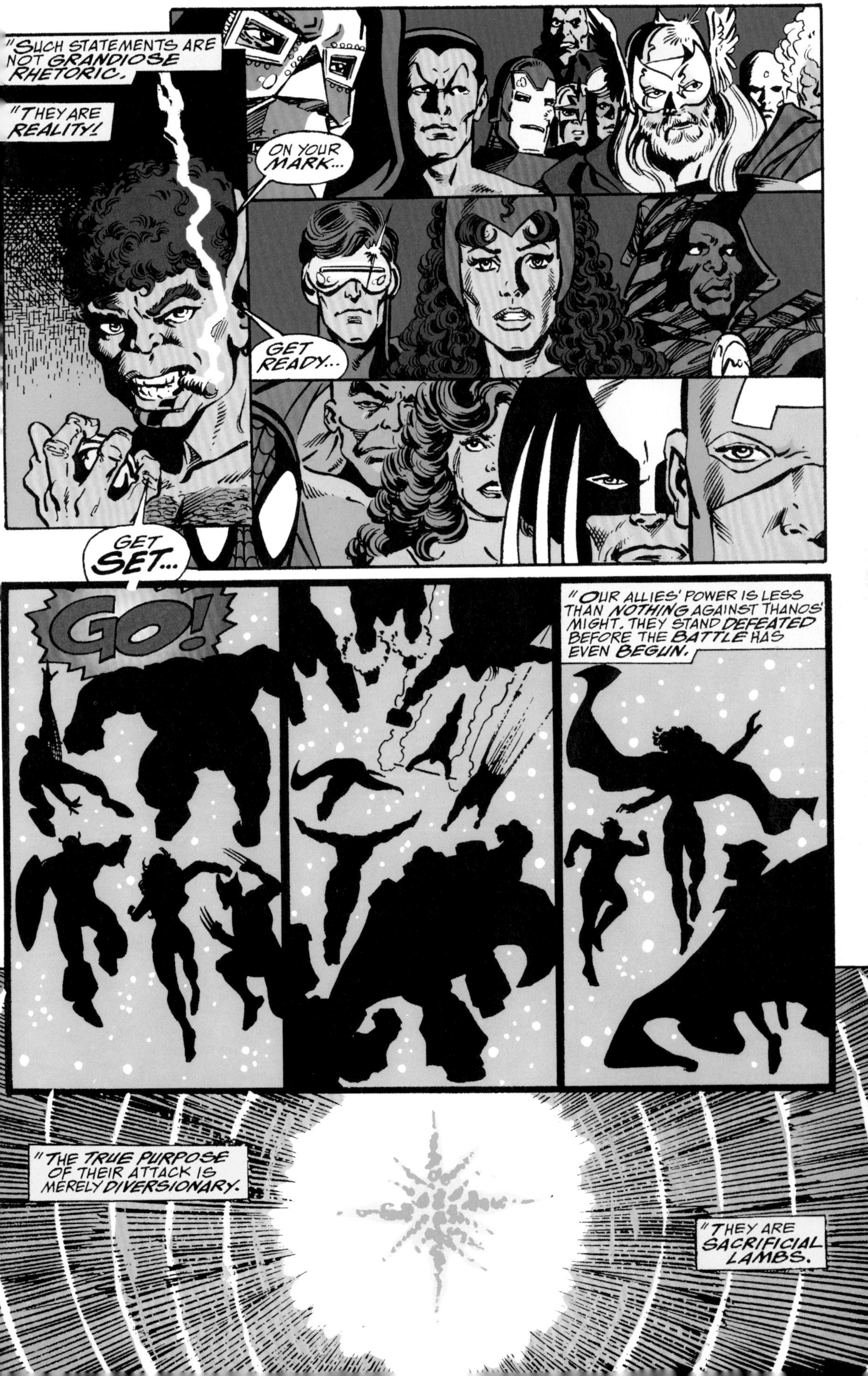
"SUCH STATEMENTS ARE NOT GRANDIOSE RHETORIC.
"THEY ARE REALITY!
ON YOUR MARK...
GET READY...
GET SET...
GO!
"OUR ALLIES' POWER IS LESS THAN NOTHING AGAINST THANOS' MIGHT. THEY STAND DEFEATED BEFORE THE BATTLE HAS EVEN BEGUN.
"THE TRUE PURPOSE OF THEIR ATTACK IS MERELY DIVERSIONARY.
"THEY ARE SACRIFICIAL LAMBS.

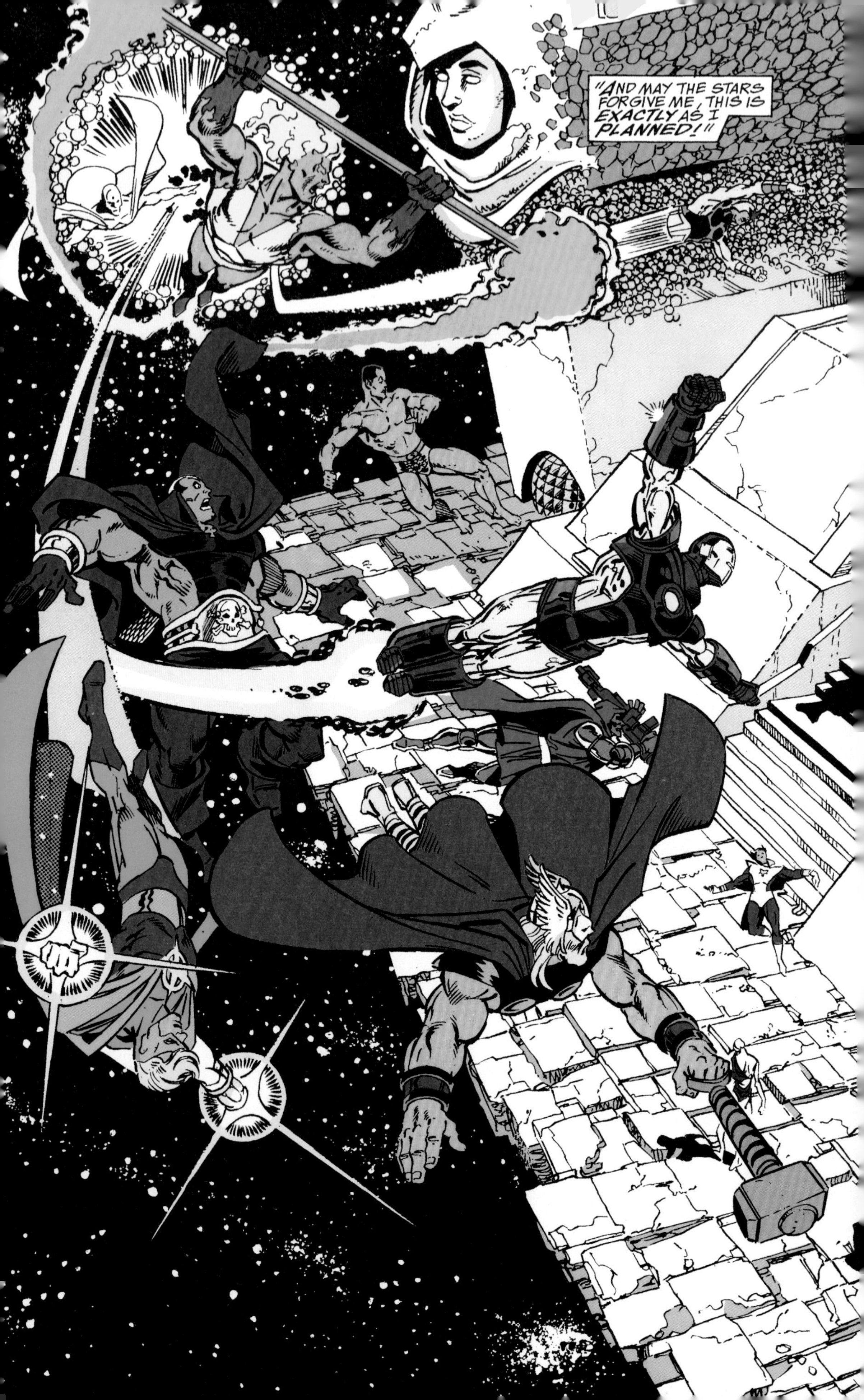
"AND MAY THE STARS FORGIVE ME, THIS IS EXACTLY AS I PLANNED!"

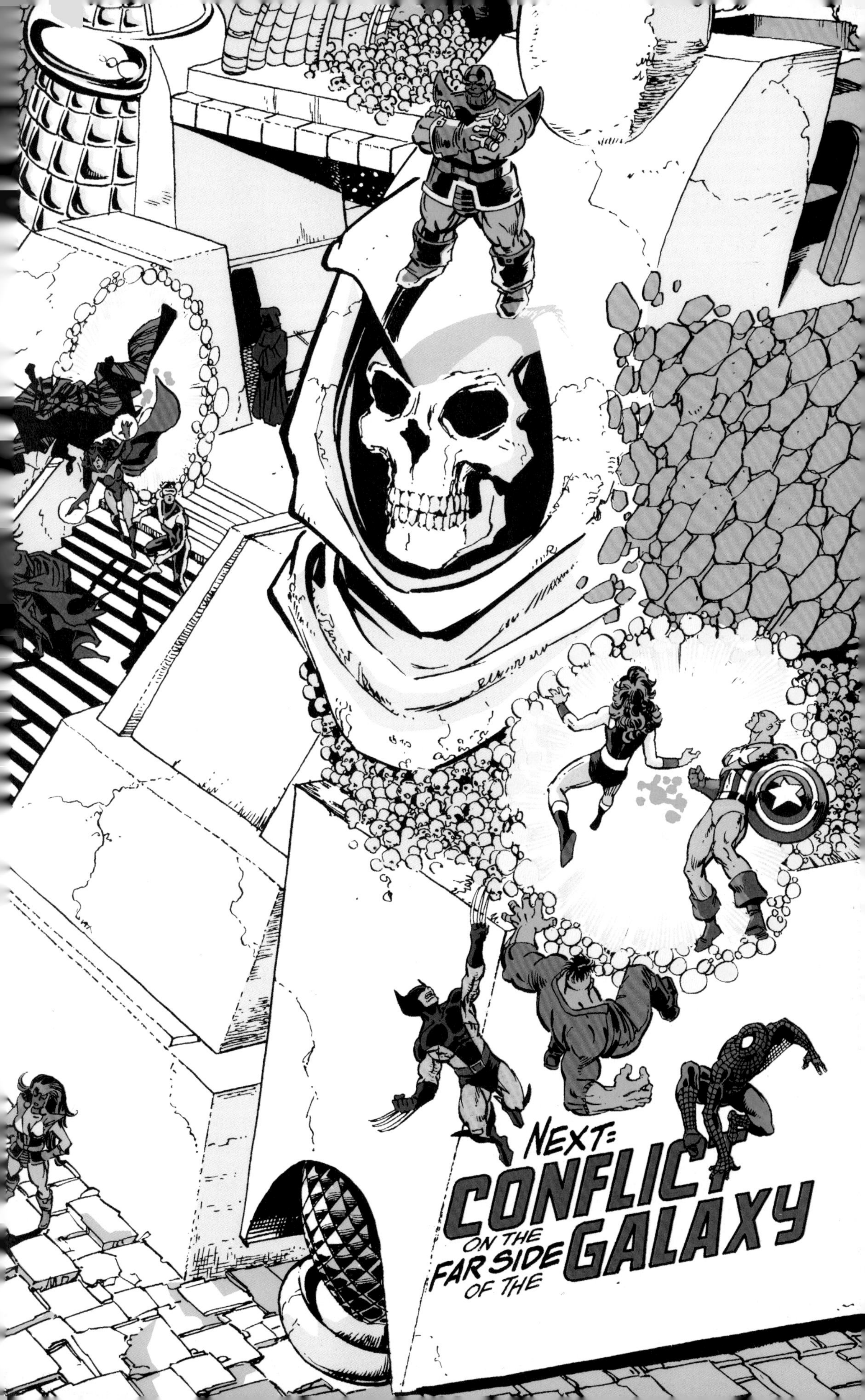
NEXT:
CONFLICT ON THE FAR SIDE OF THE GALAXY

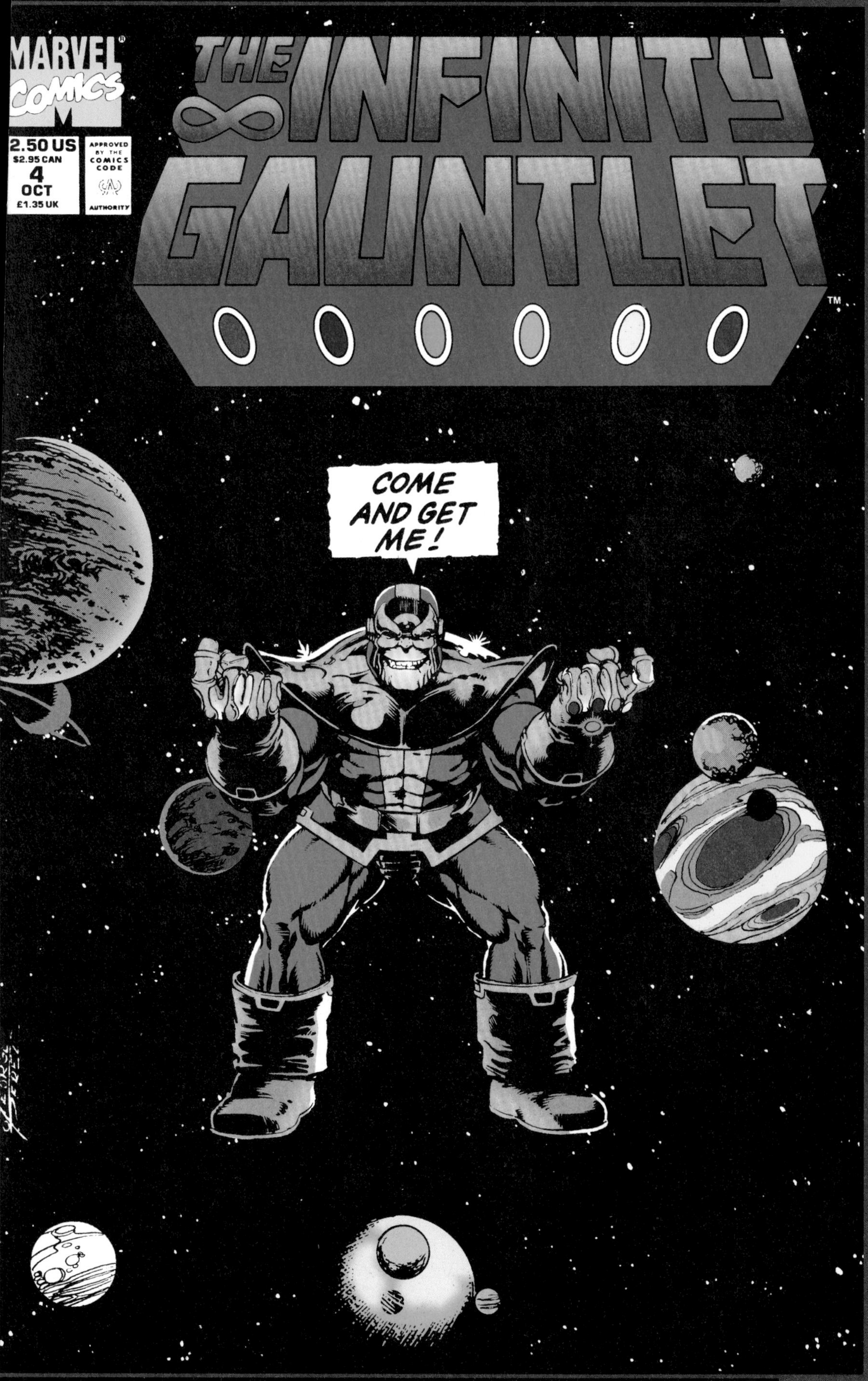
MARVEL COMICS
THE INFINITY GAUNTLET
2.50 US
$2.95 CAN
4
OCT
£1.35 UK
APPROVED BY THE COMICS CODE AUTHORITY
COME AND GET ME!

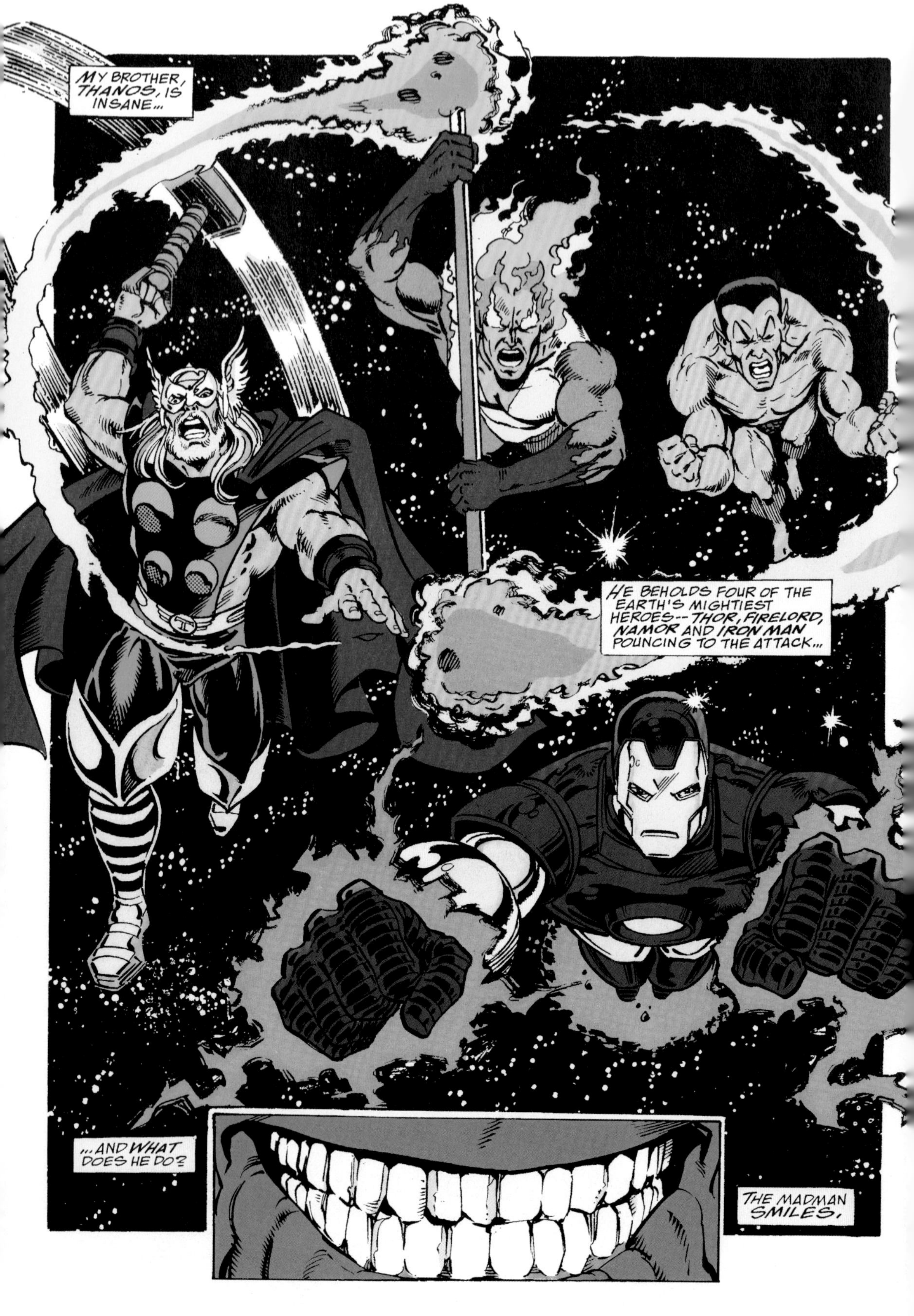
MY BROTHER, THANOS, IS INSANE...
HE BEHOLDS FOUR OF THE EARTH'S MIGHTIEST HEROES-- THOR, FIRELORD, NAMOR AND IRON MAN POUNCING TO THE ATTACK...
...AND WHAT DOES HE DO?
THE MADMAN SMILES.

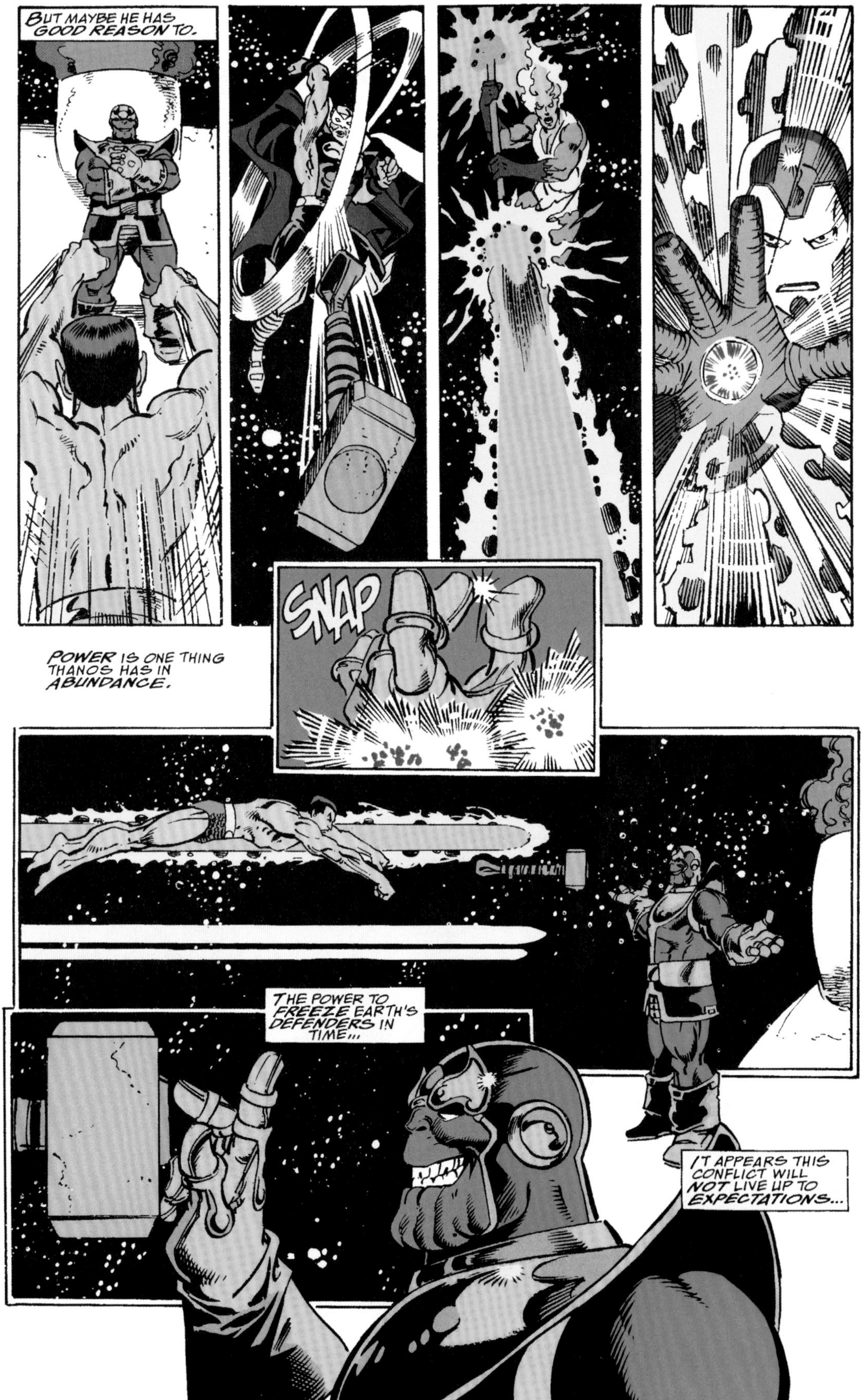
BUT MAYBE HE HAS GOOD REASON TO.
SNAP
POWER IS ONE THING THANOS HAS IN ABUNDANCE.
THE POWER TO FREEZE EARTH'S DEFENDERS IN TIME...
IT APPEARS THIS CONFLICT WILL NOT LIVE UP TO EXPECTATIONS...

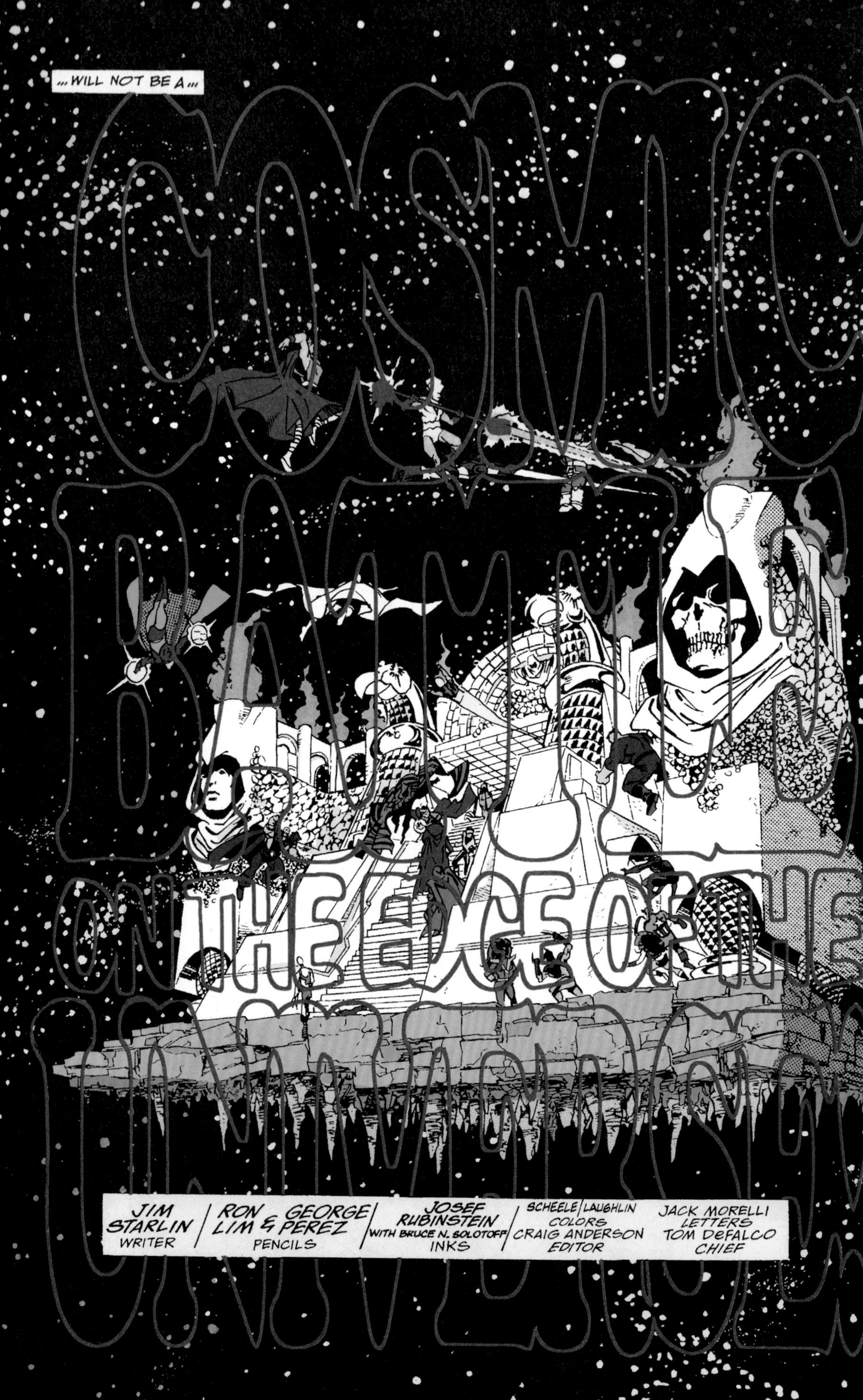
...WILL NOT BE A...
COSMIC
ON THE EDGE OF THE
JIM STARLIN WRITER
RON LIM & GEORGE PEREZ PENCILS
JOSEF RUBINSTEIN WITH BRUCE N. SOLOTOFF INKS
SCHEELE | LAUGHLIN COLORS
CRAIG ANDERSON EDITOR
JACK MORELLI LETTERS
TOM DeFALCO CHIEF

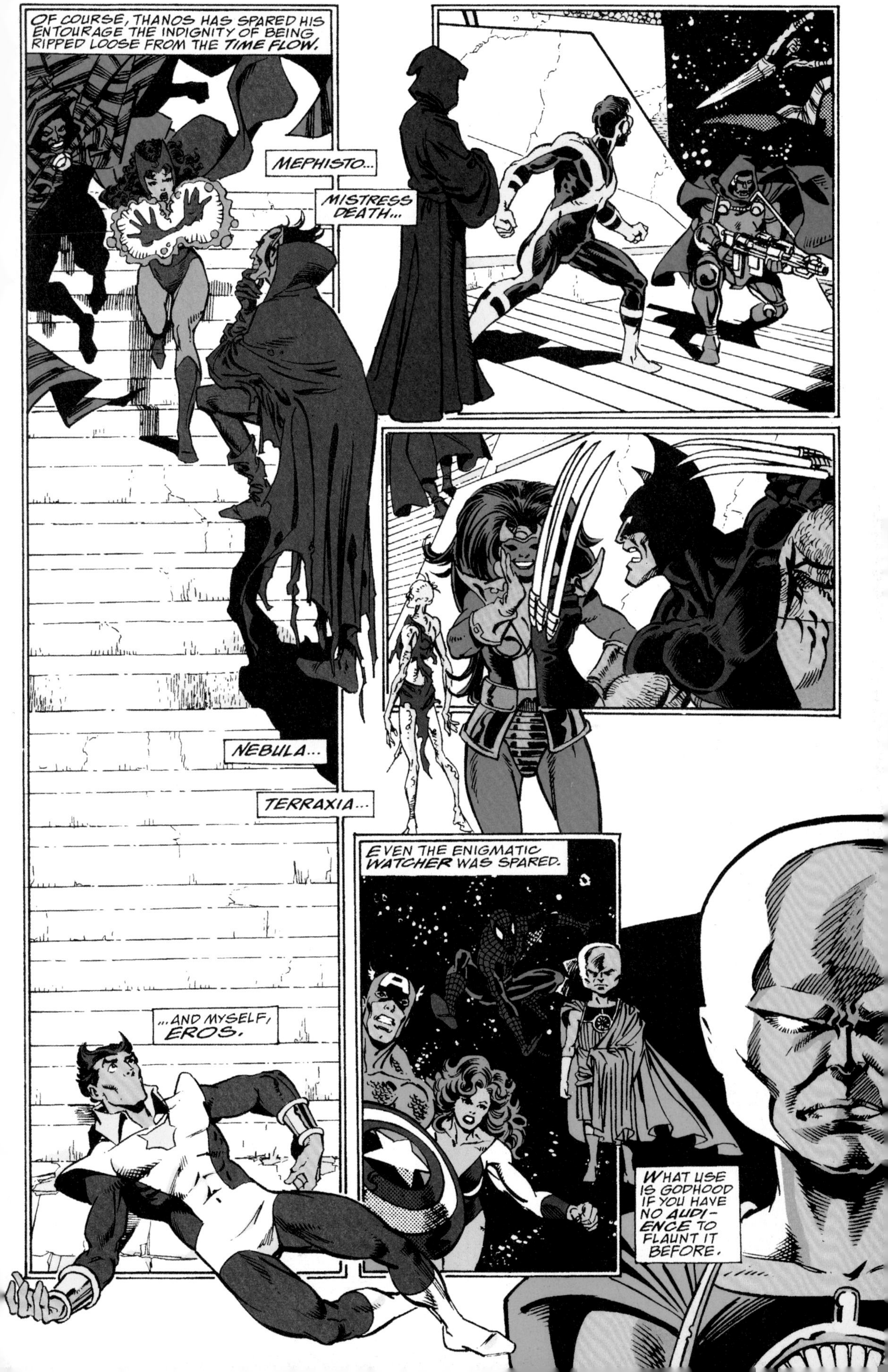
OF COURSE, THANOS HAS SPARED HIS ENTOURAGE THE INDIGNITY OF BEING RIPPED LOOSE FROM THE TIME FLOW.
MEPHISTO...
MISTRESS DEATH...
NEBULA...
TERRAXIA...
...AND MYSELF, EROS.
EVEN THE ENIGMATIC WATCHER WAS SPARED.
WHAT USE IS GODHOOD IF YOU HAVE NO AUDI-ENCE TO FLAUNT IT BEFORE.

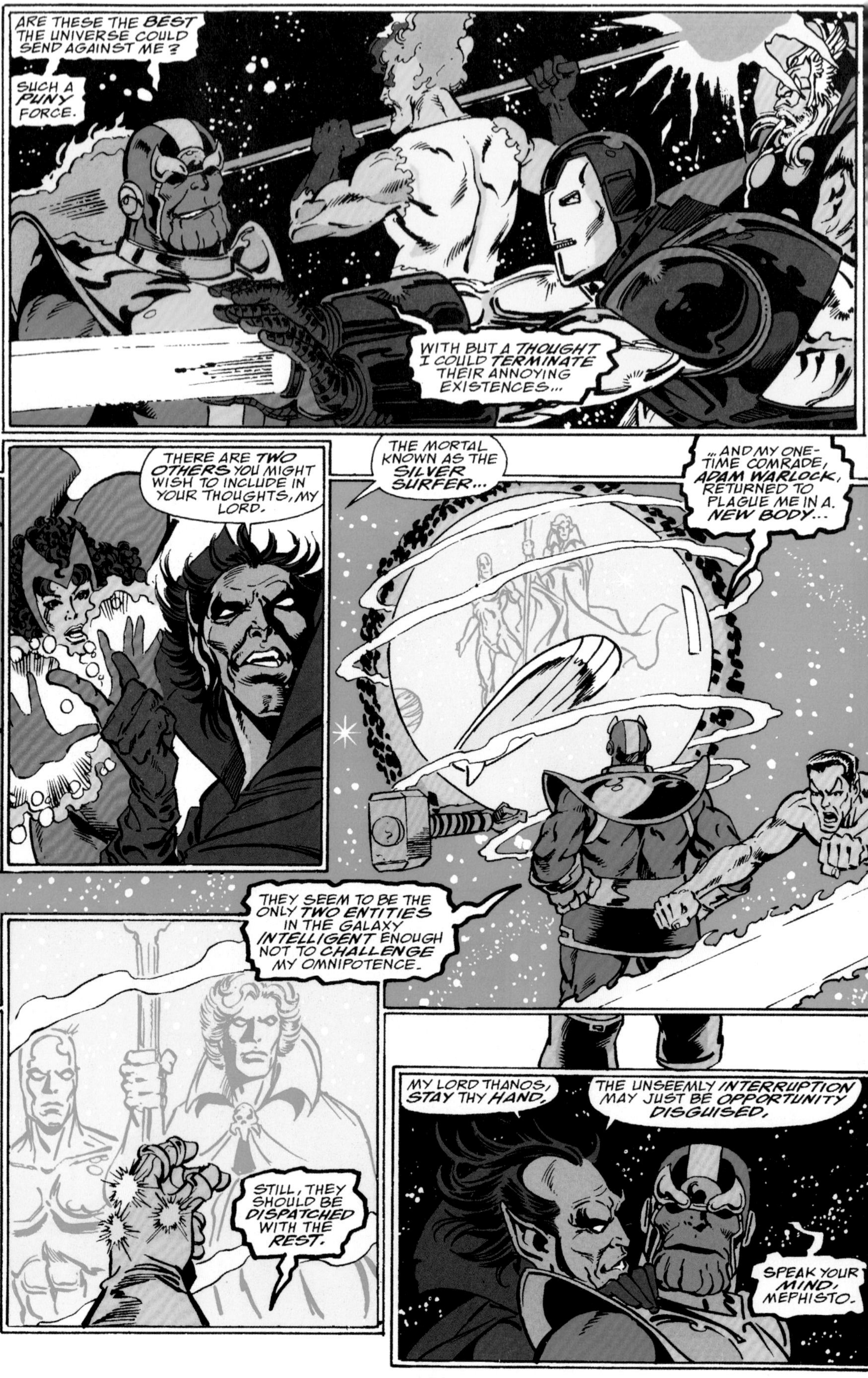
ARE THESE THE BEST THE UNIVERSE COULD SEND AGAINST ME?
SUCH A PUNY FORCE.
WITH BUT A THOUGHT I COULD TERMINATE THEIR ANNOYING EXISTENCES...
THERE ARE TWO OTHERS YOU MIGHT WISH TO INCLUDE IN YOUR THOUGHTS, MY LORD.
THE MORTAL KNOWN AS THE SILVER SURFER...
...AND MY ONE-TIME COMRADE, ADAM WARLOCK, RETURNED TO PLAGUE ME IN A NEW BODY...
THEY SEEM TO BE THE ONLY TWO ENTITIES IN THE GALAXY INTELLIGENT ENOUGH NOT TO CHALLENGE MY OMNIPOTENCE.
STILL, THEY SHOULD BE DISPATCHED WITH THE REST.
MY LORD THANOS, STAY THY HAND.
THE UNSEEMLY INTERRUPTION MAY JUST BE OPPORTUNITY DISGUISED.
SPEAK YOUR MIND, MEPHISTO.

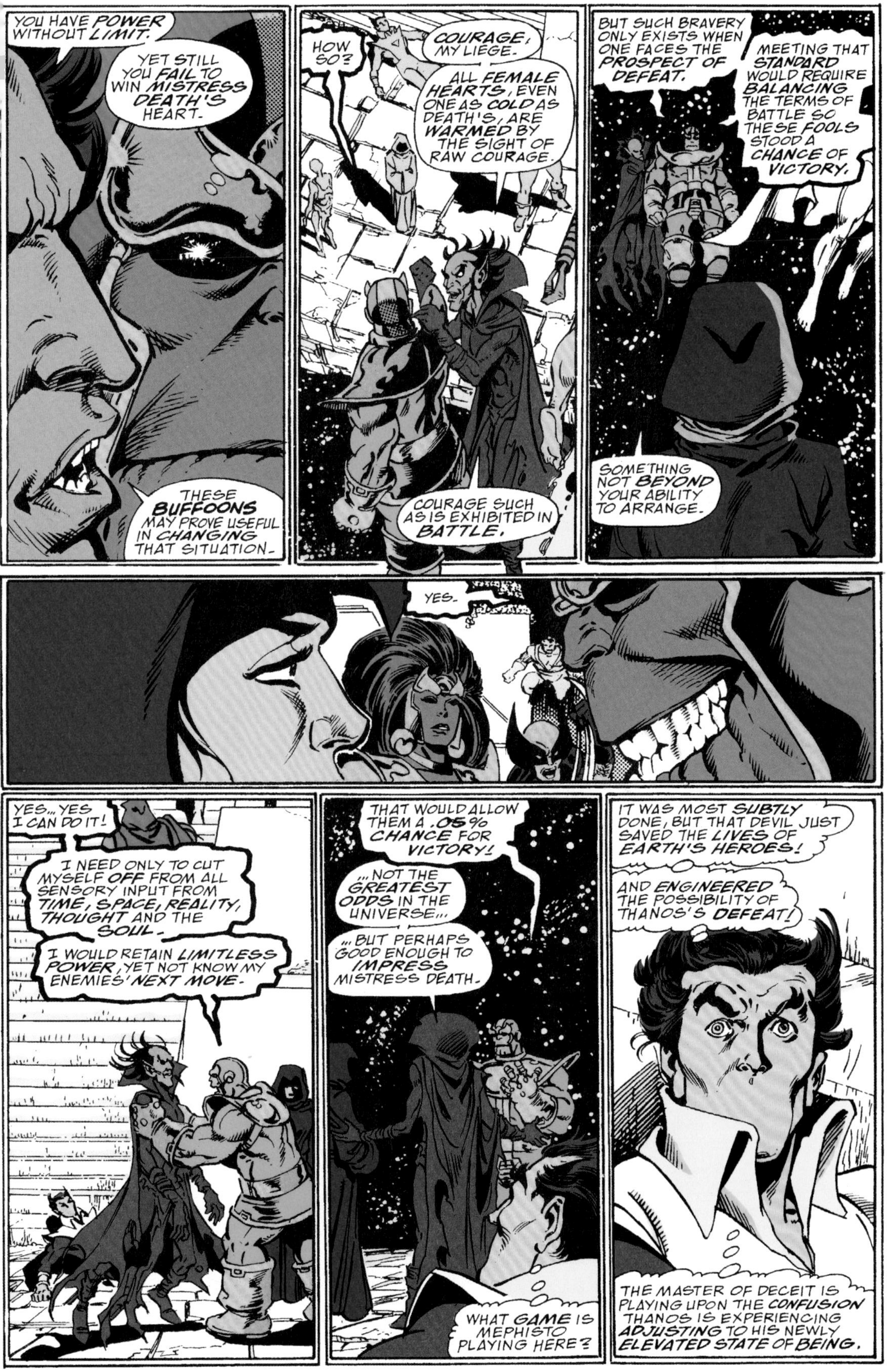
YOU HAVE POWER WITHOUT LIMIT.
YET STILL YOU FAIL TO WIN MISTRESS DEATH'S HEART.
THESE BUFFOONS MAY PROVE USEFUL IN CHANGING THAT SITUATION.
HOW SO?
COURAGE, MY LIEGE.
ALL FEMALE HEARTS, EVEN ONE AS COLD AS DEATH'S, ARE WARMED BY THE SIGHT OF RAW COURAGE.
COURAGE SUCH AS IS EXHIBITED IN BATTLE.
BUT SUCH BRAVERY ONLY EXISTS WHEN ONE FACES THE PROSPECT OF DEFEAT.
MEETING THAT STANDARD WOULD REQUIRE BALANCING THE TERMS OF BATTLE SO THESE FOOLS STOOD A CHANCE OF VICTORY.
SOMETHING NOT BEYOND YOUR ABILITY TO ARRANGE.
YES.
YES... YES I CAN DO IT!
I NEED ONLY TO CUT MYSELF OFF FROM ALL SENSORY INPUT FROM TIME, SPACE, REALITY, THOUGHT AND THE SOUL.
I WOULD RETAIN LIMITLESS POWER, YET NOT KNOW MY ENEMIES' NEXT MOVE.
THAT WOULD ALLOW THEM A .05% CHANCE FOR VICTORY!
...NOT THE GREATEST ODDS IN THE UNIVERSE...
...BUT PERHAPS GOOD ENOUGH TO IMPRESS MISTRESS DEATH.
WHAT GAME IS MEPHISTO PLAYING HERE?
IT WAS MOST SUBTLY DONE, BUT THAT DEVIL JUST SAVED THE LIVES OF EARTH'S HEROES!
AND ENGINEERED THE POSSIBILITY OF THANOS'S DEFEAT!
THE MASTER OF DECEIT IS PLAYING UPON THE CONFUSION THANOS IS EXPERIENCING ADJUSTING TO HIS NEWLY ELEVATED STATE OF BEING.

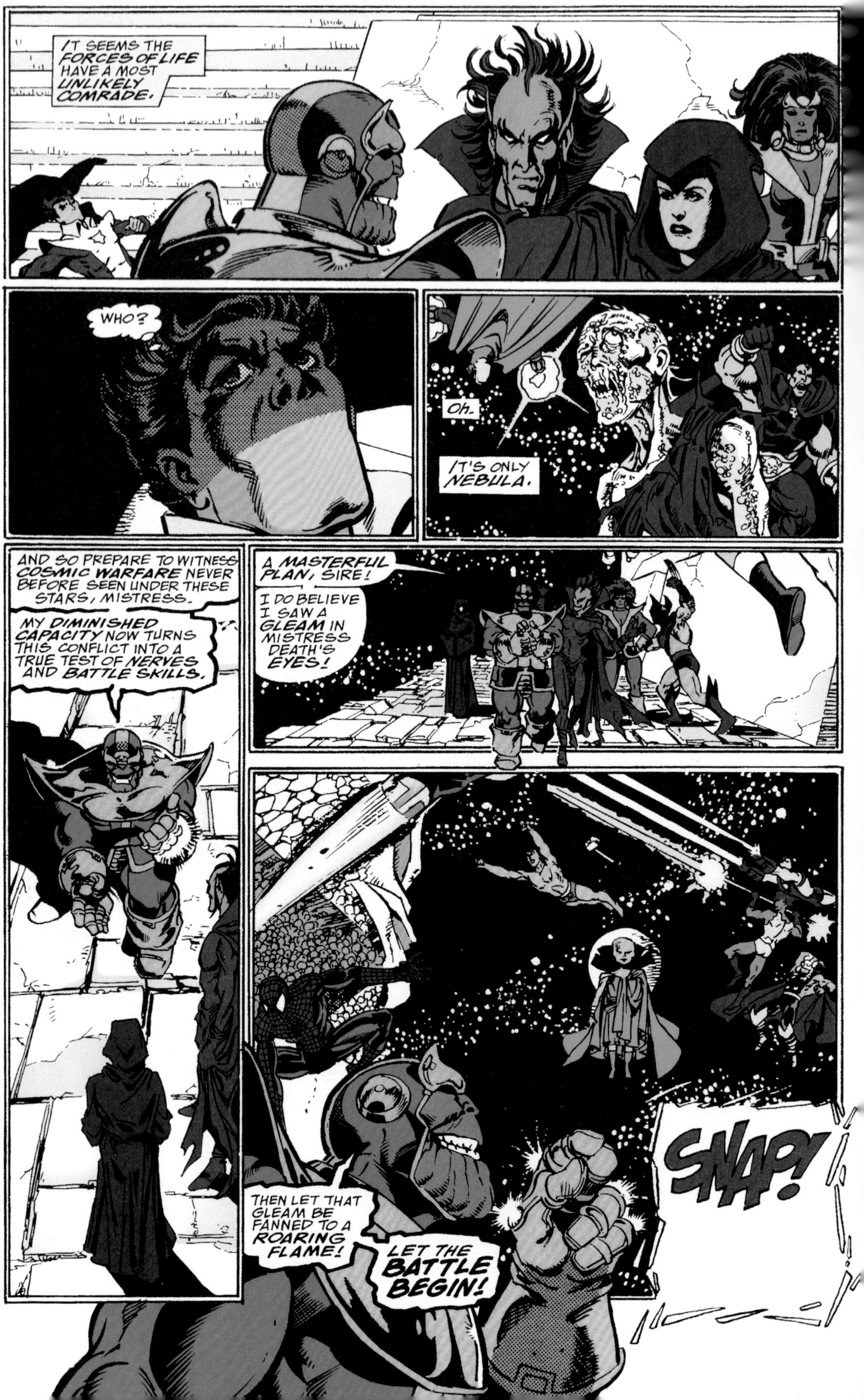
IT SEEMS THE FORCES OF LIFE HAVE A MOST UNLIKELY COMRADE.
WHO?
Oh.
IT'S ONLY NEBULA.
AND SO PREPARE TO WITNESS COSMIC WARFARE NEVER BEFORE SEEN UNDER THESE STARS, MISTRESS.
MY DIMINISHED CAPACITY NOW TURNS THIS CONFLICT INTO A TRUE TEST OF NERVES AND BATTLE SKILLS.
A MASTERFUL PLAN, SIRE!
I DO BELIEVE I SAW A GLEAM IN MISTRESS DEATH'S EYES!
THEN LET THAT GLEAM BE FANNED TO A ROARING FLAME!
LET THE BATTLE BEGIN!
SNAP!

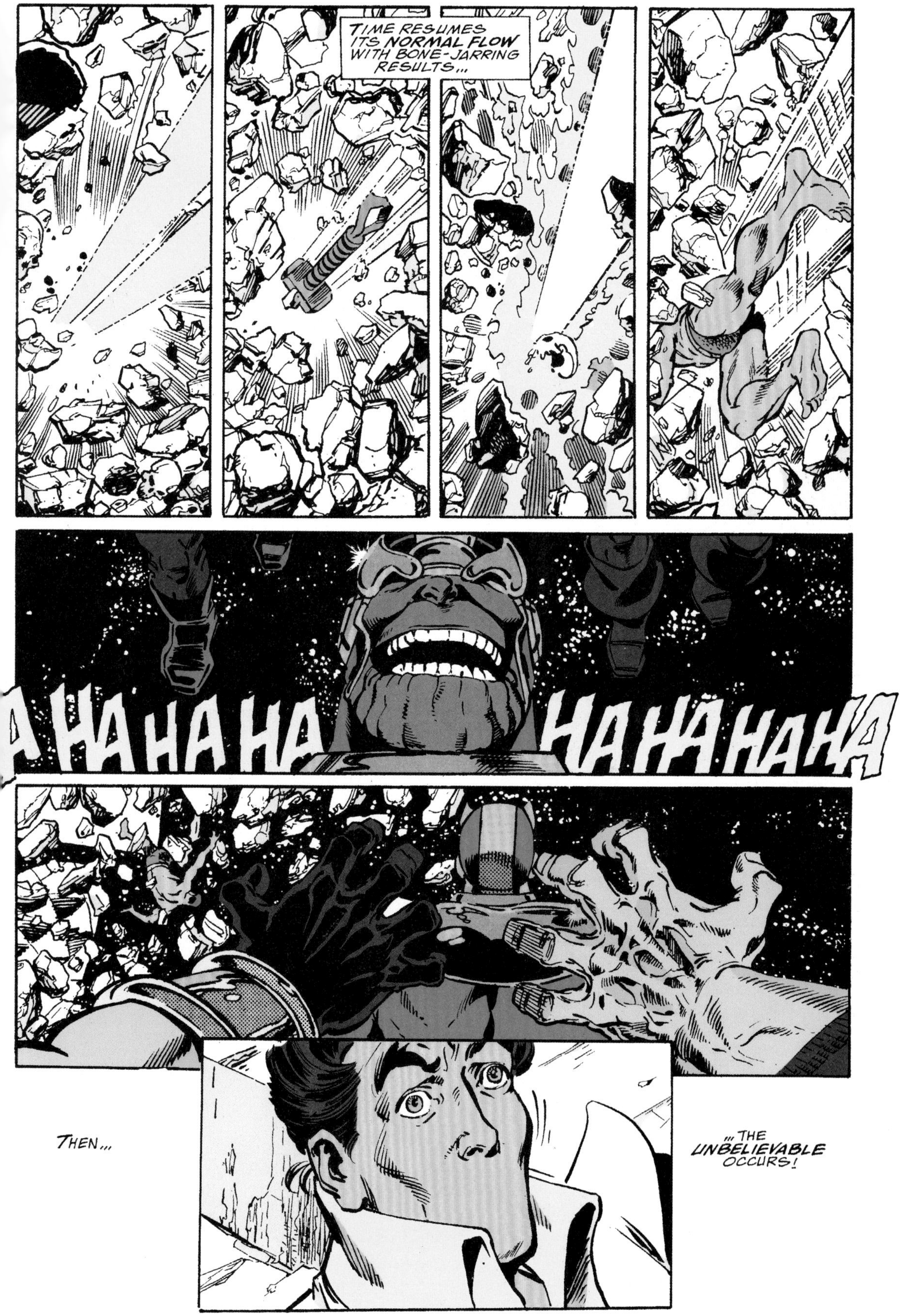
TIME RESUMES ITS NORMAL FLOW WITH BONE-JARRING RESULTS...
HA HA HA HA HA HA HA HA HA HA
THEN...
...THE UNBELIEVABLE OCCURS!

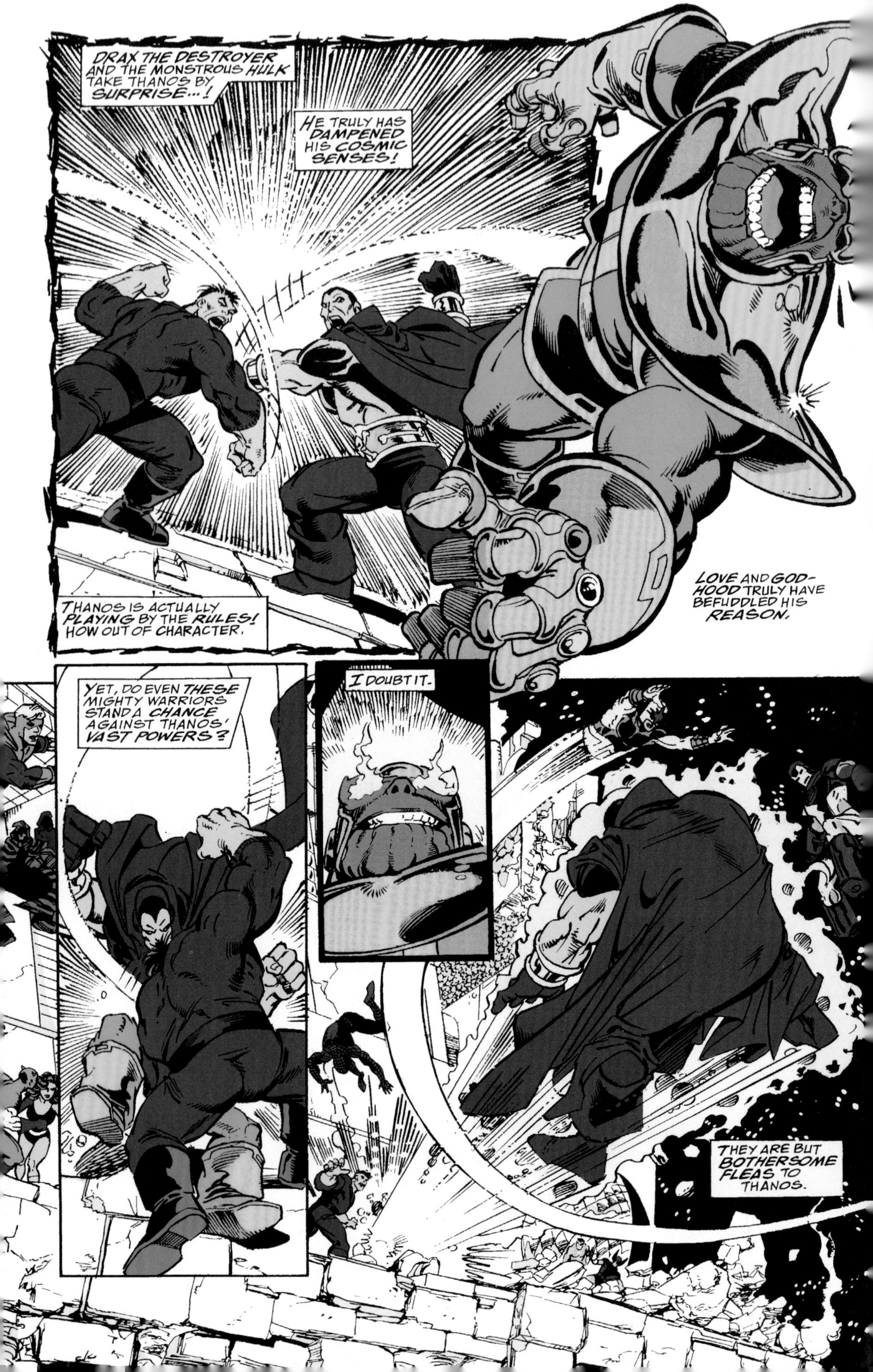
DRAX THE DESTROYER AND THE MONSTROUS HULK TAKE THANOS BY SURPRISE...!
HE TRULY HAS DAMPENED HIS COSMIC SENSES!
THANOS IS ACTUALLY PLAYING BY THE RULES! HOW OUT OF CHARACTER.
LOVE AND GOD-HOOD TRULY HAVE BEFUDDLED HIS REASON.
YET, DO EVEN THESE MIGHTY WARRIORS STAND A CHANCE AGAINST THANOS' VAST POWERS?
I DOUBT IT.
THEY ARE BUT BOTHERSOME FLEAS TO THANOS.

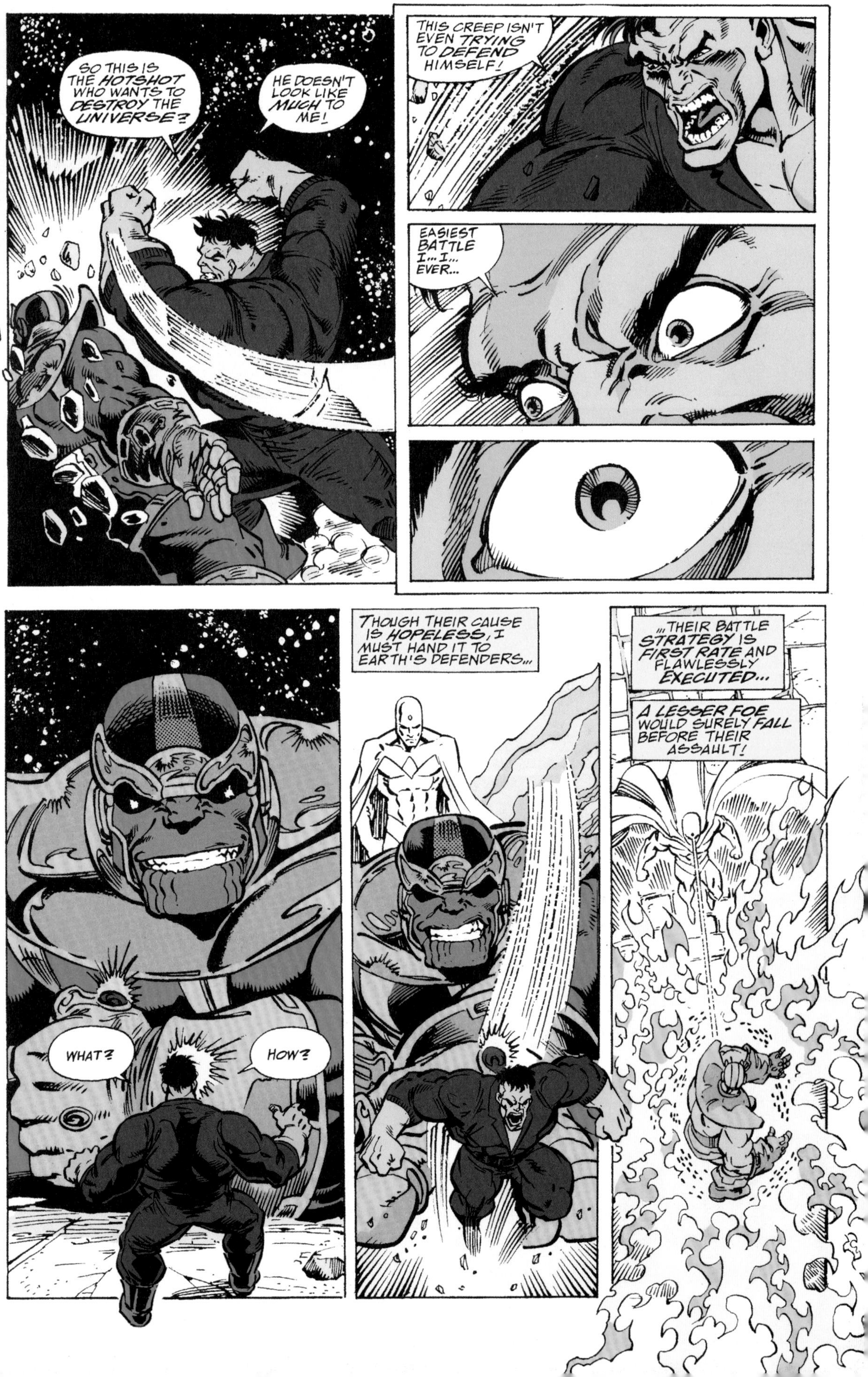
SO THIS IS THE HOTSHOT WHO WANTS TO DESTROY THE UNIVERSE?
HE DOESN'T LOOK LIKE MUCH TO ME!
THIS CREEP ISN'T EVEN TRYING TO DEFEND HIMSELF!
EASIEST BATTLE I... I... EVER...
WHAT?
HOW?
THOUGH THEIR CAUSE IS HOPELESS, I MUST HAND IT TO EARTH'S DEFENDERS...
...THEIR BATTLE STRATEGY IS FIRST RATE AND FLAWLESSLY EXECUTED...
A LESSER FOE WOULD SURELY FALL BEFORE THEIR ASSAULT!

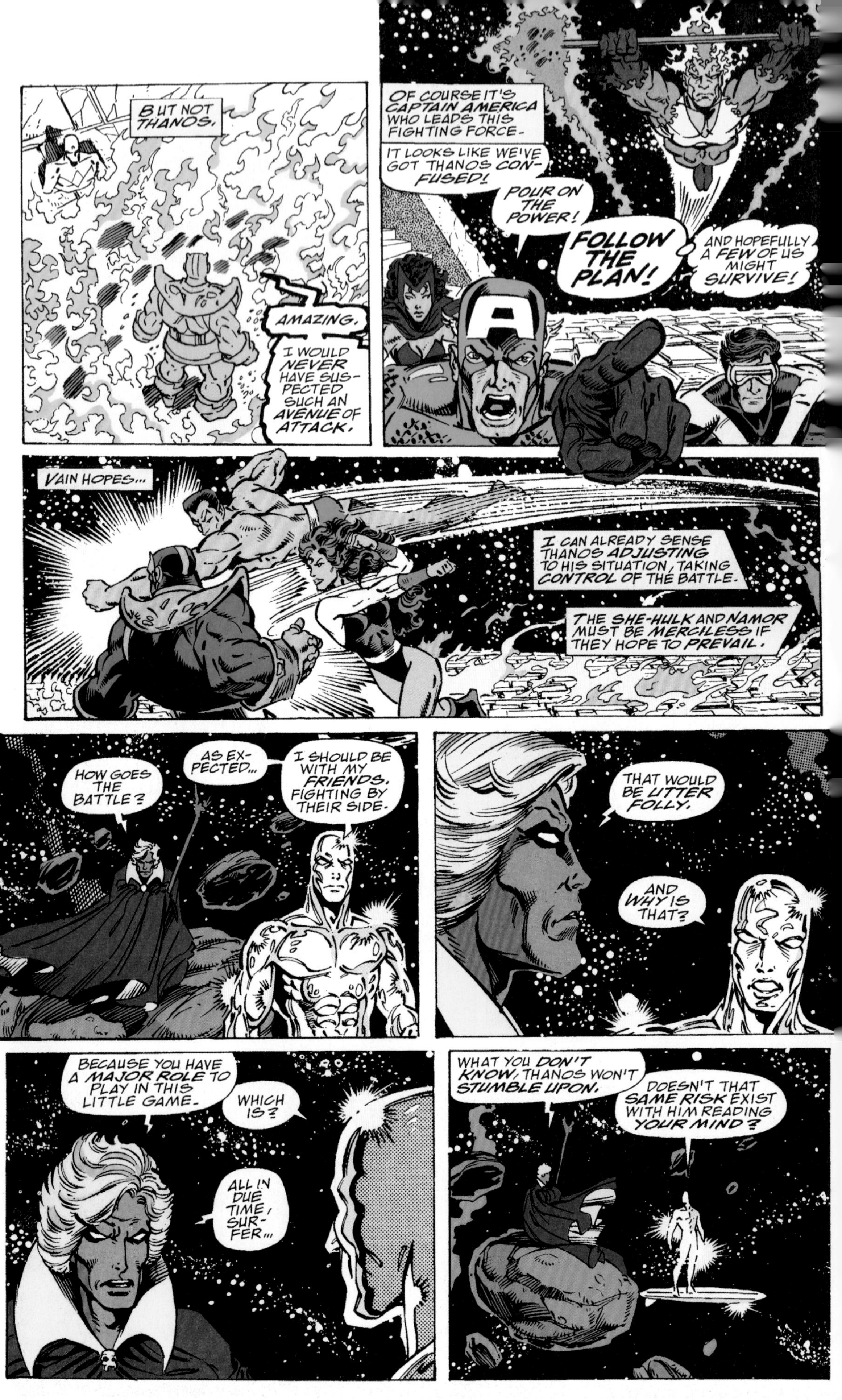
BUT NOT THANOS.
AMAZING.
I WOULD NEVER HAVE SUSPECTED SUCH AN AVENUE OF ATTACK.
OF COURSE IT'S CAPTAIN AMERICA WHO LEADS THIS FIGHTING FORCE.
IT LOOKS LIKE WE'VE GOT THANOS CONFUSED!
POUR ON THE POWER!
FOLLOW THE PLAN!
AND HOPEFULLY A FEW OF US MIGHT SURVIVE!
VAIN HOPES...
I CAN ALREADY SENSE THANOS ADJUSTING TO HIS SITUATION, TAKING CONTROL OF THE BATTLE.
THE SHE-HULK AND NAMOR MUST BE MERCILESS IF THEY HOPE TO PREVAIL.
HOW GOES THE BATTLE?
AS EXPECTED...
I SHOULD BE WITH MY FRIENDS, FIGHTING BY THEIR SIDE.
THAT WOULD BE UTTER FOLLY.
AND WHY IS THAT?
BECAUSE YOU HAVE A MAJOR ROLE TO PLAY IN THIS LITTLE GAME.
WHICH IS?
ALL IN DUE TIME, SURFER...
WHAT YOU DON'T KNOW, THANOS WON'T STUMBLE UPON.
DOESN'T THAT SAME RISK EXIST WITH HIM READING YOUR MIND?

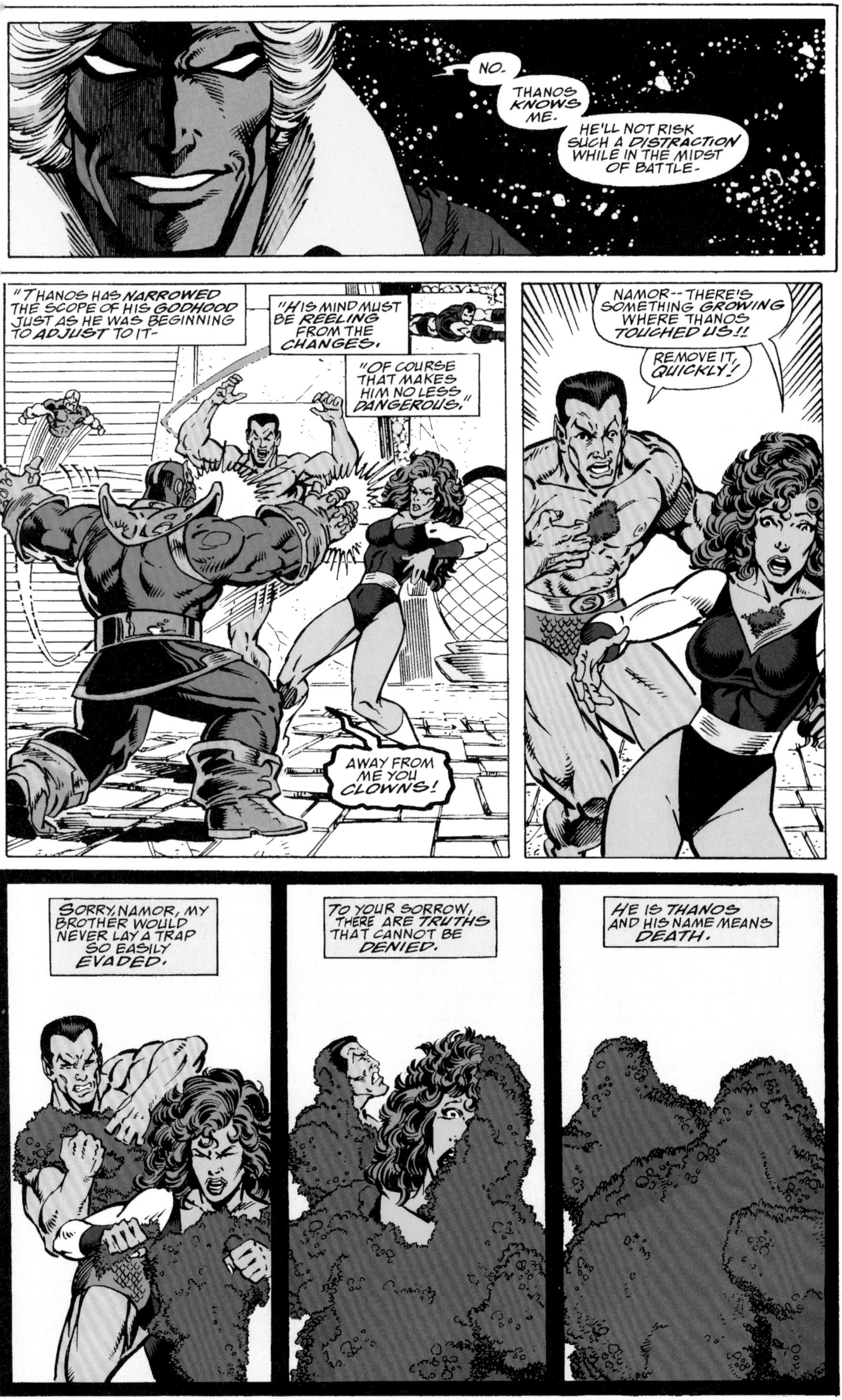
NO.
THANOS KNOWS ME.
HE'LL NOT RISK SUCH A DISTRACTION WHILE IN THE MIDST OF BATTLE-
"THANOS HAS NARROWED THE SCOPE OF HIS GODHOOD JUST AS HE WAS BEGINNING TO ADJUST TO IT-
"HIS MIND MUST BE REELING FROM THE CHANGES.
"OF COURSE THAT MAKES HIM NO LESS DANGEROUS."
AWAY FROM ME YOU CLOWNS!
NAMOR-- THERE'S SOMETHING GROWING WHERE THANOS TOUCHED US!!
REMOVE IT, QUICKLY!
SORRY, NAMOR, MY BROTHER WOULD NEVER LAY A TRAP SO EASILY EVADED.
TO YOUR SORROW, THERE ARE TRUTHS THAT CANNOT BE DENIED.
HE IS THANOS AND HIS NAME MEANS DEATH.

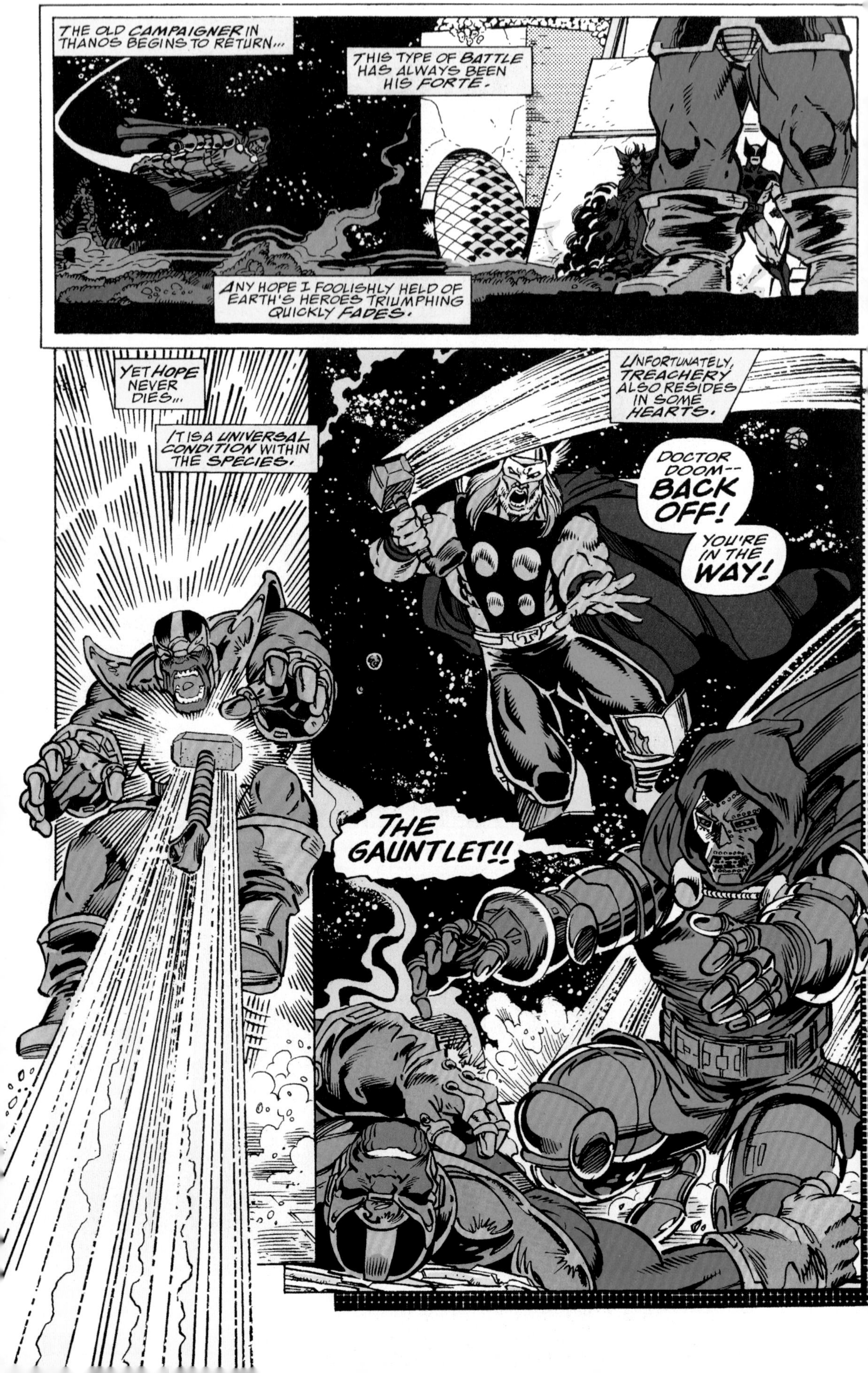
THE OLD CAMPAIGNER IN THANOS BEGINS TO RETURN...
THIS TYPE OF BATTLE HAS ALWAYS BEEN HIS FORTE.
ANY HOPE I FOOLISHLY HELD OF EARTH'S HEROES TRIUMPHING QUICKLY FADES.
YET HOPE NEVER DIES...
IT IS A UNIVERSAL CONDITION WITHIN THE SPECIES.
UNFORTUNATELY, TREACHERY ALSO RESIDES IN SOME HEARTS.
DOCTOR DOOM-- BACK OFF!
YOU'RE IN THE WAY!
THE GAUNTLET!!

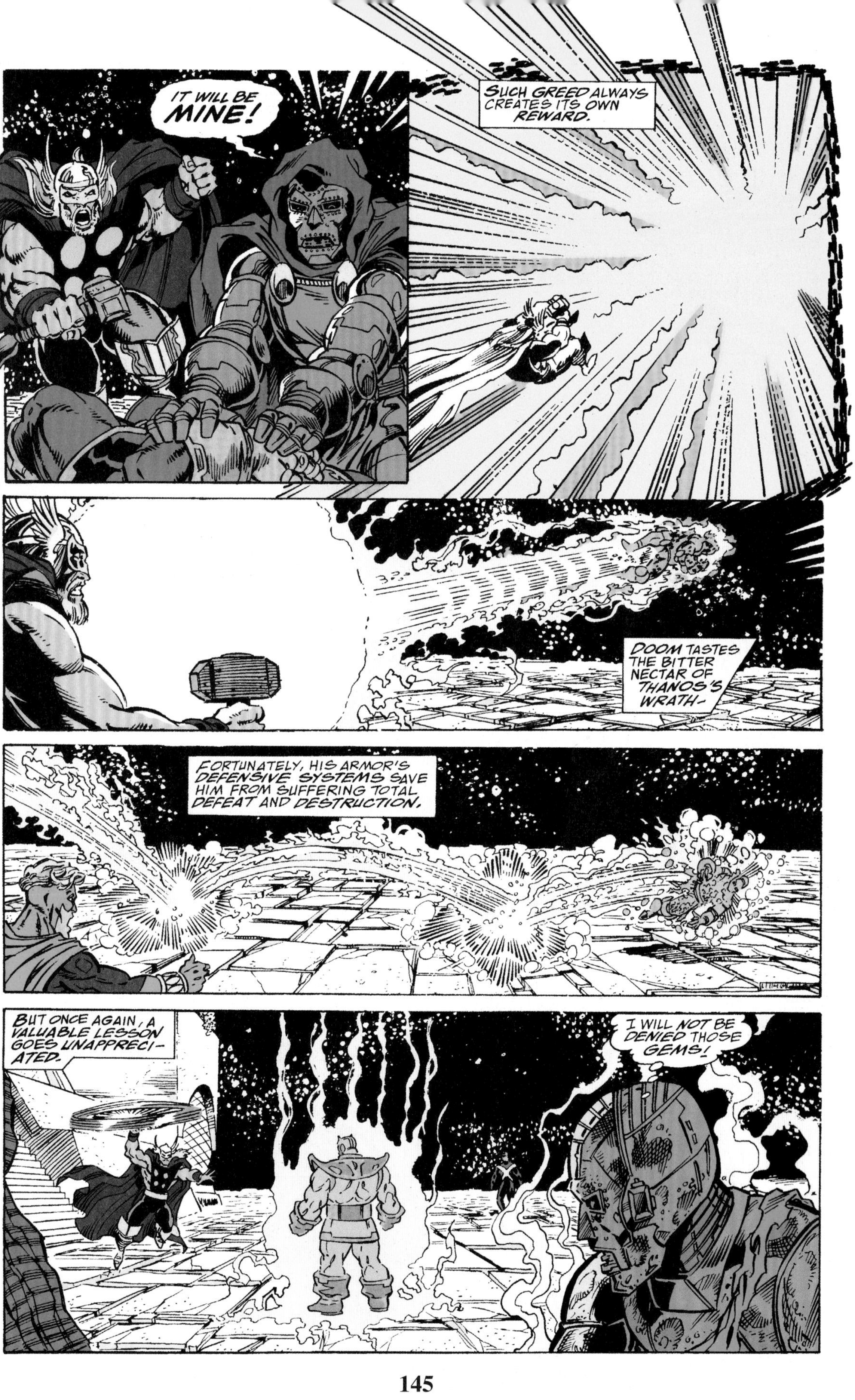
IT WILL BE MINE!
SUCH GREED ALWAYS CREATES ITS OWN REWARD.
DOOM TASTES THE BITTER NECTAR OF THANOS'S WRATH-
FORTUNATELY, HIS ARMOR'S DEFENSIVE SYSTEMS SAVE HIM FROM SUFFERING TOTAL DEFEAT AND DESTRUCTION.
BUT ONCE AGAIN, A VALUABLE LESSON GOES UNAPPRECI-ATED.
I WILL NOT BE DENIED THOSE GEMS!

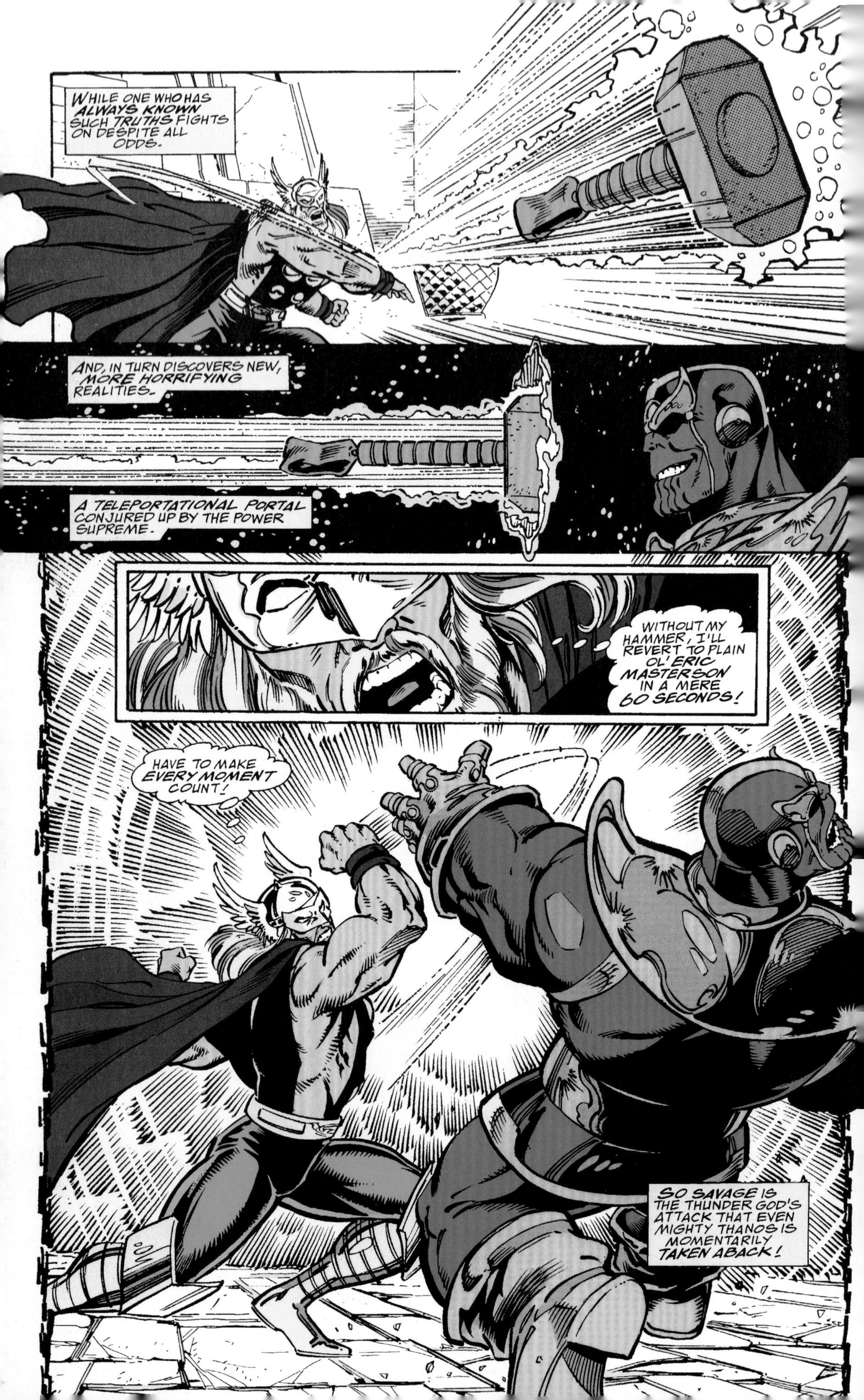

WHILE ONE WHO HAS ALWAYS KNOWN SUCH TRUTHS FIGHTS ON DESPITE ALL ODDS.
AND, IN TURN DISCOVERS NEW, MORE HORRIFYING REALITIES.
A TELEPORTATIONAL PORTAL CONJURED UP BY THE POWER SUPREME.
WITHOUT MY HAMMER, I'LL REVERT TO PLAIN OL' ERIC MASTERSON IN A MERE 60 SECONDS!
HAVE TO MAKE EVERY MOMENT COUNT!
SO SAVAGE IS THE THUNDER GOD'S ATTACK THAT EVEN MIGHTY THANOS IS MOMENTARILY TAKEN ABACK!

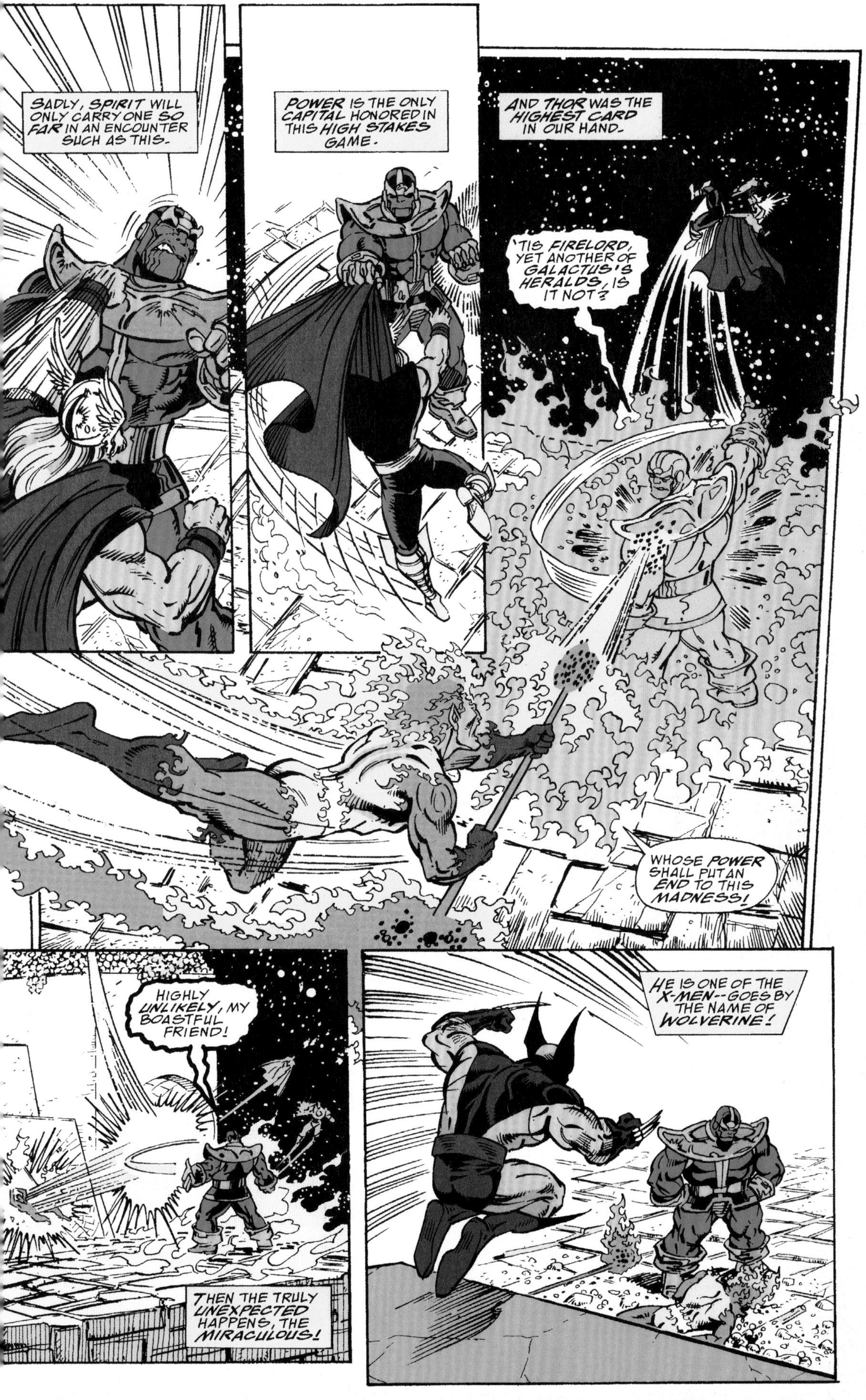

SADLY, SPIRIT WILL ONLY CARRY ONE SO FAR IN AN ENCOUNTER SUCH AS THIS.
POWER IS THE ONLY CAPITAL HONORED IN THIS HIGH STAKES GAME.
AND THOR WAS THE HIGHEST CARD IN OUR HAND.
'TIS FIRELORD, YET ANOTHER OF GALACTUS'S HERALDS, IS IT NOT?
WHOSE POWER SHALL PUT AN END TO THIS MADNESS!
HIGHLY UNLIKELY, MY BOASTFUL FRIEND!
THEN THE TRULY UNEXPECTED HAPPENS, THE MIRACULOUS!
HE IS ONE OF THE X-MEN--GOES BY THE NAME OF WOLVERINE!

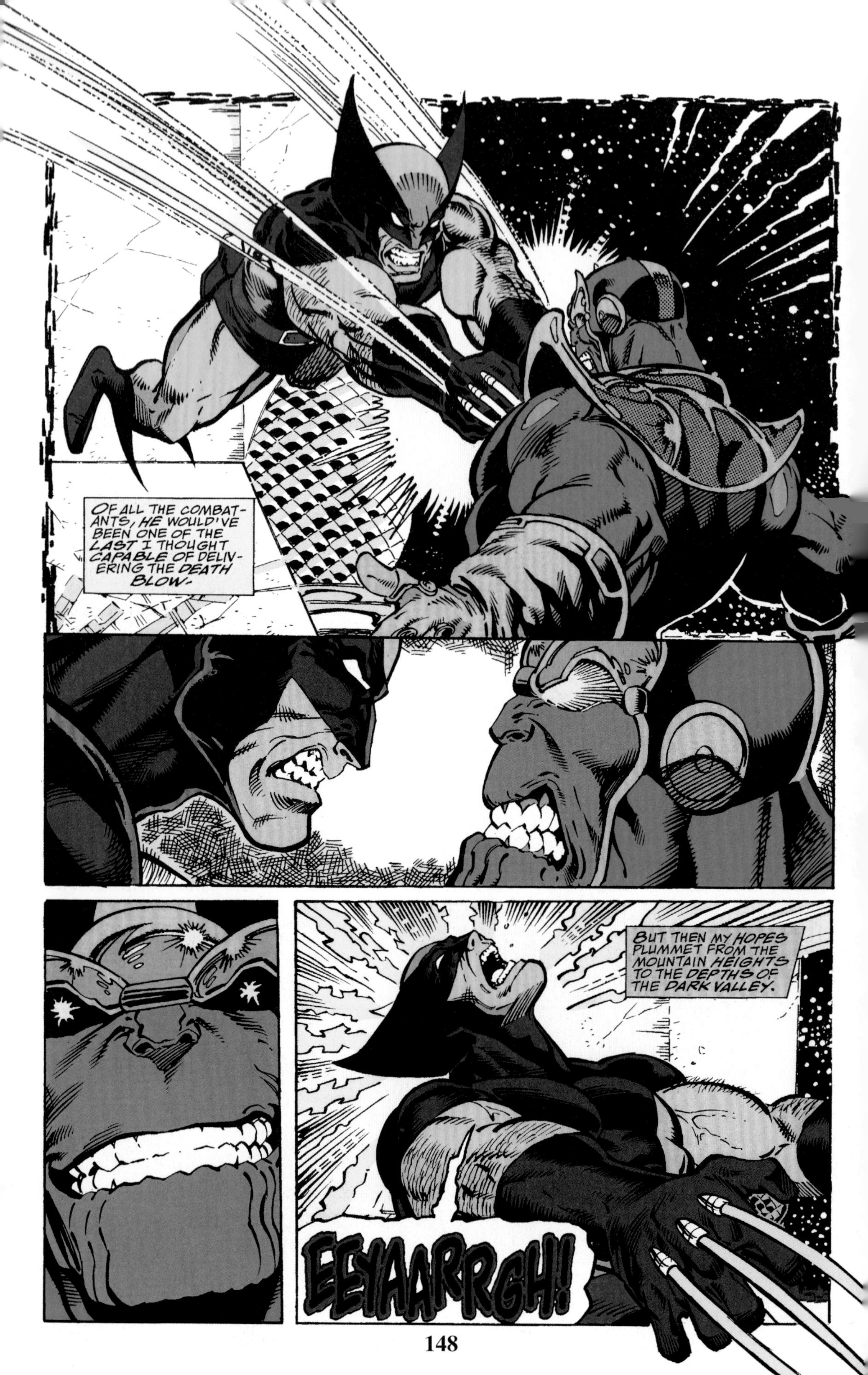

OF ALL THE COMBATANTS, HE WOULD'VE BEEN ONE OF THE LAST I THOUGHT CAPABLE OF DELIVERING THE DEATH BLOW-
BUT THEN MY HOPES PLUMMET FROM THE MOUNTAIN HEIGHTS TO THE DEPTHS OF THE DARK VALLEY.
EEYAARRGH!

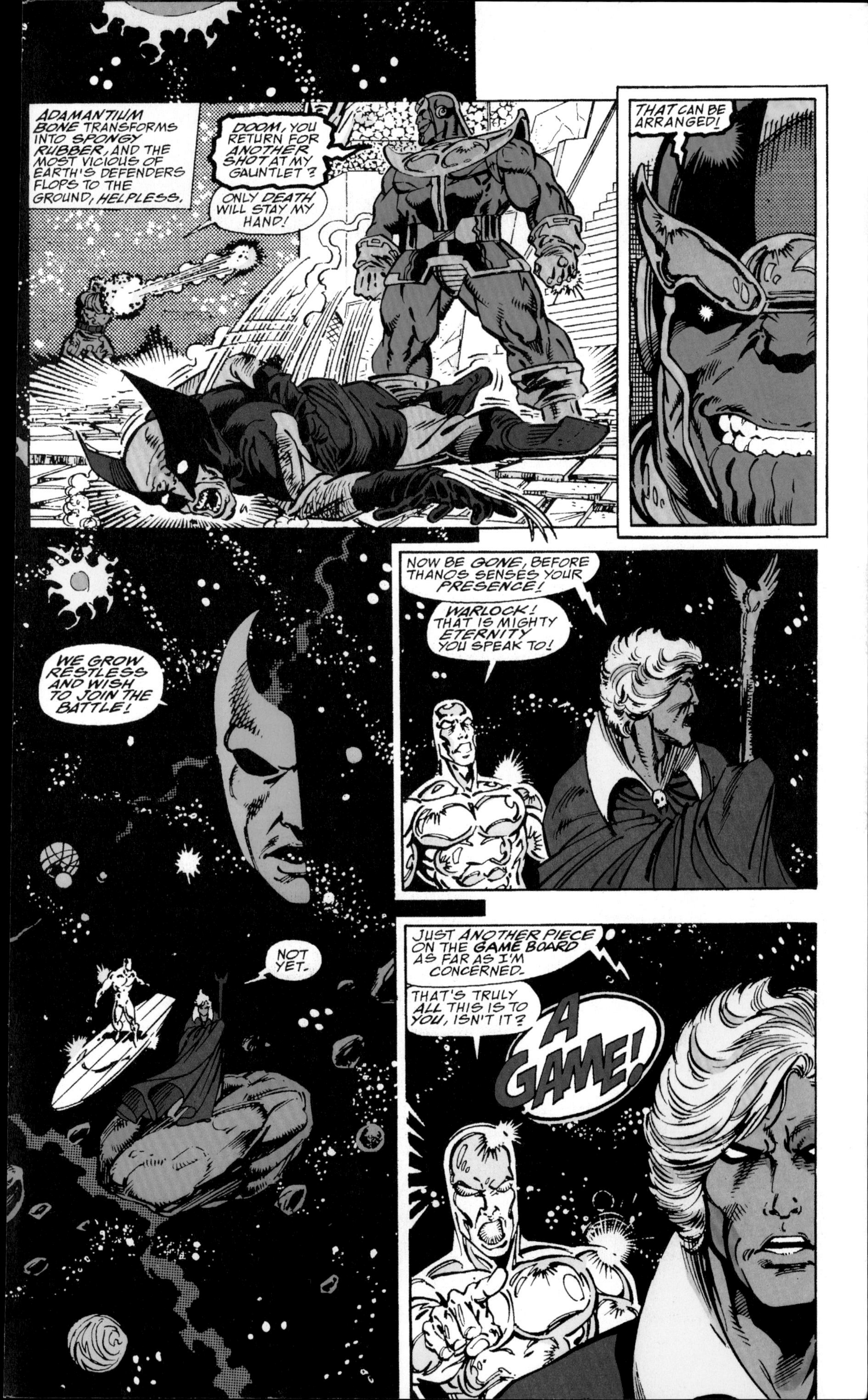
ADAMANTIUM BONE TRANSFORMS INTO SPONGY RUBBER, AND THE MOST VICIOUS OF EARTH'S DEFENDERS FLOPS TO THE GROUND, HELPLESS.
DOOM, YOU RETURN FOR ANOTHER SHOT AT MY GAUNTLET?
ONLY DEATH WILL STAY MY HAND!
THAT CAN BE ARRANGED!
WE GROW RESTLESS AND WISH TO JOIN THE BATTLE!
NOW BE GONE, BEFORE THANOS SENSES YOUR PRESENCE!
WARLOCK! THAT IS MIGHTY ETERNITY YOU SPEAK TO!
NOT YET.
JUST ANOTHER PIECE ON THE GAME BOARD AS FAR AS I'M CONCERNED.
THAT'S TRULY ALL THIS IS TO YOU, ISN'T IT?
A GAME!

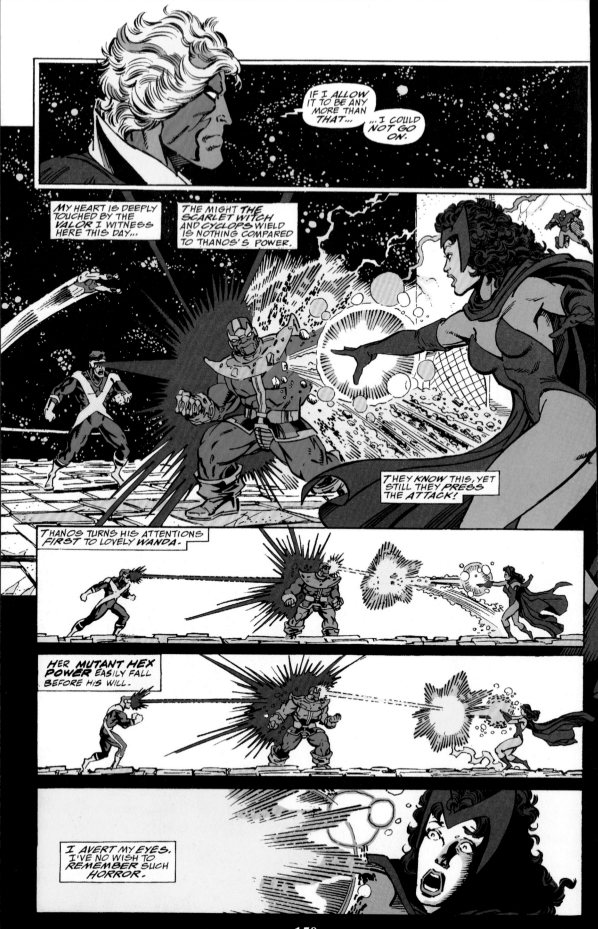

IF I ALLOW IT TO BE ANY MORE THAN *THAT*... ..*I COULD NOT GO ON.*

MY HEART IS DEEPLY TOUCHED BY THE VALOR I WITNESS HERE THIS DAY...

THE MIGHT THE SCARLET WITCH AND CYCLOPS WIELD IS NOTHING COMPARED TO THANOS'S POWER.

THEY KNOW THIS, YET STILL THEY PRESS THE ATTACK!

THANOS TURNS HIS ATTENTIONS FIRST TO LOVELY WANDA.

HER MUTANT HEX POWER EASILY FALL BEFORE HIS WILL.

I AVERT MY EYES. I'VE NO WISH TO REMEMBER SUCH HORROR.

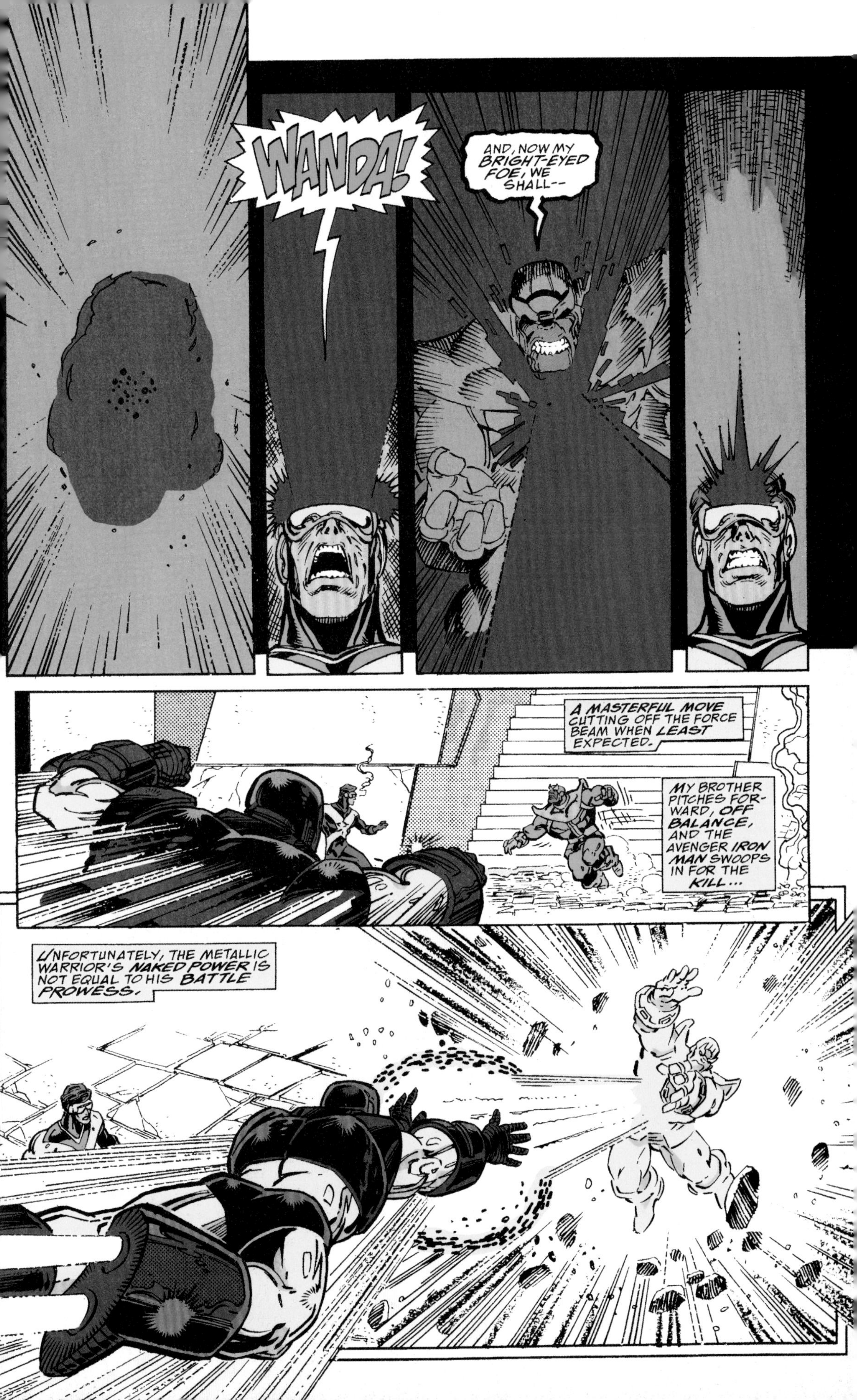
WANDA!
AND, NOW MY BRIGHT-EYED FOE, WE SHALL--
A MASTERFUL MOVE CUTTING OFF THE FORCE BEAM WHEN LEAST EXPECTED.
MY BROTHER PITCHES FORWARD, OFF BALANCE, AND THE AVENGER IRON MAN SWOOPS IN FOR THE KILL...
UNFORTUNATELY, THE METALLIC WARRIOR'S NAKED POWER IS NOT EQUAL TO HIS BATTLE PROWESS.

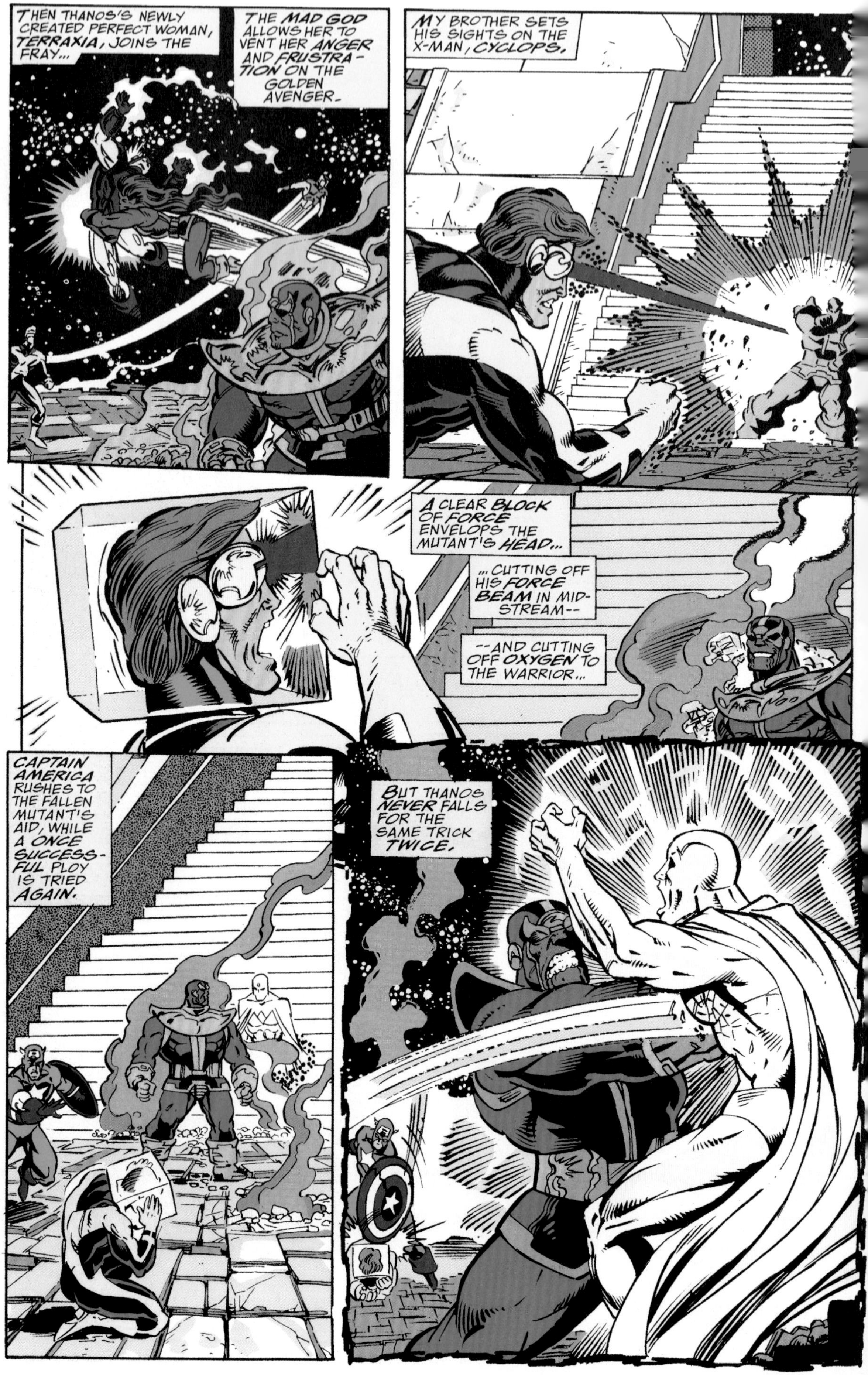
THEN THANOS'S NEWLY CREATED PERFECT WOMAN, TERRAXIA, JOINS THE FRAY...
THE MAD GOD ALLOWS HER TO VENT HER ANGER AND FRUSTRATION ON THE GOLDEN AVENGER.
MY BROTHER SETS HIS SIGHTS ON THE X-MAN, CYCLOPS.
A CLEAR BLOCK OF FORCE ENVELOPS THE MUTANT'S HEAD...
...CUTTING OFF HIS FORCE BEAM IN MID-STREAM--
--AND CUTTING OFF OXYGEN TO THE WARRIOR...
CAPTAIN AMERICA RUSHES TO THE FALLEN MUTANT'S AID, WHILE A ONCE SUCCESSFUL PLOY IS TRIED AGAIN.
BUT THANOS NEVER FALLS FOR THE SAME TRICK TWICE.

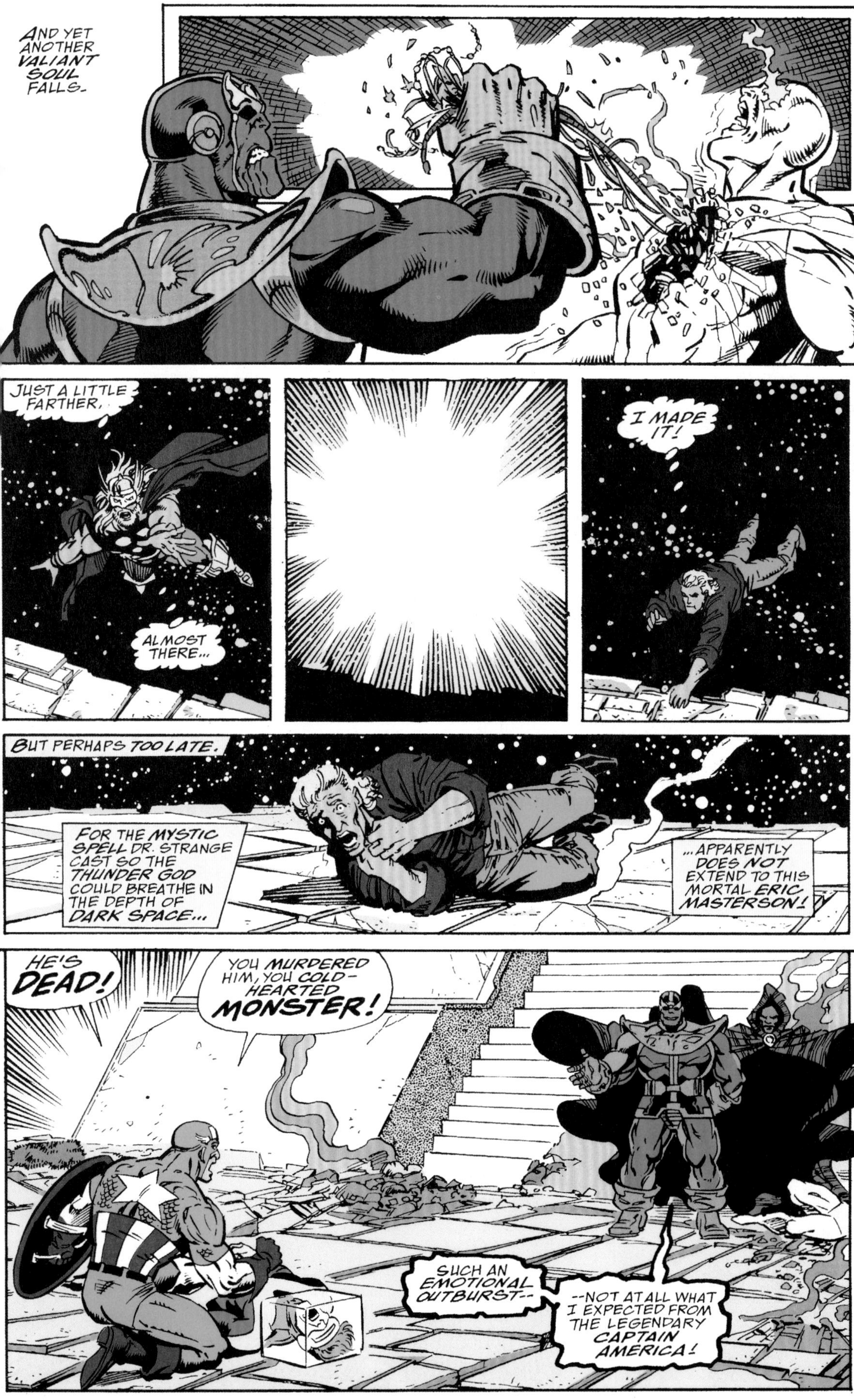
AND YET ANOTHER VALIANT SOUL FALLS.
JUST A LITTLE FARTHER.
ALMOST THERE...
I MADE IT!
BUT PERHAPS TOO LATE.
FOR THE MYSTIC SPELL DR. STRANGE CAST SO THE THUNDER GOD COULD BREATHE IN THE DEPTH OF DARK SPACE...
...APPARENTLY DOES NOT EXTEND TO THIS MORTAL ERIC MASTERSON!
HE'S DEAD!
YOU MURDERED HIM, YOU COLD-HEARTED MONSTER!
SUCH AN EMOTIONAL OUTBURST--
--NOT AT ALL WHAT I EXPECTED FROM THE LEGENDARY CAPTAIN AMERICA!

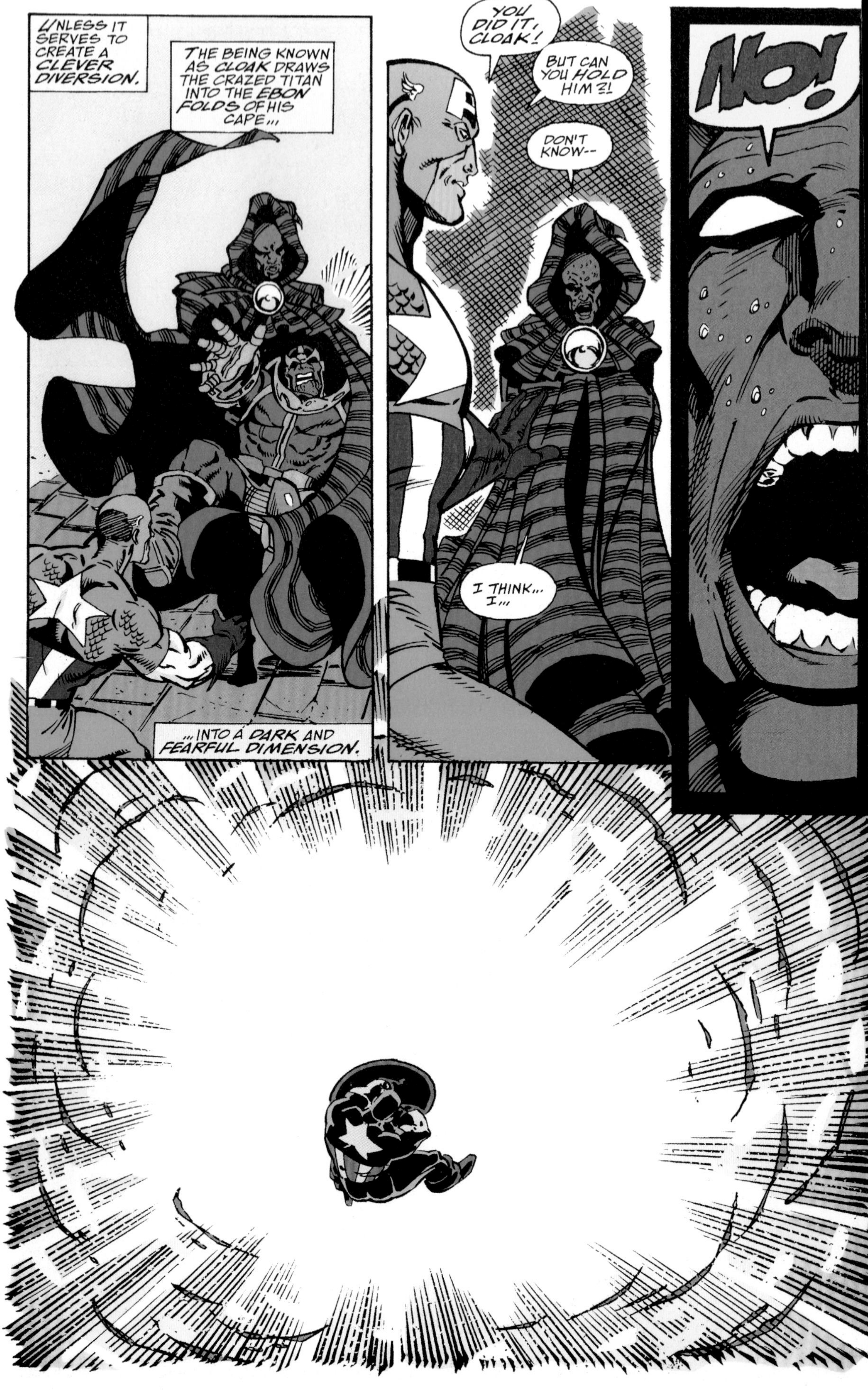
UNLESS IT SERVES TO CREATE A CLEVER DIVERSION.
THE BEING KNOWN AS CLOAK DRAWS THE CRAZED TITAN INTO THE EBON FOLDS OF HIS CAPE...
...INTO A DARK AND FEARFUL DIMENSION.
YOU DID IT, CLOAK!
BUT CAN YOU HOLD HIM ?!
DON'T KNOW--
I THINK... I...
NO!

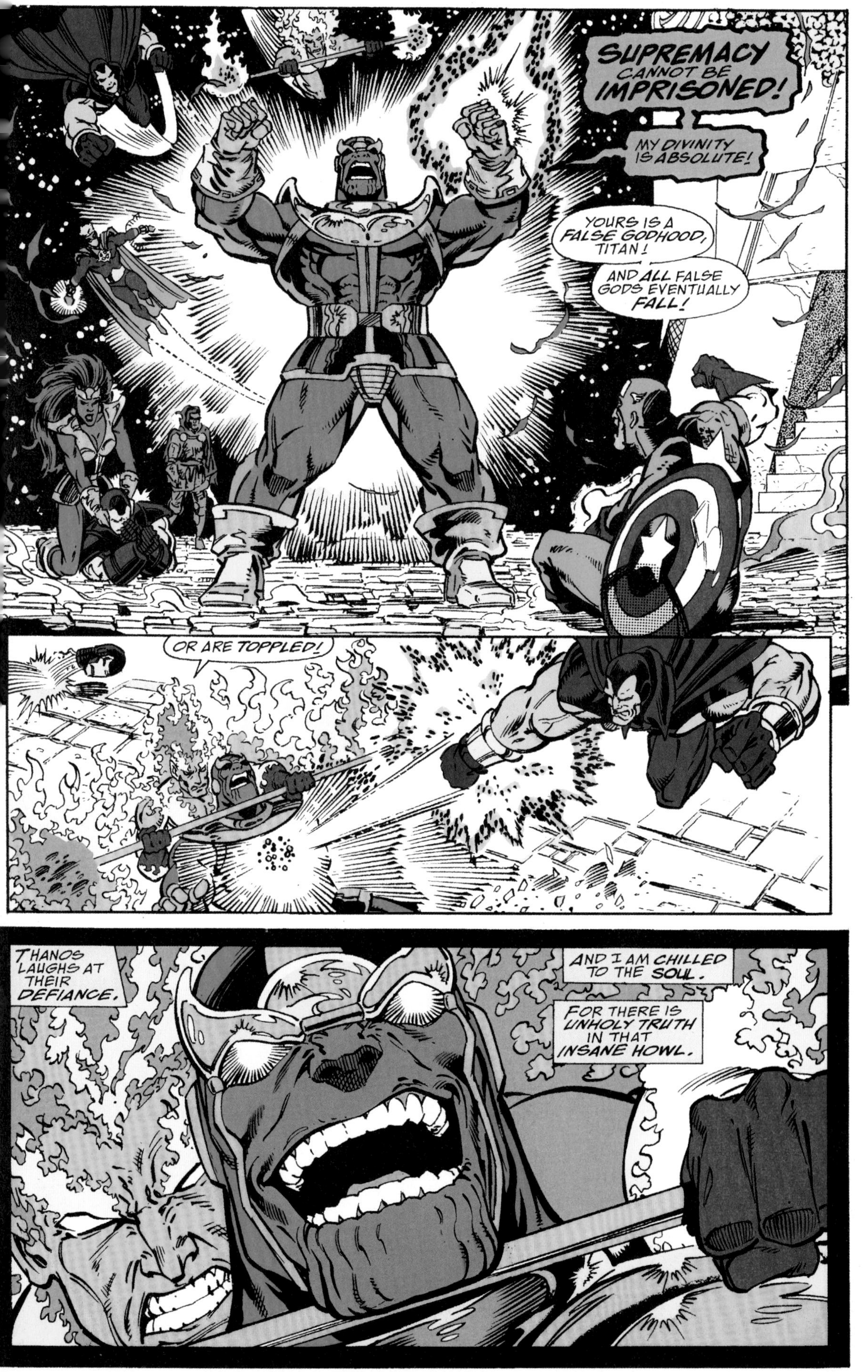
SUPREMACY CANNOT BE IMPRISONED!
MY DIVINITY IS ABSOLUTE!
YOURS IS A FALSE GODHOOD, TITAN!
AND ALL FALSE GODS EVENTUALLY FALL!
OR ARE TOPPLED!
THANOS LAUGHS AT THEIR DEFIANCE.
AND I AM CHILLED TO THE SOUL.
FOR THERE IS UNHOLY TRUTH IN THAT INSANE HOWL.

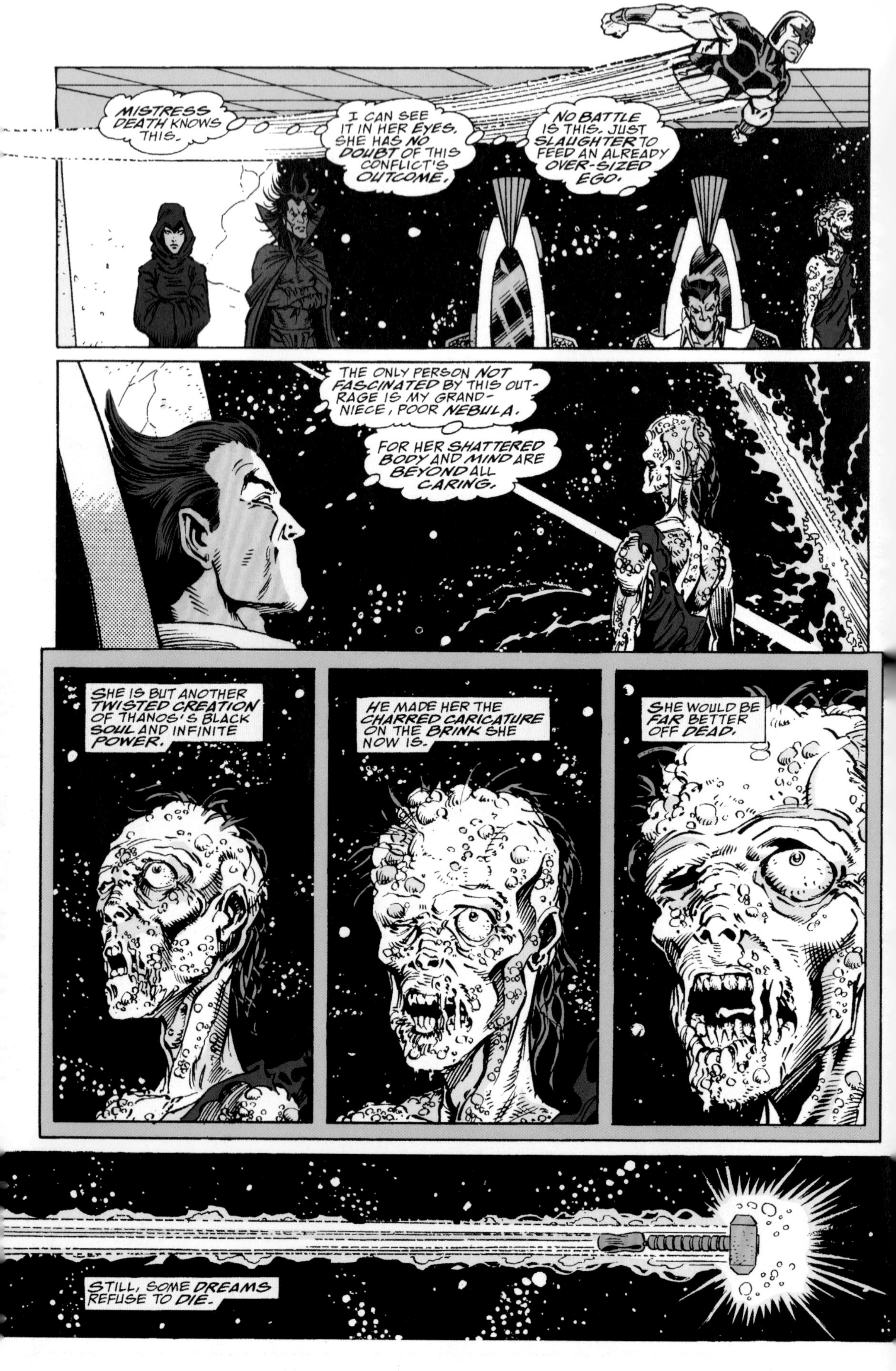

MISTRESS DEATH KNOWS THIS.
I CAN SEE IT IN HER EYES. SHE HAS NO DOUBT OF THIS CONFLICT'S OUTCOME.
NO BATTLE IS THIS. JUST SLAUGHTER TO FEED AN ALREADY OVER-SIZED EGO.
THE ONLY PERSON NOT FASCINATED BY THIS OUTRAGE IS MY GRAND-NIECE, POOR NEBULA.
FOR HER SHATTERED BODY AND MIND ARE BEYOND ALL CARING.
SHE IS BUT ANOTHER TWISTED CREATION OF THANOS'S BLACK SOUL AND INFINITE POWER.
HE MADE HER THE CHARRED CARICATURE ON THE BRINK SHE NOW IS.
SHE WOULD BE FAR BETTER OFF DEAD.
STILL, SOME DREAMS REFUSE TO DIE.

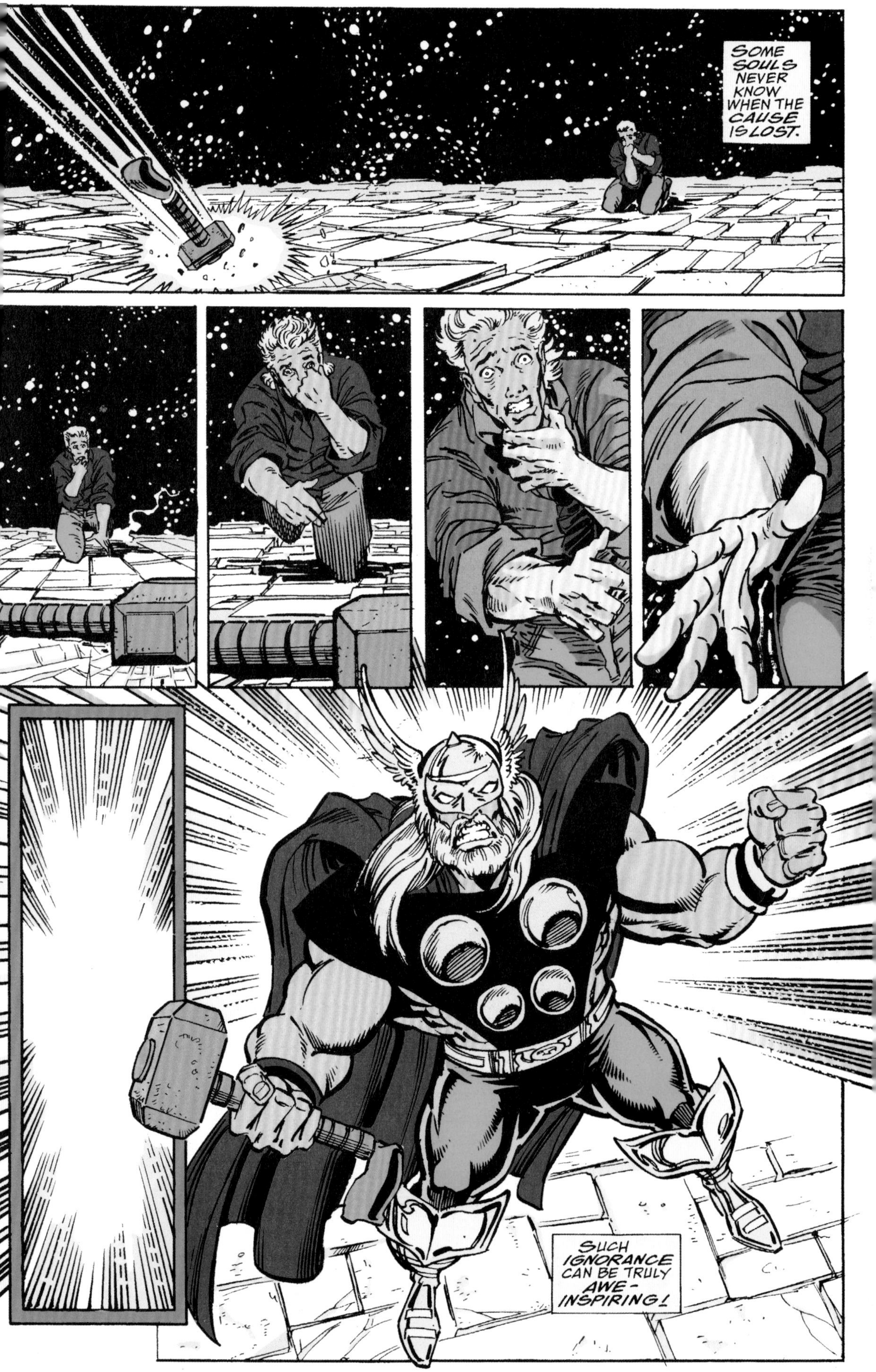

SOME SOULS NEVER KNOW WHEN THE CAUSE IS LOST.
SUCH IGNORANCE CAN BE TRULY AWE-INSPIRING!

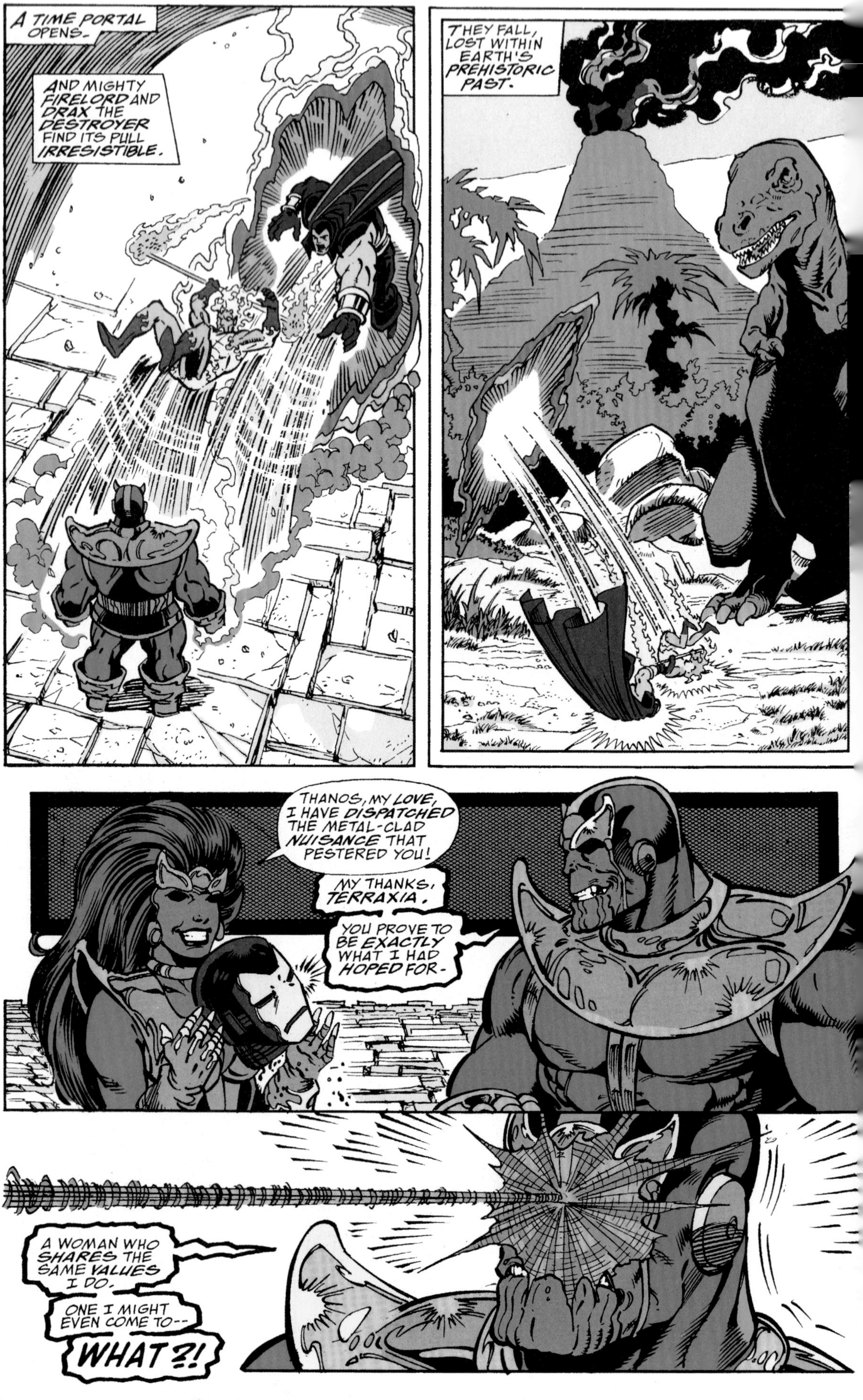

A TIME PORTAL OPENS-
AND MIGHTY FIRELORD AND DRAX THE DESTROYER FIND ITS PULL IRRESISTIBLE.
THEY FALL, LOST WITHIN EARTH'S PREHISTORIC PAST.
THANOS, MY LOVE, I HAVE DISPATCHED THE METAL-CLAD NUISANCE THAT PESTERED YOU!
MY THANKS, TERRAXIA.
YOU PROVE TO BE EXACTLY WHAT I HAD HOPED FOR-
A WOMAN WHO SHARES THE SAME VALUES I DO.
ONE I MIGHT EVEN COME TO--
WHAT?!

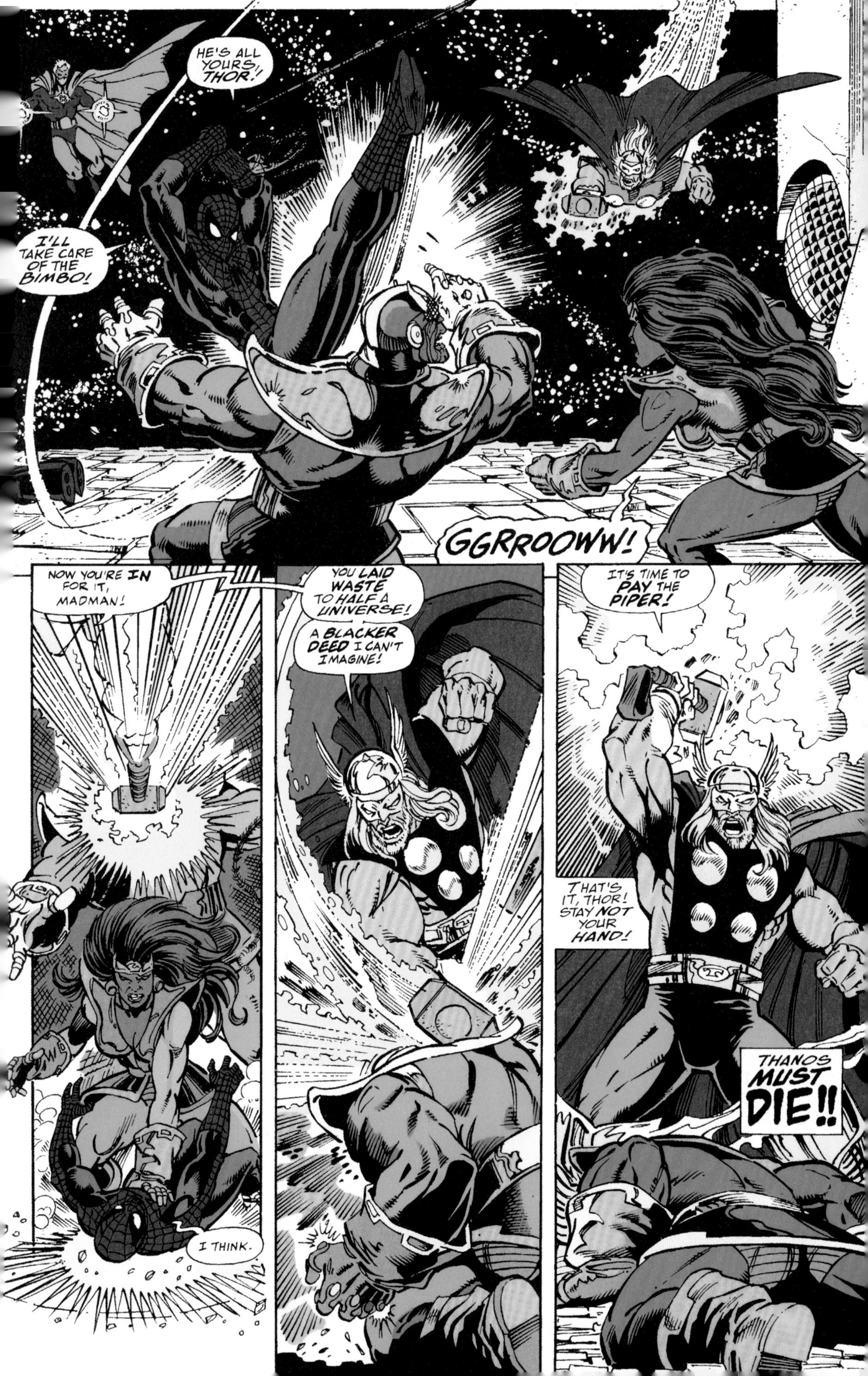
HE'S ALL YOURS, THOR!
I'LL TAKE CARE OF THE BIMBO!
GGRROOWW!
NOW YOU'RE IN FOR IT, MADMAN!
YOU LAID WASTE TO HALF A UNIVERSE!
A BLACKER DEED I CAN'T IMAGINE!
IT'S TIME TO PAY THE PIPER!
I THINK.
THAT'S IT, THOR! STAY NOT YOUR HAND!
THANOS MUST DIE!!

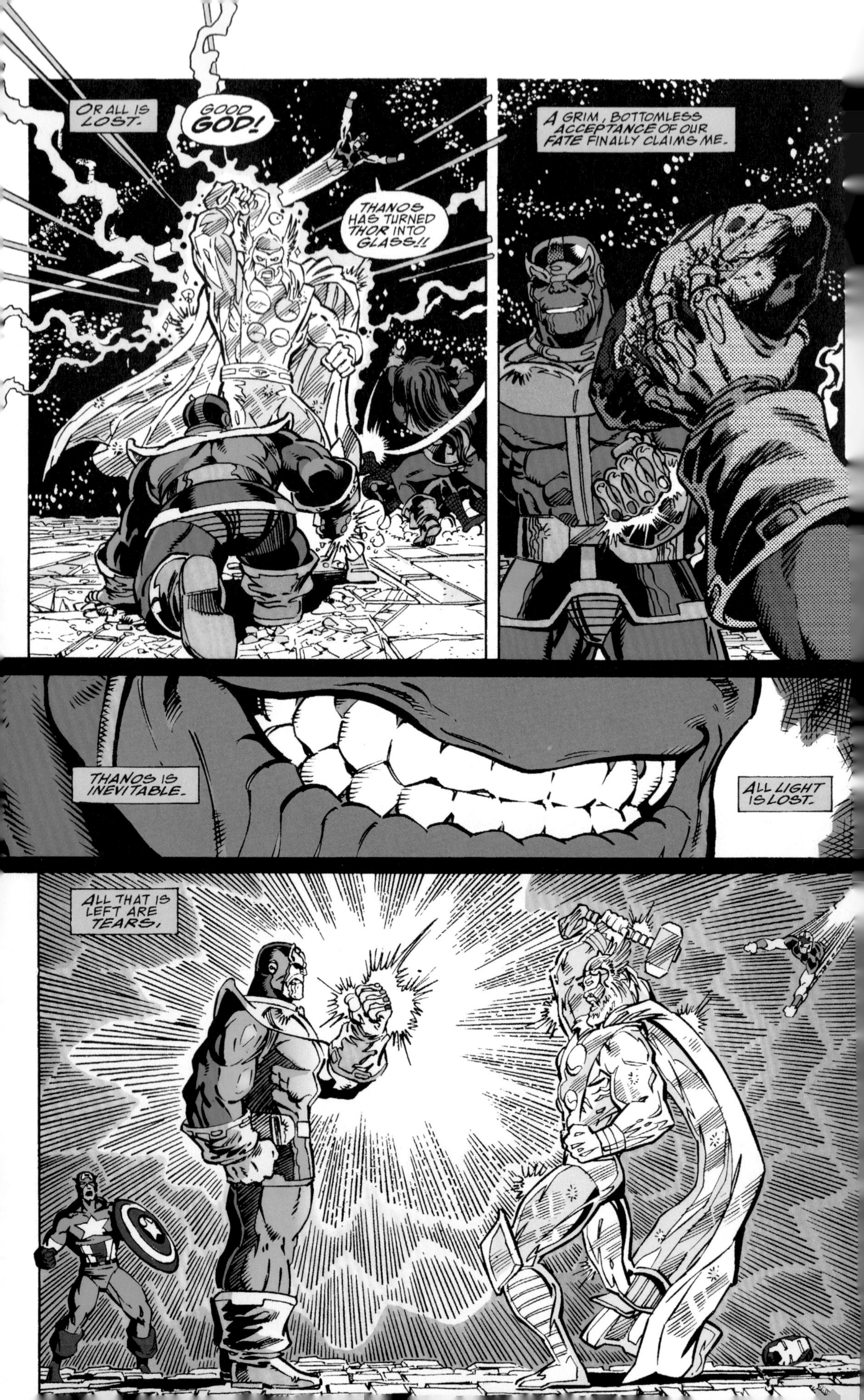
OR ALL IS LOST.
GOOD GOD!
THANOS HAS TURNED THOR INTO GLASS!!
A GRIM, BOTTOMLESS ACCEPTANCE OF OUR FATE FINALLY CLAIMS ME.
THANOS IS INEVITABLE.
ALL LIGHT IS LOST.
ALL THAT IS LEFT ARE TEARS,

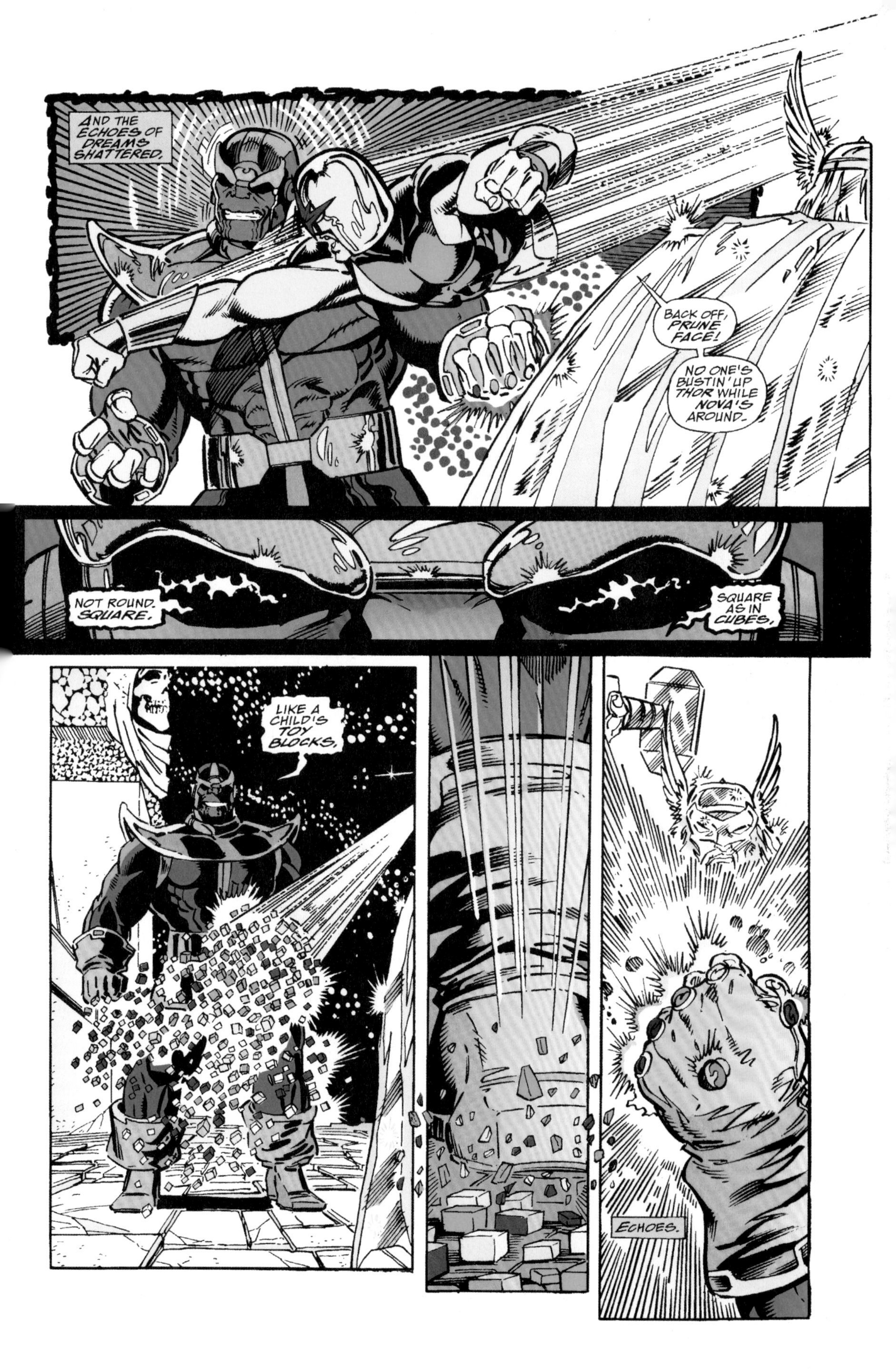
AND THE ECHOES OF DREAMS SHATTERED.
BACK OFF, PRUNE FACE!
NO ONE'S BUSTIN' UP THOR WHILE NOVA'S AROUND--
NOT ROUND. SQUARE.
SQUARE AS IN CUBES,
LIKE A CHILD'S TOY BLOCKS,
ECHOES.

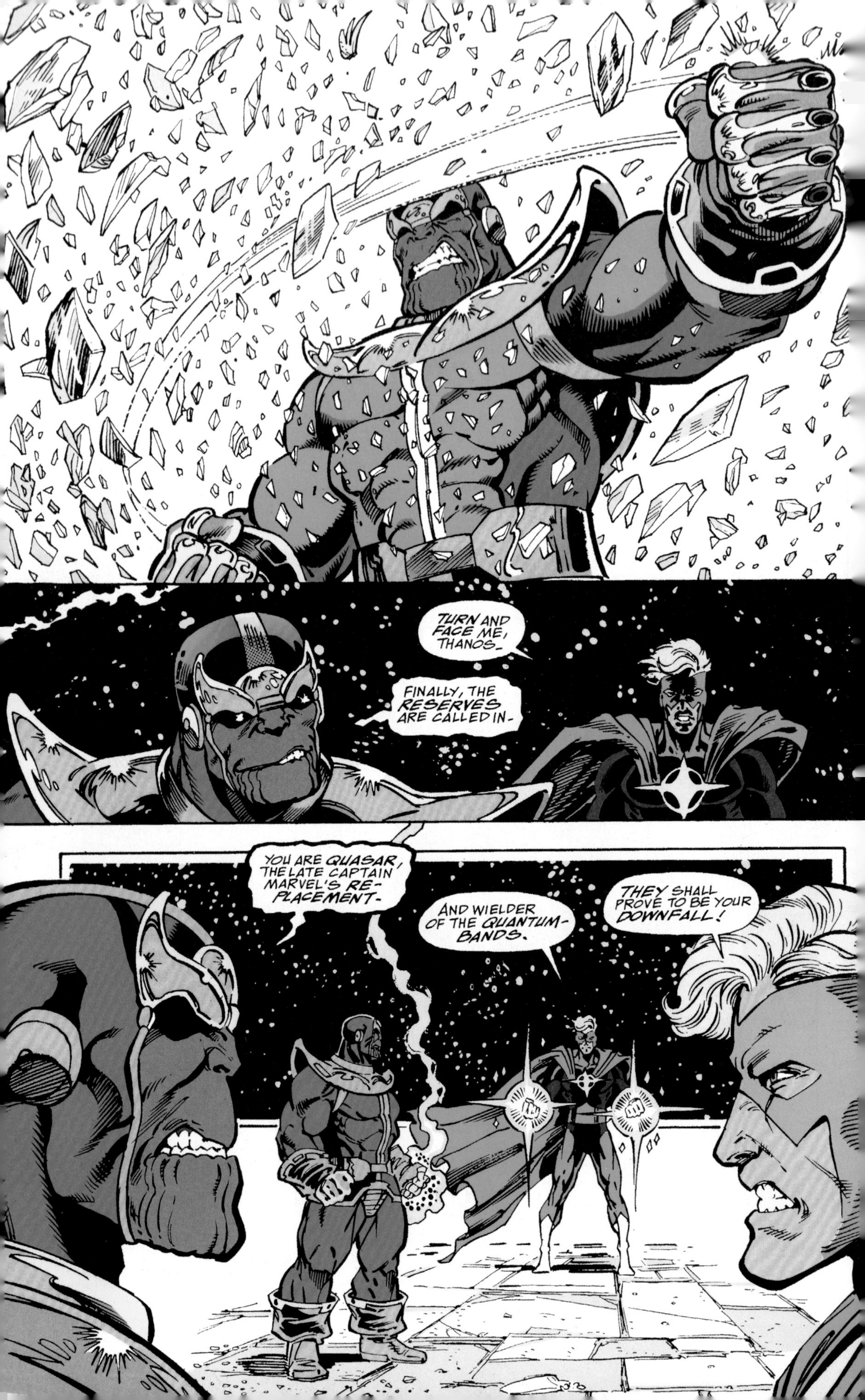
TURN AND FACE ME, THANOS--
FINALLY, THE RESERVES ARE CALLED IN--
YOU ARE QUASAR, THE LATE CAPTAIN MARVEL'S RE-PLACEMENT--
AND WIELDER OF THE QUANTUM-BANDS.
THEY SHALL PROVE TO BE YOUR DOWNFALL!

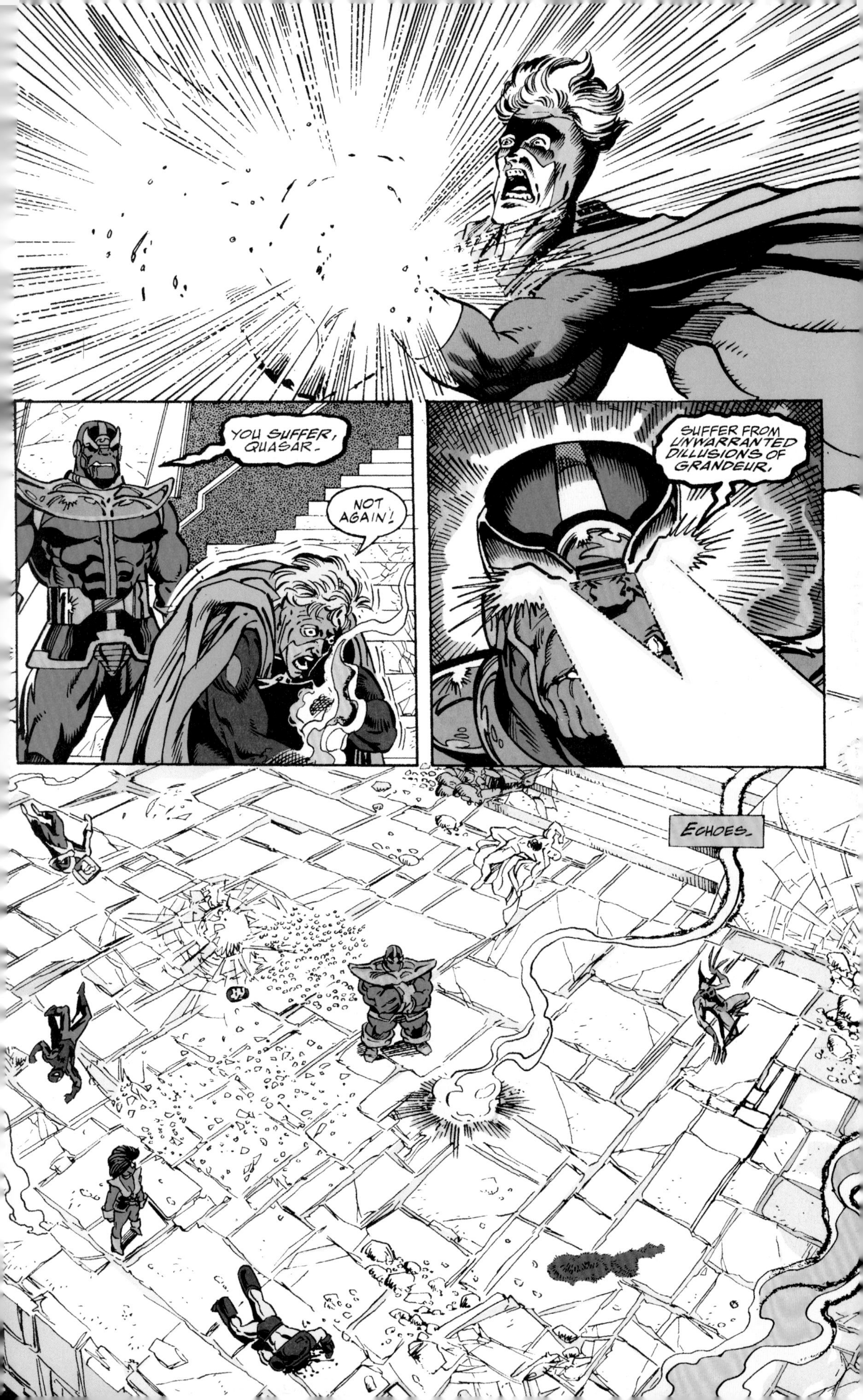
YOU SUFFER, QUASAR-
NOT AGAIN!
SUFFER FROM UNWARRANTED DILLUSIONS OF GRANDEUR.
ECHOES-

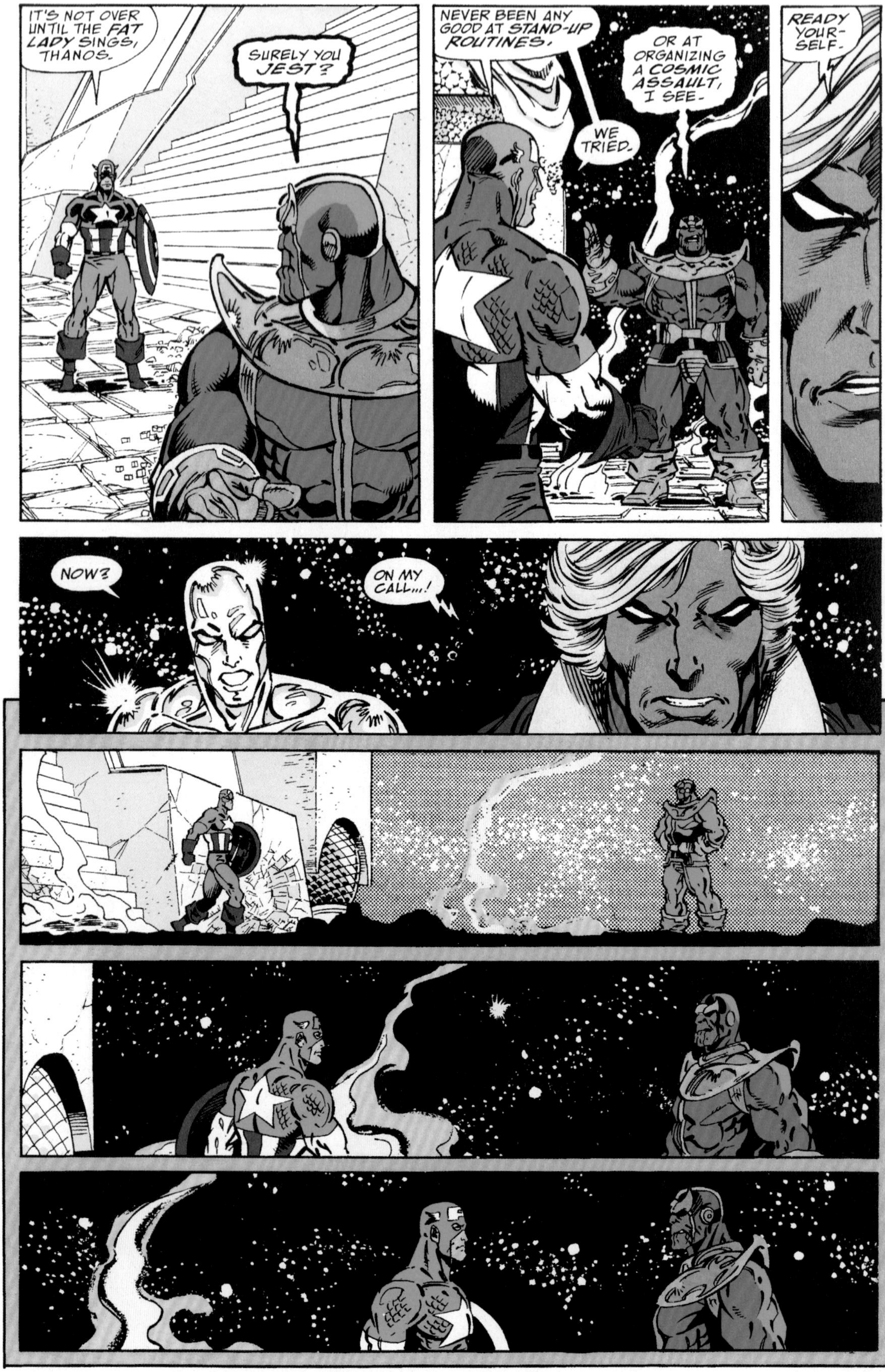
IT'S NOT OVER UNTIL THE FAT LADY SINGS, THANOS.
SURELY YOU JEST?
NEVER BEEN ANY GOOD AT STAND-UP ROUTINES.
OR AT ORGANIZING A COSMIC ASSAULT, I SEE.
WE TRIED.
READY YOURSELF.
NOW?
ON MY CALL...!

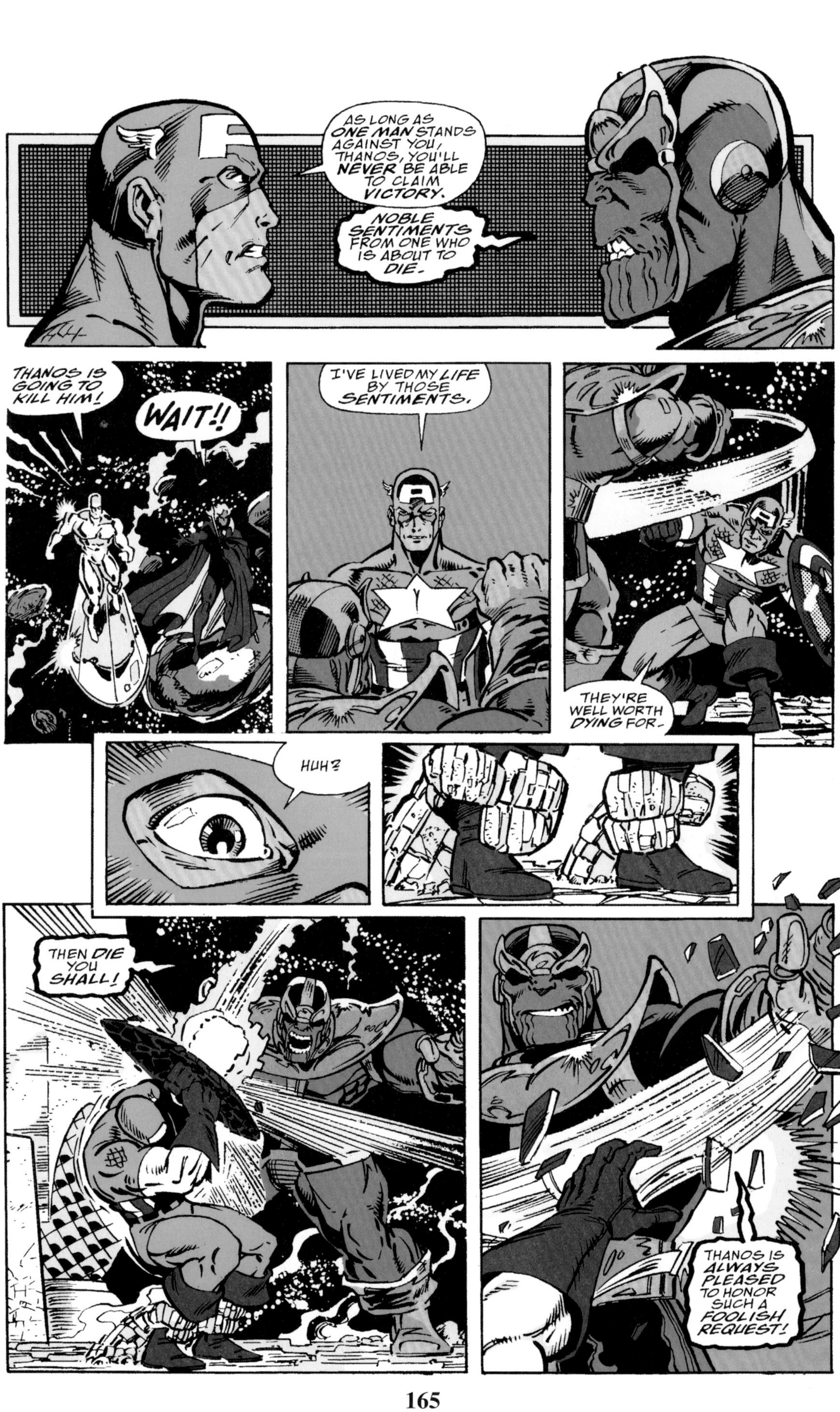
AS LONG AS ONE MAN STANDS AGAINST YOU, THANOS, YOU'LL NEVER BE ABLE TO CLAIM VICTORY.
NOBLE SENTIMENTS FROM ONE WHO IS ABOUT TO DIE.
THANOS IS GOING TO KILL HIM!
WAIT!!
I'VE LIVED MY LIFE BY THOSE SENTIMENTS.
THEY'RE WELL WORTH DYING FOR.
HUH?
THEN DIE YOU SHALL!
THANOS IS ALWAYS PLEASED TO HONOR SUCH A FOOLISH REQUEST!

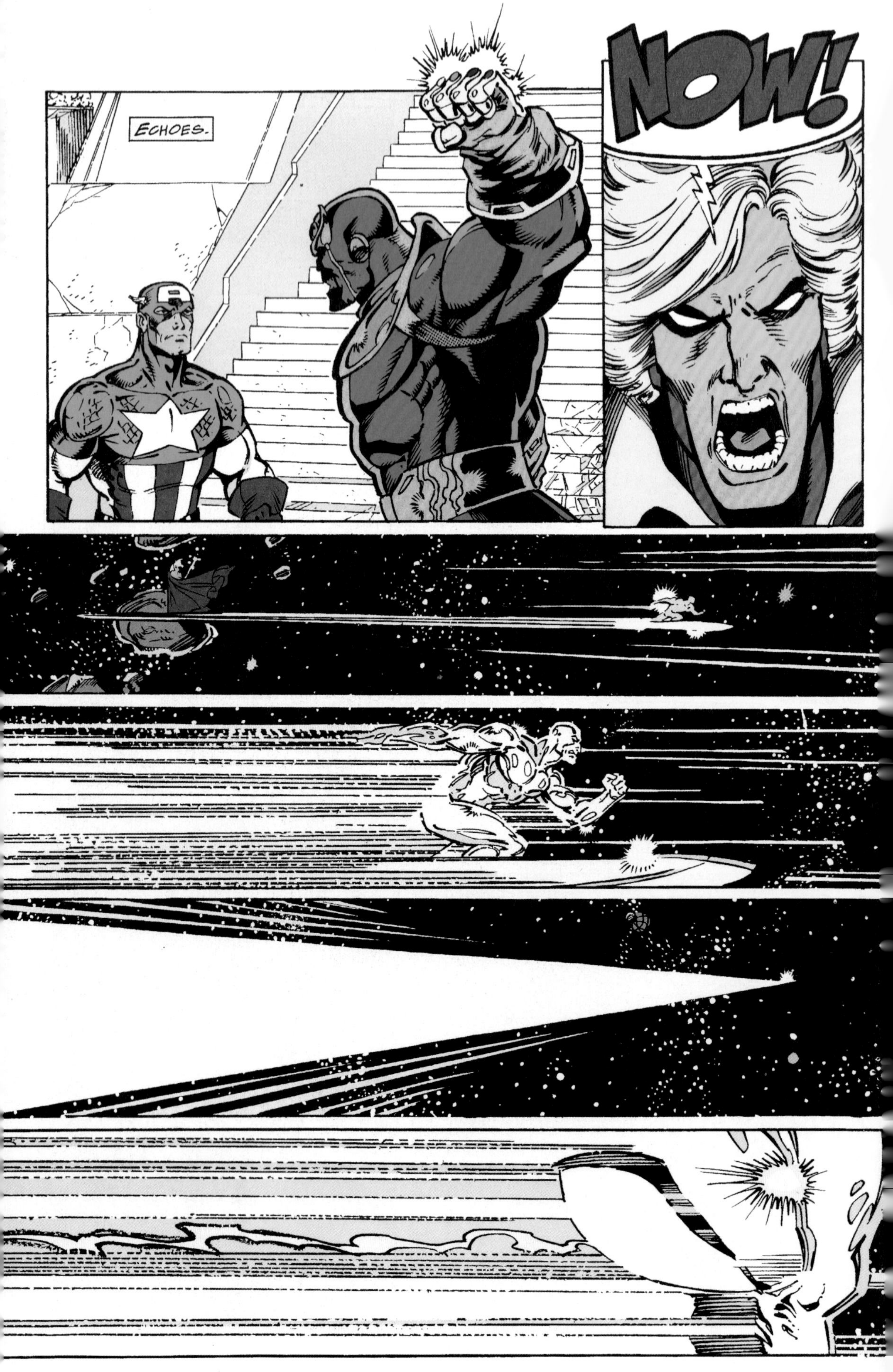
ECHOES.
NOW!

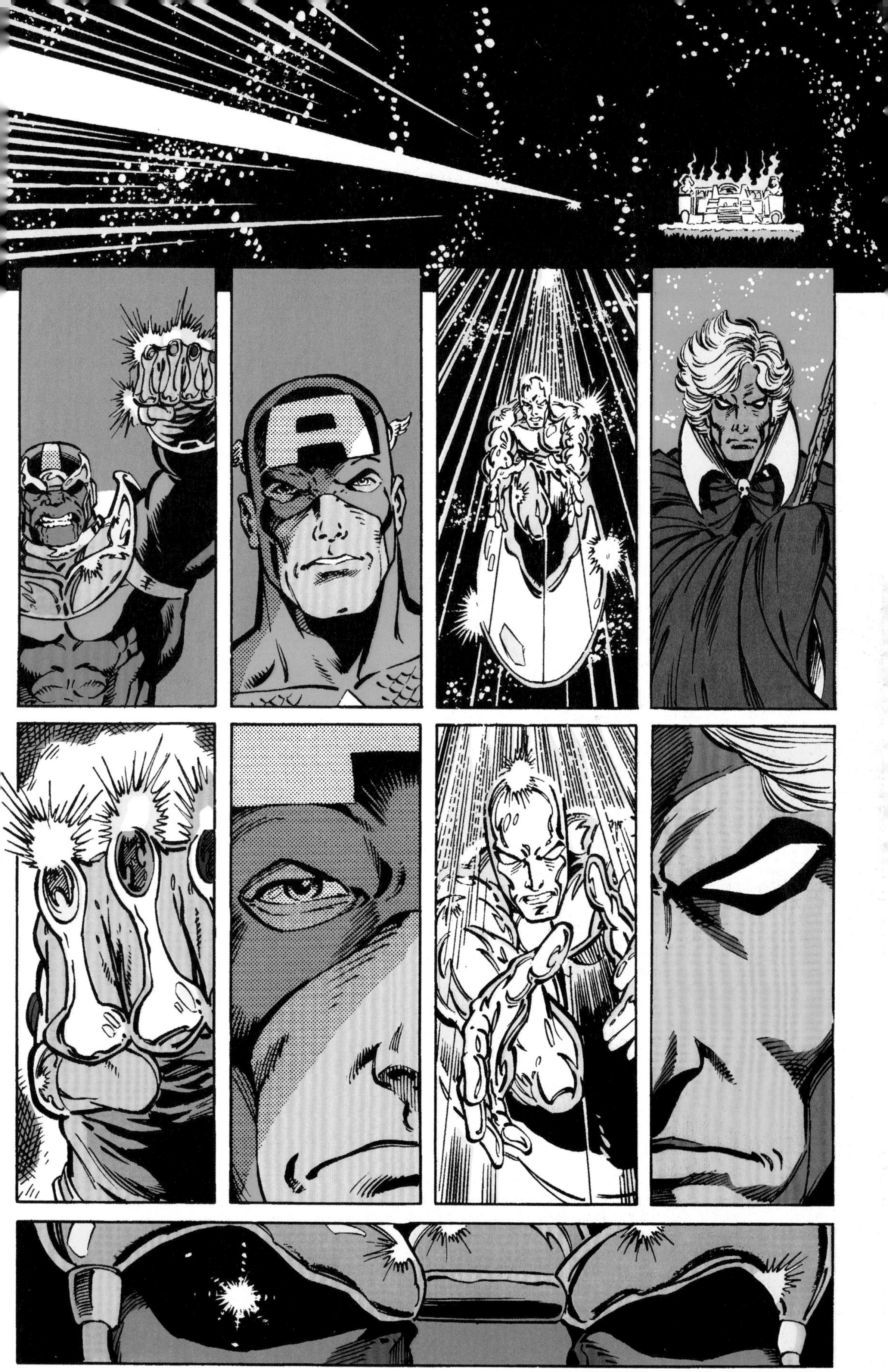

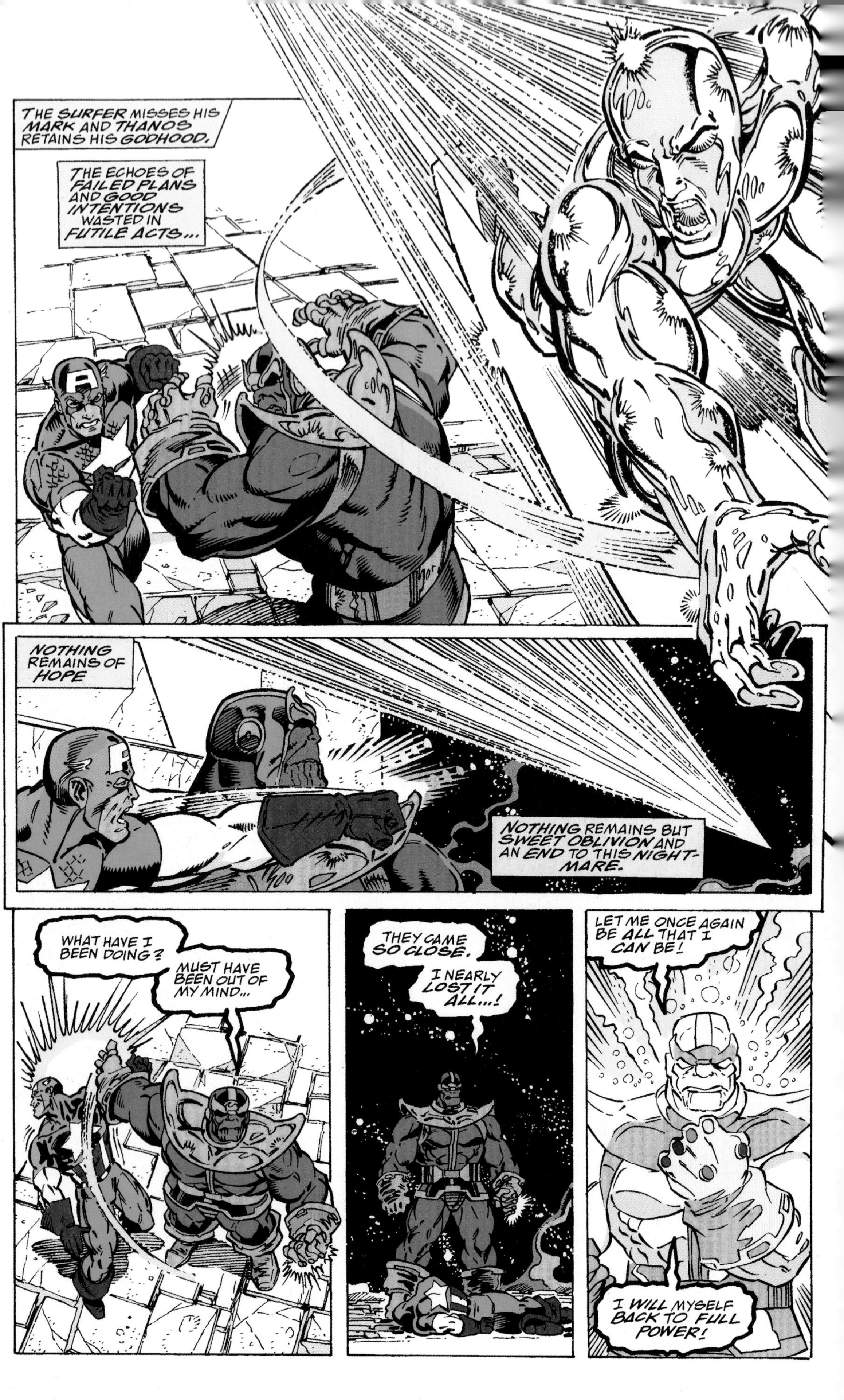
THE SURFER MISSES HIS MARK AND THANOS RETAINS HIS GODHOOD.
THE ECHOES OF FAILED PLANS AND GOOD INTENTIONS WASTED IN FUTILE ACTS...
NOTHING REMAINS OF HOPE
NOTHING REMAINS BUT SWEET OBLIVION AND AN END TO THIS NIGHT-MARE.
WHAT HAVE I BEEN DOING?
MUST HAVE BEEN OUT OF MY MIND...
THEY CAME SO CLOSE.
I NEARLY LOST IT ALL...!
LET ME ONCE AGAIN BE ALL THAT I CAN BE!
I WILL MYSELF BACK TO FULL POWER!

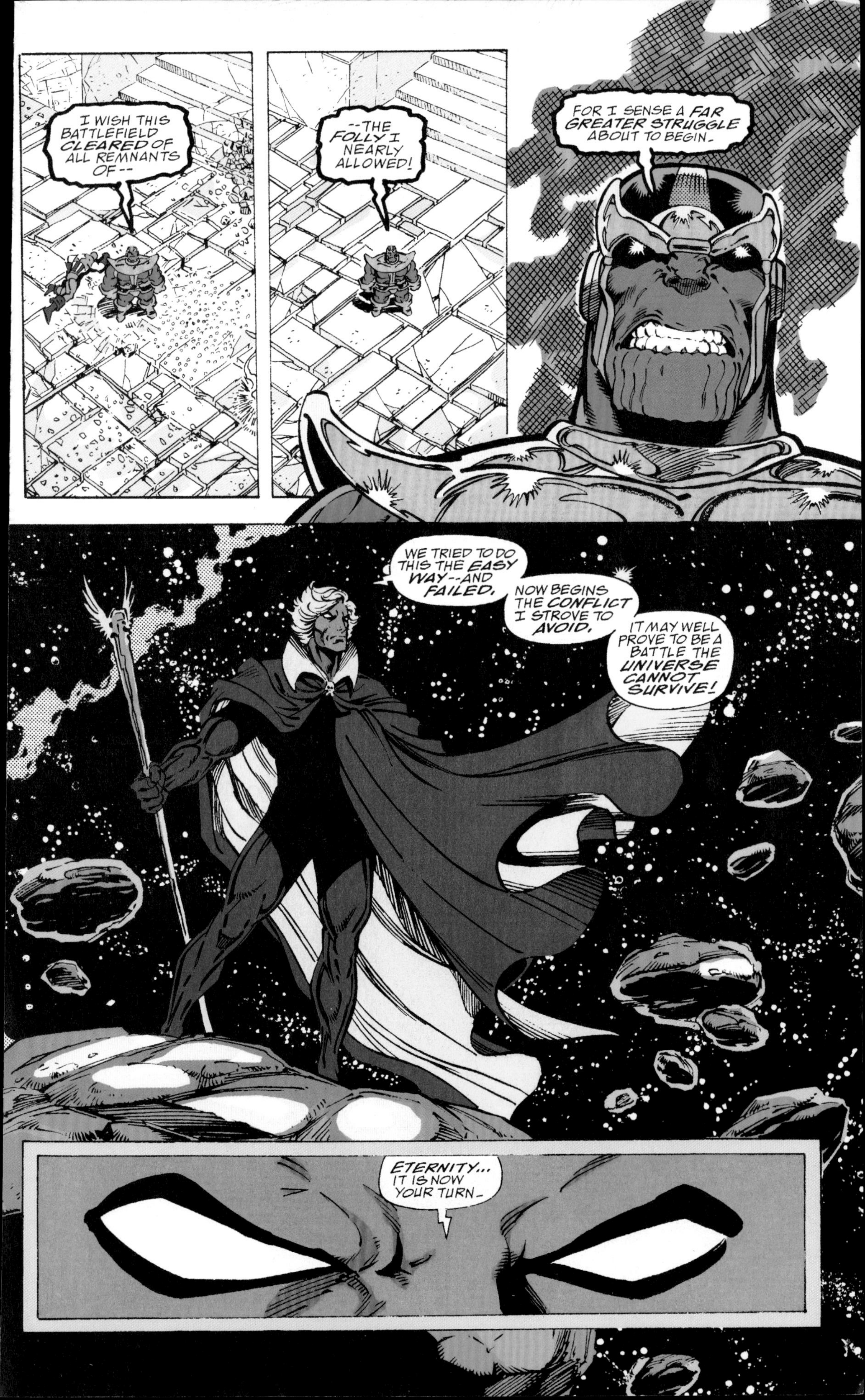
I WISH THIS BATTLEFIELD CLEARED OF ALL REMNANTS OF --
--THE FOLLY I NEARLY ALLOWED!
FOR I SENSE A FAR GREATER STRUGGLE ABOUT TO BEGIN.
WE TRIED TO DO THIS THE EASY WAY--AND FAILED.
NOW BEGINS THE CONFLICT I STROVE TO AVOID.
IT MAY WELL PROVE TO BE A BATTLE THE UNIVERSE CANNOT SURVIVE!
ETERNITY... IT IS NOW YOUR TURN.

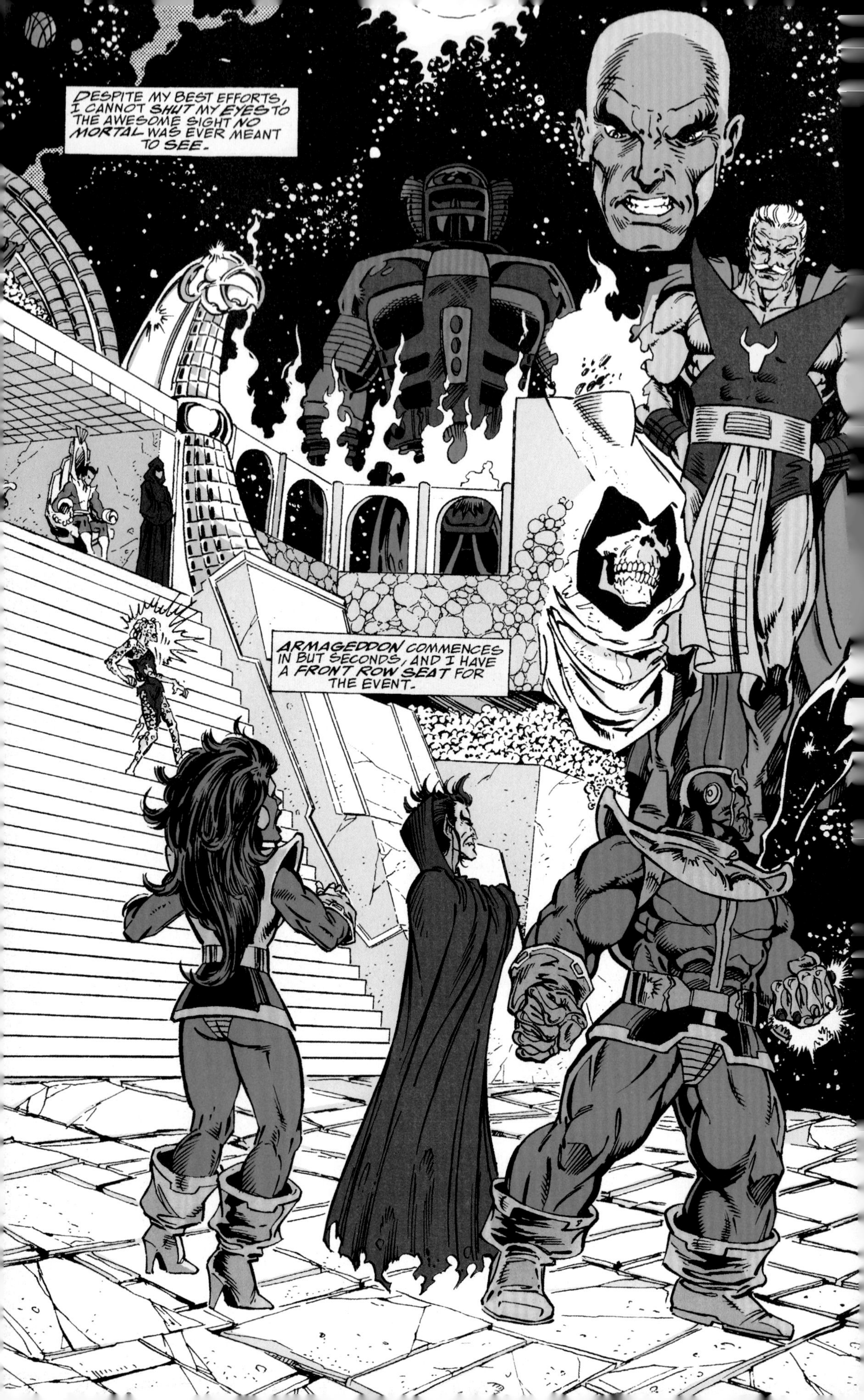
DESPITE MY BEST EFFORTS, I CANNOT SHUT MY EYES TO THE AWESOME SIGHT NO MORTAL WAS EVER MEANT TO SEE.
ARMAGEDDON COMMENCES IN BUT SECONDS, AND I HAVE A FRONT ROW SEAT FOR THE EVENT.

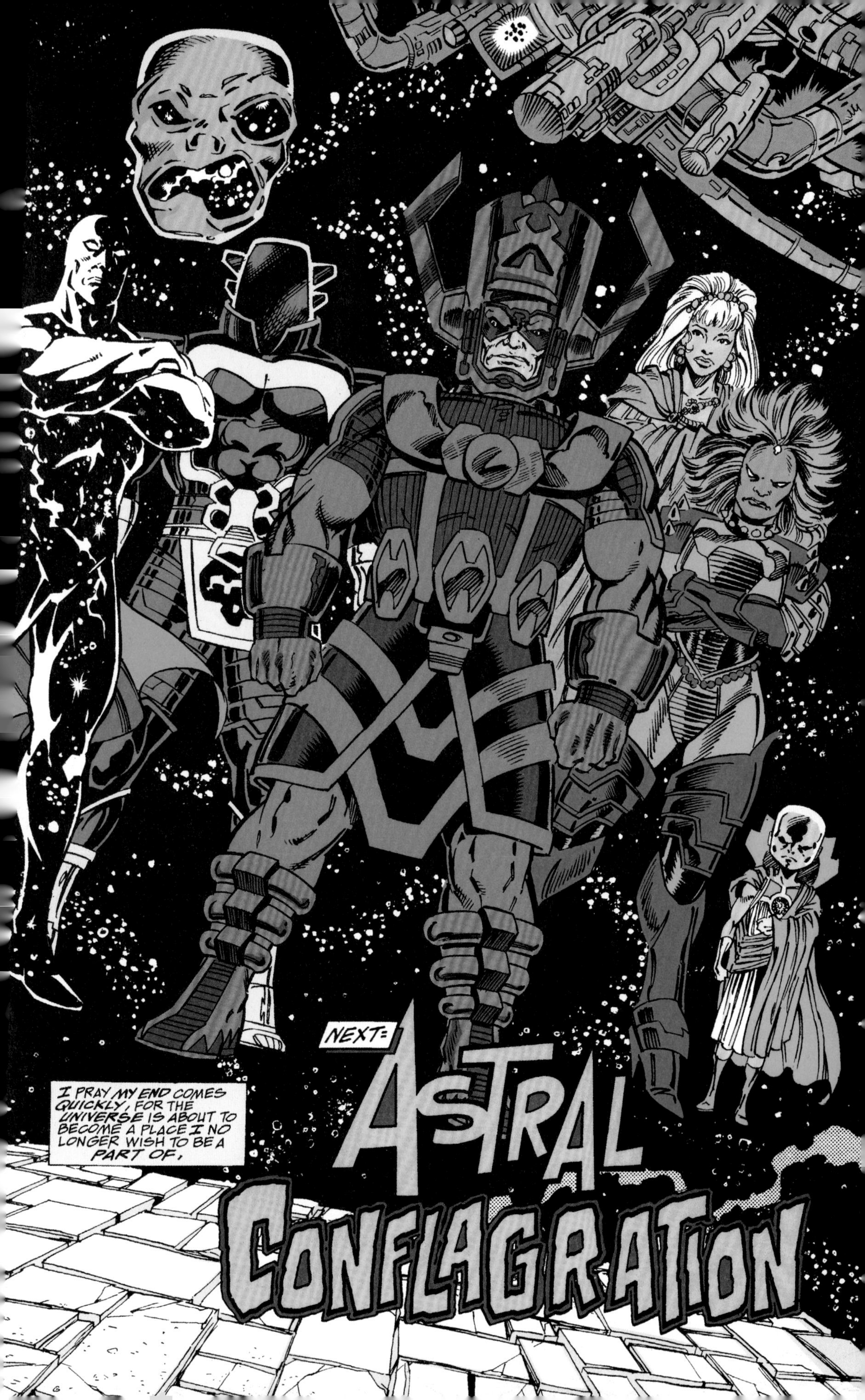

I PRAY MY END COMES QUICKLY, FOR THE UNIVERSE IS ABOUT TO BECOME A PLACE I NO LONGER WISH TO BE A PART OF.
NEXT: ASTRAL CONFLAGRATION

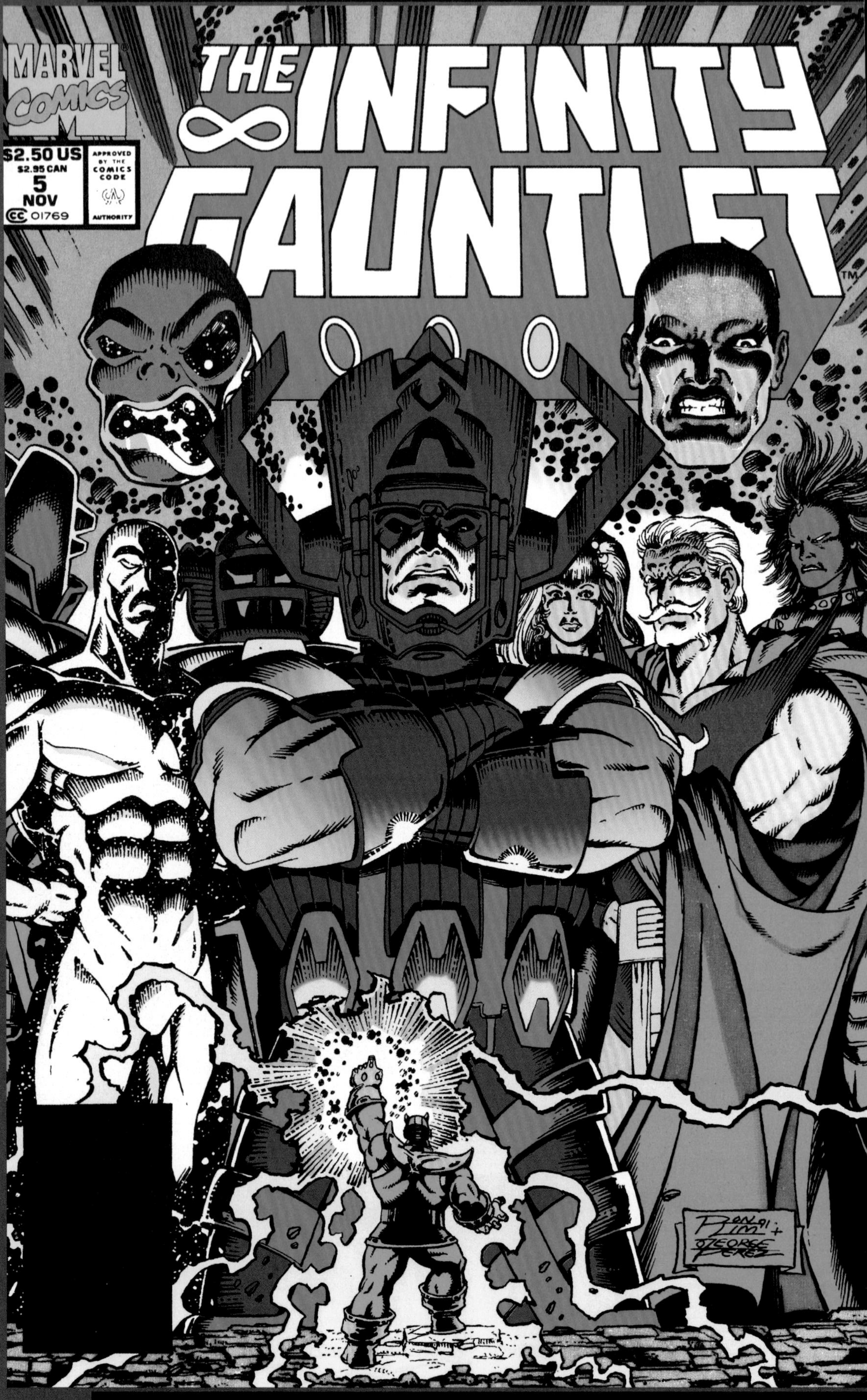
MARVEL COMICS
THE INFINITY GAUNTLET
$2.50 US
$2.95 CAN
5
NOV
01769
APPROVED BY THE COMICS CODE AUTHORITY

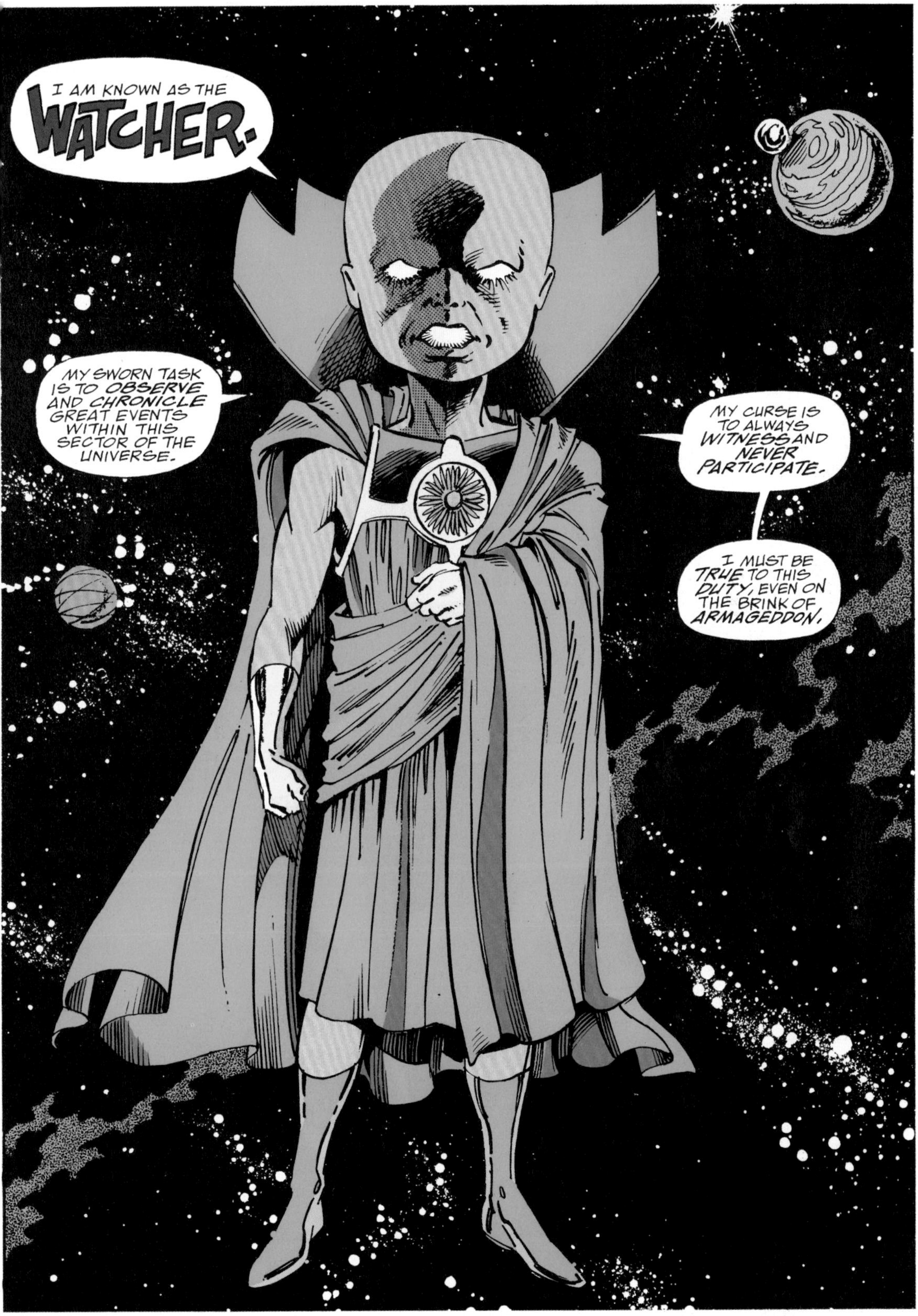
I AM KNOWN AS THE WATCHER.
MY SWORN TASK IS TO OBSERVE AND CHRONICLE GREAT EVENTS WITHIN THIS SECTOR OF THE UNIVERSE.
MY CURSE IS TO ALWAYS WITNESS AND NEVER PARTICIPATE.
I MUST BE TRUE TO THIS DUTY, EVEN ON THE BRINK OF ARMAGEDDON.

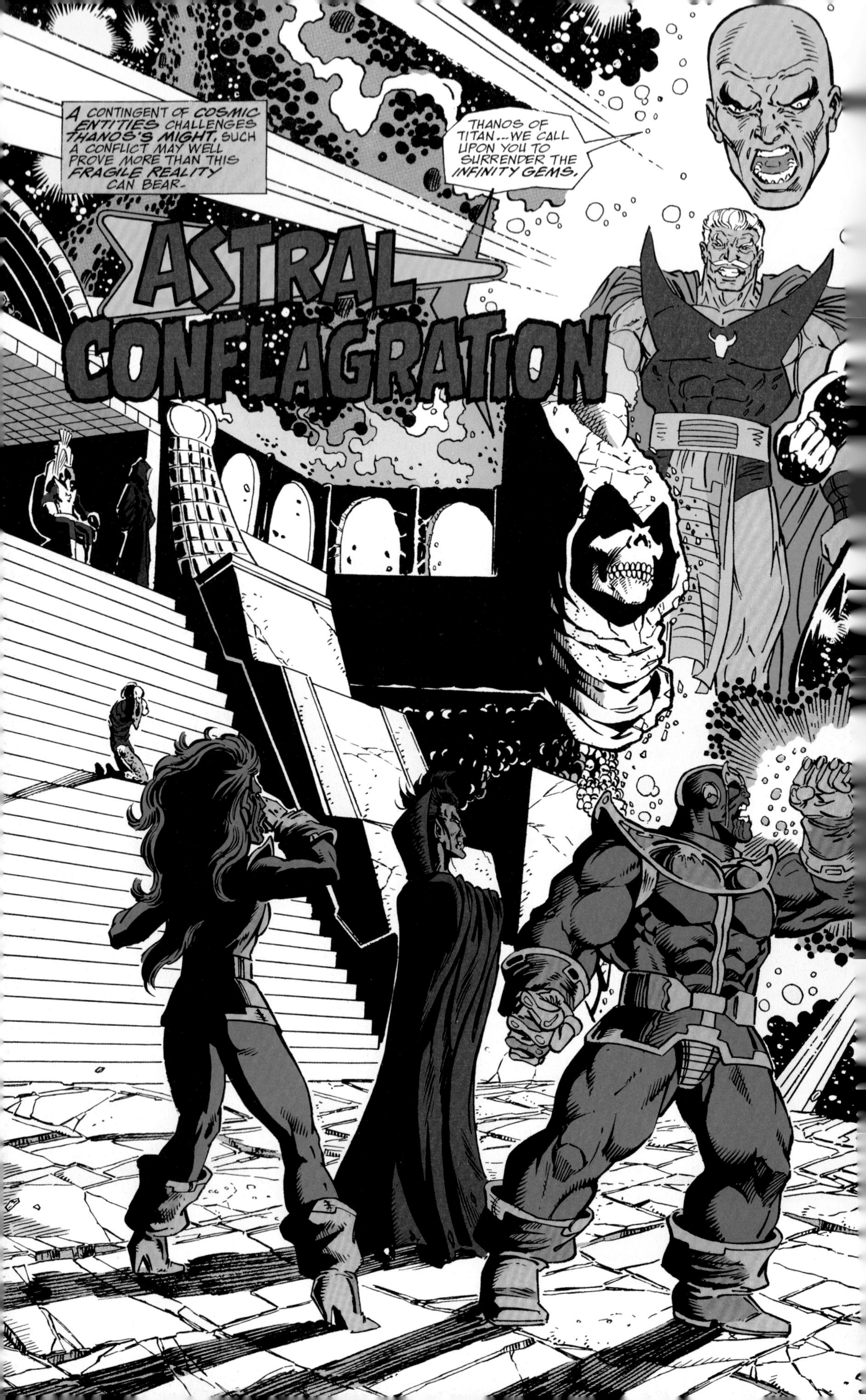
A CONTINGENT OF COSMIC ENTITIES CHALLENGES THANOS'S MIGHT. SUCH A CONFLICT MAY WELL PROVE MORE THAN THIS FRAGILE REALITY CAN BEAR--
THANOS OF TITAN--WE CALL UPON YOU TO SURRENDER THE INFINITY GEMS.
ASTRAL CONFLAGRATION

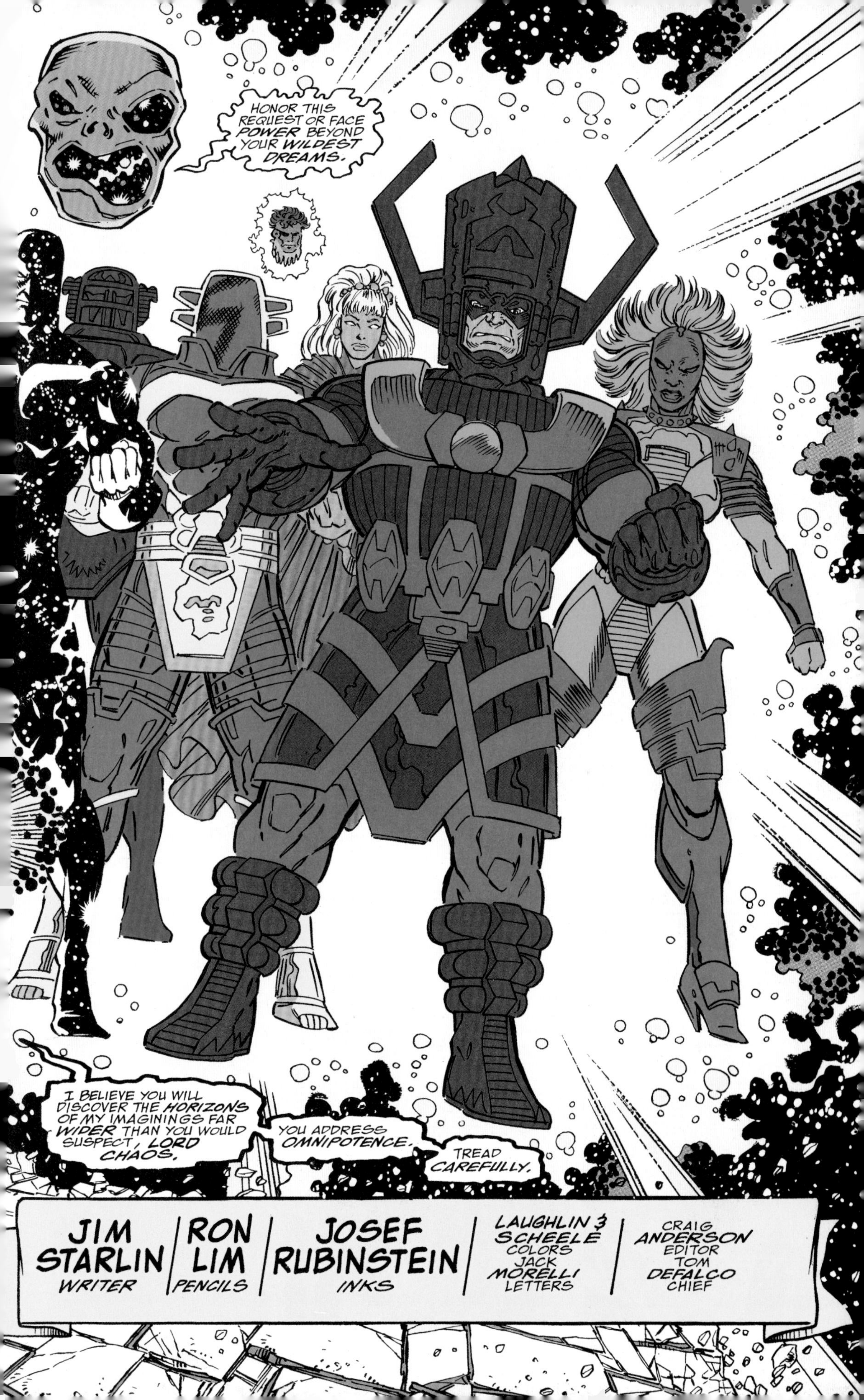
HONOR THIS REQUEST OR FACE POWER BEYOND YOUR WILDEST DREAMS.
I BELIEVE YOU WILL DISCOVER THE HORIZONS OF MY IMAGININGS FAR WIDER THAN YOU WOULD SUSPECT, LORD CHAOS.
YOU ADDRESS OMNIPOTENCE.
TREAD CAREFULLY.
JIM STARLIN WRITER
RON LIM PENCILS
JOSEF RUBINSTEIN INKS
LAUGHLIN & SCHEELE COLORS
JACK MORELLI LETTERS
CRAIG ANDERSON EDITOR
TOM DEFALCO CHIEF

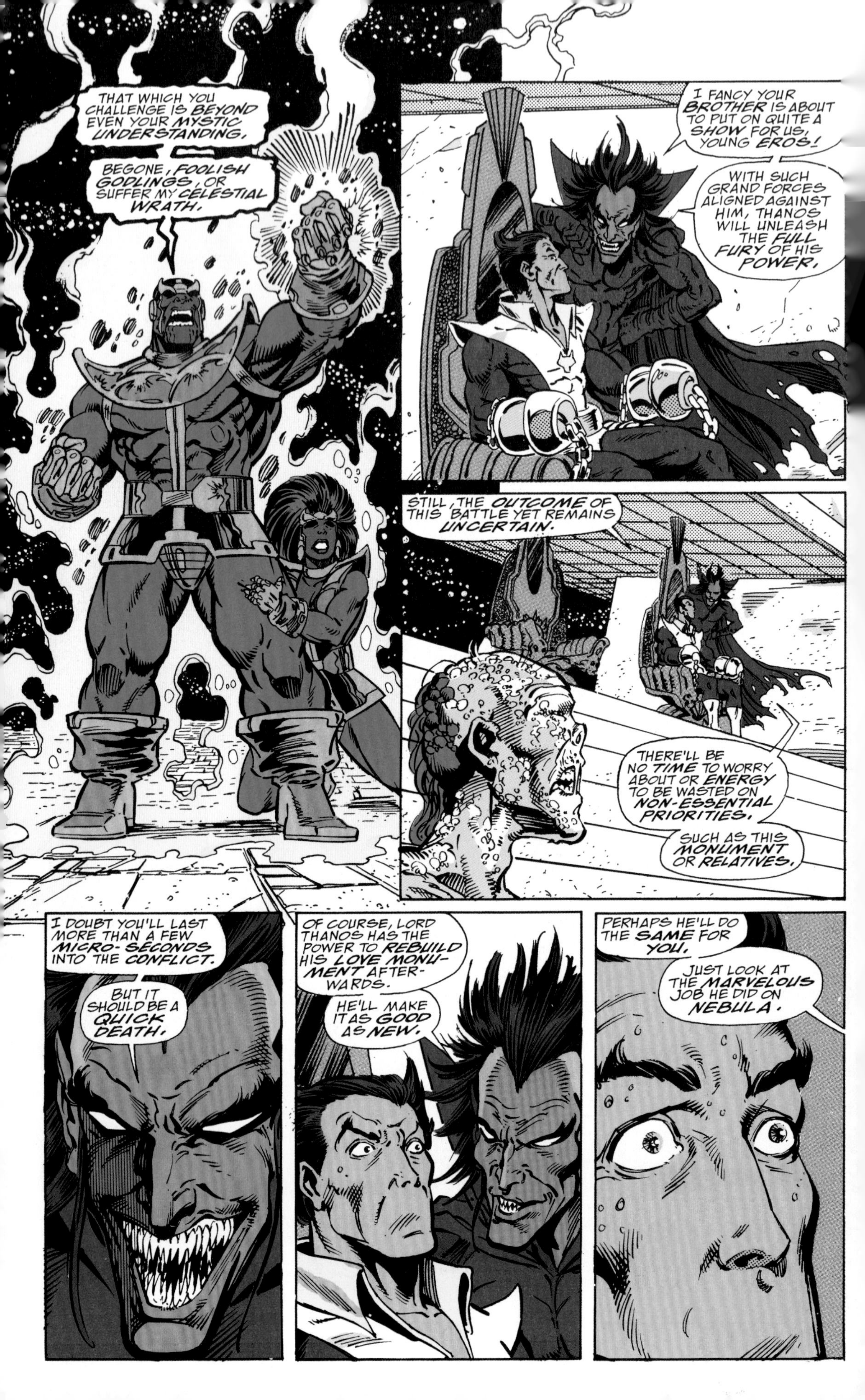
THAT WHICH YOU CHALLENGE IS BEYOND EVEN YOUR MYSTIC UNDERSTANDING.
BEGONE, FOOLISH GODLINGS, OR SUFFER MY CELESTIAL WRATH.
I FANCY YOUR BROTHER IS ABOUT TO PUT ON QUITE A SHOW FOR US, YOUNG EROS!
WITH SUCH GRAND FORCES ALIGNED AGAINST HIM, THANOS WILL UNLEASH THE FULL FURY OF HIS POWER.
STILL, THE OUTCOME OF THIS BATTLE YET REMAINS UNCERTAIN.
THERE'LL BE NO TIME TO WORRY ABOUT OR ENERGY TO BE WASTED ON NON-ESSENTIAL PRIORITIES.
SUCH AS THIS MONUMENT OR RELATIVES.
I DOUBT YOU'LL LAST MORE THAN A FEW MICRO-SECONDS INTO THE CONFLICT.
BUT IT SHOULD BE A QUICK DEATH.
OF COURSE, LORD THANOS HAS THE POWER TO REBUILD HIS LOVE MONUMENT AFTERWARDS.
HE'LL MAKE IT AS GOOD AS NEW.
PERHAPS HE'LL DO THE SAME FOR YOU.
JUST LOOK AT THE MARVELOUS JOB HE DID ON NEBULA.

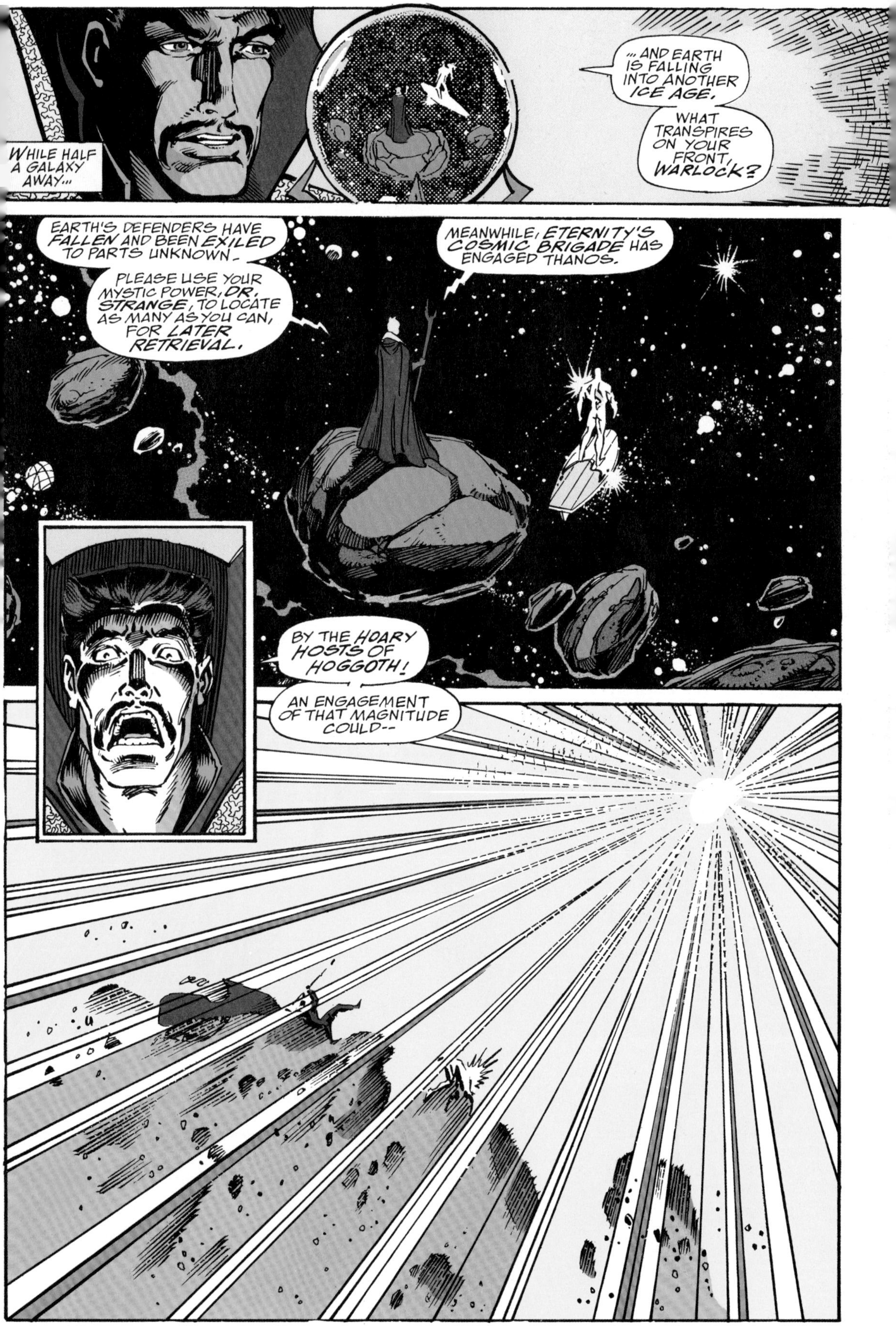
WHILE HALF A GALAXY AWAY...
...AND EARTH IS FALLING INTO ANOTHER ICE AGE.
WHAT TRANSPIRES ON YOUR FRONT, WARLOCK?
EARTH'S DEFENDERS HAVE FALLEN AND BEEN EXILED TO PARTS UNKNOWN.
PLEASE USE YOUR MYSTIC POWER, DR. STRANGE, TO LOCATE AS MANY AS YOU CAN, FOR LATER RETRIEVAL.
MEANWHILE, ETERNITY'S COSMIC BRIGADE HAS ENGAGED THANOS.
BY THE HOARY HOSTS OF HOGGOTH!
AN ENGAGEMENT OF THAT MAGNITUDE COULD--

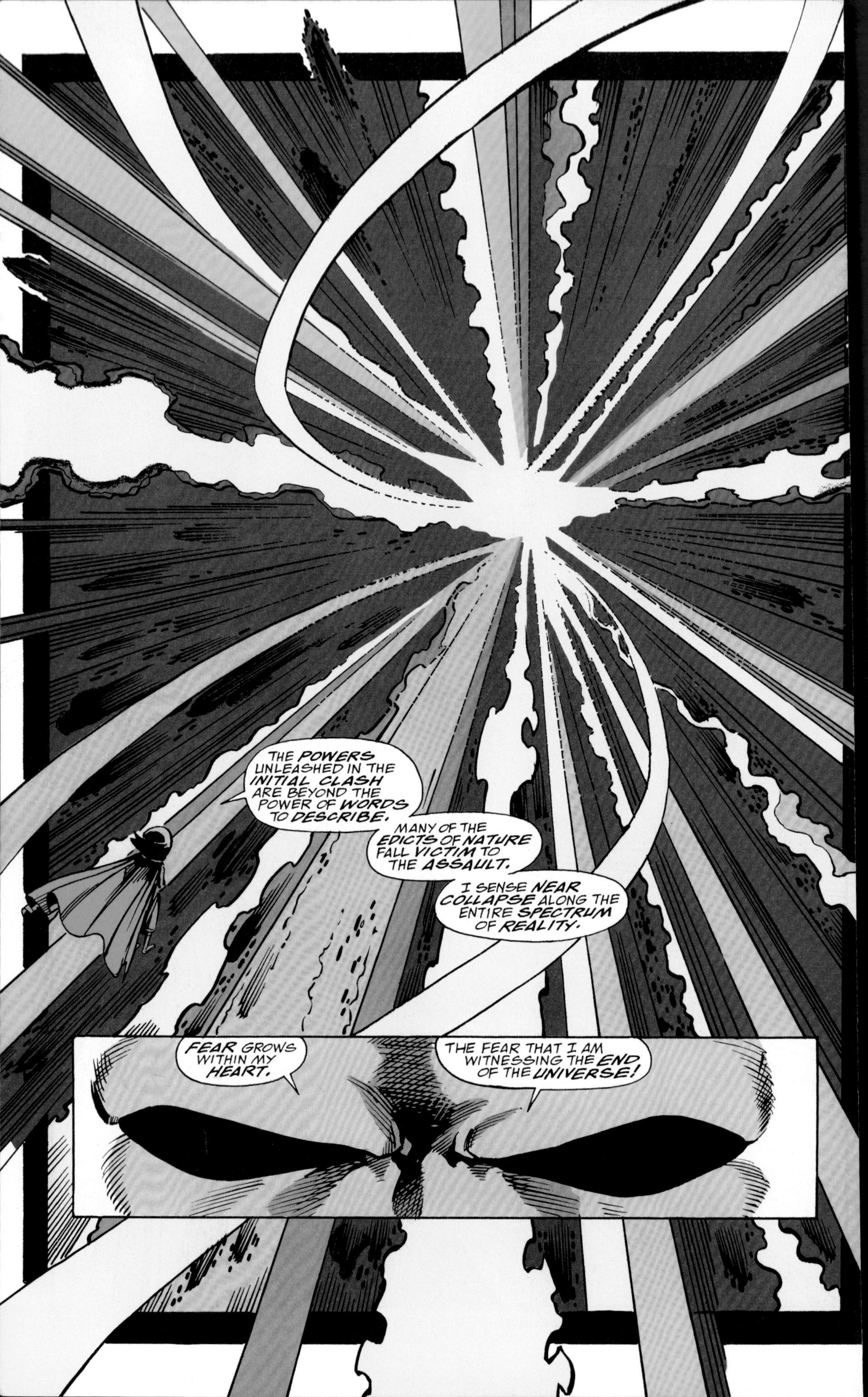
THE POWERS UNLEASHED IN THE INITIAL CLASH ARE BEYOND THE POWER OF WORDS TO DESCRIBE.
MANY OF THE EDICTS OF NATURE FALL VICTIM TO THE ASSAULT.
I SENSE NEAR COLLAPSE ALONG THE ENTIRE SPECTRUM OF REALITY.
FEAR GROWS WITHIN MY HEART.
THE FEAR THAT I AM WITNESSING THE END OF THE UNIVERSE!

ENTIRE *SOLAR SYSTEMS* IN THE IMMEDIATE VICINITY ARE *RAVAGED* BY THE EFFECTS OF THIS *CELESTIAL CLASH.*

'CALCULATING THE *BILLIONS* OF LIVES LOST AS A RESULT OF THIS CONFRONTATION WILL HAVE TO *WAIT.*

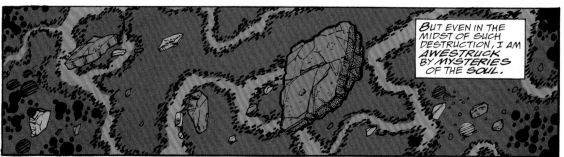

BUT EVEN IN THE MIDST OF SUCH *DESTRUCTION,* I AM *AWESTRUCK* BY *MYSTERIES OF THE SOUL.*

THE TITAN, *EROS,* FELT CERTAIN THAT *DEATH* WAS NEAR TO CLAIMING HIM·

THE ONLY THING GREATER THAN HIS *SURPRISE* AT FINDING HIM-SELF AMONG THE *LIVING*...

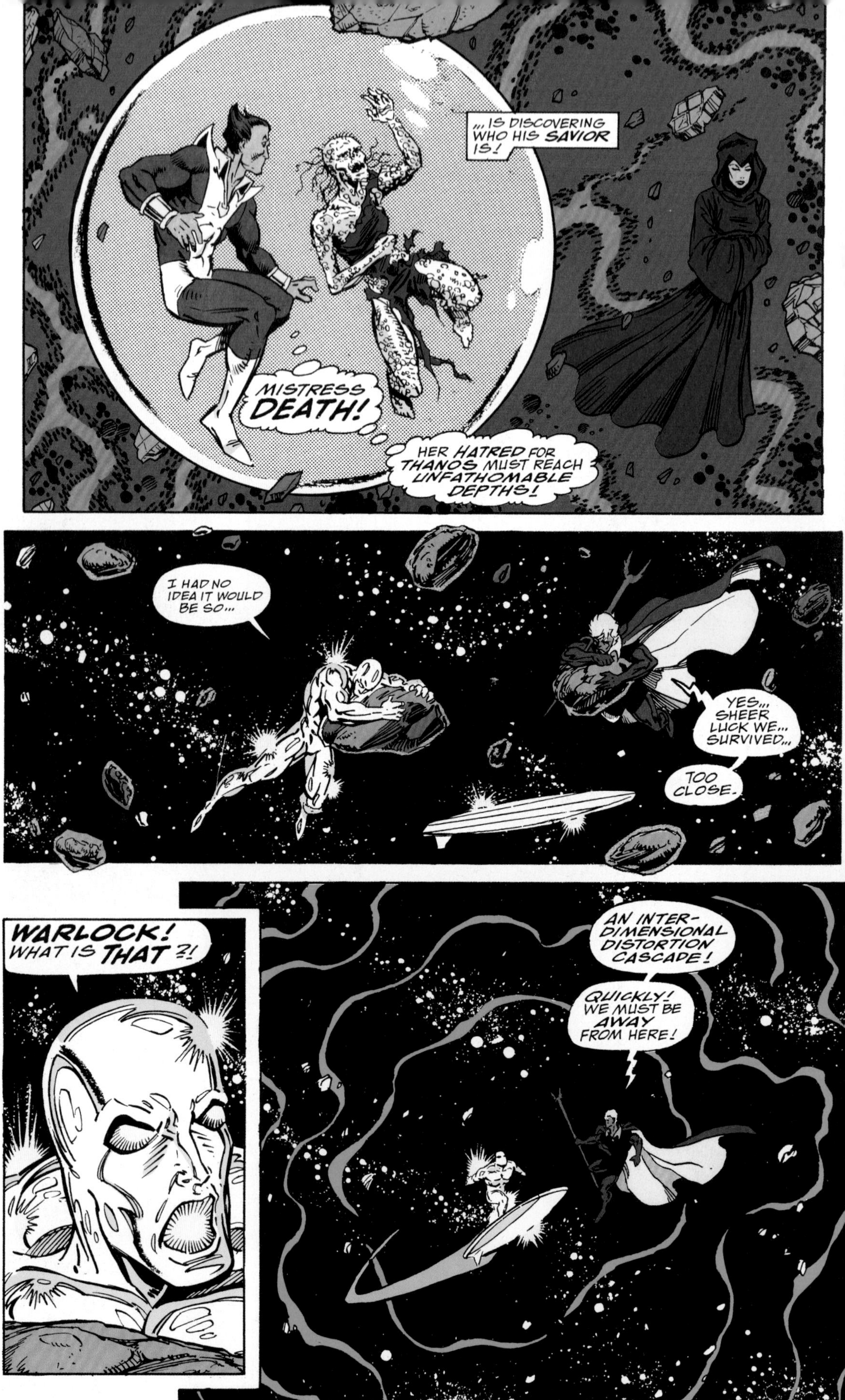
...IS DISCOVERING WHO HIS SAVIOR IS!
MISTRESS DEATH!
HER HATRED FOR THANOS MUST REACH UNFATHOMABLE DEPTHS!
I HAD NO IDEA IT WOULD BE SO...
YES... SHEER LUCK WE... SURVIVED...
TOO CLOSE.
WARLOCK! WHAT IS THAT?!
AN INTER-DIMENSIONAL DISTORTION CASCADE!
QUICKLY! WE MUST BE AWAY FROM HERE!

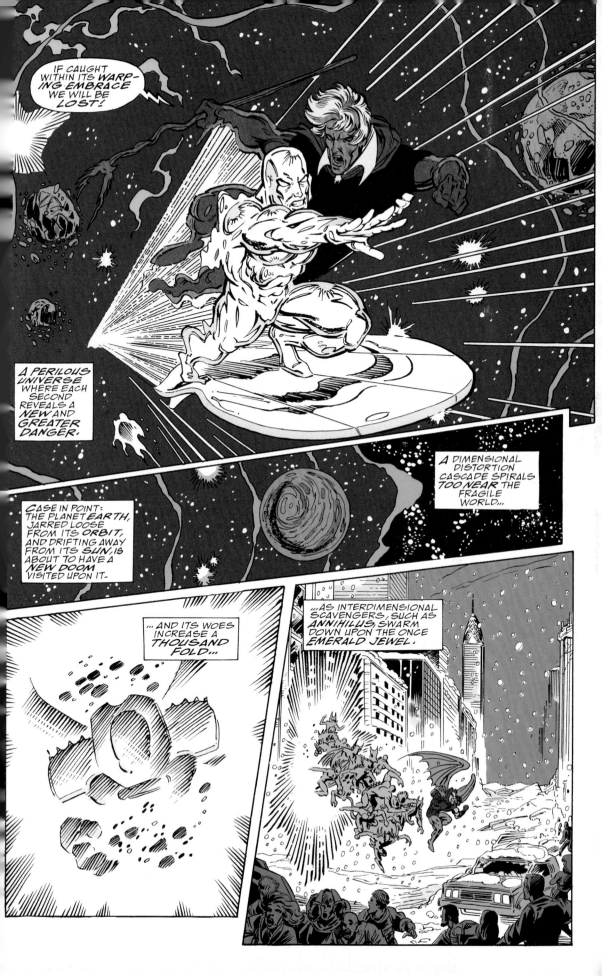

IF CAUGHT WITHIN ITS *WARPING* EMBRACE WE WILL BE *LOST!*

A PERILOUS UNIVERSE WHERE EACH SECOND REVEALS A *NEW* AND *GREATER DANGER.*

CASE IN POINT: THE PLANET *EARTH,* JARRED LOOSE FROM ITS *ORBIT,* AND DRIFTING AWAY FROM ITS *SUN,* IS ABOUT TO HAVE A *NEW DOOM* VISITED UPON IT—

A DIMENSIONAL DISTORTION CASCADE SPIRALS *TOO NEAR* THE FRAGILE WORLD...

...AND ITS WOES INCREASE A *THOUSAND FOLD*...

...AS INTERDIMENSIONAL SCAVENGERS, SUCH AS *ANNIHILUS,* SWARM DOWN UPON THE ONCE *EMERALD JEWEL.*

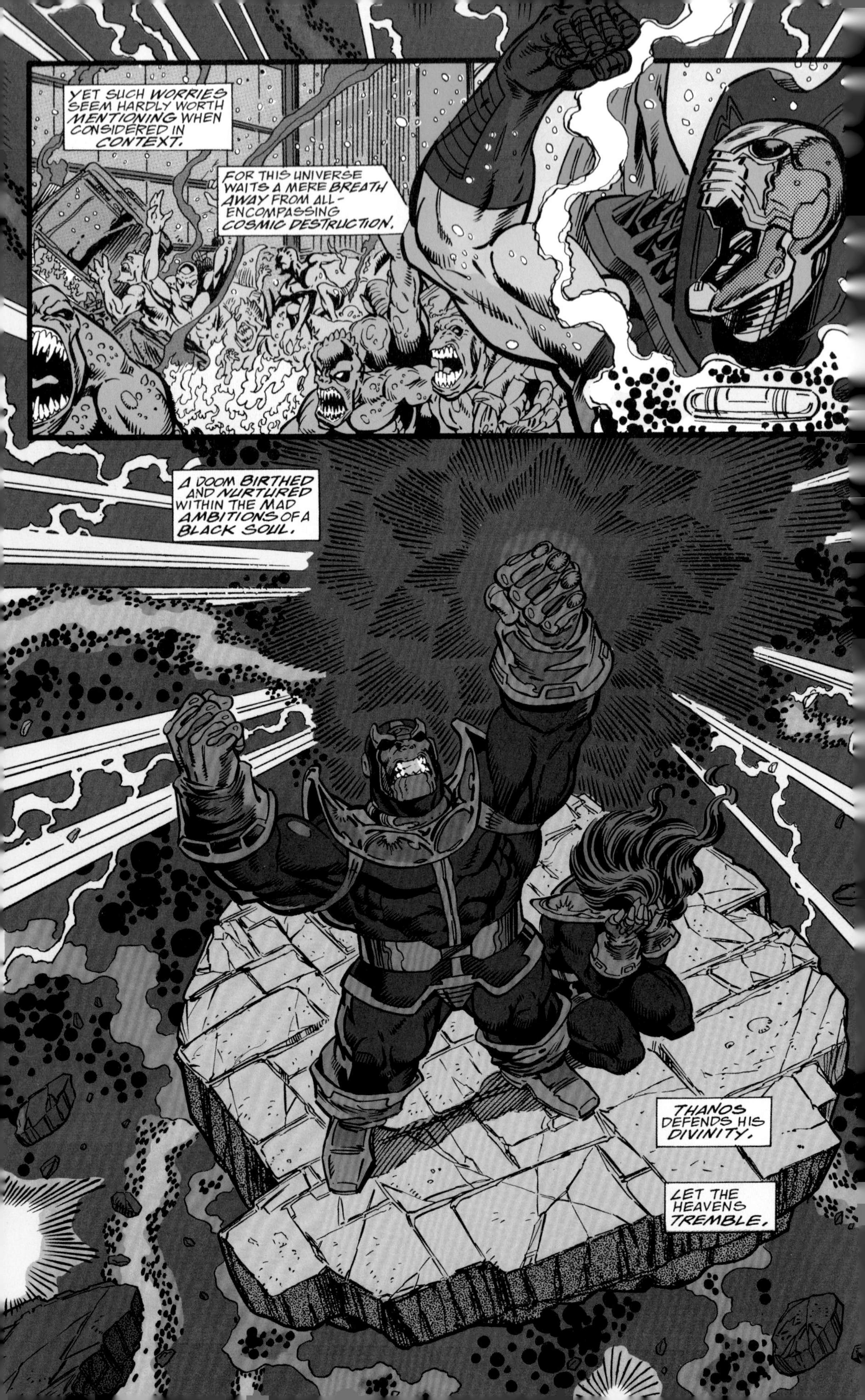
YET SUCH WORRIES SEEM HARDLY WORTH MENTIONING WHEN CONSIDERED IN CONTEXT.
FOR THIS UNIVERSE WAITS A MERE BREATH AWAY FROM ALL-ENCOMPASSING COSMIC DESTRUCTION.
A DOOM BIRTHED AND NURTURED WITHIN THE MAD AMBITIONS OF A BLACK SOUL.
THANOS DEFENDS HIS DIVINITY.
LET THE HEAVENS TREMBLE.

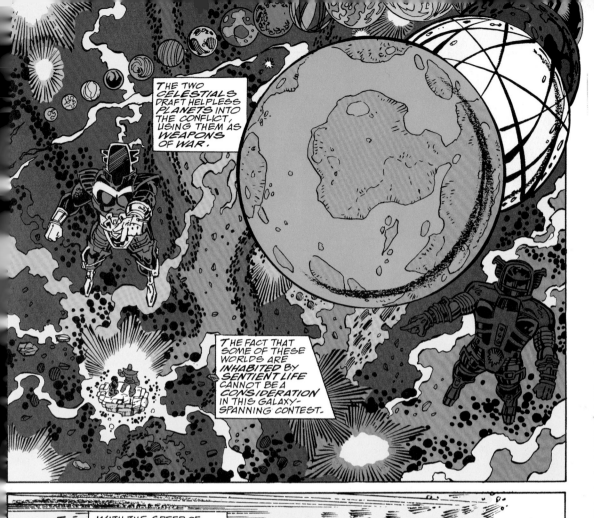

THE TWO *CELESTIALS* DRAFT HELPLESS *PLANETS* INTO THE CONFLICT, USING THEM AS *WEAPONS* OF WAR.

*T*HE FACT THAT SOME OF THESE WORLDS ARE *INHABITED* BY *SENTIENT* LIFE CANNOT BE A *CONSIDERATION* IN THIS GALAXY-SPANNING CONTEST.

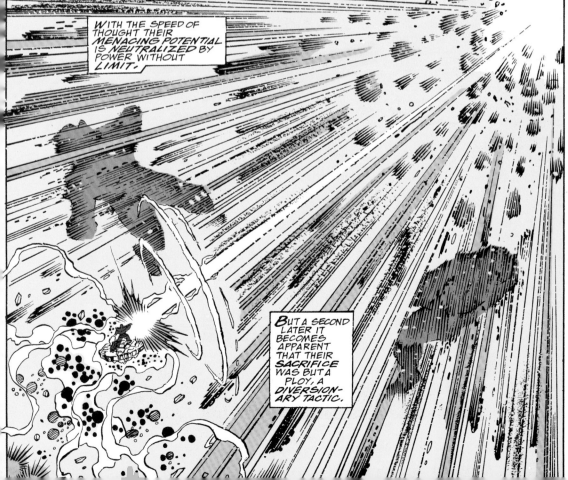

WITH THE SPEED OF *THOUGHT* THEIR *MENACING* POTENTIAL IS *NEUTRALIZED* BY *POWER* WITHOUT *LIMIT*.

BUT A SECOND LATER IT BECOMES APPARENT THAT THEIR *SACRIFICE* WAS BUT A *PLOY*, A *DIVERSION-ARY TACTIC*.

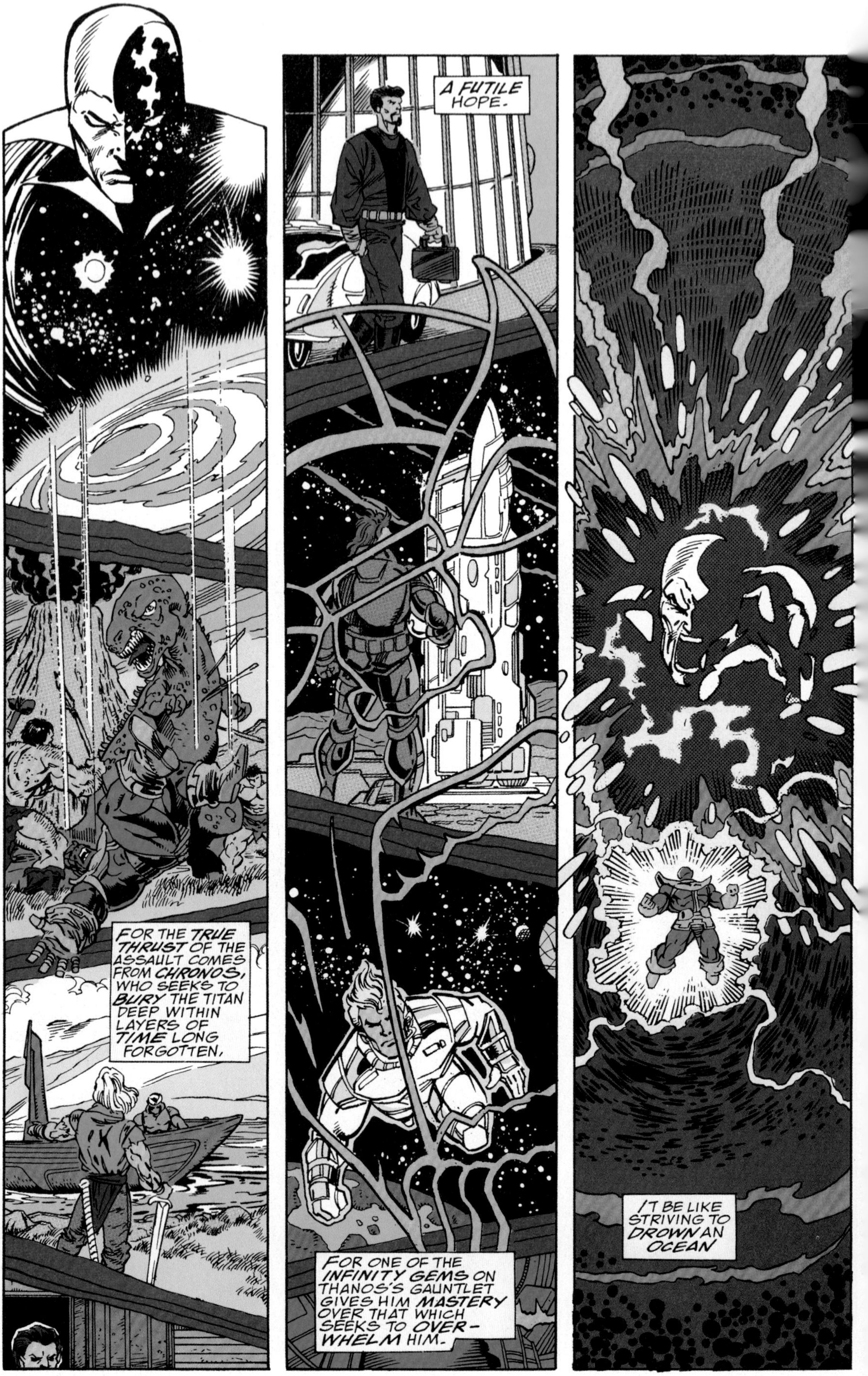

FOR THE TRUE THRUST OF THE ASSAULT COMES FROM CHRONOS, WHO SEEKS TO BURY THE TITAN DEEP WITHIN LAYERS OF TIME LONG FORGOTTEN.
A FUTILE HOPE.
FOR ONE OF THE INFINITY GEMS ON THANOS'S GAUNTLET GIVES HIM MASTERY OVER THAT WHICH SEEKS TO OVER-WHELM HIM.
IT BE LIKE STRIVING TO DROWN AN OCEAN

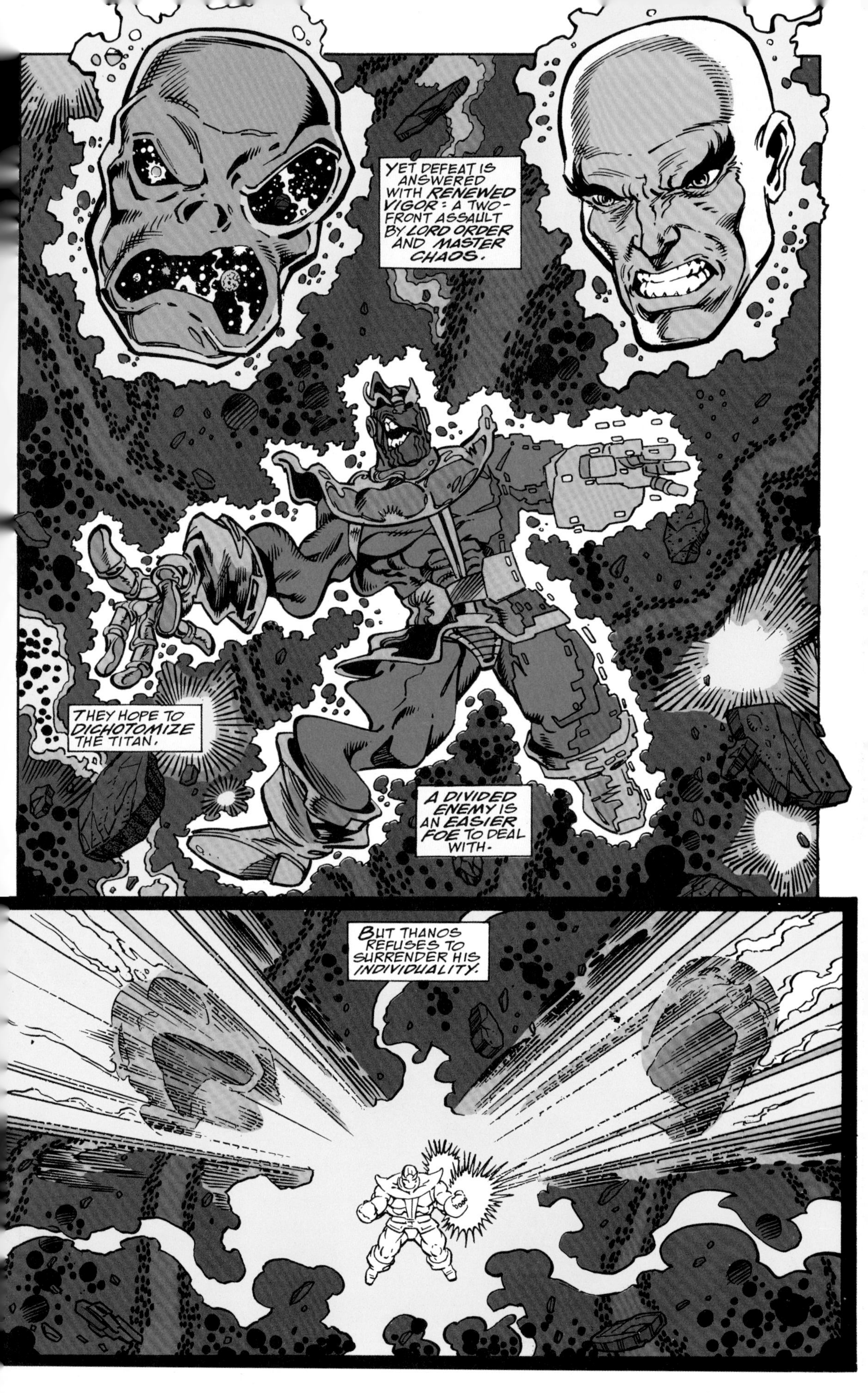
YET DEFEAT IS ANSWERED WITH RENEWED VIGOR: A TWO-FRONT ASSAULT BY LORD ORDER AND MASTER CHAOS.
THEY HOPE TO DICHOTOMIZE THE TITAN.
A DIVIDED ENEMY IS AN EASIER FOE TO DEAL WITH.
BUT THANOS REFUSES TO SURRENDER HIS INDIVIDUALITY.

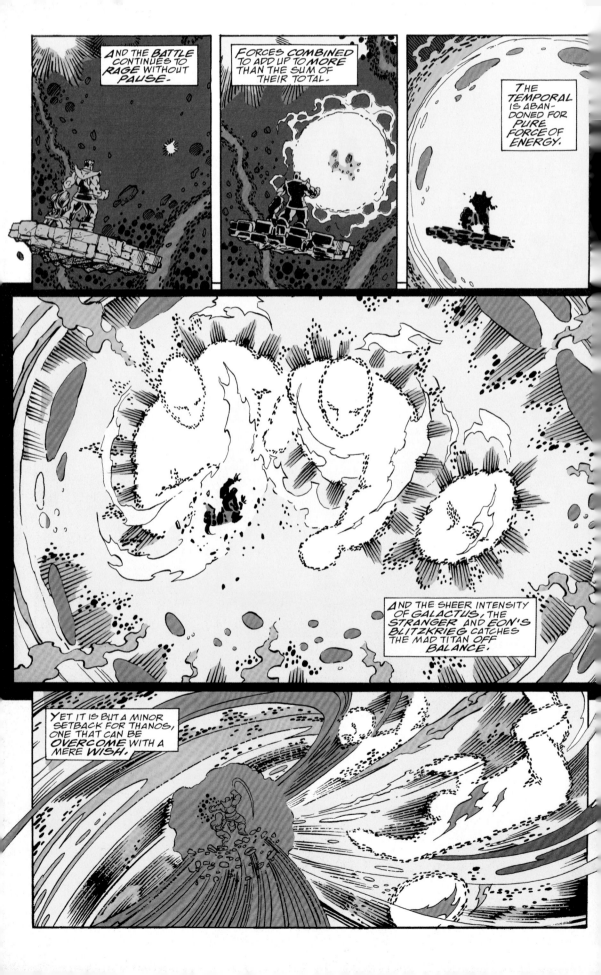

AND THE BATTLE CONTINUES TO *RAGE* WITHOUT *PAUSE.*

FORCES COMBINED TO ADD UP TO *MORE* THAN THE *SUM* OF THEIR *TOTAL.*

THE *TEMPORAL* IS ABANDONED FOR PURE FORCE OF ENERGY.

AND THE SHEER INTENSITY OF *GALACTUS*, THE *STRANGER* AND *EON'S BLITZKRIEG* CATCHES THE *MAD TITAN* OFF *BALANCE.*

YET IT IS BUT A MINOR SETBACK FOR *THANOS,* ONE THAT CAN BE *OVERCOME* WITH A MERE *WISH.*

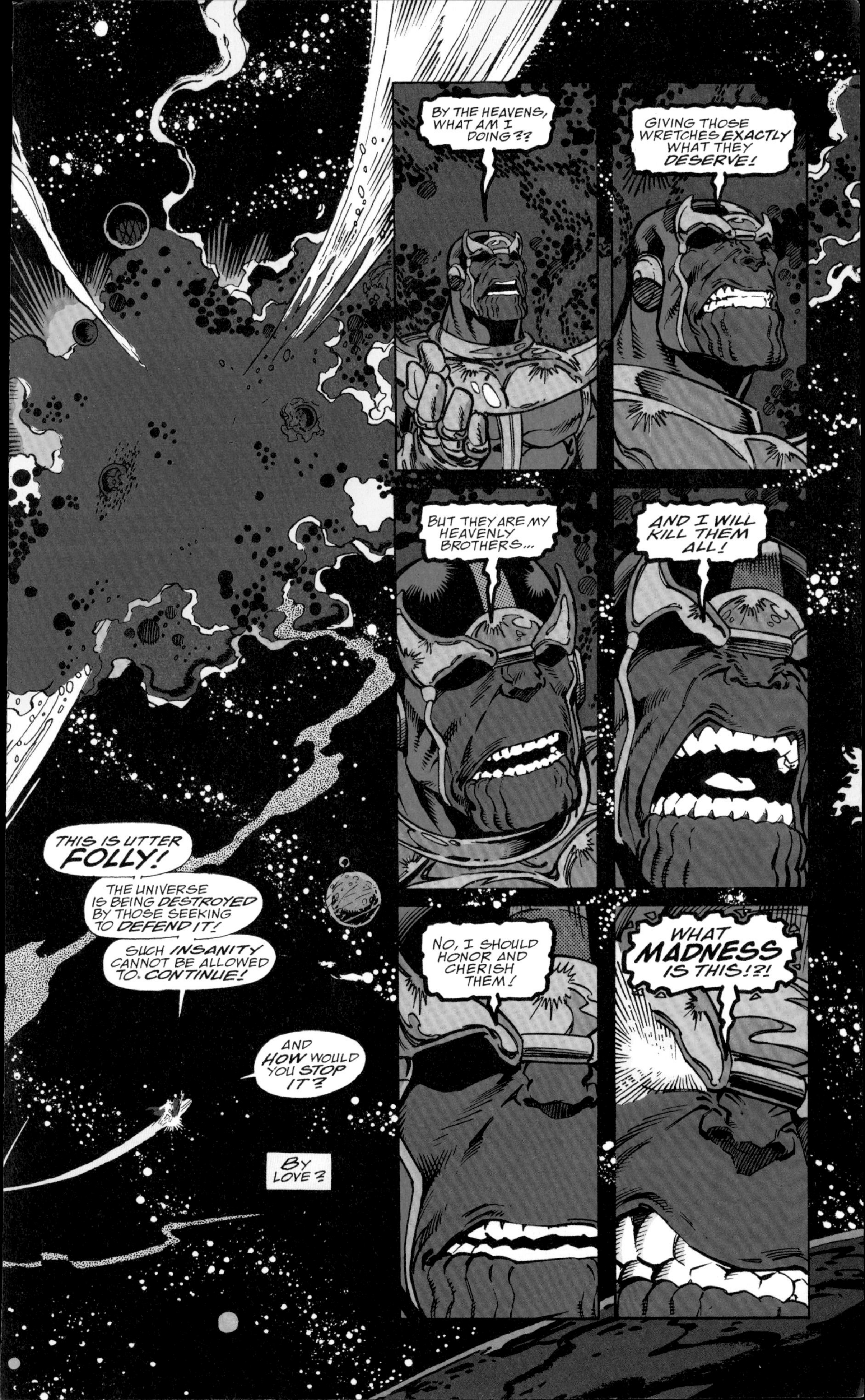
BY THE HEAVENS, WHAT AM I DOING ??
GIVING THOSE WRETCHES EXACTLY WHAT THEY DESERVE!
BUT THEY ARE MY HEAVENLY BROTHERS...
AND I WILL KILL THEM ALL!
THIS IS UTTER FOLLY!
THE UNIVERSE IS BEING DESTROYED BY THOSE SEEKING TO DEFEND IT!
SUCH INSANITY CANNOT BE ALLOWED TO CONTINUE!
AND HOW WOULD YOU STOP IT?
BY LOVE?
NO, I SHOULD HONOR AND CHERISH THEM!
WHAT MADNESS IS THIS!?!

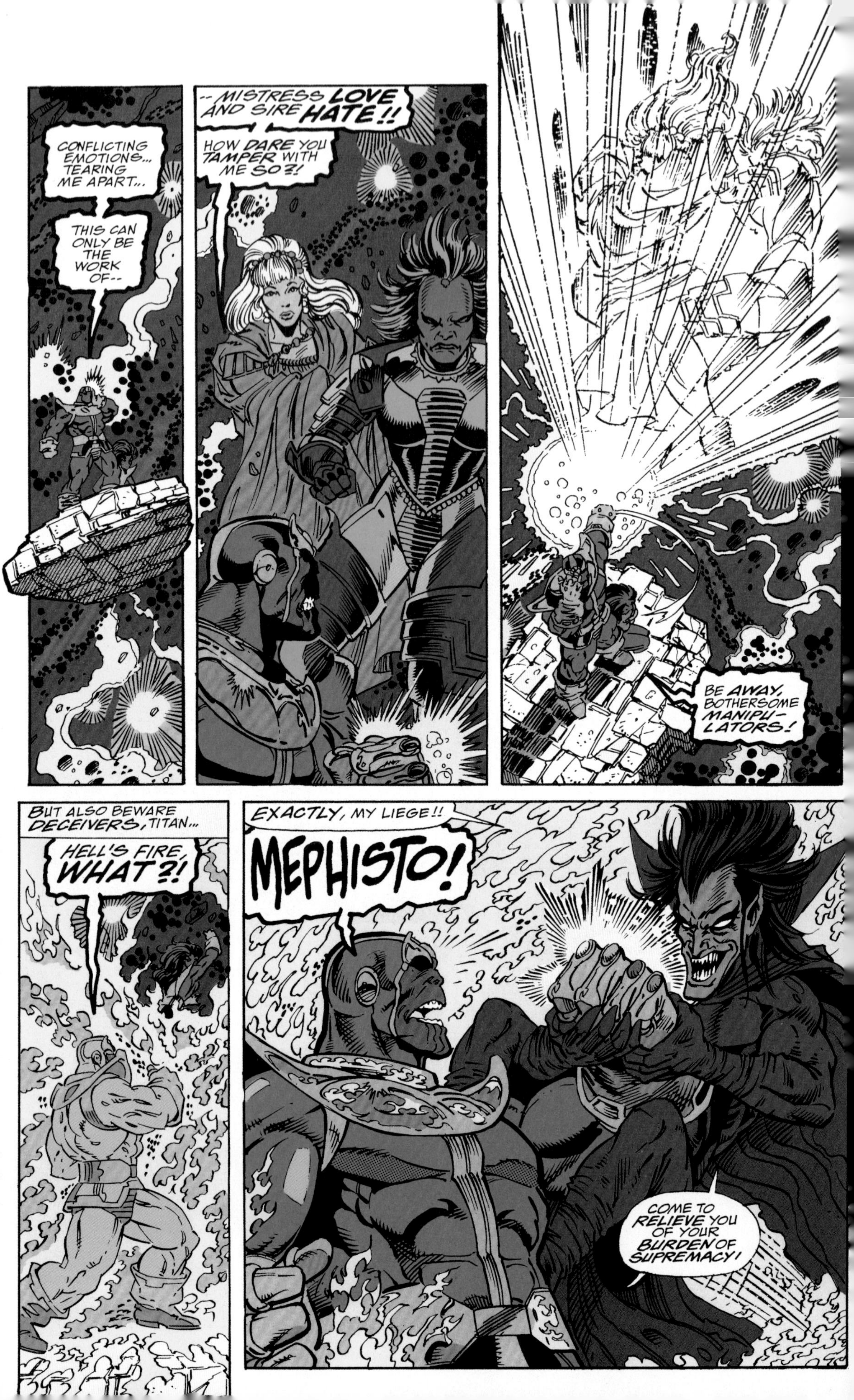
CONFLICTING EMOTIONS... TEARING ME APART...
THIS CAN ONLY BE THE WORK OF--
--MISTRESS LOVE AND SIRE HATE!!
HOW DARE YOU TAMPER WITH ME SO?!
BE AWAY, BOTHERSOME MANIPULATORS!
BUT ALSO BEWARE DECEIVERS, TITAN...
HELL'S FIRE, WHAT?!
EXACTLY, MY LIEGE!!
MEPHISTO!
COME TO RELIEVE YOU OF YOUR BURDEN OF SUPREMACY!

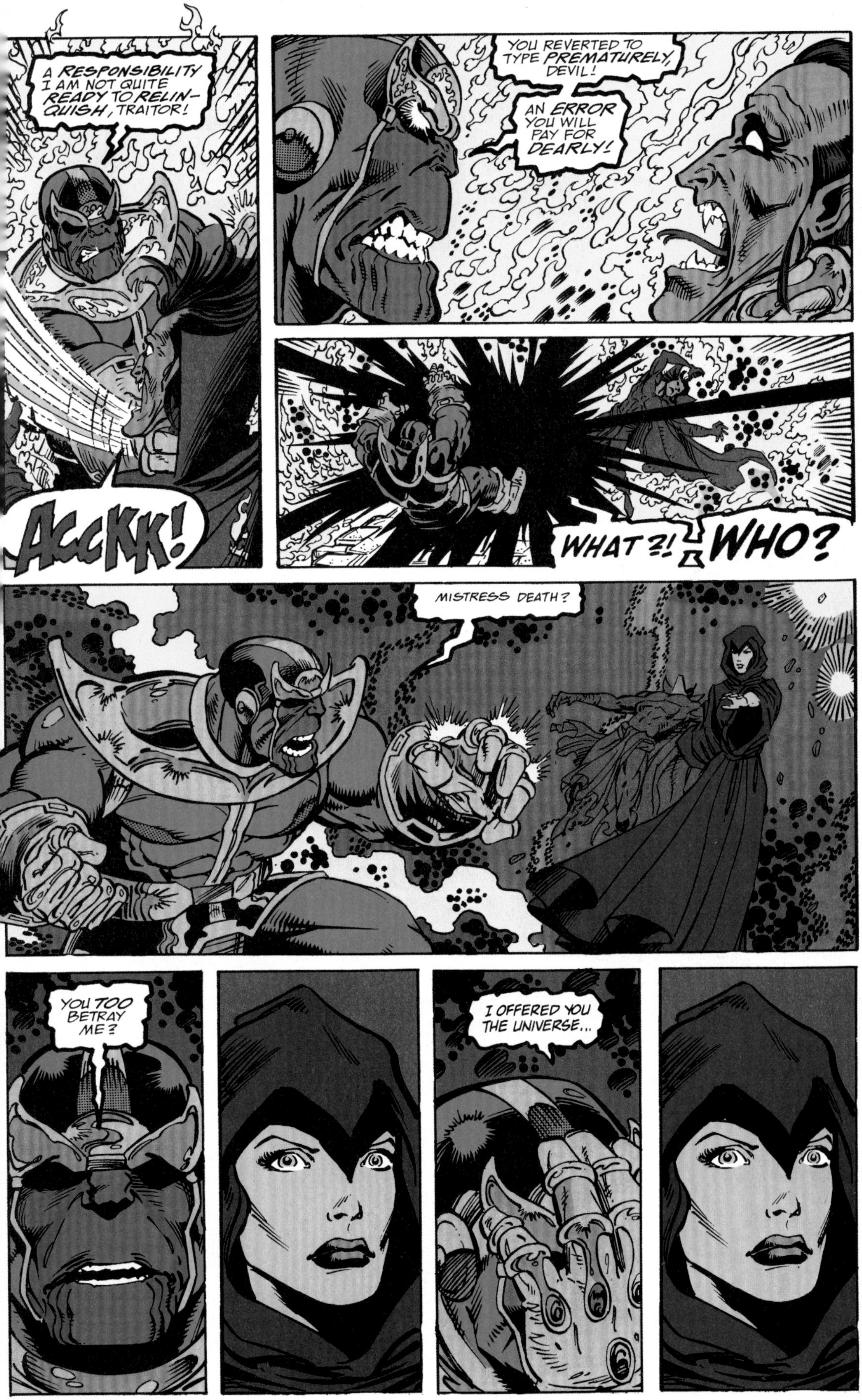
A RESPONSIBILITY I AM NOT QUITE READY TO RELINQUISH, TRAITOR!
ACCKK!
YOU REVERTED TO TYPE PREMATURELY, DEVIL!
AN ERROR YOU WILL PAY FOR DEARLY!
WHAT?!
WHO?
MISTRESS DEATH?
YOU TOO BETRAY ME?
I OFFERED YOU THE UNIVERSE...

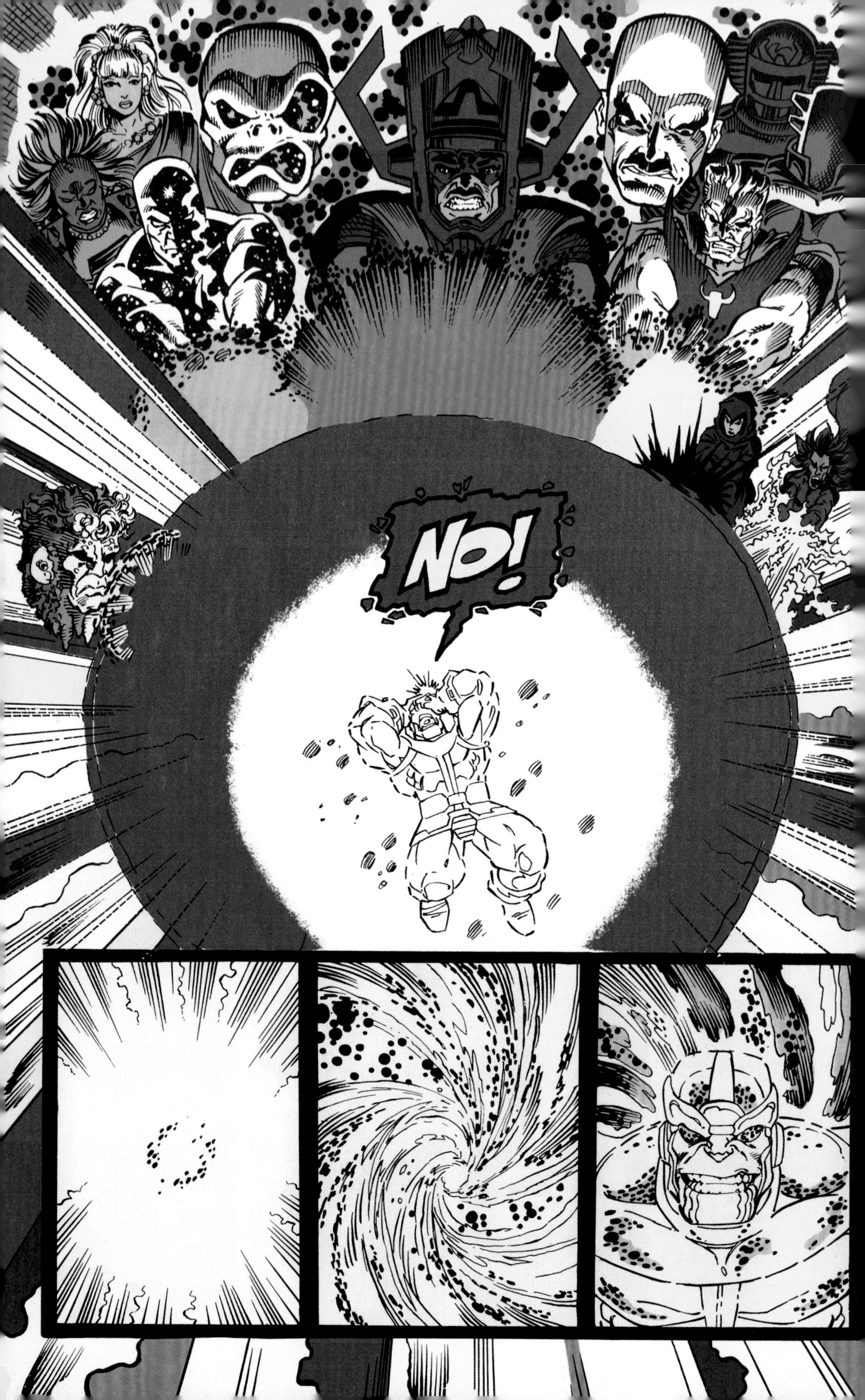
NO!

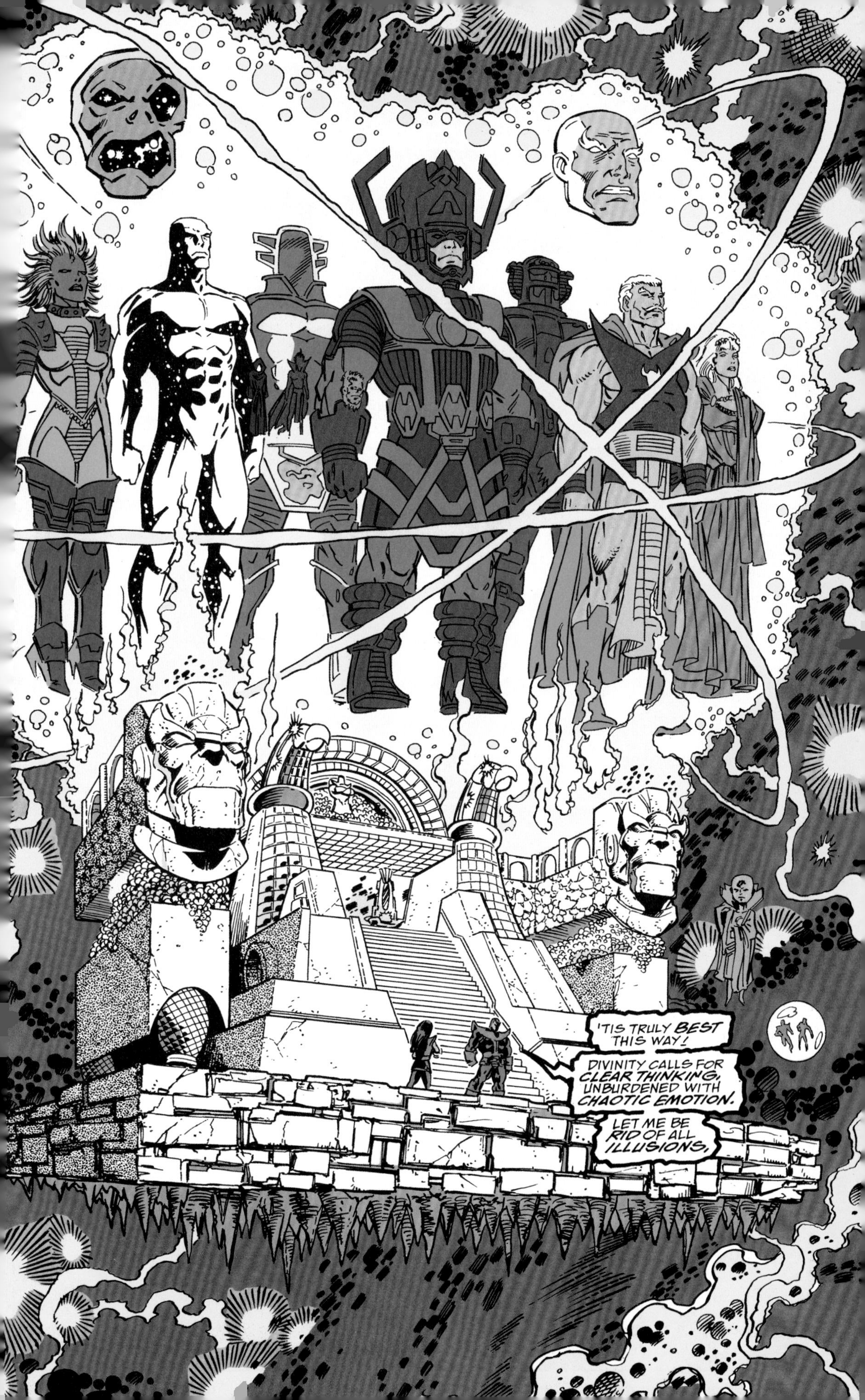
'TIS TRULY BEST THIS WAY!
DIVINITY CALLS FOR CLEAR THINKING, UNBURDENED WITH CHAOTIC EMOTION.
LET ME BE RID OF ALL ILLUSIONS,

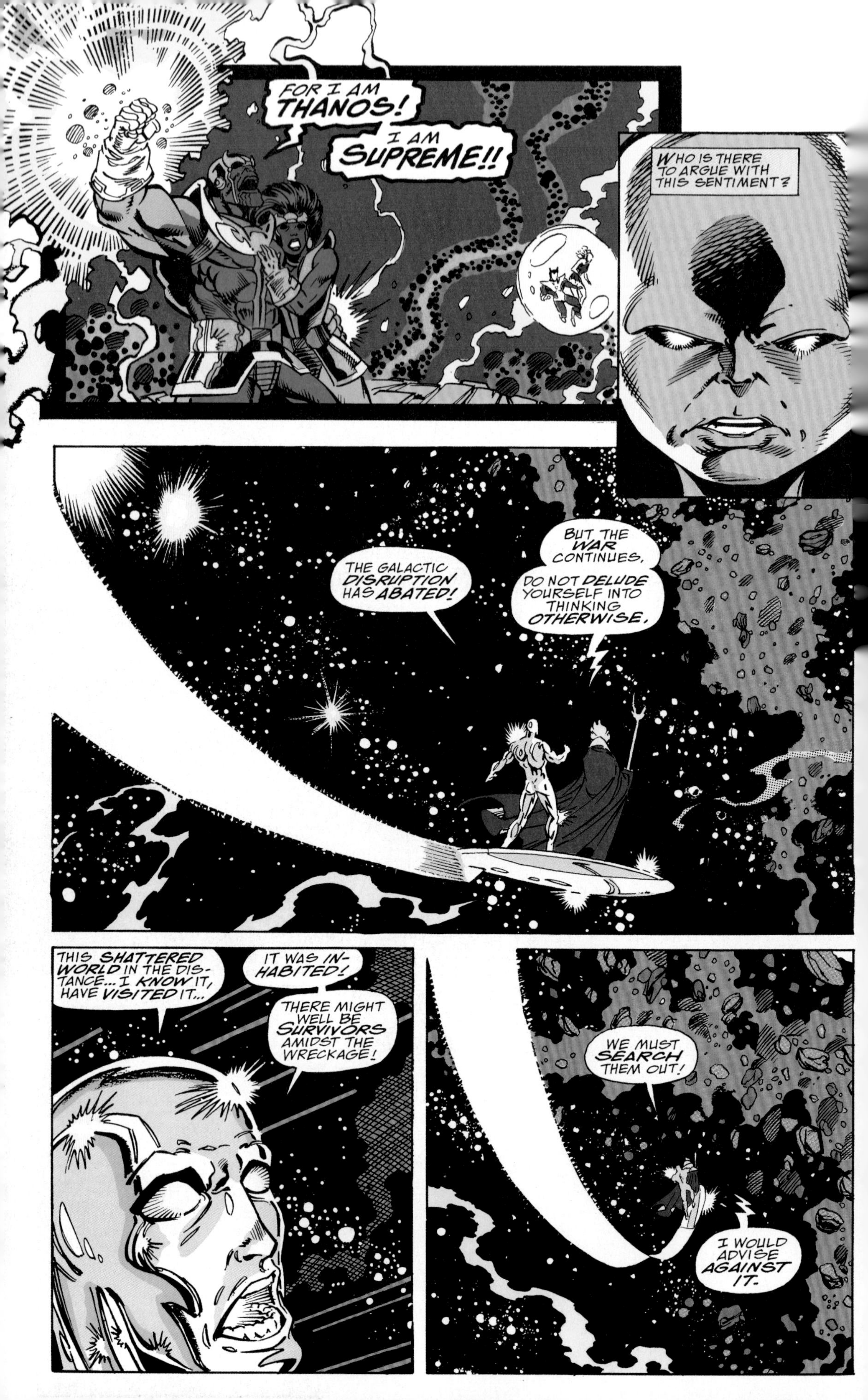
FOR I AM THANOS!
I AM SUPREME!!
WHO IS THERE TO ARGUE WITH THIS SENTIMENT?
THE GALACTIC DISRUPTION HAS ABATED!
BUT THE WAR CONTINUES.
DO NOT DELUDE YOURSELF INTO THINKING OTHERWISE.
THIS SHATTERED WORLD IN THE DISTANCE... I KNOW IT, HAVE VISITED IT...
IT WAS INHABITED!
THERE MIGHT WELL BE SURVIVORS AMIDST THE WRECKAGE!
WE MUST SEARCH THEM OUT!
I WOULD ADVISE AGAINST IT.

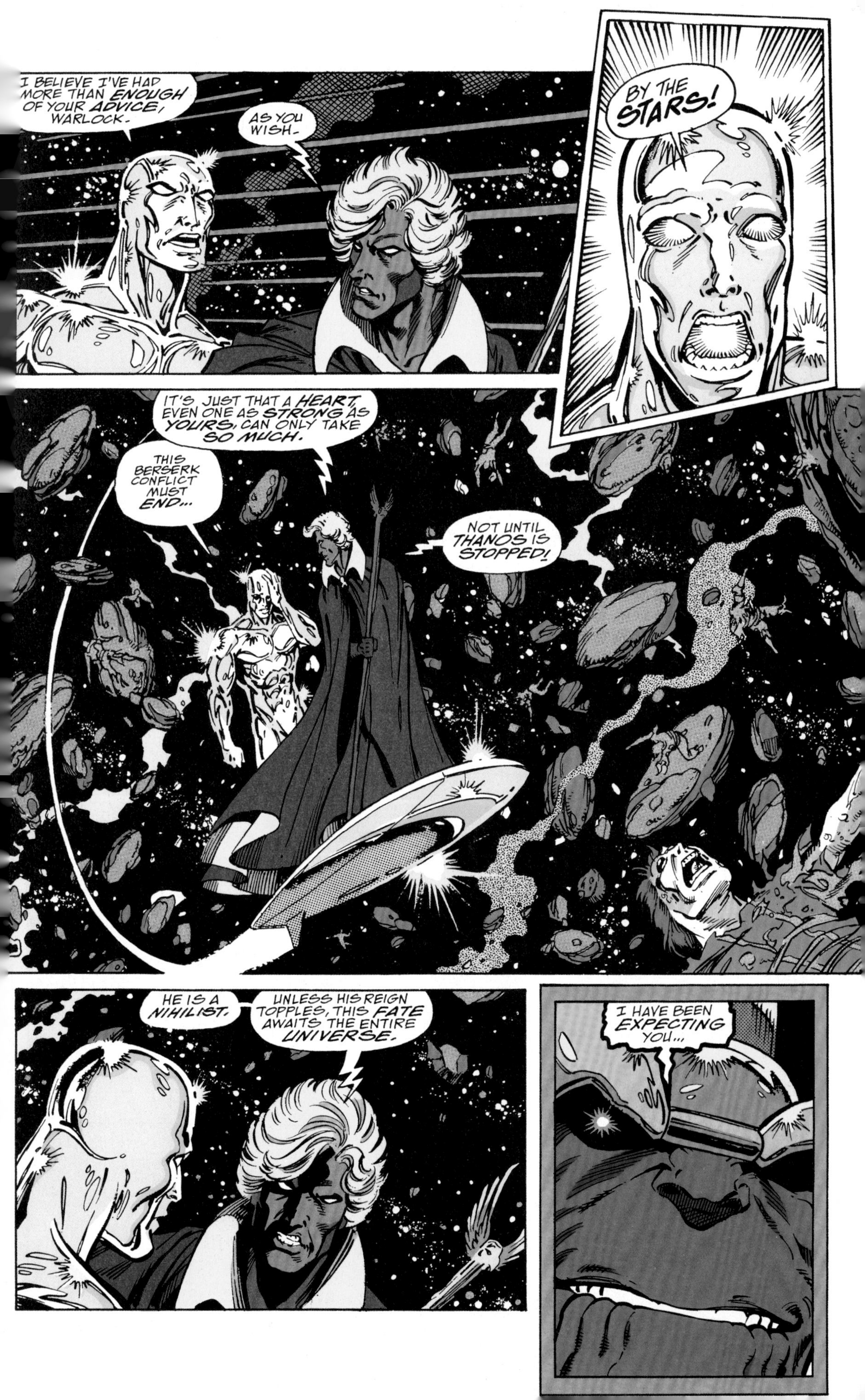
I BELIEVE I'VE HAD MORE THAN ENOUGH OF YOUR ADVICE, WARLOCK.
AS YOU WISH.
BY THE STARS!
IT'S JUST THAT A HEART, EVEN ONE AS STRONG AS YOURS, CAN ONLY TAKE SO MUCH.
THIS BERSERK CONFLICT MUST END...
NOT UNTIL THANOS IS STOPPED!
HE IS A NIHILIST.
UNLESS HIS REIGN TOPPLES, THIS FATE AWAITS THE ENTIRE UNIVERSE.
I HAVE BEEN EXPECTING YOU...

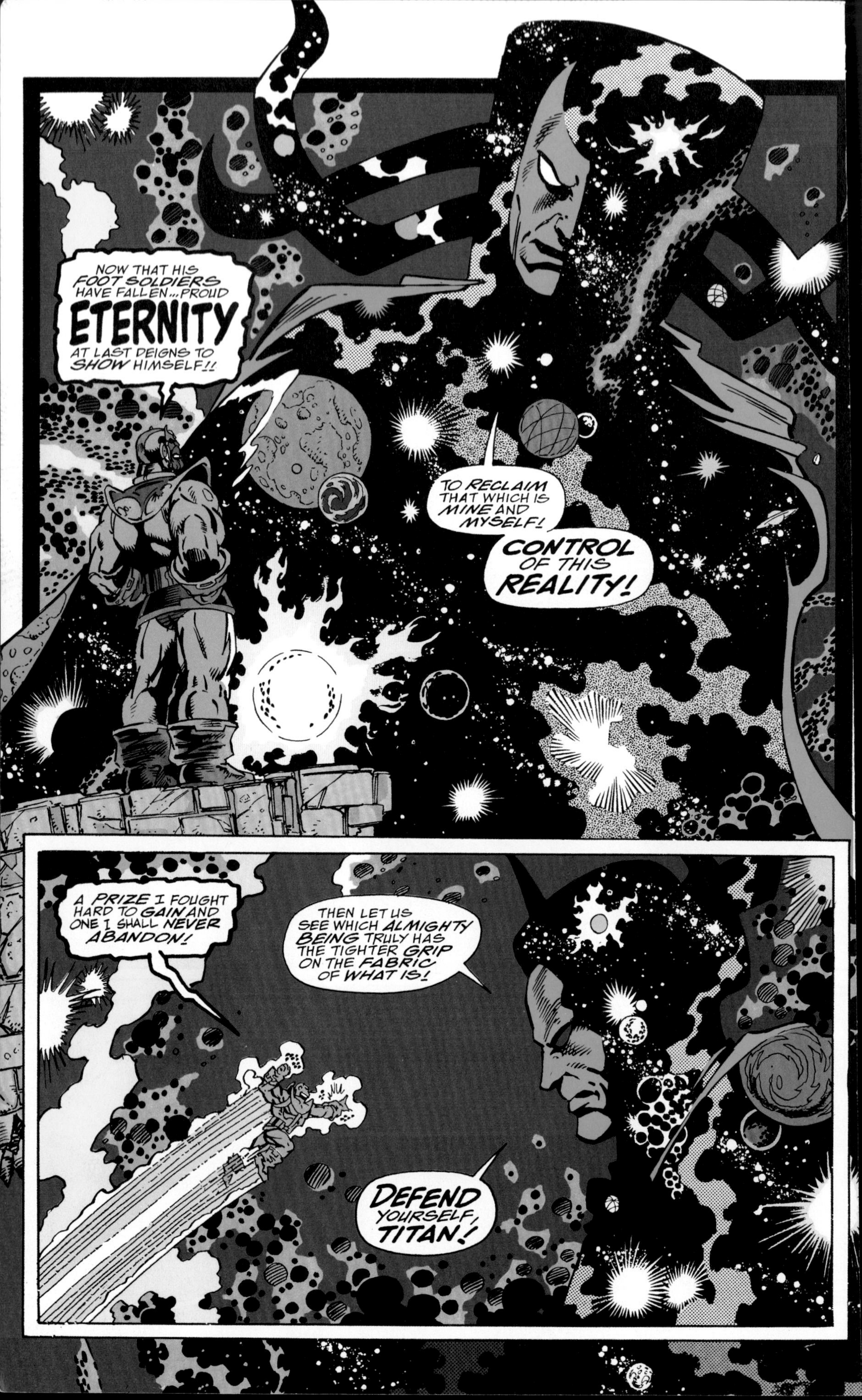
NOW THAT HIS FOOT SOLDIERS HAVE FALLEN...PROUD ETERNITY AT LAST DEIGNS TO SHOW HIMSELF!!
TO RECLAIM THAT WHICH IS MINE AND MYSELF!
CONTROL OF THIS REALITY!
A PRIZE I FOUGHT HARD TO GAIN AND ONE I SHALL NEVER ABANDON!
THEN LET US SEE WHICH ALMIGHTY BEING TRULY HAS THE TIGHTER GRIP ON THE FABRIC OF WHAT IS!
DEFEND YOURSELF, TITAN!

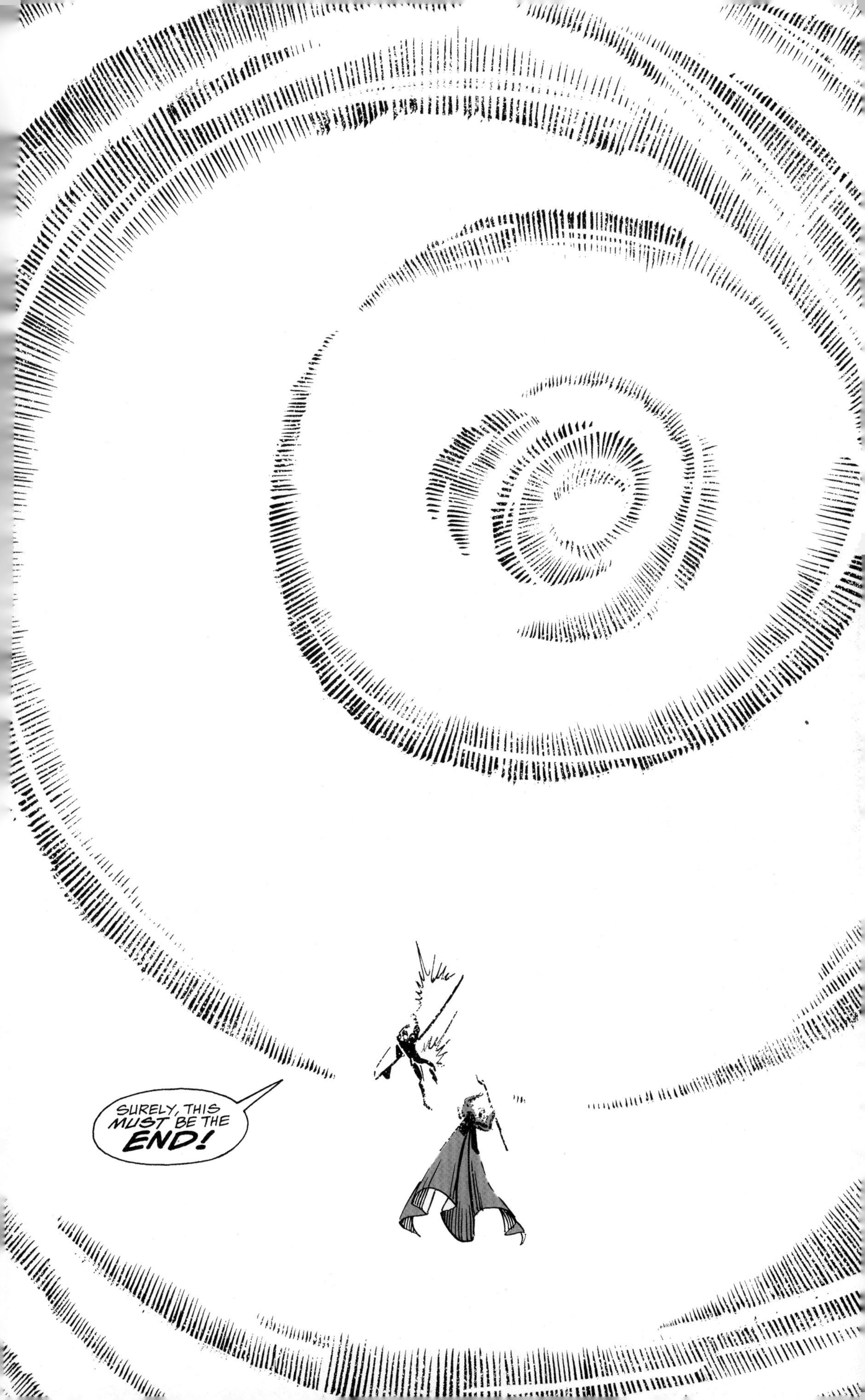
SURELY, THIS MUST BE THE END!

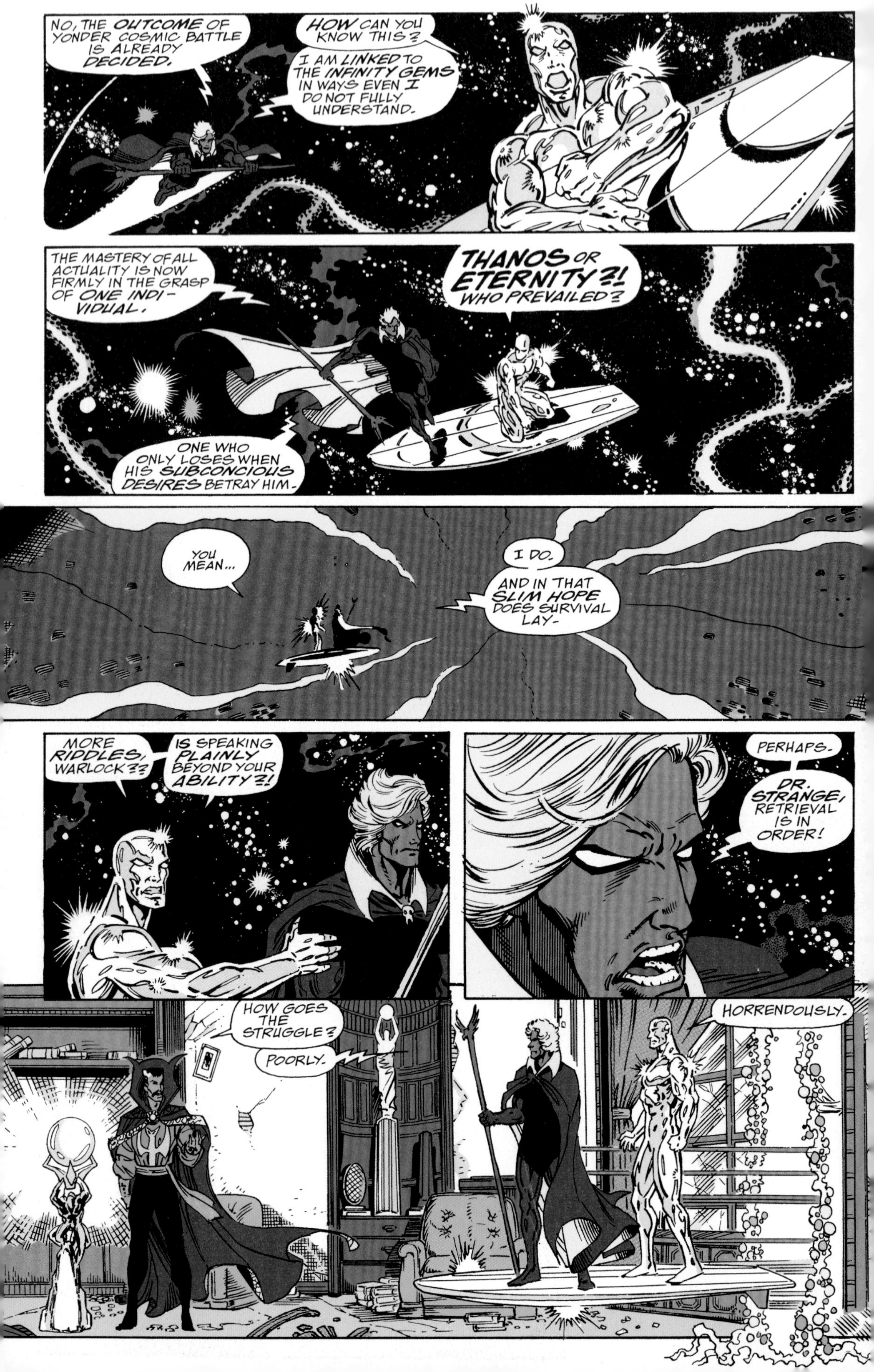
NO, THE OUTCOME OF YONDER COSMIC BATTLE IS ALREADY DECIDED.
HOW CAN YOU KNOW THIS?
I AM LINKED TO THE INFINITY GEMS IN WAYS EVEN I DO NOT FULLY UNDERSTAND.
THE MASTERY OF ALL ACTUALITY IS NOW FIRMLY IN THE GRASP OF ONE INDI-VIDUAL.
THANOS OR ETERNITY?! WHO PREVAILED?
ONE WHO ONLY LOSES WHEN HIS SUBCONCIOUS DESIRES BETRAY HIM.
YOU MEAN...
I DO.
AND IN THAT SLIM HOPE DOES SURVIVAL LAY.
MORE RIDDLES, WARLOCK??
IS SPEAKING PLAINLY BEYOND YOUR ABILITY?!
PERHAPS.
DR. STRANGE, RETRIEVAL IS IN ORDER!
HOW GOES THE STRUGGLE?
POORLY.
HORRENDOUSLY.

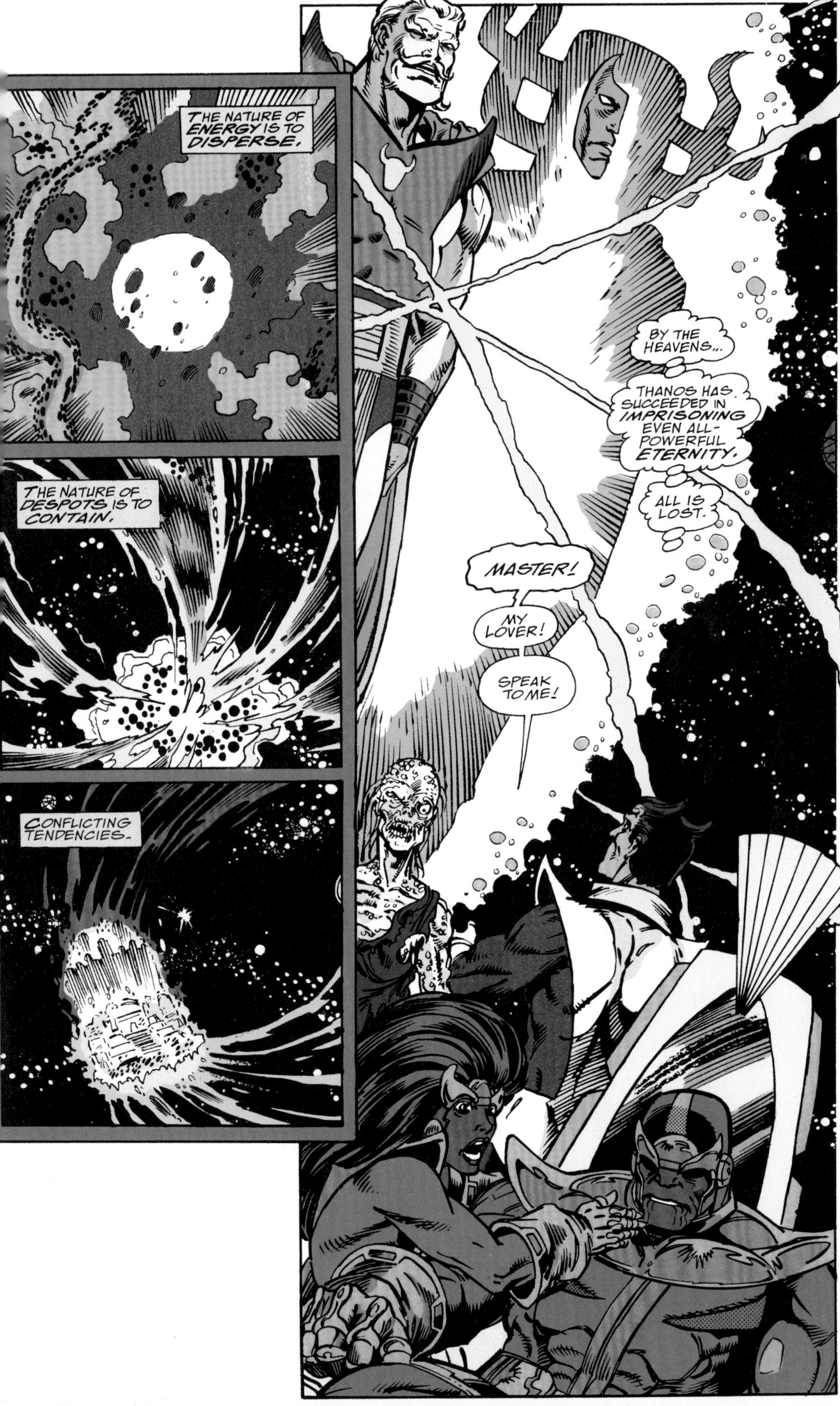
THE NATURE OF ENERGY IS TO DISPERSE.
THE NATURE OF DESPOTS IS TO CONTAIN.
CONFLICTING TENDENCIES.
BY THE HEAVENS...
THANOS HAS SUCCEEDED IN IMPRISONING EVEN ALL-POWERFUL ETERNITY.
ALL IS LOST.
MASTER!
MY LOVER!
SPEAK TO ME!

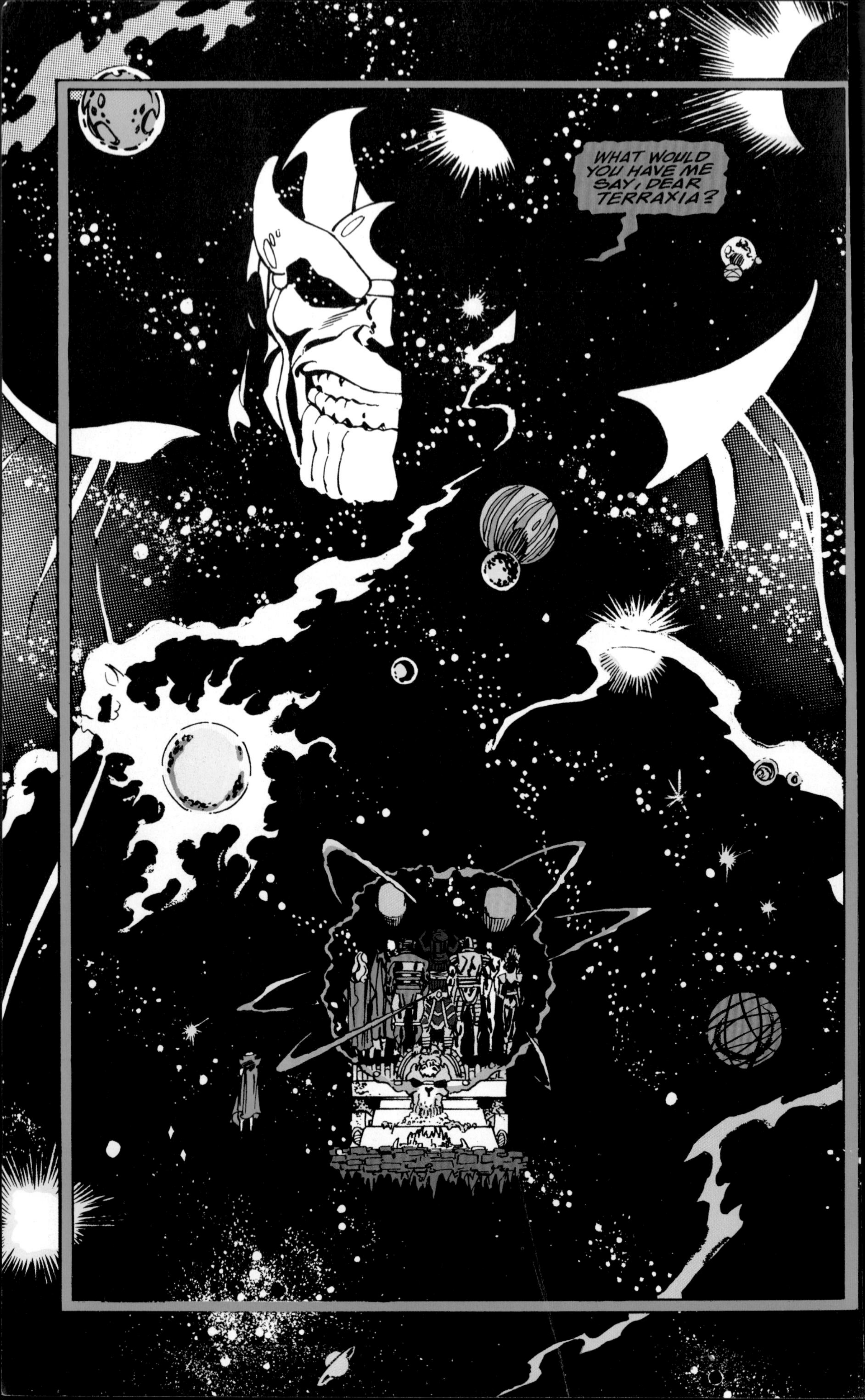
WHAT WOULD YOU HAVE ME SAY, DEAR TERRAXIA?

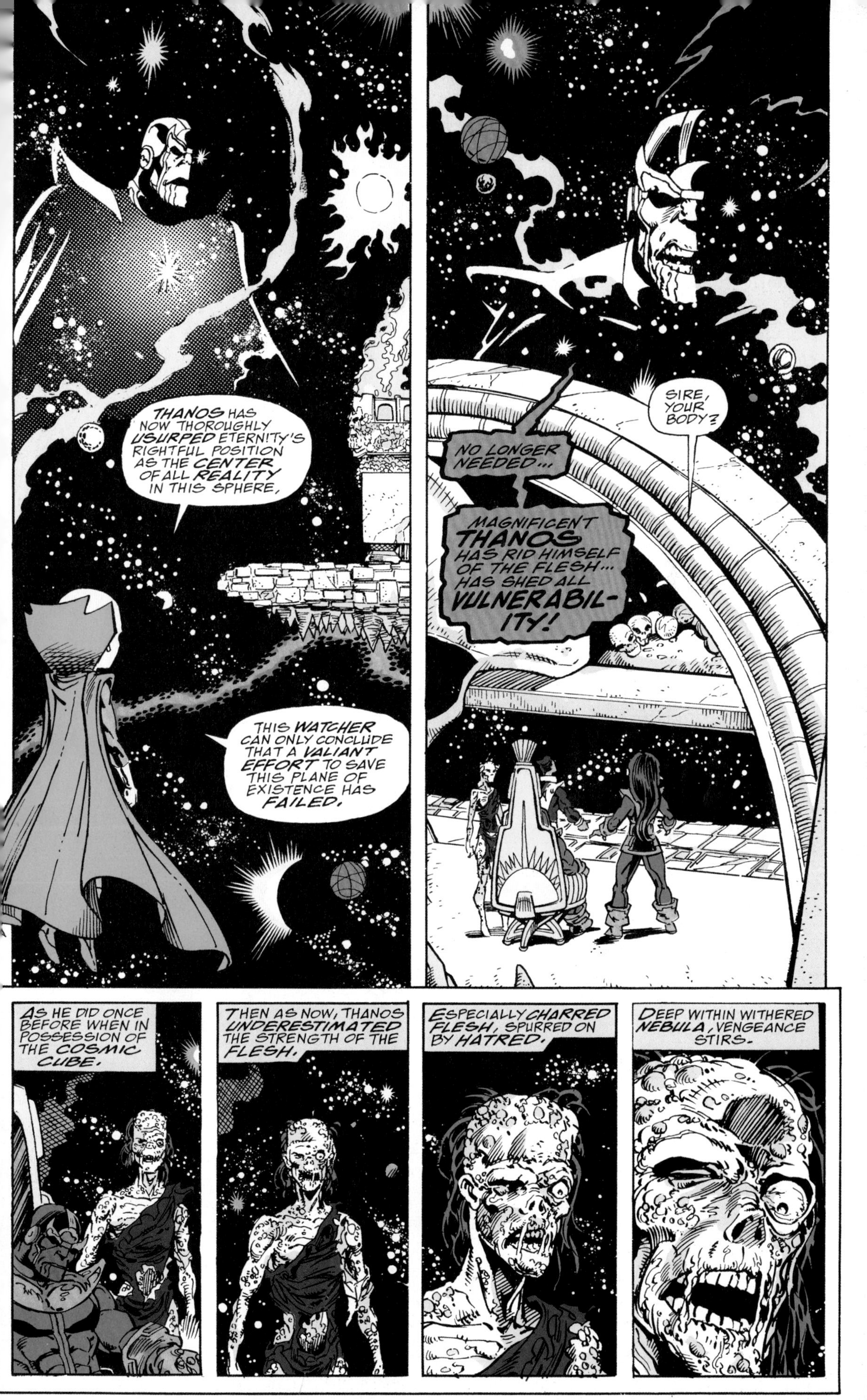
THANOS HAS NOW THOROUGHLY USURPED ETERNITY'S RIGHTFUL POSITION AS THE CENTER OF ALL REALITY IN THIS SPHERE,
THIS WATCHER CAN ONLY CONCLUDE THAT A VALIANT EFFORT TO SAVE THIS PLANE OF EXISTENCE HAS FAILED.
SIRE, YOUR BODY?
NO LONGER NEEDED...
MAGNIFICENT THANOS HAS RID HIMSELF OF THE FLESH... HAS SHED ALL VULNERABIL-ITY!
AS HE DID ONCE BEFORE WHEN IN POSSESSION OF THE COSMIC CUBE.
THEN AS NOW, THANOS UNDERESTIMATED THE STRENGTH OF THE FLESH.
ESPECIALLY CHARRED FLESH, SPURRED ON BY HATRED.
DEEP WITHIN WITHERED NEBULA, VENGEANCE STIRS.

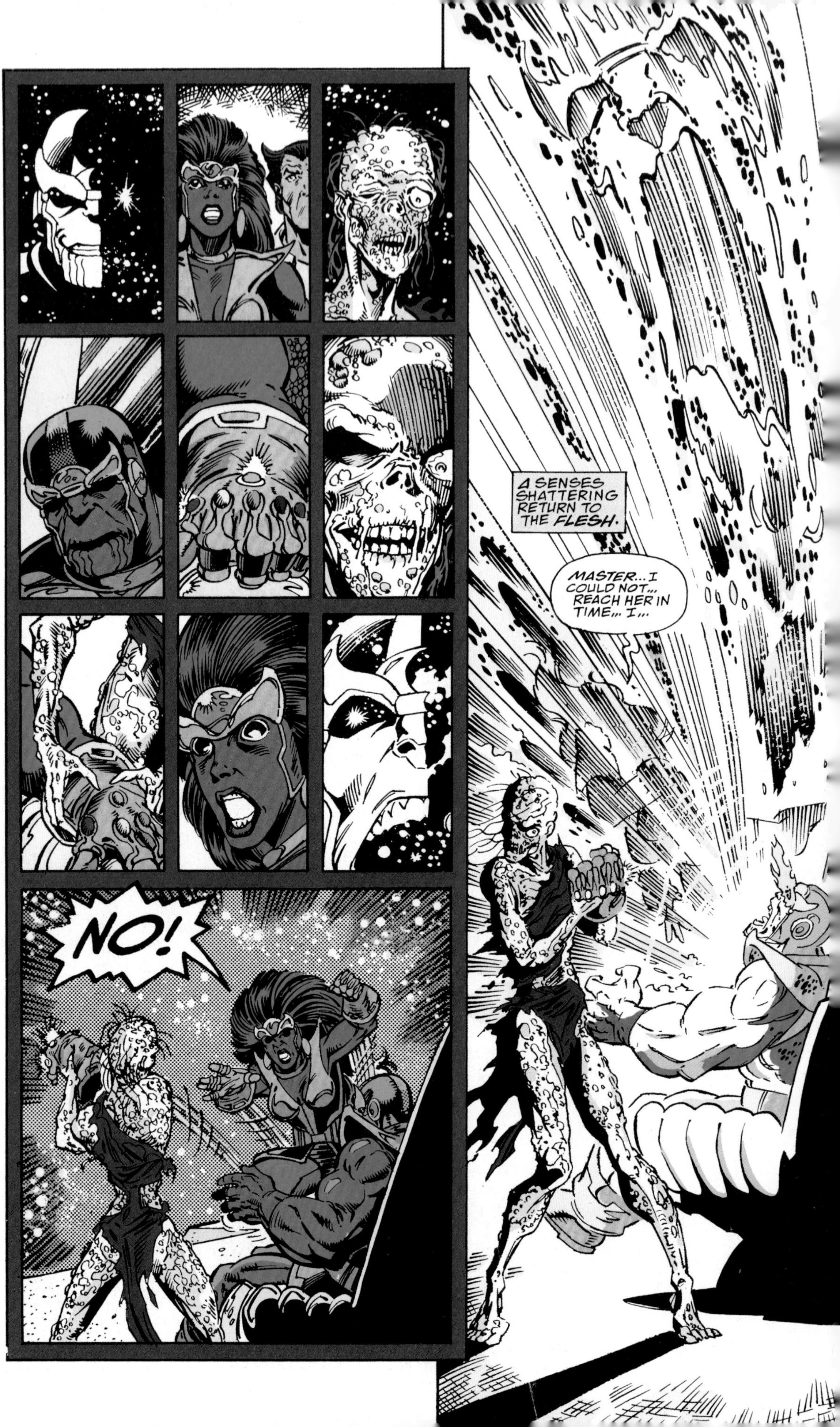
NO!
A SENSES SHATTERING RETURN TO THE FLESH.
MASTER... I COULD NOT... REACH HER IN TIME... I...

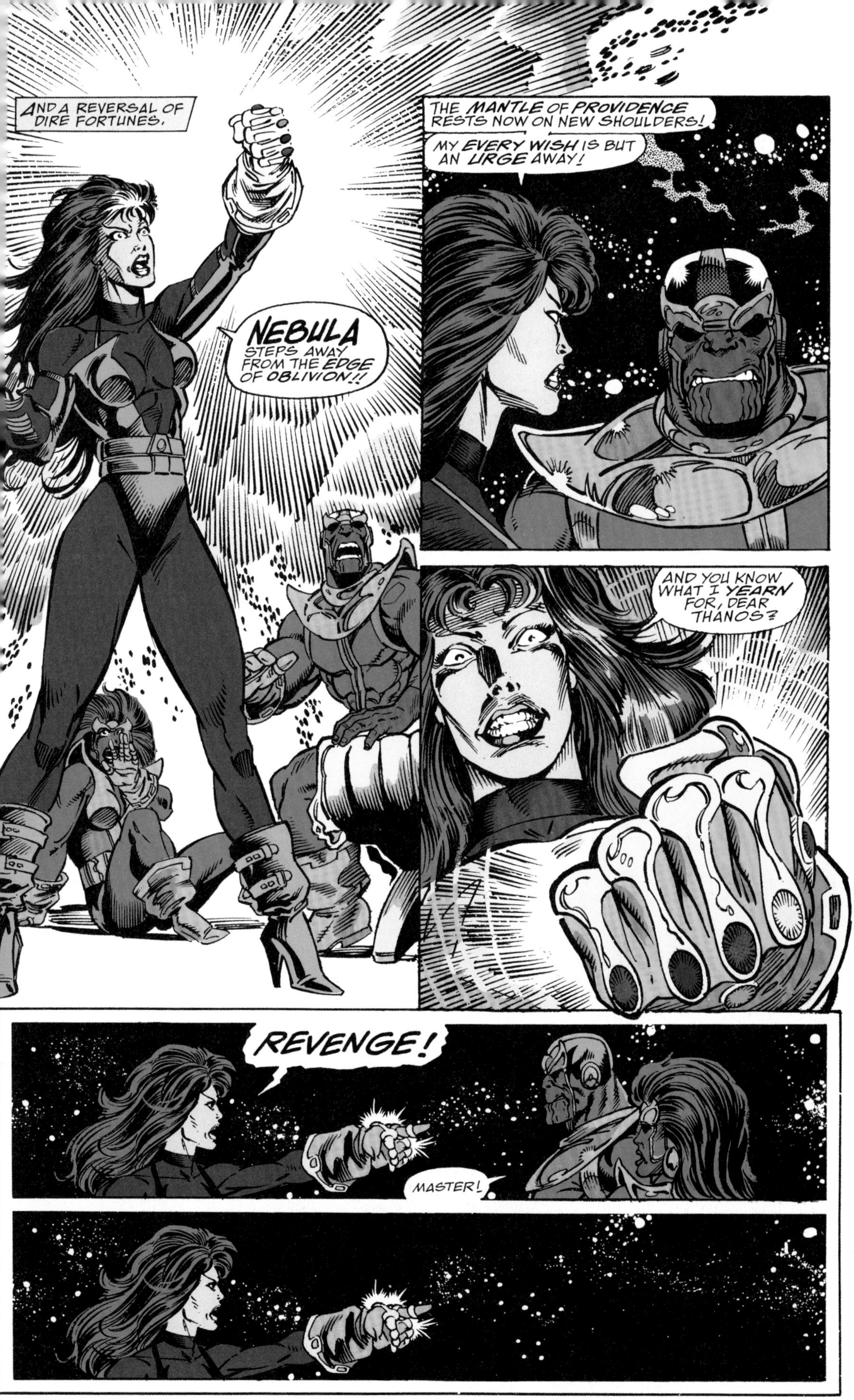
AND A REVERSAL OF DIRE FORTUNES.
NEBULA STEPS AWAY FROM THE EDGE OF OBLIVION!!
THE MANTLE OF PROVIDENCE RESTS NOW ON NEW SHOULDERS!
MY EVERY WISH IS BUT AN URGE AWAY!
AND YOU KNOW WHAT I YEARN FOR, DEAR THANOS?
REVENGE!
MASTER!

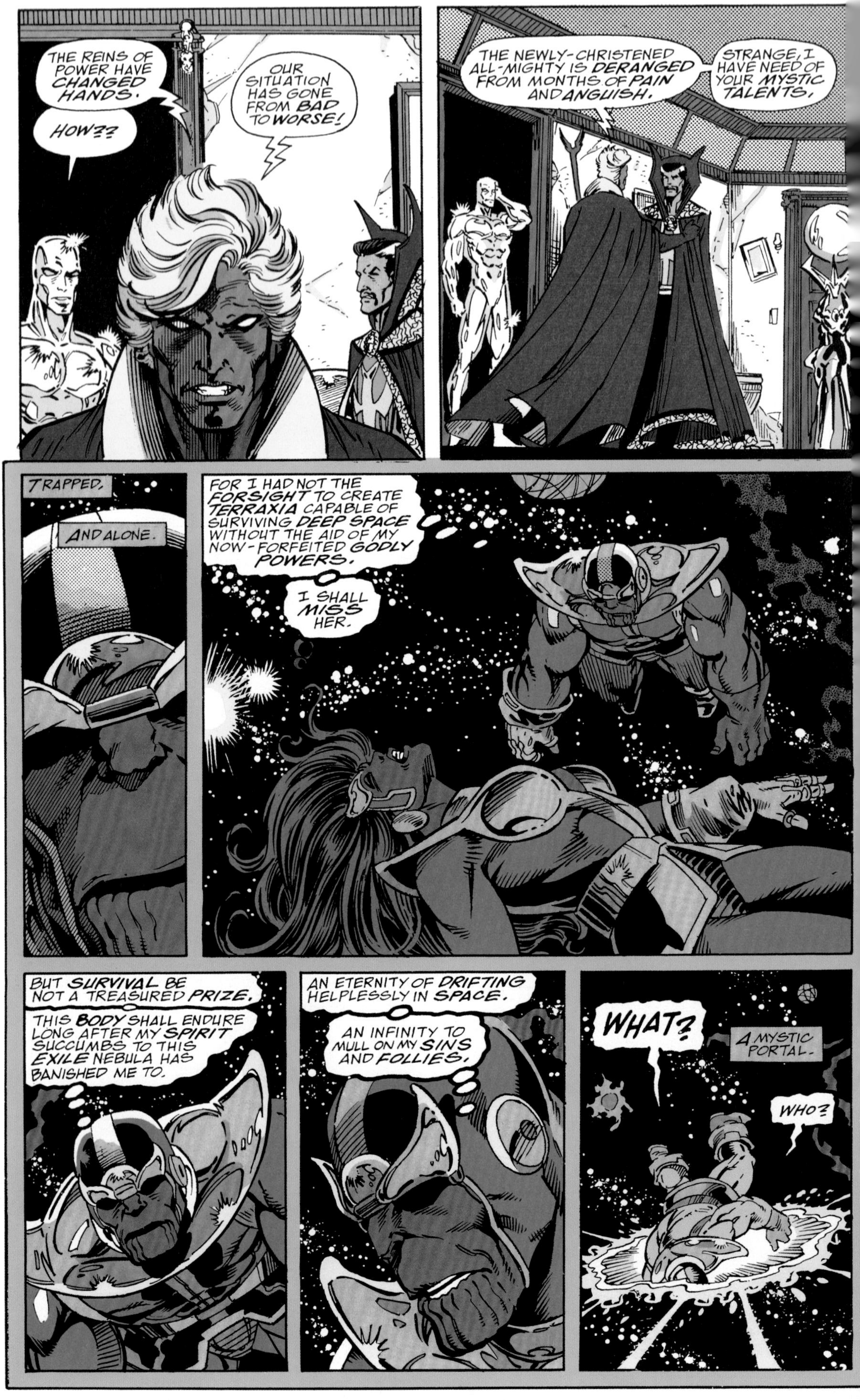
THE REINS OF POWER HAVE CHANGED HANDS.
HOW??
OUR SITUATION HAS GONE FROM BAD TO WORSE!
THE NEWLY-CHRISTENED ALL-MIGHTY IS DERANGED FROM MONTHS OF PAIN AND ANGUISH.
STRANGE, I HAVE NEED OF YOUR MYSTIC TALENTS.
TRAPPED.
AND ALONE.
FOR I HAD NOT THE FORSIGHT TO CREATE TERRAXIA CAPABLE OF SURVIVING DEEP SPACE WITHOUT THE AID OF MY NOW-FORFEITED GODLY POWERS.
I SHALL MISS HER.
BUT SURVIVAL BE NOT A TREASURED PRIZE.
THIS BODY SHALL ENDURE LONG AFTER MY SPIRIT SUCCUMBS TO THIS EXILE NEBULA HAS BANISHED ME TO.
AN ETERNITY OF DRIFTING HELPLESSLY IN SPACE.
AN INFINITY TO MULL ON MY SINS AND FOLLIES.
WHAT?
A MYSTIC PORTAL.
WHO?

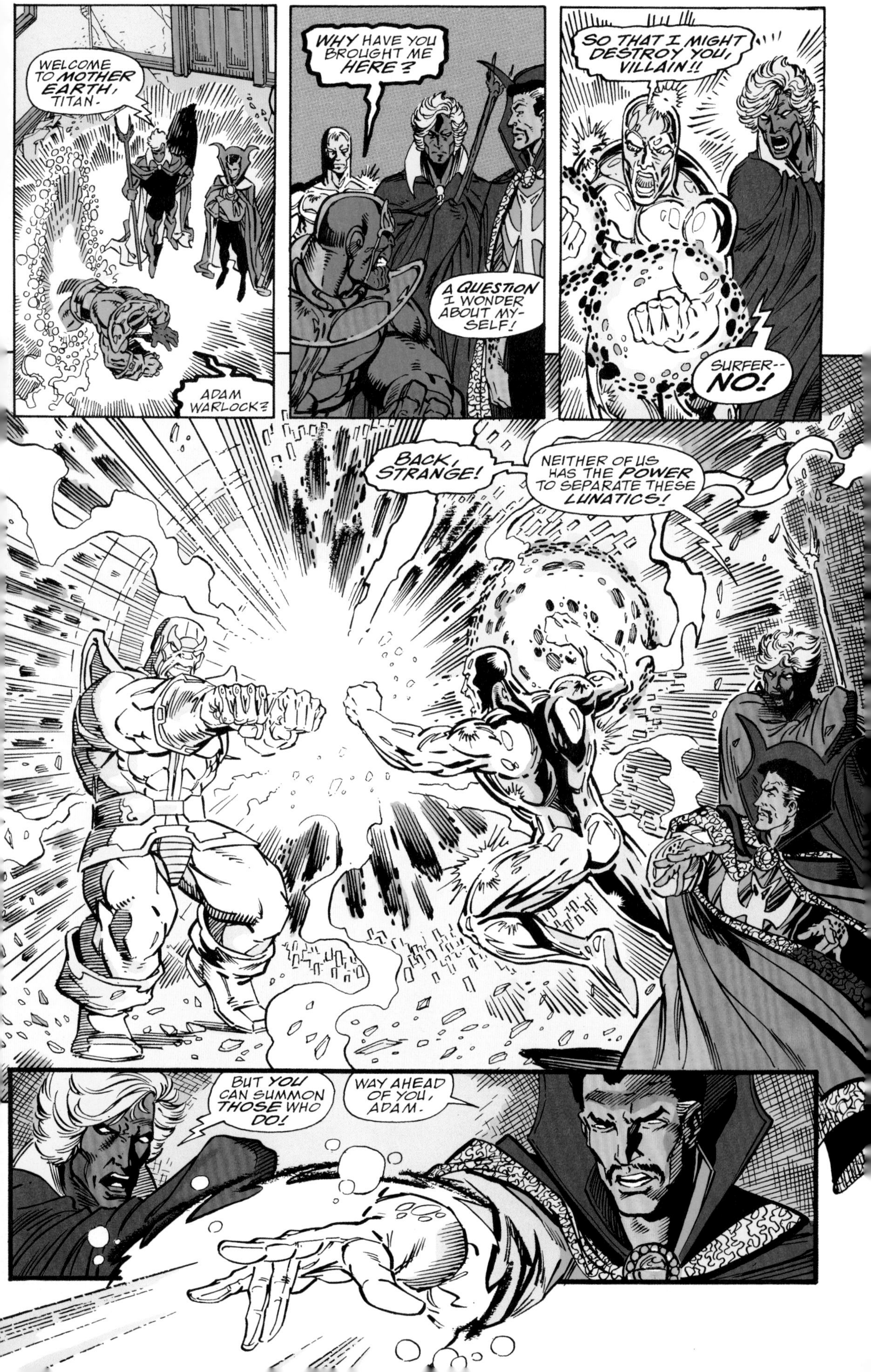
WELCOME TO MOTHER EARTH, TITAN.
ADAM WARLOCK?
WHY HAVE YOU BROUGHT ME HERE?
A QUESTION I WONDER ABOUT MY-SELF!
SO THAT I MIGHT DESTROY YOU, VILLAIN!!
SURFER-- NO!
BACK, STRANGE!
NEITHER OF US HAS THE POWER TO SEPARATE THESE LUNATICS!
BUT YOU CAN SUMMON THOSE WHO DO!
WAY AHEAD OF YOU, ADAM.

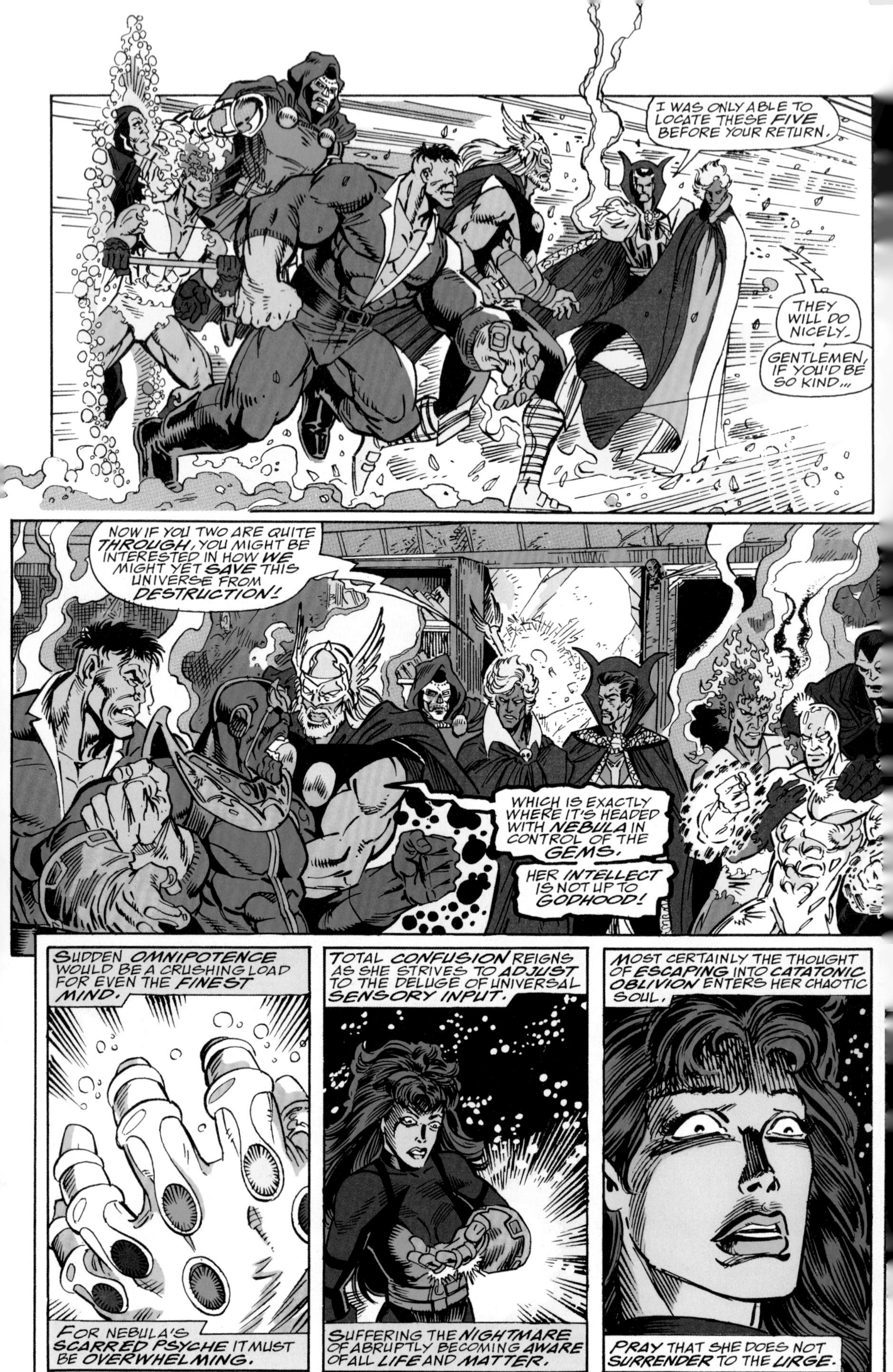
I WAS ONLY ABLE TO LOCATE THESE FIVE BEFORE YOUR RETURN.
THEY WILL DO NICELY.
GENTLEMEN, IF YOU'D BE SO KIND...
NOW IF YOU TWO ARE QUITE THROUGH, YOU MIGHT BE INTERESTED IN HOW WE MIGHT YET SAVE THIS UNIVERSE FROM DESTRUCTION!
WHICH IS EXACTLY WHERE IT'S HEADED WITH NEBULA IN CONTROL OF THE GEMS.
HER INTELLECT IS NOT UP TO GODHOOD!
SUDDEN OMNIPOTENCE WOULD BE A CRUSHING LOAD FOR EVEN THE FINEST MIND.
FOR NEBULA'S SCARRED PSYCHE IT MUST BE OVERWHELMING.
TOTAL CONFUSION REIGNS AS SHE STRIVES TO ADJUST TO THE DELUGE OF UNIVERSAL SENSORY INPUT.
SUFFERING THE NIGHTMARE OF ABRUPTLY BECOMING AWARE OF ALL LIFE AND MATTER.
MOST CERTAINLY THE THOUGHT OF ESCAPING INTO CATATONIC OBLIVION ENTERS HER CHAOTIC SOUL.
PRAY THAT SHE DOES NOT SURRENDER TO THE URGE.

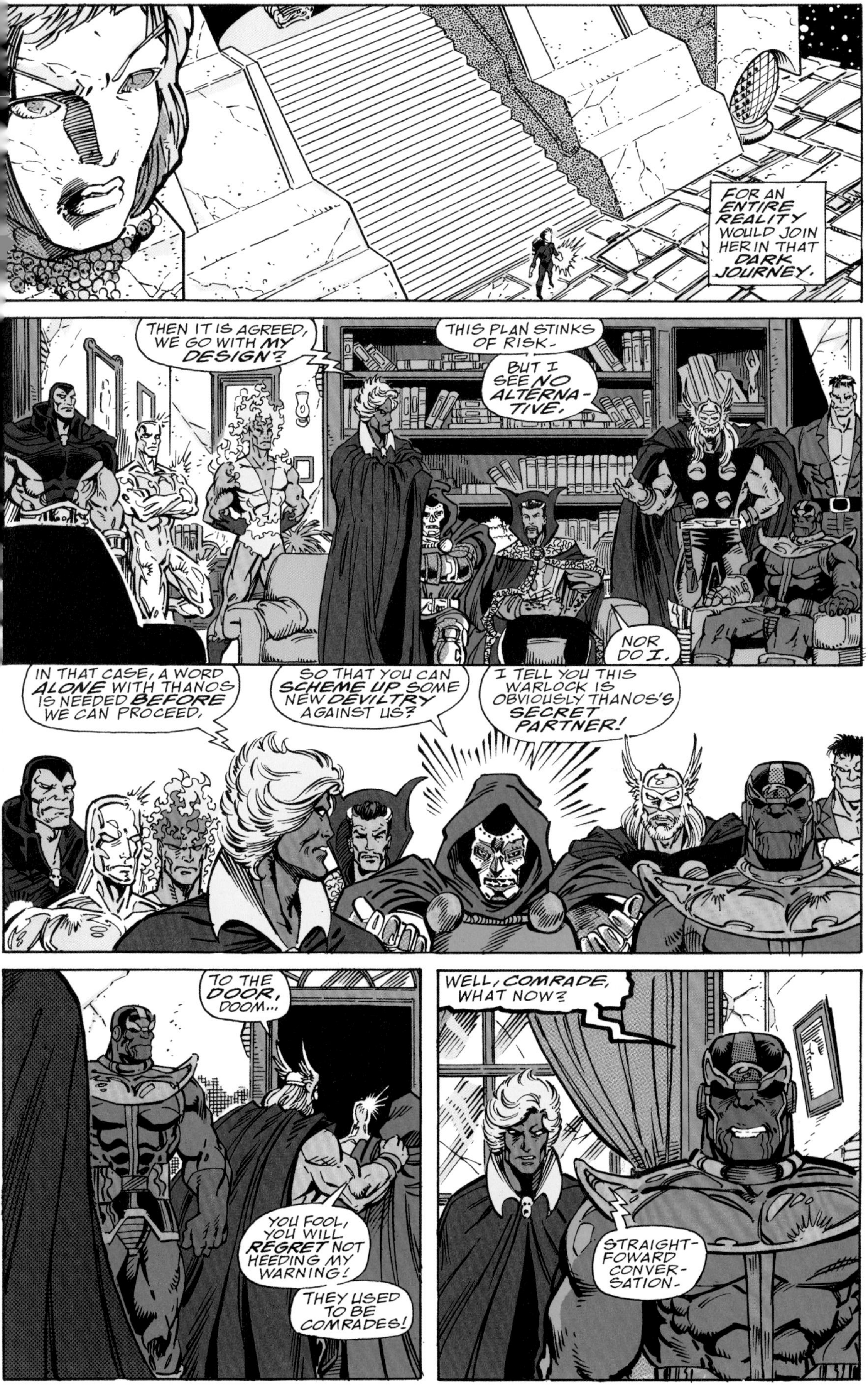
FOR AN ENTIRE REALITY WOULD JOIN HER IN THAT DARK JOURNEY.
THEN IT IS AGREED, WE GO WITH MY DESIGN?
THIS PLAN STINKS OF RISK.
BUT I SEE NO ALTERNATIVE.
NOR DO I.
IN THAT CASE, A WORD ALONE WITH THANOS IS NEEDED BEFORE WE CAN PROCEED.
SO THAT YOU CAN SCHEME UP SOME NEW DEVILTRY AGAINST US?
I TELL YOU THIS WARLOCK IS OBVIOUSLY THANOS'S SECRET PARTNER!
TO THE DOOR, DOOM...
YOU FOOL, YOU WILL REGRET NOT HEEDING MY WARNING!
THEY USED TO BE COMRADES!
WELL, COMRADE, WHAT NOW?
STRAIGHT-FOWARD CONVER-SATION.

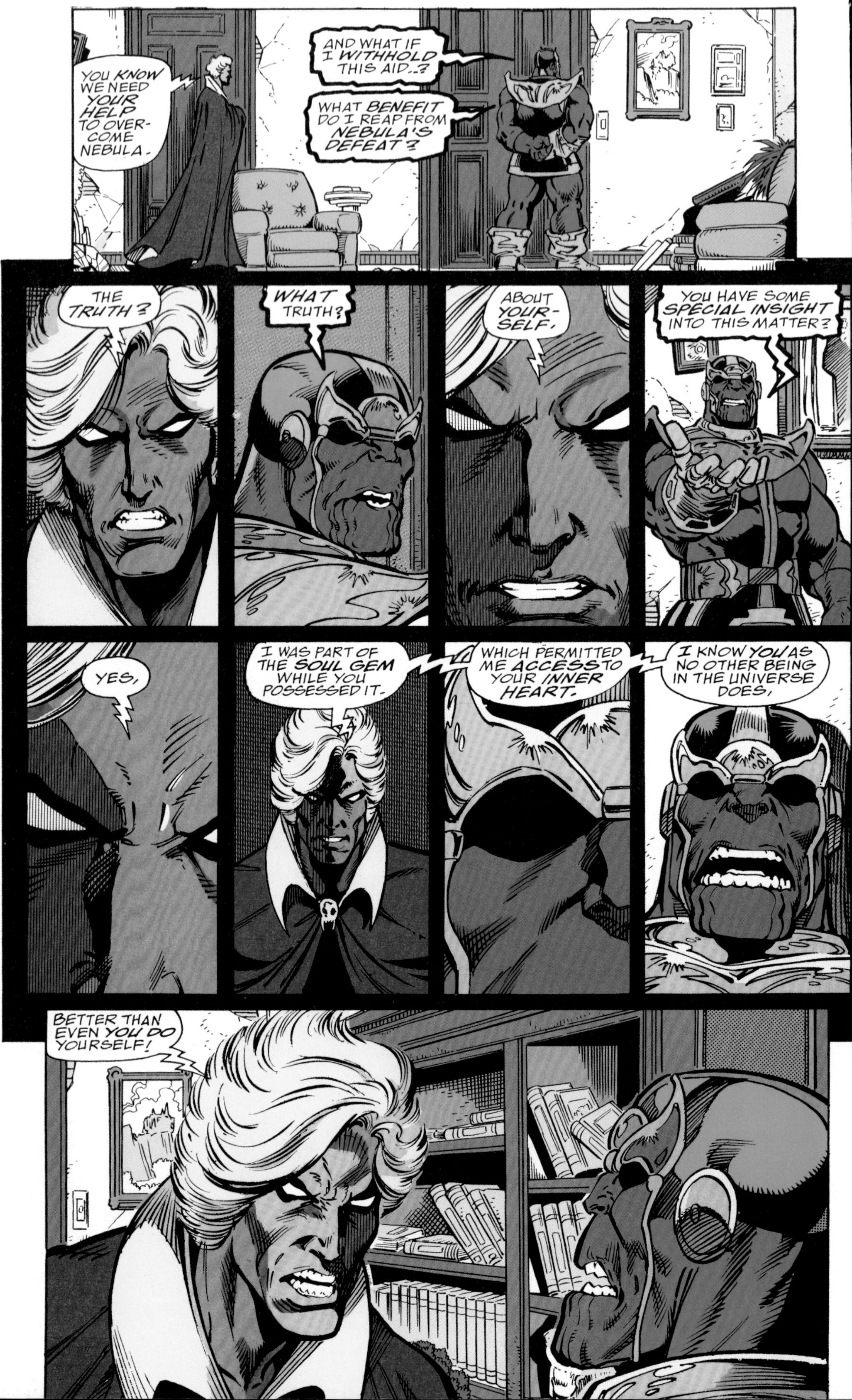
YOU KNOW WE NEED YOUR HELP TO OVERCOME NEBULA.
AND WHAT IF I WITHHOLD THIS AID..?
WHAT BENEFIT DO I REAP FROM NEBULA'S DEFEAT?
THE TRUTH?
WHAT TRUTH?
ABOUT YOURSELF.
YOU HAVE SOME SPECIAL INSIGHT INTO THIS MATTER?
YES,
I WAS PART OF THE SOUL GEM WHILE YOU POSSESSED IT--
WHICH PERMITTED ME ACCESS TO YOUR INNER HEART.
I KNOW YOU AS NO OTHER BEING IN THE UNIVERSE DOES,
BETTER THAN EVEN YOU DO YOURSELF!

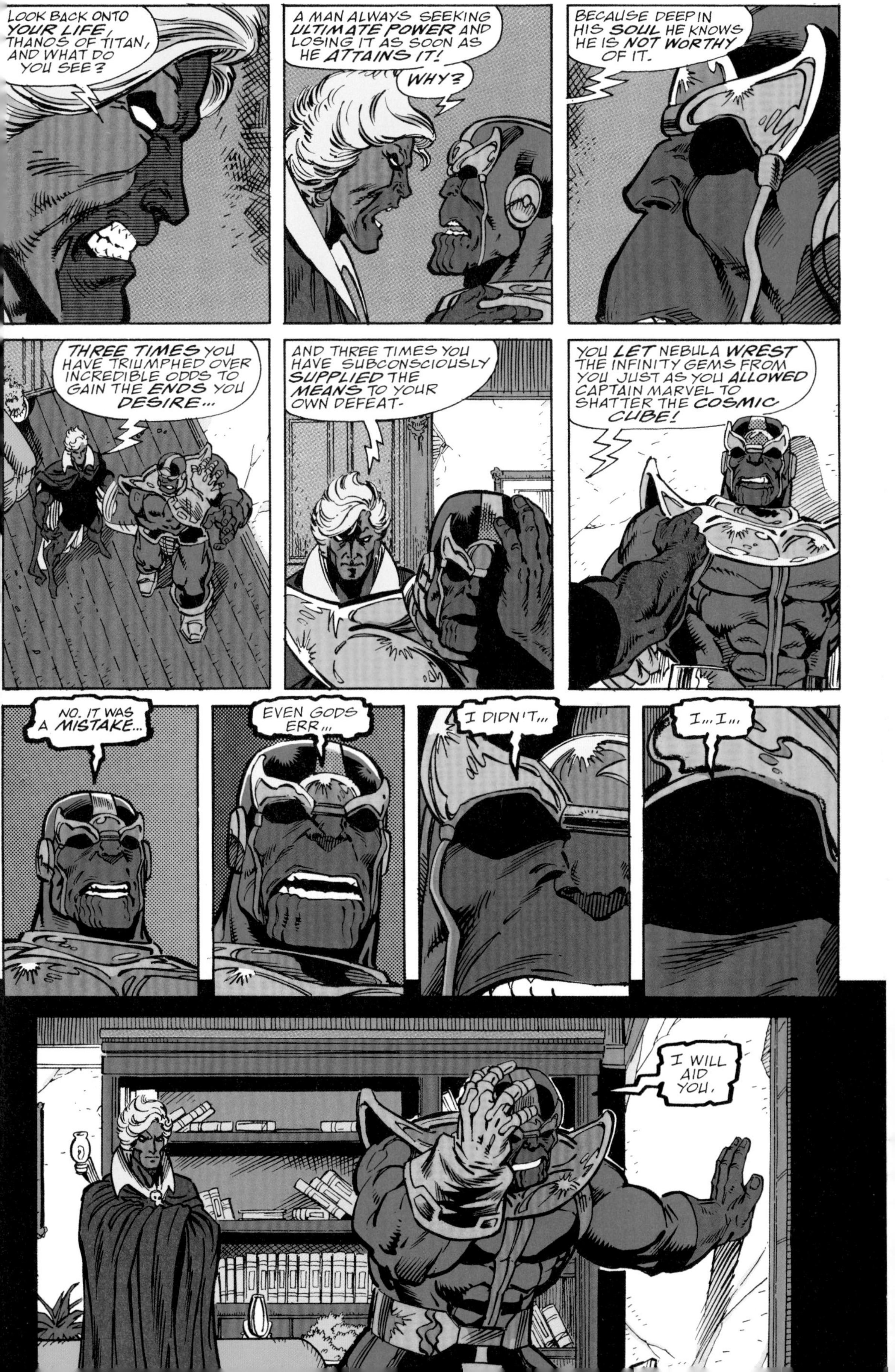
LOOK BACK ONTO YOUR LIFE, THANOS OF TITAN, AND WHAT DO YOU SEE?
A MAN ALWAYS SEEKING ULTIMATE POWER AND LOSING IT AS SOON AS HE ATTAINS IT!
WHY?
BECAUSE DEEP IN HIS SOUL HE KNOWS HE IS NOT WORTHY OF IT.
THREE TIMES YOU HAVE TRIUMPHED OVER INCREDIBLE ODDS TO GAIN THE ENDS YOU DESIRE...
AND THREE TIMES YOU HAVE SUBCONSCIOUSLY SUPPLIED THE MEANS TO YOUR OWN DEFEAT-
YOU LET NEBULA WREST THE INFINITY GEMS FROM YOU JUST AS YOU ALLOWED CAPTAIN MARVEL TO SHATTER THE COSMIC CUBE!
NO. IT WAS A MISTAKE...
EVEN GODS ERR...
I DIDN'T...
I... I...
I WILL AID YOU.

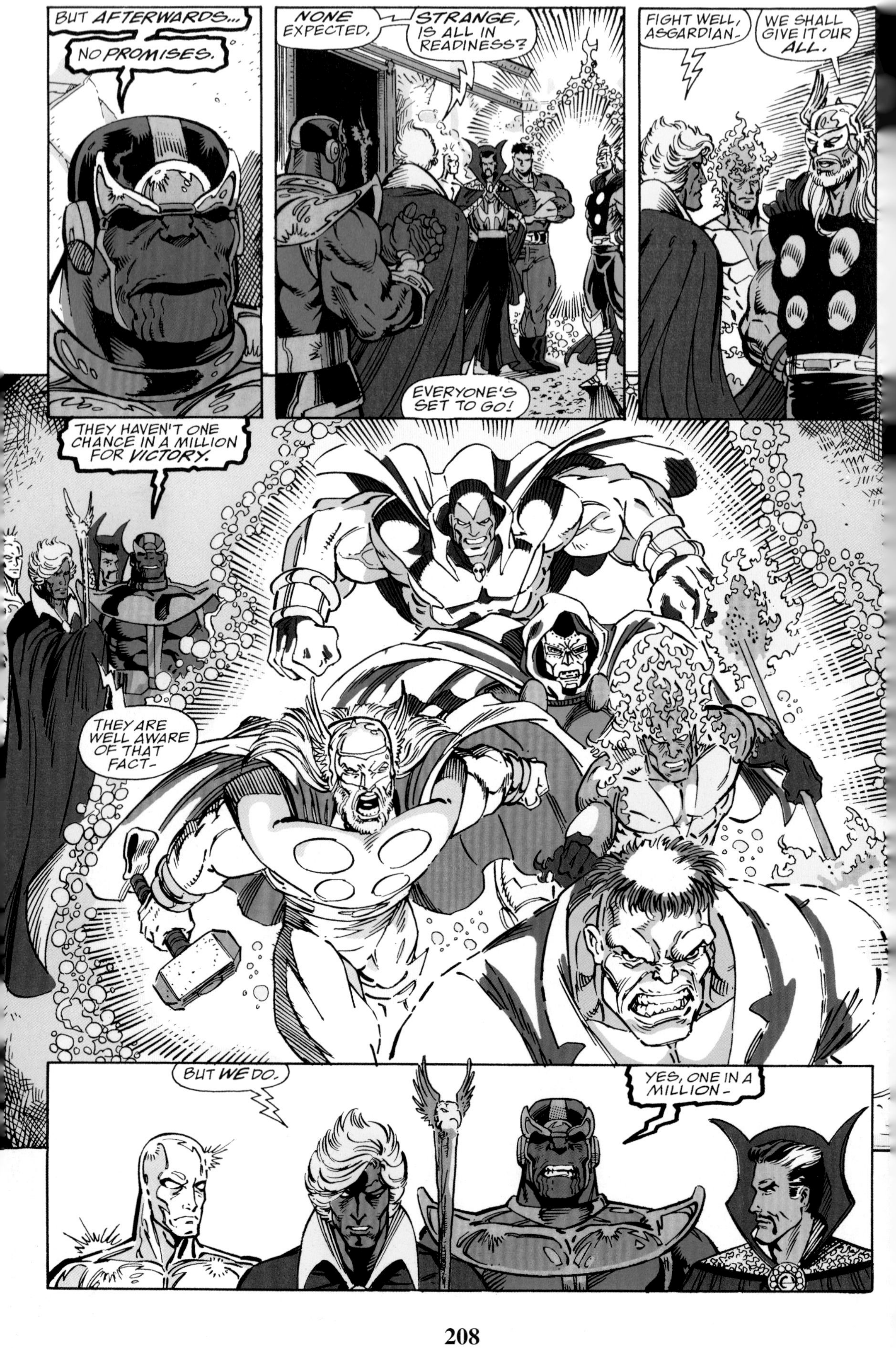
BUT AFTERWARDS...
NO PROMISES.
NONE EXPECTED,
STRANGE, IS ALL IN READINESS?
EVERYONE'S SET TO GO!
FIGHT WELL, ASGARDIAN-
WE SHALL GIVE IT OUR ALL.
THEY HAVEN'T ONE CHANCE IN A MILLION FOR VICTORY.
THEY ARE WELL AWARE OF THAT FACT-
BUT WE DO.
YES, ONE IN A MILLION-

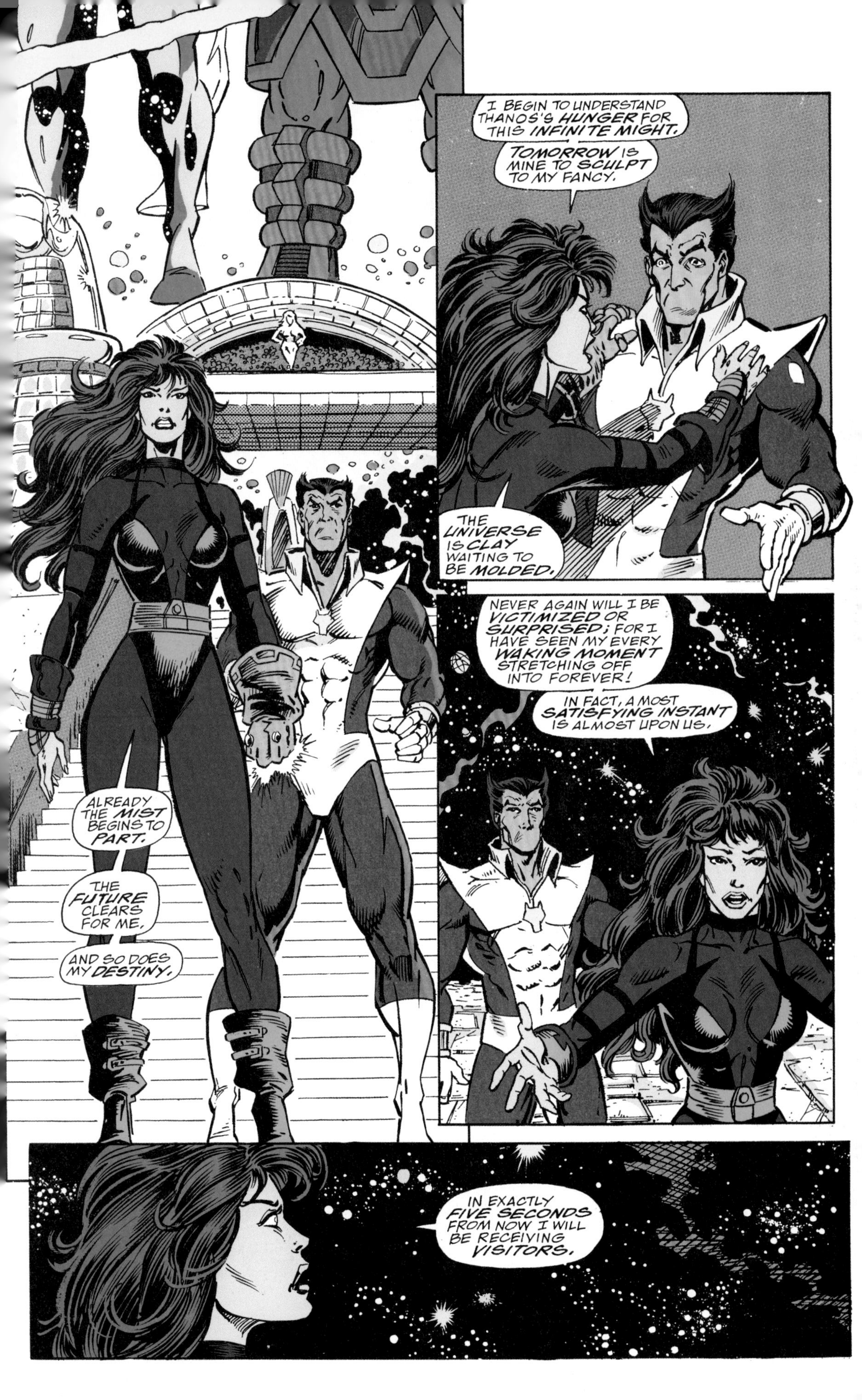
I BEGIN TO UNDERSTAND THANOS'S HUNGER FOR THIS INFINITE MIGHT.
TOMORROW IS MINE TO SCULPT TO MY FANCY.
THE UNIVERSE IS CLAY WAITING TO BE MOLDED.
ALREADY THE MIST BEGINS TO PART.
THE FUTURE CLEARS FOR ME.
AND SO DOES MY DESTINY.
NEVER AGAIN WILL I BE VICTIMIZED OR SURPRISED; FOR I HAVE SEEN MY EVERY WAKING MOMENT STRETCHING OFF INTO FOREVER!
IN FACT, A MOST SATISFYING INSTANT IS ALMOST UPON US.
IN EXACTLY FIVE SECONDS FROM NOW I WILL BE RECEIVING VISITORS.

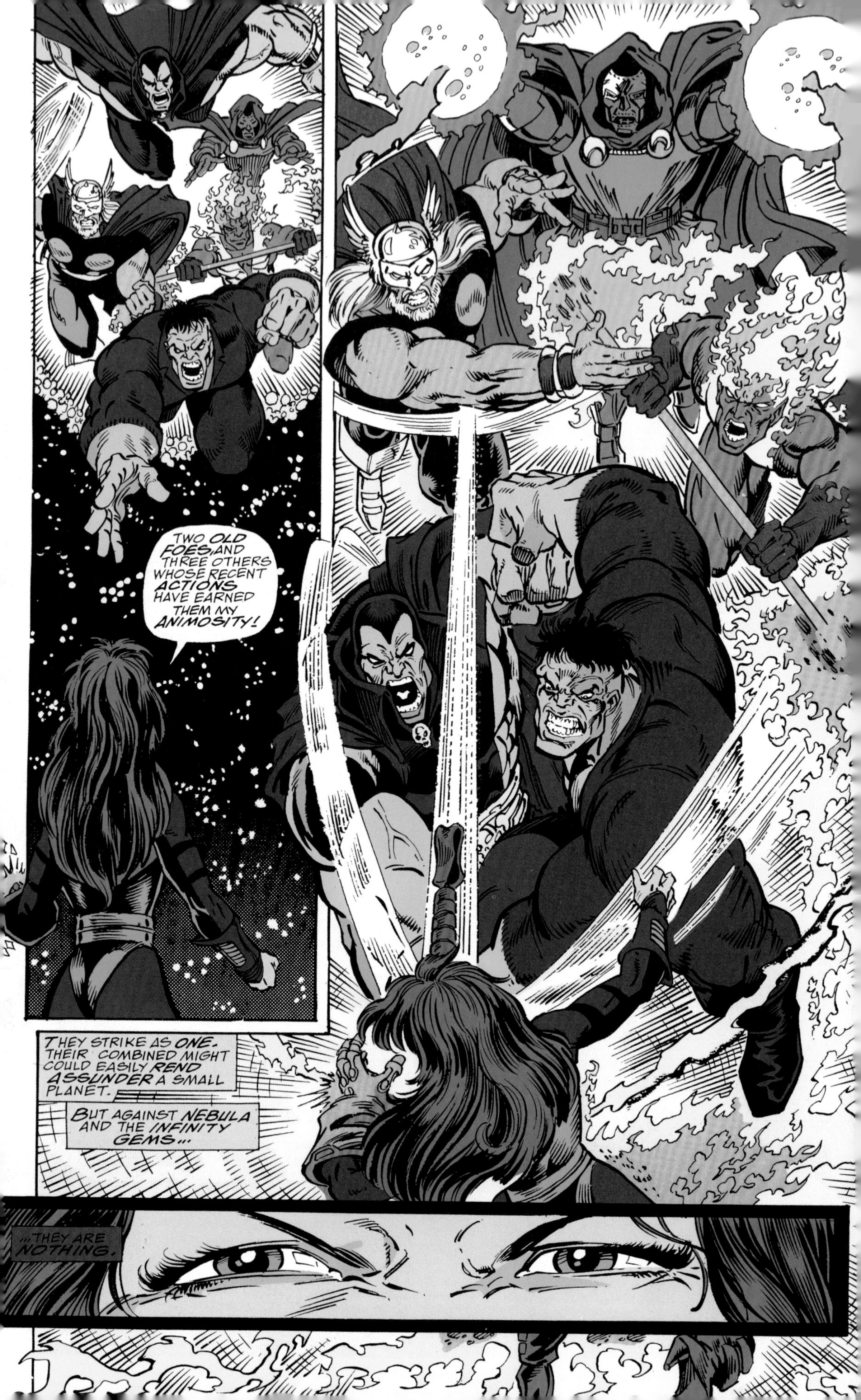
TWO OLD FOES, AND THREE OTHERS WHOSE RECENT ACTIONS HAVE EARNED THEM MY ANIMOSITY!
THEY STRIKE AS ONE. THEIR COMBINED MIGHT COULD EASILY REND ASSUNDER A SMALL PLANET.
BUT AGAINST NEBULA AND THE INFINITY GEMS...
...THEY ARE NOTHING.

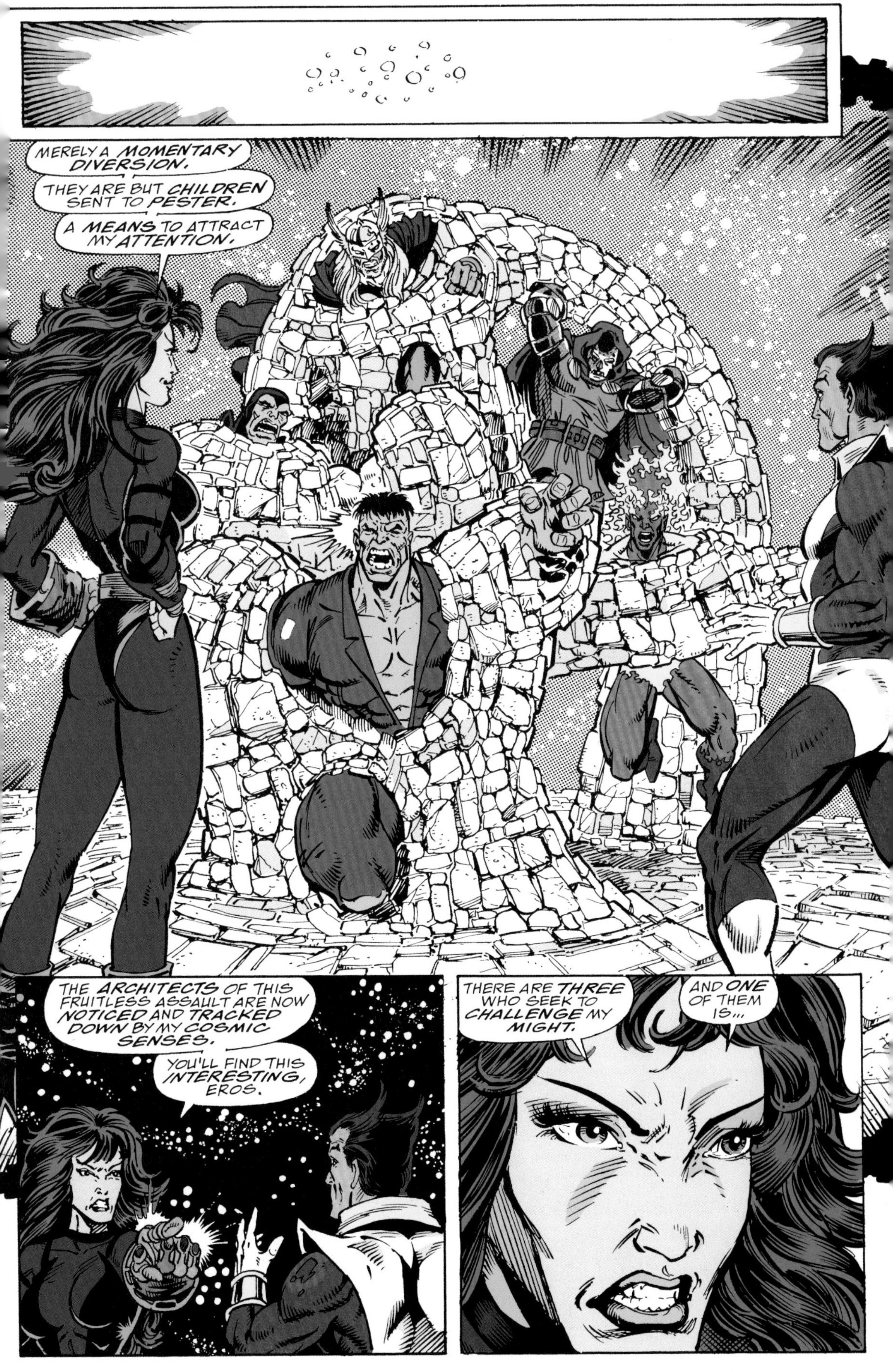
MERELY A MOMENTARY DIVERSION.
THEY ARE BUT CHILDREN SENT TO PESTER.
A MEANS TO ATTRACT MY ATTENTION.
THE ARCHITECTS OF THIS FRUITLESS ASSAULT ARE NOW NOTICED AND TRACKED DOWN BY MY COSMIC SENSES.
YOU'LL FIND THIS INTERESTING, EROS.
THERE ARE THREE WHO SEEK TO CHALLENGE MY MIGHT.
AND ONE OF THEM IS...

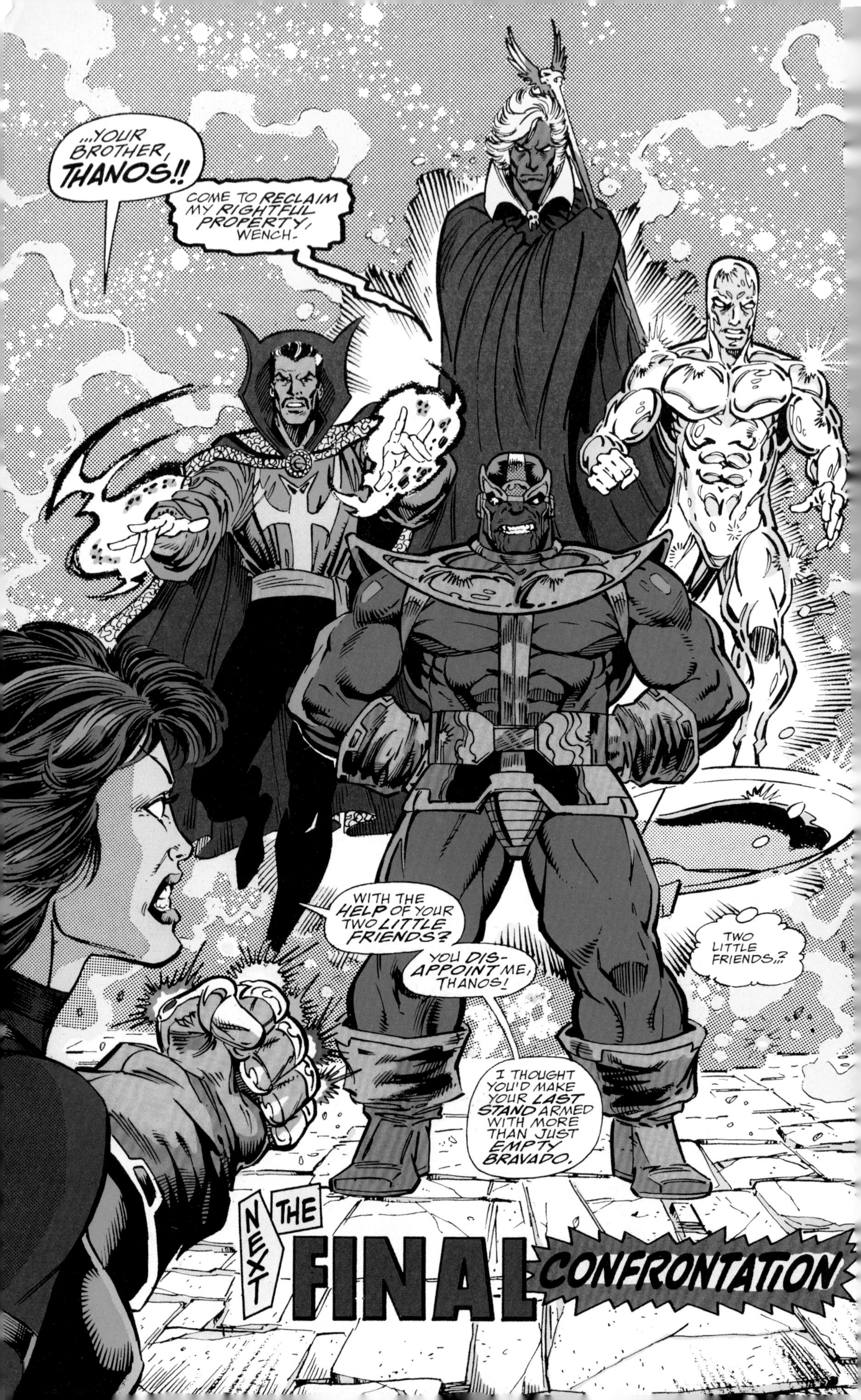
...YOUR BROTHER, THANOS!!
COME TO RECLAIM MY RIGHTFUL PROPERTY, WENCH.
WITH THE HELP OF YOUR TWO LITTLE FRIENDS?
YOU DIS-APPOINT ME, THANOS!
I THOUGHT YOU'D MAKE YOUR LAST STAND ARMED WITH MORE THAN JUST EMPTY BRAVADO.
TWO LITTLE FRIENDS..?
NEXT
THE FINAL CONFRONTATION

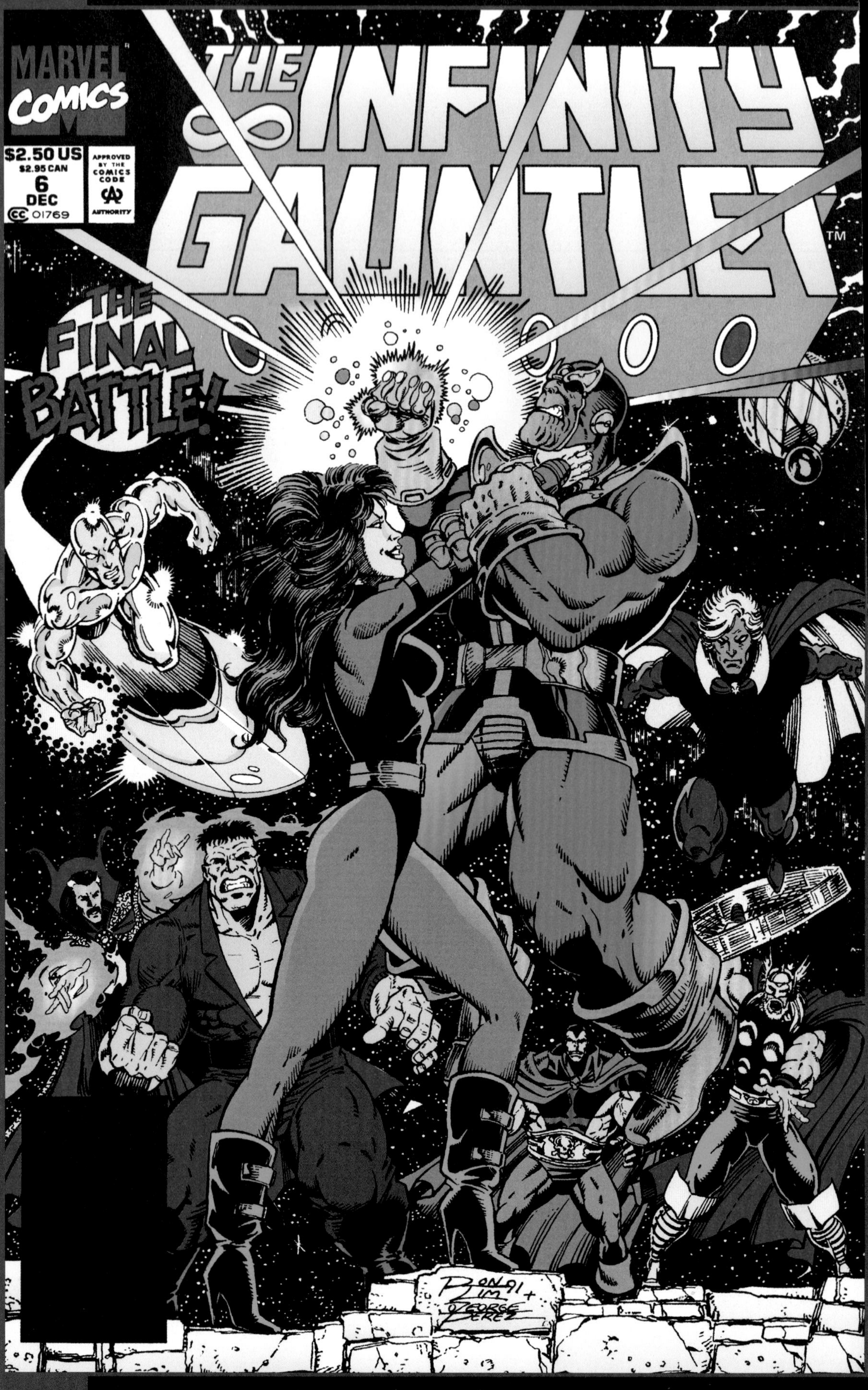
MARVEL COMICS
$2.50 US
$2.95 CAN
6
DEC
01769
APPROVED BY THE COMICS CODE AUTHORITY
THE INFINITY GAUNTLET™
THE FINAL BATTLE!

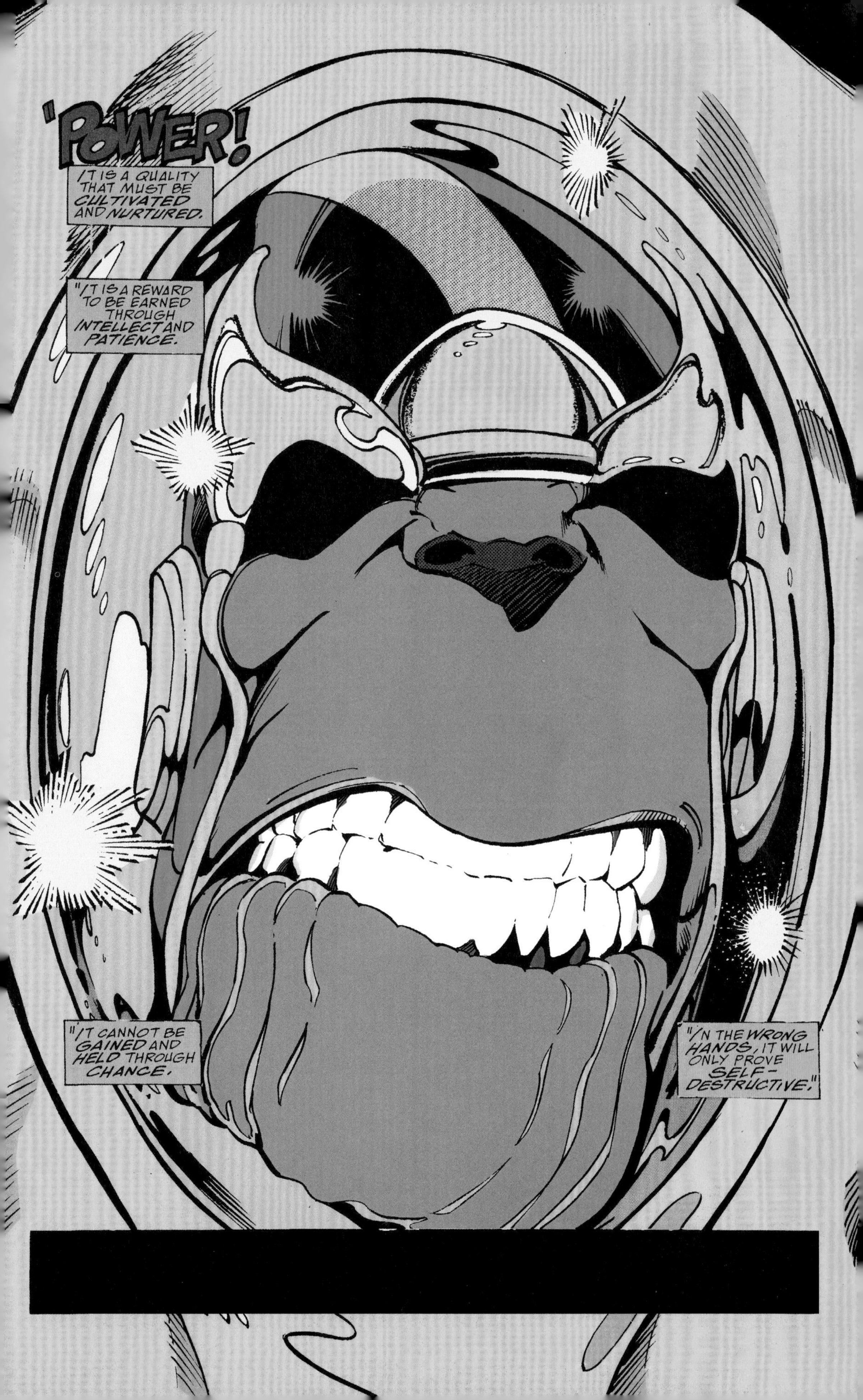
"POWER!
IT IS A QUALITY THAT MUST BE CULTIVATED AND NURTURED.
"IT IS A REWARD TO BE EARNED THROUGH INTELLECT AND PATIENCE.
"IT CANNOT BE GAINED AND HELD THROUGH CHANCE.
"IN THE WRONG HANDS, IT WILL ONLY PROVE SELF-DESTRUCTIVE."
[redacted]

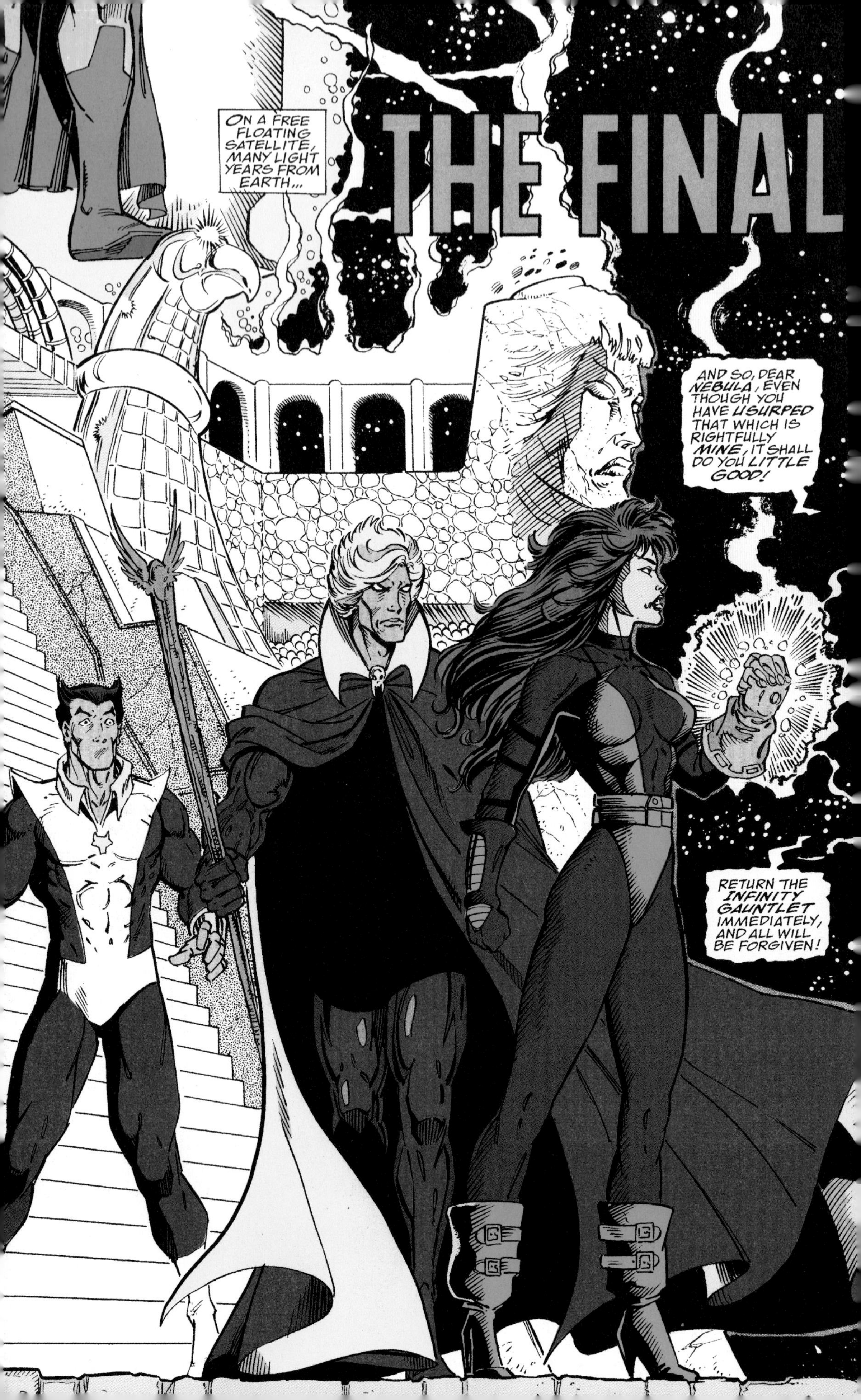

ON A FREE FLOATING SATELLITE, MANY LIGHT YEARS FROM EARTH...
THE FINAL
AND SO, DEAR NEBULA, EVEN THOUGH YOU HAVE USURPED THAT WHICH IS RIGHTFULLY MINE, IT SHALL DO YOU LITTLE GOOD!
RETURN THE INFINITY GAUNTLET IMMEDIATELY, AND ALL WILL BE FORGIVEN!

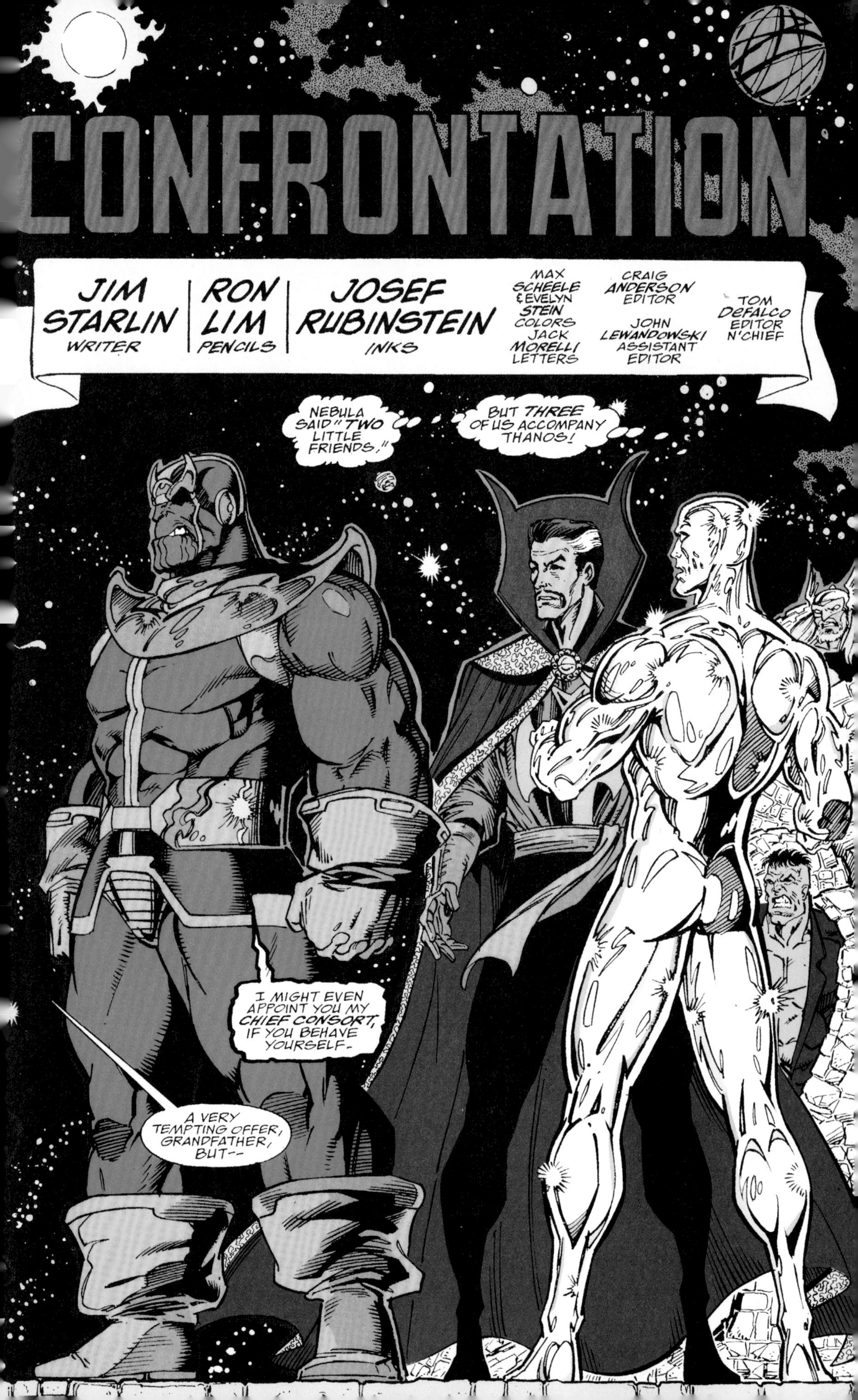

CONFRONTATION
JIM STARLIN WRITER
RON LIM PENCILS
JOSEF RUBINSTEIN INKS
MAX SCHEELE & EVELYN STEIN COLORS
JACK MORELLI LETTERS
CRAIG ANDERSON EDITOR
JOHN LEWANDOWSKI ASSISTANT EDITOR
TOM DeFALCO EDITOR N'CHIEF
NEBULA SAID "TWO LITTLE FRIENDS,"
BUT THREE OF US ACCOMPANY THANOS!
I MIGHT EVEN APPOINT YOU MY CHIEF CONSORT, IF YOU BEHAVE YOURSELF-
A VERY TEMPTING OFFER, GRANDFATHER, BUT--

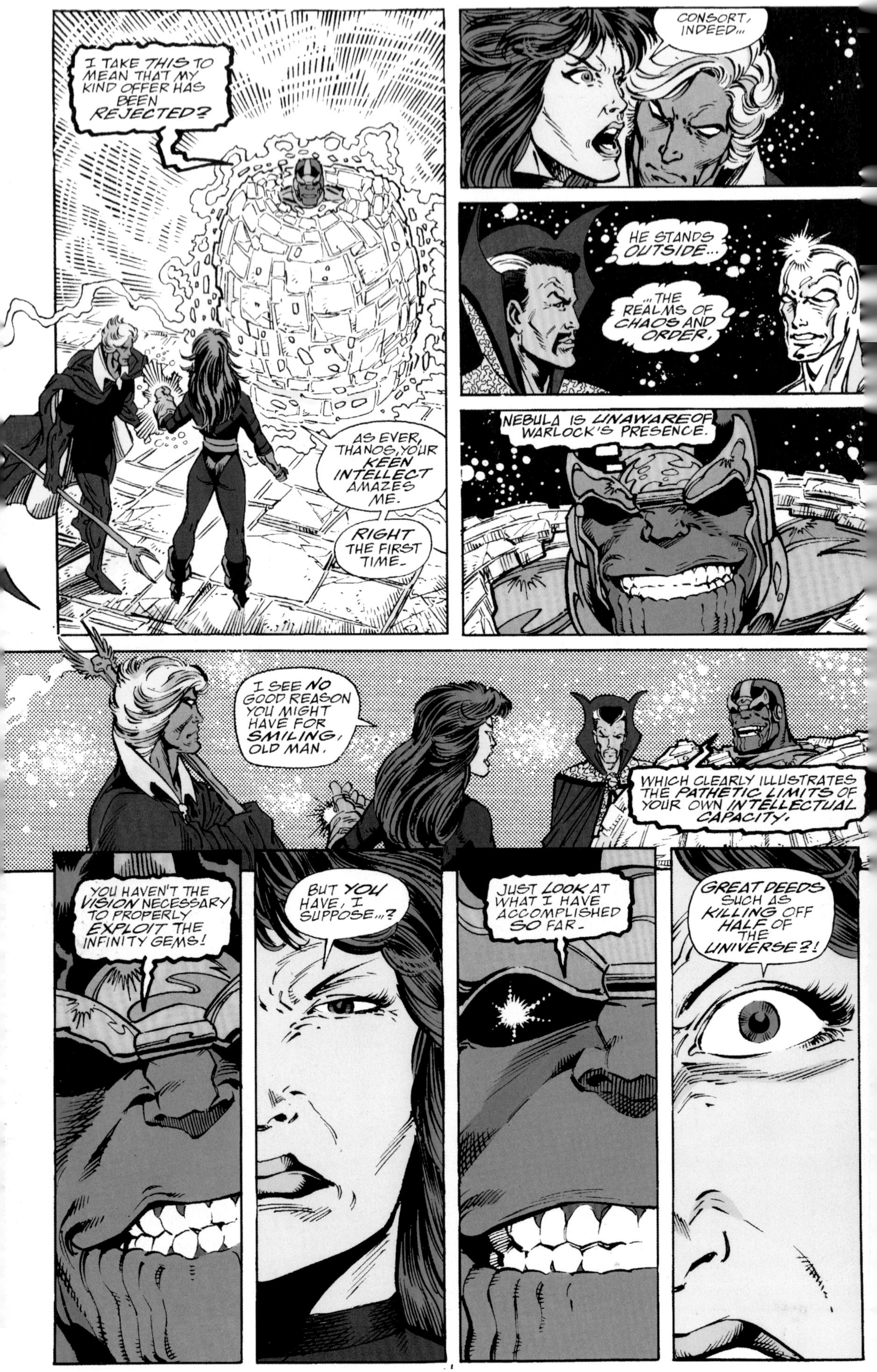

I TAKE THIS TO MEAN THAT MY KIND OFFER HAS BEEN REJECTED?
AS EVER, THANOS, YOUR KEEN INTELLECT AMAZES ME.
RIGHT THE FIRST TIME.
CONSORT, INDEED...
HE STANDS OUTSIDE...
...THE REALMS OF CHAOS AND ORDER.
NEBULA IS UNAWARE OF WARLOCK'S PRESENCE.
I SEE NO GOOD REASON YOU MIGHT HAVE FOR SMILING, OLD MAN.
WHICH CLEARLY ILLUSTRATES THE PATHETIC LIMITS OF YOUR OWN INTELLECTUAL CAPACITY.
YOU HAVEN'T THE VISION NECESSARY TO PROPERLY EXPLOIT THE INFINITY GEMS!
BUT YOU HAVE, I SUPPOSE...?
JUST LOOK AT WHAT I HAVE ACCOMPLISHED SO FAR.
GREAT DEEDS SUCH AS KILLING OFF HALF OF THE UNIVERSE?!

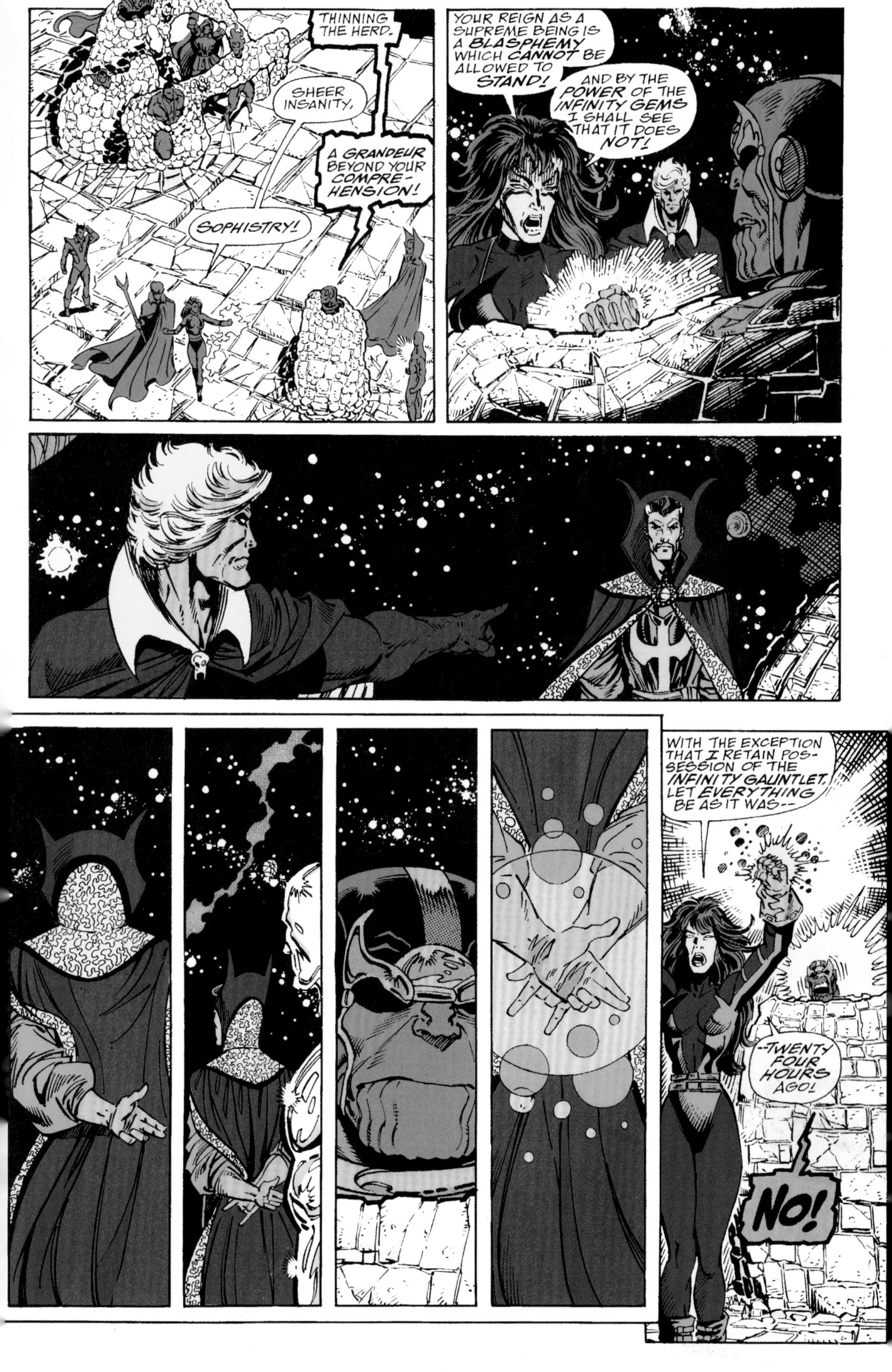
THINNING THE HERD.
SHEER INSANITY.
A GRANDEUR BEYOND YOUR COMPRE-HENSION!
SOPHISTRY!
YOUR REIGN AS A SUPREME BEING IS A BLASPHEMY WHICH CANNOT BE ALLOWED TO STAND!
AND BY THE POWER OF THE INFINITY GEMS I SHALL SEE THAT IT DOES NOT!
WITH THE EXCEPTION THAT I RETAIN POS-SESSION OF THE INFINITY GAUNTLET, LET EVERYTHING BE AS IT WAS--
--TWENTY FOUR HOURS AGO!
NO!

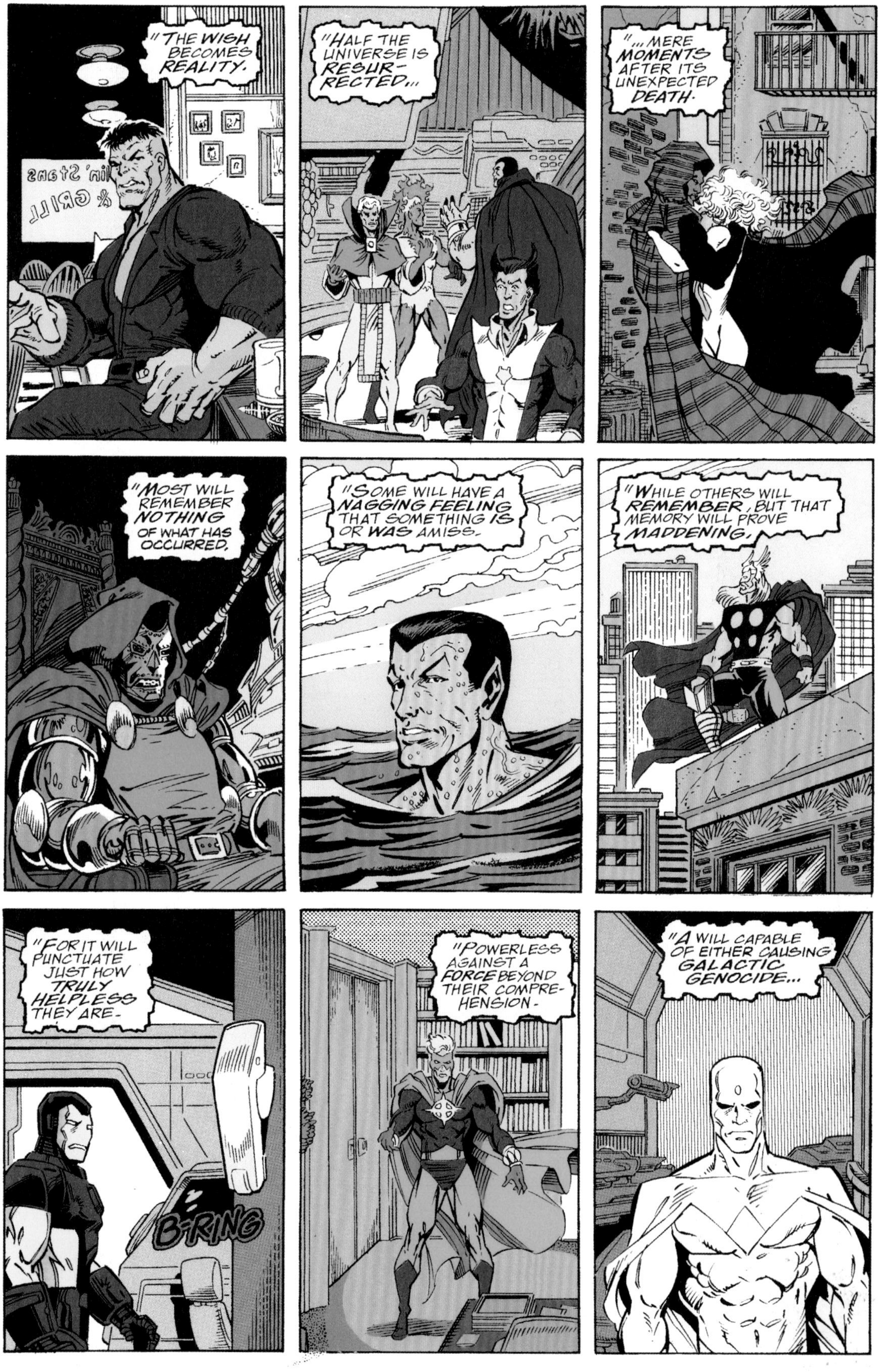
"THE WISH BECOMES REALITY.
"HALF THE UNIVERSE IS RESURRECTED...
"...MERE MOMENTS AFTER ITS UNEXPECTED DEATH.
"MOST WILL REMEMBER NOTHING OF WHAT HAS OCCURRED.
"SOME WILL HAVE A NAGGING FEELING THAT SOMETHING IS OR WAS AMISS.
"WHILE OTHERS WILL REMEMBER, BUT THAT MEMORY WILL PROVE MADDENING.
"FOR IT WILL PUNCTUATE JUST HOW TRULY HELPLESS THEY ARE.
B-RING
"POWERLESS AGAINST A FORCE BEYOND THEIR COMPREHENSION.
"A WILL CAPABLE OF EITHER CAUSING GALACTIC GENOCIDE...

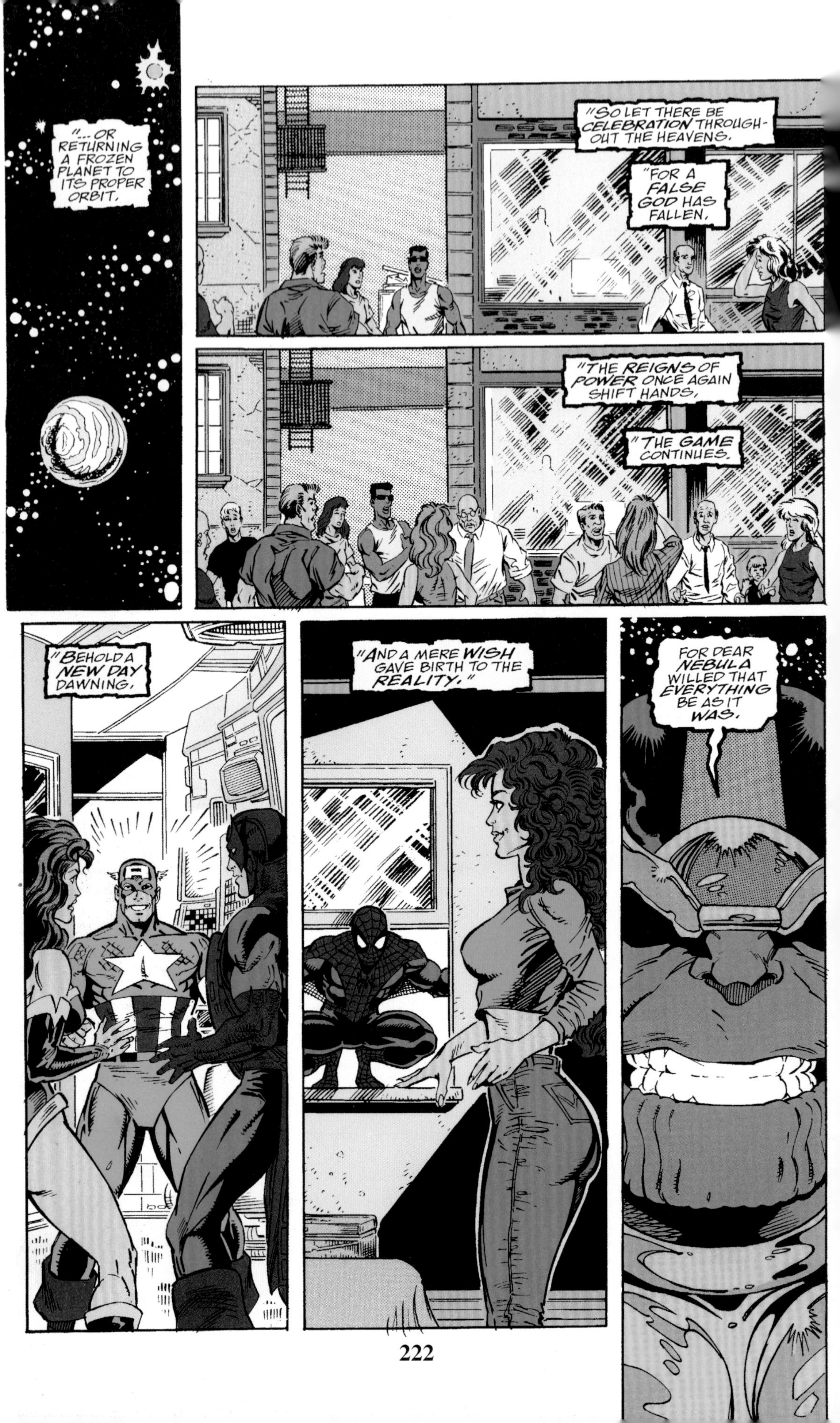
"...OR RETURNING A FROZEN PLANET TO ITS PROPER ORBIT.
"SO LET THERE BE CELEBRATION THROUGH-OUT THE HEAVENS.
"FOR A FALSE GOD HAS FALLEN.
"THE REIGNS OF POWER ONCE AGAIN SHIFT HANDS,
"THE GAME CONTINUES.
"BEHOLD A NEW DAY DAWNING,
"AND A MERE WISH GAVE BIRTH TO THE REALITY."
FOR DEAR NEBULA WILLED THAT EVERYTHING BE AS IT WAS.

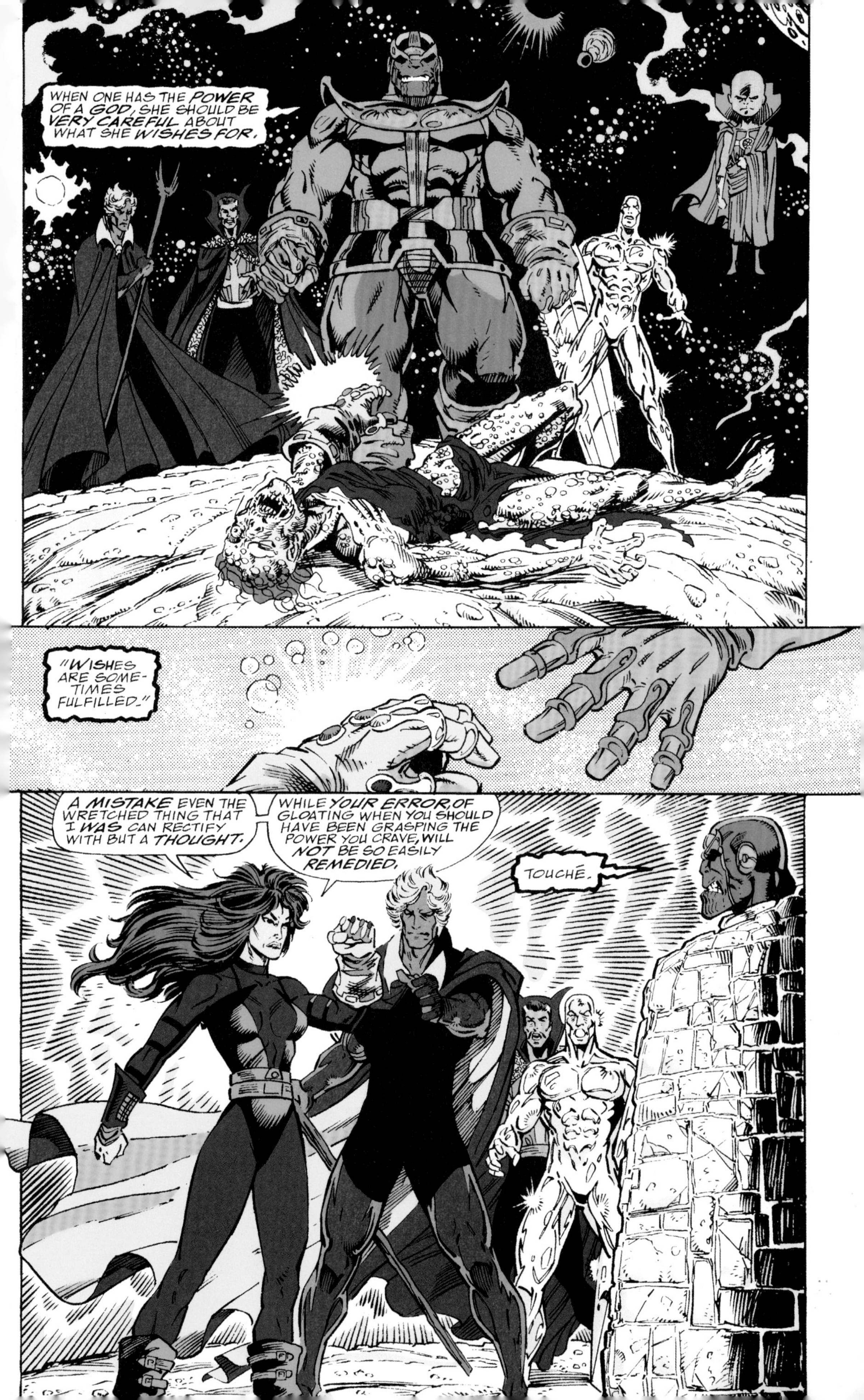
WHEN ONE HAS THE POWER OF A GOD, SHE SHOULD BE VERY CAREFUL ABOUT WHAT SHE WISHES FOR.
"WISHES ARE SOMETIMES FULFILLED."
A MISTAKE EVEN THE WRETCHED THING THAT I WAS CAN RECTIFY WITH BUT A THOUGHT.
WHILE YOUR ERROR, OF GLOATING WHEN YOU SHOULD HAVE BEEN GRASPING THE POWER YOU CRAVE, WILL NOT BE SO EASILY REMEDIED.
TOUCHÉ.

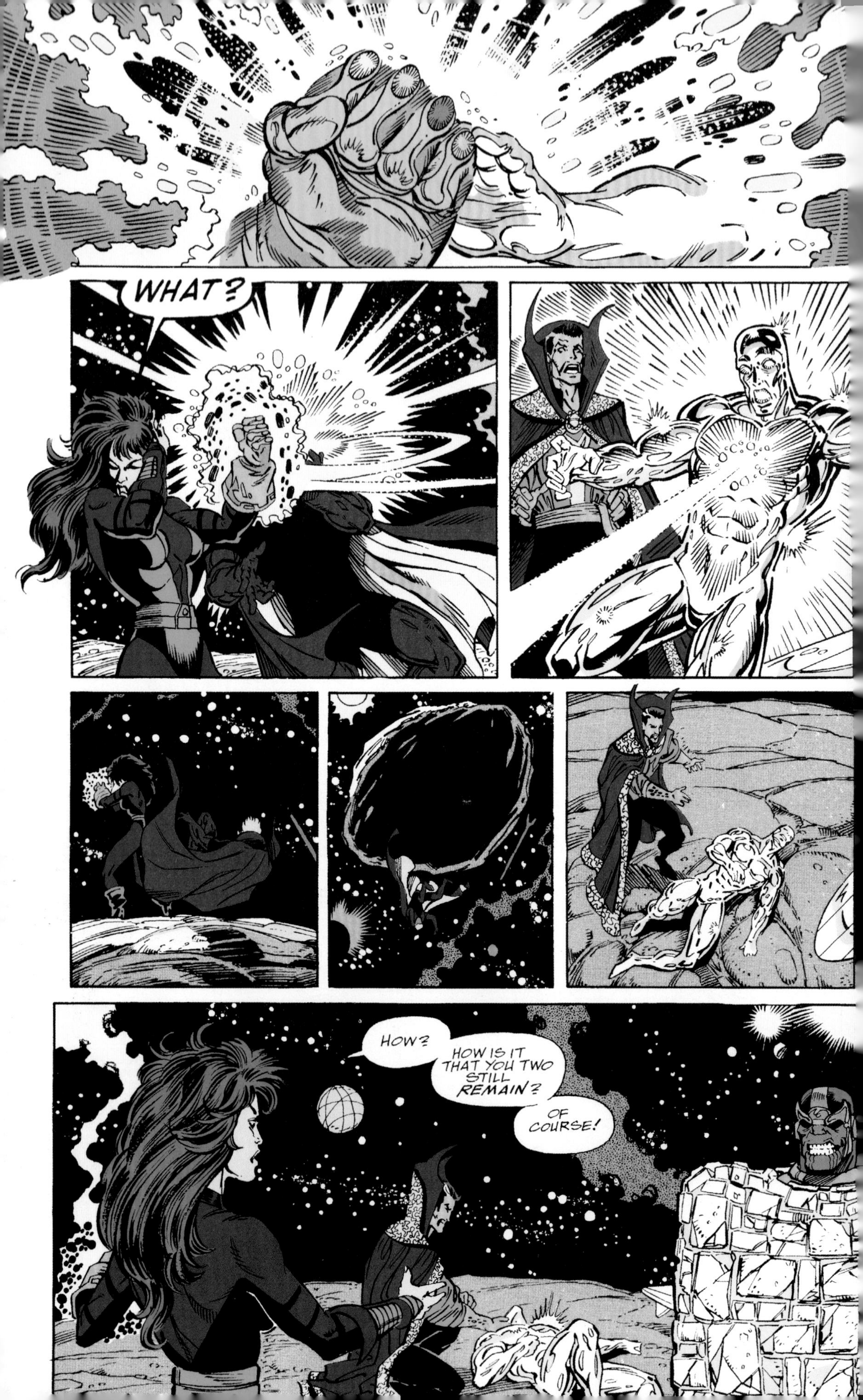
WHAT?
HOW?
HOW IS IT THAT YOU TWO STILL REMAIN?
OF COURSE!

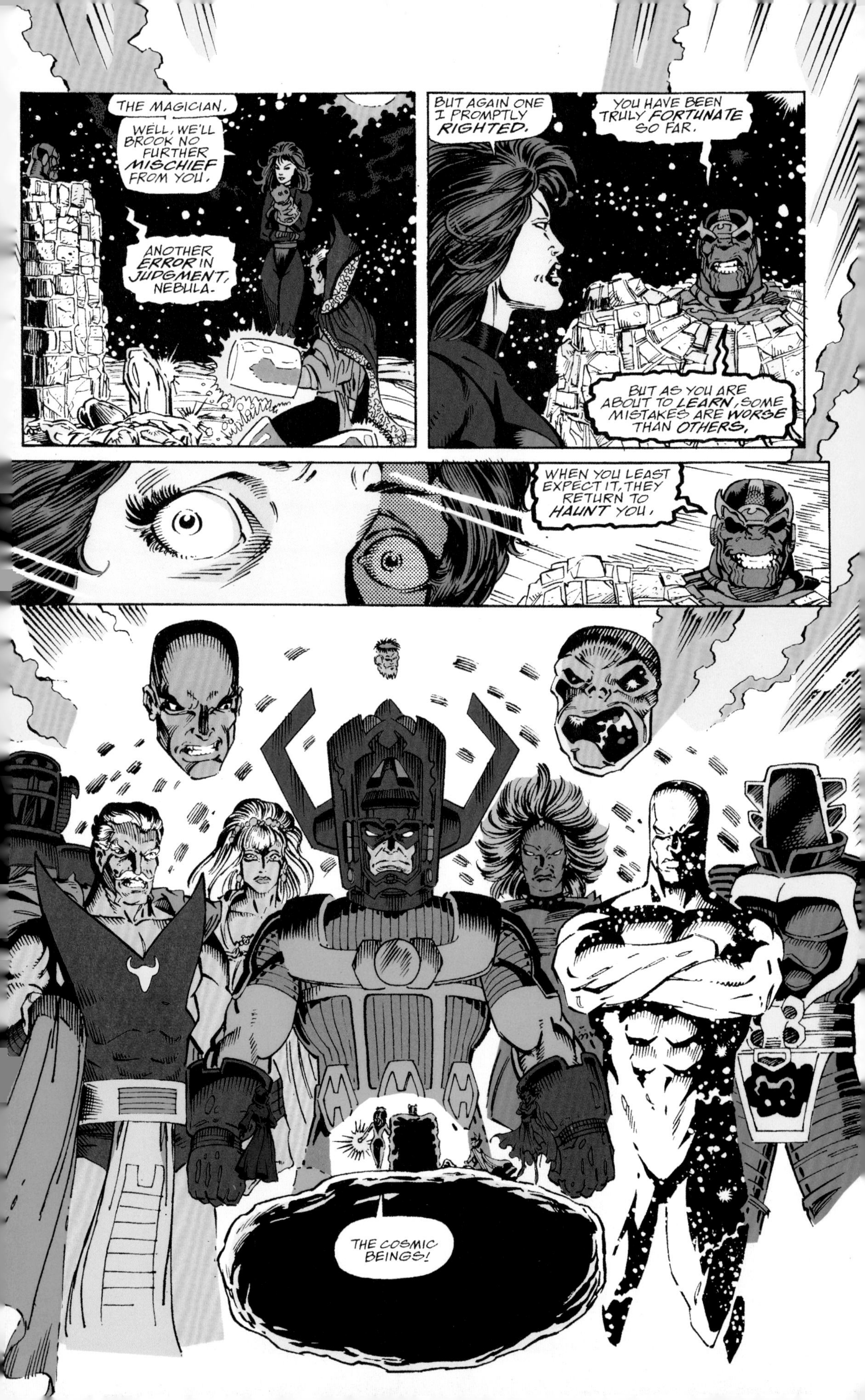
THE MAGICIAN.
WELL, WE'LL BROOK NO FURTHER MISCHIEF FROM YOU.
ANOTHER ERROR IN JUDGMENT, NEBULA.
BUT AGAIN ONE I PROMPTLY RIGHTED.
YOU HAVE BEEN TRULY FORTUNATE SO FAR.
BUT AS YOU ARE ABOUT TO LEARN, SOME MISTAKES ARE WORSE THAN OTHERS.
WHEN YOU LEAST EXPECT IT, THEY RETURN TO HAUNT YOU.
THE COSMIC BEINGS!

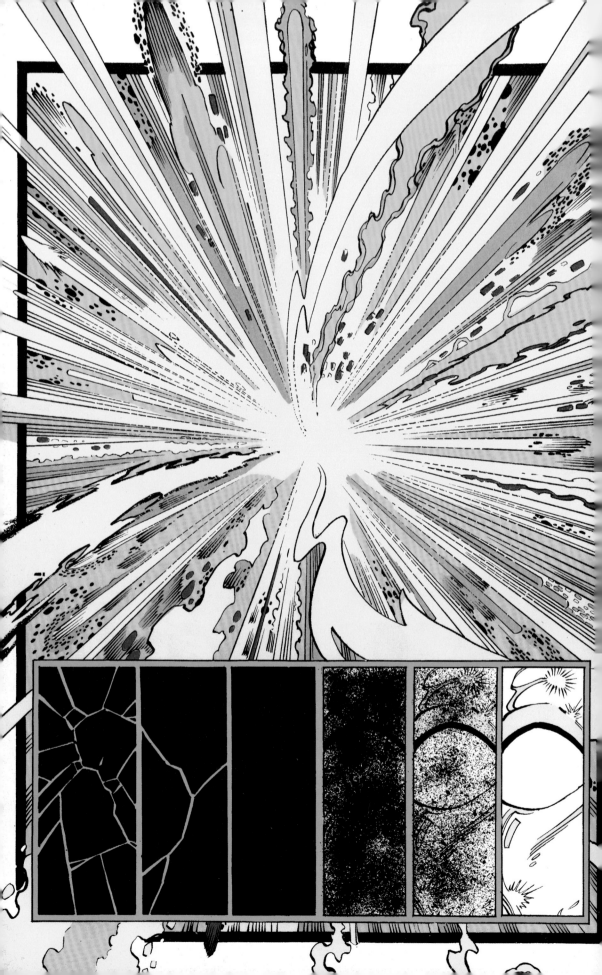

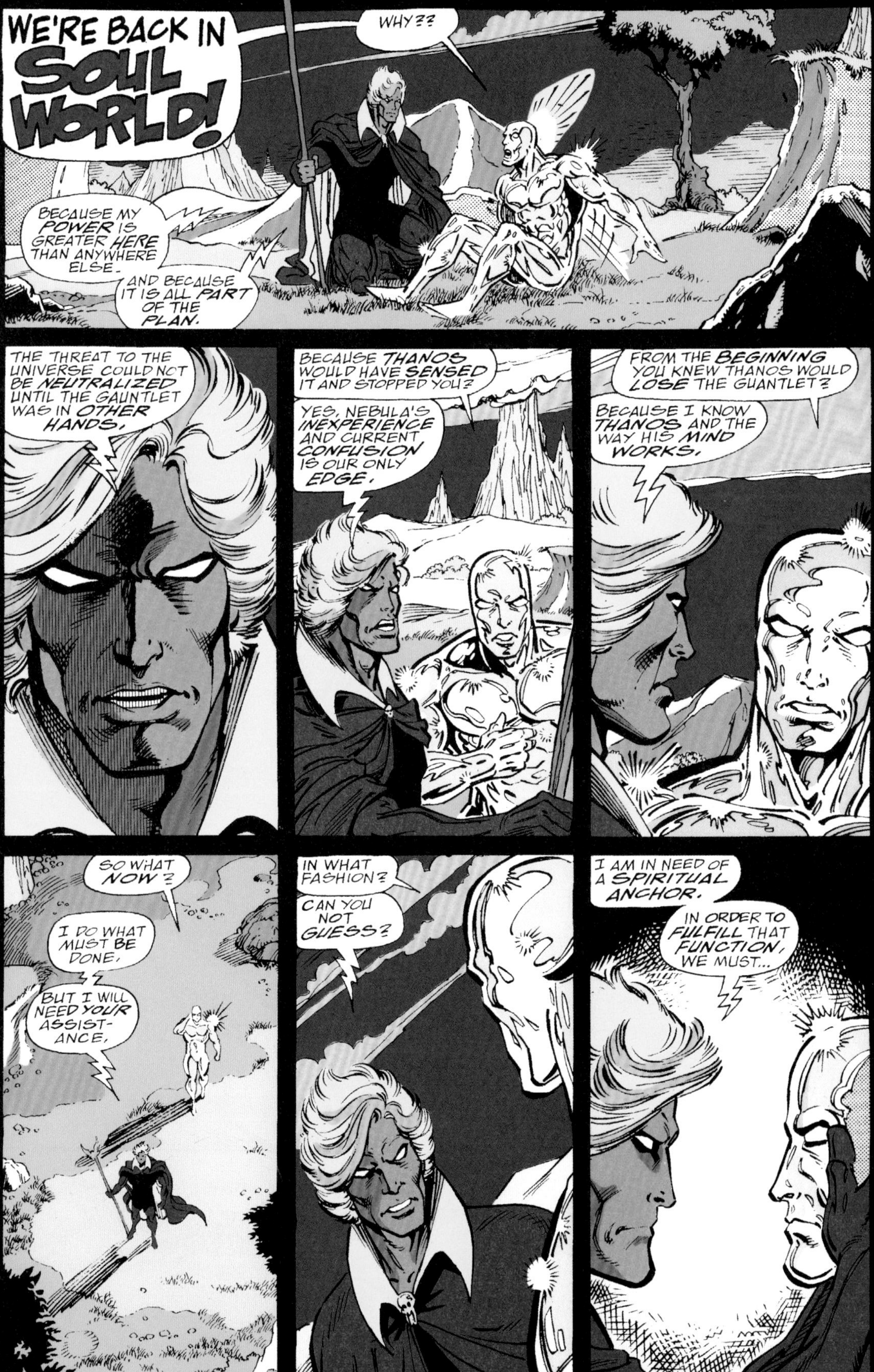

WE'RE BACK IN SOUL WORLD!
WHY??
BECAUSE MY POWER IS GREATER HERE THAN ANYWHERE ELSE.
AND BECAUSE IT IS ALL PART OF THE PLAN.
THE THREAT TO THE UNIVERSE COULD NOT BE NEUTRALIZED UNTIL THE GAUNTLET WAS IN OTHER HANDS.
BECAUSE THANOS WOULD HAVE SENSED IT AND STOPPED YOU?
YES. NEBULA'S INEXPERIENCE AND CURRENT CONFUSION IS OUR ONLY EDGE.
FROM THE BEGINNING YOU KNEW THANOS WOULD LOSE THE GUANTLET?
BECAUSE I KNOW THANOS AND THE WAY HIS MIND WORKS.
SO WHAT NOW?
I DO WHAT MUST BE DONE.
BUT I WILL NEED YOUR ASSIST-ANCE.
IN WHAT FASHION?
CAN YOU NOT GUESS?
I AM IN NEED OF A SPIRITUAL ANCHOR.
IN ORDER TO FULFILL THAT FUNCTION, WE MUST...

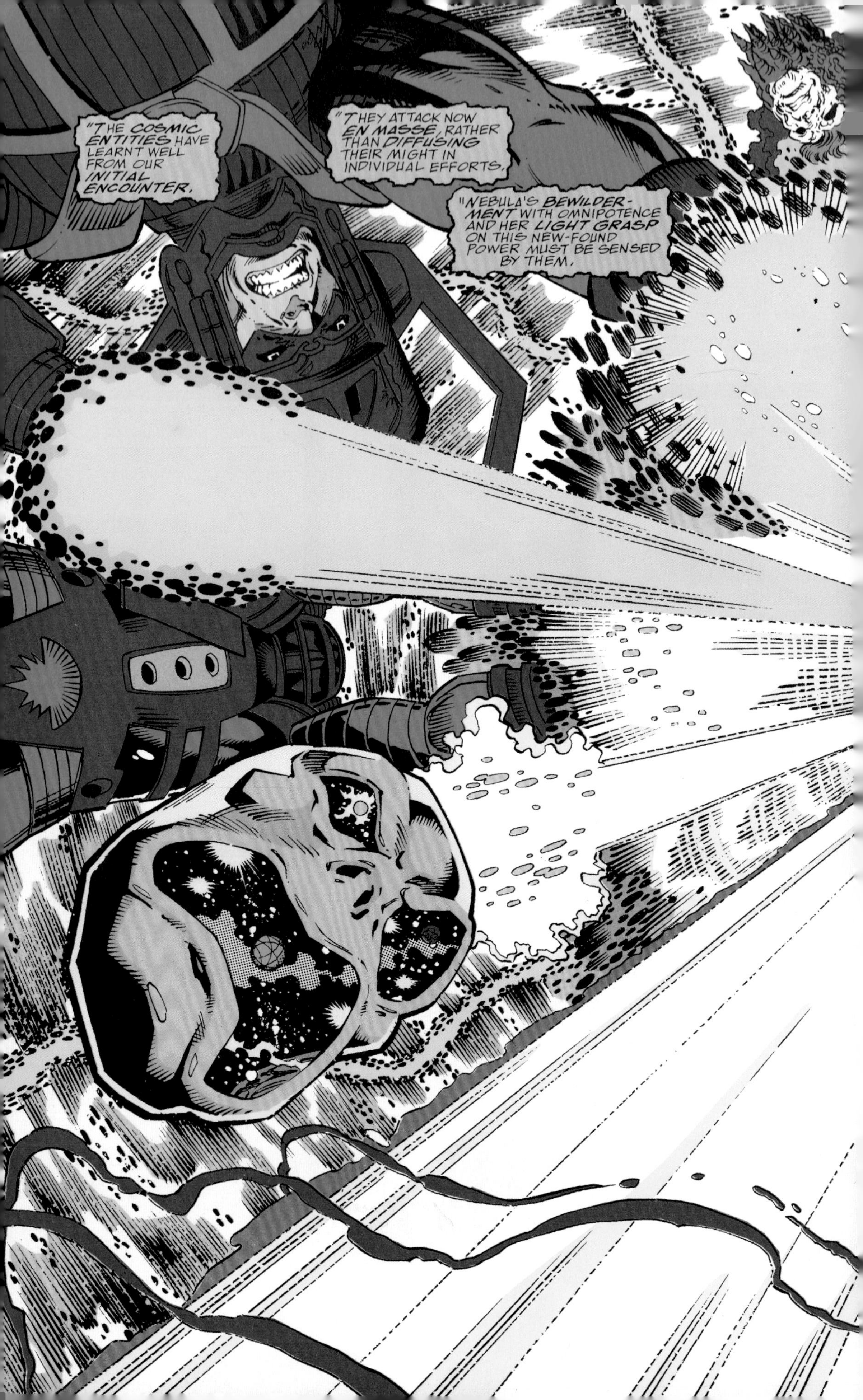
"THE COSMIC ENTITIES HAVE LEARNT WELL FROM OUR INITIAL ENCOUNTER.
"THEY ATTACK NOW EN MASSE, RATHER THAN DIFFUSING THEIR MIGHT IN INDIVIDUAL EFFORTS.
"NEBULA'S BEWILDERMENT WITH OMNIPOTENCE AND HER LIGHT GRASP ON THIS NEW-FOUND POWER MUST BE SENSED BY THEM.

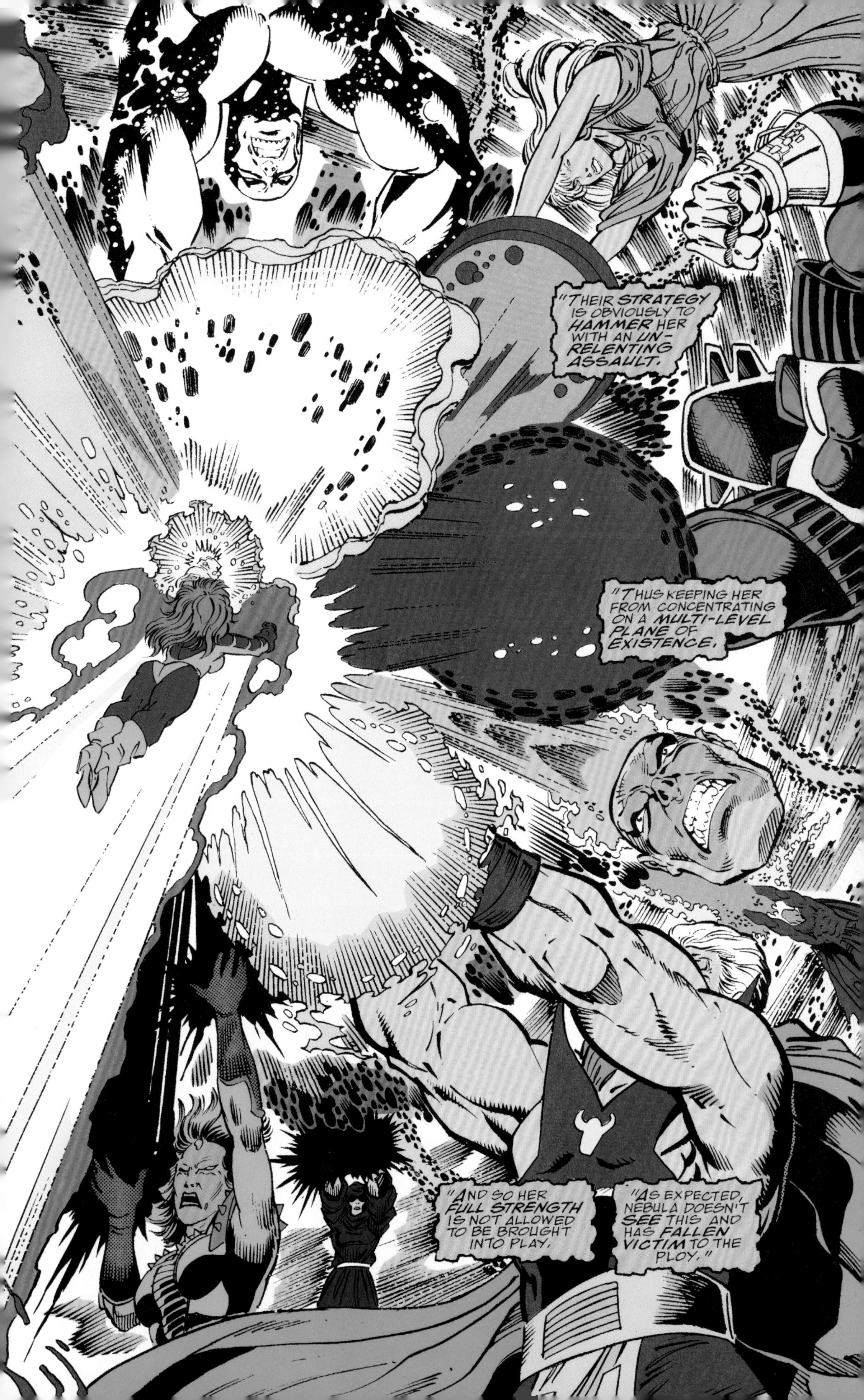
"THEIR STRATEGY IS OBVIOUSLY TO HAMMER HER WITH AN UN-RELENTING ASSAULT.
"THUS KEEPING HER FROM CONCENTRATING ON A MULTI-LEVEL PLANE OF EXISTENCE.
"AND SO HER FULL STRENGTH IS NOT ALLOWED TO BE BROUGHT INTO PLAY.
"AS EXPECTED, NEBULA DOESN'T SEE THIS AND HAS FALLEN VICTIM TO THE PLOY."

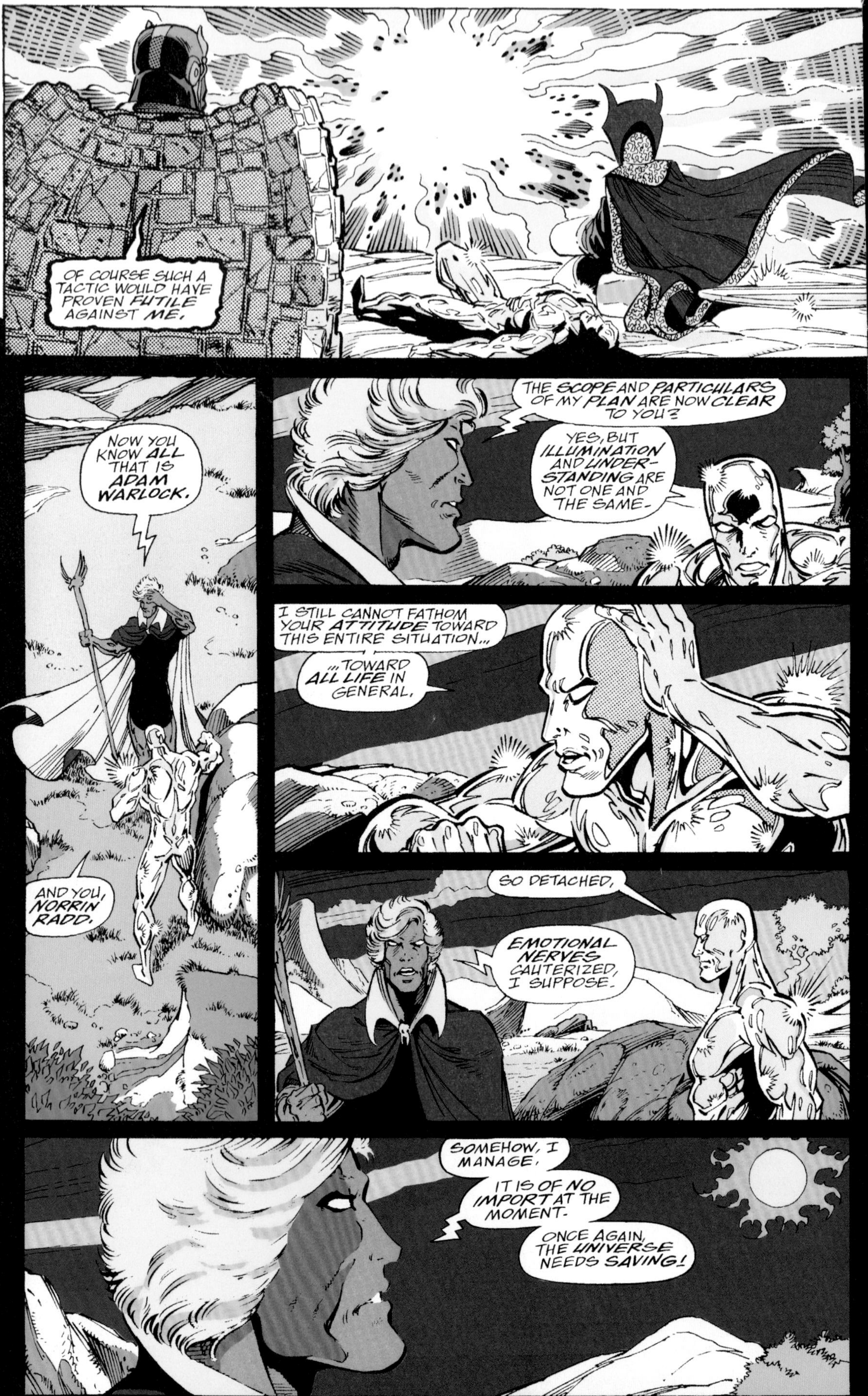

OF COURSE SUCH A TACTIC WOULD HAVE PROVEN FUTILE AGAINST ME.
NOW YOU KNOW ALL THAT IS ADAM WARLOCK.
AND YOU, NORRIN RADD.
THE SCOPE AND PARTICULARS OF MY PLAN ARE NOW CLEAR TO YOU?
YES, BUT ILLUMINATION AND UNDER-STANDING ARE NOT ONE AND THE SAME-
I STILL CANNOT FATHOM YOUR ATTITUDE TOWARD THIS ENTIRE SITUATION...
...TOWARD ALL LIFE IN GENERAL.
SO DETACHED.
EMOTIONAL NERVES CAUTERIZED, I SUPPOSE.
SOMEHOW, I MANAGE.
IT IS OF NO IMPORT AT THE MOMENT.
ONCE AGAIN, THE UNIVERSE NEEDS SAVING!

IT ALL SOUNDS RATHER *MUNDANE* WHEN SAID LIKE THAT, DOESN'T IT?

BUT THAT IS WHAT BEINGS LIKE *YOU* AND *I* DO; WE DE-FEND REALITY.

ESPECIALLY A REALITY IN WHICH A *SOUL* CAN *EXPAND* TO FILL A NEED—

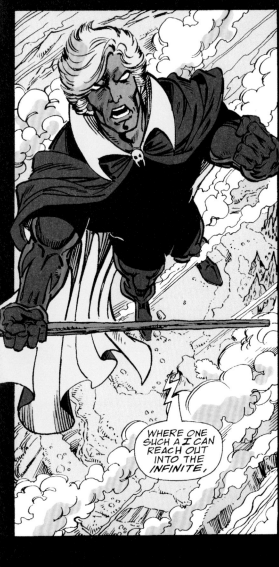

WHERE ONE SUCH A *I* CAN REACH OUT INTO THE *INFINITE*,

AND PERHAPS CHANGE THE *FACE* OF THE *COSMOS!*

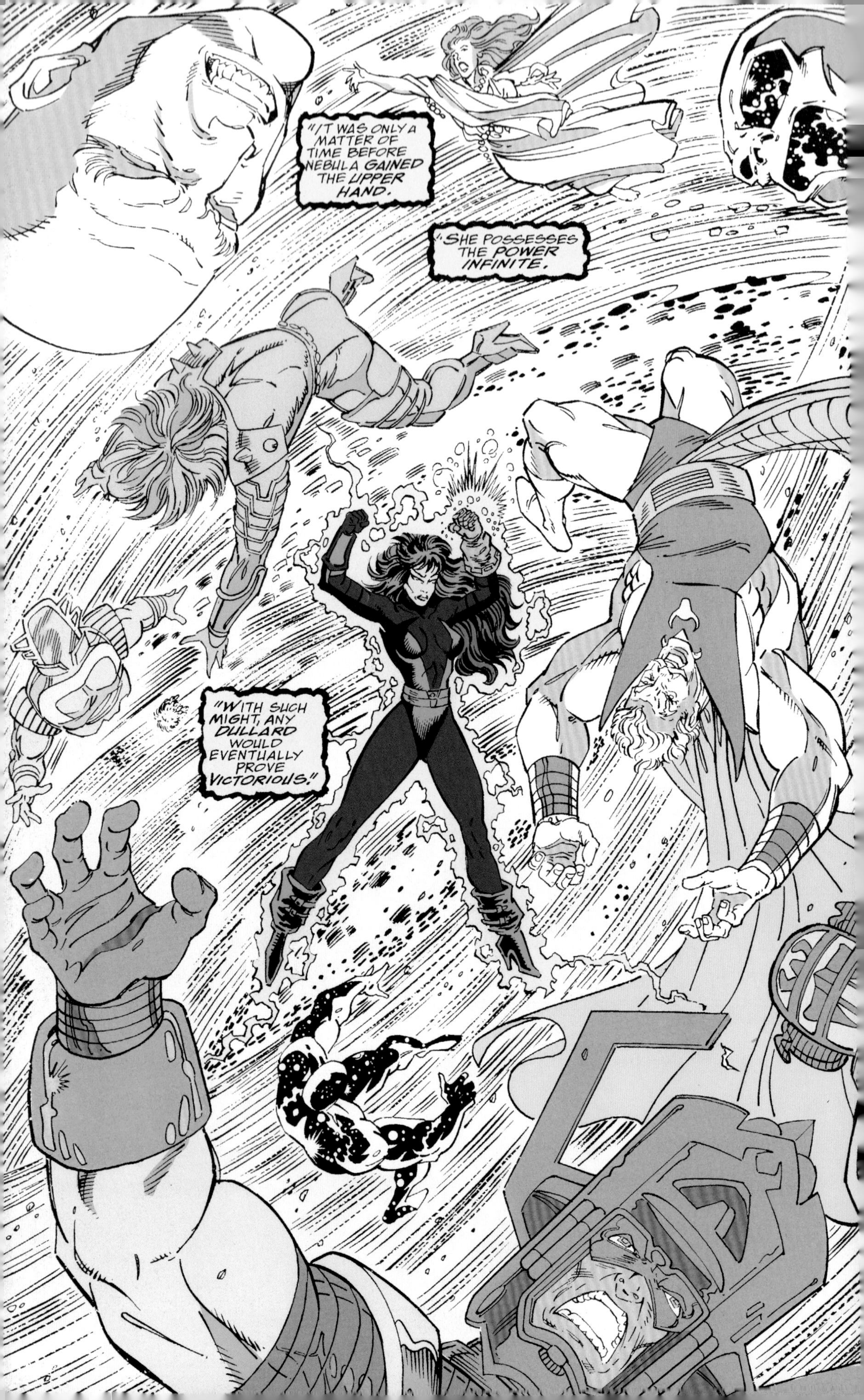
"IT WAS ONLY A MATTER OF TIME BEFORE NEBULA GAINED THE UPPER HAND.
"SHE POSSESSES THE POWER INFINITE.
"WITH SUCH MIGHT, ANY DULLARD WOULD EVENTUALLY PROVE VICTORIOUS."

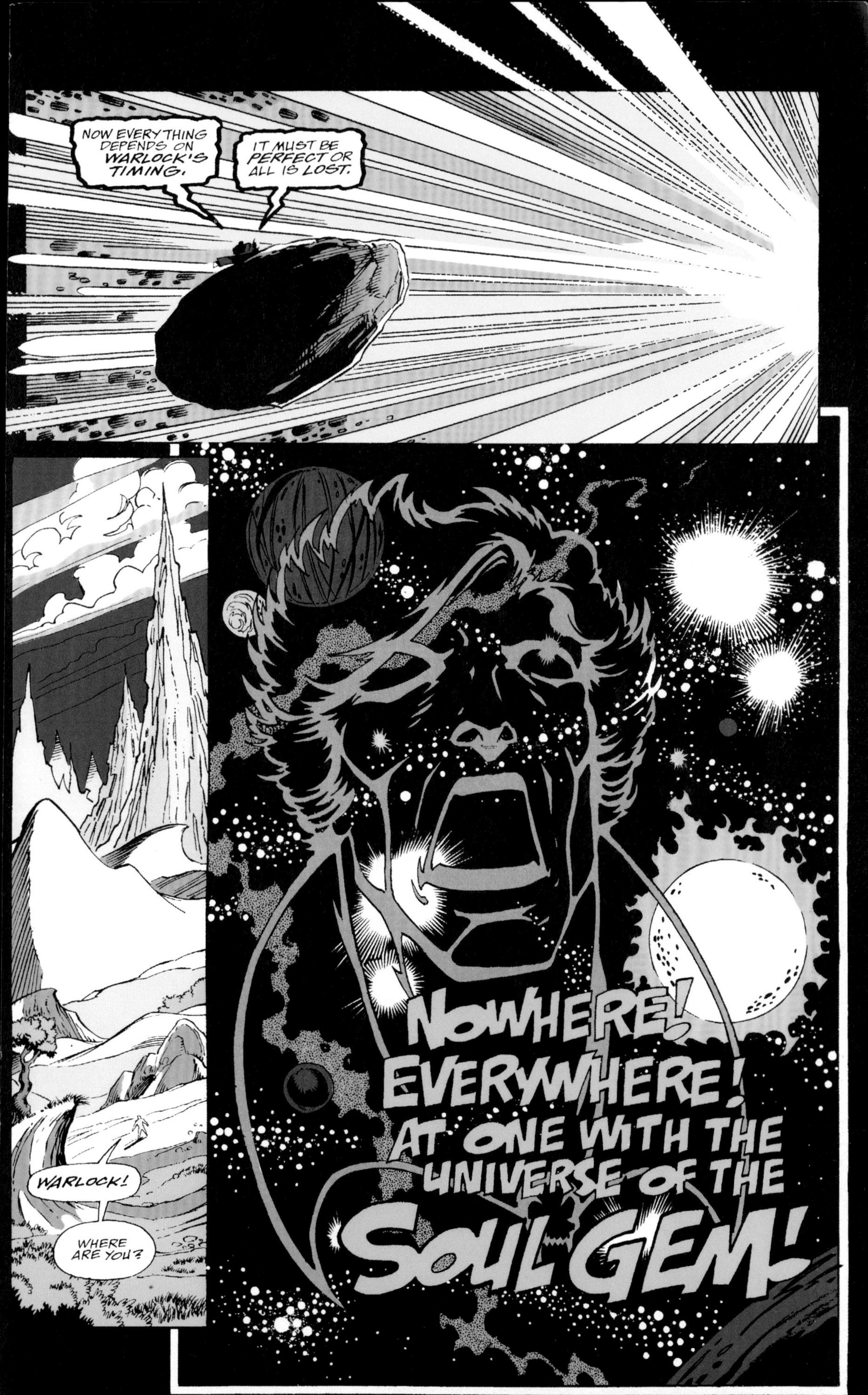
NOW EVERYTHING DEPENDS ON WARLOCK'S TIMING.
IT MUST BE PERFECT OR ALL IS LOST.
WARLOCK!
WHERE ARE YOU?
NOWHERE! EVERYWHERE! AT ONE WITH THE UNIVERSE OF THE SOUL GEM!

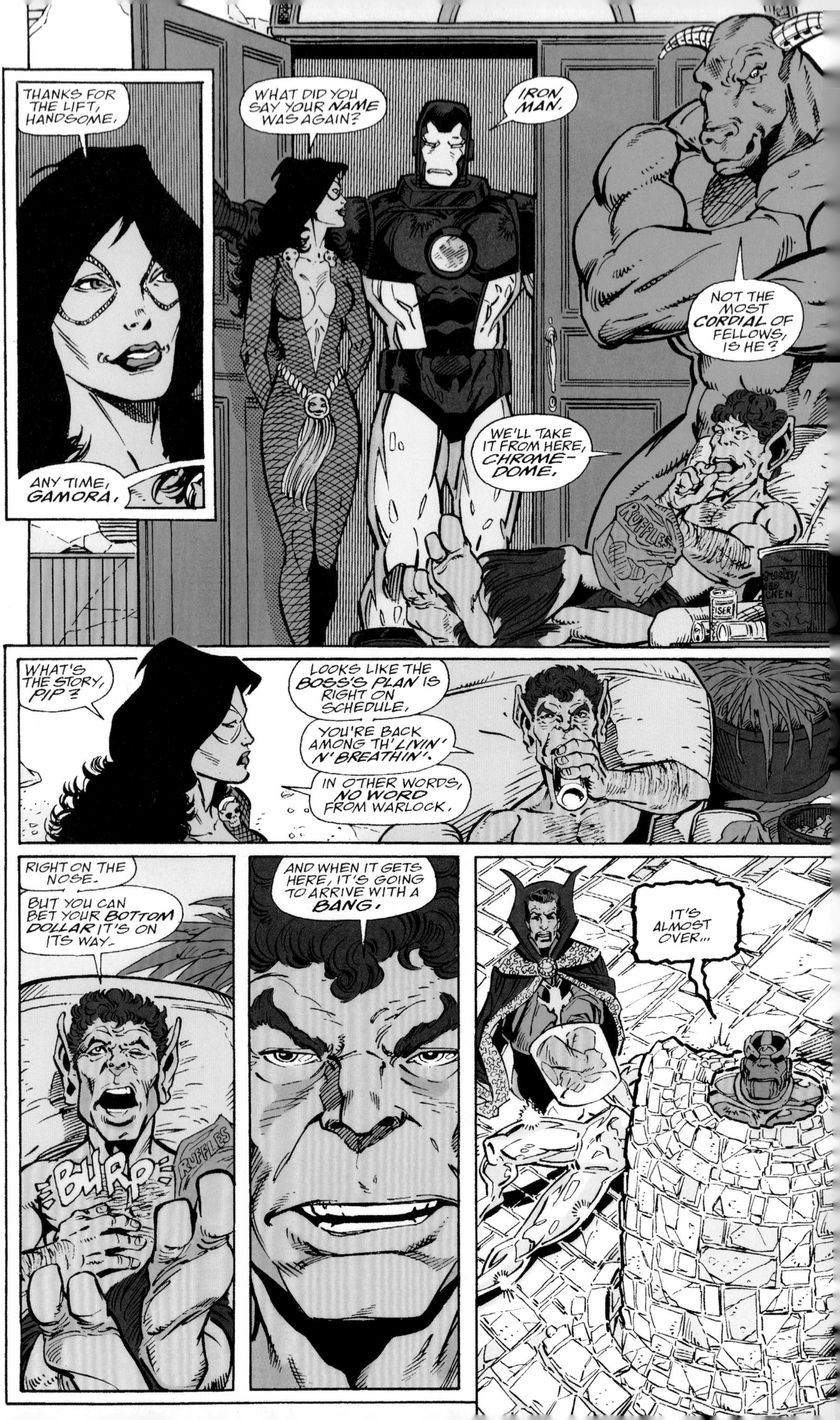
THANKS FOR THE LIFT, HANDSOME.
ANY TIME, GAMORA.
WHAT DID YOU SAY YOUR NAME WAS AGAIN?
IRON MAN.
NOT THE MOST CORDIAL OF FELLOWS, IS HE?
WE'LL TAKE IT FROM HERE, CHROME-DOME.
RUFFLES
WHAT'S THE STORY, PIP?
LOOKS LIKE THE BOSS'S PLAN IS RIGHT ON SCHEDULE.
YOU'RE BACK AMONG TH' LIVIN' N' BREATHIN'.
IN OTHER WORDS, NO WORD FROM WARLOCK.
RIGHT ON THE NOSE.
BUT YOU CAN BET YOUR BOTTOM DOLLAR IT'S ON ITS WAY.
BURP
RUFFLES
AND WHEN IT GETS HERE, IT'S GOING TO ARRIVE WITH A BANG.
IT'S ALMOST OVER...

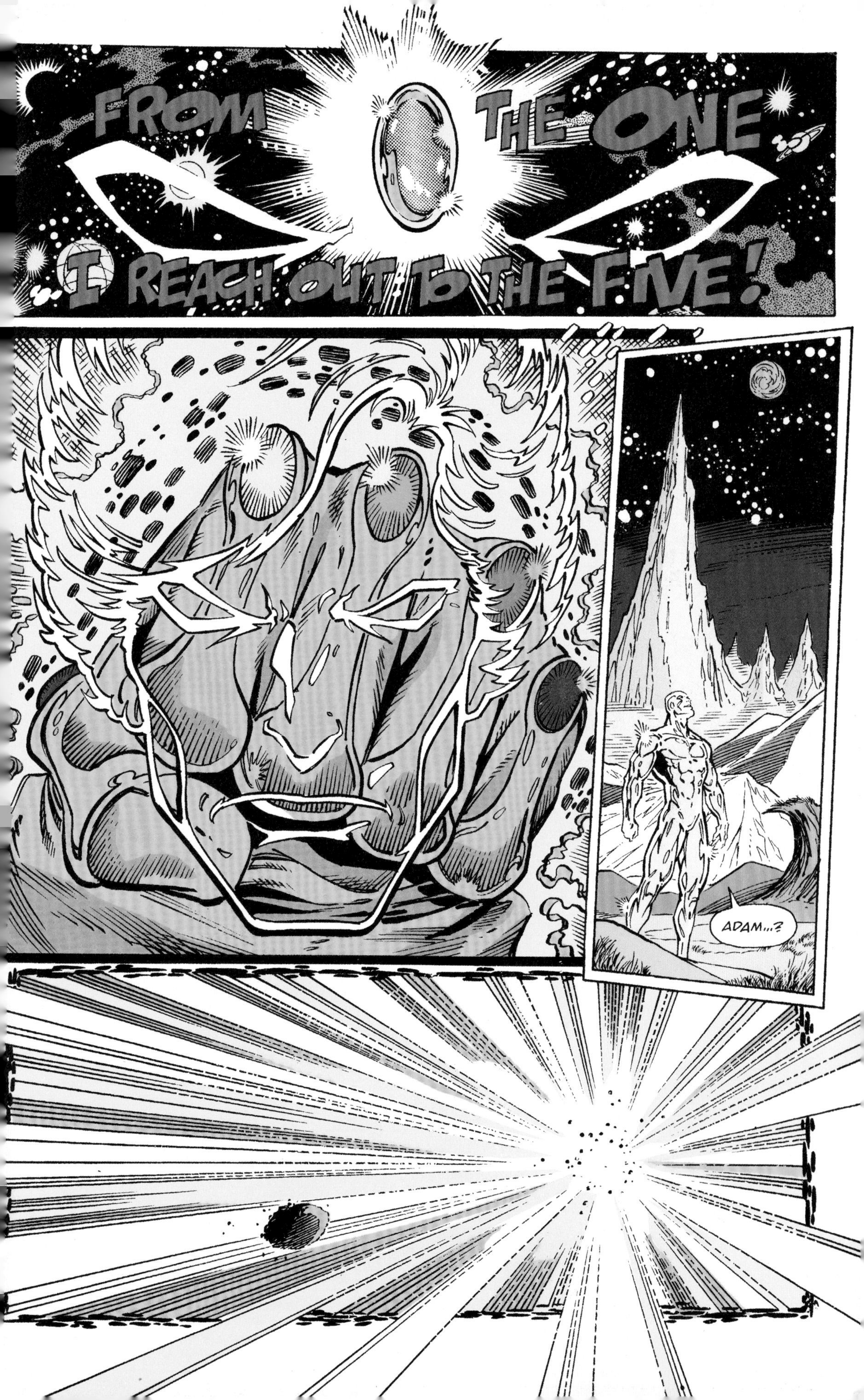
FROM THE ONE
I REACH OUT TO THE FIVE!
ADAM...?

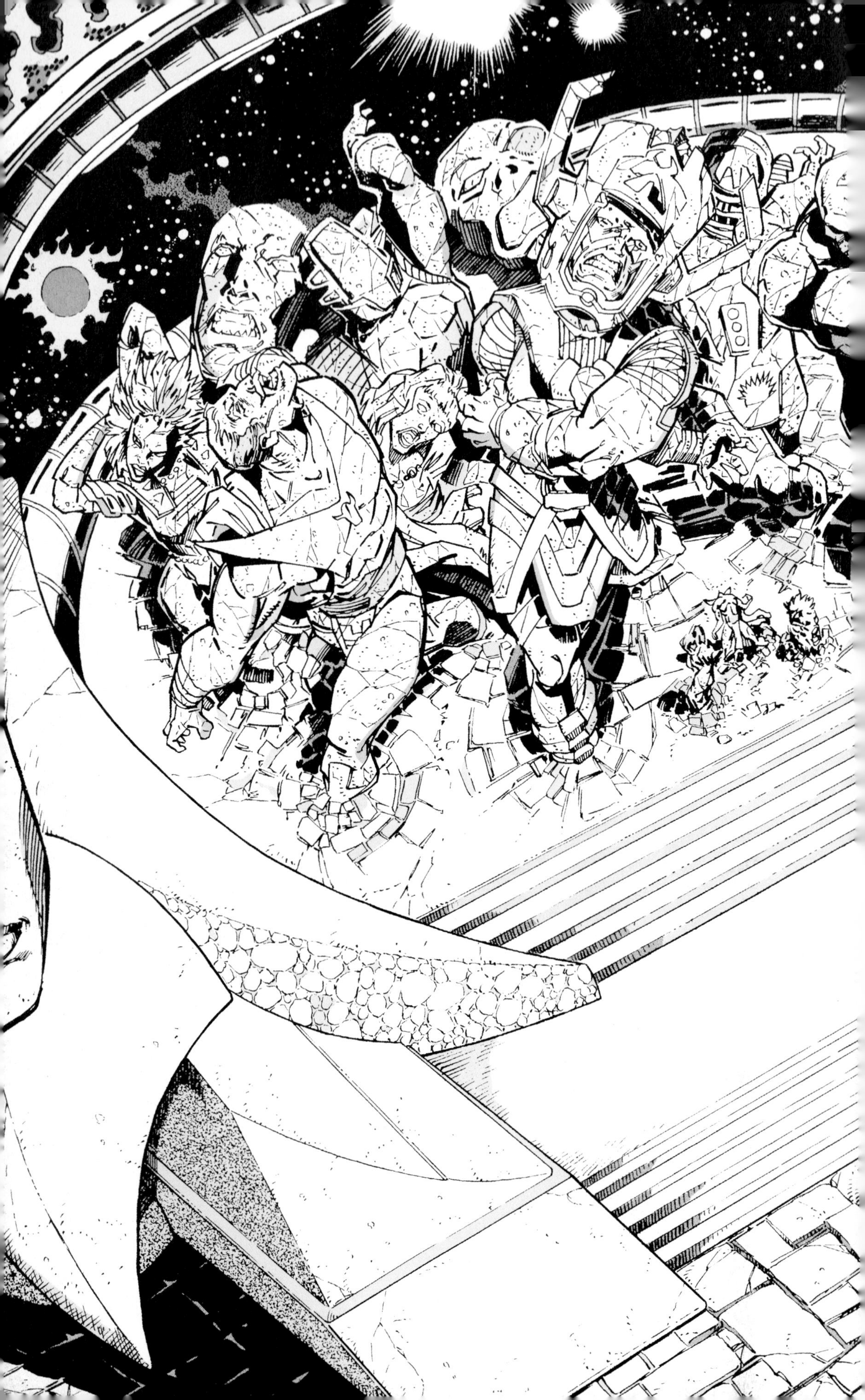

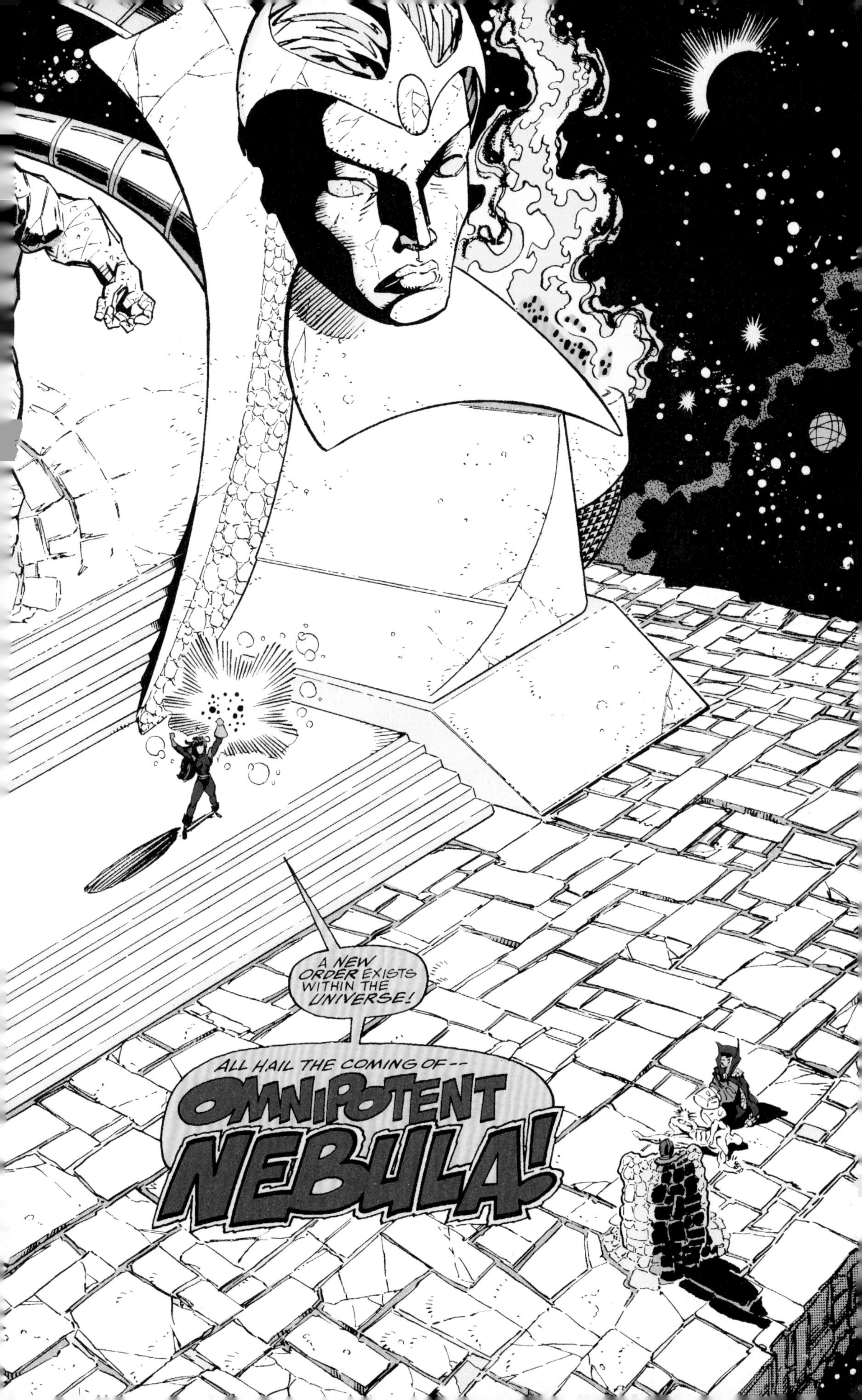
A NEW ORDER EXISTS WITHIN THE UNIVERSE!
ALL HAIL THE COMING OF--
OMNIPOTENT NEBULA!

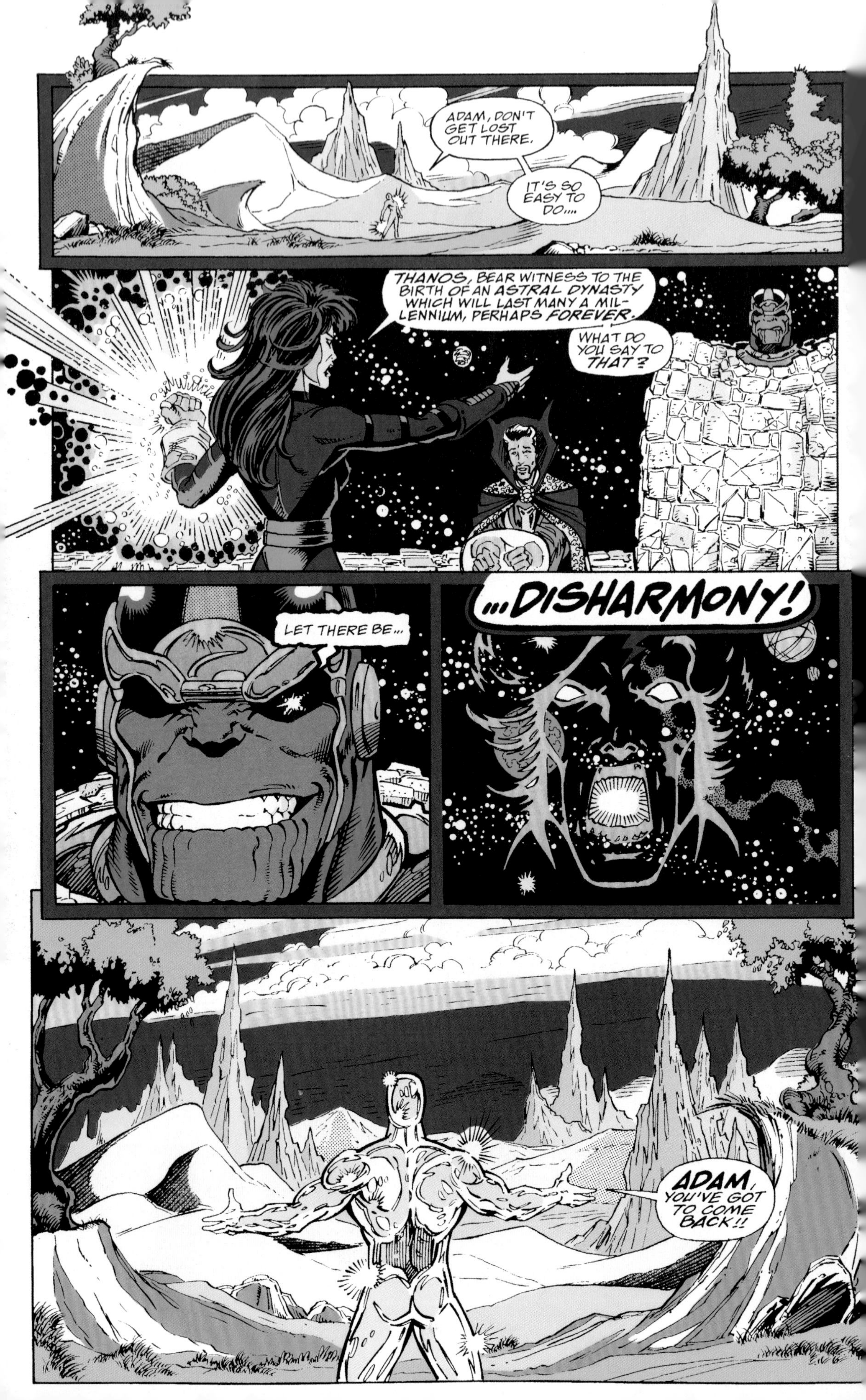

ADAM, DON'T GET LOST OUT THERE.
IT'S SO EASY TO DO....
THANOS, BEAR WITNESS TO THE BIRTH OF AN ASTRAL DYNASTY WHICH WILL LAST MANY A MIL-LENNIUM, PERHAPS FOREVER.
WHAT DO YOU SAY TO THAT?
LET THERE BE...
...DISHARMONY!
ADAM, YOU'VE GOT TO COME BACK!!

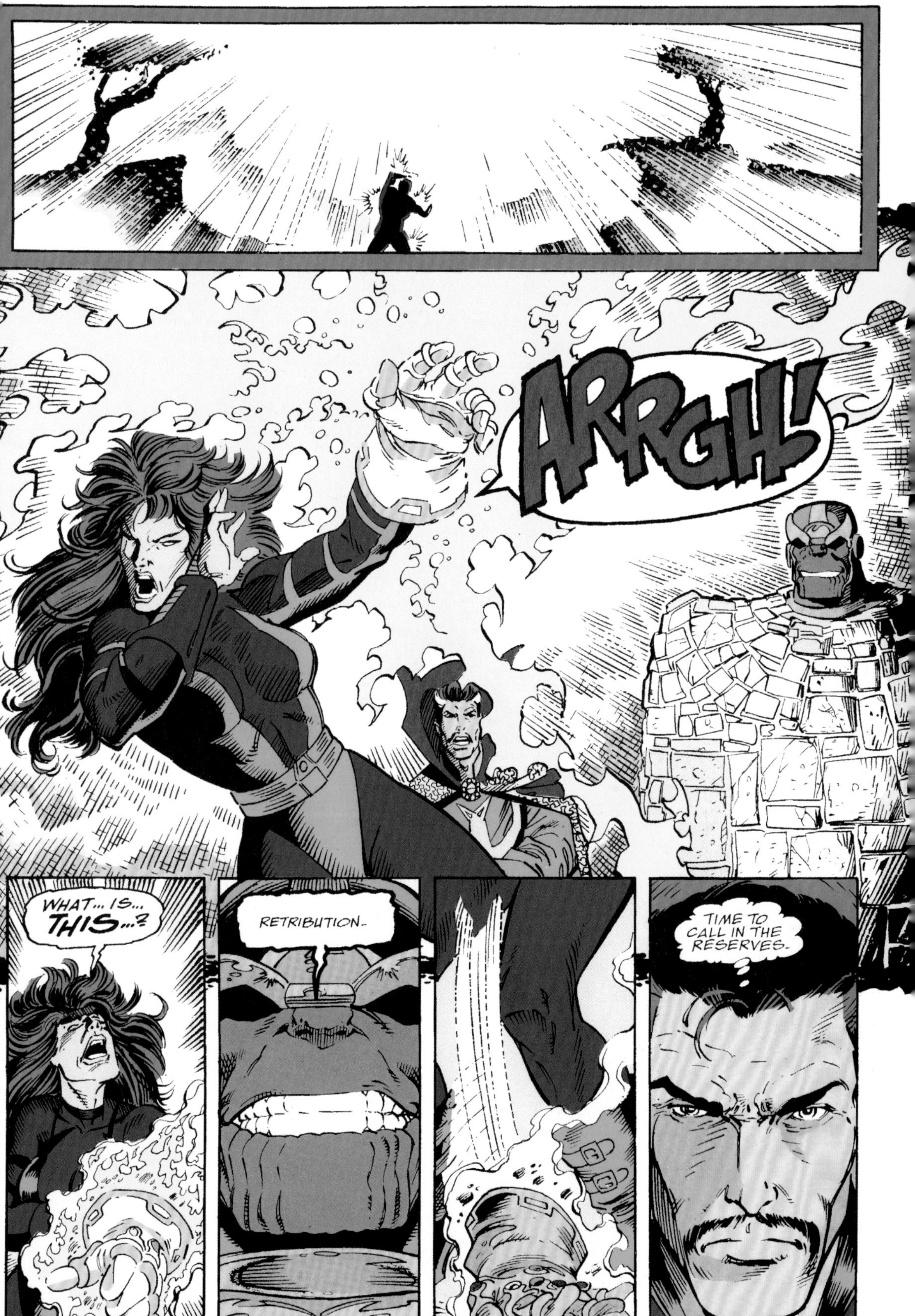
ARRGH!
WHAT... IS... THIS...?
RETRIBUTION.
TIME TO CALL IN THE RESERVES.

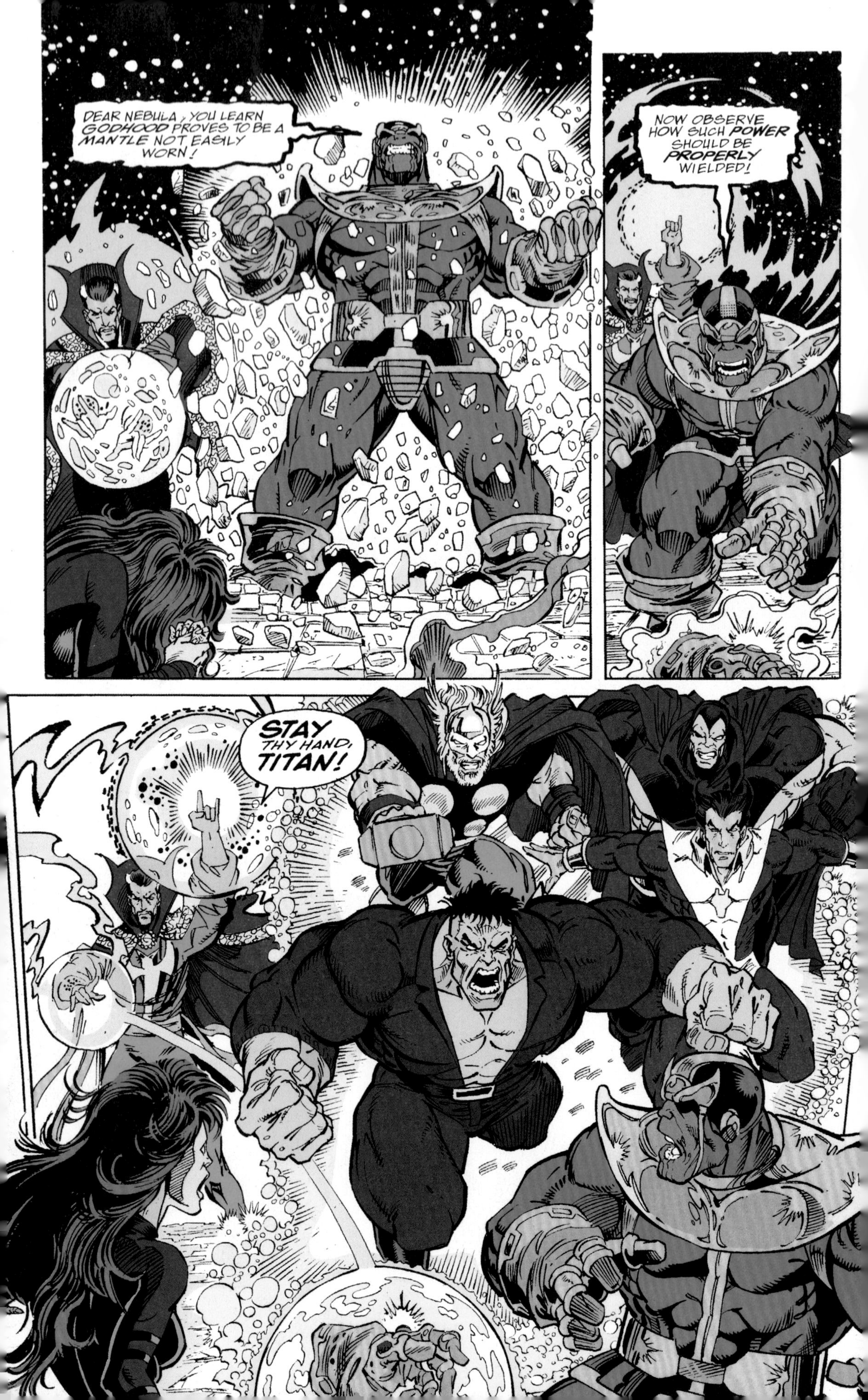
DEAR NEBULA, YOU LEARN GODHOOD PROVES TO BE A MANTLE NOT EASILY WORN!
NOW OBSERVE HOW SUCH POWER SHOULD BE PROPERLY WIELDED!
STAY THY HAND, TITAN!

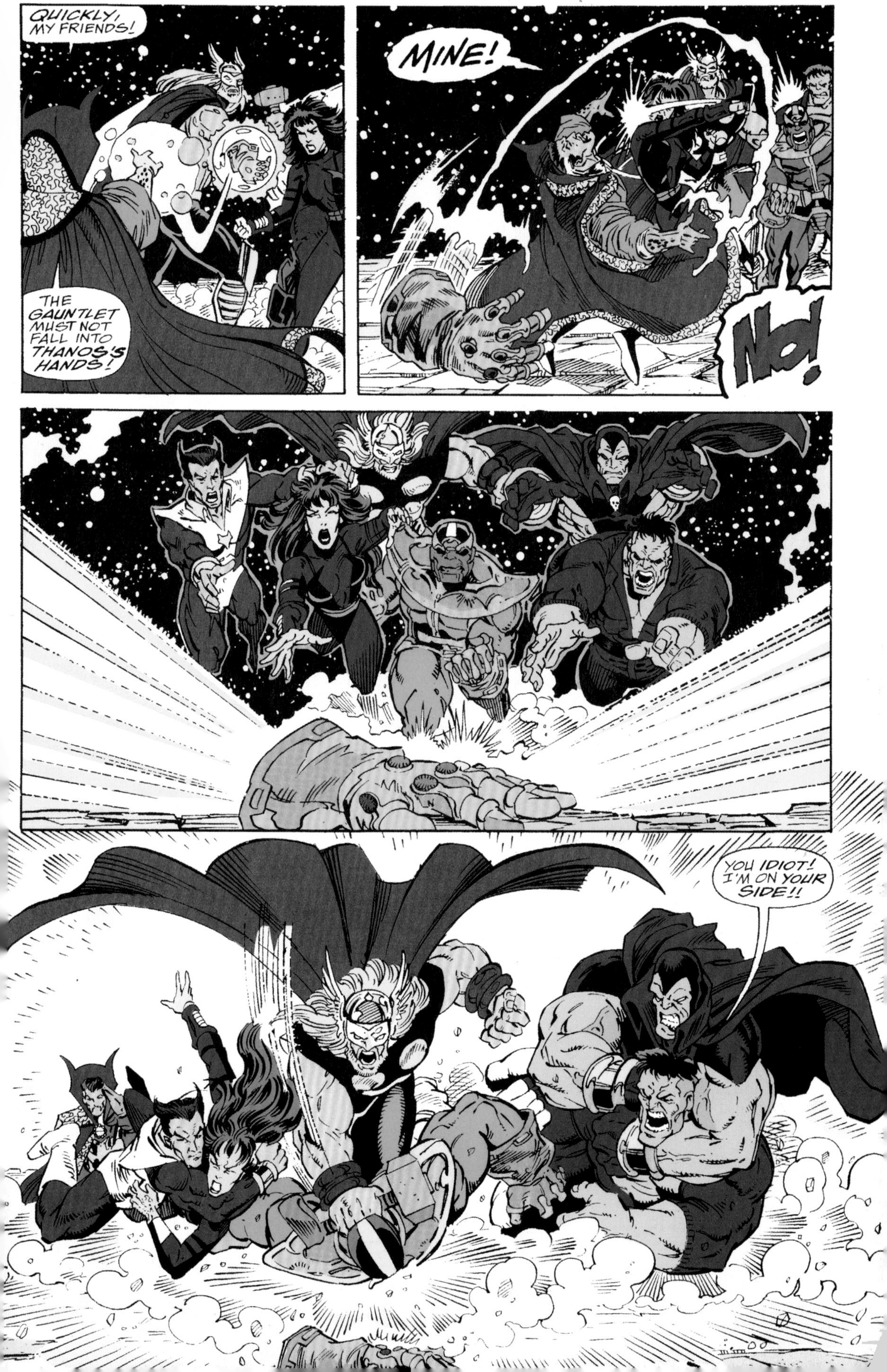

QUICKLY, MY FRIENDS!
THE GAUNTLET MUST NOT FALL INTO THANOS'S HANDS!
MINE!
NO!
YOU IDIOT! I'M ON YOUR SIDE!!

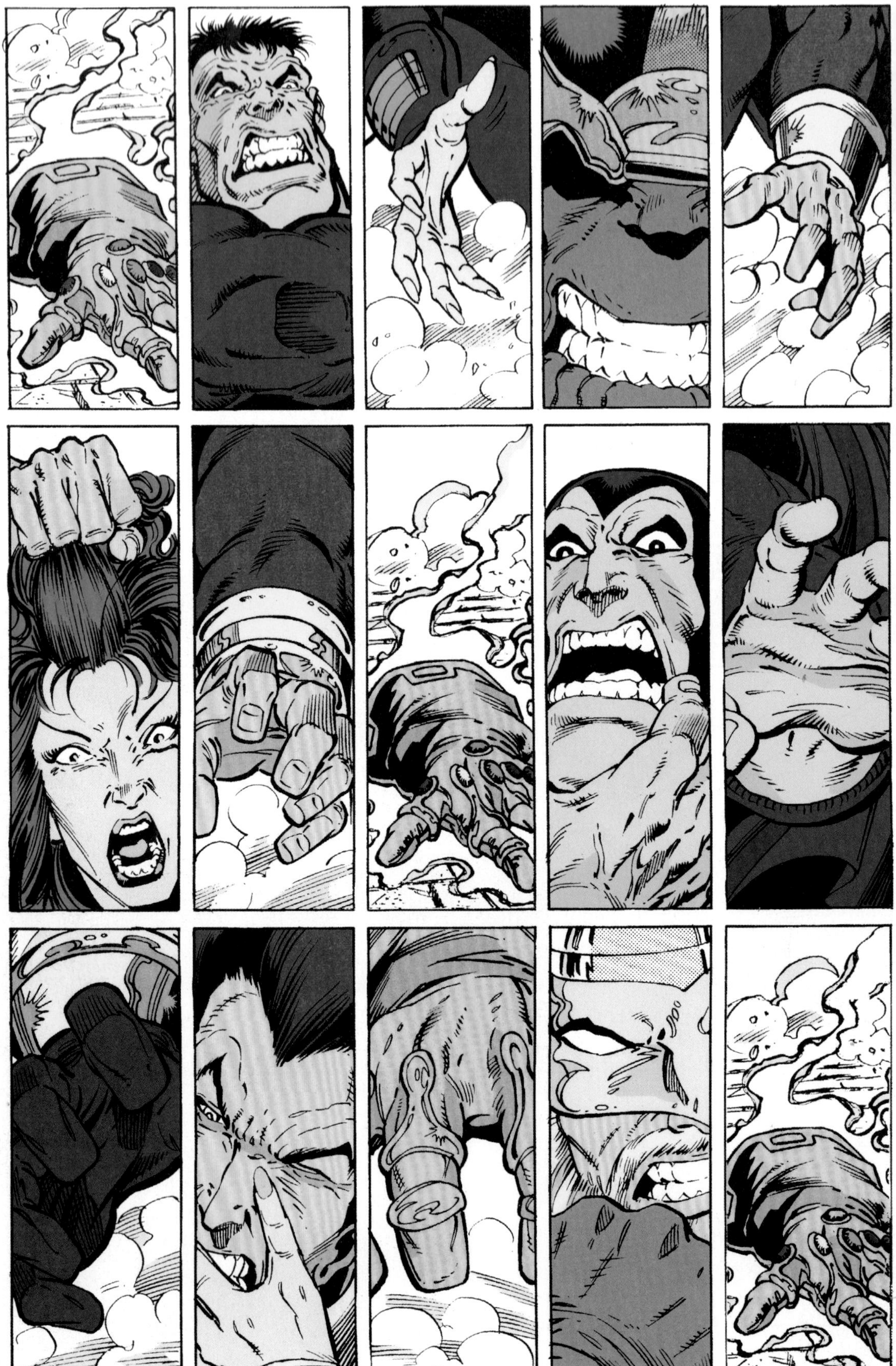

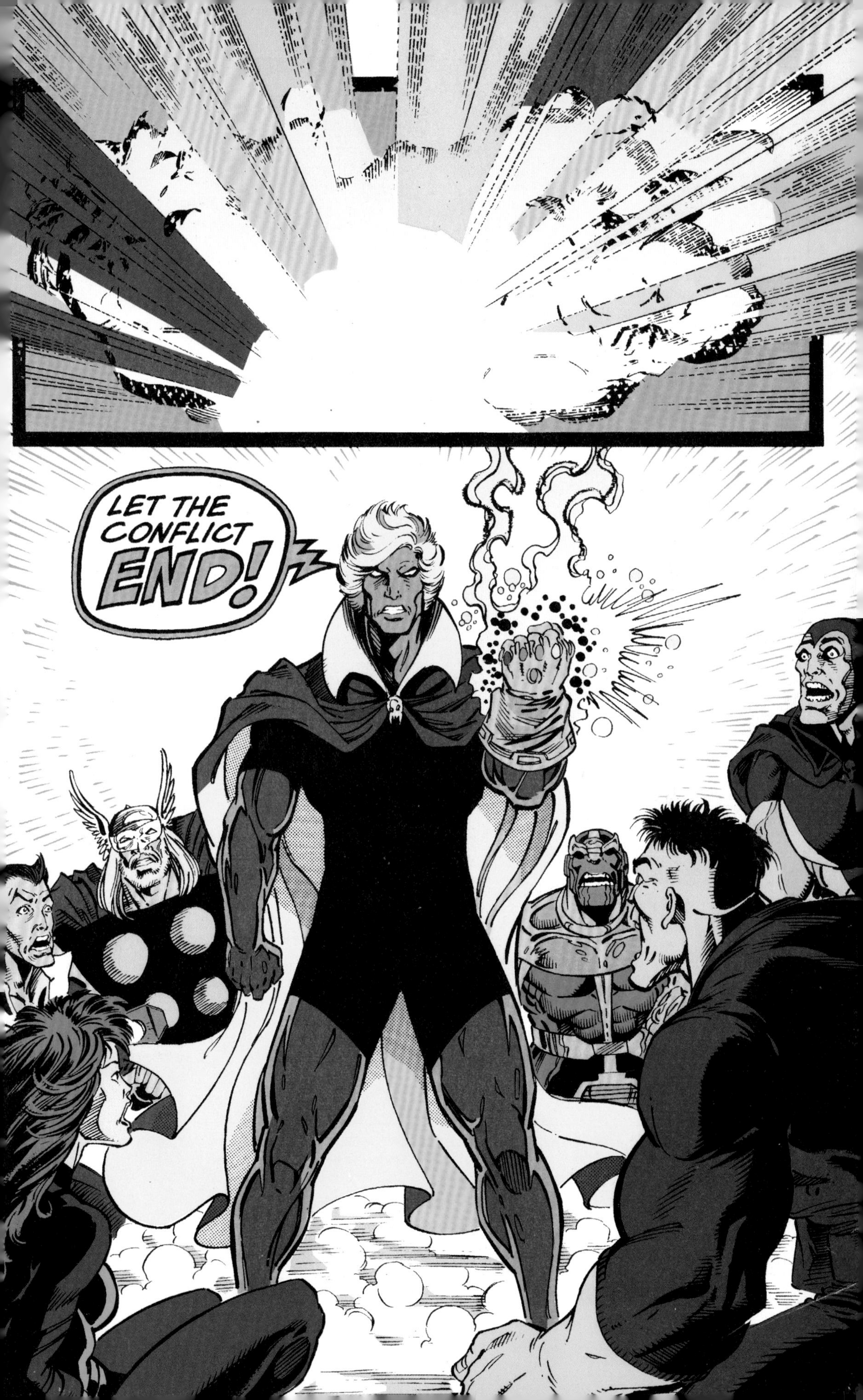
LET THE CONFLICT END!

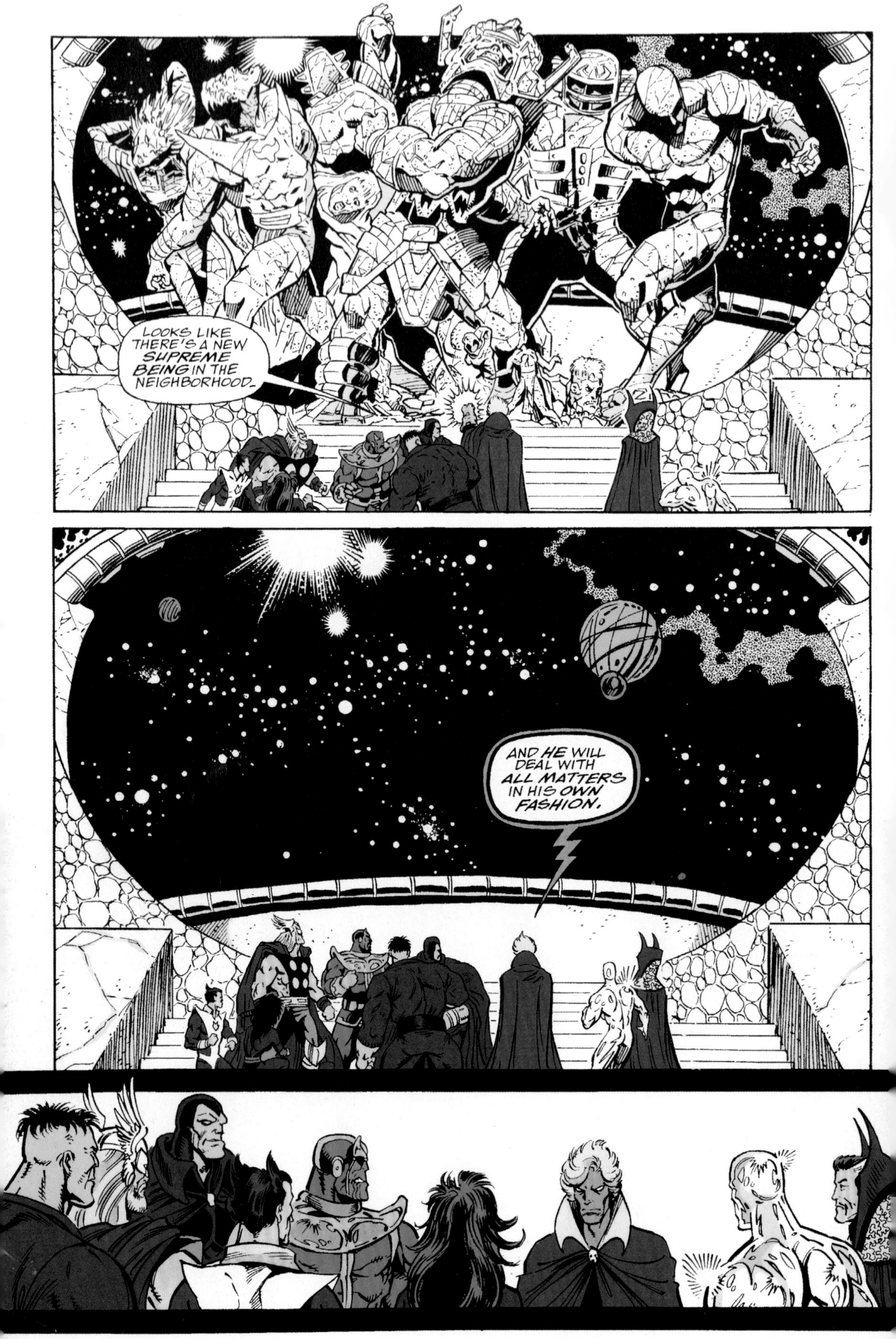
LOOKS LIKE THERE'S A NEW SUPREME BEING IN THE NEIGHBORHOOD--
AND HE WILL DEAL WITH ALL MATTERS IN HIS OWN FASHION.

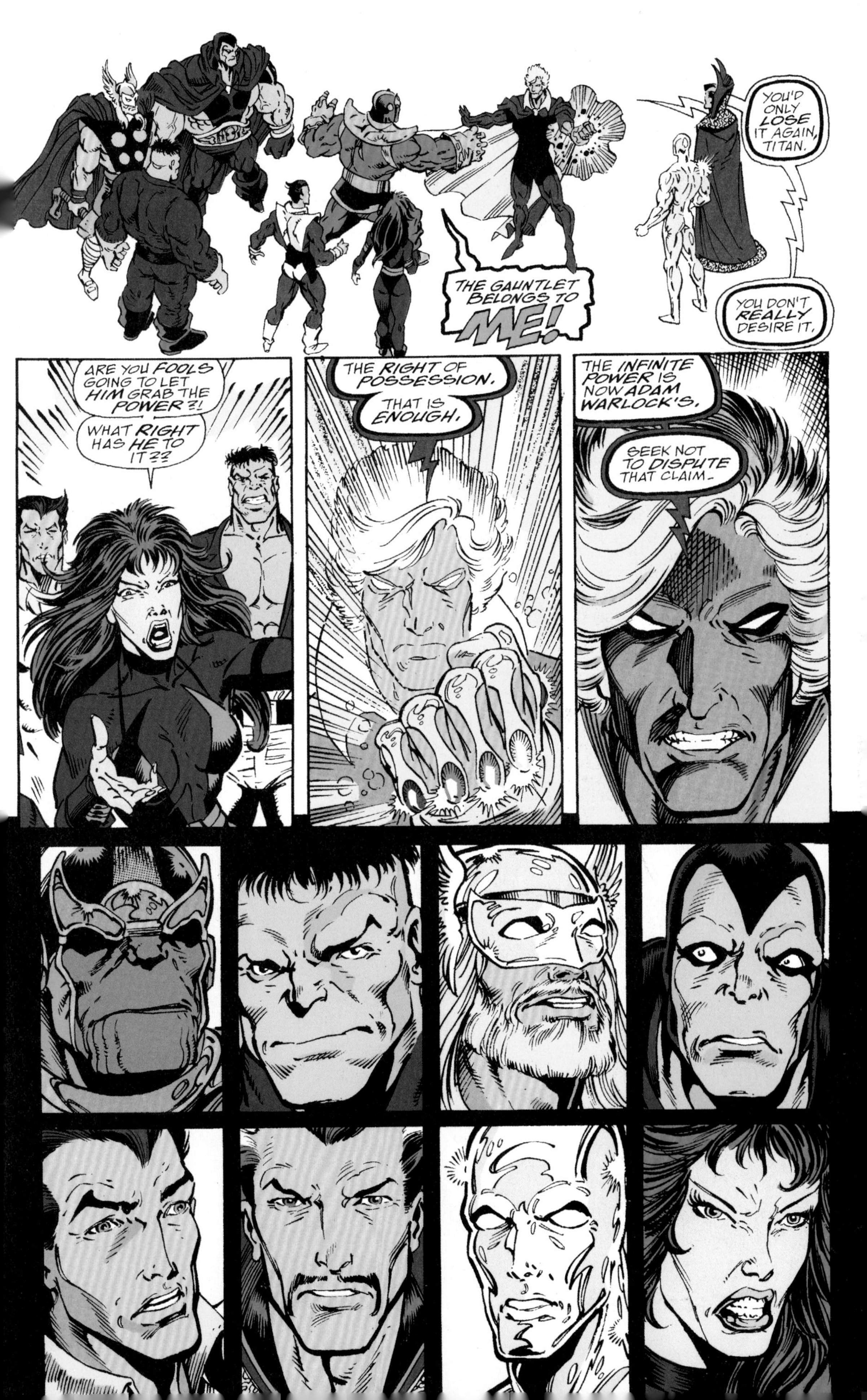
THE GAUNTLET BELONGS TO ME!
YOU'D ONLY LOSE IT AGAIN, TITAN.
YOU DON'T REALLY DESIRE IT.
ARE YOU FOOLS GOING TO LET HIM GRAB THE POWER?!
WHAT RIGHT HAS HE TO IT??
THE RIGHT OF POSSESSION.
THAT IS ENOUGH.
THE INFINITE POWER IS NOW ADAM WARLOCK'S.
SEEK NOT TO DISPUTE THAT CLAIM.

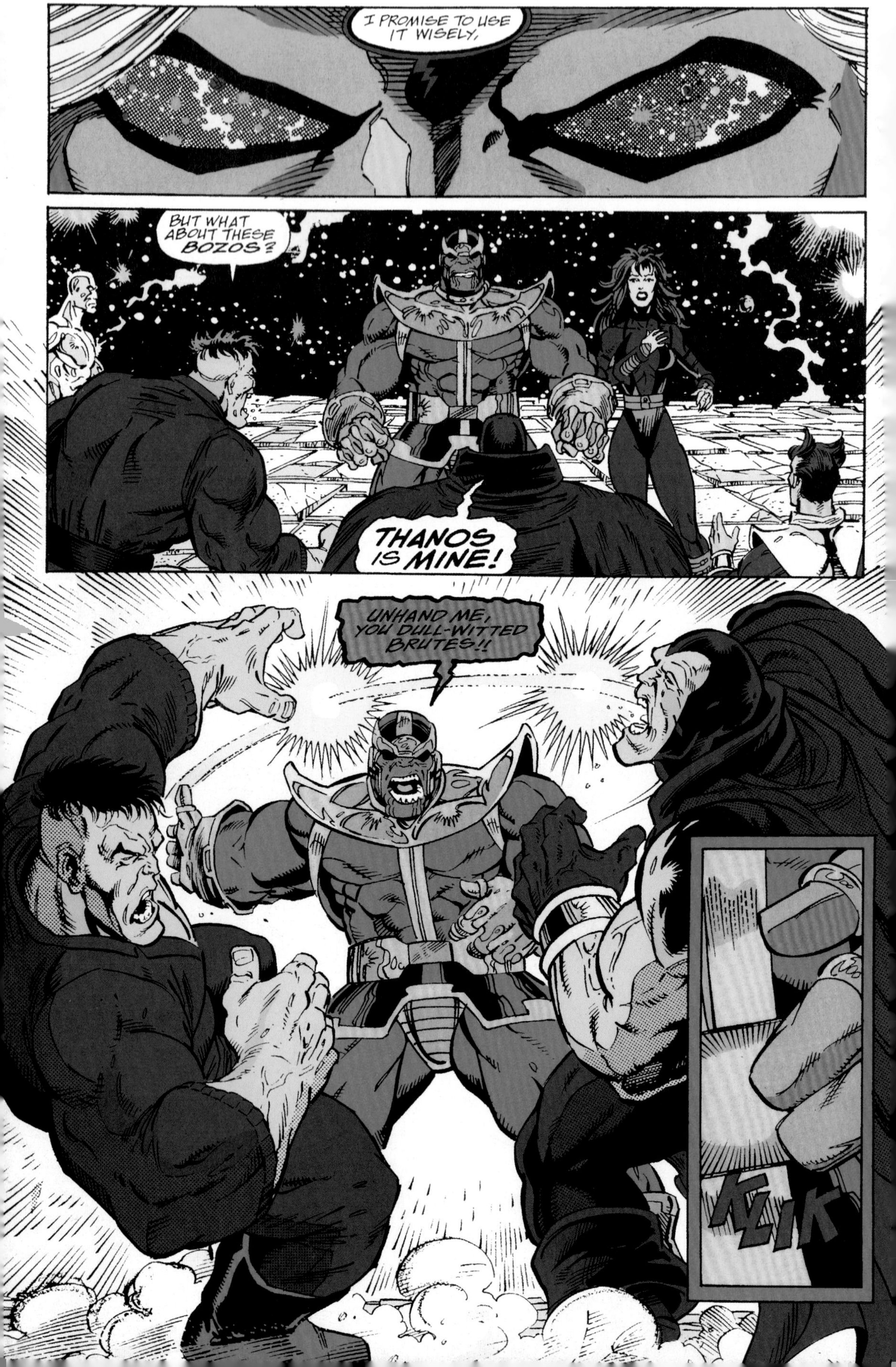
I PROMISE TO USE IT WISELY,
BUT WHAT ABOUT THESE BOZOS?
THANOS IS MINE!
UNHAND ME, YOU DULL-WITTED BRUTES!!
KLIK

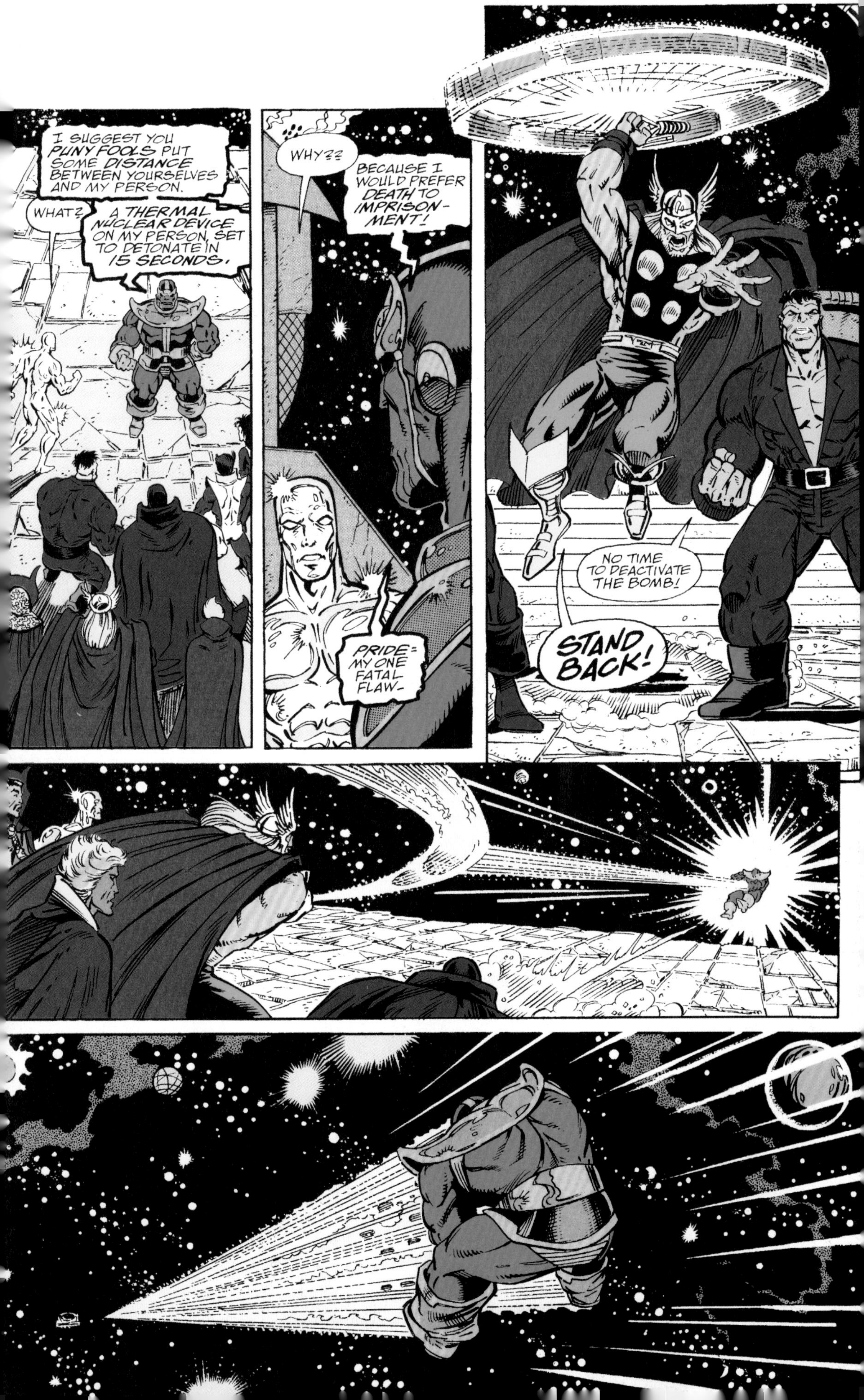
I SUGGEST YOU PUNY FOOLS PUT SOME DISTANCE BETWEEN YOURSELVES AND MY PERSON.
WHAT?
A THERMAL NUCLEAR DEVICE ON MY PERSON, SET TO DETONATE IN 15 SECONDS.
WHY??
BECAUSE I WOULD PREFER DEATH TO IMPRISONMENT!
PRIDE: MY ONE FATAL FLAW...
NO TIME TO DEACTIVATE THE BOMB!
STAND BACK!

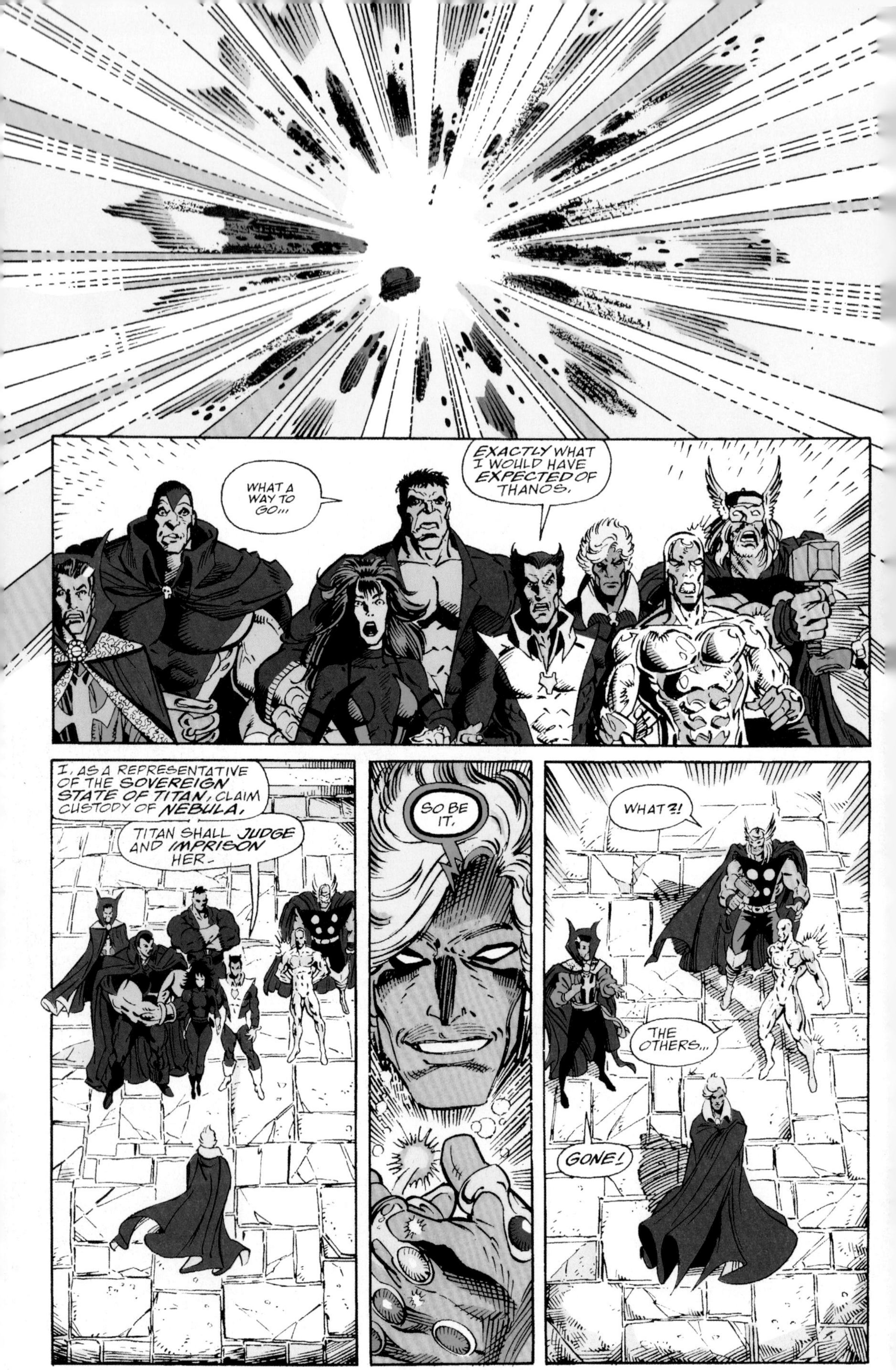
WHAT A WAY TO GO...
EXACTLY WHAT I WOULD HAVE EXPECTED OF THANOS.
I, AS A REPRESENTATIVE OF THE SOVEREIGN STATE OF TITAN, CLAIM CUSTODY OF NEBULA.
TITAN SHALL JUDGE AND IMPRISON HER.
SO BE IT.
WHAT?!
THE OTHERS...
GONE!

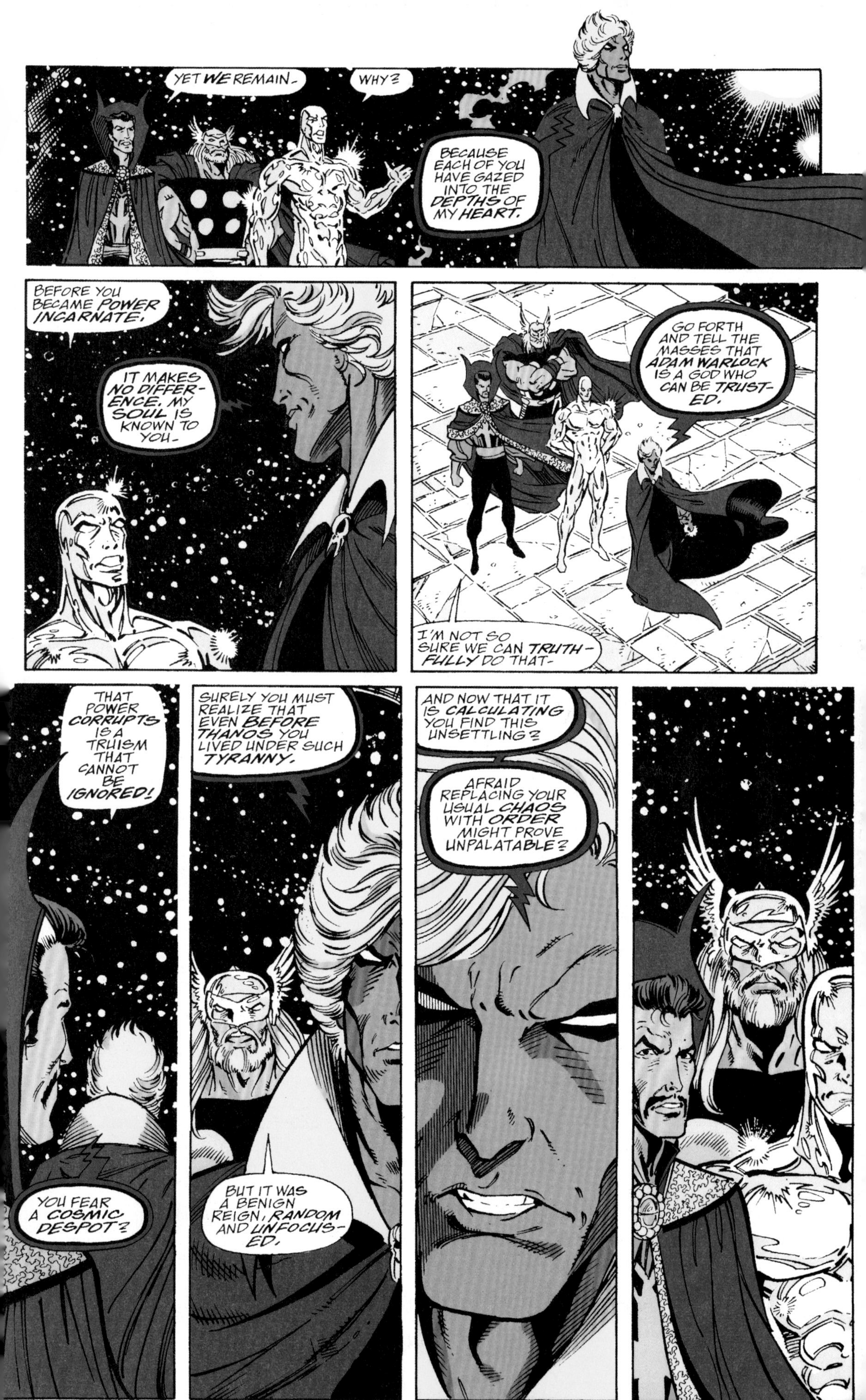
YET WE REMAIN-
WHY?
BECAUSE EACH OF YOU HAVE GAZED INTO THE DEPTHS OF MY HEART.
BEFORE YOU BECAME POWER INCARNATE.
IT MAKES NO DIFFERENCE. MY SOUL IS KNOWN TO YOU-
GO FORTH AND TELL THE MASSES THAT ADAM WARLOCK IS A GOD WHO CAN BE TRUSTED.
I'M NOT SO SURE WE CAN TRUTHFULLY DO THAT-
THAT POWER CORRUPTS IS A TRUISM THAT CANNOT BE IGNORED!
YOU FEAR A COSMIC DESPOT?
SURELY YOU MUST REALIZE THAT EVEN BEFORE THANOS YOU LIVED UNDER SUCH TYRANNY.
BUT IT WAS A BENIGN REIGN, RANDOM AND UNFOCUSED.
AND NOW THAT IT IS CALCULATING YOU FIND THIS UNSETTLING?
AFRAID REPLACING YOUR USUAL CHAOS WITH ORDER MIGHT PROVE UNPALATABLE?

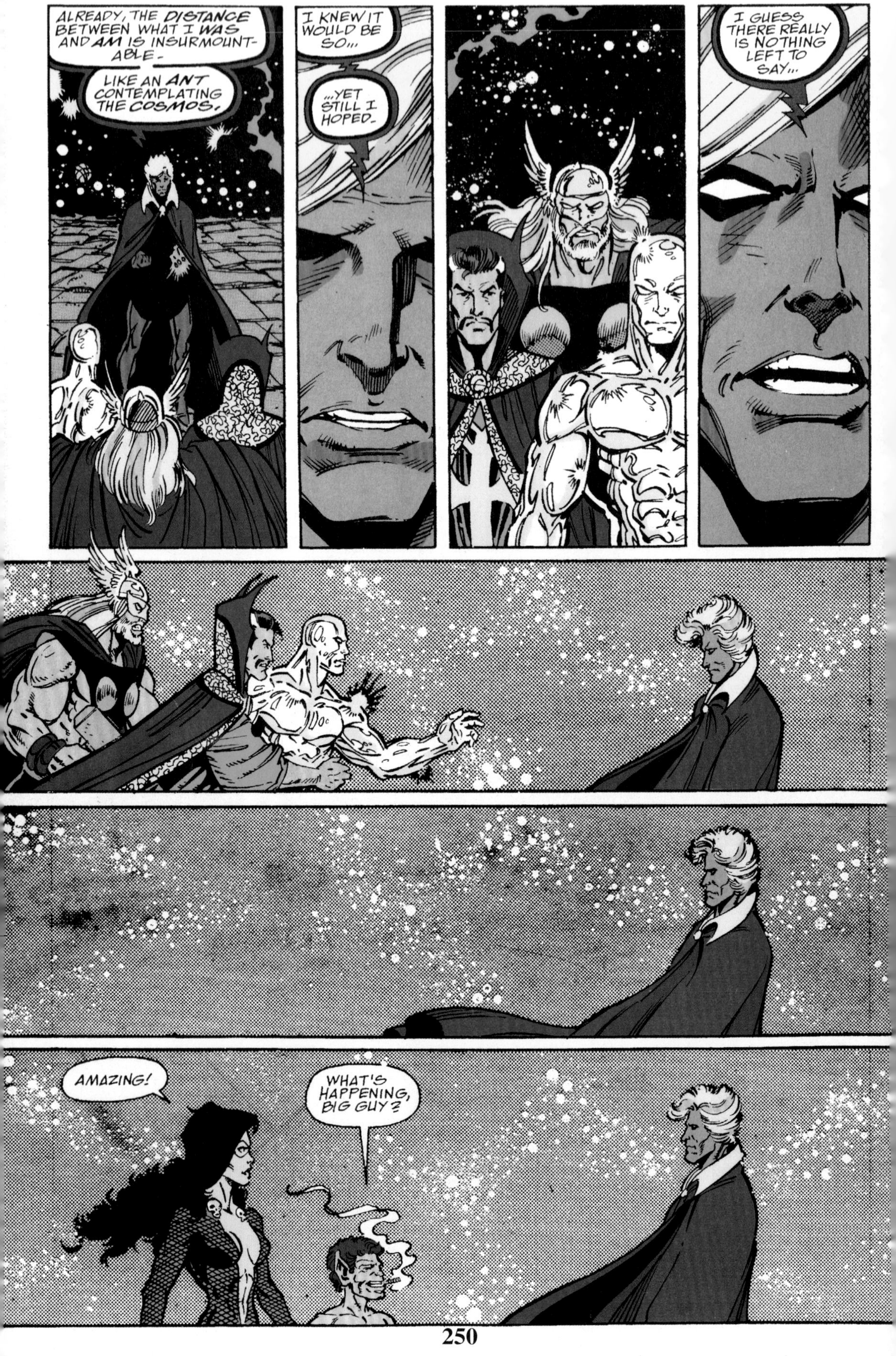
ALREADY, THE DISTANCE BETWEEN WHAT I WAS AND AM IS INSURMOUNT-ABLE-
LIKE AN ANT CONTEMPLATING THE COSMOS.
I KNEW IT WOULD BE SO...
...YET STILL I HOPED-
I GUESS THERE REALLY IS NOTHING LEFT TO SAY...
AMAZING!
WHAT'S HAPPENING, BIG GUY?

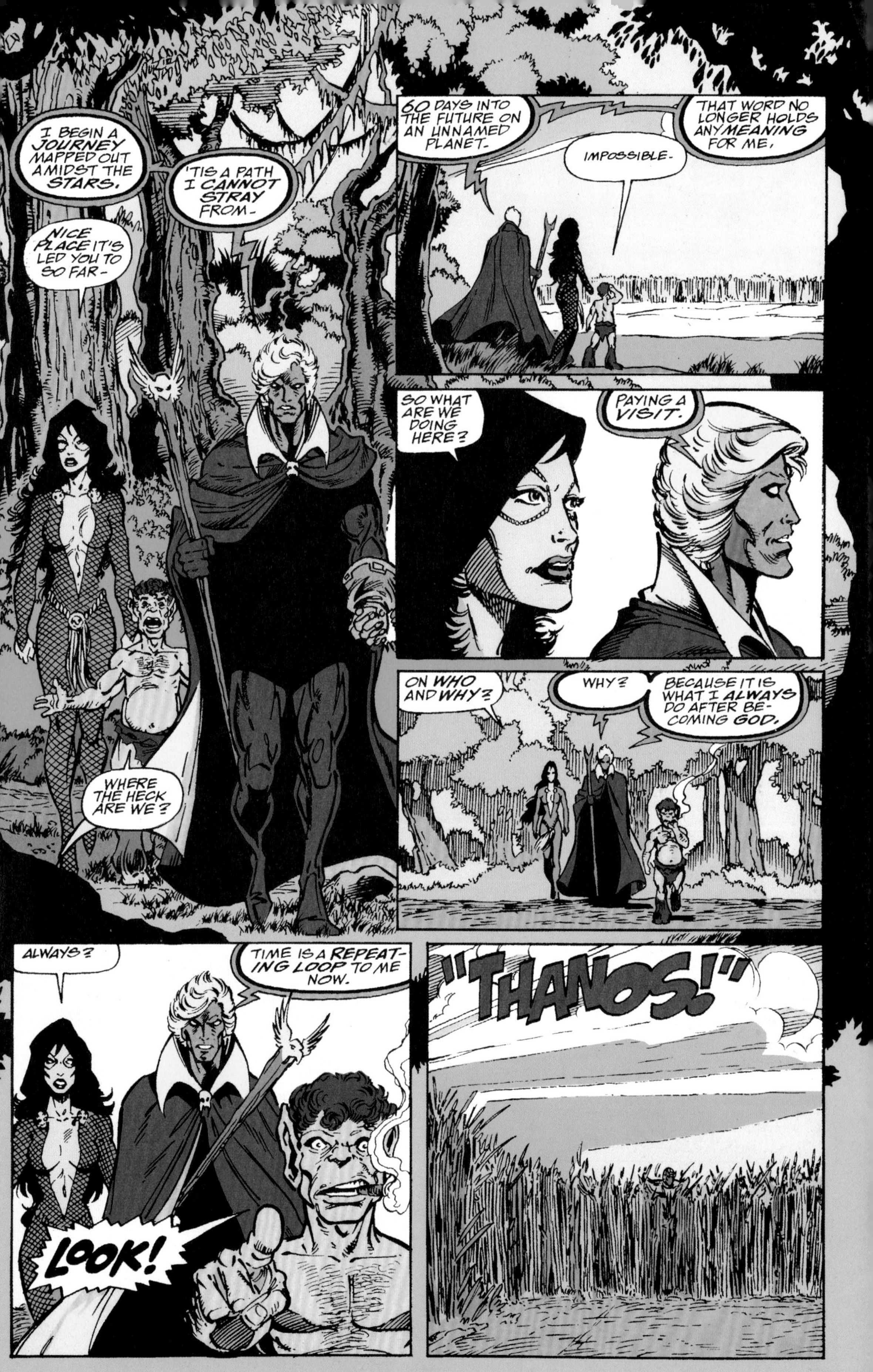
I BEGIN A JOURNEY MAPPED OUT AMIDST THE STARS.
'TIS A PATH I CANNOT STRAY FROM-
NICE PLACE IT'S LED YOU TO SO FAR-
WHERE THE HECK ARE WE?
60 DAYS INTO THE FUTURE ON AN UNNAMED PLANET-
IMPOSSIBLE-
THAT WORD NO LONGER HOLDS ANY MEANING FOR ME.
SO WHAT ARE WE DOING HERE?
PAYING A VISIT.
ON WHO AND WHY?
WHY?
BECAUSE IT IS WHAT I ALWAYS DO AFTER BE-COMING GOD.
ALWAYS?
TIME IS A REPEAT-ING LOOP TO ME NOW.
LOOK!
"THANOS!"

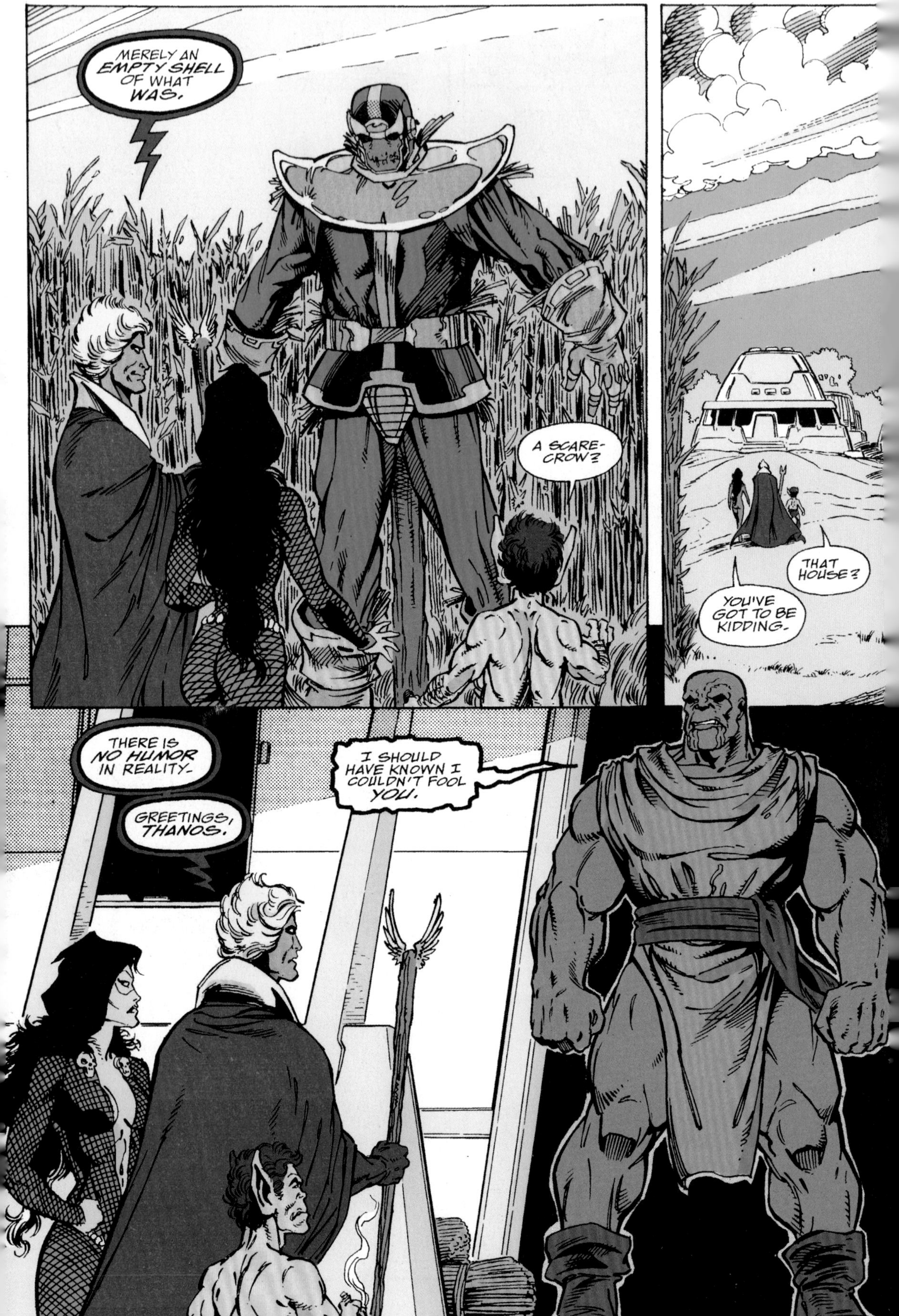
MERELY AN EMPTY SHELL OF WHAT WAS.
A SCARE-CROW?
THAT HOUSE?
YOU'VE GOT TO BE KIDDING.
THERE IS NO HUMOR IN REALITY.
GREETINGS, THANOS.
I SHOULD HAVE KNOWN I COULDN'T FOOL YOU.

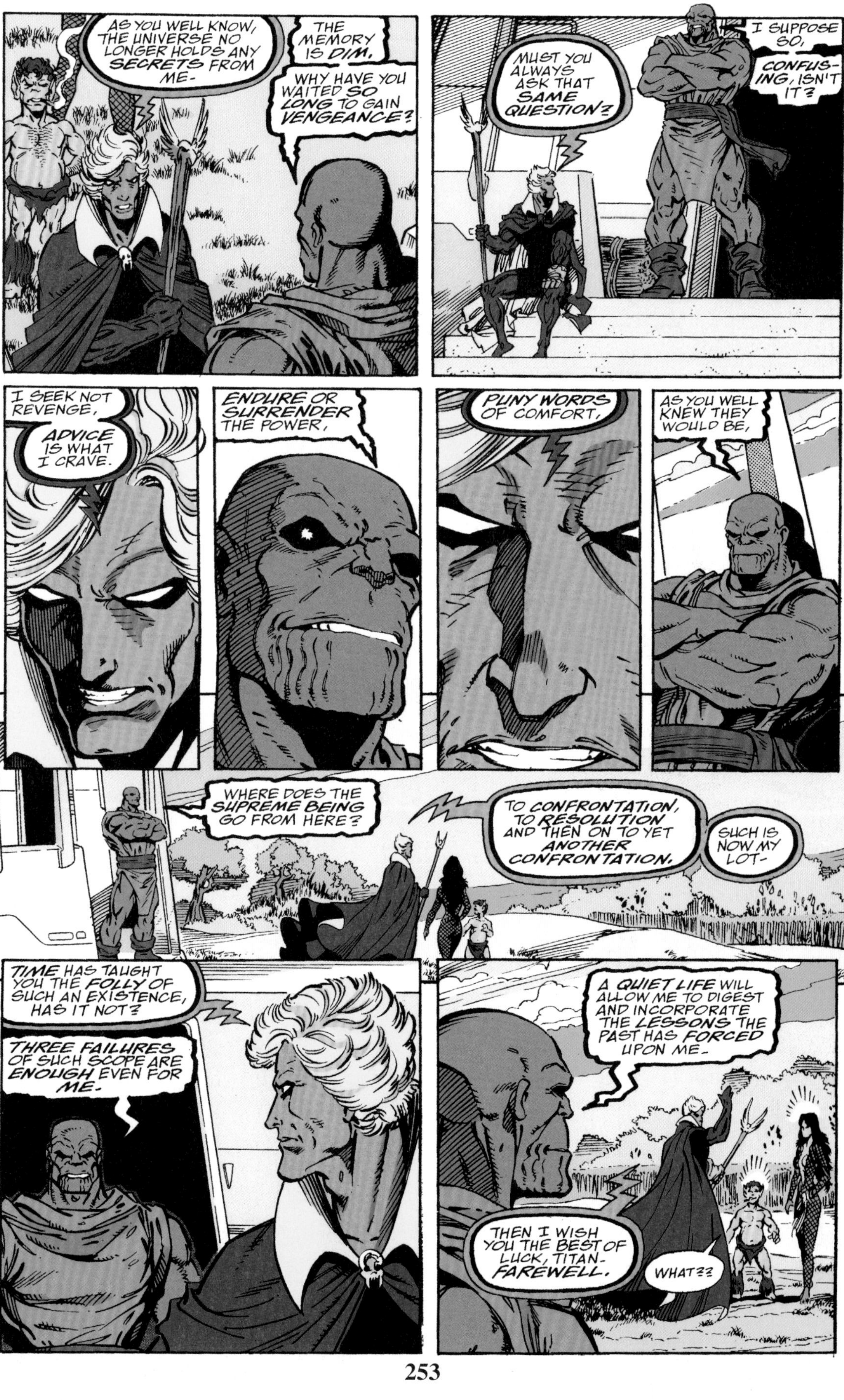

AS YOU WELL KNOW, THE UNIVERSE NO LONGER HOLDS ANY SECRETS FROM ME-
THE MEMORY IS DIM.
WHY HAVE YOU WAITED SO LONG TO GAIN VENGEANCE?
MUST YOU ALWAYS ASK THAT SAME QUESTION?
I SUPPOSE SO,
CONFUSING, ISN'T IT?
I SEEK NOT REVENGE,
ADVICE IS WHAT I CRAVE.
ENDURE OR SURRENDER THE POWER,
PUNY WORDS OF COMFORT,
AS YOU WELL KNEW THEY WOULD BE,
WHERE DOES THE SUPREME BEING GO FROM HERE?
TO CONFRONTATION, TO RESOLUTION AND THEN ON TO YET ANOTHER CONFRONTATION.
SUCH IS NOW MY LOT-
TIME HAS TAUGHT YOU THE FOLLY OF SUCH AN EXISTENCE, HAS IT NOT?
THREE FAILURES OF SUCH SCOPE ARE ENOUGH EVEN FOR ME.
A QUIET LIFE WILL ALLOW ME TO DIGEST AND INCORPORATE THE LESSONS THE PAST HAS FORCED UPON ME-
THEN I WISH YOU THE BEST OF LUCK, TITAN-FAREWELL.
WHAT??

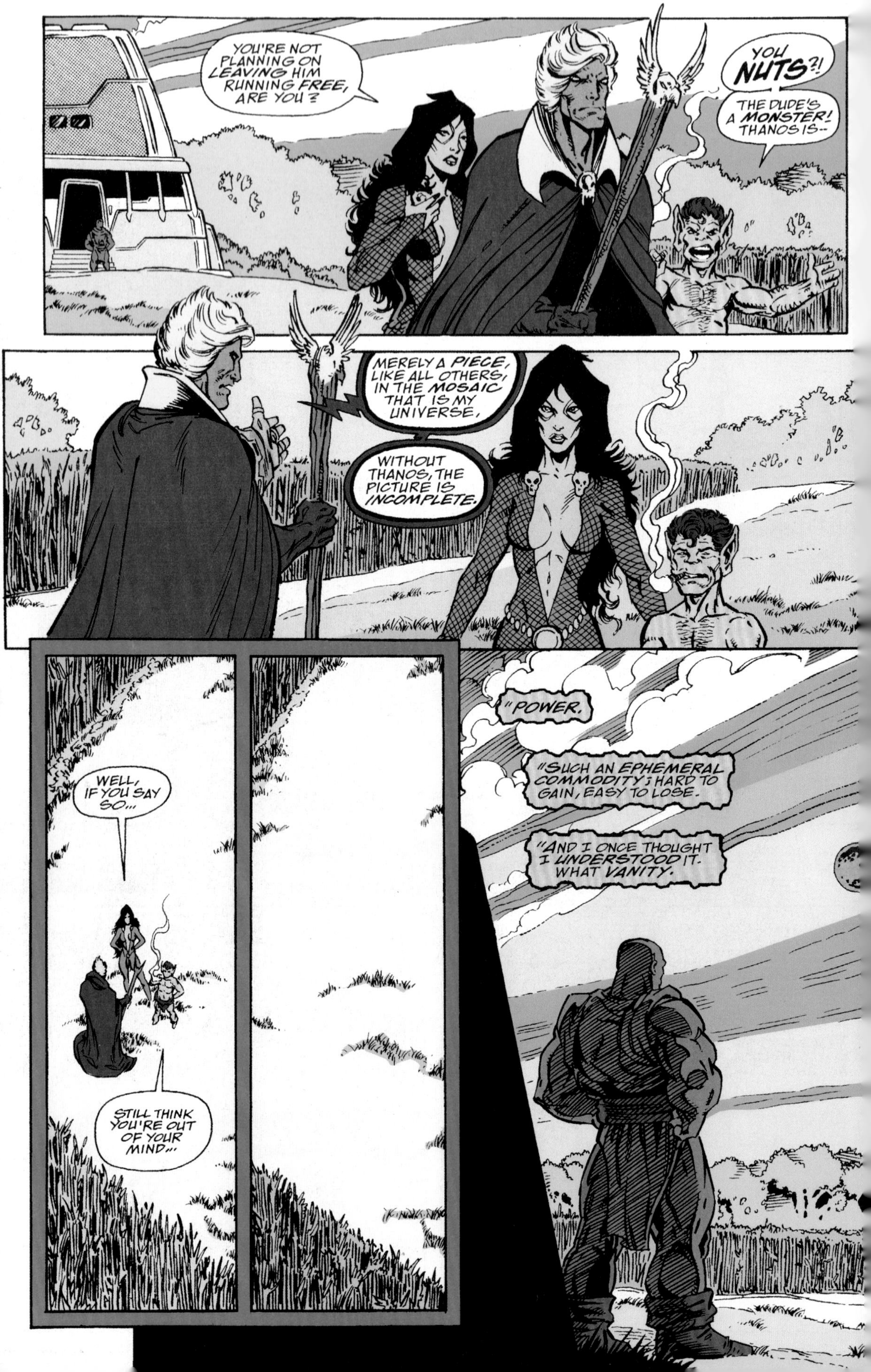
YOU'RE NOT PLANNING ON LEAVING HIM RUNNING FREE, ARE YOU?
YOU NUTS?!
THE DUDE'S A MONSTER! THANOS IS--
MERELY A PIECE, LIKE ALL OTHERS, IN THE MOSAIC THAT IS MY UNIVERSE.
WITHOUT THANOS, THE PICTURE IS INCOMPLETE.
WELL, IF YOU SAY SO...
STILL THINK YOU'RE OUT OF YOUR MIND...
"POWER.
"SUCH AN EPHEMERAL COMMODITY; HARD TO GAIN, EASY TO LOSE.
"AND I ONCE THOUGHT I UNDERSTOOD IT. WHAT VANITY.

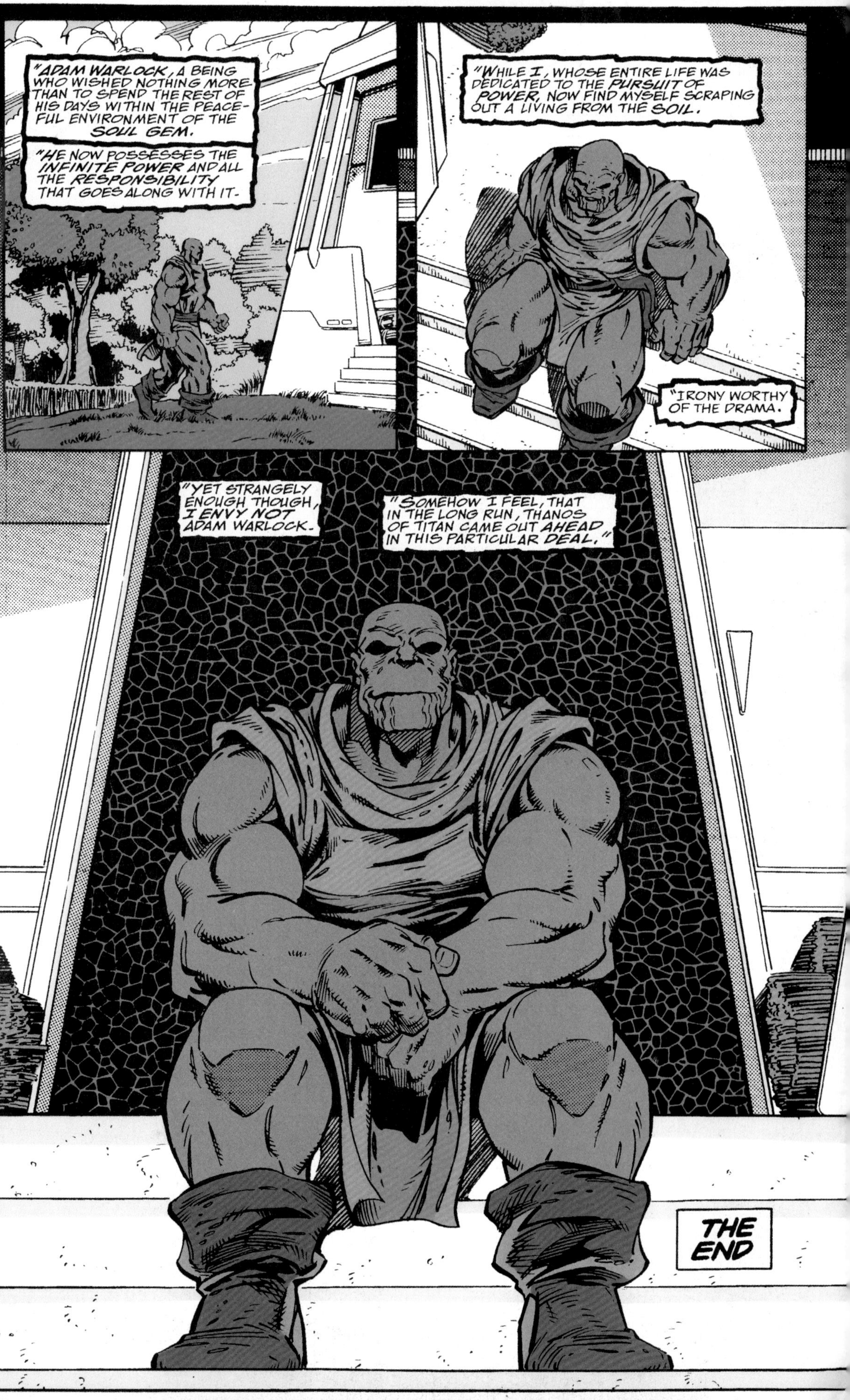
"ADAM WARLOCK, A BEING WHO WISHED NOTHING MORE THAN TO SPEND THE REST OF HIS DAYS WITHIN THE PEACEFUL ENVIRONMENT OF THE SOUL GEM.
"HE NOW POSSESSES THE INFINITE POWER AND ALL THE RESPONSIBILITY THAT GOES ALONG WITH IT.
"WHILE I, WHOSE ENTIRE LIFE WAS DEDICATED TO THE PURSUIT OF POWER, NOW FIND MYSELF SCRAPING OUT A LIVING FROM THE SOIL.
"IRONY WORTHY OF THE DRAMA.
"YET STRANGELY ENOUGH THOUGH, I ENVY NOT ADAM WARLOCK.
"SOMEHOW I FEEL, THAT IN THE LONG RUN, THANOS OF TITAN CAME OUT AHEAD IN THIS PARTICULAR DEAL."
THE END

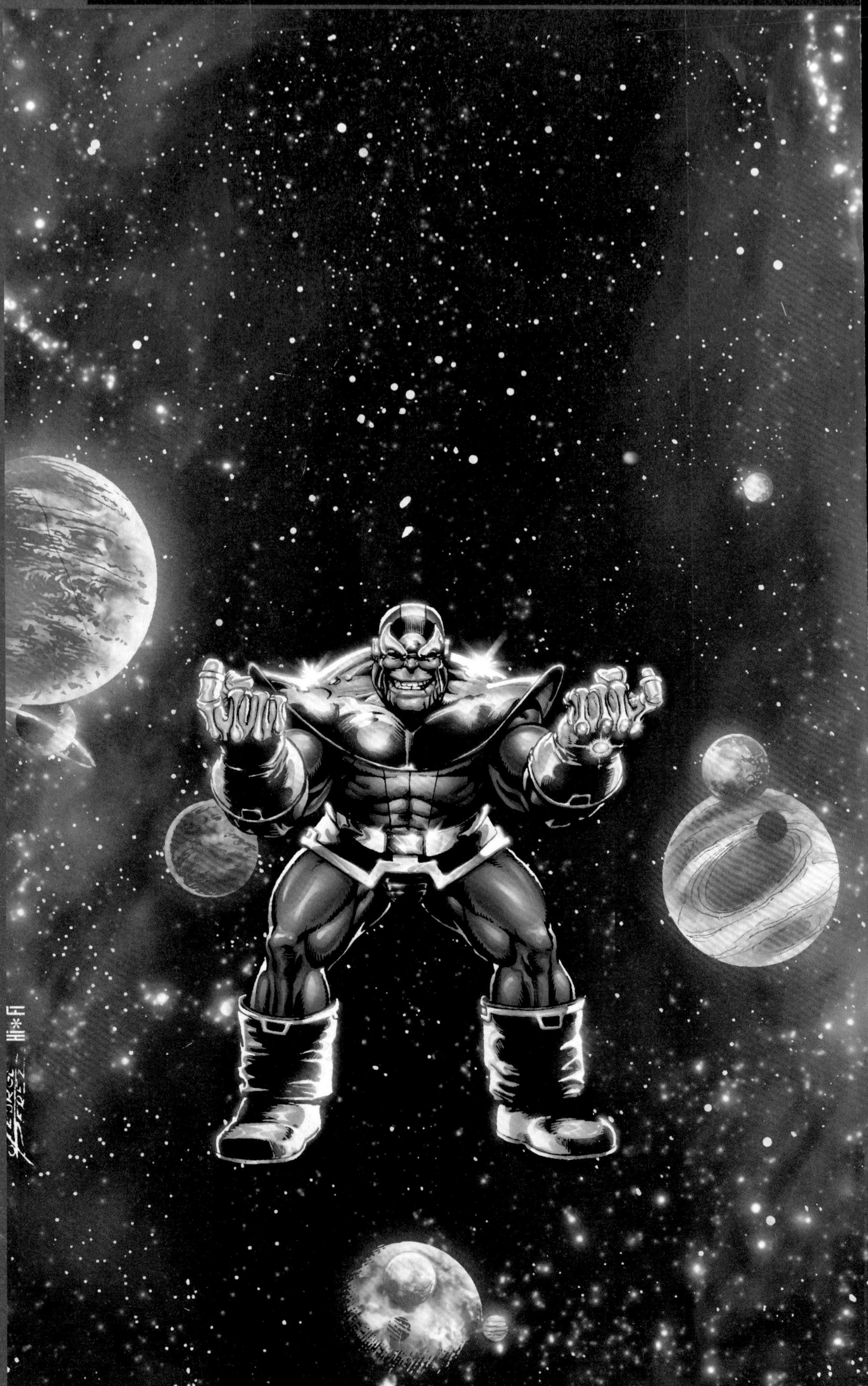